Muthologos

Charles Olson invited to read in David Ray's class at Cornell University 23 July 1962.
Photo: Lenny Lipton.

Charles Olson

Muthologos
Lectures and Interviews

REVISED SECOND EDITION
Edited by Ralph Maud

Talonbooks

Talonbooks
P.O. Box 2076, Vancouver, British Columbia, Canada V6B 3S3
www.talonbooks.com

Typeset in Minion and Myriad and printed and bound in Canada.
Printed on 100% post-consumer recycled paper.

First Printing: 2010

The publisher gratefully acknowledges the financial support of the Canada Council for the Arts; the Government of Canada through the Book Publishing Industry Development Program; and the Province of British Columbia through the British Columbia Arts Council and the Book Publishing Tax Credit for our publishing activities.

Library and Archives Canada Cataloguing in Publication

Olson, Charles, 1910–1970
        Muthologos : lectures & interviews / Charles Olson ; edited by Ralph
Maud.—Rev. 2nd ed.

Includes bibliographical references and index.
ISBN 978-0-88922-639-5

        1. Olson, Charles, 1910–1970—Interviews. 2. Poets, American—20th
century—Interviews. 3. Poetry—Authorship. I. Maud, Ralph, 1928–
II. Title.

PS3529.L655Z46 2010   811'.54   C2010-902235-1

Contents

Photographs

Introduction

From the Introduction to the first edition, 1978

With the widespread availability of portable recording equipment, taped interviews and lectures have been added to the corpus of a literary figure in recent times, whether as ancillary documents or, almost, as a separate genre. This volume collects the public voice of Charles Olson as transcribed from the surviving tapes. There is a variety of occasions presented in the thirteen transcriptions, a range of formality, from full public lectures before large audiences to conversations at ease with friends. All took place in the 1960s, beginning when Olson emerged from Gloucester, having all but finished the second and most explorative volume of his major work, *The Maximus Poems*, in order to join Robert Creeley, Robert Duncan, and Allen Ginsberg at the Vancouver Poetry Conference in the summer of 1963—and continuing up to August 1969, just a few months before his untimely death. The selections include such events as the poet's tour de force reading at Berkeley, shortly following his return from an uncertain success amidst the international art world at Spoleto (including an encounter, after almost twenty years, with his former master Ezra Pound). There are also discussions of Black Mountain College, whose success was so far out of proportion to its size and life span, and revealing comments by the poet on his own work.

If Berkeley was to be his most significant public appearance, Olson's conversation with veteran newspaperman Herb Kenny reveals most clearly his devotion to Gloucester and its heroic past. Among the more formal occasions—or those announced as such—were the lecture at Berkeley entitled "Causal Mythology," a series of lectures at Beloit College, and an address before a convocation at a state college in upstate New York. There were not that many public appearances or taped occasions, after all, even though it was an age dominated by the media. We are fortunate with what we have, in that sense. They are all rare emergences from a man who could be a commanding and conspicuous public figure, but who also had his vulnerabilities.

In only two cases was the poet aware ahead of time that transcriptions of his spoken words might be made and published. In one, with Gerard Malanga for the *Paris Review*—a series which included the likes of Faulkner, Hemingway, Eliot, Pound, Frost, Picasso, Cocteau, Williams—Olson made it as difficult as possible for the interviewer, at the same time wresting an occasion into his own hands (just as he did in his letters concerning *Origin* magazine) and remaking it according to his own sights. The other instance was the Beloit lectures, where part of the agreement in delivering them was, that should they be published in book form, an additional small sum would be paid. (It was one of the things on his mind, as a bit of unfinished business, even on his deathbed, as notes and last instructions in the margins of the book he was reading attest.) Otherwise, all the other addresses and conversations were unprepared, impromptu, intended for the moment only. Not that the "Beloits," formal as they were, turn out to be of such a different quality than the other occasions. Try as he might—and there is evidence of successive attempts among his papers—Olson was unable (and finally, unwilling) to formulate the talk ahead of time. He was an unsystematic thinker, although a persistent one, obsessive even, until an area was totally possessed by his repeated acts of attention to it. A "saturation job," he called such. Whether it was speaking or teaching or writing the poem, there was to be no "thinking it out or living it ahead of time," according to some preconception or ideal form. "Who knows what a poem ought to sound like? until it's thar?" He would throw out an argument or a tale like Babe Ruth pointing to the stands, challenging himself, to see if he could meet the pitch. It was a healthy and resourceful activism, a drama of risk, part of the spontaneously creative moment, an art which sought not "to describe but to enact." Such enactment might be the hope of these transcriptions as well, despite the inescapable limits of the mode.

George F. Butterick

Introduction to the second edition, 2010

George Butterick did not divulge in print why he chose *Muthologos* as the title for this volume. I think it was because Olson once defined the word *muthologos* as "what is said about what is said," which has a breadth that would recommend it for a volume that stands as the range of where the poet's mind went in a life-time's intent to go places. The three volumes of Athenaeus's *Banquet* were among Olson's favorite books; *Muthologos* is like the expansive table-talk of the deipnosophists, those called to the feast of the learned. The poems are allowed in as part of the banquet, but the totality is in the life, which was chiefly talk. It is in this compilation of transcribed tapes that we get what is preserved of Olson's life of talk; hence the claim, as close as it gets, to totality.

This second edition of *Muthologos*, coming some thirty years after the first, is able to add several new items: "At Goddard College, April 1962"; a second Vancouver 1963 discussion, "Duende, Muse, and Angel"; a short addition to the "BBC Interview"; "On Black Mountain (II)"; and a further hour of the conversation with Herb Kenny.

All the available tapes have been listened to again. Many of the problems have been cleared up, as explained in the Textual Notes, which also give the provenance of the tapes and the particular way in which each transcription was handled.

Another procedural difference is that the first edition separated the footnotes from the text, putting them at the back of the volume, and giving as much information as possible to supplement Olson's points. Butterick wanted to set us at ease by showing that Olson knew what he was talking about. This second edition assumes that we have acquired some faith in Olson's erratic brilliance and that we would prefer to be left more or less in the same position as Olson would expect his audience at that moment to be in, reasonably aware of things but not too prepared ahead of time. One does not usually stop a conversation (or the flow of a tape) to ask for a reference or to look something up. Sometimes, however, one is inclined not to let a puzzling thing go by, and the notes at the foot of the page of this edition are a recognition of such occasions. An annotated index will be found useful for remaining difficulties.

The two simple devices used to communicate the stop and flow of Olson's speaking manner are (1) the dash (—), where Olson interrupts his own sentence while continuing the thought with new syntax; and (2) ellipses (…), which do not indicate words omitted editorially but are reserved for when an incomplete sentence trails off or is interrupted by an interlocutor. Overall, it has been the chief duty of the editor of these transcriptions to use punctuation as skilfully as possible to recreate on the page the brilliant timing with which Olson almost always puts out his meaning when intellectually aroused.

Ralph Maud

I wish to acknowledge the considerable contribution of Shyla Seller, Lori Keenan, John William, and lately Greg Gibson at Talonbooks, in accomplishing a final digital text.

The campus of Goddard College, Plainfield, Vermont, around the time of Olson's visit.
Photo courtesy Goddard College Archives.

1

At Goddard College, April 1962

Referring to his time at Goddard College, Plainfield, Vermont, in a letter to Robert Creeley soon afterward, Olson said: "did 4 things there." Only two public appearances were recorded, a poetry reading on the Thursday evening and a talk on Melville on the Saturday afternoon. Olson mentions a Friday afternoon gathering, and there may have been further events as Olson and his wife extended their stay, finding the atmosphere at this "experimental" college congenial—with only one blip: "John Bloch was kicked out for three days for a party he threw us—and both Bet and I were haled before their Judiciary Committee on same charge, and told to abide by Community laws while there! But the sharp fact was the Supreme Court Justice, who gave me the legalistic justice, stepped outside afterwards to tell me where I cld get a drink, like" (letter to Creeley 25 April 1962 at Stanford).

As for the poetry reading, Olson had in mind to go through the poems he had written most recently, not yet fixed in print but almost ready to be sent to Jonathan Williams to follow *The Maximus Poems* (1960). Olson is at pains to point out that they constitute a "set." We should not look for the kind of medley that usually constitutes a poetry reading but a unified body of work around a theme.

Likewise, the Melville lecture is up to the minute in that Olson is rising to the challenge of an essay by Gino Clays in the issue of *A Pamphlet* that had arrived in Gloucester the week before. He reads out that whole essay as well as the two-paragraph response he had penned just before leaving for Goddard. The other pieces, as he himself suspects, are aurally difficult, but they seem to him what the occasion demanded. One can see him trying to obey the dictum enunciated in the lecture: "I myself would wish that all who spoke and wrote spoke always from a place that is new at the moment that they do speak."

Thursday evening, 12 April 1962

KRISTIN GLASER: Charles Olson is going to give a reading from his work tonight. Now I'll let him introduce himself, because I don't know very much about him.

CHARLES OLSON: Well, I'm very glad I'm going to be here for a few days, because I'd really rather talk about poetry or read somebody else's than myself, being at some stage of existence which makes that sensible.

AUDIENCE: You don't mind the tape recorder, do you?

OLSON: No. As a matter of fact I'm going to just watch it, like a fire. Let's sit here and watch that thing. What happens if it just goes on and I don't say anything? Just that problem of being—as a matter of fact, it gets to be kind of a bore because it's become performing art and you feel as though you have an audience and you're supposed to do a concert or something; and I don't think I believe in verse in this respect at all. As a matter of fact, I know I don't.

Miss Glaser asked me to introduce myself, which is nuttier than a fruit-cake. I suppose I'm here because my co-agitator, Mr Creeley, was here a year ago, and in fact I feel very much at home because that previous tape, as far as I know, of a reading—unless you've had someone in between—is Creeley's tape, which ran from this room (was it?) into our kitchen in Gloucester, directly almost. I think it was in a matter of hours. It was like hot cakes. Have you had a poet read since?

GLASER: Not since then, no.

OLSON: No. Then I see it's a trap. If I don't read you'll all be disappointed, and if I do read I'll have to be very careful because they'll have to be the poems that interest *me*, and I'm not so sure from recent experience that they're the poems which interest anyone else.

GLASER: You can do whatever you want.

OLSON: I don't feel unfree. But then, I—like, it's not a captive audience so much as a captive poet, I think. [LAUGHTER] I've been working for quite a few years on a poem which gets called *The Maximus Poems*, and this volume was published last year, which has the first three volumes, and the fourth volume is supposed to be published this year by the same publisher; and yet I'm tempted tonight, if I could feel your own experience a little more, to read you first some poems from the fifth volume just because that's more where I am than where I was. This book dates back about twelve years, I think; that's the first poems were twelve years ago, and I've no impression of how much this book is known. Can someone give me some sense of how much you know *The Maximus Poems*? I'm really fishing because, if I go to the fifth volume instead of the first, and the first is unknown, it's awkward for you, I believe.

AUDIENCE: I think probably it's fairly little known by most.

OLSON: Yeah, yeah. The general proposition is to address yourself—or I mean this creature "Maximus" addresses himself to a city, which in the instance is Gloucester, which then in turn happens to be Massachusetts; that is, Gloucester, Massachusetts. I'm not at all impressed that it's necessarily any more Gloucester, Massachusetts, in any meaningful sense than the creature is either me or whom he originally was intended as, which was Maximus of Tyre, a 2nd-century dialectician. At least, on the record, what he wrote was *dialetheia*, which we have, I guess, in the word "dialectic," meaning intellectual essays or essays on intellectual subjects. And he mostly wandered around the Mediterranean world from the old capital of Tyre, talking about one thing, Homer's *Odyssey*. I don't have much more impression of him than that. I've tried to read his *dialetheia*, and I've found them not as interesting as I expected.[1] But he represents to me some sort of a figure that centers much more than the 2nd century AD. In fact, as far as I feel it, like, he's like the navel of the world; and, in saying that, I'm not being poetic or loose. We come from a whole kind of life which makes Delphi that center. I guess I can say that amongst you and be heard. And this, I think, is a kind of a thing that ought to be at least disturbed. I stress this part of it rather than what—maybe just to make it possible for you to ignore the fact that you don't know, most of you don't know these poems, so that I might be free to read a few of the fifth volume to start us off, because what I arrived at in these recent poems is something that is a transfer for me to that vision of a difference that Tyre is, or proposition that Tyre is, as against, say, Delphi. And if I can find the beginning of this volume, I'd like to run a few of those poems.

I read in Toronto just a couple—it's a little longer than that—a few weeks ago, again after two years. Toronto is one of the great places on this continent, or was two years ago; and, in reading there at that time, I had read a poem from this volume which includes a poem of John Smith's. Now John Smith was that man, I mean, who had to do with Pocahontas, and was, as nobody seems to know, the Governor of the Virginia Colony shortly thereafter and, in an explosion of ammunition on the James River, was so badly burned he had to go back to London—in fact, almost like burned more than half his body, that sort of thing—and he went back, and he was cured, and then became the great explorer of the North Atlantic and mapped the Gulf of Maine, Massachusetts Bay, as thoroughly as he had earlier mapped Chesapeake for the Virginia Colony, and became by appointment the Admiral of New England, after having been the Governor of the Virginia Plantation. And after one voyage for what was set out for whales in 1614, he never was able to get back to America again, and in fact was refused by the Pilgrims in 1620 as an advisor. In fact, he would like very much to have been able to come over again, knowing that whole situation, as their, well, really as their Miles Standish, but it was a more complicated role. And Smith is one of my heroes, and I had read this poem, which is

1. It was in the Library of Congress in the late 1940s that Olson consulted the two-volume *Dissertation of Maximus Tyrius* translated by Thomas Taylor (London: C. Wittingham, 1804).

published in Smith's last book the year of his death 1629 or '30. And it's called "The Sea Marke":

"Aloofe, aloofe; and come no neare,
the dangers doe appeare;
Which if my ruine had not beene
you had not seene:
I onely lie upon this shelfe
to be a marke to all
which on the same might fall,
That none may perish but my selfe.

"If in or outward you be bound,
do not forget to sound;
Neglect of that was cause of this
to steere amisse:
The Seas were calme, the wind was faire,
that made me so secure
that now I must indure
All weathers be they foule or faire

"The Winters cold, the Summers heat
alternatively beat
Upon my bruised sides, that rue
because too true
That no releefe can ever come.
But why should I despaire
being promised so faire
That there shall be a day of Dome."

And when I read that, which sits in another poem, which I will read you, which sits in a poem of my own, the leading poetess of Canada[2] questioned me as to whether Smith had written it. Well, I know PhDs, and my wife and I stayed in San Francisco with the wife of a leading PhD who wrote his thesis on how many Elizabethan hacks there were who were capable of writing poems like this,[3] and that … Can you hear?

AUDIENCE: Not quite.

OLSON: Not quite. I got a very big voice; I'm just playing mouse at the moment … And we had a lovely long evening, and the whole audience was involved in my argument that Smith is one of the distinguished English poets and that with his prose and his poetry one moves from England to America that early. Now this poem goes, that is, my own poem goes on from that moment of quoting that.

[Reads parts III & IV of "Maximus, to Gloucester, Letter 15"
(1.70–71)]

2. During his stay in Toronto for a reading on 24 February 1962, Olson had arranged to see Margaret Avison, whose poetry he admired.
3. Ruth Witt-Diamant, Head of the English Department at San Francisco State University, was Olson's hostess during his two-week visit to the Poetry Center there in 1957. Her husband was Henry Diamant, a professor at Berkeley.

STUDENT: [INAUDIBLE]

OLSON: You don't follow that? Shoot. I told you that tape's goin' on.

So the first poem of the fifth volume of the *Maximus* is this, "A Later Note on Letter #15," which I just read.

[Reads "A Later Note on Letter #15" (II.79)]

That, I submit, is a poem. That was written January 15, 1962, which even further confirms it. [LAUGHTER] The next poem in this series is this [II.80]:

> 128 a mole
>   to get at Tyre

128 is not—it's like I was talking to Dick Bishop,[4] who's been our host overnight last night, and he tells me that 750 is an important number in American life, see. Well, 128 is the route that is a highway from Boston to Gloucester.

> 128 a mole
>   to get at Tyre

The third poem in this series is called "'View': fr the Orontes / fr where Typhon" [II.81]. Now that is not as obscure as it looks either; but then it's just that problem: you work for a long time on a long poem and you get involved with it, and you finally find yourself just composing *it*, see? What I really mean about reading poems is that they no longer can extricate themselves from each of themselves. Somewhere in some poem some years ago I had a whole big smash about "stepping right off the Orontes," a big congested poem ["Letter, May 2, 1959" (I.150)]. I could read you that passage, at least. Oh, yes, surely, oh yes, it's very interesting because it's a dirty poem, dirty in the sense of just messing everything up, about a bridge over a river, a very huge highway bridge which really feeds that route 128 successfully on to the island that Gloucester and Cape Ann properly is, and wasn't when John Smith charted that situation, but was when Champlain did in 1606. The beach had built up and choked the channel of this river which previously, when the Indians were in Gloucester, had been a very satisfactory connection between Ipswich Bay and Massachusetts Bay, so that the Gulf of Maine and the whole coast was really a unit. It became a great desire of Massachusetts Bay Colony to open that, get that cork out of there. Now of course it's been a great desire to put this bridge across it. And this poem has to do, in one passage, with this effect of the building of this bridge. Do you know yourselves enough of the history of Tyre to know that the only thing in the world that confronted the universalization that Alexander proposed, which I think is the great complement to the present, was Tyre? It so refused to be knocked down by this Macedonian athlete that it was the sole place in the world which bucked him. And it took Alexander, I can always be corrected, but was it three to four years to reduce Tyre? And

4. Dick Bishop was a former student at Black Mountain College who had at one point established a "Black Mountain North" in South Royalton, Vermont, not too far from Goddard College, and presumably still resided in the area.

in order to get at her he built a mole from the mainland to Tyre, like we did, by the way, to take Mexico City in the Mexican War, uh? You remember how Mexico City was …

STUDENT: What's a "mole"?

OLSON: A mole, oh, is an earth bridge, simply extending earth out until you have a causeway. We did that to that lovely City of Flowers, floating Mexico City. You remember that wonderful story of how the American, how early our characteristic intrusion upon all places—you remember that wonderful military fact of the Mexican War that we did that thing? Or am I?—it is Cortés that did it? I think it's Cortés that did it, I think. Was it? I think it was. It was, yes. Sounds very American right from the start. Well, I object to this damn bridge. And I state where I am, which is:

> Am in the mud
> off Five Pound Island
> is the grease-pit
> of State Pier
>   Go 'way and leave
> Rose-Troup

(is an English maiden, who wrote a lovely history of the founder, the minister of England, who really supported the United States before she began)

>   Go 'way and leave
> Rose-Troup and myself   I smell your breath, sea
> And unmellowed River under
> the roar of A. Piatt Andrew

(which is the name of the bridge)

> hung up there like fission
> dropping trucks the face
> Samuel Hodgkins

(who ran the ferry across that same spot)

> Samuel Hodgkins didn't show
> poling pulling 1 penny
> per person 2
> for a horse
>   step off
> onto the nation The sea
> will rush over The ice
> will drag boulders Commerce
> was changed   the fathometer
> was invented here the present
> is worse give nothing now your credence
> start all over step off the
> Orontes onto land no Typhon
> no understanding of a cave
> a mystery Cashes?

And so forth [from "Letter, May 2, 1959" (1.150)]. So this is some time after-wards:

[Reads "'View': fr the Orontes / fr where Typhon" (II.81)]

You dig? You want that again? I dunno. Call me if you'd like any one of these again. That problem of scoring is difficult in music. Like, you know, one writes music, one doesn't play it. That's that problem with this kind of a performance situation. I'm not—I'm not—I'm Beethoven, not … some-body. If you liked the score, I'd be happy to read it again, but …

STUDENT: Maybe you'd better.

OLSON: This one, I think, is not a bad score, like they say. "'View': fr the Orontes / fr where Typhon." Now I won't … I'll be back, don't worry, I'll … [LAUGHTER] There's an earlier *Maximus*, way back some time, on Columbus, in which this whole business of the fact that Cyprus—yeah, you know Cyprus?—that island just off this point of land that I'm talking about where the Orontes River comes in at the northern end of Syria …? (What is that, a pussy cat? A child? All right. Is that the Bishops' child? A child, where is there a child? Is there a child in the audience? Help! [LAUGHTER]) Well, anyhow … Mind you, it's a picture, like; there's a picture, you see. There's been several pieces of the picture put down before. One is that the island of Cyprus, which I hope I can put in your mind quickly like that, is very close to this point where the Orontes River, which was the main manageable traffic trading outlet of the whole of the old Near East to the Mediterranean and Atlantic, like—and the first step was, the first stop and first step, both weather-wise and sailing-wise, was the island of Cyprus. Well, there was a big business previously [in "The Song and Dance of" (1.54–58)] about how from Cyprus to Columbus we get here. Now, this one [II.81] is poking around in that same place, and I'm talking about those who were

the 1st to navigate
those waters
thus to define
the limits
of the land

[Rereads the poem]

Trouble? Yeah, come again. I'll be back with this—can't get rid of it, that's all. The fourth in this series—now it's one of those things you have to do in order to stay alive. And we happen to live in Gloucester, so—like, it doesn't matter where you live, like, the same people occur. This poem is called—no, it's got no name, pardon me.

[Reads "The Young Ladies …" (II.82)]

The next has an awful lot of local allusions in proper names, but I don't believe they should trouble you, because again, like, proper names are all over the place, and if any of you know a great poet who should be here at any moment, I should hope, for your sake, Edward Dorn—don't any of you know Dorn's poetry? Well, Dorn actually was living in Santa Fe, and then—you see, it doesn't matter, I mean Santa Fe is the same thing as in Gloucester.[5]

[Reads "patriotism / is the preserved park" (II.83)]

You see, I don't think you had trouble. Now, number six is—actually got a title; it's called "Bk ii chapter 37." It has nothing whatsoever to do with anything but, if you have the power of recognition or the experience of whom I am imitating, you will know. (Is that somebody speaking? Did I hear voices? It's that tape, talking back to me! I knew it would object.)

[Reads "Bk ii chapter 37" (II.84)]

Anybody recognize who that is, beside myself? No?

AUDIENCE: Is it Greek? Herodotus?

OLSON: No, it's Pausanius. It's Pausanius. *The Description of Greece,* of the 2nd century AD. Do you know that book? It's a remarkable—it's a very, very, very, to me, like, twin to Herodotus. He was a traveler, again, like the boys of—like everybody, you see, like *On the Road,* no? Really, those first two centuries, wow, talk about being knocked out; I mean, nobody was at home. And in fact they did the thing that anybody does who moves, they found very interesting things. And Pausanius, I think Pausanius's *Description of Greece* is comparable to Herodotus, I think, for our minds or our interests, yeah. You know, everything has gotten very interesting and very complicated and very intellectual and very satisfying for inquiry, uh? Honestly, expression has lost ground rapidly, and a look-see is really in business, uh? And this boy is a cat like Plutarch—y'dig Plutarch? A contemporary, by the way, Plutarch again 2nd century, crazy, crazy, crazy, crazy record. If the 20th has one resemblance—it has four, but it has one— one is the 2nd century.

STUDENT: What are the other three?

OLSON: Well, let me hold that off; we'll come to that. How many days am I going to be here? I got to lecture on Saturday; I got to have something for reserve. [LAUGHTER] I got to *lecture* on Saturday; I got to really, like, put it out. All I have to do tonight is to have a ball. I mean, what am I going to do on Saturday night? It's terrible. [LAUGHTER]

I didn't feel as though that one made it with you. At least, it seemed too obscure or something. Aw, to hell with it. Nah, it's a postcard. I'll send it to you in the mail. [LAUGHTER] Number 7 [II.85]:

> the rocks in Settlement Cove
> like dromlechs, menhirs

---

5. Olson is referring to Dorn's *What I See in the Maximus Poems* (first published as a Migrant pamphlet, Spring 1960), where Dorn compares his own situation in Santa Fe with Olson's in Gloucester.

—"menhirs," uh? Whatever that is—"menhirs." Do you know what I mean? You know those two words I'm using? No?—"dromlechs,[6] menhirs": megalithic, mostly around Brittany and, like, old Ireland and Scotland, Denmark, or those waterhenge—what is it? no, stonehenge, but smaller. The Brittany stones are smaller than those real megalithic stones of Stonehenge. Yeah, burials, burial mark, apparently. There were two forms. I love the two words. In fact, driving up here tonight for—the whole damn scenery's nothing but earth dromlechs and menhirs. At least, those words were what I kept thinking of all the time. These are clichés. I love them: dromlechs, menhirs.

> the rocks in Settlement Cove
> like dromlechs, menhirs
> standing in the low tide
> out of the back of the light,
> from Stacy Boulevard on the water
> at night

Can you get that picture? I'll try—I think it's dead, yeah—I'll try it again.

[Rereads the poem]

And the next one, dating a short time ago, November 12, I discover, 1961.

[Reads "Peloria" (II.87)]

The next poem has just recently appeared in New York and—oh, I'll try to think where it did appear, oh yes, in LeRoi Jones's *Floating Bear*, if you know this remarkable mimeographed magazine which is appearing in our time, do you know it, any of you? He's a very great editor, the greatest editor since Robert Creeley, and Jones has been putting this thing out for a couple of— oh no, maybe it's only a year—with Diane di Prima. She does the typing, most remarkable. No, don't think I'm putting her down, wow, I mean, I published the most terrible thing was ever written last year, called "GRAMMAR—a 'book,'" and it's nothing but parts of speech; and she took my typed copy and put it in mimeograph so that there wasn't a—and it's all tilted and squeezed and shoved, and the only trouble is that the mimeograph doesn't make the same effects as the typewriter, but that's not her fault. She did it marvelously; it was like the greatest publishing I've ever had was Miss di Prima. Well, this poem, for some reason everybody thinks it's awful square. But then I've had more response from it from those who— well, now I've ruined it. You never should make a pitch, you know. [LAUGHTER] Actually, it's a very quiet idea. The title is "In the Face of a Chinese View of the City." I was talking to the very man that I wrote this about, the City Manager, the other day, and I said, "I just published a poem about you, in New York, called 'In the Face of a Chinese View of the City.'" I said, "I don't know anything about Chinese. Don't mind." I said, "You remember Confucius, like?" "Oh, yeah." He'd say "yeah." [LAUGHTER]

---

6. The proper form is "cromlechs." Olson left in the mistake in *Maximus Poems IV, V, VI* at this point, but corrected himself later (III.97).

"Well, I just did it." It suddenly occurred to me that, wow, we all go around living with a past as though it had value, and here we are stuck with not value.

[Reads "In the Face of a Chinese View of the City" (II.88–89)]

AUDIENCE: Read it again.

OLSON: Yeah, and I'll read you a better version. I read the typed copy, and I got the manuscript, I see, and there's a few nice differences, I think, if I can find the second page, wait a minute. I don't. I've got most of it in manuscript.

[Rereads "In the Face of a Chinese View of the City"; then the next poem (II.90). Rereads the poem; then reads the next poem (II.91). Rereads the poem]

Thirteen. January 17, 1962.

> A 'learned man' sd Strabo
> the 'English' of the Mediterranean
> as the Greeks the Germans
> the inherited past.

I don't know, I don't even know what the hell I'm referring to—wait a minute. "A 'learned man' sd Strabo ..." I've lost touch with that one.[7] [LAUGHTER] It doesn't matter, like. Like, "learned" men we know about. You know, Strabo is, again, I think, 2nd century, the geographer who's responsible for our knowing about Pytheas at all, the man of the 4th century BC, who actually set out of Marseilles and, by the very thing which makes Strabo suspicious that he was a liar, Stefansson, who really knows— the present Stefansson, Vilhjalmur—who knows, like, the Arctic, says is the best evidence of the fact that Pytheas was really in a certain season off the coast of Iceland in the 4th century BC. Like, let's really talk, instead of crap of Irish and Vikings, like, everything was really in existence in powerful ways back before Alexander, uh? There again, I'm pushing; but don't be fooled by the universalization of the present. The work, the real work of the future has already been done, and the future that is proposed is a lie. (I didn't know I was going to get that up!) Ma'am? Mrs Hamlin?

MRS HAMLIN: [INAUDIBLE]

OLSON: I can't figure out what I'm referring to. It's a very complicated intellectual poem: [LAUGHTER] "the 'English' of the Mediterranean"— you see, it goes on. Gee, that really looks pretty obscure. [LAUGHTER] It's very important to me. I can't—I wish I could get it—catch—find out.

> A 'learned man' sd Strabo
> the 'English' of the Mediterranean
> as the Greeks the Germans
> the inherited past.

---

7. Olson is reading from a manuscript version which was much revised for publication in *Maximus IV, V, VI* (II.92).

Can you help me? What am I talking about there? Do you know what I'm talking about? "A 'learned man'": I can't figure it out. The reference, by the way, the distinction being drawn is between the Phoenicians, who are the "English" of the Mediterranean, as against the Greeks, who are the "Germans," which, wow, you know, like, that has never been said, I think, to our knowledge. I mean, I even think it's mighty, mighty, mighty important.

I think this one is the same day, yes.

[Reads "Cyprus / the strangled / Aphrodite" (II.93)]

STUDENT: Again?

OLSON: Yeah. Oh, sure. Sure, it's all right.

[Rereads the poem]

STUDENT: Thanks.

OLSON: Same day.

[Reads "after the storm was over" (II.94)]

That's a story. I, like, I think it should be enjoyed.

[Rereads the poem]

[Reads "to travel Typhon" (II.95)]

[Reads "up the steps, along the porch" (II.96)]

[Reads "people want·delivery" (II.97)]

[Reads "the coast goes" (II.98)]

[Reads the two-word poem "tesserae / commissure" (II.99)]

STUDENT: "Tesserae"?

OLSON: Yeah, the little pieces that are used in making a mosaic, they are tesserae, all those pieces of stone and glass and color.

STUDENT: What's the next word?

OLSON: "Commissure," which means "bound together," but it's a—yeah:

    tesserae
        commissure.

The "tesserae" is underlined, as a foreign word, and "commissure"— actually they're both in the Webster's, but I don't know if "tesserae" is.

That's really a kind of a run. It moves now differently. In fact, it kind of breaks a little bit. I'll read you the next poem, but the one beyond it I haven't been able to write. It's very bad, you see, it's why I said to you I've got to talk about where you get stuck, and you really get stuck. Twenty-one.

[Reads "Lane's eye-view of Gloucester" (II.100)]

And this missing poem; and then this one. That missing poem ["3rd letter on Georges, unwritten" (II.107)], by the way, is a story I may not be competent to write, but it should be a story which I know a man who wrote—I'm involved in that problem: shall I crib him or not? Very great writer, who won the running broad jump at the first modern Olympics in Athens: James Connolly. What I'd like to do is what he can do and has done, which is to take a vessel from the eastern end of Georges shoal, the northeastern end, and run it at night in an easterner and eastward through the maze of the shoals of the north end of Georges without wrecking, and getting into clear water on the other side, and making the market in Boston. And it really takes experience I don't have. So I'll have to wait, or see what I do with that problem of stealing it from Connolly.[8] It's important to me. I have published in earlier *Maximus*es some such sea stories, one of which I might read after I get through with this sequence, if you're interested, called "The Rattler" [II.19], which has been published in another one of those mimeograph magazines, from the West coast this time, *Migrant*, which some of you know, by any chance? I did it originally on a tape that Duncan and I made for Creeley for his Christmas two years ago, two or three years ago.

[Reads "Older than Byblos" (II.101)]

I've been, in these recent poems, plugging—not plugs I'd likely to get something, but getting involved with the whole damned Phoenician thing as a force, which seems more interesting than—I mean, interesting to me. And there's two stanzas and a running line.

[Rereads the poem]

You will see that in the fifth poem ahead, which will be the last one I'll read in this sequence, that language, I guess, comes home, comes to bear. This is called "Chronicles," and I guess it's two.

[Reads the two parts of "Chronicles" (II.102–3)]

[Reads "Sanuncthion lived" (II.104–5)]

[Reads "John Watts took" (II.106)]

STUDENT: Could we have that again?

OLSON: Sure.

[Rereads the poem]

And now the last one, called "The Gulf of Maine," if I can find it. It may take me a minute. Meanwhile, I'll read another poem on that subject for your, like, information, as I read it this afternoon. We had a little accidental stop on the way at a place called Dartmouth, where on Thursdays fortunately they have a very nice thing about the poets—what do they call it? "Thursday Poets"? or "Poets' Thursday"? Something like that. And I read this poem, and I've forgotten where it goes in series, but it's another one so: "Going Right Out of the Century" [II.74]. "I, John Watts ..." Oh, I should say—like,

---

8. Olson found the story in Connolly's *Book of Gloucester Fishermen* (1927), chapter 6, "Driving Home from Georges," which, with its reference to the "pawl post" (p. 128), also gave Olson the poem he next reads, "Older than Byblos."

again, we have to come back to some information—it seems to me I've handled this thing for—I've been interested in it for a long time. There was a fellow named Watts, who was a factor of this Dorchester Company, who did come over on a voyage and found this stuff stored on this island which is in the middle of Gloucester Harbor, and it had been left there by a ship from London, the *Zouche Phoenix*, and the Admiralty Courts fortunately are full of this record, and I'm drawing on that. No, not in this one.

[Reads "Going Right Out of the Century" (ii.74)]

And now with "The Gulf of Maine," if I find it, we can have a break.

[Reads "The Gulf of Maine" (ii.108–10)]

Well, that's a set. That's a set. Can you cut that for a minute while we have a little intermission?

[GAP]

This Thursday afternoon scene that I went to, it's very nice. There's one very decent guy, a man named Alexander Laing, whom all the poets I know that have come through would do anything for; which is why I really went there today, despite delaying my coming here, is simply because he wrote a letter here, which I haven't seen yet, asking if, so long as I was going to be here tonight, would I come to that thing this afternoon. His wife was a poet whom I know better than his work, Dilys Laing—previous wife—and he really is, he's one of the few—like, there's a few men in this country whom you'd touch just to—and if they said come you'd come just because they said. I know up to, say, about three, and he's one of them. And there's a great bookstore man, Cairnie in Cambridge, Mass., Gordon Cairnie, whom any of us would go out of our way for. And Laing is just this sort. And it's a very quiet small thing; it's tucked in there. He's really got nothing to do with— he's got a post at the library of Dartmouth, he's not a big-shot, like, litera- ture or any of that. And there was a very beautiful poet there, whose work I don't know, but who's a lovely man named Guthrie—do any of you know Ramon Guthrie? Uh? Gee, he was a ball, at least in person.

Well, Mr Hamlin asked me if I'd explain a little bit of what this proposed method, as far as it makes—but then I suddenly stumbled on this earlier poem on Shag Rock, written October 18, 1961, called "Shag Rock":[9]

> the positive: the mythological
> (the world, the mundus:
> round. No explanation
> All that happens is eternal.
> No examples. No 'proving'
> possible.

Almost fallen—it almost fell in my hand, didn't it?

[Rereads the poem]

9. This poem was finally dropped by the poet, and published only posthumously in *OLSON* 9 (Spring 1978), p. 58.

Which sort of—it makes the case, like, if the case can be made. I guess a lot of you are—I heard some, I got some impression that, like, the references were—especially the apparent historical was a little interfering. I don't know how much I can do about that. I mean, like I said from the beginning, this work leaves me not very much room to read poems like poems really either certainly can be and usually are and I see no reason why they shouldn't continue to be, but I seem to be off on this kick. So I can—I mean, there's plenty of them, [LAUGHTER] but like they don't do that I guess more immediate thing that one feels a poem is. I don't know. I published a book this past year, less than a year ago, published by Grove Press, which is all those sorts of poems that I've written outside the *Maximus* poems. And like Miss Glaser asked me, "Do you write poems like about those you love or live with so that a person could know, you know, without needing to have the reference, have the experience itself?" So I thought I might read one poem I think of that would give you that experience, I think, without departing from the path that I myself am on: which is called "The Librarian." I'd like to read that, and a very open historical poem, that "Rattler" that I mentioned, a solid sea story. So, you see, we could move for a little bit, for a short while, if you're still interested, a little aside from that apparently what appears to be congested 2nd century Phoenician run. "The landscape"—I always have trouble getting this one off.

[Reads "The Librarian" (from *The Distances*)]

Does that seem more a poem? I thought it might, like they say. Or here's a short poem, like a lyric, called "Moonset, Gloucester, December 1, 1957, 1:58 AM."

[Reads the poem of that title, which follows "The Librarian" in
The Distances]

STUDENT: Could you read that again?

STUDENT: Yes, please.

STUDENT: Before you begin, what's that "Cut"?

OLSON: Cut. It's that thing I mentioned earlier, the plug in the Annisquam River, which builds up and shuts it off, shuts the passage off between the Ipswich Bay and the Massachusetts Bay, and it's called "the Cut" for the necessity to cut it through. It always has to be—no, it used to be in the 17th century—like I said, when Champlain was there at the beginning it was open; when Smith was there twenty years later it was closed. It's been a—it's the chief item of whether that's an island or not, like, when it's in it's not, and when it's out it is, uh?

[Rereads "Moonset, Gloucester, December 1, 1957, 1:58 AM"]

[Reads "The Distances," the next poem in *The Distances*]

[Reads "Cashes" (II.19)]

STUDENT: You read it as a poem, but I think it's written as a story?

OLSON: No, if I did it's only a little accident at the moment; it's really a story. You see, the margin gets more—I mean, I'm interested that that piece, for example, was published where it was, and I had, that is, a response to that. That's why I mentioned that tape that I put it on. The poem was—the thing was picked off the tape I made, for publication. It's one of those kinds of things. I'm sure the man who did, he's one of the most conservative men we've got on either shore of the Atlantic. His name is Gael Turnbull, if you know him. He's a poet who is a doctor: did his internship in Canada, and comes from Worcester, England, and has been avoiding my work for years, and embarrassed because he didn't have something he could publish, but then he's published this. So you see there is a—it has to do with a poem, somehow or other it sure does.

AUDIENCE: In what way?

OLSON: Don't you think it works by itself, and yet something that what had to do with allegory, what had to do with meaning, what had to do with punching it out a little, with statement, with pushing something, makes it too—I mean, it's without being captive, that is, being free it also has a quality of entanglement or connection to. I'm talking about it as a—it's stupid but, I mean, you asking me a question, I'm even just talking about it for the first time this way sort of thing.

WILL HAMLIN: Are you suggesting in part that, if it can stand as a metaphor for something larger, then it has a quality of a poem and not a story?

OLSON: No, I'm suggesting that just such a thing as metaphor has broken down and to some extent we're involved in succeeding in picking up things which will not then behave as metaphors again, but which will put us in touch with what metaphor didn't put us in touch with and never would, because metaphor is caught in a discourse system. Would you know— where is that Greek man? Do you know Greek? I ask you to help me: *metapherein* is the verb "to carry over," or "to transfer forth" is the actual word of metaphor, yeah? In fact, if you take the Greek verb it has a great deal of meaning. Here we get into that really crazy question that's so exciting, at least to some of us today for whom language is still a part of the art of poetry, in fact is the art of poetry. Excuse me, I mean, like, that's the point: that you can't any longer, any more than you ever could, expect language to behave except current to the sources of its invention. Now, to my mind, to make metaphor mean something I would have to know what the Greek use of that word was in the—not necessarily to be pedantic to say in the "original" use of it, but in a use that began to get a little overlaminated sometime probably in the 5th century, or, if it was invented in the 5th, was already beginning to get a little over-plastic by the—well, already in Aristotle's teaching Alexander, it was already a kind of a hang-up, uh? And that in just these places that used to be called "image" or, like, "imagery," is where poetry today is really very much in business, altogether is how to make what was called an image really an image, and how to make what we inherit as a metaphor really be a metaphor. And to do it, I think you stumble towards, you get involved with places that are edges of experience rather than something that you know by making anything like an image. Fair? O.K.

HAMLIN: When I asked the question about metaphor, the sense in which I was using it is fairly much this larger thing.

OLSON: Yeah, yeah, I dig, yeah.

HAMLIN: Story stands, to my mind, as poetry in the fact that it suggests or has outlines similar to things which are other than it and larger than it.

OLSON: Right. Now, I suddenly think of a poem which I could read you, a very short one and, I think, a pleasure. For example, so—at least let me speak for myself—that this Cashes shoal that this thing happens on is one of my places in the poem. I, in some of that stuff I read earlier, I did mention Cashes. On that Typhon, that earlier Typhon poem, I left off on Cashes [1.150]. But let me read you a thing which *Floating Bear* published originally, a short one, just to suggest how I'm just reluctant to let this thing go away from where I think you'll find anything to be, if I can labor it a little. It has to be resisted, to leave it where you find it. Yeah, that would be a real thing. Just to punch that "Cashes" thing, let me read this one. "All My Life I've Heard About Many" is the title [11.7].

> He went to Spain,
> the handsome sailor,
> he went to Ireland
> and died of a bee:
> he's buried, at the hill
> of KnockMany
>
> He sailed to Cashes
> and wrecked on that ledge,
> his ship vaulted
> the shoal, he landed
> in Gloucester: he built a castle
> at Norman's Woe

I lose some of the lilt of that. I should do it lighter.

[Rereads the poem]

Steve?

AUDIENCE: In that case I see it. Just the way the poem goes kind of imitates the action you're talking about; it's kind of direct experience.

OLSON: That's right, that's right.

AUDIENCE: But in the one that you read before that, the one about the wreck of the ship, I didn't get the same thing.

OLSON: No, I don't want you to. And, in fact, I'm only suggesting in answer to Mr Hamlin—not to him, but in furthering what we're talking about—

that I think that you get inventions—I guess sort of like that—of all sorts of rhythms and faces by letting this thing stay back where you find it, and then going back there, that kind of a thing, almost like an atavism rather than an image. Very much so, as a matter of fact. I believe completely in magic practice.

AUDIENCE: Would it be part of the "Rattler" poem for you that it is as it might have been told by some persons who had heard about it?

OLSON: Oh boy, oh boy, as a matter of fact, the point of the writing—I think one of the other ways to say it is the reason why the "Rattler"'s had some publishing attention is due to the fact that I think here I hit one of the real problems, which is that that thing doesn't have idiomatic language, yet doesn't give that effect of how it well might be reported and with no … One of the boring things about most writing in America is slang, whether it's local or national or—like, in fact, the complement: our cultural speech is a form of slang; that is, that deadness of our cultural, of our universal speech is just so dull it's like dialect, uh? I hate it. I would clean every—I myself would wish that all who spoke and wrote spoke always from a place that is new at that moment that they do speak and not hung up on any of the places from which they may have acquired their speech, whether it's putative, purposed, or personal. And I think really that's why I think Turnbull really dug this poem. This thing was—some way or other I'm getting somewheres a language thing there which is … well. Who was sitting there? Did she just go? She asked me something, and I went back to you, and … Oh, here she is. Excuse me, for—you had a question which I missed.

STUDENT: You were saying something about the edge of experience. I was trying to connect that with geographical points that you mentioned.

OLSON: Yeah, yeah, absolutely. Well, while you were out I got to the point where I was saying that I believe even—I read another poem on that Cashes shoal, and said that I almost would return to the very place that somehow or other caused the fermentation. Yeah, let's talk wine, that kind of a thing. Each year you grow the damn grapes and make the wine from the same vine, don't you? You really do; so you go back. That's not a bad image. Like, we got a wonderful conversation this afternoon on—I tried to read a poem of Duncan's from *trobar*, and I held this thing up, and this guy Guthrie, who's a learned man (sd Strabo), he gets—oh, he comes on strong because I guess he published a book called *Trobar* or something, and so [LAUGHTER] immediately a very live thing occurred: What does "trobar" mean, like? And we both had no trouble in saying "to find"; but then I said, "Well, isn't the meaning really 'to find on a guitar the tone'?" "No," he says, "as a matter of fact, so and so (like Dilys Laing or somebody it was) did a book on the diseases and cures of birds and was called a 'troubador' for having done it, because it was a 'trovar'." In other words, it means "to find out something"; which just knocks me for a loop, because my whole poem is—well, let me read … You asked me about the sources of that "Gulf of

Maine" poem, let me read you the stiffer—stiffy—that opens the last of the three books, number 23. It's just a big pitch; I avoided reading it tonight, but I guess I'm stuck again. I always seem to read the damn thing every time I read that "Gulf of Maine." And I would read this again as a question of finding a language in the moment of dealing with the poem that presents itself to write, which is of the character of language new to that moment of writing that poem.

[Reads "Letter 23" (1.99)]

Well, my mind flipped. I thought it was in that statement: "I would be an historian as Herodotus was, looking for oneself for the evidence of what is said"; but it was in that first poem I read tonight ["A Later Note on Letter #15" (II.79)], in which I say "'*istorin*, to look … to look …" It's the first paragraph of Herodotus's *History* which the word is used for the first time, I believe, the verb '*istorin*, from which we draw "history"; and it means "to look, to find out for yourself," in other words, exactly what *trobar* (which is the basis on which we are all poets, like, since the Provençal, uh?) is "to find out," like this guy did the diseases and cures of birds. I hear it that way: it means that he's a troubador because he found out about the diseases and cures of birds. I should say that too, but my god we're talking all over the lot now, I mean, like a fix in the geographical sense, an atavatism of that place, but then also that constant alertness that you do find out for yourselves every time you find out anything anyhow, if you do, and that each time you do, you the next time find out for yourself, because that's what the next time is, so that there's this, yeah, that kind of a …

AUDIENCE: Could you just define *muthos*?

OLSON: Myth. It's the source of our word "myth." Miss Harrison says it's *muth* "mouth," *muth* "mouth"; and *logos* actually is "words," but words—it got that dumb meaning. *Muthologos* actually meant "the man who finds out the words." Herodotus called Homer the *muthologos*; in turn, Herodotus was called a *muthologos*, like a *trobar*, a *trouver*. Comes out crazy, today it comes out crazy to me: the Provençal, and this point of Greek. Gee, it's too much, I should go home now. I mean, like, today, the third is today, it really is today, where we are, I swear, is founding, finding, founding, finding, founding, finding, like that, in one sentence.

Well, look, why don't we—I mean, it got a little not as light as I thought, and I'm going to be—we're going to be here for a few days, and you'll have another—or you'll put up with me again, if you do, on Saturday, so why don't we call it quits officially, or formally, now, and cut that tape off—see, my friend is getting tired too—and talk further closer if you like or we could have a drink or something.

Saturday afternoon, 14 April 1962

GLASER: All right, today Charles Olson is going to give us some kind of talk or discussion about Melville.

OLSON: It was curious that I wrote a thing last week,[10] and again he walked right into the middle of it, so that's why I was laughing was the fact that I had again been involved in him. And I thought, before I came, that it would be an interesting way to suggest how much he has stood for and stands for. I don't have too much sense of how much of Melville you all know. Like Paul Winer says, he hadn't realized that *Moby-Dick* had become a school classic, like Lawrence said it was. My father gave it to me when I was a kid, and that's a lucky way to get it if you can, I guess. And it wasn't in schools, as a matter of fact. I wonder when it came in the schools. I didn't know it was a school book. But then, you see, I said to Paul, "Well, that's fine, there's a lot of other books." How, just off hand, how much do any of you have, even, say, like *Moby-Dick* or beyond him …? Yeah. So it's a little difficult talking about him without honestly your having read him, or having a beef about him, like Paul does. I guess so, don't you, Paul?

STUDENT: From Junior High School?

PAUL WINER: Yes, Junior High.

OLSON: Junior High, yeah. I suppose it's become a—it's probably a cut-down edition, I guess. Like my son has read it in that wonderful one—what do you call those illustrated classics today? Comic strips, those beauties, they're really the best of all, they really have some meat in 'em, those things. But I started this piece: "I hate the spirit of streets."

> The spirit anyway of this nation went away at some point of time between 1765 and 1770 and a man born about then, therefore a son rather of those men who made the Revolution was already, in the first years of the Nineteenth Century crying us down accurately—James Fenimore Cooper, that early. All which writing including the hump-up of the Middle of the 19th Century did insist upon and Melville had already passed American art out into the geometry which alone— until time re-entered, about 1948—was what was making things possible again.
>
> What it was which did break in the moment of time in the Eighteenth Century must have been what Gino Clays has said I'm sure as well as anyone, that when men are still putting down houses to live in and work to make food the earth is still lived on. When that breaks—Captain Somes' house on Lower Middle Street is the possibility at its last moment here on the new continent—when it broke all had to be begun again. The critique by Cooper was so complete all

10. An untitled MS (Storrs Miscellaneous file 112) from which Olson will read was expanded to "A House Built by Capt. John Somes 1763" (*Collected Prose*, pp. 351–52), which is dated 10 April 1962, and was first published in *A Pamphlet* 3:7 (12 June 1962) "for Ted Crump," the editor of that Pocatello, Idaho, magazine.

after was simply going to live it out, until today—or at least until 1949. Any change, any new chance, had to be toward earth not (again Gino Clays) not across.

And that is provoked by an article by a guy namèd Gino Clays in a lesser sheet than *Destiny*, but a similar sheet and done very similarly, which came in this last week from Pocatello, Idaho, which is called *A Pamphlet*,[11] and has no advertising, but otherwise is exactly like what Winer is doing here. It's done because everything that the college does at the University of Idaho, the editors of this magazine find, doesn't equal the need, so they now have—in fact, this issue is to publish three poems of Edward Dorn, whom I mentioned to Ernie yesterday among the younger poets, and I think you have his last book, *The Newly Fallen*. But suddenly in the back I was reading this thing, and here's a piece by a former editor of *A Pamphlet* called "Omnia Mea Mecum Porto," which I'd like to read to you.

Nate sat in his room staring at the same walls that probably his father had stared at all through Europe and he thought perhaps there is a room some-where in Austria or Hungary just like this one with the faded blue plaster crumbling and peeling and the stained water murals. One generation American who is now leaving the shell that was destroyed long ago before there was electricity and television. I didn't last long as long as my ancestors remained in Europe but then they were still building buildings for shelter and working for food and what have I to do with a hammer but set off a chain reaction and they still had dreams of fortunes and Junker estates along the Donau and Strauss waltzes captured in Mosel Wine and I can hear them shout build that house plant those crops the Huns have left us long centuries ago and deposited their seeds in our soil and a new generation later one of my ancestors put rosin on his eyes to decrease the epicanthric fold and requested a visa to Oberammergau. And they were still building when Herr Schickelgrüber came marching over vineyards shouting Heute hört uns Deutschland und morgen die ganze Welt and loaded up boxcars of dreamers with Alle Rader müssen rollen für den Sieg written on the side and deposited their ashes over the pastures of Deutschland and the years following the winecrop was excellent. So my father singing to himself omnia mea mecum porto traveled across ashes with a rifle in his rectum and spent tormenting nights in hotels such as this telling himself that America would be different. And when the boat left Lisbon he lived like a pig in the bottom deck crammed in with eight hundred other visioners and at eight knots a day across the Atlantic while German planes above were skywriting demn die todten reiten schnell. New York City is a blackout and the war became a reality he found all the ghettos completely filled and someone said foreign-ers are not allowed but then this is war and you should try Jersey and my father found a job and procurred a wife in a cafe next door and then the apartment was filled with a screaming youth who thought his mothers teat was paradise. But the war did not end in 1945 and I was fighting with gravel in my elbows and wiping the blood from my nose and my father said that

11. *Destiny* was a mimeographed series of Goddard student papers, edited by Paul Winer. The quoted essay, "Omnia Mea Mecum Porto," appeared in the 19 March 1962 issue of *A Pamphlet*. Olson on the tape refers to Gino Clays as Guy Clay, until he corrects himself at the end of his reading of the piece.

things will be better with a college education but I found out early that no one really respects education but only for the pragmatic diploma that lets you sell life death hospital car accident baby home crop failure insurance and what can be insured when no one is living and there are no crops and I saw man's exterior crumbling and the psychiatrists treating the interior when there was no interior to treat. There is no home to build father the ground is sterile, the people impotent and I instinctively headed West for I saw no purpose and I kept going as my greatest grandfather did as he chased dreams across the Gobi desert and what did he find but no purpose and so I kept chasing myself until I reached San Francisco and this room with some understanding of inseparability with the universe and with no purpose I was liberated and I checked on a boat to the Orient where Tin Sung was waiting for me inside Buddha's triple body with no ego and where there is an innate trust in good and evil and here is balance and not the land of used car salesmen and was flowers over dead people that had always been dead because the Westward migration of man had been too soon based on greed and wealth and exterior pomp and so I am leaving America in the womb of a saline world of Pacific for I am going to be reborn inside the world and I knew that the circle would be completed and the last of man's migration for the next migration would be inside of the world and not across.

STUDENT: Whose is that now?

OLSON: A guy named Gino Clays, who was the previous editor, according to this: "Gino Clays, former editor of *AP*"—meaning *A Pamphlet*—"back from Europe, blistering Baghdad and Pont Neuf." Well, I let it … that's it, hm?

    My interest in actually doing that book on Melville, it's some years ago now, was to arrest, arrest the West. In fact, I was so disappointed when everything didn't stop it knocked me out for five months. I couldn't imagine how the world could have this book and not catch up, so since then I've been continuing to write things on Melville. All sorts of things happen once you do that, like in 1951 they were going to have a centennial celebration of *Moby-Dick* at Williams College; so I wrote, and we published at Black Mountain, a poem called "Letter for Melville 1951"; and that's in that volume *The Distances*, and I was amused to see some reviewer attacking that book in the *Hudson Review* or something, saying, "Boy, that Olson has to look around for subjects if all he can find to complain about is a meeting of the Melville Society in Williamstown."

STUDENT: Can you read that one?

OLSON: I can't find a copy. I must have lost it since I've been here. Somebody got my *Distances*? It may be in here. Ah, here it is. Instead of reading all that sort of stuff that was at the moment valuable *occasionally*, which was the whole attack upon the academic side, myself would rather go to the part that was what you were writing the poem for, which was just to write a poem about Mr Melville. Except it's a little hard; the thing is composed so that it's a critique and an essay and a poem in one. Let me just read little pieces of it before I want to read you a later thing, the last thing I've written on Melville, just so we're closer to the present, and to Gino Clays, I think.

[Reads a fifty-nine-line passage from "Letter for Melville 1951"
from "Timed in such a way" to "once before you," as found in
Collected Poems, pp. 235–36]

Well, this goes back to—I was talking to Melville's granddaughter, who took me once to Pittsfield many, many years ago when, long before this celebration, when I was a kid, and Mumford gave the main speech at a banquet to Herman Melville, and drank water, toasted—this was what murdered me was that toast in plain drinking water … So I go back to … . But then I wanted to really slice at some of all—there's quite a few critics of Melville, as your friend well knows. There's been a tremendous—it's become an academic industry. Another reason why this subject of Melville today—thank god I'm here in this situation, we can talk about it with some life, because really there's been this tremendous thing. Again, like, when I first went there to Pittsfield there was no Melville Society and there was no organized business, and it was simply a bunch of friends; but then, even then, like, there was drinking water. So I won't read this long smash against one guy in particular, who has been the editor and has written most of the Melville books of the last few years.

[Reads an eighty-nine-line passage from "Letter for Melville
1951" from "Myself, I'd like to extricate …" to the end of the
poem, as found in *Collected Poems*, pp. 238–41]

Now, some time after that I did two pieces in *The New Republic* on Melville, of which the title was "The Materials and Weights of Herman Melville." That was a year later, and I, by this time, like, I was involved in quantity much more clearly than I had been when I wrote *Ishmael*. And about three years ago, when the *Chicago Review* was changing into the *Big Table*, and there was the whole shove of Zen Buddhism upon the nation, I was asked to review for the *Chicago Review* a new book on Melville by another one of those fellows, but which had the greatest reach of title I think has ever been tried on Melville. Melville once, I think it's in *Moby-Dick*, characterized Solomon's wisdom as "the fine-hammered steel of woe"; and this guy writing a PhD thesis at the University of Illinois wrote a book called *The Fine-Hammered Steel of Herman Melville*, which I was asked to review. And just to—I want to read this, and then we can throw this thing open a little to further talk or questions. And this is the last thing I've done, got on him that I can think of, except for that reference in that paragraph this week. To some that were there yesterday afternoon I promised to bring these matters up. I see that not all that were there yesterday are here today but we'll carry it forward as though they were.

We were talking yesterday on this situation of language again, and talking with Chuck—was it Chuck? yeah—I referred to John Keats and tried to get somebody to help me quote him, and now I find out that Chuck, I found out later last evening that Chuck could have quoted "The Eve of St Agnes" easily, but the son-of-a-gun he never opened his trap at the moment.

[Reads the first five paragraphs of "Equal, That Is, to the Real Itself" as printed in the *Chicago Review* (Summer 1958) and as found in *Collected Prose*, ending with a quotation from the book under review]

He writes, in summary of what he takes it Melville did prove:
that the naturalistic perception in the years of the modern
could and must take from woe not only materialism but
also the humanism and the deep morality of social idealism, which are the true beginnings of wisdom.

I'd like to repeat that. This is Stern's, this is the heart of this whole naturalist concept. I'm using that word "naturalism" as it's classically used, and I hope some of you are acquainted with it. I think it's not actually, as a tag-word, used today, but much that's going on today I think is simply further naturalism. And it's not Nature, it's not the early use, after Thoreau or somebody.

[Repeats the quotation and continues with the next four paragraphs of the review, up to the reference to Francis Bacon, whom Melville called "that watch-maker brain"]

This is one of the great passages in *Pierre* is Melville's attack upon Bacon, that's Francis Bacon. I guess none of you have ever read *Pierre* in this room, have you? This is a novel that, if you pretend at all to be, like, at grips with writing in your society, I swear that you couldn't—I mean, it's unbelievable, this book, it's a broken book of life in Vermont and New York City, written by Melville right after *Moby-Dick* and just absolutely busted by having done *Moby-Dick* and carrying four children, and keeping a farm down here just below us in the Berkshires and trying to make it; and really broken after a year and a half of writing *Moby-Dick* he rolls right on into this book, and he actually went off his rocker as far as anybody knows, because Dr Oliver Wendell Holmes was called one night, and the family finally got wise and got together and sent him off to Europe, but by this time he'd written four more books, so it was obviously a lot later than *Pierre*; so he suffered much for several years, and then had this damn thing that I mentioned in that poem of having fallen off the farm wagon when it turned on a rut and he had what they used to call sciatica; he obviously had hit one of his vertebrae or something probably. So he really was never much good—I mean, he was plenty good: he lived to be seventy or more, seventy-two I think, and worked for twenty years in a customs house in New York thereafter. But this *Pierre* is really a—I couldn't possibly suggest a book that will both take away the curse of *Moby-Dick*, in the sense of how that's been over-circulated … But only those who care, really, and then if they stumble onto *Pierre* they're done for, and *The Confidence-Man*, which he wrote before he went on a trip to … I mean, I'm suggesting that Melville's critique of Bacon applies directly to Newton's *Scholium*.

[Reads, without interruption, the rest of "Equal, That Is, to the Real Itself," as found in *Collected Prose*, pp. 122–23]

Well, I'm sure that's much too written for the page, I suspect, to be read out loud, and especially—really it must sound like I'm trying to be a philosopher, if you haven't read Mr Melville. I think that the thing is very relevant to Melville. I myself find it more interesting than *Ishmael*—than the book I wrote—simply because it feels to me it's more in on how he was a poet and a writer. Because he *was* also a poet. I think it's one of the other crazy things that's happened in recent years that, not only has *Pierre* and *The Confidence-Man* risen in value, but there's been a number of poets that have found Melville's poetry interesting to them. I'm not one of them, but I respect some men that have found that verse important to them.

Those verses come late in his life. He wrote a whole book of poems on the Civil War called *Battle Pieces*, which includes, say, half a dozen that are among the poems that these men I speak of value; and then, when he got this job in the customs house, he occupied himself for some years with a two-volume novel in verse called *Clarel or A Pilgrimage to the Holy Land*, which almost nobody reads, even these people I speak of. I thought I had succeeded in getting Grove Press to publish that as a paperback, which was about as wild a—I mean, that was getting a publisher to risk his money! I was hoping it would work. I was asked to do an introduction to it, but I decided the best thing to do was to just get them to get it out. But I haven't seen it; I guess they really fouled me up. They didn't do it.[12] That's a crazy book, a two-volume novel in verse, dig that. And it's written in tetrameters, which contradicts—I mean, it doesn't contradict, but it shows you how difficult it was for him to get at the problems of verse for himself. And then in the last year of his life he did publish two volumes which I think are beauties. One is called *Timoleon*, a little paper book smaller than that, and much thinner, I mean, about so big. And *John Marr*. *Timoleon* and *John Marr*, two volumes of late poems, among which is a very great poem called "After the Pleasure Party," which I wish I had my hands on at the moment, I'd read it, but I don't see any Melville arrived. Look, I suggest you—that's a wow, that's one of the—now *there's* where I really pick up on it. I think that poem is one of the greatest ever. It's written to a woman in Italy, whom he obviously met at a dinner party, and he gets her called Urania in the poem, which again sounds like him to make her a goddess of astronomy, I guess, isn't it? Sure. And it opens with these beautiful lines on "Amor Threatening"; and in the middle of the poem he breaks out with a passage: "shy the fractions through life's gate." If I can get any of it, wait a minute. I can't at the moment. "Shy the fractions through life's gate." In terms of what I'm talking about here, both in statement and in image and in feeling and in dropping into the mass-matter-ishness of the spirit of life, where, if John was here, I'd now say the *Wahrheit* lieth, the poem is all, is everything going in a whole, in a whole, in a little thing about five or six lines, just a knock-out. I always know those lines, I don't know why I can't quote 'em, I've lived

12. See *Poet to Publisher: Charles Olson's Correspondence with Donald Allen* (Vancouver: Talonbooks, 2003), pp. 22–26.

with them for … The only line I can get is "Shied the fractions through life's …" O.K.

Well, that's enough, I think, for me to shoot off about. I'd like very much now to deal with any questions you have, or do anything else. I could read you a story which isn't very long, I think, the opening of the *Ishmael*, which is the closest I ever got to being successful in the movies. In fact, this book had a great history, because it brought me to Hollywood, where I sat around waiting for Mr Warner to return from the Côte d'Azur, and then interrupted by his desire to see the World Series, meanwhile I had little money, but then here was my golden chance, because I was going to be asked to advise on John Huston's *Moby-Dick*, because of this book, which was about as silly a—then, you see, there are some people that might think that *Ishmael* has something to do with existenz, and at least Mr Huston was interested in existenz, as you know, his movies like *The Treasure of Sierra Madre*, which you'll see tomorrow night. But, curiously enough, the real success I had was with a much more interesting director, who read this story and said, "I'll make it into a movie, if you'll write it as a movie." And, if you want to hear it, it's one of the desperate stories I think it's possible to hear. But it's a sea narrative, and that's always kind of palatable. The director was Jean Renoir, and, as a Frenchman, it was clear that he didn't understand. Would that be a good way to—unless—how would that sit with you all?

STUDENT: That's good.

OLSON: We can cut out, or do otherwise, if you'd like. I don't have time, I'm running. Can anybody tell me what time it is?

STUDENT: Four o'clock.

OLSON: It's four? Oh. I think this takes about fifteen minutes, I should think. It's seven pages of … I open the book with it. It's called "First Fact as prologue."

> [Reads "First Fact" from *Call Me Ishmael*. After a break in the
> tape, the conversation continues concerning Melville's grand-
> daughter, Eleanor Melville Metcalf]

In 1921, when Raymond Weaver wrote the first biography of Melville, he went to her for materials, and one night they went up in the attic and opened that cake box for the first time, and there was the manuscript of *Billy Budd*. It was never published, and never known to exist, until then. I've looked at that manuscript, but I've never made the studies that a man named Freeman, in particular, and Jay Leyda have made of it. And Freeman published a book, which you can buy now, I bought it myself in paper. The paperback edition of *Billy Budd* is Freeman's edition, originally published by Harvard Press. It's a very interesting study, I think. I've reviewed that, by the way, in a piece of prose that's going to be published in this book, for *Western Review*. And I argue a big case there. The title of the piece is called "Hawthorne, Homosexuality, and Hebraism." No, it isn't. The title is "David Young, David Old": but the real pitch is Hawthorne, Homosexuality, and Hebraism, because *Billy Budd* is a novel of a pretty boy who is loved by a

Master of Arms aboard a ship, and the love is scorned by Billy, and the Master of Arms accuses Billy of being the ringleader of a mutiny aboard the ship; and Billy, who's a completely unflawed apple of cheek and everything else: Virtue. But he has one impediment, his speech: and as a result, his muscles act faster than his mind. So he clouts Claggart, and kills him. So then the Captain is stuck with the problem of trying this thing not only as possibly the mutineer but actually as a murderer aboard a vessel. So he hangs Billy from a yardarm. It's a parable, allegory, everything else. And I myself think that Freeman's argument that it was originally a short story, and that as a short story it was very powerful; then Melville decided to try to make it a short novel, which he did, and the manuscript is the second thing, the short novel ...

STUDENT: It's not *Redburn*, is it?

OLSON: *Redburn* is before *Moby-Dick*. It's a beautiful—you know that book? It's a knockout.

STUDENT: In relation to *Billy*?

OLSON: Yeah, I think not anything of meaning at all, really, again by that fact that a whole Hawthorne thing, that whole homosexuality thing, and that whole Hebraic thing is all on the later story. And *Redburn* is marvelous, simply as a story of an American boy of his period who goes to sea and is therefore just shoved right down into the filth of life. And it's actually, it's called—the title of that book is called *Redburn*, which is the name of the boy, *Or, the Story of a Gentleman*. It's a funny subtitle, because the whole story is the bitterness of Melville's having, from his own point of view, fallen, due to his father's failure in business in Albany, from a social class that he was born into to becoming simply a normal—I mean, like, in this damn society, I mean, mind you, the democracy is an old thing, like. I think it's a marvelous book. In that poem again, "Hey! Jackson!" is a smash out of that. Jackson is the Claggart of *Redburn*. There are those kind of fictional relationships between the two books.

STUDENT: Charles, do you know is it Maxwell Anderson who did the play of *Billy Budd*?

OLSON: No, no, it's two young men, Louis Coxe, who's now at Bowdoin, and the guy who's now the head of the theater at Harvard, Robert Chapman. They wrote the play of *Billy Budd*.

STUDENT: What did you think of that?

OLSON: I never saw it. Don't know a thing about it. Never read it either. No, don't know a thing about it.

STUDENT: *Billy Budd* I know has been touted by some people as being Melville's peace with the world.

OLSON: Yeah. Well, when I said in that piece I read that only once did he manage to skip out of that prison of the Semitic notion of Transcendence—

believe you me, Melville's problem with God was somewhat an old-fashioned Puritan concept of God. But then, Melville was a big psyche, and the Old Man up there was his own old man, like, and that kind of stuff, and he was wrapped up. And *Billy*, the interesting thing about *Billy* is the Captain, De Vere, who again, if John was here, listen to that for "Truth": Captain Truth of the vessel. And Pa and God and Truth were all authority. By the way, if you ever want to get Melville where he's younger and less organized in a sense, as he is in *Billy*—*Billy* is the only organized sort of a managed formalized literary achievement, in a sense, yeah? Otherwise, his forms are open forms—but "The Lightning-Rod Man," a short story by Melville of a guy who sells lightning-rods up and down the Berkshires and the Vermont area, you ought to read that, because actually it's clearly Zeus [LAUGHTER], and the story is just the most wonderful manipulation of allegory, again, because the guy is no more than a guy going around from farm to farm up and down these valleys selling lightning-rods to farmhouse wives when their husbands are in the field; and, gee, it's too much, that story. Another one, by the way, of his is "I and My Chimney," which has to do with his house in Pittsfield, which had this chimney. The biggest chimney in New England, I think, still, is that one down there. I've been down in the basement of that house; it's a pyramid that chimney, and the base of the pyramid is wider, is almost as wide as the cellar. It starts with a base that you'd never have seen, and it goes up on an angle through the house, and he writes this—well, a very beautiful scholar on Melville named Sealts from Yale has written the most interesting—almost equal to Lawrence's great passage on "The Cassock," the chapter called "The Cassock" in *Moby-Dick*, which is one of the greatest pieces of scholarship that—in fact, Lawrence is one of the greatest Melville scholars for having written that chapter alone. Nobody caught on, I think, like Lawrence did to what Melville was up to in that chapter called "The Cassock," marvelous essay by Lawrence. But Sealts on the "Chimney" is just too much again on this subject of Captain De Vere and the Poppa, Poppa, Father, and God thing.[13] He was Justice, you know, like the problem of justice in the world, like, that's De Vere's problem. He loves Billy. Billy's his son in the novel. Billy's perfect. He's just the captain of a vessel; but he's got responsibilities, yeah. So he hangs Billy; and boy, it's a man hanging his own child, there's no question about it. And Melville gets himself a big rise in being hung. You can feel that. That ending of that thing, which is pure Crucifixion, by the way, stolen right out of it, just, I mean, he's spreadeagled on a, isn't he? I think he's hung that way, he's spreadeagled, isn't he? But at least—or he's hung from, I guess he's just hung from a yardarm, but ...

AUDIENCE: Yeah, but the sun comes out.

OLSON: Yeah, the sun, yes, exactly. It's a resurrection, sure. Big moment, boy.

AUDIENCE: Melville never quit, even as an old man.

13. "Herman Melville's 'I and My Chimney'" is included in Merton M. Sealts, Jr, *Pursuing Melville, 1940–1980* (Madison: University of Wisconsin Press, 1982), pp. 11–22.

OLSON: No, no. No, no. Oh, no. Lord, no.

AUDIENCE: Did you see the movie that they made with Gregory Peck?

OLSON: Oh, sure. Yeah, sure.

AUDIENCE: How did you like the way they handled it? Did you have any reactions?

OLSON: No, unnaturalism. But then, if you know Huston's movies, like the one I'm always thinking of is, rather than *The Treasure of Sierra Madre* or the *Moby Dick*, is one with Katherine Hepburn and Bogart on that—*The African Queen*. Or the one he made, *Beat the Devil*, I think it is. He's a p-poor novelist, Huston; he really should have been a writer. He was a writer, you know, like. And if he'd only had to meet the problem where he really can't get away from trying, I mean, wishing he could, which is in novels, instead of making movies—I think always the literary is so present that even if he's a marvelous movie-maker that dishes the film, or you feel that statement thing coming in from existentialism. He really is, he's just a guy who admires Camus and Sartre and that vision of life; and it's hardly, it seems to me, got a goddamn thing to do with Herman Melville, as they say.

STUDENT: Do you think there's anyone else in American literature who's anywheres like Melville? I wonder if Crane wasn't sort of influenced by him very much.

OLSON: Yeah, sure. Yeah, absolutely. Yeah. Crane, of course, had the misfortune, in a sense, to be living at the time that naturalism was at its height, like, he's one of the great naturalists we have. But then "The Blue Hotel" is something that'll make your skin stand up.

STUDENT: There's a passage in "The Blue Hotel" that exactly parallels a passage in *Billy Budd*. Beautiful connection. It's a …

OLSON: Well, just think how few years there are between the writing of those two stories, do you realize that? Well, no, it's about ten to fifteen years, but it's a relatively small amount of time, yeah. It's very close. I've always, or due to Duncan, I've always—since I heard Duncan make the most beautiful piece on Gertrude Stein I've ever heard—you realize that Melville was alive until 1892 and writing—1891, I think—writing right up to the last minute, one of the manuscripts being *Billy Budd*; and Miss Stein's *Three Lives* is 1903. You know, I think it's hard for us to realize that the 19th century is woven into our lives, because we feel Miss Stein or Stephen Crane as being, belonging, similar to us; and Melville sounds like—surely most everybody has one of those, oh dear, even Henry James is closer than Melville.

AUDIENCE: Stein sort of makes an example of …

OLSON: Yeah. Yeah, well, that's the great date. If I'd mentioned *Three Lives*, I'd rather mention Planck's theory, it's 1901 or '2, isn't it? Maybe even 1897 is that. I stress this only because, really, I don't think we're disconnected at all, and those little years don't break at all. If the Melville line, if you feel the Melville line, for example, as against Whitman, I mean, I think he's a beautiful poet and all that, boy, I don't mean—that sounds, light, like I honestly—like, Whitman's just as alive. It's only in that other, the things that I've been talking about, that Melville seems more, feels to me more relevant, but …

AUDIENCE: Do you see any relationship between Conrad and Melville?

OLSON: Almost none, except the fact that they were both superb seamen once, obviously. I mean, they went to work on the sea, didn't they? Oh, absolutely none whatsoever. Bet and I were up at Maine summer before last, I guess, and I stayed with an old friend of mine whose son is a lobsterman, and in the house we had for a few days there was a copy of *The Nigger of the "Narcissus"*, which I had never read, so I'm really quite fresh on Conrad, I could talk—and it's painting. It's got nothing to do with literary art; it's just incredibly good painting, it's better than all sea painting, that's what it is, yeah, I mean, storms, and …

STUDENT: Have you read *Heart of Darkness*?

OLSON: Yeah, sure.

STUDENT: I've always had the feeling that it's great painting and yet he was doing more than that.

OLSON: Well, you know, every man eats, you know. Suddenly, now that you say it that way, I'm thinking of a man who read in Gloucester the other night; he's been a friend of ours for years, and he's a statistical analysist for Gorton-Pew Fisheries, and they had—I thought Duncan was going to be in, and I set up a reading for Duncan and he never showed up and I never heard from him. So I was going to go in and read him and Creeley; and the other people in town thought it would be better if they asked three writers to read, three other writers, and they did. And this guy read a thing called *Prologos*, a chapter, the opening of his novel; and this man believes in Conrad, I mean, has that feeling for Conrad. I suspect Conrad's really his master, and this piece of a novel I'm going to try to get published, it's so crazy good, like.[14] What does, you know, what does it make? Who's your man? If he's your man, that's the lot. These values are really, you know, like, that's literary history and literary criticism. I don't think it relates. For me, Conrad is not at all as interesting. Psychologically, I think he's a bore of character; physically I think he's got the sea and the painting world, you know, these things. And, like, Mr Melville turneth me on, that's all.

WINER: You mentioned the homosexuality in *Billy Budd*, not a physical contact, but a feeling of love towards one of his own sex. Does this permeate Melville's work, because I seem to recall several references of this nature in *Moby-Dick*?

OLSON: Oh, tremendous. And if you know *Clarel*, the novel, or the poem on the death of Hawthorne, the poem called "Monody":

14. *Prologos* by Jonathan Bayliss was finally published in 1999 by Basilicum Press, Ashburnham, Massachusetts, as part of his "Gloucesterman" series.

To have known him, to have loved him
   After loneness long;
 And then to be estranged in life,
   Ease me, a little ease, my song!

And the second stanza is, because Hawthorne died up here at Crawford Notch and is buried there, and he's buried in the snow, and the vine image is "the vine that hid the shyest, cloistral grape." The imagery of vine and grape—the leading character of *Clarel*, outside of Clarel, the story-teller, the hero and story-teller, is Vine. Melville is a man of such archetypalism, by the way, that his—again, if we only had—why didn't a person like Chuck not come today? It's dopey. Probably he spent a whole afternoon on these problems and we can pick it up again. Let me come—I'm just answering you: is that the proper nouns, like Vine and the image "shyest, cloistral grape" are where Melville's, where the seams in his psyche that had to do with homosexuality are all—they flow towards, they flow like in his lifetime and friendship, towards Hawthorne, they flow right on the same vein out to David and Jonathan, which is the biggest imagery he's got as of the relationship of men. He cries out in the middle of *Billy Budd*: "I can't use David as my hero because you've all lost touch with the Old Testament, so I got to use Lord Nelson as my image of the authority that De Vere has to use. You know that marvelous passage right smack out still in the novel. It's such an angry passage about how completely crippling the condition of man is now that he's lost touch with the Old Testament, which had all that imagery and all that swell and swelter in it of the possibilities of life in a human being.

AUDIENCE: Was this caused primarily because of his sailing?

OLSON: Well, I'm sure he got a good—he must have had his—he must have had his ... No, no, on the contrary, oh boy, oh boy, there's no evidence whatsoever that Herman was a homosexual in the active sense.

AUDIENCE: No, I meant that he was involved.

OLSON: Well, I'm sure that, like Billy, he was a very—well, I describe him in that poem, he was—don't think Herman wasn't a little beauty. And you don't think a few seamen on board those vessels all those years weren't interested in said fact.

AUDIENCE: In the opening scenes, when he goes to bed with Queequeg.

OLSON: Yeah, I think that's always abused in ...

AUDIENCE: D.H. Lawrence pointed it out; he sees the beauty of the thing.

OLSON: He certainly does. Absolutely. Yeah, and I think that one is—but that's often abused, that passage, in this homosexual thing. All this other place that I'm working at the moment to answer Paul is really where it's really true, and where it's much more meaningful, and where Melville was engaged for his whole lifetime crucially. Believe you me, that friendship with Hawthorne is so beautiful simply because once in his life—you know, by the way, *Billy Budd* is inscribed to Captain John Chase of the maintop of the U.S. vessel, the *United States*, who was Melville's maintop captain when Melville was a sailor coming back a year and a half from Honolulu to Boston, and John Chase, I mean, John Chase is so obviously the figure of a man whom he really loved. Whatever furtherance that love had one doesn't know, but clearly there was another man beside Hawthorne in his life for whom the whole thing was going, and that was Chase, who was an older man than he by, I think, about ten years at the time they were aboard that vessel.

AUDIENCE: Do you think that if society had then condoned homosexuality, this would have changed both his writing and his personality?

OLSON: Not at all, not at all. Absolutely no. I don't believe that social change has anything but superficial effects upon these matters. I think these matters are locked in nature and reality and in life. And I don't even care for a human race that would be removed from them by becoming a new species, personally.

Charles Olson and Robert Creeley at Warren and Ellen Tallman's house in Vancouver, summer 1963. Photo courtesy Karen Tallman.

2

On History

Robert Creeley had been visiting lecturer at the University of British Columbia for the year 1961–62 and Warren Tallman was on the permanent faculty: the two of them set in motion the month-long summer course which in the annals of the New American Poetry became known as the Vancouver Poetry Conference of 1963. The reverberations of this event might be measured in the fact that the audience for this discussion of history on the morning of 29 July 1963 included not only local writers George Bowering, Judith Copithorne, Lionel Kearns, Gladys Hindmarch, Daphne Marlatt, Robert Hogg, Jamie Reid, and Fred Wah, but also Linda Wagner, Edward Van Aelstyn, Michael Palmer, David Schaff, Drummond Hadley, Larry Goodell, Clark Coolidge, Ronald Bayes, and David Bromige, all of whom, it is safe to say, would declare the occasion memorable. (Extracts from some of their notebooks were published in *OLSON* 4.)

Robert Creeley, Robert Duncan, Allen Ginsberg, and Philip Whalen were also at the table, but this was Olson's moment, and his intention was clearly to found the summer community from the start on the principle of immediacy: it is present facts that are the reality, and history is only what you can bring into the room from the past that is meaningful to yourself and can be made useful to others. Olson offers as text for the day a recently published piece called "Place; & Names," prose as dense as poetry and formatted as such, but included all the same in the *Collected Prose*. The one place mentioned, the "Place Where the Horse-Sacrificers Go," shows the extraordinary dimension Olson is giving to the immediate. It is the "horizon where the sky and the sea meet, between the two shells of the world egg" and there is union with Brahman at the back of the sky, through a gap "as broad as the edge of a razor." This comes from Jung's *Symbols of Transformation* (p. 422). It is this kind of "experiential" place which is "worth more than a metropolis—or, for that matter, any moral concept." From the university's promontory at the Pacific's edge, a break-through was imminent.

CHARLES OLSON: Why don't you pick up from where you last left off? Where did you leave off on Friday?

ALLEN GINSBERG: I was joining the Communist Party.

OLSON: You were? All right, go ahead. That'll start it.

ROBERT CREELEY: I would like to center on the question of context, in what context does language operate, in terms of what is the ground that you literally walk on, in no metaphoric sense, but actually. Because I think the first day we were here the poems were still isolated from quote "actual events" unquote, and I'd like to take it not so much into the whole business of what you can do with a poem, where you can put it or hang it on the wall, but where, what is, "history"?

OLSON: Why don't I kick it off by reading a short piece, which is the last sort of feeling or thought of my own, as far as that kind, which was published in—it was written January 5, 1962, I see—but was in *Yugen* 8, I think; was called "Place; & Names."

> a place as term in the order of creation
> & thus useful as a function of that equation
> example, that the "Place Where the Horse-Sacrificers Go"
> of the Brihadaranyaka Upanishad is worth more than
> a metropolis—or, for that matter, any moral
> concept, even a metaphysical one
>   and that this is so
> for physical & experiential reasons of
> the

(which is the only thing I don't like in this thing)

> the *philosophia perennis*, or Isness
> of cosmos beyond those philosophies
> or religious or moral systems of
> rule, thus giving factors of naming
> —nominative power—& landschaft
> experience (geography) which stay truer
> to space-time than personalities
> or biographies of such terms as specific
> cities or persons, as well as the inadequacy
> to the order of creation of anything except
> names—including possibly mathematics (?)

(a question mark there)

> the crucialness being that these places or names
> be as parts of the body, common, & capable
> therefore of having cells which can decant
> total experience—no selection
> other than one which is capable
> of this commonness (permanently
> duplicating) will work

"Story" in other words is if not superior
at least equal to ultimate mathematical
language—perhaps superior because of
cell-ness (?) In any case history
(as to be understood by Duncan's Law
to mean a) histology & b) story)
applies here, in this equational way
& severely at the complementarity of
cosmos (complementary to individual
or private) and not to cities or
events in the way it has, in
a mistaken secondary way, been
understood.

Right, now, I'd like to answer any …

GINSBERG: I don't understand what you're saying. [LAUGHTER]

OLSON: Well, let's find out, then. Let's find out, Allen. Let's see if we can make you understand.

GINSBERG: What's that all about? First of all, what's Duncan's Law? I never heard of Duncan's Law.

OLSON: Well, I immediately state it. Obviously the word "history" is a word, unless you take it to root, which doesn't have any use at all. And the root is the original first use of it, in the first chapter if not the first paragraph of Herodotus, in which he says, "I'm using this as a verb *'istorin*, which means to find out for yourself; and this is why I've been all over the goddamn Middle East and down into Egypt, been taught by the great Fathers of Egypt the ancient learning, and have learned everything I possibly could about the Persian War, and now I'm going to tell you about it." So, what he starts off to tell you about is history before the Trojan War, which is how the first Helen was taken by somebody and brought out from some place to that place, and then there was trouble because this woman was seized by these plundering sailors, and that was the beginning of that. In fact, in the moment of the invention of the word, you get almost the moment of the invention of some supposed division between Europe and Asia. It's a very curious fact that you can even peg the thing down to the word's moment of first use and the division of the so-called continent on one side and a continent that's coming on the other. And what Duncan did, it seemed to me, in that—was that a letter to me?[1] He divided it into—it's a hell of a lot further than any pun ever was—histology, or the study of cells, and story, story in the sense that the only thing that really counts, again, is what's so exciting. After all, Herodotus goes around and finds out everything he can find out, and then he tells a story. It's one of the reasons why I trust him more than, say, Thucydides, who basically is reporting an event. We all go through this all the time, don't we? I mean, we have the Thucydidean. Not

1. Duncan letter to Olson, 18 December 1961. Olson replied on 22 December 1961: "I am wholly prepared to accept your division of that wild word history into histology and story: I never could force that word *'istorin* on even myself!"

too long ago, if you went to war you had a story. Oh boy, isn't every war sup-posed to produce a new literature, I guess. Well, it'll produce a Thucydidean literature. But a good old-fashioned man like Herodotus, he just went to find out really what was up, what's going on, what was said about the thing. And, in fact, as you well know, he's talking about a war that the Greeks went through themselves in his—no, not in his generation, one generation earlier, the Persian War. So, that idea of breaking that word so that we don't talk about a concept "history"—that's why I offered the damn thing is to break up that word immediately, break it back to either a verb of Herodotus, which, as some of you know, I've put a whole lot of weight on in working on a longer, a "long" poem, like they say.[2] And I found that, when Robert took that split and did introduce the idea, that the minuteness that you're after is the histology, and the result that you may come up with is story. O.K.?

Because, honestly, many of the conversations we've had, as I said to you last night, is all political history. And, unless I'm in great error, political has to turn out to be also an etymon of great power, a word which I don't want to mention, but it is the word on which the word "politics" also exists. I mean, either we're men of language in the real sense that language is the life that we're producing—and, by god, to my mind, the event of language—I would say that the thing that we're after is etymons, all over the place.

GINSBERG: What?

OLSON: Etymon. The right word. The root. The word in its rightness of its root. Not at all the usages, the behaviors of the word, but the actual thing that it is. Yeah? And that thing in itself is where we really have a chance to put our hand out and grab ahold of something. Otherwise we're simply getting caught in the event either of the society, which is one form of what's boringly called "history," or the event of ourselves, which is also that damn boring thing called "personal history." Now, mind you, at any other point, if I could support it, I think the piece can be always be exposed by the same rule of order: that it is "logographic," it's made up of words. That piece is made up of words.

GINSBERG: Was history made out of words too?

OLSON: Not at all, absolutely not. We've missed the point again.

ROBERT DUNCAN: This is an event in words, which is different from an event in history. This swings back to the other day. Someone here asked a ques-tion about care and attention, and we did get that the only place you have any care or attention is right where you are, right where you are in the poem or right where you are in the event. That's why you're misled if you're asked to participate in an event where it isn't there. Which you're always asked. This is the great shuffle game of cards: how do you feel about—but you aren't there. You can't be responsible to any event except the one you're in.

CREELEY: Williams's dilemma in *Paterson*, in terms of this context, was that he was straddling. He was trying to make up a city. He was involved with

2. *The Maximus Poems*, especially "Letter 23" (1.99).

histology, but then he'd get involved with concepts prior to looking. It's like saying, "I know what's there," but you don't know what's there unless you're walking in the particulars of what's there, or here—there's no "there" in the context of history. There's only "here" you can only walk in the facts.

GINSBERG: What to do, then, with what is called "past history" that's not going on right now?

DUNCAN: There's no place that the past can take place except right now when we consider it. The past has no other existence. It has only existence as it is right present. I've quoted enough times Whitehead's lovely "The congress of saints is a great august body and it had no place to meet except right here." No place else in the universe to meet. It can only happen now. The future can only happen now. Both of these things are very, very real only because they're present.

GINSBERG: In other words, I don't have to worry about …

CREELEY: Any more! [LAUGHTER]

OLSON: Well, it's fun, because Allen said to me he thought that one of the things he wanted to do, besides joining the Communist Party, was to go to Laos. And not at all "to see a war." But to see: Is there a war? Was it a war? Is it? Whatever. What is it? And that seems the real act which one is talking about here, which is you just want to find out for yourself what really this whole thing amounts to, and the only way you can do it is go there. I told that story in a letter to Creeley.[3] I walked into a store in Lerma, Yucatan, one night, to get some cigarettes. The people had closed those double doors, but I knocked. I could see the light through the crack, and they allowed it was a gringo, so they let me in. The husband and wife were just knocking off for the night, and they were looking at this Mexico City paper. They were obviously utterly fascinated. For the first time here was a television ad, double page normal American spread for TV, with one of those things pictured and something, action on the screen. And the guy says, "Gee, you—" Like, I had no Spanish, but I listened as well as I could. But he says, "You know. You could tell us. Yeah, you're an American. *Posible vídeo la guerra?*" I mean, with great excitement: "This means we can all be watching the war going on on the battlefield?" It seemed to me the wayest-out incitement of what you might call the natural human impulse, which you seem to be following by going to Laos, Vietnam, that was hoping that, "Gee, with this new thing we can really all sit down and watch the goddamn thing being fought out." And in a curious way that term was very exciting to me because I realize what expectations we all have from the facilities that have—and actually the great hunger is still that marvelous one to get there and find out, uh? And all that's really going on at this moment, as far as any of us are concerned at this moment, is just what's going on here, with all the recidivism or anything else that we're carrying.

3. Letter of 20 February 1951 in *Mayan Letters*, reprinted in *Selected Writings*, p. 76 and *Olson-Creeley Correspondence* 5, pp. 32–33.

PHILIP WHALEN: There's a lovely song about let's watch World War Three on pay TV, before the television melts away. [LAUGHTER]

GINSBERG: Actually, you see, we're talking all the time at home, so half the conversation is now elliptical here. But what was linking up was we all came in and said we were all bankrupt to begin with. Like, our history was finished, mine, say, as a Beatnik; Creeley as a writer of exquisite little poems [LAUGHTER]; Duncan as a nasty old aesthetician; and Olson as some kind of father figure has now become a great baby. [LAUGHTER] And I don't know what's going to emerge out of "monster" Whalen. Our history is finished, so now we've decided everybody's is. Has anybody any objection to this total abolition? [LAUGHTER]

OLSON: I, absolutely.

DUNCAN: The main thing that's happened in Ginsberg's world is that from a vocabulary that consisted of "we" and "they," it has now gotten to the place where it's all "we." [LAUGHTER]

CREELEY: As late as the forties at least, when, say, Allen and I went to school, history was the justification of all attitude. I think what has accumulated is that this as a measure is no longer accurate. I'm curious to know why. What Charles was saying the other evening is that McNamara, Secretary of Defense, can now, by all measures that exist—and they're pretty accurate in terms of these relationships or in these areas of concern—can now say nothing will or can happen …

OLSON: I think many of you must have seen it. I twist it a little bit, because what I do say he says is that nothing is going to happen to us in our lifetime. It isn't quite what he said, but as far as I can see it's just exactly a guarantee that really all our worries and fears and the danger has been really organized and set aside, so that there is nothing in our lifetime.[4] And it's said with that—really, you just really think: "Yeah, I guess you probably know, like." Number one. And two: "I guess you're in the position—if you are there, you is the guy we's expecting to write this guarantee." And, like, he does come out of the Second World War; he learned all that new comptometry that developed in the Air Force Ordering Service of the Second World War; and he proved that you can take that thing anywhere. Well, he took it here now. That seems to me to pair exactly again with that song you're quoting, and the expectations of those wonderful Lermeros. We can save all the trouble: we can cut across and be free from any of that stuff.

CREELEY: There's a double action. This again reinforces the sense that there is no other occasion, no other reference for measure except that which is "to find out for yourself." There is nothing that can propose a reference beyond this context.

OLSON: But Bob, may I interrupt you to say that I think there's one dirty thing that's happened now to that thing, that "finding out for yourself": it's got a

4. The *New York Times* of 5 April 1963 had reported Robert S. McNamara as predicting that the Soviet Union would not equal the U.S. economically or militarily "in our lifetime."

patent on it. It sounds as though, if you find out for yourself, you then can do anything. To some extent it's true. One of the exciting things I think that Allen is referring to when he says we're all bankrupt is that we all have become really new, in a crazy sense that we have this patent. My own experience is that most everyone, say, in this room already has proved that they do have plenty of competence to do some things, which they do remarkably, and better, probably, than single individuals of the human race did just a short while ago, in practically any other form. I mean it in your word "context," I think: a thing which held, or proposed, or supported, or shaped. Like, McNamara does not support us in that remarkable protection, right? It just doesn't support us at all. In fact, on the contrary, it accomplishes the end of destruction, which is it destroys us sitting right here. It really just says we're all dreaming right through into some moment later, when this sort of thing will have gone away. It's—what is it?—it's wish-magic, brand new modern wish-magic. Just get rid of it. I think there's a deep split. And the only thing I'm interested in is what do you do. I mean, what do you do that I—if you find it interesting, that's O.K., but there is a production point: what do you do that's interesting to somebody else?

WHALEN: That Williams quote: "not what do you do but what are you doing now."[5]

OLSON: Aw, I hate that participle. I think it's gone the other way entirely. I can prove in case after case—I've seen it even over this weekend—people of absolute interest and importance in what they got their mind on and what they're doing. Well, let's take it on the basis of what we're here for. Show me your paper, and my judgment may be utterly wrong but at least I can experience what you put on a piece of paper. If that's what you're here for, then that at least is what we're here for to do. Again, we come back to the business that this is the incidence of which we are a part at this moment. I think there's a big choice question here. Does anyone need to write? Why write? I mean, really, unless you do? And why do you write? I heard that the first day Robert and Allen sat here saying exactly the mechanics of how they write, what they prefer to have around them. Magic, again. Setting. What situation is the one that you like best? That's great. What else have we got to talk about except how is it that you are around that you get something done with? And if you don't produce writing that's interesting, then I'm sure you ought to be doing—or haven't found out, even if, maybe.

WHALEN: Well, suppose it came to Allen to write about the war if he hadn't taken the trouble to go look at it?

CREELEY: These journals, these poems that Allen's now writing are operating on the very same principle as Pausanias's walking down the street and seeing what's there. That's the way they work.

5. "In Europe [as opposed to the American 'What do you do?'] they would ask ... What are you doing now?"—William Carlos Williams, *Paterson*, p. 60.

GINSBERG: The present event is also, in a sense, TV and other media coming in on us.

OLSON: Yeah, sure. But I think now again we're back at the very important thing that Duncan is talking about when he quotes that Whitehead on "the congress of saints." You are only capable of doing that because you are yourself in the experience of that other purpose. It isn't because you're a historian. I mean it in the best sense: it isn't because you're a historian.

DUNCAN: You really have to be enacting in order for this thing to be. So any place, with any kind of data, including looking at or hearing the *muthos*, what they say about it—Vietnam has got to happen in you or happen in me for it to happen, but it's also going to be happening—you can be in the middle of even an explosion, and if you're not interested, it isn't happening. For you. Everybody else can watch you to pieces, and clap, but ... The thing Charles is talking about: when it's on paper there, the poem has really moved out so that not only I can look at a poem but you could also look at a poem of yours. But one thing that happens with poets is—and especially at the beginning—the poem's there, then they aren't interested in the poem; so, as far as they're concerned, the poem doesn't happen. I've had people's poems happen for me that never happened for the people concerned. Then they say: "How did you see that in there?" Well, you say: "If you'd look, you'd see something in there, but you're obviously not interested in the poem you wrote, which is interesting." There's not a damn piece of writing that isn't interesting. Where the writer's not interested, you just have to take that piece of writing and you really do have to become a super-detective, because everything has been obscured, twenty million interferences have happened. You decently go as far as you can to know as completely as you can. I asked that guy Crick what criterion is there. Well, he said he thought science had the criterion of completeness. I went, and sat home and thought, "What is completeness?" Well, all right, but here we can say a poem can be given the same criterion: that you are working toward completely knowing what is present in this poem that you're looking at. And when you completely know, any other human being can; because it isn't a matter of clickety-clickety, big brains, little brains. It's simply a matter of being concerned with the event that's there. Bob and Allen said they were stuck in school in history; but in school they never saw history. They weren't stuck in Herodotus when they were "stuck in history." This is what we're trying to get around. "Chronology" I guess they were in. Williams gets mixed up between the history, which he gets, but he also thinks that he's responsible to chronology. In other words, he gets his story false because he is tied to "this happened after this happened after this happened" is a story. Well, it is a story, at a level; but that isn't the story he's after. Just like he's tricked by taking over from *Finnegans Wake* all the business about the head is this part of the city and the feet are this part of the city and the body, all of that. Why he loaded that on, it was just a carapace for the thing, a surrounding; because he wasn't going to go at it straight. And then he's going at it straight: when he discovered the library, and that there was a fire, that's a discovery. That has nothing to do with the beginning, the end, the middle sort of thing. There was a fire. All right, then that date counts everything about it, that he gets that library right, and, wow, he's away. That would be the particular—but the false one is … You've got your falsies on …

OLSON: Well, all right. You call it the false one; but a hell of a lot of *Paterson* is this false one. As a matter of fact, I think that was probably where Bill was much more himself involved in his poem than in his successes; in the sense that what he was searching for in trying to create this man of the Falls, that Mr Paterson or whatever he calls him, that figure, yeah, was a thing that was for Bill, inside, of greatest moment. I think if he knew how to get that identity, or stature, Mr Paterson is a figure which will give him himself the satisfaction of filling. And in fact the "falsie" is obviously a little more of a thing to him than a "falsie." I think you can talk with great dryness and literalness about how come he was on that search, and what it requires to be on that search. And we'll come back again to the histology, cell matter, not in that dumb completeness sense but the completeness for Bill Williams of his figure.

DUNCAN: All his particulars work. He found so-and-so leaped from the Falls. It operates everywhere; everything he found in that thing works.

OLSON: Right, and there is that crazy last passage of the river washing all to the sea, where the thing suddenly becomes one of the craziest clichés.

DUNCAN: As long as the river's language, as long as the river's the rhetoric, that works.

CREELEY: Let's take, say, three instances of an attempt to find the order of event on the one hand and the order of recognition on the other. Go back to Eliot's *The Waste Land*, where you have a very simplified chronology, where history is …

DUNCAN: I don't think there's any history in *The Waste Land*. Listen, Jessie Weston was the one who was a historian, so he borrowed. I don't think that *The Waste Land* was concerned with history. It was concerned with telling the story of the adultery, and masking it because it was painful. He's got contained in there his own fury: he's working at the bank, and his wife, who is a nymphomaniac, is … And he can wear the mask: it's a play; it's a charade is what it is, and a charade is not history. But this doesn't make it not genuine. Let's say its interest in history is minimal. It wears historical costumes, and that's not the same thing. There was a dominant idea in the twenties that they were in a wasteland, which shows that it had historical force too.

CREELEY: You can't be in a wasteland without having history. I wasn't thinking of it in terms of the method, but rather of how to place oneself.

OLSON: Yeah, well, now let's talk about "currentness." As a matter of fact, I think, on the contrary, that what really hides in the word "history," and actually "political history," the dopey meaning, is more in truth today than it was when some of its sense was actually in lives. There's no sense in lives today. There is suddenly this enormous thing, "currentness," which is actually placing people around only in their own behavior and expression of energy. And in the future of that lies actually any chance to both change this society and to emerge again into history in the sense that I feel the word has (which I don't believe Bill in his great works ...): "to tribe." I mean, let's not forget that that guy wrote that *American Grain*. Remember the time when you showed me that Sam Houston passage? I think Houston, by the way, was kind of the real poppa of Bill; that is, he was the guy, of all the American heroes to Bill, who seemed to do what Bill would like to have done, in that funny way in which he became an Indian. He lost his wife, didn't he? Isn't he the one that gave up the governorship of Tennessee because something didn't go on between them? And he allowed her to divorce him, and therefore became no longer a valuable political property. Then went back. Having been a Cherokee, I think, at fifteen, he then took off for the West and became a Cherokee again; and then re-emerged in the Texan Rebellion, and became the first President of the Texas Republic before she'd been brought into the United States. Now, the shifting, the very beautiful shift ... John?

JOHN KEYS: Wasn't it Houston that left the Alamo too? Wasn't this an important point?

OLSON: Oh, I was—you've stolen my thunder, man. O.K. Jesus, I'm here to give as much as I can. Yeah, it's a beautiful story. How many miles away can you hear the guns, by the way? What's earshot when you do it like he did it? Do you know the story that we're referring to? Houston did one of those beautiful things. The Alamo was really a lousy story, like. Here these guys were, and the whole goddamn Mexican army is going to come and smash 'em. Well, Houston rushed off to the provisional capital of Texas, at that time, which was over east, and I've forgotten how many miles away. And he got nothing out of the Representatives, so he said, "Jesus, we can't stay here, we're going back." He took himself and his orderly or friend or guide, and they were going to go back at least to be there when that thing happened. And he was scared because he knew the time to even go and get a force to help was small, and he was nervous. I think they traveled about three or four hours till sunset, and he got off his horse—as I remember the story, it's a hundred miles from the Alamo—and he put his ear down on the ground like a well trained Indian, and he read the actual moments of the Alamo battle's end from his ear on the ground. He could tell from the cannonade of the final charge, and then nothing happened, then he knew from that cannonade that Alamo had fallen. Do I have it fairly within range of the actual report of this thing?

KEYS: Well, yeah. The question arises now: Is that *'istorin* or is that Herodotus reading from the ground? I mean, is it of that importance?

OLSON: Oh, I think it's terribly important. It's relevant exactly to each one of us. What are we capable of in terms of really catching, with what means we got, any possible message or event, if we're interested, if we're an interested party, like. I want to bring the Houston case to bear on Bill Williams, because Bill's search for some figure or "measure," to use that word which I guess he invented, uh? Because really the measure in Bill was not in the verse question at all. It was in this other place. Now, the real question, it seems to me, that's mooted here is: Do you think there's a measure that has in it this thing that has been called story and histology? Is there in that thing a measure? You can kick it or not, I think.

CREELEY: Robert Duncan told me, in a letter that he got one time from him, Williams spent the whole body of the letter discussing "measure." The real measure consisted of a P.S. at the very end saying: "What are your family arrangements?" [LAUGHTER] This was the measure. And I was thinking Charles, in a book called *Mayan Letters*,[6] states that the ego system, in other words, Pound, is the company he keeps, the words he develops for this company, all the ways he tries it on, his insistent qualification of activity coming up to some degree of *intelletto*. But yet, that always depends upon the quality of the man speaking, which is finally not good enough. It's man-standing-by-his-word. All these measures are arbitrary to the actual life which may be going on along with this premise. So, what I'm getting to now is: "to find out for one's self"—what can we use for measure this time? You said it was "completeness." What is "completeness"? There is no "completeness."

OLSON: That's a beautiful thing when Pound recently said: "All my life I thought I had something to say."[7] And that's a very powerful thing, because it seems to me that we can even use that to speak of all that we're talking about right now; in fact, to meet that lady who's talking about those three men, who talked all the time, by the way, as far as I know. I don't know how much Buddha talked, but certainly Socrates and Christ talked like mad. As far as I know, that's what they did. Their life was a life of talk. Let's not make a literaryism to get in here at all; it's silly. There is this tremendous record of Christ's talking. He was obviously one of the sharpest talkers that's been on the earth yet, and what he had to say is worth listening to, and we got the record of it. What's the concern about the literary, the problem against having something to say? I don't think there's anybody here that's writing that isn't doing it because they feel they have something to say; and if it should break down, you won't write; but you also won't have anything to say, I do believe.

WHALEN: Well, that reminds me about Gertrude Stein, about "Some day there will be a history of each one who is now living." How does that go?

---

6. *Selected Writings*, pp. 81–84; *Olson-Creeley Correspondence* 5, pp. 49–51.
7. Olson had seen a *Time* magazine report (12 April 1963) of an interview with Pound where he said: "I was always wrong. I lived all my life thinking I knew something; then a day came when I realized I didn't know anything."

DUNCAN: God, it goes on for ten pages. [LAUGHTER] I used to be able to recite it because I had the record.

GINSBERG: Isn't that: "A history of each and everyone down to the minutest particular"?

WHALEN: But anyway, the idea that history is some place ahead, like we were talking about the other day: Some day history will be.

OLSON: I think that has come, as a matter of fact. And I think one of the errors of our whole conversation is that we're leaving out what transposes that, which is exactly that the minutest particulars are now the only thing that's interesting, and that if you don't get that registered—and we're all in the process of finding out how the hell can you make language and/or act register that. It's curious that Crick should use that word "complete," because I'd like to take it all away from him and science, where it's really been, by the way; and in fact the terror of that registration that you're bringing up is that it's possible today to produce human beings who are— the history of that person is so completely known that everything they're going to do for their whole lifetime is usable. In fact, that's just the intention of the men who are getting the Nobel Prizes. There was five of them, about six months ago, in the *New York Times Book Review*, they all spoke out and said exactly what kind of an absolutely dependable human being—and I don't mean in that bullshit of industrial employment—I mean the real creation of a species who has a history so well known that they are without fear, they are utterly capable of anything that's called human, and that the biggest hang-up, the proposed biggest hang-up of the human race is that it's still primitive because it knows fear, and it's about time we got rid of that one. And these boys are in laboratories getting rid of it. I mean, I think the "completeness" is completed. And the completeness that we really are opening up here is the only thing which matters, which is that you damn well have something to say and/or do that is of such effect that it is complete in its occurrence, and it just bombs—to use the verb the way we use it—it bombs the thing right then and there, and frees it for any person that isn't yet themselves complete. And those who are "complete" in that other sense are really not here; they aren't going to be here, unless we effect a real change of the society or of the imagined human thing; so that we topple in on them, as I think those men that lady mentions sure toppled in on what- ever was going on at their time. The direct line is the lesson of the master to you, isn't it? How did the man called Christ drop off between Tuesday and Thursday and come back in on Thursday? One knows damn well that he made some decision in Bethany that caused him to walk right back in Thursday and take what he had himself provoked. No? I think we can be rather precise in this whole story. Paul recorded his experience of Christ, and actually the four previous men were the story of Christ; and he created his history, Pauline Christianity, as against, by the way, the great unspoken critic, Peter. Petrism is one of the biggest un—I mean, it took Dostoevsky to create Shatov to give you any lead at all on Peter, this enormous figure, who

is the biggest opacity, blockhead, shape. But, lookit, he's the guy whom Christ really did choose. I mean, he said, "That's my man, that Peter." But nobody got a story about Peter. The only thing we know is he crucified himself upside down; except we do have only those pieces of him that come into the Christ story. It's wonderful to talk Petrism, instead of these—these are religious arguments instead of interesting relevances of where we are. I believe that one could take a good shot at saying that history is the way time has a character of which we are the representatives. That is, there isn't any other way that you can get your hand on time as an interesting matter except by that word "history." It has the great advantage of giving a name to time that is really our name for time.

AUDIENCE: Do you think a person is responsible to history, the events around him?

OLSON: Not at all. What he does to history is where that history that has any meaning is occurring. What he does. That's why you do talk about those men who have imposed themselves upon time so that they changed it.

WHALEN: The responsibility is to persons, and not to this big abstract thing.

OLSON: All right, Philip, but don't worry; the abstraction isn't going to hurt nobody. I think without the damn word you're not going to have anything that's going to meet this. Time is going to slip away if you don't have that good, old-fashioned meaning of … Oh, god, I'm so obvious. How many centuries has history simply been the obvious means of the advance of national politics? I've always said it starts with Thucydides; and it was reacquired some time in what century?—the latter part of the 13th, I would think, almost to a tee.

DUNCAN: Yeah, when you pass chronicles, which were just events. Gregory of Tours, who writes a history to the French kings that we've got, and from there on everybody wants to have history.

OLSON: What's his date?

DUNCAN: I don't know. Flunk me, like they say, in Chronology. [LAUGHTER]

OLSON: I mean it only in the sense that there is a big piece here, that the 13th century—I mean, god, every one of us is educated with all this business of Aristotelianism coming in from Arabs in Spain, and the Bollingen are now publishing that goddamn Arab's historian, whom all those people say is the greatest …

DUNCAN: You mean Khaldun? He's better than *National Geographic.* All I remember is that Sicily had water rushing all over the place.

OLSON: I mean, it sounds just like Toynbee. And that's just what's happening: these big historians, epiphanic historians, are suddenly occurring all over the place; and actually it's worthless. We can date its coming in; we can date its source as much as that statement about Aristotle being what did come in at the same time. But that's not told us. We're told that Aristotle came in and created modern mind and science; but we're not told that history came in and created modern history. One of the things I'd love to do is to be sure that little trick and secret is exposed: that we've been riding for a long time with a history which is manipulated, and is probably the biggest hidden trick in the wicket. It's certainly been out from the second half of the 13th century until the middle of the 20th; and it's all over. But most of us are still cluttered with that exact six hundred years of shit. I would like to try to say that you do have to have a word on time that gives you this, and it isn't that thing at all that we've had for six hundred years.

GINSBERG: How did history come in and create history?

OLSON: I tell you, I have only one little phrase—I've used it—it's from John Smith, and it is: "History is the memory of time." I find that thing I carry around in my pocket, and it's the only thing that yields light to me on this thing. It holds all that seems to me that's in the actual importance and possibility of the word, is that curious, pale statement: "History is the memory of time." I don't know whether it hits anybody, but it sure is the one that's hit me the most, and that I've carried to throw whatever it does for me.

GINSBERG: So history is not, in that sense, an existent thing, as we are. It is merely a memory.

OLSON: Yeah, but it is our memory. I mean, you take any one of the three words; the binding of the three words in that statement, it seems to me, becomes the whole lot. For example, if you act so that you are memorable, it is because your memory—and you have made it history—has imposed itself on time, which covers that wonderful intrusion of men in their time upon time. There is that beautiful idea of the Muslims that you're walking towards that angel—the actual occurrence is on Cinvat Bridge in the text. There is this angel who's coming towards you as you are coming towards him. And there's a moment when you pass through your angel and become the creature, not of the two, but of the fact that you are without any chance involved with another figure who is you, who is coming towards you in time as you proceed forward in time. And at the moment that you pass, you then are something that that angel was, and you're no longer that thing that you were. It is, again, one of the pictures that for me has had as much power on me as that funny statement of Smith's.

AUDIENCE: Isn't that the same idea as Themis, you really get the sense that …?

OLSON: I have trouble with that figure of Themis. I'm not sure we know even from Miss Harrison what that woman, Themis, is.

DUNCAN: Let's read the "Place; & Names" again.

CREELEY: Yes, relocate.

OLSON: I will. And in the light of what we've been talking about, and Robert's statement that if Allen did what he said he would do it would be like Pausanias, a curious thing happened. There's a poem which appears in published form as though it was the proof of the proposition. And for the hell of it, as long as I've got the proof in front of me, I'll continue, after rereading it, and read you the poem which is called "Bk ii chapter 37" and is simply a secret statement that it is book two, chapter thirty-seven of Pausanias. So, "Place; & Names":

> a place as term in the order of creation
> & thus useful as a function of that equation
> example, that the "Place Where the Horse-Sacrificers Go"
> of the Brihadaranyaka Upanishad is worth more than
> a metropolis—or, for that matter, any moral
> concept, even a metaphysical one

In other words, I think the lesson of that Upanishad is worth much more than any of the—that is, that becomes then a place, as such, and is of such teaching and use for me—and I believe for others, then, if it is of that order, that it's a greater chance and measure than, say, all the things that we call "place" usually.

> is worth more than
> a metropolis—or, for that matter, any moral
> concept, even a metaphysical one
> and that this is so for physical & experiential reasons of

(And I'd like to cut that next line.)

> of cosmos beyond those philosophies

That is just lousy cosmos, by the way. One can cut that thing in a million pieces. I mean, it's not far enough back, and it isn't true of now, by Duncan's law.

> of cosmos beyond those philosophies
> or religious or moral systems of
> rule, thus giving factors of naming
> —nominative power—& landschaft
> experience (geography) which stay truer
> to space-time than personalities
> or biographies of such terms as specific
> cities or persons, as well as the inadequacy
> to the order of creation of anything except
> names—including possibly mathematics (?)

In other words, I'm suggesting that I believe that names, and that certainly is our names, yes, and in fact, finally, it's your name, each one of our names, on that Angel Rule, is the only thing that really is a true thing equal to all that language that mathematics includes. There is really here something which is much more exciting than mathematics, which is that name that we are, and that we bring about.

DUNCAN: And that name is not general.

OLSON: Is not general. It's so specific that there ain't no other way that we as an individual really is, except that name.

> the crucialness being that these places or names
> be as parts of the body, common, & capable
> therefore of having cells which can decant
> total experience—no selection
> other than one which is capable
> of this commonness (permanently
> duplicating)

I'm just trying to get that commonness reduced to the very exciting truth that we are also simply duplications at the same time that we are this utter, utter particularity that nobody is going to take away from us, unless they do, right? But the other great thing is that we got the chance of it, and that's really where it's at.

> this commonness (permanently
> duplicating) will work

> "Story" in other words is if not superior
> at least equal to ultimate mathematical
> language

And that would be "story" in the sense that you are keeping journals or something. You prove it; you prove that your journal intrudes and changes everything that has happened up to now, so that things will happen differently in the future. That seems to me to be what that "story" is.

DUNCAN: Then they become part of the story.

OLSON: Yeah, in the real, in the very terrific sense that the story is to be carried on. We are going to tell the story, believe you me.

> "Story" in other words is if not superior
> at least equal to ultimate mathematical
> language—perhaps superior because of
> cell-ness(?)

Again, I'm really led to think that it's much more interesting than that school "histology," that cell-ness. That wonderful word of Whitehead's: "concretized," uh? That ugly, wonderful word that he uses: "concretized."[8] That the cellness is of such an order of completeness that, if any one of us gets even a portion of that in operation for ourselves, we really are going.

> In any case history
> (as to be understood by Duncan's Law
> to mean a) histology & b) story)
> applies here, in this equational way
> & severely at the complementarity of
> cosmos (complementary to individual
> or private) and not to cities or
> events in the way it has, in

8. It appears that Olson is slightly misremembering Whitehead's word "concrescence," which is used throughout *Process and Reality* for a fundamental operation of the world, where "the actual entity is the real concrescence of many potentials … and that every item in its universe is involved in each concrescence" (U.S. edn, p. 33).

> a mistaken secondary way, been
> understood

Well, I don't know what that means. It sure felt good when I wrote it.

GINSBERG: No, that works in with everything we've been doing.

OLSON: I think so, yes. So, let me end my pitch with a poem, uh? "Bk ii chapter 37." It's from the *Maximus* poems [11.84].

> 1. Beginning at the hill of

Yeah, I'll just read the numbers. I'm doing it that crazy way. I think it's three numbers; it's really the way Pausanias—I don't know why they used to do that number thing within the text, do you, why the Greeks did that? But they sure did.

> 1. Beginning at the hill of Middle Street the city
> which consists mostly of wharves & houses
> reclines down to the sea. It is bounded
> on the one side by the river Annisquam,
> and on the other by the stream or entrance
> to the inner harbor. 2. In the Fort at this entrance
> are the images of stone and there is another
> place near the river where there is a seated
> wooden image of Demeter. The city's own
> image of the goddess also in wood is on a hill
> along the next ridge above Middle Street
> between the two towers of a church called
> the Lady of Good Voyage. There is also a stone image
> of Aphrodite beside the sea. It explains the
> annual ceremony of Phryne appearing before the people
> and going into the water in her full and original
> beauty. 3. But the spot where the river comes into the
> sea is reserved for the special
> Hydra called the Lernean monster,
> the particular worship of the city,
> though it is proved to be recent
> and the particular tablets of Poseidon
> written on copper in the shape of a heart
> prove to be likewise new.

Allen Ginsberg and Charles Olson at Warren and Ellen Tallman's house in Vancouver, summer 1963.
Photo courtesy Karen Tallman.

3

Duende, Muse, and Angel

This was the second of the two group sessions during the Vancouver summer of 1963 in which Charles Olson took stage center. The date was 14 August 1963 and the circumstances were the same as for "On History," except that just Ginsberg and Duncan were his fellow panelists. "Duende" is Federico García Lorca's word, and the participants had all probably been familiar with his essay at least since its publication as an appendix to *Poet in New York* (1955) by Grove Press. The translator Ben Belitt offered a useful footnote there (p. 178): "Characteristically, Lorca took his Spanish term for daemonic inspiration from the Andalusian idiom. While to the rest of Spain the *duende* is nothing but a hobgoblin, to Andalusia it is an obscure power which can speak through every form of human art." If this information had been on the table in Vancouver it might have reduced a great deal of speculation; but it would have undermined the value of the discussion arising from the interplay of minds coming through to a sense meaningful to that time and the company present. The subject was initiated by Denise Levertov in a class earlier that week when she began quoting Lorca, and Duncan picked up the "Duende" essay and read quite a bit from it. Olson was not present that day. Two days later he was ready to have his say on the subject.

ROBERT DUNCAN: I think Lorca tells us what to think of the Duende in relation to—and he just said it was a daemon. And I don't think it's a personal rhythm; daemon's a real spirit, who attends you, and a resource outside yourself—although I know it's now supposed to be inside the psyche, but I've never quite believed that.

CHARLES OLSON: Well, do you have any problems with that division?

DUNCAN: No, not at all. Only inside and outside.

OLSON: Right.

DUNCAN: Except it's more fun if it's outside. Like wanting to go to haunted houses.

OLSON: Matter of fact, if he's inside, damn well put him outside so that you *can* heed him there where you have to deal with it. Trouble with that damn Socrates' appropriation of him …

DUNCAN: He's walking around with him in his pocket!

OLSON: … was that he kept a dirty little secret there on him.[1] And, in fact, as it's been often said, the whole trouble is that suddenly all that used to be called *muthologos* died in that moment. Socrates didn't know a goddamn thing about the stories of the past. Absolutely. Story would have died with Socrates. He didn't even know what the hell the point of it was of Helen hanging herself from a tree while he saw her, somebody, somebody getting a dirty piece of ankle or something.[2] Literally the rational imposes itself here.

DUNCAN: So the daemon was given a rational place to live, outside of any story, who, as it turned out, was in philosophy—like, he was in philosophy.

OLSON: Mind you, inside or out. Any story, inside or out. Right.

ALLEN GINSBERG: Is it evident you can get any kind of personal physiological rhythm out of the Duende for use in poetry? Is that right?

OLSON: It isn't. But is it? Doesn't Lorca—I used it in that review of Creeley's book, at the end[3]—doesn't Lorca literally propose three poetries? A poetry of the Duende …

DUNCAN: … of the Muse, and …

OLSON: … and the Angel. In other words, the *Geist*, for example?

DUNCAN: He opposes the Muse absolutely, which for him's French poetry. Apollinaire, he says has a stinky Muse …

OLSON: Well, I can agree on that, but …

DUNCAN: … and he wants to arrive at the Duende all alone, and he doesn't want any of those Angels in there.

OLSON: I think it's an enormously helpful division, and much more interesting than that one of Pound's, which lasted awfully well for half a century, the one which I heard you read into even in instructing somebody about phanopoeia.[4] I think we ought to really treat that one below its formulation,

1. Olson knew Plutarch's essay "A Discourse Concerning Socrates's Daemon" and the tradition that the daemon's job was to nudge Socrates to desist in an unworthy course of action if the temptation arose.
2. There is one version of the death of Helen in which she was hung on a tree by Furies (Pausanius Book III, chapter 19); Olson seems to be embellishing it.
3. "There are three poetries, I believe it was Lorca's neatness to specify. There is one of the muse, one of the angel, and that which I suppose was his, of the duende, is it? Creeley has one of these all to himself"—last paragraph of Olson's review of Creeley's *For Love* in *Village Voice* 13 September 1962, reprinted in *Collected Prose*, p. 287.
4. "Phanopoeia," as Ezra Pound defined it in *ABC of Reading* (1934), relates to the visual imagination in poetry, while "melopoeia" is the musical element and "logopoeia" the conceptual. Duncan expanded on these terms in "Notes on Poetics Regarding Olson's *Maximus*" in *The Black Mountain Review* 6 (Spring 1956), included in his *Fictive Certainties* (1985).

as well as take the Lorca thing as a formulation which really can be sort of felt out rather than to go below it.

GINSBERG: What is the technique for going about feeling out the Duende, or feeling the Duende in you? Is there any way of conjuring it up? Or conjuring it in you?

OLSON: Well, you're—yeah, I don't know. I mean, are you—would you call yourself a Duende poet?

GINSBERG: Yeah. Duende.

OLSON: You would? Well, what would you call yourself?

DUNCAN: Well, what will you cheat? [LAUGHS] I find I'm not calling the ticket right now.

OLSON: No, but just for the hell of it, use the tickets and see what you would. If I was shipping Allen to Lorca, to Spain, what ticket ...?

DUNCAN: I'd call myself a Muse poet, except for some complications.

OLSON: Well, we know about the complications. What about the simplification?

DUNCAN: The simplification, I think, is a Muse poet.

OLSON: I think I call Creeley a poet of the Angel, if I'm not mistaken, in that review, didn't I? I said that he—did I not? And I don't mean you're a ... Well, I'm not sure, as a matter of fact. Your interest is on various things.

GINSBERG: If you want to make it with the Duende, just you got to stamp your foot while you're making a poem.

OLSON: I think it would be extremely valuable if everybody in this room sort of understood to some extent which of these three roads they most naturally are traveling on, at this point of time, anyhow.

DUNCAN: I have some definite earmarks that would indicate the Muse was in question. For one thing, melody and memory being as absolutely essential to my movement in poetry, so that if we were looking at it detective-wise it'd make a pretty good ... And the appearance of—although I don't trust the appearance of Apollo. That's the trouble with what you evoke: you can't always be that sure ...

OLSON: You don't trust the appearance of Apollo? Well, I don't think you should, as a matter of fact. I can prove to you that Apollo and Aphrodite are god and goddess of a particular hour of twenty-four, and it's been—we've lost great lengths of strength because of the failure to specify the—how do you say it?—the canons of mythology. We've really lost it, and we play around with something which really has much deeper and tremendous plant, or fix, for both life and work, in just this point: the birth of the two of them, even in the island they were born in and the conditions under which they were born, which is, whew, a title of both of them. It's rather hung back before they became sort of those dopey sniveling ...

DUNCAN: Before they became Olympians.

OLSON: I mean, you've got to be statuary rather than—I mean, you know, the wickedest thing in the world is what happened to those ... It's a little island, just off the coast. It's a double island, and she was born first, so she rowed her mother over to help her in the birth of Apollo; so Apollo gets born on one little island ...

GINSBERG: Those on Rhodes?

OLSON: No, no. I'm so stupid, you see. And its very great title they both carry.[5] But the point I was—I would wish that you would be always sure about the damned Greeks. And you can get it in an enormous fashion by looking at Clark's book on *The Nude*. There's one moment—I think the date is 476 BC—in which the damn model, the modeling, the model modeling, stenciled stamps, much as the American Express Company, imposed itself upon all of this, stiffened it up, made it ideal, long before the three thinkers came along. The whole vision of nature and man was just put in a freezer like a popsicle. And even if it's beautiful, it still is—became a popsicle.

DUNCAN: Beauty was limited to the popsicle at that point.

OLSON: Well, that's when beauty again got all ...

DUNCAN: Absolutely closed, and everything else was out of it.

GINSBERG: Where did that happen?

OLSON: It's exactly in the statue of who had been Kore and became Venus, and who had been Kouros, a Kouros ...

DUNCAN: And became Apollo.

OLSON: ... and became Apollo. And these two were really great creatures of youths instead of what they come out as: everything *we've* ever had, which is simply Beauty, male and female, or Love, male and female. And they really are—they're gooped off from that point themselves. It's very hard to get at them because of that, because they—Venus becomes Callipygos, right? And Apollo becomes Belvedere.

DUNCAN: Like Belvedere Rose, or whatever.

OLSON: O.K. let's go to the Hotel Apollo! It's an enormous stiffening, which I'm not sure we today are not just simply the other end of. We're now sucking the popsicle down to the stick. But, quickly, I mean, get rid of the ...

DUNCAN: And waiting for the message on the stick.

OLSON: Which has a message. Which again gets me back to ...

GINSBERG: You get another free popsicle. [LAUGHTER]

---

5. The title is "Delian." Olson is trying to remember what he had read in Robert Graves's *The Greek Myths* (rev. edn, 1960) vol. 1, pp. 55–56: "Leto at last came to Ortygia close to Delos, where she bore Artemis, who was no sooner born than she helped her mother across the narrow straits, and there, between an olive-tree and a date-palm growing on the north side of Delian Mount Cynthus, delivered her of Apollo."

DUNCAN: Yeah, you get another free popsicle, and you're back on the same round again.

OLSON: Which gets me back to the advantage of not talking poetry as though it was that melopoeia, logopoeia, and phanopoeia were three sort of styles. But that does come up in Pound ...

DUNCAN: But it doesn't work that way at all.

OLSON: And it doesn't work that way. And, in fact, the bases on which any of us are really both living and writing is much more in Lorca's idea of the Muse, the Duende, and the Angel. What is his word for Angel, by the way? He just says Angel?

DUNCAN: Angel. Angel, straight on. And he dismisses it. But the thing is that the church—Mohammedan and Christian and Jewish churches had all dismissed the angels, officially. That again has a time when it couldn't fit in at all.

OLSON: Yes, except that in the first half of the 13th century, Ismaili nationalism is really rediscovering the Angel like mad, is rediscovering an anthropology as well. It has a time in there which is as great as the recognition by Whitehead that we're living only in an electromagnetic epoch, which may be five hundred million years long, but what a sort of a quick point that makes: that you don't exaggerate this great condition of the present. I mean, it is only one of other alternatives. So that suddenly you've found Duende, Muse, and Angel both on some baseline, which is interesting, as well as give yourself a chance to appropriate some anthropology or angelology which makes sense to you. And I swear the Muse somewhere is an anthropological mantra, is that eidolon, and now mantra is a sign, gesture as sign?

GINSBERG: Mudra. Mudra.

OLSON: Mudra. A mudra.

GINSBERG: Yeah. But the Indians have Sarasvati, goddess of Learning, Poetry, and Muse; they have a goddess, with a mandala.

OLSON: Yes, that's right. But we're not really *there*. Now that's phanopoeia and melopoeia, isn't it? That's when we're talking that.

DUNCAN: Yeah, anyway, but these Muses weren't goddesses. They danced around the figure, so that you could name one, one part of it, or one another, but they were a ring, dancing.

GINSBERG: Can you invoke Muse, you know, in its form?

OLSON: Oh, and how! Literally. Certainly. I don't mean in the poem, but in the feeling and attitude. Oh, I got a Muse, and I just call her up, because I happen to know who she is. And I just think about her, and whew! No? I mean, it's that literal.

GINSBERG: I just wondered what you did.

OLSON: Oh, sure.

DUNCAN: Sometimes she calls you up, in the middle of work.

OLSON: Well, then I don't answer. I won't answer. I won't take any telephone calls; no telephone calls.

DUNCAN: Certainly there's been—take Swedenborg, who thinks that angels are people and that people are essentially angels.

OLSON: Well, I believe he's got a great idea there.

DUNCAN: Yeah, the self should be an Angel; or the self should be a Duende; then should self be a Muse? No. That's very disturbing.

OLSON: No poet thinks so at all. That's why you have what's called the Muses.

DUNCAN: What's clear in my mind is the sense that the Muse is the music, and they dance; and that's it.

OLSON: But equally Duende and Angel are objectifiable, too. There's three— I'm totally convinced that we really are talking three roads in and out, which are all on different planes, three different planes. And you may be invoked or inspired by any one of those three, according to some peculiar corpuscular character of your own self. But the nine are late; the nine are late; the nine are like Ezra again.

DUNCAN: And the poet always says there's *a* Muse.

OLSON: That's right. And if that is really true ...

DUNCAN: And that may be Mama.

OLSON: Usually is. It is, as a matter of fact. It's that little wife of Zeus, who— daughter? It's tough to say. Was she a daughter or was she one of his girls? I think she was one of his wives, in fact one of the very earliest was Mnemosyne. No? Pretty sure.

DUNCAN: Was Mnemosyne ever in that Orphic order where the gods are out of the picture?

OLSON: Well, I don't know. The great passage on the Muses, by the way, you can read is in Pausanias's visit to Helicon, where he actually sees the statues of the three Muses, not the vain—the nine is like the Olympian system. There were three, and they're wonderful, they're like, you know, like Graves's bullshit about the triple goddess, but they clearly are three powers, like you were talking *poiein*,[6] and you're talking some other thing to arouse both yourself and anyone else.

DUNCAN: This is the thing that's called rhetoric, which is not only that it can flow forth but that it persuades.

---

6. In a lecture at the Vancouver summer conference, Duncan spoke of "three primary entities that have merged into one: one from the Roman-Greek world, which is *poiein*, which is 'to make the poem,' ... the second is a very definite one from the Bible, from the Jewish source, which is to speak with God's voice ... and a third one, and that is the Celtic-Bardic poet" (typed transcription in Simon Fraser University Library Special Collections).

OLSON: That's right. And rhetoric is, as you know—that's why I was teasing you the other night. We've been having—no, we haven't: don't think we have big, secret conversations. We have the same conversations, only in a different aspect. We were reading Wordsworth, we were fighting a battle the other night of Wordsworth and Shelley, and Allen wants to say that Shelley—"Listen to this rhythm!" And I said, "Oh, Christ, forget the rhythm. You make rhythms." But it's true, rhythm is really great if you take it on the level of the word *rhetor*, because *rhetor* is the same word as "rhythm."

DUNCAN: *Rhetor*.

OLSON: *Rhetor*, right. That's quite true, but those—I've forgotten the literal names, like Melicertes and …

GINSBERG: Melpomene?

OLSON: No, no, that's all that lot later. I believe that we're terrifically advantaged because everything that was that rational discourse structure that came in absolutely at 476 and showed itself first in the marble—yeah, the marble, really, right—has not only broken but we really have tremendous opportunity to walk around now in the areas where the Indo-European peoples first put their hands on the real thing.

$$\begin{array}{c} \text{Angel} \\ \text{Duende} \overline{} \text{Muse} \\ \text{Serpent} \end{array}$$

AUDIENCE: … the fourth corner?[7]

OLSON: Oh, of course it's the Serpent. But we don't mention him. I mean, there is always a quadratic, behind the three, but—uh? Sure, we can treat Serpents properly these days. That drawing is very important, like. You carry that four where you can manage to carry 'em, and try it on 'em, that's all. See how well you can do with number four.

DUNCAN: These would be unstable if it weren't for the fact that there's a Shadow up—I mean, there's another triangle.

OLSON: Very much there.

DUNCAN: They would tend to fly apart, and two of them would mate, and the third one would interfere, and everything would go. I mean, you'd be in one of those triangles, like they say, in soap operas.

OLSON: You'd better put that line back, otherwise …

DUNCAN: Yeah, I'd better. Yes, I know, that's what I put that for.

OLSON: Oooooo! Oooooo!

---

7. The blackboard diagram is found in Daphne Marlatt's notes on this session, included in "Excerpts from Journal kept during the Summer of '63 Conference, Vancouver" *OLSON* 4 (Fall 1975), p. 84. The word "Serpent" was added underneath "Angel" with a horizontal line of separation, apparently deleted during the discussion, and then restored.

DUNCAN: Taking that line away is part of what them magicians want to do; they keep wanting to get …

OLSON: Very much.

DUNCAN: That's why they're not poets; I mean, that's why they're not writers.

OLSON: I don't trust magicians for that reason. They're playing without that line.

DUNCAN: No, as a matter of fact, they look very silly; and they keep thinking if we took the line out, it would be one big open house.

OLSON: It's not like tennis, but it's like marking off your steps. How many yards did you make? What lines do you draw?

GINSBERG: Now, wait a minute. Are we involved in drawing lines?

OLSON: No. But we are divided, in a sense, from union. We are divided from union. By the way, statue here gets tremendously important: that's why I would talk "mudra," or whatever we want to talk about. That word "image" is marvelous because it also does mean "eidolon," something which is objectively represented, or presented, right? And that was the great concept of an object: that it was something you either could carry, that you had in your house, or was in the public square. I mean, if you take that *David* by Michelangelo, standing in Florence, it's an enormously great figure, but I don't believe it carries any of this characteristic of object.

DUNCAN: First, it was stone, wasn't it? I mean, first it's a real gift to make, that's the thing. And every bit of its shaping …

OLSON: Very much so. I never saw it so rude, by the way, as in Yucatan. One of the great advantages, to my mind, of Amerind civilization is to see how a city like either Uxmal or Chichen, which has enormously elaborate architecture—you remember that kooky pigeon house, say, at Uxmal? Or the Governor's Palace, right? Which is what? It's like one of them damned French things.

GINSBERG: So is the elaboration of hell.[8]

OLSON: Well, that's a fake, like an architectural fake, but the Governor's Palace is an enormous building that this university and everybody else isn't any better with. And right in front of it was a phallus of stone just absolutely, literally, stuck there in the ground; and all over the place is this enormous jump between this image of nature, which is that thing we've just been talking about, and this incredibly literal building of any city anywhere in the world, for offices or so. It's an enormous picture that you get when you— you can't see it; the damned palaces have been removed, but …

DUNCAN: If you take that first stone that's given, it could be said: "This is she." If you get to the Greek image, the one that Charles is talking about that sucked us in, by that time: "This looks like her."

---

8. Ginsberg's allusion seems clear to Olson, but has not yet been identified.

OLSON: Yes, quite. Very much, very much.

DUNCAN: Once "This looks like her," then "she" is an idea, and then "she" floats all over the place: she's Beauty, she's anything they want to name.

OLSON: Right.

DUNCAN: As a matter of fact, when they dig it up they know—and that's what first things are—that this is "she," and she proves to be a stone, including all the things she was up here, Beauty and so forth. And even "idea" means "to see it," and must go back to that seeing the stone. But between that stone and the cut stone, the shaped stone, that's the danger; and when you come to "idea" poets, and Shelley's certainly one of them, and it's beginning in Wordsworth in parts, you are coming to a separation again between the statement "This is she" and "This looks like her."

OLSON: I think so, very much, because Wordsworth's weakness—as, again, you were quoting Yeats to me last night—is not at all that he had a system of thought, but that nature had become a substitute for this thing that we're now talking about. Like, literally nature: you go out and you see—or he gets scared by a looming shadow out on the boat on the lake. I don't think that's—he ain't being scared by a looming shadow out on the lake on a boat, he's being scared by some funk in himself. And we know these things: one of our chances is to be sure that we get to place the funk where it belongs, and not distribute it as though we were dealing with a formal character of the real. The real is only things. You got to be awfully sure that you got that fixed in your mind. Things. No, I mean, literally it only means it, and that's all it is. Otherwise, you're going to poeticize, tragedize, do a hell of a lot of "-izing" to what really has a greater impact. And in fact you are yourself a more critical problem because you're really independent of that enormous system. Yeats himself should be calling names! Like, ahah! Let's talk about where *he* is. I mean …

GINSBERG: When you said the universe or the real is only things, or only in things, the problem there is you can have things without having them real also. I mean, you know, the eye doesn't see them.

OLSON: You can't take anything away, Allen. You get nervous, I think, in saying that, 'cos you won't lose anything by just treating the universe as real.

GINSBERG: No, that's true enough, but …

OLSON: It ain't going to go away, or it ain't gonna suddenly crack in.

GINSBERG: Righto, but when done doctrinally, then the feeling of the thing is lost. I've seen that operating in Williams sometimes. Or from Williams.

OLSON: Yeah, that's right. Williams sure has the danger.

GINSBERG: Or many of the young poets who are now writing "thing" poetry. "No ideas but in things" is completely without …

OLSON: Well, I don't myself believe that Bill's adage is holding up now as interestingly either, because of the—because of how you said it: the "formulation?" What did you say for that stiffening that occurs when you've made a mold?

GINSBERG: Become doctrinal.

OLSON: Doctrinal, right. I think the doctrinal in Bill's—I've even, not a month ago, felt—I can't get the feeling back now, but I felt some way that that statement can be now stated with a …

GINSBERG: Well, of its time in its functioning it was quite perfect and will last, understood for what it was.

OLSON: Well, I asked Rony and Phyllis when we were driving back from the radio station[9]—just to bring this home, like—I mean, "What do you do with the persons of your dreams?" The persons of your dreams: because that, to my mind, is a tremendous place that we are now free to possess in a way that—I mean, like

> For al so siker as *In principio*,
> *Mulier est hominis confusio,*—
> The meaning of this sentence is,
> "Womman is mannes joye and al his blis."

Which is that wonderful answer about dream that is in "The Nun's Priest's Tale" about—to fix it as real, I mean, he's really saying, "You know, like, you're a damn nuisance, but I'm going to tell you you're beautiful." I mean, I would say you've got to treat the persons of your dreams, who are always (aren't they?) whom you know, I mean, essentially, I mean that level of dreaming which always is the persons you know: what do you do with those people? To bring this whole muth-mythologicalness in. Because the out seems to me much more—I don't know, from seeing it, for me it's much more easily demonstrable than the evidences of the same thing within. It seems to me we're absolutely exploded and required to reveal all that's in our chest: "Let your hot heart burst!" I mean, Ahab's great statement: "Burst his hot heart like a crater" or something "on the whole of it." I mean, that's a marvelous agony and anger, in his instance, violence; but, essentially, it's where *we* are, isn't it? I mean, to get it out, not to play as though there's two, there's an in and an out: that's no longer interesting at all. I'm struck at how the whole idea of dreams as wish-fulfillment, for example, is so essentially interesting if you take it the old definition of the gods was that their *wish* was will. That's so exciting to me: that they were so called and have powers because their wish was will. There's no second start. The ordering is a single order of wish and will. That's beautiful, to my mind, and it releases the whole dream thing, so that you get an absolute one to one with the dream condition of the universe. You can call it "race" and you can call it "dream," because that wish/will thing is just an instant of power.

I think one of the craziest examples of this is the greatest Angel known to man in the Greek system is Hecate; and I could prove—I could read

9. The well known Canadian poet Phyllis Webb recorded an interview with Olson for the Canadian Broadcasting Corporation, where Olson speaks of Pound in a dream. See Addendum to this volume.

you—I did for that Bollingen translation a long supposed translation of about fifty lines of Hesiod. There's fifty lines in *The Theogony* on Hecate, which ought to forever put an end to this use of her as the frightful goddess, the goddess of fear, which is one of the damnedest clichés we have, really, is the idea—she's been a bore for how long? But in fact she is the great "angel" of her father; she does the real stuff. Whenever a real thing has to be done, she's sent to do it. It's an amazing fact that Hecate was really like, gee, I don't know, in our system, like Michael? In the Christian system, who's the …? The archangel, the archangel. She's the archangel, early, look, a woman archangel. And, you know, she became, in some curious dumb problem of fear and fright, this monster. But she's no monster.

DUNCAN: That's when they made that division, I'm sure.

OLSON: Yes, it is, completely. Oh, sure, absolutely.

AUDIENCE: The way Hecate is connected in my mind to what we were talking about before is that she is supposed to have three faces, isn't she?

OLSON: No, that's the junk; that's the junk. That's the junk; that's the triple goddess junk of Robert Graves and *The White Goddess*. That's not …

DUNCAN: That's the later Demeter-Kore-Hecate.

OLSON: She is called, really, *kourotrophos*, she is the nurse, the nurse of man and a nurse of life. Not the mother; the nurse, the rearer, the carer, the other thing entirely. And, as such, I mean, she is the instructor of all nursing; and she comes to the aid of those who need to lend somebody care. But she's tied, of course, tremendously to the Demeter-mother, because when the mother loses her daughter it's Hecate that really knows where she is, not the people that saw Pluto take her, but *she* knows because that's her business, that's her world business. And she's in and out all the time because that's her function and responsibility, as Zeus's principal daughter. She's a wow, that woman; and I wish I had that passage with me because—I threw it away as verse, but, wow, it's unbelievably interesting material.[10] It's easy to find, actually: it's in *The Theogony* under Hecate.

RONA HADDON: Is there anything special …? [INAUDIBLE]

OLSON: Well, I could talk about it. I had a literal visit of my Angel to me this spring. Talk about a dream! I mean, he literally came; he was carrying a— he was behind the counter. I was having a cup of coffee with Dan Rice, who's a friend of Creeley's and mine, a painter, and another person who I've forgotten; and this fellow, this Angel, was the counter-man, and suddenly held up this fish, and the fish in—it was, by the way, that beautiful story in the Bible of Tobias and the angel, is it not? Is it Tobias? Yeah. It was absolutely. I could confirm to a tee the Tobias story, and, in fact, even to this:

---

10. The poem "There is a goddess" was included in the posthumous *A Nation of Nothing But Poetry*. It is based on the Loeb Classical Library *Theogony* of Hesiod pp. 109–19, where Evelyn-White translates Hecate's epithet *kourotrophos* as "nurse of the young."

you remember the gull-shit that blinded—how's that get in there? Isn't Tobias blinded by gull-shit?[11]

AUDIENCE: Sparrow.

OLSON: A sparrow, right. Excuse me, I've made my ...

GINSBERG: *Yeshiva bucher.*

OLSON: Huh? *Yeshiva bucher.* Right. [LAUGHS] Well, I've forgotten at the moment all the details of the dream, but, believe you me, the Angel comes straight to you, literally, and tells you everything. Just like under the mushroom or something, you're absolutely told, on the moment, where you are, what you're not quite taking care of, and where you must get busy. It's valuable instruction, absolutely; and all you are asked for is obedience, which is the thing we most are disgruntled to give; but it is the thing that's asked all the time.

DUNCAN: I take it that imperatives that appear are really coming from there, and they can appear in a poem, imperatives of ...

OLSON: I don't know that you can get any deeper than the Lorca formulation on the instructional level of the poet to his work, actually, on it. That's what I think you're asking, Rona, is to get between life and reduction. And the truth is that these are the three terms that actually operate in the mystery of things to carry that, to carry all this thing: the Muse, the Angel, and the Geist. Would "Geist" be fair for Duende or no?

DUNCAN: No, because Geist, I think is like one's guide.

OLSON: Tell me, what does *duende* literally mean? Can anybody ...? Hawkins, do you know? But what is *duende* in Spanish? "Technique"? "Craft"?

AUDIENCE: Craft.

DUNCAN: Well, then, it's fire. Then it's Hephaistos, fire. We got to go back to the daemonic; it's the fire.

OLSON: It's crazy.

GINSBERG: But in Chiapas, *duende* is used for the people that come out at night and steal your cows, or start the horses neighing and running around and around.

OLSON: Well, then we are back into the Celtic, yeah.

AUDIENCE: Don't we use *duende* in the way a singer sometimes has an electrifying air that comes into effect ...?

OLSON: Yes, sure, sure.

DUNCAN: So Duende first was a flash of lightning, and a fire.

OLSON: Or it's your ability, in that sense. Is that a legitimate ...?

11. The poem "I met my Angel last night," included in *A Nation of Nothing But Poetry*, records Olson's dream of the weekend of 1 February 1963.

GINSBERG: I heard the word *duende* used many, many months, over and over and over again.

OLSON: Well, it's an invasion of forces outside in, isn't it?

GINSBERG: Well, it's just sort of like a spirit comes in that makes the horses run around in the pasture in the moonlight.

OLSON: Right. Right, well, that's a lowering of the idea, but it's a perfectly good case.

GINSBERG: *Hay los duendes en el potrero porque los caballos están rodeando.*

OLSON: It sounds awfully much at all points here that we're talking a release of one's ability.

GINSBERG: Yeah, because it was a released god.

AUDIENCE: It's pretty hard to translate it into …

OLSON: Yeah, I don't think we need to. We've gotten the essential meaning out of it. I don't find any problem in calling this the Holy Ghost, because the Holy Ghost was absolutely a practical manual of how to speak; and that was what he was to do, and does.

Inside the International
Foundation for Internal
Freedom house in Newton,
Massachusetts.
Photo: Ivan Massar for
the *Saturday Evening Post*.

4

Under the Mushroom

On 16 November 1963 Olson with his wife Betty was invited to lead one of
the discussion meetings held periodically at the home of Bill and Harriet
Gratwick in Pavilion, New York, some forty miles east of Buffalo, where
Olson had just accepted a post at the State University of New York. He had
obtained the use of a small house on the Hooker estate in Wyoming, New
York, close by, and thus entered the rather select society of well-off
intellectuals. The subject for this evening was not poetry but Olson's
experiences with Timothy Leary and Allen Ginsberg in December 1960
and February 1961 in the early experiments with psilocybin. "Under the
Mushroom," the title given by George Butterick to this tape transcription,
is a phrase used several times by Olson to refer to these two experiences
(there were no others), notably in the illuminating essay "Experience and
Measurement" printed along with the first publication of this discussion
in *OLSON* 3 (1975), pp. 59–63.

Documents on the table during the discussion were (1) the current
issue of *Playboy* (November 1963) with three perspectives on "The Pros
and Cons, History and Future Possibilities of Vision-Inducing
Psychochemicals" by Dan Wakefield, Alan Harrington, and Aldous
Huxley; (2) the recent *Time* (25 October 1963) with a report under
"Religion" on Leary's International Federation for Internal Freedom and
a photograph of their "headquarters" in Cambridge, Massachussetts,
which has the appearance of a church, with altar and stained glass; (3) the
current *Saturday Evening Post* (2 November 1963) with John Kobler's "The
Dangerous Magic of LSD," reporting on Leary in Mexico; and (4) *Main
Currents in Modern Thought* (September–October 1963), which includes
U.A. Asrani's "A Modern Approach to Mystical Experience" and a
substantial article by Willis W. Harman, "The Issue of the Consciousness-
Expanding Drugs," where Harman quotes at length from a previous paper
he did with J.N. Sherwood and M.J. Stolaroff, "The Psychedelic
Experience—A New Concept in Psychotherapy" in *Journal of Neuro-
psychiatry* (1962) on the three stages of the psychedelic experience, quoted
in turn by Olson.

The other work which was a common point of reference among several members of the group, including Olson, was a first draft of the schematic philosophy of Arthur Young, the inventor of the Bell helicopter. This was circulated for several years in typescript before book publication as *The Reflexive Universe* (Lake Oswego, Oregon: Robert Briggs Associates, 1976) with its full account of the seven-level grid of the atomic and molecular kingdoms (pp. 84–88) and chapter 15, "Process as Described in Myth."

HARRIET GRATWICK: … And he's taught at Clark University, at Harvard and Black Mountain College—I think most of you know about Black Mountain College—and he has written several volumes of verse, and *Call Me Ishmael* is prose, is that correct? Yes, and this copy is out of print and he had his last copy stolen from his car the other day. (This is very dramatic!) Anything that I have forgotten, you can say. We figured he might talk tonight about his experiences with the Harvard group and his philosophical position that he presently holds. Is that about right? All right, you're on.

CHARLES OLSON: And to do that solely to have something for us to chew on, really. I don't—it's of such a vast aspect or subject that we really are involved in that I would start simply by giving testimony. One of the great examples of the—one of the great advantages of what has now arisen is the—I mean like "visible truth"[1]—is that all you can do is show your own experience and actually, literally report how true you think it is.

VOICE: Well, you're going to have a piece of paper we're going to sign up here, aren't we?

OLSON: No, I don't believe in—like any of us that are involved today in membership …

VOICE: Oh, shucks, we can get the train and go right out.

OLSON: Yeah, I agree—well, as a matter of fact, I can put you on to many churches and combos that are desirous of rushing right ahead, especially in the next decade. For example, the Harvard bunch have really gone—I saw that—did you see that picture—was that in that *Playboy*? Who read that *Playboy*, said that they had? Was it there they had the picture of the actual church condition of the Learyists today? It was in one of the big national magazines. Was it *Time*? Well, they actually use that text that some of you have been reading, *The Tibetan Book of the Dead*, as literally almost a Bible of this scene. In addition, they have a physical layout which is literally churchy. In that picture, for example, what were the objects that was in that picture which made it churchy?

GRATWICK: Was it a church?

OLSON: No, I say "churchy." But in the very early days, which I will refer to just to get us started, the idea—you know the Swedenborg Church in

1. Olson is quoting Melville's letter to Hawthorne, as he does later: "By visible truth we mean the apprehension of the absolute condition of present things."

Cambridge on the corner of Divinity Avenue? It sits alone still by the big Memorial Hall. And the idea, very hardly thought of, was to purchase the Swedenborg Church to have the Center, because, as you know, the Center of Personality Research is just a half, well, less than a third of a block down from that corner, so … And there was obviously going to be the rupture that has happened. In fact, that was so evident to me the first day I went in for drinks with the department that I realized instantly, because the head of the department was McClelland from Wesleyan, who is a professional psychologist and teacher of psychology and is now head of the new Honors College at Radcliffe, and he's clearly a normal, ambitious, and successful professional academic, and I knew him at Wesleyan, which is my own college; and it was perfectly clear that McClelland was gonna funk! I mean, he just doesn't have the reasons of life to risk the changes that activism involves us all in. And it's risky, I mean risky in both respects: to what you are doing with yourself in the first instance, if you have a risk doing it, and secondly you do run up against attitudes of this society, which was so well said in that Harman article that you spoke of, beautifully, in fact.

VOICE: What is this eerie whistle we have? I think it's the tape recorder.

OLSON: Over there. It's you! [LAUGHS] It's right over there behind you.

GRATWICK: We'll let it go unless it gets louder.

OLSON: But I must have been involved in the first week of the actual use of the mushroom as it was derived at the Sandoz Laboratories into Psilocybin 39, I think is actually the name of the so-called drug. Actually, it could be a synthetic, about the size of an old placebo, which was even smaller than an aspirin, and looks very much like those fake pills we always were given, if you remember, if we needed a cure, like saccharine in tea, just a little pink thing about so big. In fact, when I took it I was so high on bourbon that I took it like as though it was a bunch of peanuts. I kept throwing the peanuts, and the mushroom, into my mouth. Actually, as you know, the mushroom as such, the natural mushroom, was the source of all this, and it was *amanita muscaria*, the basic poisonous, so-called poisonous mushroom of history, which was actually taken just about a year earlier by the two—I call them "personality psychologists," or, say, let us call Leary what he really is, a "psychologist of personality," and the other fellow, Barron—who's now on the West Coast and has, I think, generally failed to carry out the same sort of a program that Leary was trying at Harvard—is actually an enormous horror which lies around in this whole area. He's a professor of creativity, and in fact is the, I guess practically the first. Frank Barron. He is a well trained, almost like hospital psychologist, very similar to Leary I think in training. No, he's a lot younger even. He comes from Pennsylvania and Leary comes from Springfield, Mass. And they both, independently of each other I think, got ahold of a bag of this mushroom as used in Mexico by the *curandera* or *curandero* of the back country. Barron told me he took the first bag of it he ate—he was about to leave for Europe the next day and he had a date with a girl and he thought it would be fun to go under the mushroom together. So he'd chew the mushroom and then feed it to her like gum, and actually he ate the whole bag and she took the chewed mushrooms, and he left for Europe the next day and said that the ripples lasted the whole time he was in Europe, that is, ten weeks. He said he never talked to people like that, and he never did such things in his life. He talked to people he never would talk to, he experienced things he'd never experienced, and it was very exciting actually to hear it, because he must have taken a beautiful dose. That's a long ripple for the mushroom is ten weeks. As you know, the Indians actually figure—it's been so long in use by certain people in the human race, among them the Central American Indians, that they know exactly how long it takes for the hair to grow and the beard, so that it's about three weeks that you return for a shave and a haircut. And the *curandero* or *curandera* business is so solidly organized on the basis of when the ripples run out that they can expect a volume of business to return each three weeks, and so therefore it works out under the calendar year.

GRATWICK: Do they take it that regularly?

OLSON: Oh very much, as, literally, I want to put it on the basis of barbers and bars, because I think myself I'm such a protestant or protagonist of the mushroom, at least, that I think it's a wretched shame that we don't have it in the common drugstore or as a kind of a beer, because it's so obviously an attractive and useful normal food. We were even kidding those in that half a block between the Center of Personality Research and the Swedenborg Church on, say, the Food and Drug Administration. It's very interesting that in both Massachusetts and in the nation the actual administrators of this are responsible officials of food and drugs. The true equivalences are right in that administrative title. And it was the FDA—let me get to the end and then I'll go back—the last thing that blew up in the administrative face was that the common morning glory, as you probably all know, was discovered to be a great—I want to use one of those technical words, con—what is the word I'm looking for?—like not contrary, but con—*construct* to LSD, in fact, that it's blown up the whole idea that LSD is simply chemically a derivative of rye and the ergot. The ergot thing has turned out to be chemically now very much more interesting, because it turns out morning glory in its simplest form, the Heavenly Blue, the most attractive form, is the same chemical substance and puts you on in almost identical form to the LSD. And the kids were buying it all over the nation in those little packages and they were tearing them open and piling them up until they got a liter or something. But the Leary group was buying bales from all over, and suddenly the FDA realized that something's up and ...

VOICE: Bales of what?

OLSON: Bales! They bought directly from the seed companies; they bought out the Heavenly Blue! And they had about three-quarters of it in the nation baled up in Newton to be sure that they had at least some drug. You know the censure or the prevention or the cutting off at source is now almost complete, as far as I know. The mushroom is no longer made, LSD is not made, and the only one that was left practically was Heavenly Blue. Am I not right? Something like that has already happened. That is, the administrative has actually moved in so severely that you can't today enjoy these privileges that I speak of as though they were at the drugstore. Which was true, by the way, in those earliest days, and it was one of the advantages that psilocybin was being produced by the Sandoz Laboratory on a research basis. I've got in my house in Gloucester old mushroom pills—it's a shame—which I just didn't use. Which brings up that other point which I'd like to have you ask me about: why, if it's so great, you don't go to the barber every three weeks yourself?

So, to come to Hecuba, I was waked after this night in which I just ate these things like peanuts, by Mr Leary and Mr Ginsberg, who had asked me to enter the research. Both of them came rushing in to wake me up and ask me how was it, and I said, "Well it was great, it was …"

GRATWICK: Will you tell us about it?

OLSON: Yeah, well, I'm gonna tell you. My answer was, "It's a true love feast and a truth pill." And that seemed to satisfy them, as they rushed me into … That was the end of it, as far as I—but, like, all I was left with was the ripples from that point on.

And I went under the mushroom another time, as a kind of *curandero* myself, but rather like a football player, to run Arthur Koestler, whose work you may know. Certainly you must know his novel *Darkness at Noon*, which was of such power in the forties, reporting on the Stalin trials. But he's since become one of the most useful journalists in the world, certainly, and has in recent years got joined to the scientific research into neuro—how would you say that?—physio-psychology? How do you say that thing that's up, of which the Swedes are such marvelous leaders? That's the reason why he was in the country and they wanted me to do a run with him was that he was in San Francisco for the first showing by a Swede of the model of the human brain which works, and it's of great—to that wing of today which is, like, hard science, if you want to call it that, this had gotten so far that the actual dupli—the model of the human brain had been accomplished. The only trouble with it is if you were going to do more than, say—I think he'd, for example, modeled one cell or something—it's such a project in magnitude, I mean literally size, that is, to duplicate the human brain in model form would occupy so much space and involve so much money, way beyond space programs and way beyond sums of money …

GRATWICK: You mean to get everything into it?

OLSON: To get everything, to actually do the brain total, you haven't got enough earth. It comes out that kind of a marvelous elephantiasis or cancer of the brain. What's that stuff in corn where the corn all—what do you call it when the whole ear is there and each kernel is actually turned into an enormous horrible thing like Mexican kids' eyes? Blast, isn't it? Blast. Well, it would be like that. To make the brain is like having blast of corn ear, going all each unit brrt, brrt, brrt. And that was a very bad experience. It was a very crucial political fact for Leary and the group because they wanted to capture Koestler, who, as you know, was then publishing that book, *The Lotus and the Robot.* Yeah.

VOICE: A terrible book!

OLSON: Terrible. Who said that? Oh, it's utterly terrible, but, one of the great factors in the politics or journalism of the present, probably had a great effect upon the closing down of the manufacture of the drug, because he's such a useful publicist.

VOICE: One of the most unsympathetic books I ever read.

OLSON: Very much. Well, and that's what I had—I'm supposed to be euphoric under the drug, and I was supposed to make him feel he could be comfortable and confident. The unfortunate thing was he was late for the session and I was sitting at the kitchen table with Leary's kids and the girl was studying mathematics, and the kid had his guns and wanted me to try them out; and just as Koestler came into the room I was holding two guns. [LAUGHTER] Complete lovely synchronicity of time, right? So we started out badly. He's a little man and they never thought—nobody ever thinks about that. That's a great problem. But he was very brave and he tried as many pills as any of the rest of us for a while. I have the session record, I kept the book that night, and I can watch my own handwriting go down the page. And I was fluid. I was trying to lead him and at the same time stay with him. No, I mean lead him so that he'd stay with us, and then at any point we were all free to go further if we wished. He did up to about ten, I think, eight or ten of the units of the old psilocybin, which rides you pretty far. That stuff all depends on your own size, literally, I mean quantity size. He's a little man, so ten would give him a jump up to about fourteen, fifteen maybe, say, for me. Eight or ten he took. And he was on, but the resistance was so strong that he finally after about an hour, stood up, and there was eight of us, say, in the session in a room something similar to this, and he stood, he definitely made a move to leave, and he stood so that all were aware that he was, and he said, "As John Donne said, 'With a great sober thirst, my soul attends.'" And turned and left. He left and went upstairs. And had a hell of a time, because he walks into his own room and he found a couple making love on the bed in the darkness so he had to go to another room, and he couldn't get the window up and he put the light on, so that he actually recreated the—if I was holding a gun on him like a Nazi or a Fascist American, when he left us he put himself in a concentration cell, and stayed there all night long unable to open the window, again pure accident, like they say, and with the lights on, because he could not—he was high enough to have to go through the time of the mushroom. And we all went up, knocked on the door, begged him to come out and have breakfast, bacon and—all night long we moved to help him, and he wouldn't come out. It was one of the most exact examples of how willful will is.

And I do want to call your attention to that article that Mr Carlson put in Mrs Gratwick's hand which is here, which if you haven't read you ought to. I think the best summary of this whole thing is that Harman article. It's marvelous, and specifically on this point, because Harman is the first man to identify the three real stages—how do you say it? It isn't stages in the developmental sense, but the three actual problems or—he calls them "states." One is those who buck. The second is those who really have the experience and find the sensations are great. And the third is those for whom it is really a vision. I think it's just really—that's very beautiful because that's really true: there are those three experiences, and they're equally valid. And his point is that—and as such, it's quite long and it's cut out of a paper by him and two other men. It's very recent, it's just been out. You ought to look—I mean it's too long to start with at this moment, but it is a marvelous study that they did.

VOICE: I thought from the very little of it that we heard that there were also people who had terrible experiences but who might not be people who had bucked it.

OLSON: Well, I think that's part of the rumor mill. I've run into it again this summer from one of the women of the Leary group, who did her thesis on Gottfried Benn, the German poet, and she and her husband came to Gloucester because they were going to buy Jack Hammond's sister's 17th-century houses on Dolliver's Neck for another center and possibly the center that they'd work from. And so we met, Bet and I, the whole bunch of them again this summer.[2] And amongst them was this very gifted German woman who—and we walked away from the group. They were looking at the real estate thing, and we walked away and sat on a rock and talked, and she said that—she said, like, from the insides, that was true. But you know, curiously enough, I kind of think most of this is what Harman says it is. It *is* where there's a buck. The buck may be so deep, only, that you get—did you read the Harman article?

VOICE: I don't think so, no.

OLSON: Well, the great question—really, I could read you the first, the evasive stage he calls it, where he argues how the schizophrenic and other states, paranoia sort of suspicion and anxiety arises. The interesting thing is, again, always the test is the person and what they do. If we could get that straightened out, no matter who, we could add a great deal to the whole story. The great generalization is that everybody is what they are. Which means what you do and what you are is exactly where all this best applies and where in fact its future lies. But I mean it is that kind of a ...

2. There was a visit to Gloucester by Timothy Leary and others including Alan Watts, in the spring (as is mentioned elsewhere). This visit can be pinned down to 24 March 1963. If a group came again in the summer, the exact date is not known. The Germans mentioned are Rolf and Elsa von Eckartsberg (see *Guide*, p. 509).

GRATWICK: You mean it accentuates what you are?

OLSON: Certainly. And it requires you, as both the material and an agent—so that if there is anything in the whole thing as a revelation it's simply that in the end you act differently because the vision is true. But otherwise all the time one ought to be pursuing it solely in what one does and is. In other words, there is that literalness that is terribly crucial here that I would love to see if I could get across tonight, and seems to be mostly left out of even as great a job like this, which is a summary job, is the question of how literal, or how literal true subject, how—to traverse is all. I mean, all—series of literalnesses that cover everything would be worth stressing forever for each of you and for us and for any of the future of all this change of the discourse of man. That's how literally it seems to me that we gotta talk if we're gonna talk. So let me use this girl, because the funny thing is that when they had that big, big experience in Mexico within six weeks of this scene, she was out; she pulled out and left her husband behind. In other words, there was a tension at some point in her even, who was very excited and very truly a part of it, and her paper on Benn or Benn's paper, "The Provoked Life," which is in the first edition of the *Psychedelic Review*—you've seen that? Well, Benn was a German medical poet of the—who we all first translated in Boston in 1950 in *Origin* magazine, I may be proud to say. Benn was first introduced to America by a magazine which I was connected with. He was a very beautiful poet, a very hard-headed medical German, and he's written, or she translates, this beautiful essay. But somehow or other, I suspect that she even, not rumor-wise, but like Koestler, determinedly-wise, she said that too. Yeah? I see no evidence, and I don't know anybody that can testify. The best evidence I have is Tim Leary himself reporting the last night in Mexico. I've forgotten the identity of the man, but he's a considerable man, a West Coast scientist or something. Can you help me on exactly who that guy was? In L.A. or San Francisco. I mean, a really very, very highly trained man who came in under LSD in Mexico and blew up. And really blew up! As a matter of fact, when Leary came back to talk to us he had the most ugly bruise on his elbow from the guy throwing him down so harshly.

VOICE: He became violent, you mean?

OLSON: Very. I mean, really went way out, and became—and he took the Lord's Prayer and attacked God and used everybody present, and did it physically. He let go of a beast—not a beast, but a giant of a man just released itself. And then nobody could touch him. And Leary was very unhappy because he took the advice of the psychoanalyst that they always had. What was that drug that you can knock a person out with? I've forgotten what it is, but it's a drug you can hit a person with to be sure that if they go extreme you can get them back under control. And he took the advice of that psychoanalyst and gave this guy a shot. And he regrets it very deeply because he feels that night was a true night of the outburst, again synchronically, with this moment of time—I mean, that moment of time.

VOICE: For that man, you mean?

OLSON: For that man and the whole group and the whole being in Mexico because of the United States had turned them down and being on LSD instead of mushroom or not having yet reached Heavenly Blue. I mean, I would stress the term "politics" here. I would even say that today if you aren't sure that you've got a triad of politics, theology, and epistemology you'd better get out of this business; that those three are so tight, and they are so truly woven, the strand is woven of those three things and nothing else. So that if you don't use the—if you're not careful that you have that triple weave going on ...

VOICE: What are these three again?

OLSON: I said politics—and I'm using them in a reverse order—politics, theology, and epistemology.

GRATWICK: Well, explain epistemology, it's ...

OLSON: Oh, how you know. Or the belief that we—that there is knowing. And it was invented by a man named Plato. *Episteme* is his invention and it's one of the most dangerous inventions in the world is the idea that there is such a thing as knowledge. But if you take it the process way, again, to talk like any of us here that comes to this point in the century, Young here is wonderful talking how I mean process, basing that whole study of his on the fact that the whole universe is process. I think he loses the other thing, the Real, by saying it, and involving himself with words like "determinism."[3] But that's O.K., I mean one is apt to overfall today because the work is so crucial.

But I do say that that instant—and I'm sure I know enough about how agile an American Leary is that, without him being able to say that's politics, what he really meant was that he should not have interfered with the universe. If this man killed everybody present, that's O.K. There is a point at which you—"This thing is dangerous?" Like, ha-ha! I mean, and really is very—I don't believe that myself, to tell you the truth, but you've got to be sure that you're including the danger. I don't mean danger. You've got to be sure that this whole thing might—you suddenly might have to deal with a man who is going to kill, because of his own problems, yeah? Instead of back out.

VOICE: I wonder if this man felt that he had problems when he began?

OLSON: Obviously he did. I mean, it was a man of considerable status and accomplishment in life, who came into this group to be helped. Hardly anybody except us who were first in the experiment really are clean in that sense, that we were there simply because we're free.

VOICE: You didn't do it for a purpose.

OLSON: That's right. Now I don't say that to put down the later stuff at all, as a matter of fact; actually, again, here's where you do get the advantage of pursuing that thing. But mind you, the initial stage of something is really

3. Arthur M. Young, *The Reflexive Universe* (NY: Delacorte Press, 1976), pp. 7–8 and passim.

where it's complex. From there on you get revelations of or go further; in fact some advantages, too. But initially the complex exists.

VOICE: Are you suggesting that what happened that night was due to the complex of the total situation—this man was acting out the total situation rather than just his own?

OLSON: No, he was himself. No, he was his own. But the point was—in fact Leary said that very beautifully, didn't he?—that this was the third case in three days with the Mexican FBI present. It was like Armageddon—he used even a better—he used the negative: that the negative was so in the air, because the State of Mexico was going to fly them out the next morning, bundle them into planes, and took their tickets away—their traveler's visas, traveler's permits for Mexico, and they had to fly off in three chartered planes, get out!

VOICE: Well, then, he would be acting out the total situation.

OLSON: He would be, exactly, but the total …

VOICE: But you think it's synchronicity rather than …

OLSON: Oh, completely. If you argue total situation without today assuming that, say, politics is synchronous too—that's all I'm trying to say. Which we tend to regard as what? We tend to regard politics as an area of choice or purpose, a progressive situation. Well, it certainly is not. I think it's of such an order that I would say it's equal, as I've said, to that which we call the divine, and to that question of ourselves, what is knowing. I would say there are three great terms, and I want to use those lesser or drier or university words, epistemology, theology, and politics, to cover it.

VOICE: Excuse me, do you feel that if Dr Leary hadn't given him this drug which more or less brought him out of it that the man would have helped himself?

OLSON: One doesn't know. You know, this is that wonderful thing. Again, one of those things that you've got to say when you examine, say, myth as Young does, is that the story is there. Who knows what the end of a story is?

VOICE: But I mean if he was in a destructive vein in which he was destroying and murdering everybody, possibly, is that helpful for him?

OLSON: Well, it's very uninteresting unless it's true, right? I mean, who cares about helping another person? This is a big doubt in this, yeah? I think it's again one of the things we inherit is the idea that people should be helped. I mean, kill 'em first, rather than—most people shouldn't be helped at all. That's a bore. But I mean the point is that we don't know where that guy would have gone. And in fact it might have turned in a split second. What the guy needed, probably, was simply—this is a transit question: how far does any of us need to go to arrive? When we are there, we know already; we go back, or we're there, which is where we wanted to be. I mean, I would even argue that's a discourse question. We have a very bad discourse system.

We do, as a society, for a long time. We don't know much about transit, why we will go from one place to another. By the way, Young is wonderful; he's got a formula for that: A B + sigma. Now the point in this case, all you gotta treat that man as is how far does he have to go, really? Well, he was gonna rape a woman, they thought. That was the moment at which somebody rushed out and said, "We gotta stop this guy," one of the nicer women of the place. It wasn't anything extreme, you know. [LAUGHTER] Well, but, you see, you just tie that to that position. The FBI of the Mexican government was there. I can see Leary's mind thinking, "Well, gee, if we get a rape case on our hands we'll really be booted out." You know, somewhere in Leary the thing was operating too. So he chucked it.

VOICE: Say, how come you don't think the nice lady was part of the synchronicity too? [LAUGHS]

OLSON: I do. I got no …

ANOTHER VOICE: Do you think if the FBI had not been there they would have permitted the thing to run its full course?

OLSON: Oh, they were planning actually to make that one of the centers, homes, or session places of the further development of the research.

VOICE: I meant the man.

OLSON: Oh, I think so. Because Leary himself had been absolutely so cruelly harmed by the guy, that I'm telling you I never saw such a terrible thing. It was ugly, what was on his elbow from the smashing that the man. But he was a giant. Better to say it that way. The unleashed forces of his being, you know, were just out.

VOICE: What's the man's present state?

OLSON: I have not heard, I don't know. I heard that he was very angry that he'd been cooled, and desperately angry, felt he'd been cheated of his scene and he really did—huh?

VOICE: He hasn't arrived yet, then?

OLSON: Obviously he was cut off. No, clearly that was a great loss. That's the opposite of the Koestler story, who wouldn't come in, huh? And that third case, that girl. Her husband is still one of the editors, heads of this *Psychedelic Review*. What's that fellow's name?

BETTY OLSON: The German? Ilse?

OLSON: Elsa, yeah, what? I mean, there's three. Let me name the people because it's the first facts …

VOICE: This is something that I've asked a number of people and have never really gotten an answer that I thought was satisfactory. People under alcohol, which is a similar situation, I suppose, react differently and someone once said that either they become, I mean if you're really, really drunk, you become somebody else quite different or else just moreso of yourself.

Now, from what you've indicated of some of these reactions under LSD would you say the same thing?

OLSON: Not at all. No.

VOICE: Is that quite a different thing?

OLSON: Oh, it certainly does.

VOICE: It changes you completely or brings out something quite different?

OLSON: No, it makes you exactly what you are.

VOICE: Well, under alcohol some people just become more of what they are.

OLSON: Yes, that's true, that's true. I'm glad you brought this up because I would like to stress—which I don't think any of that literature that I've seen that you people have at least some acquaintance with, some of you do—the autonomic nervous system. In fact, it's a curious fact of the condition of the last five years as they've progressed. Is it five years now? Four. '60? Was it fall of '60 or fall of '59? Fall of '60, wasn't it? It's only three years ago I'm talking when things started to mess up. Am I not right, that the first use of psilocybin was fall of '60?

VOICE: You mean in this country?

OLSON: Yeah. LSD had been used—huh?

VOICE: '42 or '43 LSD was first introduced.

OLSON: Oh yes, that's right. And it was introduced by Dr Max Rinkel, who is on the staff of Massachusetts General, but does his research in Boston. And it was used, with great care, among a bunch of psychoanalysts throughout the nation. And Rinkel—for some reason I can't understand why nobody says this and I'd like to talk to you about it at some length, because again this is the other place, besides the literal, that I think you'd better talk very solidly is what it means to say "the autonomic nervous system." These things are called the "hallucinogens," and that's a name which really applies to those of the second stage, those for whom the threshold of sensation is, in normal reasons of life, low, and that what they discover is that they got better sensations than they knew and it goes to their head. They suddenly realize color, and then on personal power, a whole theory—we could specify that. I'm running tonight, so it don't matter, just to cover the area. But you can specify that rise of the level to what can be nothing more than a normal, real, true character of senses. That word, therefore, is false, that "hallucinogen" word. What actually happens, however, why they can be isolated as a series of drugs—and there's only what, four of them, if I'm not mistaken, four or five at the most, that are in a class? That is, it's pot, it's mushroom, it's LSD, it's mescaline and it's *ololiuqui,* to use the old Indian term for the—for the …

VOICE: For peyote?

OLSON: Peyote, but peyote is the same as pot, is it not? Isn't peyote pot? I'm not—my point is that those all do a very simple thing: they click on the autonomic nervous system. Now, I'm using—this is Rinkel's physiology, and I can find nothing that not only doesn't verify it, but that my own experience being under the mushroom is just that experience.

VOICE: I misunderstood you to say it puts you off or on ...?

OLSON: No, it puts you on your own autonomic nervous system, as against the motor. That is, that we do—I mean, it's been—it's truth is long now in this part of physiology there was two nervous systems, right, the sympathetic or parasympathetic system and the motor? Now, alcohol goes to the motor system, so does coffee. And Rinkel for example, in Gloucester, took the position he thinks the human race should never have anything else than coffee and alcohol. He's a tight little guy, who had a hate of the advantages of the very things like LSD that he brought to this country. Very curious kick-up, kick-off. I don't think he's ever taken it, myself. By the way, this is a very important thing. I don't think any of us should be talking if any of you haven't taken any one of the hallucinogens, because you really don't know, you're really just talking academically, because you ought to have the experience, that's all. I mean, we'd be much better off actively if I had had the supply and you were all on now. We'd all be better off, because we'd be real and we'd be comfortable, free, and we'd be true. That's the important thing. And we aren't, because this is an artificial situation.

VOICE: Is it possible to achieve this, though, without the aid of any of these agents?

OLSON: Oh, I believe, utterly; I do. Certainly I do. Otherwise I'd be using that stuff I've got in Gloucester. I'd go for a haircut, but I don't go. I think so, too. But it's not easy to achieve. And certainly the human race has been so bereft of its autonomic system for so long that you can practically talk that we're green. In fact, I would think almost that you have to talk about the species today as green, individually and socially, not at all how you say it the way we tend to talk from our progressive or evolutionary or developmental past as though we've now got to take this step. It's not some step that you take easily, or that even to take the step means anything more than you know without taking the step, if you stop to think about it, because you're just who you are: what you do, if it's any good, is true, and you are capable of being alive because of love. I mean, it's about as simple as some simplicity's offerings, and that's it. Well, like, it may not be so easy to come to believe as absolutes, imperatives, and universals. In fact, on the contrary, we've been encouraged to think that there is some universal absolute or imperative which we seem to be missing out on. But that autonomic thing is very crucial. And I don't know what it means. I've heard—as a matter of fact, so much does this seem the exciting thing that another funny thing even in that Harman report is the absolute absence of the word "cells" throughout, no mention of cell. Did you notice that in the Harman article? Literally.

VOICE: Of cell or self?

OLSON: Cell. C-e-l-l. That's very interesting. For example, if you know Rinkel's original—Rinkel got into notice because Cary Grant had been the subject of that early use of it in Zurich. The only place I've ever seen this mentioned was in *Time* magazine in a footnote on Rinkel, where he's quoted as saying that his belief from LSD experiment is that every cell—not every cell in the individual's body, but that the cell as a principle of the structure of the human body is of an order equal to the brain. That is, that any given cell holds in itself—oh, I have been told by somebody in the last week that Rinkel has now said that he's tied that evidence to the DNA, the DNA of cell structure. But the crazy thing is that he lectured to us one night in a library in Gloucester, actually to Lansing and myself—that was the prepared thing, and some others were a little prepared—on what he said is what seems to happen, for example, with the hallucinogens: they go directly to the cells involved. He made the parallelism to both the discovery of adrenalin and the power of adrenalin in the motor system: that what happens is that there's a physiological unit in the cell similar or parallel to adrenalin, which is backed in, like a—I mean, it comes alive, light goes on and it comes out or it gets affected. And the cell then suddenly is both receiving and transmitting through that eye or ear thing of special existence there interior linked to the cell, which only occurs, now I suppose we have to say, not in danger, like adrenalin, but in the opposite of danger. I would say this must be the love unit, if you like, in the cell that comes on because here …

VOICE: How does that fit in with some of Dr Puharich's experiments?

OLSON: Yeah, well, Puharich was early in the whole lot, as we know. But Puharich's first book is pretty sort of cheap or tawdry. The only thing is, he was marvelous on that Alcoa program, demonstrating—excuse me?

VOICE: Pardon me, it wasn't the mushroom book I was thinking of, it was his later one where he is …

OLSON: On the ESP rays.

VOICE: Yes, but he used various different so-called hallucinogenic agents like glue-sniffing I guess was one of them. But it's pretty well itemized at the back where he …

OLSON: I didn't know. I don't know that one. I did see him on Alcoa produce the effect of the mushroom, on a national television program, which was remarkable. That must be about two years ago in the fall, if any of you saw that Puharich taking that guy that runs the Alcoa program and testing him first, before giving him mushroom, on his ESP cards and reading a picture blindfolded. And then he bumps him with two mushrooms as a matter of fact, two—literally he eats them, you watch him eat two *amanita muscaria* and zing! he runs the test again. And it's one of the most beautiful jump-ups you've ever seen. I mean, the guy knocks those cards into place about seventy-five or eighty percent and then he reads, blindly, like that woman that's reported out of the Soviet Union today,[4] a picture with his fingertips,

4. Rosa Kuleshova was reported in the *New York Times* of 26 January 1964 as being able to sense colors through her fingertips.

and he hits it. It's a waterfall picture, isn't it? And he hits this falling water thing almost to a tee with his fingertips. Which again puts you back to Rinkel, I believe. I think we're awfully close to cell research here which ought to pay off like mad.

VOICE: That's what Dr Puharich is trying to do in this.

OLSON: Is doing. Well then, I better just slow up.

VOICE: Adjusting it to adrenalin and a physiological aspect. That's what he was primarily trying to do.

OLSON: O.K.

GRATWICK: Is this a kind of seeing through the fingertips?

OLSON: It comes out literally. Or hearing through the—or hearing. I guess you'd want to say hearing and seeing, wouldn't you? I would, on the basis of a belief that etymology is even behind mythology as the secret of the universe. Etymology. And there's only two forms of knowing that I can figure out exist. One is GNA and the other is VID, and VID is seeing, and GNA is *prajna* and is apprehension that I think you can only call oral, in the sense of sounds, therefore language. Yes, therefore language, therefore eyes, and that's all. There's a double, there's a staple or two of the agents, the division: one is the eye and the other is a knowing which is, well, I would even say oral but I don't want to press the point. It is GNA, though. Leave it just in the g-n-a, which is the basic root of "knowing." K-n-o is g-n-a, actually, simply slipped. Kna, kno. And VID, because we all use the word— again this is where the vocabulary matters, because we all use the word "vision." We fake all—at least that's where we get—where the danger of the mystical is, for example, is vision. The vision is even—it's just a word we're used to is "vision," for all the great demonstrations.

Now I'd like to close my remarks, and so we can throw the whole thing open is to read you the one statement in this which is really something I can verify and is the one that is considered the mystical statement of stage three. And you'll see it's like I said I went when I found out about the mushroom, when I woke up and I said to Leary and Ginsberg, is that this is simply what this guy records.

> One individual writes: "During this stage ... comes that experience called by the mystics 'the realization of God within us.' This comes to many under these drugs, and is an indescribable, piercing, beautiful knowledge and *knowing*, which goes beyond the body, the mind, the reason, the intellect, to an area of *pure knowing*."

I mean, we could knock the words about for a long time, but ...

> "There is no sensation of time. God is no longer only 'out there' somewhere, but He is within you, and you are one with Him. No doubt of it even crosses one's awareness at this stage. You are beyond the knower and the known, where there is no duality, but only oneness and unity, and great love. You not only see Truth, but you *are* Truth. You *are* Love. You *are* all things! It is not an ego-inflating

experience, but on the contrary, one which can help one to dissolve the ego. It gives one a splendid flash of what *can be*, and what one must surely aim for. It resolves the goal, and the goal is found worthy of pursuit. The consciousness or awareness is expanded far beyond that of the normal state. And this level of consciousness, which actually is available to us at all times, is found to be that part of us which, for want of a better way to express it, might be called the 'God-ness' of us. And we find that this 'God-ness' is unchangeable and indestructible, and that its foundation is Love in its purest form … Utilizing this inner Self as the working basis of your life, you realize fully that nothing can ever hurt you or bother you, not even death. It gives life a completely new meaning, and one which is indestructible, and which fits in with the scheme of things. You no longer find yourself an outsider, separated from Nature and separated from God, and separated from your fellow beings."

This is Harman, this engineer's report, who is the one I spoke of who did "The Issue of the Consciousness Expansion Drugs." That, by the way, is the single testimony I would subscribe to or say is quite—and considering the problems of voicing that, this person, whoever it is, has come awfully close to saying it in the rational language that we have inherited. I would say that it's better to put this in action, but if you need a capsulated statement of what seems to me to be the real truth, or love, of the thing, there it is.

VOICE: And you experienced these three as such?

OLSON: That's what I happened to get. That's why I said, when they asked me, I said, "It's a love feast and a truth pill," the mushroom. Well, here's this fellow who must have drunk just similarly; he went on the same way like I did. There's nothing there, except for the sort of juiciness of the language, that's not perfect.

GRATWICK: Did you have to go through the other two stages first?

OLSON: No, no. And I don't think—and that's very decisively true: you can't say that they are development, that you have to get rid of the one to get to two to get to three.

VOICE: Do you think that all of these different hallucinogenic drugs, as they call them, produce the same …?

OLSON: Oh yes, absolutely. And the only differences are the length of time of the high. The quantity doesn't seem to be as interesting. That is, you bump at a certain point and that's it. I found, for example, that the recent research on the recent use of LSD disproves the old argument that LSD in quantity is wholly dangerous. You know, it was so—Puharich, for example, was involved in that early research by the Army about eighteen years ago up in Maine, where the Army tested out LSD just after its introduction, as a weapon of war.

VOICE: Weapon of war!

OLSON: Yeah. Well, the Army was way early; the American Army at least was in on this so early that they're the original researcher-testers.

VOICE: Were they going to bring peace to everybody?

OLSON: On the contrary! It was knocking a city out for nine hours, which is the term of LSD anyhow. And it just was thrown away by the Army because, it turns out, that tactic—technically, you can't move an occupation in in nine hours, so it's not as good as other forms of … [LAUGHTER]. Pretty cool, huh, pretty cool? We live in that world. That's pretty nice, actually, that's excellent research results.

GRATWICK: I think it would be more expected if they decided to make peace that way.

OLSON: Well, you see, basically, H, that was the push of the early mushroom experimentation and it's now disappeared as such an end, I think. But Leary, for example, used to argue that this was the decade of the mushroom, and if we didn't get peace from turning everybody on, the race would be destroyed. I think now that that's no longer true, and I myself think that was thin politics to begin with, myself.

VOICE: Well, having experienced this, can you recapture this thing? I mean, does it somehow become a part of you then?

OLSON: Well, I would meet that two ways. That if you use the drugs you will want to recapture it when the ripple runs out. And that's very good for the folks. I think the folks should have a ripple which runs out.

VOICE: Did you find that you have to take, or require, less and less each time?

OLSON: No, I think that's not true, but you see I've only been under any of these drugs twice in my life, except for smoking pot a couple of times. And that's twice under the mushroom. I've never taken LSD.

VOICE: Was it the same each time?

OLSON: Absolutely. Yes.

VOICE: But then you must have felt no need to take it again, as you said.

OLSON: Yeah, yeah. I don't have any great—I don't rush, I wouldn't rush. By the way, this is a great—now you're getting into an interesting problem. I don't believe in the use of the food except in a session, anyhow. See, I'm very Indian here. I don't think you should do this without company and in company and at a place where company is expected. That it is truly social, uh? And it's not excusable itself. For example, the first time I went under the mushroom I went into a big hall longhouse take. I discovered a great truth of the Indians of this territory, who discovered the longhouse principle late, as you know. But we don't know too much in anthropology yet about the history of the longhouse before the Dekanawidah epic. The epic may itself be the result of an Indian experience which hadn't solidified itself before the longhouse.

One is now talking typology of constructs which are ahead of us for sure, and we pick up—in fact, I think you could almost isolate the places you can pick up this kind of typology from, and the Indian here in this state is one place, on the longhouse thing. I, under the mushroom, was absolutely a peace sachem, holding, as chief, a longhouse ceremony, and I said it in so many words. It came popping out of my mouth. The moment the peanuts affected me I started talking longhouse talk, and created, because I was the responsible person, I was the victim, or whatever you want to say, in that instance, I was the tone, I created the tone of the evening; and it was absolutely a pure ceremonial set.

GRATWICK: Then did others that were taking this with you, did they fall into your pattern?

OLSON: They took it. But you see, the great experience of this is you're individual. Like this guy says, your ego goes and your self is on. So everybody is themselves. There's none of the social problem. There's none of the individual problem either. There isn't the ego or the rational, or even what we're doing here, which is sitting and being intellectual about it. It's in, it's soul, that's all! It happens to be, that's all.

VOICE: Does every self belong in a longhouse?

OLSON: I don't know. The only thing I'm trying to say is that there is a typology of a social set that I think is required here. The *curanderos* practice it exactly the same way.

VOICE: What do you mean "the same way"?

OLSON: That there ought to be a house and a leader to whom you go just like you go to a barber, for a shave and a haircut or to have your hair done, a beauty parlor. It should be a house which is the House of the Rite. That is done in all places where it's actually been experienced for years, for centuries, and is known for what it is.

VOICE: And it is set apart?

OLSON: It isn't set apart, no. Now, that's important. It is another house on the street, functioning like other houses on the street, but with this purpose. Yeah? You gotta say it very carefully: it's not set apart. That's right, it's not a temple. In fact, I think I could show from my own research that the church, the temple, never was supposed to be the same as this. You've got to be very careful. Religion is not the same as this, and it never was. It tends actually to obstruct this, that's true, but it never was intended to be anything but a form of its own. I think you could, for example, you could correct Frazer's great founding statement of the 19th century on this, when he says that man goes through three stages: magic, religion, science. If you remember, that's Frazer's absolute fixed statement of why he's writing *The Golden Bough* is to show how man was once in a magic stage, then was caught in religion, and now is in the stage of science. Well, that's only one term wrong, the stage of magic, so-called magic. That's inaccurate. There was no such stage as magic. But you can really talk about the function of religion, the function of science, and the function of mythology as though they were absolute, distinct functions. And one just happens to be primary and, as I said earlier, the prime is complex. I think that's very true and we're about to discover that again. And it's one of the advantages of this whole thing coming into existence in our time.

VOICE: Prime is not primitive, is it?

OLSON: Not at all. It's utterly complex. It's one of the biggest mistakes we've made is that the prime is elementary. Well, as a matter of fact, take what physics has proven, what we found out about matter. Phew! I mean what physics has shown us, where the whole thing got where it got, which is that the initial units of creation are unbear—well, I don't think unbearably, but for a while they seemed unbearably complex in the sense that they were much more powerful than we ever dreamed that we are.

VOICE: Excuse me, I was just wondering if under the mushroom one has a feeling of knowing more about one's own unconscious self?

OLSON: Completely. Completely. I would—I thought if we could do the other thing—I actually myself am a poet. I'd be perfectly happy to read you some poems that are, from my point of view, examples of what the so-called experience of the mushroom is, as well as how action for any person, when it's their own, is going in the direction of revealing this, this whatever this is that we say is true. It's that easy.

VOICE: May I ask another question? I'm still trying to get a feeling of what this inner relationship is under the influence of these drugs. If the feeling is one of complete unity, which we hear and read so much about, then it must be a little bit like a field experience.

[GAP]

OLSON: ... first came on, Leary was sitting there watching me, and he's—he then was obviously central, didn't even—the thing was his coach's whistle at football, calling the formal plays, and I suddenly watched him and was listening, and whatever a person said I said, "Did you say that?" Everybody started to laugh, but I thought, "Why, that's the most remarkable thing I've ever heard!" And all they said was "Could you pass me another ...?" [LAUGHTER] The truth is that it really is so that just exactly what you do say is who you are and that happens to be the tricky little thing. I don't know how to give you the conviction there, unless, say, you've got to get yourself under an hallucinogen.

VOICE: How do we do that?

OLSON: Well, this is easy, I mean, except it is illegal now, isn't it? [LAUGHTER] I don't know how you do it. The actual supplies have become criminal. It's a very terrible thing that's happened.

VOICE: When was that law passed?

OLSON: Oh, it's been tripped out. Sandoz is—who stopped Sandoz manufacturing psilocybin? Who stopped the manufacture of LSD? One has only one guess. The companies were threatened, if they didn't, that's all, by obviously, well, like you can start with the Food and Drug Administration. They must be the operators in the field. Somebody here must be much more knowledgeable about the recent events in this thing than I am. I was surprised, for example—I got to Vancouver this summer, and a kid had written to me from Alaska, from Seal Point,[5] and asked me—through the mushroom people—they knew I was going to be in Vancouver and he'd written to them saying that he'd like to go into a drug session, and they wrote back and said, "Well, get Olson, who'll be in Vancouver." And he went around picking up all the Heavenly Blue, and immediately the Royal Mounted was aware, and they sent a guy to say to this kid, "Look, either get out of town or we'll pick up your Heavenly Blue." And he came to me rather disturbed. I said, "I don't want to go under the damned thing." I said, "I haven't got the time." You see, it's nine hours in the session and then the next day you're rather—they tell you that under the morning-glory seeds, like LSD, the next day you really are—you've got a big ripple. You have a big ripple under the mushroom the next day—and in fact, by the way, to be fair, to tell the opposite side of the Koestler thing, the next day after that session, I was—my nerves, my neural, my whatever aggressive—I don't think so, but that's the way he described me in the London newspaper as a horrible American hotrod gunman that he had to take on![6] [LAUGHTER] So maybe it was true, because the next day I backed my Pontiac into a brand-new Cadillac right in front of the Personality Center, and I billed the Personality Center for seventy-five dollars for repairs, because I said I'm transporting your host's customer and he's given me such a terrible day after the mushroom that all the benefits of benefit have been lost! Here I am trying to drive an automobile and this idiot, and I backed right into a lovely new Cadillac.

VOICE: Would you define "ripple" for me?

OLSON: Yeah. I don't know what—it could—by the way, the other thing about the cell that Rinkel says is that when that stuff goes on—I think it's known that this is true as of adrenalin, isn't it, that there's a clearance system in the cell that operates to pull the adrenalin out after it's done its purpose? That is, to clear the adrenalin. Is this so or not? Is there a doctor in the house? Is that so or not?

VOICE: It's a metabolic degradation.

OLSON: It's just a degradation of that unit? There isn't another operator in that.

VOICE: An enzyme split.

5. John Hill, a historian of the Silk Road, lived in Sand Point, Alaska. He now resides in Australia, and retains in his possession several letters from Olson.
6. Olson is embellishing a clipping from the *Sunday Telegraph* for 12 March 1961 which had been sent to him because of the following description in Koestler's article "Return Trip to Nirvana": "… an American writer whom otherwise I rather liked began to declaim about Cosmic Awareness, Expanding Consciousness, Zen Enlightenment, and so forth. This struck me as obscene, more so than four-letter words, this pressure-cooker mysticism seemed the ultimate profanation. But my exaggerated reaction was no doubt also mushroom-conditioned, so I went to bed." Koestler could, however, have been referring here to Allen Ginsberg, also present.

OLSON: It's an enzyme split. Well, do you know enough about what Rinkel's argument is about this side of it, the autonomic cell system, afterwards? But in any case, you've got it if you say "degradation." It clears out. And apparently that clearing out is the ripple stage. That is, slowly your cells lose the bump-up of the unit that is, say, unisolated yet but comparable to—at this point, by the way, you're just talking chemistry, and there's a lovely piece of work by Schultes, the Harvard botanist, on all this drug stuff in this issue, "Drugs and the Mind," the *Harvard Review*. And this is cool, because Schultes gives actually, literally, the chemistry of all the drugs involved. And all that we don't have is, I guess, a comparable chemistry yet of the physiology of the human system and possibly, from that point on, of such organic units as cells anywhere in the creation, right? Is that fair to say? Sounds vague and large and quick, but it's only because it's quick. Don't mind anything I say that sounds rapid; it's only because we've got one evening. This is work which the human race is going to go on doing for a long time, until it gets this stuff set.

VOICE: So "ripple" means duration of the effect?

OLSON: Degradation of the effect, I should assume, if one may accept your— that is, that the degradation of the bump of whatever it is that comes on in the cell just lasts over a period of time, slowly goes away.

VOICE: So it's the duration of the degradation?

OLSON: Right. That's right. And there seems to be quite a long—and, even on my own experience it lasted, say, four or five days, maybe.

VOICE: Does it smoothly decay or …?

OLSON: Yeah, very. Oh yes, very. Oh it's a nice, little slow …

VOICE: I wondered why the word "ripple," then, which would imply that there might be …

OLSON: I don't think, by the way, it's my use of the word or Barron's. Nobody as far as I know has talked about this in any of the reports is the length of the time after the session in which the stuff generally gives you a buoyancy. It's a buoyancy, it's a feeling that you've been there and that was fine, and you feel fine, and, gee, that's all right. And yet things still stay a little bit freshly different. I don't know why—I don't want you to be beaten by that, because, it could be easily—that again is discourse. We don't have any discourse yet on that.

VOICE: Just once more, when the ripple has expired, are you still connected with the experience?

OLSON: Oh yeah. Oh boy. Right now as I talk to you I'm still right there. I know. Now there again is that great question of transit: you stay where you were. We don't know anything—we know what that's called, we call it memory; but we don't know what memory power is.

GRATWICK: Has it affected you as it creates your work?

OLSON: No, not at all. In fact, that's one of the bullshits in this whole—this whole creativity thing is one of the things that ought to be kicked in the face. I think it's one of the unconscionable social products of quote "creativity" talk.

GRATWICK: Well then, you don't worry about that artist …

OLSON: No, I read that article in the Boston newspaper.[7] That stinks.

VOICE: Oh, why?

OLSON: Because I don't think it has—I mean "creative"—you know, creation is man's work. Ah, you got to be hard-boiled about that word. It sounds like juicy and wonderful and all that stuff; in fact, all it is is that you do, and can do, what you propose to do. It's as solid as that. And to start to call it something is one of those—gee, aren't we a society and a nation that would just do that today, call it "creativity," call it "culture," call it "technology," call it "art"?

I mean, agh! I mean, at this date? This is just what we need not one inch more of! The less the better! Because of the very things that it's brought us to the point where we're on. And it's gonna kill the thing as sure as the letter killeth the spirit. Here it is, again.

VOICE: Excuse me. One does read in some of these accounts of people who have taken amounts and suddenly, for no particular apparent reason except that it may be clued or something, they turn on what they call automatically or maybe with a suggestion or something. Have you ever seen this happen, to be turned on without taking the drug?

ANOTHER VOICE: When a person says he's been to the light is that the same thing?

OLSON: Now we're into the great area of vision, aren't we? Even the word "turned on" is turn on the light, and light is—and now we can talk Dostoevsky and epilepsy, and talk saints; we can talk St Anthony in the desert; we can talk of whether or not, say, sense deprivation doesn't turn you on. As a matter of fact, Lilly, the dolphin man, who's been making himself like a dolphin very carefully, refuses to tell anybody how horrible it is under his experiences of sense deprivation. We're now talking in all the unexplored areas of sense and sensibility which have existed as long as man. And you've got to take each individual there on his merit and his report. And we certainly know objectively when it's true. There is that, when a person is on, we know. Now, if you've read Dostoevsky's reports on what it was like in his—how do you call it?—in his mouth, boy, I mean I think that's a witness that you believe. He says exactly what I guess actually now has become textbook medicine probably, in studied cases. But again, I think it's awfully important that Dostoevsky did that. We have that evidence and he is a literary artist, therefore you can trust what he says in words, that's all. Now I don't know whether that meets what you're saying about somebody being on?

7. This article is not at present known.

VOICE: No, not necessarily. I can't recall actually which report it was where this was specifically mentioned, but someone walking along the street having perhaps not had LSD for a week or so, or even longer, might suddenly, without seeming provocation, be what they called or termed "turned on." And of course some of those people walked in front of cars and things like that. It seems somewhat dangerous.

OLSON: Oh yes, I would think so, but I don't even know if there is such a reported case.

VOICE: Yes, I'm positive I have.

OLSON: You have seen one?

ANOTHER VOICE: I think it was in the *Saturday Evening Post* article.[8]

VOICE: Oh, was it in that one?

OLSON: Well, I—you know, we—it may be better—it would settle an awful lot of questions if you would care to read this thing yourself, to read the three stages as defined by Harman. And the other thing that's worth it out of this magazine, which has really got two marvelous articles on all that we're talking about, is to read this Hindu guy here on, say—it's one of the nicest statements of some—say, for example, that there's four ways that human beings may experience, like, the same thing. It's out of the drug thing entirely this guy's talking; he's talking the four basic yoga. And it's very beautiful to see it stated at this point parallel with the Harman article, which is who is an engineer, a professor of engineering at Stanford, and this guy Asrani is simply a—he says "thirty-five years I've been in the practice of that form of yoga called Jnana Yoga Sadhana," which he likens to—that is, that's the yoga that seeks the stage in the Bhagavad Gita which is called "the Sthita Prajna state." And that's remarkable itself, the passage that he uses to—as a Tantrist myself, that's a pure dandy, pure passage. I mean I wouldn't touch the drugs because I'm a Tantrist. I know how books put you on. Like, literally, the book puts you on. The poem puts you on. Literally, the poem puts you on.

VOICE: What about the *Tibetan Book of the Dead* in connection with …?

OLSON: Yes, I don't know it. I have avoid—I purposely stay away from it because I have my own book.[9] I don't know, I got projects. I actually can't afford the time to try to find out if that's as good as Leary. I told H that they're all so hopped up on this thing they're preparing a new translation. The problem for me with, say, *The Tibetan Book of the Dead* or any of these, is translation, is whether you've got the thing true.

8. John Kobler's hostile article "The Dangerous Magic of LSD," in the *Saturday Evening Post* (2 November 1963), pp. 31–40.

9. This book could be *The Secret of the Golden Flower*; or, alternatively, *Man and Time* (Eranos Yearbook, 1957), especially Henry Corbin's contribution, "Cyclical Time in Mazdaism and Ismailism," which presented Olson with an angelology he had used in *The Maximus Poems* since March 1961. It is this text that Olson refers to later in the discussion as providing him with a feeling for Mohammedism from 15th-century Spain and Iran.

VOICE: Are they doing it from the Tibetan?

OLSON: Yeah. And, boy, when they throw something at it, I'm telling you, they are a body of contemporary actualist-scientists or activist-scientists. This is one of the reasons why they got fired at Harvard is because they slopped the activist principle. What are you going to do as against the taxonomic? It's all—there's a big, big struggle on today. It's right across our society. We've moved rapidly from the taxonomic, forced out by the developments of the 19th century in physics and in geometry, and now we're in a stage of hard science which is purely an investigation of active states. Now what are you going to do with soft—which isn't soft at all, but which is the science—what did you call them, the "rejected" sciences? We used that word as of the work that Arthur Young went into after having been an engineer, an engineer or inventor, when he writes about things that I would call business that I've spent my life on, like mythology. That's a soft science, if you like. It's soft because it's literary or something. Bullshit. It's the same hard as that hard, only we don't know that, we've had no—we're just beginning to start again on that experience. I don't mean that experience, but I mean on the discourse, the language we use in that area of knowing, and we don't have anything, practically, yet, in terms of tooling.

VOICE: Could you read a poem?

OLSON: Yeah, I'd like to. It's a little—how long—we shouldn't—I think we might do that another time. If there's any questions left in your minds I'd rather land on the subject tonight than, say, give you examples. What is it, 9:30?

VOICE: Are the three stages the political, the theological, and …?

OLSON: Politics, theology, and epistemology.

VOICE: Are these the three stages that Harman mentions?

OLSON: No, oh no, not at all. Let me keep that book, 'cos I think that's very valuable. He's only talking about literally under all the drugs, and his experimentation, his and his fellows', is in LSD. And this re-think thing is stated in their article, J.N. Sherwood, M.J. Stolaroff, W.W. Harman, "The Psychedelic Experience—A New Concept in Psychotherapy," *Journal of Neuropsychiatry*, 1962. And this is their summary.

VOICE: But his three stages have nothing to do with the three which you were talking about?

OLSON: Oh, not at all. I'm talking discourse there, curriculum of discourse, when I say that—I'm saying that the only three studies that you ought to have today is epistemology, theology, and politics, as a study, like literally. I'm talking like Plato did when he wrote his bloody book, and, in fact, that bloody book is what we're talking about. If we had a lot of hours I'd now take a mid-stage in this thing before I read my own poetry to talk about what Plato says about poetry, that it must be driven out of society because it prevents people from the real. And I agree with him completely. Plato's argument, took in reverse, is now true, tremendously true. Plato says absolutely, and it is utterly true, that you cannot have society because poetry—and what he means by poetry is all art as practiced at his date (now mind you that's a damn good date) is wrong because it keeps people from the real. And he's absolutely right. We're talking the real here.

VOICE: Is it in the transcendentalism you mean ...?

OLSON: No, not at all. No, no. That both its means and its experience is wrong. It enables people to, not project, but to—it enables people to have their experience by mimesis, and therefore their experience then becomes mimetic. Most human beings live mimetically anyhow. Most of us all live our lives mimetically instead of—I don't want to use the word which may occur to you as the opposite of mimetic ...

VOICE: What happens if you give one of these drugs to an animal?

OLSON: Oh, it's being—it's now being used to take care of elephants' nails or something. Have you ever looked in a tiger's eyes? I think they're in it all the time. [LAUGHTER] I once had an affair at the Washington Zoo with the wife of the tiger, and the tiger looked at me as though I was really casting eyes at his woman. I got the hell scared out of me. And they were two beautiful tigers. And I really thought, my lord, it's truth going on here! Those eyes, you know those eyes. They're marvelous, because they're so big. By the way, I met a woman once in a railroad station that literally had—I never forgot this in my life. In Harrisburg Railroad Station I once saw a woman that had eyes twice as big as the normal eye. And I wish to god I knew who that was. She was sitting at a lunch counter and I completely felt the same experience I had in the zoo. So I don't know. [LAUGHTER]

VOICE: Going from tigers to children, there was an article in the *New York Times* that LSD had been used on children to great advantage and that they do not have the bad reactions that apparently, shall we say, warped adults have.

OLSON: Right. Right. I should think so, because of the condition "child," anyhow. Wouldn't you? I mean, literally, the stage "child" is such a superior—like a stage—that it should respond to it.

VOICE: Why has this resistance sprung up to the manufacture of the drugs?

OLSON: Well, again Harman is marvelous on that. He says in so ... Beg your pardon?

VOICE: Is someone against euphoria?

OLSON: It's more serious than that. What happens if you can't do the—how does he say it? It's so marvelous. Can you help me here, Mr Carlson? Do you remember that point where he says out at some length why the resistance exists even?

MR CARLSON: No, I don't remember, except the point that just because it's called a drug it's lodged in many peoples' minds with danger.

OLSON: That's right. And in fact, by the way, this is another thing that you ought to know and it applies to what you're saying. I mean, I've had—we've had friends that use drugs indiscriminately. And they end up damaged. Now, let's not kid ourselves, I mean it's a perfectly obvious fact that ...

VOICE: Isn't this a little more subtle than that? Now when you read earlier the summation of this paper, the thought ran through my mind that most people had a great deal to unlearn in Western society, and naturally ...

OLSON: Yes, very much. In fact we all do, let's be quite flat about it.

VOICE: Yes. In Western society I think it's bolstered by people who don't want to have the facts.

OLSON: That's right. He says it so much altogether across the board, though, at some point here, that I just—I'm not trying to avoid answering it. It is something of that order that, really, it would upset the ratio basic to our whole procedure of life.

VOICE: Well, just the idea of God within oneself is contrary to ...

OLSON: Well, sure, I mean that guy was off the lists the moment he made the sermons.[10] And that was the second half of the 13th century. And he was already wrong, by the way. So there you are. He had it within. When we've got it—I'd like, by the way, I'd love to make a very great case for, say, the Americans here. I would love to—rather than read myself, I'd love to read you Walt Whitman's "Crossing Brooklyn Ferry," say, which the argument is made, in the greatest sermon I know as a poem that exists in the world, as to where does lie the sources of the true. But I can capsulate it by a contemporary of Whitman's who wrote in a personal letter to Hawthorne—and that's Herman Melville—"By visible truth we mean the apprehension of the absolute condition of present things." That we have, as a people, preparation of inordinate order already in these areas of non-mimetic imagination, of doped-up perceptions, of serious—a totally serious art has been done by Americans for a hundred years, completely clearheaded on the question of the changes of discourse. Because when Melville says "by visible truth I mean the apprehension of the absolute condition of present things," this is all that you can say is the absolute condition of present things. That fellow's saying, that I quoted as a testimony, is actually saying simply the absolute condition of present things. And in fact, as far as I can see, the advantage of the autonomic drugs, if I may call them that, is simply they restore the fact that we live in the auto-nomic system, which, as far as I understand, is to preserve our organs from our will. This it seems to be, if you will accept that, as a man of this knowledge—that's why we call it autonomic, as a matter of fact: it's without the interference of a will. It has a will and is the will of free—that is, that

10. Olson picks up quickly on the phrase "God within" as reminding him of Meister Eckhart (d. 1327), the essence of whose sermons Olson summarized as "God is interested in *me*; the Mass is his participation in me" (*Olson-Boldereff Correspondence*, pp. 197–98).

which the organ itself requires to be permanently in function within the terms of creation.

VOICE: Where does instinct or intuition then fit in here?

OLSON: I'm trying to avoid those words. By the way, I would knock 'em right down by using Jung's four functions. I think that nobody has improved on Jung's declaration of functions. These are functions. The four functions are intuition, sensation, thinking, and feeling—which I notice that Young in that article slips and makes "emotion" instead of feeling, which is a terrible error. The great advantage of the definition of feeling is wholly scientific. "All is there for feeling," for example, to take Whitehead's, that enormous statement of Whitehead's about the character of creation. "All is there for feeling." That's not emotion; emotions are strictly a personal business and hung-up stuff, which disappear the moment that you touch the real.[11] The Aztecs called the mushroom "God's meat." You bit God when you took the mushroom. This is literally *carne*, the earliest Spanish translation of the Nahuatl for the mushroom. When you buy meats in the store it's *carne*. God's meat. Literally, the "quarter" of God. That's beautiful, that's so literal that you can't beat it, I think.

VOICE: Were you starting to tell us how we could have this experience before I interrupted you?

OLSON: No, I wasn't, I was just talking the technical ways of getting a drug session, if you'd like. And that would seem to be quite—I mean, Leary is just down here in the state. I'll tell him that you people are interested, and see if he'll come up and give you a run under his—he's a beautiful *curandero*, that's why I suggest it. He's a highly trained man with beautiful *curandero*'s power. He's one of the best, probably one of the best trained Western or American or North American leaders of a session, Leary, the guy who got fired by—the man who has now become a saint, a notorious person.

VOICE: Yeah, I thought he'd gone to the islands or something.

OLSON: No, as a matter of fact, they're preparing—the bulldozers are in the islands. The Gagarines is now supposed to be where we're all—where they're all going.

VOICE: The Grenadines?

OLSON: The Grenadines, excuse me! [GENERAL LAUGHTER] There you are! Aren't I beautiful! There you are. See, you always say, "Did I say that?" [LAUGHS]

VOICE: Have you run across Alan Watts at all?

OLSON: Certainly.

---

11. Olson is echoing *Process and Reality*: "Every reality is there for feeling: it promotes feeling; and it is felt" (U.S. edn, p. 472). Jung's four functions are dealt with in his *Psychological Types* (1946) and elsewhere in his work. Arthur Young has a section called "Emotional projections" in *The Reflexive Universe*.

VOICE: What can you tell us about him?

OLSON: Well, Watts as you know is one of the theologians of the psychedelic movement, along with Gerald Heard, Huxley, and that actual literal theologian at Boston University, the fourth one of the team. What's his name? There's a paperbook by him on the philosophy of religion recently out. He seems to be the most sort of, well, academic or rational.

VOICE: Not Huston Smith, surely?

OLSON: Yeah, that's it, Huston Smith.

VOICE: Oh, really? Oh, amazing!

OLSON: Those four are the real—they meet every Monday night in a pique. I was asked one night to go as the fifth wheel. [LAUGHS]

VOICE: Huston Smith's the only reason I send money to MIT.

OLSON: Well, he's it, and he's the guy that goes with the others.

VOICE: Why have you only had this twice if there's been such a wonderful experience?

OLSON: Because it simply can corroborate with my own experience. And believe you me, I would want it only on the highest social terms. And it's not easy to get that. This society doesn't have any place where I can go if I wanted to, instead of drinking or dancing or making up to a girl or something. I mean, where do you go? It isn't yet established; the longhouse just doesn't exist.

VOICE: It sounds as though four men are starting a tent somewhere.

OLSON: Well, they can't get a—did you see the wonderful case in Newton where the mushroom house was attacked on the basis of—how do you call it?—the problems of building a house. You've got to get a permit.

VOICE: Multiple housing or something.

OLSON: Yeah, it was. Whether they were a family unit, because there were seven men and four women, or seven women and four men and thirteen children in the house. It was a marvelous case, by the way.

VOICE: Alpert was the one that did that.

OLSON: Yes, it was Alpert—no, Alpert owned the house. Alpert is a—well, his father actually tried the case. His father is the former president of New Haven Railroad and he beat them; he went into the court in this case and defeated the—what do you call it?—the zoning. Zoning was the argument, and they didn't lose that one. But it'll come up again. In fact, I bet you seriously it'll come up so that there will be definite changes in zoning laws.

VOICE: Well, the thing that disturbs me about this: this experience has gotten into the realm of, you might say, the common man's gossip, and it never should have been allowed. Why has this happened? Why have these people let this get out? Now, of course it leaked out of Harvard via students apparently.

OLSON: Go on! A whole gang, a bunch of criminals moved in. Sure, they were selling LSD, laced sugar cubes of LSD for a buck. And the kids were just gobbling it up. The black market operations. I could answer you on Watts very simply. I said to Alan last spring in Gloucester, "You really want to be a member of the syndicate." He does. He's ragged, he's going ragged as a human being because he really wishes to be a member of the syndicate. And I said, "Why don't you become the drug boss, drug peddler of the syndicate? You're knowing on the mystical area, you're knowing on the theological area, you're competent within the group; why the hell don't you go, why don't you go"—go what? What?

VOICE: Go commercial.

OLSON: Go commercial. Right, absolutely. He really is, and it's showing up badly. His reporting gets worse and worse. Worse and worse. That last book of his, the one on LSD is—why, I'm sure if Arthur Young were here, with the work he's done already in mythology, he could call the shots on Alan's reports on it.

VOICE: You mean *The Joyous Cosmology*?

OLSON: Yeah, absolutely.

ANOTHER VOICE: I was alarmed by what Alpert and Leary had to say in that book.

OLSON: Oh, so was I. Oh, completely!

VOICE: The point in it that made sense to me, and which ties in to what you're saying, is when Watts compared our existence to the two crusts of a loaf of bread.

OLSON: I know it. Absolutely. That's why one talks language. That's why I want to, really—if I can get one point across to you tonight: be happy in what you do, because the errors here are not doing what they're doing. This is a most simple thing. Rushing into print or rushing into vision, or trucking in the reports of vision or of action, instead of just doing it. But it's a terrible temptation. I mean activism; the active is now of such an order, and the enemy is so huge and so strong. I heard Leary the first night he got up before the Soc Rel Department and the boss of the department, which was in this new building, was the chairman of the meeting. Riesman was in the back of the room. And the other guy on with him was a current powerful researcher in social anthropology or psycho-anthropology. And Leary makes this dumb speech about how "knowledge today has to move into the active, we cannot examine anybody except in their being, in the context of their own place and behavior and pattern, and that's what the study of personality must be." And it sounded like just lush and trash. But at the same time the heart was there, and he wasn't a fool, but he had to make a fool of himself to even mention what he considered the study of man today—or the study of study today, it's even better than that.

VOICE: You've mentioned two extremes and I'm disturbed by this. You talk about the syndicate on one hand led by Mr Watts …

OLSON: [LAUGHING] No, wishing to be!

VOICE: You also say that this isn't connected with religion, and yet the only time in history when it seems to have worked properly was when the high priests controlled it. So how do you avoid commercialism?

OLSON: Yes, I know, I hear you, I know.

ANOTHER VOICE: I don't quite understand the nature of the problem here.

VOICE: Well, he suggested, to which you would be inclined, it be a syndicate type operation. The other thing, it can't be a religion …

OLSON: No, no. Mind you, I had said that Alan Watts's condition as a human being is deteriorating because he himself has a heroism of the criminal man, and he hides it. And actually, in fact, I was simply suggesting a way that he could implement his own entrance into the syndicate, was to become the drug—the pusher of the syndicate. In the new activism, by the way, see? One of the reasons why the whole thing blew up was that we have no activism, literally, except the session. That's why I say to you, this is an idle thing to be doing tonight except that we should be under the drug, that's all. We're doing a secondary thing.

VOICE: Participation instead of saying.

OLSON: Yes, or direct experience. I mean, to use a great word of the transcendental mystical world, the direct experience of said so and so, yeah? The direct experience means what it says. It's a very straight thing. And as of your business of the high priest, I myself say that I don't think we know the typology of the forms that are required for us to now restore, for those who want it, the experience, the direct experience that this thing includes. I don't think we've invented yet the typological form. For example, I can testify the only one I believe in, personally, and from an image, say, is the longhouse. But then I can give you a very good example of the long race's experience of the use of the *curandero* in both the Mexican, the Mayan, and Peruvian society.

GRATWICK: What is it?

OLSON: Oh, it's simply the very same thing that Leary was and isn't any longer, I fear, but probably is competently enough to hold a session here if he'll come.

VOICE: Isn't that what he meant, then, by saying that we have to take into consideration our social and cultural patterns of the moment?

OLSON: Yes, I suppose he does. But, mind you, in saying that, he's already trading with the enemy! I mean if you mention the social and political …

VOICE: Then you admit that we don't know yet how to do it?

OLSON: Yes, better to be, really, illiterate. In fact, it's very crucial today in these areas to be sure that you stay illiterate simply because literacy is wholly dangerous, so dangerous that I'm involved every time I read poetry in the fact that I'm reading to people who are literate, and they are not hearing. They may be listening with all their mind, but they don't hear. Recently I read a whole lot at Brandeis and I got so damn offended I backed up against the wall and said, "You people are so literate I don't want to read to you any more," and stopped. And the moment I said it of course the shock was so great that I could read from that point on as long as I chose. Everybody needs to be bumped like mad on this point. But if you're talking in terms of creating agency, which he is—Leary, for example, wants very much to create social and political agency for the drug. That's really what he wants to do. He believes, as I've said to you, this is the decade of the mushroom. Now he believes that this is the century of the psychedelic. But it's work to be done, and he can do it.

GRATWICK: You ought to tell us more about the longhouse. We keep getting off the ...

OLSON: Well, I meant only that there was an image for me, literally, in practice, of what I would trust as a typological form. It's perfectly clear, I think, that the Iroquois never used drugs and that the point of the session was rather the very opposite, that by talk alone you arrived at a condition of decision. By the way, this whole thing was political decision, so far as I know. Solely political and social decision, only made in the longhouse. There was no, there was not at all that "high" sought, if I'm not mistaken. And I'm saying that the other one I do know that's practical is the Indian scene. And as far as I know we don't know anything equal to that either.

GRATWICK: Have you taken it in an Indian situation?

OLSON: No, I'm saying that the one in Newton in the mushroom house under the drug for me was a longhouse, and I so said. "My god," I said, "here we are. This is longhouse. Let's ... Oh, wonderful," like, and we started to improvise.

VOICE: Did you ever see the longhouse ...?

OLSON: No, I never saw a longhouse till last week we went over to Letchworth, and that's a bad longhouse. I'd hate to sit in that longhouse! That's an uncomfortable place. And I talked to an archeologist who says it's rather questionable that Letchworth can claim that it is a true Seneca longhouse. So I think it isn't. So I'm happy to have the picture restored.

GRATWICK: Well, let's have a poem or two and then we'll have some refreshments. If you'd like to.

OLSON: It's hard. I ...

GRATWICK: Maybe we're not listening well.

OLSON: No, it isn't that. I'd rather read poetry without this condition around, yeah? That's what I suddenly realized we were—I could stand it as an example and you become the thing which it is. I'd rather read you a letter I got this week from a boy named Sassoon, who was at Vancouver, quoting suddenly to me a French philosopher named Merleau-Ponty. Unbelievable passage! Because we did agree that night that philosophy is very important, at least to this group, or to myself at least, and you used the word too. And you really meant the "consolation of philosophy," I think.

GRATWICK: Consolation?

OLSON: Yeah, to use Boethius's—Chaucer based his poetry upon Boethius's *The Consolation of Philosophy*. But this man is a part of—there was apparently a great magazine published in Buffalo until last year, *Philosophy and Phenomenological Research*. Any of you know that thing, which went away with the guy who edited it to Pennsylvania?[12] Apparently some figure he left because this thing he got attention with, but he went to Pennsylvania. But this fellow—I see that this Merleau-Ponty is one of those. I would read it simply to suggest how completely today, from another point of view, the whole question of object, the object, I mean the objective world, is being completely fed into a discourse. Let me read you one paragraph at least of the thing, because it's kind of interesting. Instead of a poem, really. One paragraph in particular is so exciting as of so much that I believe is true, whether or not you have anything to do with drugs or anything else. Or, say, that whole thing I'm trying to reverse, if I could only find it there, on empathy and mimesis or the imitation of a personality that's supposed to be stronger than humanity.

> If on the other hand we admit that all these "projections," all these "associations," all these "transferences," are based on some intrinsic characteristic of the object, the "human world"

(This is interesting as of God's *carne*, for example.)

> the "human world" ceases to be a metaphor and becomes once more what it really is, the seat and as it were homeland of our thoughts. The perceiving subject ceases to be an "acosmic" thinking subject, and action, feeling and will remain to be explored as original ways of positing an object.[13]

This is the first time I've heard those tones in professional philosophy, and it's like a birth!

> If on the other hand we admit that all these "projections," all these "associations," all these "transferences," are based on some intrinsic characteristic of the object, the "human world" ceases to be a metaphor and becomes once more what it really is, the seat and as it were homeland of our thoughts. The perceiving subject ceases to be an "acosmic" thinking subject, and action, feeling and will remain to be explored as original ways of positing an object.

12. Marvin Farber, Professor of Philosophy at Buffalo, author of *The Foundation of Phenomenology* (NY: Paine-Whitman, 1962).
13. These and further quotations that Olson reads from Richard Sassoon's letter can be found in Maurice Merleau-Ponty's *Phenomenology of Perception* (1962), pp. 21, 22, 24, and 30–31. It is not clear that Olson consulted the book for himself.

Which would seem to me what we mean by active, activism, arising from the whole picture. Then he goes on:

> The relationship of "figure" and "background," "thing" and "not-thing," and the horizon of the past appear, then, to be structures of consciousness irreducible to the qualities which appear in them.

In other words, as I read that, he means that we're undoing the qualitative, that the relationships "'figure' and 'background,' 'thing' and 'not-thing,' and the horizon of the past appear, then, to be structures of consciousness themselves, not reducible to the qualities which appear in them." Which is a great breakthrough again, say, if you work in, like they say, the arts.

VOICE: Would this connect at all with Jung's archetype type of thing, or am I completely off?

OLSON: It would, at a certain point, it sure would, I guess. If you're going to talk cosmic instead of acosmic you're gonna bump, you're going to have to deal with that. That's why I said "typology" earlier to avoid that particular word, but I mean it. I don't think there is any typology except archetypology. It's inexcusable to use the word except as a "blow" or "imprint" which is upon creation.

VOICE: What is typology then?

OLSON: It's archetypology. But we've used it always the other—our rational discourse treats typology as relational and statistical instead of initial. "Imprint." It means "blow."

VOICE: Does it?

OLSON: Type—our word "type" comes from it. Our word "type." [TAPS ON TABLE]

VOICE: Did he say that it's irresistible?

OLSON: No, I think he—"that the relationships 'figure' and 'background,' 'thing' and 'not-thing,' and the horizon of the past appear, then, to be structures of consciousness" *not* reducible to the qualities which—we do nothing but put qualities in where they should be out, and if your action has value it has quality. But that's not the same thing as that which you are experiencing and seeking.

VOICE: Is this saying that the archetype does not have quality, have its own inherent qualities?

OLSON: No, one would say, then, that the archetype is the hidden secret of something which is quantity, as very much as well or perhaps vaster than quality. We're now talking that whole problem of the extensive continuum, which has completely come into existence again. You can't treat quantity and quality as though they are opposites.

> If finally it is conceded that memories do not by themselves project themselves upon sensations, but that consciousness compares them with the present data, retaining only those which accord with them …

(The translation of this man's book is obviously poor. This is a Frenchman, I guess, and this is the English translation published in London last year. It's pretty bad.)

> If finally it is conceded that memories do not by themselves project themselves upon sensations, but that consciousness compares them

(compares memories)

> with the present data, retaining only those which accord with memories, then one is admitting an original text which carries its meaning within itself, and setting it over against that of memories: this original text is perception itself.

Which again is a tremendous gain to me and is quite close to your statement about archetypes: that you could talk arche*text* at the point that you talk arche*type*. And that I'm convinced of myself, being a Tantrist; I utterly believe that you can talk language, literally, human language as recorded from text. Literally, from text. God's a bookman, as well as the other things he is. Or the subject is a condition of the universe, and that "this original text is perception itself." Which gets us really home if you talk poetry. "At the same time"—and this is the last one, this is the longest one and the worst translated, but I think it's …

> At the same time as it (the object) sets attention in motion, the object is at every moment recaptured and placed once more in a state of dependence on attention. It (the object) gives rise to the "knowledge-bringing event," which is to transform it (the object), only by means of the still ambiguous meaning which it requires that event to clarify, it is therefore the motive and not the cause of the event.

VOICE: Hm, you'll have to read that over again!

OLSON: I will, that's a stiff one! But mind you, listen …

GRATWICK: Why don't you say it in your own words?

OLSON: Well, listen to what I wanted to say. I just didn't say, for example, that that's true that there's an archetext. The two things that you'd want to say about an archetext is that it tells a story, or has the character-action of story, and that it has the character-object of image. These are the two big powers that one deals with in, say, words, is that they have an action which we call story and they have an action which we call image. And this is the whole damn philosophic, possible metaphysical statement right now, being supplied to us by a hotshot French metaphysician, in this whole concept that the object does set attention in motion. I think you'd have no trouble with that, because almost everything that you do that your attention is called to is an object, huh? "The object is at every moment recaptured and placed once more in a state of dependence on attention." That is, attention as a mobile fact constantly is re-mobilizing the object that sets itself in motion. Then he suggests that the object itself "gives rise then to the 'knowledge-bringing event,' which is to transform it (the object), only by means of the still ambiguous meaning which it requires that event to clarify"—which is that beautiful concept of Whitehead's, the eternal event that strikes across all object and occasion,[14] that, literally speaking, behind the object is the motive that is—that we do not know, we're not so sure, but we feel we're experiencing or participating it. But this guy's point is that the object gives rise because the attention is brought to bear on it, on "the 'knowledge-bringing event,' which is to transform that object only because the still ambiguous meaning which it requires lies in that event to clarify it." In other words, that the narrative that gets started begins to be the story that will yield from the object a *raison* that causes us in the first place to give our attention to it. And it is therefore, that is, the object therefore is "the motive and not the cause of the event." Which is very exciting, to get the whole thing reversed, so that we don't have *cause* anymore; we have *motive*. And again we inherited a complete system of discourse for two thousand years which has absolutely crapped motive. We have lost motive almost entirely out of our mental capacity and have had cause instead. So that the tendency of the objective world to go away from us has been extremely strong, because the objective world won't be treated that way. It just doesn't happen to be causal, it happens to be motible, mo—, mo— motible.

VOICE: We make the motive ourselves, really.

OLSON: We do. But don't—again, don't use that word. Say "attention." Give ourselves that great quality. Simply, to start with, say "attention." That *attention* gives us ...

GRATWICK: Yes, remember in the *Psychedelic Review* that Gerald Heard felt that that was the most important thing that LSD did for him.

OLSON: Yes, I didn't remember that, but I hear you, I hear Mr Heard.

GRATWICK: Quality of attention, intensification of attention.

VOICE: I don't know that I completely comprehend what this is that you've just read, but is it right that if you focus your attention sufficiently then on an object that is ...?

OLSON: You're already saying it too subjectively. *You* don't focus your attention. Attention, which may be the source of our very existence as being human beings—one almost wonders about tigers, for example. They don't have anything else to do! They are not involved with attention. They are attention. [LAUGHS] I'm sure that Young's seven levels, for example, do have to involve themselves with that question. Some of you, I know, do know some of Young's writing and theory of his grid-like thing. I'm not trying to make a classification comparable to his, but I mean there is that crazy question. We gotta be awfully careful today.

VOICE: Is attention itself the motive?

---

14. The "eternal event" is Olson's term to sum up one aspect of *Process and Reality*. A notable use of the phrase is in "A Later Note on Letter #15" (*Maximus* II.79).

OLSON: No. No. His argument is that the object that the attention does pick is the motive. We are reversing the whole field of premise that we've used mostly.

GRATWICK: You mean, the object is the motive that starts our attention?

OLSON: No, the moment that the attention picks it you never get it back then. The advantage of the attention is the great thing, that we select. That is why, for example, in a room under the mushroom, believe you me, like I say, what everybody does, is, and says, is pure, pure utterly marvelous divine existence; in other words, that the experience outside is definitely identical with the experience inside. If I hear some of you thinking or if I hear you say something, you happen to say exactly what you should say. That gets to be terrific! Your discourse improves immediately. [LAUGHTER]

VOICE: It would seem to me that it was cycles within cycles that refer to but don't stand for anything.

OLSON: No, I would think that the static is much more crucial. We're restoring the static, by the way, tremendously. I mean, one of the great factors, possibly, of our lack of vision has been our inattention to the static, to the literally cosmic. I think it has been acosmic.

VOICE: You don't mean that the cosmic is static?

OLSON: Well, there is a way to say it. I'm using "static" deliberately to avoid the true meaning of it, yes? Well, what about it's "eternal," in that sense, is "eternal" as instantaneous or material?

VOICE: I thought it was without beginning or without end.

OLSON: Well, that's not true. Eternal simply means of an age, right? Of an epoch. We live, for example, in the electromagnetic epoch. That simply defines this particular universe that we are supplied as an executive type, but it has nothing to do with eternal time, for example. Nothing whatsoever. It may be stained with eternal time or it may be a wonderful example or symbol of eternal time, but it's simply electromagnetic epoch. Fufft, fufft. I mean, in outer time, like in outer space? Unimaginable! Epochs. I'm talking now like a Mohammedan, but, believe you me, one needs very much to bring some Mohammedan feeling into this area. We abuse the word "eternal" the moment we use it in our mouths. There is such a powerful difference of that condition of things if you drop that time term and get up a time term equal to what we're quite familiar with, space, a time term which is equivalent.

VOICE: I'm not thinking of it like your scientific term.

OLSON: Well, I'm not either. But your word "eternal" is a powerfully ...

VOICE: What is this Mohammedan analogy or relation which you speak of?

OLSON: No, they just supply a complete narrative to epochs, so that you've got time stretching out as far out into outer time as we think, more easily, of space stretching out or, as they say, expanding.

VOICE: Did he figure that one out? Is that part of his writings?

OLSON: I don't think so. It's a development of his text but I don't think it's Mohammed himself. I get it mostly from the 15th century, both in Spain and Iran.

GRATWICK: When you think of archetext would you put myth in there?

OLSON: That *is* myth. You were wrong: I teach a course in "Myth and Literature." But bless you, that's just pertinent, at the moment; yes, that's pertinent at the moment. I'm professionally a mythologist, that's all.

GRATWICK: Well, tell them what you're offering as your field.

VOICE: At the new state university.

OLSON: I'm a Research Professor in Mythology, so that that is clear that that's the subject of the research, and Visiting Lecturer in Poetry, so that I always have an out, and I can keep my income tax based upon fifteen dollars a day per diem, so that I can reduce it to zero. 'Cos I don't have—under the state law of New York you need to have fourteen dependents, is it fourteen? They don't say dependents, they say exceptions, exemptions. Is it fourteen to get zero?

VOICE: I don't know.

OLSON: Yeah, I think it is. That's federal as well, I think.

VOICE: Perhaps these drugs would help with income tax problems.

ANOTHER VOICE: You gonna take them or feed them to the tax collector? [LAUGHTER]

OLSON: There we are, right back at the whole problem. Leary wants to feed 'em to Khrushchev and Kennedy. I think that politics stinks, myself.

VOICE: What does Dr Leary feel would happen if this were used on a large scale?

OLSON: Oh, he thinks happiness would descend upon the earth. [LAUGHS] He said so, in the best interview I've seen, where somebody challenged him as being a causer of trouble, and he said, "Look," he said, "this is the only way I know that guarantees happiness. If you've got a better one, I'll take it."[15] And he's right, you know. He's talking euphoria.

VOICE: Well, what is happiness?

OLSON: It's the state of confidence that you're alive and in life.

---

15. Olson paraphrases Leary as quoted in Kobler's piece in the *Saturday Evening Post*, p. 40.

Olson talking to students at the end of the "Causal Mythology" lecture. George Stanley is in the background. Photo: Jim Hatch.

5

Causal Mythology

Olson was to give a lecture at the Berkeley Poetry Conference on the morning of 20 July 1965. There was excitement in the air, for he was flying directly from Italy, having been to the Festival of Two Worlds in Spoleto (where, it was said, he had seen Pound for the first time in twenty years). With a side trip to a PEN conference in Bled, Yugoslavia, and returning via Caresse Crosby's castle, Roccasinibalda, near Rome, for once in his life Olson had been a jet-setter.

Jet-lagged or not, Olson set himself a most difficult task with his lecture: to make his points entirely by means of poems. The idea was that if the poems were worth anything they would create a total vision of the cosmos in a way that discursive exposition could not. He had a grid of four categories within which to place the poems; but close attention reveals that he never explains anything, even while giving a sense of doing so. Secretly, this is a poetry reading, a reading of four poems of which the poet is immensely proud. And just to test their worth he is interested to see if they can fill out the categories of his cosmology, to see, as he puts it, "if by any chance the relationship of, say, the four terms to the four poems will not destroy the poems."

Another thing Olson does not explain is the title, "Causal Mythology." We should perhaps take it at its simplest: that this is a mythology that causes life events, that motivates, because it is from the Cause, some greater power. This does not have to be mystical. Though the epigraph for the lecture comes from a mystical text, *The Secret of the Golden Flower*, one can think of "causal" mythology as what Robert Duncan meant when in his introduction he called Olson "the Big Fire Source."

ROBERT DUNCAN: To give testimony to something that is in the area of fact for me in relation to poetry: some things are appreciations, some things are tastes that change, but in a letter I had to write and give some sort of a—as you would in a witenagemot, the statement of the way things are—and I was keying in to a passage in Shelley's preface to *Prometheus Unbound* in which he spoke of poetry when it becomes a text that you know you have to study, and at that point I had no doubts at all. I said this is no longer anything that I feel a matter of my sensibility, a matter of my intelligence; it's a fact. Now that Williams is dead, and H.D. is dead, there are five poets left that I study. I know I study them because the fact is that at every turn I am back at those texts to find something that now exceeds poetry, to find the substance of my own inner life. They were very clearly to me: Ezra Pound, Louis Zukofsky, Charles Olson, and then two that I feel are contemporary, Robert Creeley and Denise Levertov. Now, I return to them to find secrets, I return to rob them, you know. If I had to steal fire I know where you go, and there isn't any confusion. Everywhere else I might be stealing anything. I like to steal; I'm a jackdaw. But I know when I'm coming home with a nice piece of glass that I need in the upper corner, and where I'm going for the fire. Now I don't have to say anything else, the big fire source is the man who is about to talk to you. And if he doesn't blush and walk around when he's been called the Big Fire Source—but we can laugh, too, because us Indians like to put people on the spot. [APPLAUSE]

OLSON: You know, I'm very obliged to get rid of that rap for being Zeus. I never knew I was Prometheus until now. It's a fine thing. I've been a father figure too long. [LAUGHTER] And I've begun to suffer so completely that fate of that other fellow that what I propose to do today is to expose myself, as he was, on a rock. And, in fact, if I can accomplish anything it's simply because there's a little of my liver left from overnight, like I think his was. [LAUGHTER]

In fact, what I would like to do, actually, is to do that sort of a thing. I mean, the announced subject was "Causal Mythology," so obviously Mr Duncan has prepared me perfectly. And it's very exciting to be home here; at least it feels strange and nice to be in Berkeley this morning, especially because of so many of you here that are the ones that I've lived mostly for, and with, and by, myself, and care the most for in the world.

It's very strange because I suddenly was presented to Ezra Pound two weeks ago, after twenty years. And that was like—I don't know, it was not like your father or something, it was like having an Umbrian angel suddenly descend upon you and ask you to be, and be more than, well, just what you'd like to be. It was very beautiful the way the fierceness of Pound has settled down into a voiceless thing, which only responded twice to me. Once I told a story of Ed Sanders, who had a beautiful picture that Pound at eighty would have a revival of life and have fifteen further years of power. The difficulty of talking to Pound is he doesn't talk anymore, and he sits in his almost catatonic fix in silence. And the one word he said after I said that Sanders had that sense of him, he said, "Sanders has a sense of humor." [LAUGHTER]

The thing that I would like to do instead of what sounds like a subject like "Causal Mythology" is actually to talk four things:

> The Earth
> The Image of the World
> History or City
> and The Spirit of the World

and do those four things under a ... epigraph? yeah, which would be:

"That which exists through itself is what is called meaning."

And the reason why I say that is the desire to suggest that the four terms that I'm proposing are—the Earth itself, for example, is curiously today a thing which can be seen for itself. And I think that that's so completely changed the human species, literally, that it's almost like the old blessing of the Pope, that it is an orb; and, in fact, I likewise am pairing the city, which if you remember in his blessing was the *urbs*, as that pair. And the other pair I'd like to call instead, in Latin, the *imago mundi* and the *anima mundi*. And in doing this I would like to use four poems. They're four poems written, in fact, in a run, and I'll read them not that way but read them in a series and see if by any chance the relationship of, say, the four terms to the four poems will not destroy the poems. These will all be from the *Maximus*, written about a year ago, and some have been published. The first one [III.37] is an attempt, actually further attempt, to speak my own sense at that date of the condition of the earth.

> Astride
> the Cabot
> fault,
>
> one leg upon the Ocean one leg
> upon the Westward drifting continent,
>
> to build out of sound the wall
> of a city,
>
>   the earth
> rushing westward 2'
> each 100
> years, 300 years past
> 500 years
> since Cabot, stretching
> the Ocean, the earth
>
> going NNW, course due
> W from north of the
> Azores, St. Martin's
> Land,
>   the division
> increasing yet the waters
> of the Atlantic
> lap the shore, the history
>
> of the nation rushing to melt
> in the Mongolian ice, to arrive
> at Frances Rose-Troup Land, novoye
>
> Sibersky
> slovo,
>
>   the Wall
> to arise from the River, the Diorite Stone
> to be lopped off the Left Shoulder

Now, deliberately I'd like to go over, almost like an exegesis of text—if you'll excuse me, as I said, I have arrived at a point where I really have no more than to feed on myself. Unfortunately I didn't bring a *Maximus Poems*. Would anybody have one that I could borrow or …? Thanks, thanks. I'd like very much to literally do a—for example, that "Frances Rose-Troup Land," that "Mongolian ice" stuff, I'd love to just talk about the Earth in these terms. I did do an earlier passage on this particular English woman historian in a poem in 1959 ["Letter, May 2, 1959"]. I'll pick a section out of it [1.147–51]:

> then to now nothing
> new

(That would be from the 17th-century persons referred to just previously.)

> then to now nothing
> new, in the meaning
> that that wall walked
> today, happened a bull-
> dozer discloses
> Meeting House Hill
> was a sanddune under
> what was valued for
> still the sun makes
> a west here as on
> each Gloucester hill
> why one can say what
> one can't say is
>
> when did the sea so
> roll over as later
> the ice this stuck-out
> 10 miles Europe-pointing
> cape, the lines of force
> I said to her as of Rose-
> Troup go to as one line
> as taught as uroboros ar-
> row hooped crazy Zen arch-
> er fact that arm of bow Frances
> Rose-Troup English maiden
> lady told this city what

And then goes on into what she told Gloucester about how persons first got there. Now, this then goes on to—well, let me read that, because that is my point of the relevance of taking the Earth as a one, by the old law that a one is only so if it produces a one. This would be, then, if you talk a causal mythology, the simplicity of the principle "that which exists through itself is what is called meaning" will be that one produces a one. The Earth, then, is conceivably a knowable, a seizable, a single, and *your* thing, and yours as a single thing and person yourself, not something that's distributed simply because we are so many and the population is growing, or that the exploitation of the earth itself is increasing.

... fact that arm of bow Frances
Rose-Troup English maiden
lady told this city what

marchants Weymouth Port Book
No. 873 if East and West the
ship first employed was,
the date everything that
the local get off it Glous-
ter the old railroad joke
from the smell, the lovers
in the back seat the conductor
waking up from a snooze don't
look out the window sniffs
and calls out gloucester glous-
ter   All off

      Take the top off
      Meeting House Hill
      is 128 has cut it
      on two sides

      the third
      is now no more than
      more Riverdale
      Park

      and the fourth?
      the west?
      is the rubbish
      of white man

      Up River,
      under the bridge
      the summer people
      kid themselves
      there's no noise,
      the Bridge
      's so high.
      Like hell. The Diesels
      shake the sky

            clean the earth
            of sentimental
            drifty dirty
            lazy man:

            bulldozer,
            lay open
            the sand some sea
            was all over the
            second third fourth
            meeting house,

            once. I take my air

where Eveleth walked
out the west
on these hills
because the river

it's earth which
now is strange The sea
is east The choice Our backs
turned from the sea but the smell

as the minister said
in our noses
I am interfused
with the rubbish

of creation I hear
the necessity
of the ludicrous reference to Wm Hubbard by the
tercentennary preacher that

the finny tribe come easily
to the hook

                    Fishermen
are killers Every
fifty of 'em I pick off
the Records seek
the kame I was raised
on and are startled,
as I am, by each granite
morraine shape   Am in the mud
off Five Pound Island
is the grease-pit
of State Pier

                    Go 'way and leave
Rose-Troup and myself   I smell your breath, sea
And unmellowed River under
the roar of A. Piatt Andrew
hung up there like fission
dropping trucks the face
Samuel Hodgkins didn't show
poling pulling 1 penny
per person 2
for a horse

                         step off
onto the nation   The sea
will rush over   The ice
will drag boulders Commerce
was changed the fathometer
was invented here the present
is worse give nothing now your credence
start all over step off the

> Orontes onto land no Typhon
> no understanding of a cave
> a mystery Cashes? ... "but that these times of combustion
> the seas throughout have hindered much that work" so sayeth
> so early ...

Quote from the tercentenary preacher. And then it jibes, and I want to still come to that passage where I get this same "Siberskie slovo" job. Wait a minute, I may have gotten ahead of myself here. Excuse me. Hmmm, isn't that funny? I'd have sworn that was right ... Well, you see, if Duncan had studied me he could tell me. [LAUGHTER] If I had done it too, you know, like.

DUNCAN: Then I've still got to do it, because I can't find it either.

OLSON: No. I can't. Well, I don't know how I lost that one. Sure was there once. Well, it's somewhere.[1]

But I want to go back now, really building the—coming back to that original poem that I read. In fact, I'm really trying to explain that I don't believe I'm obscure. [LAUGHTER] In fact, really, I enjoy these terms so much that I obviously, as I said, have no reason not to try to explain them or, this day at least, lay them open to you. Let me go over the poem again and at least allow that—oh yes, really I can do it by catching the passage where, earlier in that poem [1.146]:

> Mellow and enclosed both the local and the past
> N.G. not the point not here I am not here to
> have to do with Englishmen (in habit, but
> canoes dugout as found Indian means or hauling
> marsh grass by gundalows possibly old Venetian
>
> > who came out of their marshes likewise
> > to change the commerce of NW shifting
> > man—it ends, as Stefansson couldn't
> > stomach the dead end of his own prop-
> > osition, in the ice
>
> dogs of the present don't even throw anything back The sea
> it isn't 67 years yet that the First Parish Unitarian) preach-
> er of the anniversary sermon ...

And so forth. So I'm really suggesting how much this poem, which was written in '59, is very loaded, again, simply because, say, I find myself constantly returning to that unit, Earth, as orb, as though it was as familiar to me as the smallest thing I know; and it's really, actually, to suggest that if there is any legitimacy to the word that we call "mythology" it is literally the activeness, the possible activeness and personalness of experiencing it as such.

[Rereads "Astride the Cabot fault"]

---

1. The phrase "novo siberskie slovo" appears in the prose part of the poem on the following page (1.151).

By the way, I'd be happy to be interrupted on any of each one of these four parts this thing will constitute itself as, and I'm at the moment I'm running part one out, at this moment. But I'd be happy to be picked over by anybody that wants—is unfamiliar or is unsatisfied with any of either the information or this other thing that I'm trying to do which is the connectivity of same to other poems, or of the *Maximus* at least.

BOBBIE CREELEY: What do you mean by "the Diorite Stone lopped off the Left Shoulder"?

OLSON: Yeah. That I would like, Bobbie, to hold a little back because of the fourth of the ... I do have a board, don't I? It might be easier to do ...

[Olson writes on the blackboard:

THE EARTH
IMAGO MUNDI
HISTORY
ANIMA MUNDI]

Can everybody see that? The first poem that I read is called "Astride the Cabot fault." I learned that, by the way, luckily in Vancouver, from one of the Vancouver people that I think isn't here today, Dan ...? Dan McLeod. I don't think he's here. He showed me in Vancouver a thing which I had never realized, that there's a split in the Atlantic Ocean, a fault which runs just where all my own attention has been, northeast, and that she runs right straight through Gloucester. This was for him very exciting.[2] [LAUGHTER] Again, like, by the principle of the *imago mundi* or the Prometheus figure, you get stuck with all this stuff. I wouldn't propose what I'm proposing to anybody because you end up obviously being eaten by Zeus's eagle only, and you're nobody, you're not even a hero. You're simply stuck with the original visionary experience of having been you, which is a hell of a thing. [LAUGHTER] And, in fact, I assume that the epigraph that I've offered today is my only way of supporting that, which is that [WRITING ON THE BOARD] "that which exists through itself is what is called meaning." All right? I don't have any trouble stealing that,[3] as Duncan never has any trouble stealing, because he has original experience which prompts him to reach out for just what he knows he wants. I was very lucky once to have what poets call visions, or—and they're not dreams, as several superb poets in this room know. They are literally either given things or voices which come to you from cause. And I won't quote, as one never does, one's own secrets (that's why you steal from others), but this one is an awfully good duplication.

2. McLeod had given Olson a photocopy of J. Tuzo Wilson's article "Cabot Fault: An Appalachian Equivalent of the San Andreas and Great Glen Faults and Some Implications for Continental Displacement," *Nature* 195 (14 July 1962), pp. 135–38.

3. The epigraph is adapted from the first sentence of one of Olson's companion books, *The Secret of the Golden Flower* (London: Kegan Paul, Trench, Trubner, 1945), Richard Wilhelm's translation of a Chinese sacred text attributed to Lao Tzu.

And the reason, Bobbie, I'd like very much to wait on the—no, I can answer the question very well: the diorite, uh … In fact, wow, this is marvelous, Allen. I'll read the one that you, for the first time, came on on in Vancouver. That's a fun, huh? It was that one? Yeah. If you remember, Bobbie, I did read a poem in Vancouver which has me as the Diorite Stone on Main Street [11.51]. I don't know whether I could just hit it and read it, but if I could I would. [LOOKS THROUGH MS] "I stand …" I can't remember the damn thing, don't even know where it is. I will. Hold on. The advantage, by the way, of coming in fresh is that even if you're unprepared it's more fun for me. I hope you won't mind me dragging a little … Can't remember where it is. Anyhow, "I stand on Main Street like the Diorite Stone" is as I remember it.

I'm going to spend some time in this fourth thing on the poem from which I myself steal that, which is "The Song of Ullikummi." Actually it comes to us as a Hittite version of a Hurrian myth. It's called "The Song of Ullikummi," and it's the story of how this aborted creature, whom the poem calls the Diorite Stone, started growing from the bottom of the sea, and grew until he appeared above the surface of the water and then, of course, attention was called to him, and he continued to grow, and he became so offensive to the gods, and dangerous, that they had to themselves do battle with him; and "The Song of Ullikummi" is actually the story of that battle and who could bring him down. Because he had a growth principle of his own, and it went against creation in the sense that nobody could stop him and nobody knew how far he might grow. It's a marvelous Hesiodic poem. In fact, I prefer it to those passages in Hesiod that include the battle of Zeus with the giants and eventually with Typhon, because this creature is nothing but a blue stone, and the stone grows. I would hate to start talking mythology so much as to mention that among American Indians, the Sioux, for example, believe that a stone is—I mean, this is not alchemy, mind you; at least there's nothing in what Chief Stony Brook, or whatever, Sioux Stoop, or, I forget, Crazy Bear or something, whichever was the old guy that said it, but he does say that the stone is the truest condition of creation, that it's silence and you know, like, it's solidity and all that. Well, I like that. I mean, I think the Earth is nothing but a pebble, a marvelously big stone. Big Stone. Why not? Let's call the Earth "Big Stone." And the Diorite, for me, this Diorite figure is the vertical, the growth principle of the Earth. He's just an objectionable child of Earth, who has got no condition except earth, no condition but stone. And, as you know, in alchemy this is great stuff, the lapis and all that stuff, but one of the reasons why I'm trying to even beat the old dead word "mythology" into meaning is that I think that it holds more of a poet's experience than "mysticism"; and I myself believe that this principle [TURNING TO THE BLACKBOARD] seems to me again to state that the only interest of a spiritual exercise is production.

BOBBIE CREELEY: What is the "lopped off of the Left Shoulder"?

OLSON: Yeah, well, this is how he finally was destroyed. I've forgotten which one of the younger gods, but it would be a character again like Prometheus, who finally took on—the old boys couldn't handle it, the women were all upset. That was cutting out, by the way, organic principle: biomorphism is absolutely knocked flat by this figure. I mean, we don't need any longer to put up with that business, if you could get this guy back in business. Nor do we need to put up with Zeus, either, and those big-shot figures. This young other guy, like Enki or some crazy fisherman-type person, finally goes down, just like, by the way, in that beautiful early—the other poem which I still respect from prehistory is the Gilgamesh story, and here it's the opposite way. And I think we live in a time when the future lies as much in the genetic as it does in the morphological. I just happen to be a form-ridden cat myself, but I respect all that action the other side of the whole. The right arm I respect as much as my own disabled left. I wish also today to read—well, I might do that right now, as a matter of fact. Let me read you another story. I would like to read stories today anyhow. But I'd like to read a very beautiful little story about the condition of the two angels:[4]

> He who succeeds in leaving this clime enters the climes of the Angels, among which the one that marches with the earth is a clime in which the terrestrial angels dwell. These angels form two groups. One occupies the right side: they are the angels who know and order. Opposite them, a group occupies the left side: they are the angels who obey and act. Sometimes these two groups of angels descend to the climes of men and genii, sometimes they mount to heaven. It is said that among their number are the two angels to whom the human being is entrusted, those who are called "Guardians and Noble Scribes"—one to the right, the other to the left. He who is to the right belongs to the angels who order; to him it falls to dictate. He who is to the left belongs to the angels who act; to him it falls to write.

Again, I mean, I wasn't as pat as to realize I was going to read a passage loaded on the Earth. But, again, it is why, when I talk more intellectually about mythology, I use a word "dipolar." Well, this double that we're talking about is where this Earth thing seems to me to yield. Again the Diorite Stone is sort of the child of Mother Earth, dig? And I will—the reason I sort of said that was that I want, actually, to end by reading a poem I read, unhappily, I guess, because nobody ever said a word, in front of Ezra Pound two weeks ago, in honor of him. And it fell dead, and I'd like to read it to you today as the last poem, and it's on the nature of the assault upon the rock that fathers and mothers us all, sort of thing. And it's a slipped piece of the whole story of the—it's "*From* The Song of Ullikummi." In fact, I read it as a translation, trying to honor the fact that I thought Mr Pound really, justly, freed the languages of the world. It's interesting to me because it is a

---

4. Olson is reading from p. 148 of Henry Corbin's *Avicenna and the Visionary Recital* (NY: Pantheon, 1960). He reads carefully from this source, but for the word "genii" he substitutes "genius."

translation from Hurrian into American, right? Obviously that would interest me to succeed in doing that. So that "the Wall / to arise from the river, the Diorite Stone / to be lopped off the Left Shoulder" would be the fact of—again let's be really pedantic and do this: the wall of the city, "to build out of sound the wall / of a city," right? In the earlier section of the poem, "The Wall / to arise from" (the "Wall" here is capitalized): "The Wall / to arise from the river, the Diorite Stone / to be lopped off the Left Shoulder." In fact, as I remember—I may be here inventing—but, as I remember the Hittite Hurrian myth, it turns out, eventually, that the damned thing that grew up was actually nothing but a carbuncle on the left shoulder like of Atlas, but of the Earth. I mean that this thing just rose; this blue stone just rose like a skyscraper and overtopped the walls of the gods. So that they were frightened it was all going to topple down on them, as indeed I am that neo-capitalism as well as communism is going to do that to the Earth.

I steal that phrase "neo-capitalism." I don't know it as American jive. I was quite interested in a communist poet that read—in fact, I gave the stage to him in Spoleto—Pasolini, a young Italian poet. And it's very jivey talk, apparently, in Italy today, because Italy is like ourselves; it's jumped into that new gear. Don't mind my talking history and politics currently, because we have an objection to you, Allen, Wieners and I, because when we flew into Rome we said, "Why doesn't those sons-of-bitch poets tell us [LAUGHTER] how exciting experiences are?" Like just how exciting it is to fly into a city. Not that you haven't, but as a matter of fact we used you, as so many people do, as a target of objection because you don't tell us all these wonderful things like the condition of a poet like Pasolini, talking with his claque, breaking up a whole damn reading in honor of Ezra Pound, rushing out and having a press conference. It was one of the worst things I've seen. Typical lousy job! [LAUGHTER] But the poem he read had this very exciting phrase which is just—it's new to me—calling the whole present shove that's on, "neo-capitalism." It sounded marvelously true. It seems just what has happened in the last ten years. The whole world has just done that big push that we call "the species." But I'm old-fashion enough to be—not scared, wish that the Earth shall be of another vision and another dispensation. And not from the past but from the future. O.K. I didn't mean to make a pitch.

O.K. I'm going to quit this Earth thing as part one, now. Geez, I'd better, unless somebody wants anything more on that one poem? O.K. Now, my argument would be, then, that the way that the Earth gets to be a pea is that we are born, ourselves, with a picture of the world, that there is no world except one that we are the picturers of it. And by the world here I don't mean the Earth, I mean the whole of creation. And it seems to me that I don't know enough, but I think that the phrase *imago mundi* is as legitimate as the better known phrase *anima mundi*. And I'd like to oppose that, really, to a condition of writing which is all based on what I do, or what others do, rather than comes from the darkness of one's own initiation. Again I'm suggesting that even the overt spiritual exercise of initiation is initial in us: we are, *we* are spiritual exercise by having been born; and that this involves one in something which Blake alone, to my mind, has characterized. He, in one passage, I've forgotten where,[5] asks that man, in fact, declares that man is—that there's the ugly man, who would be the rational one, that there's the strong man, who would be wholly strong, that there's the beautiful man, and the fourth; and of these forms the Son of God. I think I have that reasonably right. And in the period, the day after I wrote this poem I read you first, I wrote this other poem. It was refused by the *Paris Review*, so I'm happy to read it. [LAUGHTER] It's never been in print.

It also is a footnote, like it's an example of another side of the literal study of mythology, which I spend a lot of time on, which is really archae-ology on one side or etymology on another. I found that in Crete, or in Greece at the time of Mycenae and Pylos and Tiryns, that the god who we know of as Ares or Mars was apparently called Enyalios. In this poem I abuse his name by using "Enyalion." But the poem is based on the word "Enyalion." (I think you've seen that, yeah.) And it's directly connected now to the struggle of the *imago mundi*, as a child of Earth, with the bosses. I published a long poem in the *Psychedelic Review*. Due to Allen I was brought into that early mushroom experience and the *Psychedelic Review* was one magazine that issued from it, and in order to, almost to, put another kind of a plant in there, I put this poem ["Maximus, from Dogtown–IV" (II.163–72)]. Literally, it led Ed Sanders to ask me to translate Hesiod. But I told him I knew no Greek, it was just cribbed from a good translation of Hesiod. But it does have that big war there between Zeus and the giants. And this starts from that, this is a later poem [III.38–40] coming from there.

                    rages
                  strain
               Dog of Tartarus
             Guards of Tartarus
          Finks of the Bosses. War Makers

                    not Enyalion. Enyalion
    has lost his Hand, Enyalion
    is beautiful, Enyalion
    has shown himself, the High King
    a War Chief, he has Equites
    to do that

                Enyalion
    is possibility, all men
    are the glories of Hera by possibility, Enyalion
    goes to war differently
    than his equites, different
    than they do, he goes to war with a picture

5. Olson is remembering Number V, "The Ancient Britons," in William Blake's *A Descriptive Catalog of Pictures, Poetical and Historical Inventions* (London: D.N. Shury, 1809), from his copy of *The Portable Blake* (NY: Viking, 1946).

    far far out into Eternity   Enyalion,
the law of possibility, Enyalion

the beautiful one, Enyalion

who takes off his clothes

wherever he is found,

on a hill,

in front of his own troops,

in the face of the men of the other side, at the command

of any woman who goes by,

and sees him there, and sends her maid, to ask,

if he will show himself,

to see for herself

if the beauty, of which he is reported to have,

is true

he goes to war with a picture

                          she goes off

in the direction of her business

      over the city   over the earth—the earth

is the mundus   brown-red is the color

                     of the brilliance

                     of earth

he goes to war with a picture in his mind
that the shining of his body

        and of the chariot
        and of his horses
        and of his own equites
     everyone in the nation of which he is the High King

he turns back

into the battle

               Enyalion

is the god of war   the color

of the god of war   is beauty

               Enyalion

is in the service of the law of the proportions

of his own body   Enyalion

             but the city

is only the beginning of the earth   the earth

is the world   brown-red is the color of mud,
the earth

shines

but beyond the earth

far off Stage Fort Park

far away from the rules of sea-faring   far far from Gloucester

far by the rule of Ousoos   far where you carry
the color, Bulgar

far where Enyalion

quietly re-enters his Chariot far

by the rule of its parts by the law of the proportion

of its parts

over the World   over the City   over man

That seems to say what the image of the world, at least for me, has been. I can, therefore, move, I believe, to what I there call "History." And I'm happy to use the word to stand for City. [LOOKING FOR CHALK] I did have a piece … Well, if I said ORB here, huh?

VOICES: There's some way over on your left. To the left. Left.

OLSON: Point made. [LAUGHTER] I mean, I'm nuts on numbers because, it seems to me, I'm a literalist; and I wished only to bracket these two things, and these two hooked obviously by words alone.

[On the blackboard joins IMAGO MUNDI to ANIMA MUNDI
and ORB TO URB]

But, I mean, the city of the earth, which as far as I know on this continent arose in Massachusetts, and was, as you all know, quoted by—in fact, the only time I found Mr Kennedy interesting, verbally, was when he made his appearance, just after his successful election, before the General Court of Massachusetts. I don't know how many of you would have known that he, immediately after Los Angeles—no, after his victory—appeared and made a speech before the General Court of Massachusetts and quoted that remarkable phrase of Winthrop's that "this colony shall shine like a city on a hill." I may garble it, but some of you that know the speech may remember it. That's the one time I was moved by Mr Kennedy. And I, a day after this previous poem, wrote this one [III.41–42]. And I would like to use it to—I mean, I'm excited by this series of four poems. They represented for me an outbreak of much that the *Maximus* had been approaching for me for the ten, fifteen previous years, yeah.

7 years & you cld carry cinders in yr hand
for what the country was worth broken
on the body

> on the wheel of a new
> body
> a new social body
> he was broken
> on the wheel   his measure
> was broken   Winthrop's
> vision was broken he was broken the country
> had walked away
> and the language
> has belonged to trade or the English
> ever since   until now once more JW
> can be said to be able
> to be listened to: wanax
> the High Governor
> of Massachusetts   John
> wanax who imagined
> that men
> cared
> for what kind of world
> they chose to
> live in
> and came here seeking
> the possibility: Good News
> can come
> from Canaan

[LAUGHS] O.K. But I'm having so much fun [LAUGHTER] I would like to read "Some Good News," a poem in fivers that is this poem previously.

[Reads "Some Good News" (1.120–27) to applause]

I'd rather like to read you one pair poem to that, and one that's the third of the set, to come back to the one I read you, like, as of what I consider both the city and ourselves. I don't know whether I can do this one too good. Why don't I jump the Winthrop poem ["Stiffening in the Master Founders' Will" (1.128–32)] and go to the one that nobody, I think, seems to have been particularly interested in, but I'm so fond of it. These are all written in—I may have punched that out a little bit—they're all written in what I call "fivers," the three of them. And the third one is called "Capt. Christopher Levett (of York)." "Quack," that reference in the previous poem, is the old name for Casco, the old pronunciation for Casco, and Casco is now Portland, and Christopher Levett was the first person to put down there.

[Reads "Capt. Christopher Levett (of York)" (1.133–35)]

That makes me feel as though I ought to jump right into neo-capitalism. [LAUGHTER] I didn't realize I was putting down so much. I feel, as a matter of fact, that this later poem that I read you first, which let me now read like I'm summarizing.

[Rereads "7 years & you cld carry cinders in yr hand"
(III.41–42) to applause]

And now, if I believe that these two things are mundane and these are the realer things, I'd like finally to end with the spirit of the world, which I have never been able to see as other than the figure of a woman, as she is such in the very phrase *anima mundi.* I will just read this fourth poem, fifth actually of the days that these poems were written, which is the translation I promised of this section, "*From* The Song of Ullikummi." For those of you who heard the poems I read in Vancouver, some of which have appeared in print since, the poem has also a connection previously.[6] It would be impossible, I think, to read the actual transliteration. I'm actually translating the very first tablet of "The Song of Ullikummi." It opens up on Kumarbi, father of all the gods:[7]

Of Kumarbi, father of all the gods, I shall sing.

Kumarbi wisdom unto his mind takes,
and a bad "day," as evil (being) he raises.
And against the Storm-God evil he plans,

And against the Storm-God a *rebel* he raises.

Kumarbi wisdom unto his mind [takes]
And like a bead he sticks it on.

When Kumarbi wisdom unto his mind had taken,
from (his) chair he promptly rose.
Into (his) hand a staff he took,
Upon his feet as shoes the swift winds he put.

And from his town Urkis he set out,
and to *ikunta luli* he came.
And in *ikunta luli* a great rock lies.

6. Olson is presumably referring to a series of poems (*Maximus* II.22, 143, 148) based on Charles G. Leland's *Algonquin Legends of New England* (1884), p. 225.

7. Olson introduces his poem by reading from the transliteration of the tablets by Hans Gustav Güterbock in "The Song of Ullikummi: Revised Text of the Hittite Version of the Hurrian Myth," *Journal of Cuneiform Studies* 5 (1951), pp. 147–49. It is the next seven lines of the transliteration that Olson uses for the poem itself:

Her length is three leagues.
                but her width is one league and a half league.
What below she has,
upon this his mind sprang forward,
and with the rock he slept,
and into her his manhood flowed.
And five times he took her
and again ten times he took her.

The non-English words in the poem are taken from the Hittite of Güterbock's transcription. "*From* The Song of Ullikummi" is found in *Collected Poems,* pp. 600–2.

And that's where I picked it up.

    fucked the Mountain
    fucked her but good   his mind
    sprang forward
and with the rock he slept
and into her he let his manhood
    go five times he let it go
          ten times he let it go

        in ikunta luli she is three
     dalugasti long
            she is one and a half
        palhasti wide. What below she has
up on this his mind sprang upon

When Kumarbi his wisdom
he took upon
his mind
   he took his istanzani
   to his piran   hattatar
   istanzani   piran daskizzi

Kumarbis-za   istanzani piran hattatar
daskizzi
       sticks wisdom
unto his mind   like his cock
into her
iskariskizzi

      the fucking
of the Mountain
  fucked the Mountain   went right through it and came out
the other side

the father of all the gods
from his town Urkis
he set out
and to ikunta luli
he came

    and in ikunta luli a great rock
    lies
    sallis perunas
    kittari   he came upon
    What below she has
              he sprang upon
    with his mind
        he slept
    with the rock   kattan sesta
    with the peruni

      and into her misikan X-natur
    andan his manhood
       flowed
  into her

> And five times he took her
> nanzankan   5-anki das
> and again ten times he took her
> namma man zankan   10-anki das
>
> Arunas
> the Sea

Thank you. [APPLAUSE] I see I'm short. If anybody wants any more, I'll—I mean, not any more of that—but, I mean, if this lecture isn't complete I can complete it.

RICHARD BAKER: The clock is fifteen minutes slow.

OLSON: Oh, it is? Oh, good. [LAUGHTER]

RICHARD DUERDEN: Could you give a different shot at that *anima mundi* as woman, did you say?

OLSON: Yeah, I just meant the rather classic figure, which I—well, for example, in the Tarot deck it's the El Mundo, it's card XXI is the Anima Mundi. She's the Virgin, she's the whole works. I mean, she's it.

VOICE: Well, why do you go to another culture to get your myth?

OLSON: Well, you knock me out if you say that. I just thought I bridged the cultures. [LAUGHS] I don't believe in cultures myself. I think that's a lot of hung up stuff like organized anything. I believe there is simply ourselves, and where we are has a particularity which we'd better use because that's about all we got. Otherwise we're running around looking for somebody else's stuff. But that particularity is as great as numbers are in arithmetic. The literal is the same as the numeral to me. I mean, the literal is an invention of language and power the same as numbers. And so there is no other culture. There is simply the literal essence and exactitude of your own. I mean, the streets you live on, or the clothes you wear, or the color of your hair is no different from the ability of, say, Giovanni di Paolo to cut the legs off Santa Clara or something.[8] Truth lies solely in what you do with it. And that means you. I don't think there's any such thing as a creature of a culture.

DUNCAN: That culture's in a test tube.

OLSON: Well, I think we live so totally in an acculturated time that the reason why we're all here that care and write is to put an end to that whole thing. Put an end to nation, put an end to culture, put an end to divisions of all sorts. And to do this you have to put establishment out of business. It's just a structure of establishment. And my own reason for being, like I said, on the left side and being so hung up on form is that I feel that today, as much as action, the invention—not the invention, but the discovery of formal structural means is as legitimate as—is for me the form of action. The

---

8. Olson is thinking of plate 27, *Scenes from the life of Saint Clare,* by Giovanni di Paolo, in *Paintings from the Berlin Museums* (NY: Metropolitan Museum of Art, 1948), which he picked up at the exhibition itself in 1948 in Washington, DC.

radical of action lies in finding out how organized things are genuine, are initial, to come back to that statement I hope that I succeeded in making about the *imago mundi*: that that's initial in any of us. We have *our* picture of the world and that's the creation. I mean, with some deliberateness I should expose myself. I shrank everything that I feel and know about mythology into those four in order to offer today to you at least that best shrinkage I know at this moment. Is that fair?

VOICE: Yes, except it seems to me you're inviting the locusts of future generations to analyze all this, and you take it away from the people.

ALLEN GINSBERG: They're trying to analyze *"Berishis Bori elohim."*

OLSON: They're trying to analyze what? [LAUGHTER]

VOICES: "Berishis Bori elohim … Berishis Bori elohim."

DUNCAN: Charles, I think I can swing back to that as poets we have to find the term that stands for what we have known that's there. And it might go all the way back to—I mean, it certainly, this last one, goes back to the one place you found where it is, to know.

OLSON: Yeah. That's right.

DUNCAN: Now you don't care if you found it yesterday. You found it there. So you have to go there.

OLSON: That's right.

DUNCAN: And you recognize it; you read through miles and you recognize that this thing's it.

OLSON: Yeah. That's all. And believe you me I know everyone has their own recognitions, which Duncan knows so well too. This is one of the exciting things about something that the word "myth" used to mean. And it's a big drag to use it. But, like I say, I found—in fact, I've got a poem in this new book: "Wrote my first essay on myth, like at Kent Kunt circle" [II.129]. (I remember reading that in B …) It's that dipolar for me. I find that what we call "mythology" is the inclusion of all this that you're speaking of, the recognition. And I don't believe there is a single person in this room that doesn't have the absolute place and thing that's theirs, I mean places and things that's theirs. That's again why I say I think the literal is the same as the numeral. I don't believe that every one of us isn't absolutely specific, and has his specificity. I don't know what your use of the word "analysis" and the words you use, but I would use the other word "reductive." The reductive is what I'm proposing. I don't think you can get your recognitions by going out. I think they come from within. I mean, that sounds too easy to say, but …

EDWARD DORN: Now that you have chalk, would you draw the brackets?

OLSON: Oh yes, I do. I had it all the time in my pocket, Ed. [LAUGHTER] Well, I do want to, really, use that papal blessing, which I still, as a Catholic, am impressed by. You do all know that: that after his election each pope is required to come to that door, in that horrible building by Michelangelo and Raphael, and bless the city and the world. And I really—I mean, that moves me, like. That's where I'd say the mundane is recognizable too. [WRITES ON BLACKBOARD] And the other bracket, which I do put on the left, don't I, is that one. And I don't mind proving—I mean, it's fun to do this today, to take poems and do what nobody—I mean, just let them be proof, test them as proof. I think poems and actions both should stand that. If they fall down, then it's our intellectualism only that's been exposed.

VOICE: Which of these mythological elements do you think the establishment, trade, and war is an expression of?

OLSON: I would say that, when it comes to war, you have Beauty. That's why I read—let me put those poems [WRITING ON THE BOARD], or let me put him where he belongs, as Enyalion. And trade would be certainly this; and politics would certainly be Mr John Wanax of Massachusetts. By the way, if anyone thinks I'm being obscure there, or writing like an advertisement for Johnson's, *Wanax* is the linear B name for High King of Mycenae. Agamemnon was *Wanax* of the forces at Troy. And what do you do with this woman poem, this screw poem? *Ikunta luli.* Yeah. I got you, though; I answered you. Really. Trade? Yeah. The Earth is goods! That beautiful thing. I mean, the world can have, everybody can have, goods today. This thing is—I would just take that great Blake statement. This is "Ugly"; this is his "Reason." This is his Urizen, isn't it? Sure it is, isn't it? Al, isn't that Urizen? Sure. Trade. The Earth is Urizen. I mean, he was as clear-headed on reason and the rational as anybody I know.

[The blackboard diagram as added to:

(1) THE EARTH	ORB⌐	TRADE, UGLY, RATIONAL
(2) IMAGO MUNDI	⌐	ENYALION, BEAUTY IS WAR
(3) HISTORY	URB⌐	POLITICS, POLIS—JOHN WANAX
(4) ANIMA MUNDI		IKUNTA LULI—WOMAN]

Well, I answered you, I think, huh?

VOICE: Yes, I think so.

OLSON: And I would say, by the way, I would—that was what I wanted to do on the Blake thing. This is the fourth, I think, that Blake doesn't mention, and says the four constitute the son of God. I swear he does. You know, he's got a marvelous just blank there; he just doesn't finish his fourth part of man. The ugly, the beautiful, the strong, and the … constitute the four, who is the son of God, that's what he says. And he doesn't mean that the fourth is the Son of God. He obviously doesn't.

Well, the clock is fifteen minutes slow, so it's after twelve. Thanks.

[APPLAUSE]

Olson on the platform at the Berkeley reading. Photo: Jim Hatch.

6

Reading at Berkeley

This reading in Wheeler Hall at the University of California on 23 July 1965 represents the climactic moment of Olson's private-public life. Some people present dissented, but to listen to the tape is to hear a man at the height of his powers, pushing to the limit of a total vision the particulars of his life and writings. What this transcription cannot always communicate, unfortunately, is the engaging laughter and good humor by which Olson conducted himself throughout.

ROBERT DUNCAN: As I think all of you, or almost all of you, must know, the man I am introducing tonight is visibly a large man. [LAUGHTER] And he has had to find in poetry—a phrase came up in a seminar of his: suddenly he was saying he was trying to find a position inferior to language. Every American impulse from the beginning has been to use it right away, and cash in on it, no matter what it was. What I want to suggest is, if you find difficulties in Olson, they're because he knows that the only thing in poetry for him is going to be found in a struggle, and, because his knowledge of language is such that its usability seems everywhere, I keep thinking he'll never find how to take a hold of that so it isn't usable. We're absolutely baffled. But when he does, we have, the rest of us poets, been confronted with some amazing dimension, in which we find the—will "bedrock of poetry" do?—I mean, the really resistant thing, the poem.

He has had to occupy an area in history big enough for some spirit size. You know, it's like he's trying to find clothes big enough for him. The spirit which can roam all over anything it can imagine, and then imagine one that is still restless because it can't find a space big enough for it to exist in: we, this evening, will attend a poetry of this order.

One thing I find, for those of you who may really find yourself having to go along with something that will leave you feeling like you could have fitted it in a much smaller space and time, the other thing he delights in sometimes are really beautiful songs. And then you discover that, whatever this huge size in space, in time, he occupies, he also occupies beautiful and discrete, almost ordinary areas.

So, may I now get from the back of the room there, Charles Olson, who will take over? [APPLAUSE]

CHARLES OLSON: Thank you. It feels like a convention hall. [LAUGHTER] And I never was running for anything, fortunately. Oh, would somebody loan me a *Maximus Poems*? I haven't a copy. Thank you. [PROLONGED PAUSE AND SHUFFLING OF PAPERS] Gee, I did it again. I left something in the room. Yeah, that's right. How the hell do you prove what you always ...? Hm, wow, that's crazy. That's a funny one. Where the hell did they go? Somebody took 'em. Would by any chance, Robert Creeley, you have ...? Oh, here it is. I got it.

I'd like first to read a—thank you, Robert, for that word "song." In the face of the poets that have read here, since I've been here, at least, and I missed Mr Duncan and Mr Wieners and Mr Sanders and Miss Kandel, and a lot of others, Mr Berrigan, and all of last week, but since I've been here I have had an experience.

DUNCAN: Charles, would you put the microphone on?

OLSON: Oh. Did *you* say that? [LAUGHS] How do you do this if there ain't ...? just connect ...? You see, this is life. [LAUGHTER] I mean, I either am the Hanged Man, or ...[1] [LAUGHTER] Where do you put that, like? Where does that go? There's no hole! Where do you put it? You'd better show me, Mr Baker. Able Baker! [LAUGHTER] You see, security. Thank you. That's what we got our nation for. That's why the rest of us are, fortunately, as Mr Creeley proved last night, free. And there's really no worry about the land of the free, 'cos it's been replaced. [DRINKS] Like Allen did! [LAUGHTER] Instead of drinking to you and me, I'll drink to that, hm?

But I would like to read first what for me was kind of an experience of writing a song. It's called "The Ring of," and I hope it's, if my memory is right ... Mr Creeley? That you did ...?

ROBERT CREELEY: Yes, I did.[2]

OLSON: Yeah. O.K., that's why. I mean, that was so much a matter of support that I felt ... Here it is.

> It was the west wind caught her up, as
> she rose
> from the genital
> wave, and bore her from the delicate
> foam, home
> to her isle

---

1. Olson, in having trouble attaching the microphone cord around his neck, is likening himself to the Hanged Man, card XII of the Tarot. This theme of the helpless one runs throughout the evening's performance. Richard Baker, who helps him here, was the organizer of the conference for the Continuing Studies Department of the University of California.

2. Creeley had included "The Ring of" in the *Selected Writings of Charles Olson* (1966), which was at that moment in production at New Directions.

and those lovers
of the difficult, the hours
of the golden day welcomed her, clad her, were
as though they had made her, were wild
to bring this new thing born
of the ring of the sea pink
& naked, this girl, brought her
to the face of the gods, violets
in her hair

Beauty, and she
said no to zeus & them all, all were not or
was it she chose the ugliest
to bed with, or was it straight
and to expiate the nature of beauty, was it?

Knowing hours, anyway,
she did not stay long, or the lame
was only one part, & the handsome
mars had her   And the child
had that name, the arrow of
as the flight of, the move of
his mother who adorneth

with myrtle the dolphin and words
they rise, they do who
are born of like
elements

Hm, thank you. [APPLAUSE] I just learnt it from you last night. And it didn't quite, but O.K., we're off! I mean, the horse is at least on the track. See if we can win.

I also wrote a poem which I'm sure neither Creeley nor I would include in anything, but I want to read it. I'm going to read three poems first: that one, this one, and then "Letter 9" of the *Maximus* poems, which has to do with this same book, this beautiful book, which I love … because that design on it was done,[3] and then, I don't know how many years later, enormous years later, I, after Creeley had criticized me and taught me everything one night, when I was burned up that he let a class go to go down to Peek's to have beer, and I thought the whole of Black Mountain was going to fail if we didn't get those windows in before the freeze that night, and long after, he said, "Don't flip your wig, man." And that made me, that brought me up to time, eh? I mean, he knocked any wig I ever had off my head that night. And it was beautiful, because he knew exactly what he was saying. And he was right. But I was not up, I mean, I was obviously, like they say, not with it, not right. But, curiously enough, it was so many years

3. The design of the first edition of *In Cold Hell, In Thicket*, published in Mallorca by Robert Creeley at his Divers Press in 1953, was done by Creeley's wife, Ann, using a pattern of horned cattle heads which Olson refers to later as "Indical" i.e. Indo-European. "Letter 9" of the *Maximus* poems, which he subsequently reads, refers to his first receiving the book in the mail. It is the same book he has with him on the platform, found in his book bag after some initial difficulty.

after even that, that I was left alone at Black Mountain, with my wife and son, and with the beach wagon, which Wesley Huss had acquired just, fortunately, before we closed Black Mountain, in fact, within, I think, three days, so I had a beach wagon, which I sold myself as Rector of Black Mountain for a hundred dollars, nominally, which I have never paid. I mean, the car is zero, too, now. But the point was that in that station wagon, which had been previously, and before Wesley Huss, who is here tonight, left (and this is the first time I've seen him since, as a matter of fact—not to dig you, Wes), but I bought double glass, that stuff, you know, like in there. In fact, if I had my right jacket on, I'd show you my passport, my identification at this moment in history, if you can see that slice, the repaired slice of my forefinger. On the left hand, I call to your attention. Thank god, too. That was another lucky break. Maybe I'll make it in the end. Because it's exactly true, what Duncan says. Or maybe I hope he's all wrong already just before now. For the first time, I mean, I hope I ran faster than Peter Rabbit. [LAUGHTER] Right now, in this hall, as I'm in front of you, I hope so. So I feel even comfortable in reading what I consider, and I guess everybody else does, a bad poem, which I wrote as a Christmas pageant or something, a poem for Christmas at Black Mountain. Ha ha ha! Because I suppose Allen Ginsberg still thinks I'm Santa Claus.[4] [LAUGHTER] I'd like him to say, "No!" [LAUGHTER] Or I'll run you for whatever you—what do I want to run for, Allen?

ALLEN GINSBERG: Read the poem and I'll decide.

OLSON: No, I'm going to—O.K. that's I guess why I'm reading it. It's called "An Ode on Nativity," and I don't believe it's ever been read. I've never even, prac—except for this morning, I thought I'd look at it and I liked it, you know how you do. I don't think anybody has ever … By the way, did you reject, did you even bother to consider it, Bob? [LAUGHTER AT TROUBLE WITH MICROPHONE CORD] How far can I come with this tether?

VOICE: Go ahead and read it, read it.

OLSON: Oh, I'm going to do it. Look, this thing is so bad, I can't ruin it. The only thing I can, as Allen says, is it might turn out to be how it sounded to me t-t-today … What did you say, Bob? Excuse me, will you please let Mr Creeley speak?

CREELEY: I thought that …[5]

OLSON: No kidding. I guess that's really how it feels for me tonight, or this morning. Now I got to shove it, right? O.K.—and therefore he didn't use it. Well, I got my chance. "An Ode on Nativity," the first part:

> All cries

No.

---

4. During the psilocybin sessions in 1960–61, Allen Ginsberg, it is reported, saw Olson as Santa Claus.
5. Creeley's remarks cannot be heard on the tape.

> All cries rise, & the three of us
> observe how fast Orion

Naah, that's too poetic.

> All cries rise, & the three of us
> observe how fast Orion

Geez, I'm losing it all, and my voice already. Big voice. Shit! [DRINKS] This is going to take—you see, you shouldn't talk; you should just read the thing.

> All cries rise, & the three of us
> observe how fast Orion
> marks midnight
> at the climax
> of the sky
>   while the boat of the moon settles
> as red in the southwest
> as the orb of her was, for this boy, once,
> the first time he saw her whole halloween face northeast
> across the skating pond as he came down to the ice, December
> his seventh year.
>   Winter, in this zone,
> is an on & off thing, where the air
> is sometimes as shining as ice is
> when the sky's lights ... When the ducks
> are the only skaters
>   And a crèche
> is a commerciality
>
>   (The same year, a ball of fire
>   the same place—exactly through
>   the same trees
>   was fire:
>   the Sawyer lumber company yard
>   was a moon of pain, at the end of itself,
>   and the death of horses I saw burning,
>   fallen through the floors
>   into the buried Blackstone River the city
>   had hidden under itself, had grown over ...

I, by the way, am celebrating the city of my birth, which I have only done, I believe, in this poem, which is Worcester, Massachusetts. And the River Blackstone is the Richard Blackston of the *Maximus Poems*, who grew the Blackston apple, in fact, on Beacon Hill, before Boston was.[6] And exactly, in fact, because of his care of choice of that side of the hill, towards the Charles, and protected from the weather by the Trimount, which was cut off by bulldozers in New England not long after Boston was settled. Trimount, that beautiful thing, which I will—I mean, I intend tonight to close, if I can

6. The name is William Blackstone, though his apples were called Blackston's. Disliking the dicta-torial style of Winthrop's Puritanism he moved to near Providence, RI, where the river named after him, which begins in Worcester, runs into the sea.

drag my full length there, with a poem on Triporta.[7] But I'm happy to call to your attention that Boston lopped off the top of three hills to make that single hill, on which—Mr Kennedy really doesn't know this; therefore, from my point of view, cannot quote Mr Winthrop right, when Mr Winthrop said, almost in the first act of the legislator of Massachusetts, "Let man live in a city," meaning a society, "which shall shine as this city does upon its hill," or something like that, but ... That is my dream, of creating a city, which shall shine as such. And this is only what I am, is the builder of that dome.

But at this point of time, I find myself—and I'm nervous, like, 'cos I'm reading this poem, and I'm finding it all right, right up to this point I've stopped. How about it, Allen? Right. You're with me, I think. And I will read, after the third poem, a fourth poem, which says why and how a woman at Black Mountain asked me, and explained to me, or ... I don't know. I mean, we were talking about Paul X entering here, whose cigarettes I'm smoking, and I said, "He's simply invidious."[8] And I don't say that again to get into an argument, like they say; but, I mean, I don't still know why that woman asked me the question which the poem contains.[9] Fair enough? This would be, from my point of view, what really is argument: is the fact that we live out, until there isn't any, the argument of our own being. That's why I believe, as I've kept saying this week, and I'm enough up to say now, why I think the private is public, and the public is where you behave. And that's its advantage. [DRINKS]

That river, the Blackstone, or Blackston, is an apple in the *Maximus* poems. As a matter of fact, it's what must turn out obvious by now to be the romanticism which I must put to bed tonight. Because I don't know why, but in the last three days I've found it possible to discover this poem. And if Mr Creeley says what he says is why he never mentioned it, I'm extremely happy, and I hope I'll end up in agreement with him.

That is, you can hear: I'm just extrapolating an instance of childhood, when I came with my skates on to the ice of Elm Park one night just at the hour of the coming of night, and the moon, a hot moon, which it always is when it rises, and big. You know that problem of the optical bigness of the moon at horizon. And I went on to that ice, and I looked as I went to the ice, and there was another ball of fire, but it was fire, striae, normal fire, not a ball, a halloween face. It was

7. Boston's "Trimount," or more strictly "Tramount," reminds Olson of "Tripura," the goddess of the three towns which comprise the universe—see Heinrich Zimmer's *Myths and Symbols in Indian Art and Civilization* (1953)—as celebrated in "Poem 143. The Festival Aspect" (III.73–75). Here Olson says "Triporta," a slight and presumably deliberate variation. The layered meaning was added to when Olson wrote in a postcard to Zoe Brown 22 February 1966 that she should take it as "Trimurta" the trinity of the Hindu gods.
8. Paul Xavier, "a young anarchist barefoot poet, thin handsome face and whispy bearded, climbed up on window sill from outside summer grass to hear Olson's earlier lectures, and thus led prophetic revolutionary-poetic-street people group in objecting to the economic formalism of the poetry convocation"—Allen Ginsberg (personal communication, 4 September 1969).
9. The question asked Olson by Dori Billing of Black Mountain College was, as it is phrased in "Letter 3": "Did you know, she sd, growing up there, / how rare it was" (1.10).

(The same year, a ball of fire
the same place—exactly through
the same trees
was fire:

      the Sawyer lumber company yard
      was a moon of pain, at the end of itself,
      and the death of horses I saw burning,
      fallen through the floors
      into the buried Blackstone River the city
      had hidden under itself, had grown over

And at any time, & this time
a city

jangles
    Man's splendor
is a question of which
birth

End of section one.

The cries rise, & one of us
has not even eyes to see the night's sky
burning, or the hollows
made coves of mist & frost, the barns
covered over, and nothing in the night but two of us
following the blind highway to catch all glimpses
of the settling, rocking moon

        December, in this year
is a new thing, where I whisper
bye-low, and the pond
is full to its shores again, so full
I read the moon where grass would not reveal it
a month ago, and the ducks make noises
like my daughter does, stir
in the crèche of things

(His mother, 80, and we
ate oysters after the burial: we had knelt
with his sister, now Mary Josephine,
in the prayery of the convent of the church
where my mother & father had been married

And she had told us tales of my family
I had not heard, how my grandfather
rolled wild in the green grass
on the banks of that same now underground river
to cool himself from the steel mill's fires
stripped down to his red underwear

she was that gay, to have seen her daughter
and that the two of us had had that car
to take the Sisters downtown and drop them
where they had to go

> I had watched them
> swirl off in their black habits
> before I started the car again
> in the snow of that street, the same street
> my father had taken me to, to buy my first cap.

Gee, I'm moved. Wow, I never wrote about Gloucester like this. Do you think I've been wrong all this time? I belong in—my subject is Worcester! Shit. [LAUGHTER] Isn't it amazing? I mean, how long does it take? I was born in 1910, as even the—they keep saying that. Jesus! I'd like to start, you know. 1910? Like, right at the moment, baby, you're watching baby, that's all. 1910? Shit. [LAUGHTER] The second section ends:

> At any time, & now, again, in this new year
> the place of your birth, even a city, rings

> in & out of
> tune

> What shall be
> my daughter's second
> birth?

That's the only thing that's wrong in the poem: "What shall be *my* birth." That was the only error. And, by the way, that's an error of my condition: I am a perfect father until I'm not. And that's another thing I hope is happening tonight, Robert. And I know that beautiful story, which was told to me, that you said a thing which cleared me when you told Richard Duerden, "Olson's not your father. You *had* a father." Am I right? That quote of Duncan's. God, that gave me—that's only about a year ago I heard that, or a year and a half ago, and it brought me here tonight, or it brought me here Tuesday, for sure.

> All things now rise, and the cries of men to be born
> in ways afresh, aside from all old narratives, away
> from intervals too wide to mark the grasses

> > (not those on which cattle feed, or single stars
> > which show the way to buy bad goods
> > in green & red lit stores, no symbols

> the grasses in the ice, or Orion's sweep, or
> the closeness of turning snows, these
> can tell the tale of any one of us stormed or quieted
> by our own things, what belong, tenaciously,
> to our own selves

> > Any season, in this fresh tune

("time" is what I wrote)

> is off & on to that degree that any of us miss

—or "abuse." Rhyme! I got a rhyme after Creeley last night! He puts me back [SLAPS LECTERN]. He puts me back to the fact that that man is as, oh, wow, unco.[10]

as any of us miss

the vision, lose the instant

(or "the infant")

and decision, the close

—and I mean "close" in the medieval sense: the quarter, or the holy quarter, which you can't get out of, or won't go out of, or asked never to leave, and to stay in there, as a discipline.

the close
which can be nothing more and no thing else
than that which unborn form you are the content of, which you

—which is a pure, marvelous, brilliant theology. Thank you. Thank you, Mr Olson.

which you

alone can make to shine, throw that like light
even where the mud was and now there is a surface
ducks, at least, can walk on. And I

have company
in the night

In this year, in this time
when spirits do not walk abroad, when men alone walk

when to walk is so difficult

when the divine tempter also walks
renewing his offer

("stalks"—I'm adding)

—that choice

(parenthesis)

(to turn
from the gross fire, to hide
as that boy almost did, to bury himself
from the fearful face—twice!—that winter

to roll like a dog or his grandfather
in the snowbank on the edge of the pond's ice

to find comfort somewhere, to avoid
the burning—To go to grass
as his

("as *he* now suckles.")

as his daughter now suckles. Some way! he cries out
not to see those horses' agonies:

10. As well as Robbie Burns, Olson may have had in mind the quotation from Hubbard's *History of New England* which refers to "the unco guid" spirit pervading early New England history as quoted by Herbert P. Adams in "The Fisher-Plantation at Cape Anne," *Historical Collections of the Essex Institute* 19:4–6 (1882), p. 85.

> Is light, is there any light, any
> to pay the price of
> fire?

Then "IV":

> The question stays
> in the city out of tune, the skies
> not seen, now, again, in
> a bare winter time:
>
> is there any birth
> any other splendor than
> the brilliance of the going on, the loneliness
> whence all our cries arise?

[APPLAUSE]

Thank you. Thank you. You see how embarrassed you can be. I really was embarrassed the night I read that, and I have never looked at it again until this morning. And I, at the moment, in that wonderful fact that you're here, and I am making it, just that, think it's one of the most beautiful poems I ever wrote. And, in fact, it makes me feel as though I've been wrong, as I said. Jesus. Wow. And I don't even want to do that. My daughter has obviously been my representative until this hour, that's all. And that's what made me feel sentimental: which is your whole point, like. But how, god, long. I mean, it took me fifty-four years, as I stand here tonight, fifty-four and a half years old, like, drinking a bottle in front of you. Well, excuse me, as both Mr Ginsberg and Mr Creeley would ask you to. And I'm almost going to finish it; so we might finish earlier than you think. [LAUGHTER] Maybe I'll read a third poem and we can go home.

I mean, the rhyming. Excuse me, but, honestly, to be in the clime of rhyme. After all, I missed all that last week, but, god, think of the poets whom I love whom I've heard this week! I mean, you want me to be a poet? No. I will simply be a result of having listened to those guys. And I feel like that. And I'm proud, honestly, to have written that poem. Huh! I never thought I'd say that.

I don't, daren't, take the next step. That's the misstep. Gee, maybe you shouldn't have, you know? Here we are again. The poem I want to read is the poem *Maximus* "9," "Letter 9," and it sounds literary. I could read "Letter 5" too, by the same term. But it wasn't Mr Creeley's fault that the *Maximus* poems were written. In fact, on the contrary, what is so beautiful is that this book, with its utterly Indical cover, for me, all those years later, which, by the way, are Ann Creeley's drawings of the cattle of paleolithic. Some of you may know these rock scratchings. What do they call 'em today? I mean, that's why I attend to what's scratched in the two cans of Telegraph Avenue, as it dead-ends, now a block further, unfortunately. I don't know … That plaza, I think, is the whole thing today. That plaza is not Europe. And I think our radicalism is of that order, as against the necessary radicalism of being Americans. Not that that block, from Sather Gate, Peder Seder Gate—it sounds Jewish, like that beautiful poem of yours on Sather Gate, that god-damn "Green Automobile," right?[11] O.K., just continuing our conversation. O.K.? I mean, I believe that the public is the same. If we can't make love right now, as I do with Robert Creeley and Robert Duncan and Ed Dorn and Ed Sanders and a girl in the back of the room and Kenny Tallman—and I don't mean in any sloppy sense. I mean love is both as extricable and as multiple as what I've been talking about all week to many of you, about how many words there are in Indo-European for ... [TROUBLE WITH MICRO-PHONE CORD] I almost lost it. I feel as though I'm chained to the Catholic Church [LAUGHS]. And I am, and I have been. And, in fact, if it's become a mike, with the condition in which I am tonight, I'm lucky.

But, *leik*,[12] you dig? I mean, this is the universe. And, you know, there's no revolution left. Wow, I mean, it's happened. That means that "new" is really what Whitehead said it was: simply "novelty." The radical is simply novelty. God, ain't that a good thing to say? I hope it might be. Let any of you that think that there's a cause realize that it's creation. And not in any big shit sense, Paul X. Simply this sense. And that Philip Whalen isn't here tonight, or is he? Because the reason why Phil thinks I put him down is because he laughed when I said that God is the organ of novelty. And maybe he did or didn't know that I was simply quoting Alfred North Whitehead in a very careful statement, and laughed at "organ."[13] Was like that thing that—Suzanna and I ended up in some joint. I mean, you can't even go out at night here and get into a real—I mean, where you can drink and dance—because of this university. And this university is Berkeley, California. Jim's place, Jimmy's somebody, down on Shattuck, right? Jimmy, what, closes at two? The goddamn restaurant knocked us out at 12:30. I mean, it's worse than Buffalo. No, in fact, Buffalo is better. [APPLAUSE] No, Buffalo is three. And, you know, New York, the last time I was in New York I had a terrible time. That was when I was there with John Wieners and Edward Dorn and my wife, who is dead, staying at LeRoi Jones's. And goddamn it, that son of a bitch Dan Rice—as he's done it to Robert Creeley, I think, too—he used his thing on me. And we moved uptown, took a hotel uptown and my wife went back to take care of our children.

Gee, really, I guess I'm too much of a story-teller. [LAUGHTER] I don't mind. If we never read another poem, I'd like to finish this story. As a matter of fact, thank god, I think that poem I read *is* a story. And I never realized that, and you told me that years ago, baby. Two things have been told to me. William Carlos Williams, thank god I found out from Robert Creeley, said

---

11. Ginsberg's poems "Sather Gate Illuminations" and "The Green Automobile" had appeared in his recent book *Reality Sandwiches* (1963).

12. Olson here completes the sentence "how many words there are in Indo-European for *leik* [i.e. love]." In the past year he had received and annotated (copy at Storrs) an article by J.A. Walker, "Gothic *–leik-* and Germanic **lic-* in the Light of Gothic Translations of Greek Originals" in *Philological Quarterly* 28 (April 1949), pp. 292–93.

13. "God is the organ of novelty"—*Process and Reality* (U.S. edn, p. 104). Whalen quoted this with some edge in "Philippic, Against Whitehead and a Friend" (poem dated 8 May 1961) in *On Bear's Head*, p. 221.

that I did resemble, or that my care or interest in the sea resembled the founding, or the late, European poet, Mr Homer.[14] And Creeley did that simply because he was so damn offended at these letters that Jonathan Williams (whom I wish was here, so that I'm not talking behind his back) had sort of pumped out of poor Bill, who really never really was my man. I mean, Bill don't believe in me. He really included Allen because Allen was different, and he really believes in that guy. It's on the record. And in those wonderful ways that we live politically ... [INTERRUPTION] Oh god, do you forget that he copyrighted his *Autobiography* also in my name? I feel as though I'm in *Paterson* like you are. I wish I were in *Paterson*, but I don't mind being in a copyright office. Do you know that? The *Autobiography of William Carlos Williams* is copyrighted on the title page by William Carlos Williams, and with the permission of Charles Olson for the "Projective Verse" piece. And, you know, I didn't know that that was done. Bill did that, like. I felt as though, wow, I mean, like ...

LEW WELCH: So what? I mean, what does that mean?

OLSON: Oh, I'll tell you, Lew, and you need it, baby. You need to know that experience and society is a complex occasion which requires as much wit and power as only poets have. It's become so evident. And it's become evident right here this week. And it's only because we've all arrived at 1965, I swear. Because the very same poets, plus some others, who were in Vancouver two years ago, had that place mixed up from the first day, before I even came in, and I only added to the confu—to the conviction. But Dunky and Ginzap and Bob had already said that they didn't know what they were doing, or some—I mean, they came on on a broken step, no arsis or verses, two years ago in Vancouver, but a preparatory state which is the condition of conviction. If I may talk the theology of a—[INTERRUPTION] Oh, Lew, you don't even—by the way, you ought to get busy, man, and do the same thing we do: just read, in order to write another *Wobbly Rock*. And you've stopped reading because you succeeded in writing a very beautiful, simple, I mean, a poem with simplicity.

WELCH: I may have stopped publishing. There's quite a difference.

OLSON: Well, O.K., the same thing, baby. Writing is publishing. Any one of us in this room will prove that to you. There is no publishing—I am not published for many years, because I was not writing. I am now publishing, tonight, because I'm talking writing.

WELCH: Right.

OLSON: Well, now don't say "right" so easily. That's like work. This is wonderful ...

WELCH: I read forty-seven times last year. Forty-seven!

14. "It is a work of art which has distinguished such poems as the *Odyssey* in the past"—William Carlos Williams on *The Maximus Poems 1–10* in a letter to Creeley, quoted to Olson in a letter of 21 August 1954 (at Storrs).

OLSON: Reading? This is a—? Are you kidding? You think this is anything but a—I mean, I think this is a political occasion.

WELCH: Nobody's getting at you on that ground.

OLSON: From my point of view, I am addressing a convention floor. The only convention I care of in the whole earth is occurring tonight. I mean, it isn't a month or two ago that Mr Sanders, laughing like hell, with me and John Wieners and others, Jack Clarke, who gave me Blake … I quoted Blake the other day, I was astonished, in the face of men in this room for whom Blake has meant something. And he says I'm running—excuse me, what?

VOICE: Read some poems.

OLSON: Aw, sure. I mean, come on. Either we do, or we stay here all night to hear the poems. I mean, how much of a feeling do you have for convention? Or congress? How much political action is there in your being? Did you even see that great, like, dumb, stupid documentary on George Norris? Did you see that thing, written by that smart Harvard cat that does the great, supposed great documentaries of television? What's his name?[15] What's that guy's name that really is one of the examples of why we're here, and why we're as political as we are, and why, in fact, we're better than Madison Avenue, those of us who are. And there's some men in this hall that surely are. And I wouldn't mind proving tonight that I belong where I have been, in Madison Square Garden. Dig this! Yeah, let's do that! Why not? I mean, let's get rid of that fucking stuff right now. And I'm perfectly happy to be the party of Johnson, as well as any other citizen that doesn't, like, get rah. I mean, literally, let's be … you know, it's wonderful, you do be literary. Isn't it wonderful? The community is that extensive. That's another reason why I had occasion to say today I don't know any poetics except the poems that the poets who read there this week: that's the only poetics I know. Plus those who didn't read because they're absent. But not too many. I mean, most of them are over on the other side of the bridge or something, one or two. That's how crazy it is. Is that true? I don't mean to be smart, or cute, or like a politician; and I can be.

But you know whom I—? I mean, I did, with a guy named Lew Frank, who was a secret—I mean, it wasn't a secret to me: I wouldn't speak to him for one year across a desk in Washington, sharing the same two secretaries, because I said to him, "Until you acknowledge that you're a member of the Communist Party"—By the way, Ralph, are you here? I mean, is Ralph—is there a Communist in the house? I mean, until you say you are …[16] It's like the LeRoi problem: you know, we're stuck with the very thing that's claimed! You can't gain by the argument. The rest of us, as though we look advantaged … You know, I'm a wealthy man. I got fifteen thousand dollars

15. Robert Saudek, producer of the "Omnibus" programs for early television, wrote the documentary on Senator George B. Norris (1861–1944) for the NBC *Profiles in Courage* series, 28 March 1965.
16. Olson is referring to the Feinberg Certificate controversy at the State University of New York at Buffalo. Ralph Maud with four other faculty had initiated a court case which ultimately led to the U.S. Supreme Court's abolition of all such communist loyalty oaths. See *Selected Letters*, p. 300.

salary as a professor at Buffalo. I got a key in—it's not this pocket—to a safety deposit box, which makes it possible for me not to bother for two years with Buffalo.[17] I mean that kind of wonderful power. Wealth! [SLAPS TABLE] Wealth! Wealth! And Allen and I talking yesterday about, like, he wants to be in jail. Jesus, I've been spending my life—I don't know how to say it—I mean, I never been in jail. I'm a good boy. I never did a thing that would get me in jail, because I never—well, like anybody else, I was never found out, literally, in one or two not very big cases. [INTERRUPTION] No, I wanna talk. I mean, you want to listen to a poet? You know, a poet, when he's alive, whether he talks or reads you his poems is the same thing. Dig that! [APPLAUSE] And when he is made of three parts—his life, his mouth, and his poem, then, by god, the earth belongs to us! And what I think has happened is that that's—wow, gee, one doesn't like to claim things, but, god, isn't it exciting? I mean, I feel like a kid. I'm in the presence of an event, which I don't believe, myself.

Well, you know my image. The only time it ever happened before is when poets had the right, because some woman wanted to—as I read that poem on Tuesday—either some woman wanted to have a look at whether Cuchulain looked as good as they said he did, you know, like the braggart champion of Dogtown ...[18] The bull, actually, the young bull was what was good-looking, but Merry thought he was, you know. Like me, hm? Then I lost my hair, and I got to be older. And I feel like crazy today. I feel like young, younger than the young. In fact, may I address the young? They ain't enough of 'em here, see. I don't have the audiences that ... [INTERRUPTION] Aw, come on, what are you talking about? They busted their wind to be here for other poets. And look at me: I got a paucity audience, except for the ...

WELCH: They climbed through the window.

OLSON: Except, my dear, for the best. And that could be a lot smaller. But I want the whole thing, huh? [LAUGHS] Right?

GINSBERG: Shining city!

OLSON: What?

GINSBERG: Shining city!

OLSON: Absolutely! In the sense of the population explosion: the whole terrestrial angel vision, baby! [APPLAUSE] Like, if I get to be President, I told you about who was going to be my Secretary of State for Love. [LAUGHTER] To talk like Ferlinghetti thinks the President talks, Colonel Cornpone, you know. "It takes two of yuh tuh make a troika, or something, on the Fernandez" or some shit like that.[19] I mean, is there or is there not a Great Business Conspiracy called America and Russia? It was proved by a

17. Harvey Brown's generosity is noted by Clark (p. 347): "$5000 subsidy checks sitting un-cashed in a safe-deposit box back in Gloucester."
18. Olson is comparing James Merry, the handsome bull-fighting sailor of "Maximus, from Dogtown–I" (II.2–6) with the Irish hero Cuchulain, who figures in the Enyalion poem "rages / strain" (1.76–78), included in his "Causal Mythology" lecture.

West German, writing in 1946 or '7, in *Der Dinge Zeit* or something, a great man, a man who most of you, because you don't read enough, don't even know. And the guy was dying. You will remember this story, because I just couldn't help telling Creeley. I read this goddamn thing, and I wrote a god-damn fourteen-page letter, and I got a letter back that the guy couldn't even answer it because he was probably dying of something. His name was Ernst Zander. Talk about *Zander to Sanders*: that would be much more important than *Confucius to Cummings*. Dig![20] I mean, value let's talk! Words are value, instruction, action, and they've got to become political action. They gotta become social action. The radicalism lies from our words alone. And if they're not right—and I'm not talking Mr Williams's "republic of words."[21] I'm talking our selves here in this week, the poets of America. And I don't mean America: I saw Ezra Pound, like an Umbrian angel, listening to any-thing that's said, going to see LeRoi Jones, which … I saw it. John Wieners wouldn't go. John Wieners had an impression about that play of Jones's.[22] So I went to see it anyhow. I wouldn't try to avoid Jones, so I could go see it with no problem. I just walked in, thank god, 7:00, after the readings in the Teatro de something, Melisso. Jesus, Melisso, Melissa, Memelis. Doesn't it sound like honey and sweet song? Yeah, exactly. Melissa, Caio Melissa, Teatro Caio Melissa, Spoleto: which means "spoiled." And what did that lousy Ferlinghetti—if you'll excuse me, because he knows I said it—do, in that scene, in all this luxury: "What about Vietnam? I'm gonna read my Colonel Cornpone. I mean, I'm mad. I'm fightin'." O.K. [LAUGHTER] I'd rather fight in San Francisco. Because I don't think that's culture. I don't think San Francisco was culture from the beginning. I mean, "John Wieners of San Francisco," John Ashbery writes in the *New York Herald Tribune* … [TO SOMEONE LEAVING] Gee, really, you know, it's wonderful. If you don't know, brother, that poetics is politics, poets are political leaders today, and the only ones, you shouldn't have come, and I'm happy you left. If there's a world to be left, it's simply society. And the poet, not only can he do it, but he's proved himself the only engin-er, if I may use my earliest poem read this week, which refers exactly to the power of the Anima Mundi.[23] And if I'm born tonight, it's simply because I might have a chance of standing here as an Imago Mundi. And if I can talk right now, it's simply

---

19. At the Spoleto gathering, Lawrence Ferlinghetti had read his poem "Where is Vietnam?" which satirizes President Lyndon Johnson as "Colonel Cornpone."

20. *Dinge der Zeit* was the German periodical with which Ernst Zander was associated; the sister publication in London was *Contemporary Issues* (founded 1948), for which Zander wrote many pieces including "Documents of 'The Great Business Partnership'" in vol. 2, no. 7 (Autumn 1950). With *Zander to Sanders*, Olson is proposing an anthology to supplant Ezra Pound's *Confucius to Cummings* (1964).

21. Olson is remembering William Carlos Williams's letter to Robert Creeley of 3 March 1950, pub-lished in *Origin* 1 (Spring 1951), p. 34: "To write badly is an offense to the state since the government can never be more than the government of the words. If language is distorted crime flourishes."

22. The play performance at Spoleto was LeRoi Jones's *The Dutchman*.

23. "*From* The Song of Ullikummi" was read in the "Causal Mythology" lecture (the earliest poem historically, being Hittite) under the rubric of Anima Mundi, the female spirit of Mother Earth. So a poet might be considered an "engineer" of "her."

because I'm on, huh? I mean, on; not high, babies. I'm high, but, wow, am I on! I've never been on like this. Then I can write poems again.

WELCH: You're doing it every …

OLSON: Aw, sh—no, that's not true, baby. God, again, Welch, you gotta get going, man. I love you. And you know who reminded me of the letter that Ferlinghetti wrote with you to me? Lawrence, of course. And you remember I answered you,[24] and I said tell Ferlinghetti I was very happy to be asked. Because, you know, I said to Ferlinghetti, the moment we sat down in a restaurant in Spoleto, the *Maximus Poems* was first reviewed in the *San Francisco Chronicle.*" Number one, that beautiful, beautiful book,[25] which I had to read from, that marvelous thing, done on the paper of Matisse's sons. I don't mind being cultural, only if it's interesting. [LAUGHTER] And printed in Stuttgart, by Dr Cantz'sche whatever they call a printery in German—*Druckerei*—and published by Jonathan Williams when he was a soldier in the U.S. Army in Germany, when Mr Conant, former President of Harvard, then recently President of Harvard but, in between, having been, with Compton, the President of MIT, the two university whores on the Atomic Energy Commission, which supported …

VOICE: Bravo, bravo!

OLSON: Bravo is right. But you got to get the bravo at the same place that we live. I mean, the difficulty is to get the bravo around at the back end, as that gentleman, whom I hope is here tonight, who's been in my seminar this week, who must be older than me—I say that hopefully. [LAUGHS] Are you? I mean, so beautifully for two days, no, for a day—in fact, Paul, now let's really get intimate, like they say. Paul, if Lew was the usher on that side, the usher from Vietnam, and you were the window kid from USA, in between that curious wonderful thing that happened, that colloquium of three, four, but three always, as Blake says: "I'm not a part of that colloquium." If I'm not dogmatic, and the one who has, simply because I have lived, and I don't mean longer, the authority, the fourth term of the Son of God, the hidden term, which Blake, because he's utterly—in fact, god help us, if I'm bold tonight, I told Allen Ginsberg, it's simply because I've discovered, in the presence of the poets and, like, ourselves, on having lived, how to be modest, I mean, to be modest, to realize that Charlie Olson, shit, he made it. Pfhm! I mean, he's got to still do it if he can, or he's nothing. That's that marvelous thing: you just get there, and you get your piece, and it's the whole thing, and you're absolutely—if you then know you're just as able as you are, and no more. And those other guys, god, don't I think I wish I were they? And I mean it: every goddamn poet I've heard tonight, except myself, and tonight, in those two poems so far, I think I've entered their company. And that's what I mean, and I think Creeley and I do mean, by "home." And

24. Olson's letter seems not to have survived, but Lew Welch's letters to Olson are included in *I Remain* (1980).
25. *The Maximus Poems 1–10* (Stuttgart: Jonathan Williams, 1953) was reviewed by Lawrence Ferling (pseud.) in the *San Francisco Chronicle* for 14 March 1954, p. 17.

that's both life, the earth, the universe, if the fourth term, ourselves, any one of us, can feel this way. Excuse me, I don't mean to be showin' off. I ain't showin' off, I hope, to anybody. I mean, just I feel good like this. And I don't feel good in some easy way, because, boy, I've … I mean, I'm happy to have … to feel good.

By the way, on Madison Squares Garden, like they say, [LAUGHS] the two men that I was responsible for presenting in "Everybody for Roosevelt," a program organized actually, musically, by Yip Harburg, who's not unknown now again, were Frank Sinatra, and the only man that I think I have seen do things that Robert Duncan … Beg pardon?

VOICE: She's going to the head. She'll be right back again.

OLSON: Oh, that's all right. You don't think I'm nervous, man? If everybody left, I'd still talk. Thank god I don't want your votes. [LAUGHTER] I don't want a damn vote in, like, at all. Really, isn't it wonderful? And believe you me, I could have asked, up to almost tonight, anybody's. I don't want your vote. [DRINKS] What did you interrupt me in? What was it I was saying, sir? Yeah, yeah. Was that marvelous guy, who played in *The Boys from Syracuse* as one of the twins, one of the Dromios, but was the guy who used to do "Starting a Heat Wave." He had two songs in vaudeville. If Astaire used to knock you out—'cos I was too young; I mean, my dentist was knocked out by Astaire in the Metropolitan Theater in Boston. Thank god I can say I'm younger than Fred and Adele Astaire! That gives me eyes, I mean hope, huh? But my dentist in Worcester, when I was grown up, when I had practically no teeth left, he was the one that was a friend of Astaire's and told me that Fred and Adele really were just like vaudevilleans at the Metropolitan in Boston.

But I'm speaking of Jimmy Savo! M-mm-ah-ah! I mean, let's toast Jimmy Savo, who lost his legs in an automobile accident, if I'm not mistaken, or they were shot off by the Mafia or something. It doesn't god-damn matter in America how the hell you lose all your … I mean, there was a time, you know, when Robert Duncan and Robert Creeley and I were identified because we have what's called "cosmetic optical difficulties." He's cross-eyed; that's my guy; and I got four eyes, ah-ha! That just makes it more difficult. You know you got to spend—you know when it happened to me? I was eleven years old, and I was a ballplayer, like Kenny Tallman wants to be, and I had to put those things on. You know what turns out to be true? A ball never busted my glasses. Only a—well, I don't want to say it, 'cos some of you would know the poet. Some of you were there the second time, but none of you were there, except Vincent Ferrini and Betty. Who did break my gla—? Oh no, then there was that other thing when Tom Field and Rumaker were there: that's the only other time. That's when I fought, huh? But was John Keys! And who's absent tonight, as against Vancouver? All the East Side, except the King of it, the ethnic power, the knowledgeable one, who's somewhere here, and was going to introduce me, simply because we thought (and if you'll excuse me, Tom Parkinson, if you're here), we thought he was going to introduce me, and I just thought, "He introduced Allen Ginsberg," and, I wanted to be introduced by another person, that's all. So we thought, "Ed's the guy. He's the barker." But I'm very happy you did.

So I can go back. It only took about what, an hour, to say that? We got all night long to run through the States. Believe you me, you don't get this stuff done by Averell Harrimans. [LAUGHTER] I don't believe it. I think Harriman is a stooge, like I think Conant was a stooge, of a creation of a false state, the West German state. And I'm going to read you also "Maximus 10" after I read you the next poem I propose to read, which is "Maximus 9." But my point is I want to read you "9" because of Robert Creeley, but I also want to read you "10" because Jonathan Williams published that poem as a soldier of America, after having been a conscientious objector because of Kenneth Patchen and Kenneth Rexroth and Henry Miller. The first publication that Jon … I mean, really, O.K., I'm a particularist. I am a localist. I'm a continentalist. I believe in the end of the world, in the sense that it's knowable. I also believe that the only thing that offends the end of the world—and that's exactly the only thing that—I mean, that's what war is: the way we offend the end of the world, those who win when the end of the world is accomplished. As of what I said—and somebody picked me up on it—about why, at the end of eighty-two billion years, the earth starts again. Oh, it was you, Allen, about epochs and things, yeah, Aion. The only thing—and it's in; and if I was reading poems tonight, instead of running for power, I'd read you the poem I published in the *Psychedelic Review* [11.163–72], which I think is—and John Wieners is one of the persons that has had, like, you know that way he is to say it to you so that you feel, "Gee, that's just what I intended." I wrote a very impossible to read (and probably I couldn't read it tonight) poem. But I should say that Ed Sanders still recognized that it was absolutely a reduction of Hesiod. If this sounds egotistical, please, I mean, anybody is free to leave.

VOICE: Is that "Across Space and Time"?

OLSON: No, no. It's a long, turgid … You know, Allen, when you said "prolix," baby, I mean, isn't it nice? I'm turgid. I'm not obscure, I'm turgid! [LAUGHTER] No, I am. Today proved it. [INTERRUPTION] Aw, that's too easy, baby. That's what I thought about this poem until tonight. Isn't it funny? That's feeling; I thought that was too easy in feeling. It isn't, is it, Al? Is it, Robin? No. But I still think that "Across Space and Time" is too easy. I feel as though I could do that because Jung supplied me the material. Or, better than that poem, I'd rather, when I'm hot, do somebody's Tarot. I really would. Or be on, like I felt I was—in fact, I kissed Lenore Kandel today with that feeling. Christ! She came up and said, "You're clear," like. I think she used the word "lucid," wow. Considering the poem that she put beside Ed Sanders's poems in *Fuck You*—I mean, *Love You/ A Magazine of the Arts*, huh?, published in Lower Madison Avenue. [LAUGHTER] By the way, if that sounds like a cut, I know Ed doesn't think so. I mean, right here, or right now, "fuck" and "love" have been added to.

It's the same goddamn thing that happened in Vancouver. There was a party of seventy-five of us, right next to the Royal Mounted Canadian Police. No kidding, it was a narrow little walk to get to the Wah apartment, Fred and Pauline Wah. And we were all asked to come bringing our whiskey, because the Wahs haven't yet got any money. And we had a party there, all of us; many of us are in this room tonight. And none of us know who the kook was that wasn't a part of the party. And he came to others as well as to myself. And I remember him, 'cos three times, when I was on the bed—I don't mean, like I said to you, Paul, in copulation, but I had five women in my arms, and that's the best I've ever done! [LAUGHTER AND APPLAUSE] And among them were some of the women who are here in this room too. The only missing one is Denise Levertov, practically. And Robert Duncan was also behind me, like a Sabine or a Catullan feast. [LAUGHTER] Wonderful ... Gee, isn't it great? They came for poetry, and I've been a talker. Happily. [LAUGHS] Not much of a drinker; not much anything else but talk, talk and poetry. I expect that the reason why once I caught on that I tell stories and also have to do with prose (which is a compliment from Mr Creeley) ... So I'm going to do that too. I mean, I don't care if it gets late, or the rules obtain, I'll be happy to read like as though we was going to drink and talk, dance, or screw, until eternity! O.K.? [APPLAUSE] I mean, you know that the—what I have thought—and I've listened to utterly amazing, unbelievable, and beautiful poems by poets whom I didn't—I think we all—I mean, each of us is a poet if we were those poets by having made themselves this week ... Drunk? I'm really drunk! Like Omar Khayyam? That son of a bitch really should be added to the masters.

GINSBERG: Anacreon.

OLSON: Huh?

GINSBERG: Anacreon.

OLSON: Well, gee, you know, that's what Ed said he'd say if he introduced me, was that goddamn Pindar.[26] I mean, I put Pindar down. I plan to read that "Letter 23" in honor of Robin Blaser. I will, for those of you who will stay. Or is Anacreon? I don't know, maybe I don't even know Anacreon? I don't think I do. I'm confusing two poets, ain't I? Am I, Robin? Tell me. Show the people how unknowledgeable I am, how ignorant. Please do. Because, look, I sound so goddamn intellectual, and so knowing, and so literate ...

JOHN KEYS: You're the boss poet here, daddy.

OLSON: Huh?

VOICES: Boss poet ... boss poet.

OLSON: Moschus? [LAUGHTER] Robert Kelly called me a dirty name in the

---

26. Ed Sanders's *Catalogue* #1 (Peace Eye Bookshop, June/July 1964) describes "Maximus, from Dogtown–I" as "one of the most beautiful poems since Pindar's 1st Olympian."

best piece of writing he's ever done.[27] That, I've never gotten over. By the way, I bought that book, like I bought Sappho. I read Sappho.

VOICE: Boss poet.

OLSON: Boss poet? Well, I guess I'm just showing off boss tonight instead. That's not a bad—I mean, the Mafiosi is us. [LAUGHTER] If that crazy Sanders gave me a "conspiracy" in the new *Fuck You*, god, was I, like, envious.[28] He lists in the *Village Voice*, an interview three weeks ago, his masters. And he starts, of course, with Allen. Then he mentions a professor, and I, like, jesus, this is puttin' me down. I'm a professor. And I don't know who this guy is, this professor he mentions after Allen. But, you know, I found out who he is since, in Europe. I don't remember his name, but … [INTERRUPTION] But don't be too quickly satisfied, Lew Welch. You and I and—Ed Dorn, if he doesn't know, he will. Like I told him to, in 1955: there's an awful lot of guys you got to chase down, as well as, well, we know also, hm, *cherchez* … [LAUGHS]

I mean, there was some wonderful verb in that poem which knocked me out, right at the end. What was the verb that sounded all right, like? The second poem I read this evening. It knocked me out. I mean, I felt good about it. I don't mean "tune," which I'd even appropriated earlier, forgot I wrote it. "Choice." Dig that! "Choice!" That goddamn word of my life, like your "grace," baby. Hm? That wonderful fucking thing. So I'm "hung up." Bullshit. I mean, Corso, in that conversation with you years ago in Venice, like, or in that book, *The Unholy Barbarians*, or *The Holy*—which is it?[29] We know Spengler predicted them … Us? I believe so. I believe I am as violent in my repressions and in the conditions of my inefficiency, shynesses; I mean, literally stupid, huh, my metabolism, a whole series of things. And, boy, this is no *apologia mea*, or *confessio meo*, or *imitatio* anybody.

CREELEY: Charles, read the poetry.

OLSON: Huh?

CREELEY: Read a poem.

OLSON: What d'you say? Come on, Robert, what d'you say? "Leap hard?" I do. As a matter of fact, somebody asked me to read "Leap onto the land …

27. In a letter published in *Floating Bear* 11 (1961), Robert Kelly wrote: "what's 'wrong' with Ausonius is right with Olson." Ginsberg explains his own interpolation as intending to "throw in Anacreon among the masters because of his delight to drink and dance among the young and 'gracefully be mad'" (personal communication, 4 September 1969).

28. *Fuck You/ A Magazine of the Arts* 5:9 (June/July 1965) is dedicated, among others, to "The Charles Olson Conspiracy." Olson's expressed envy is over an interview in the *Village Voice* (17 June 1965) p. 2 where Sanders is quoted: "I borrow from crooks, hustlers, queers, dope-freaks, amphetamine-heads, poets, Ginsberg, Professor Frank Peters, Charles Olson, the Ted Berrigan Conspiracy, and other sources." Frank Peters taught Classics at New York University, where Sanders attended.

29. Ginsberg is quoted in Lawrence Lipton's *The Holy Barbarians* (1959): "Actually I think they're hung up on authority, like Ezra Pound … except that they're so open … And it comes to a great extent from Olson's influence. Because Olson is like a great hip intelligence." To which Gregory Corso responded, "No. It's aggression. It's terrible. It's an aggression against themselves and nothing else" (pp. 132–33).

Orontes," and all that, "Maximus from Dogtown–II" [11.9–11]. I'd love to, but, you know, when you can do it you don't want to write any more about—as you were saying so carefully last night about a poem in which you were writing a poem instead of doing it.[30] I mean, I'm embarrassed. I think I've written the *Maximus* practically up to date, except for the poems I'm trying carefully tonight to select, to avoid the things any of us does because we can. Poetry must never be in that lousy, I can tell you even the fucking word, "rubric," which, as a priest once pointed out to me in Hammond's Castle, a beautiful guy, who is the only man I know who has sinned, and every night that he goes to bed has to think, "God will judge me tonight." And if I use that voice, it's not for reasons of mimesis; it's just to emphasize the condition of Father Haggerty, who finally, after all these years, has a church in Brooklyn. But the Church, you know how carefully she is about homosexuals. Father Haggerty not only has a brother who's one of the—I don't know where he lives in New York State, but he's …

Gee, if this is—if one inch up to this moment is gab, any one of you should really get outta here. And my feeling is not one damn letter is yet wrong, and I'll stop the moment it is. And that's, to my mind, the law of the poem. The reason why I don't need to read the poems is I haven't written them yet, that kind of a thing.

But Haggerty, who, by the way, was so goddamn bright—I use his brother because he's one of Wall Street's and New York State … And, by the way, may I remind you that, despite the power of the vote of California, the enormous productivity of New York State—and, like, I'm not saying this for any—I mean, Gloucester is my home, is it for me; but just so that we know, like, what Haselwood (if he wrote that) has said in that preface to *Human Universe*: I talk, like, "economic" something?[31] Did I—? Do I know—? I can only read you, and I will read you tonight, one poem, a late *Maximus*, which I think none of you have ever heard—I think I didn't even get tempted in that sort of jazz session of a non-competent player in Vancouver to read the *Maximus* written, made of proper nouns alone [11.23]. Or did I? But it's an economic poem! So here I am, I'm talking economics, right now at this moment … And somebody get me back. Why did I get off on economics? That's O.K. Let's go!

Let me read you *Maximus* "Letter 9" [1.41–44]—which it's easy to do the *explication du texte*. The reference in it to a book which comes in, with its print, which is so brown, in this spring, which is so red and green, happens to be that book from which I read you those two poems. And it isn't these brown cows of paleolithic and south of France (which is now my passport privilege, like my puss), but it is the color of that print on that paper, which is hand-set, curiously enough, in Mallorca, by Mossén Alcover. And,

30. Robert Creeley in the previous evening's reading had commented on his poem "Song" (*Words* p. 78) that it seemed "coy": "I suspect because it's more interested in how it is saying something, more interested in what it wants to say than in what it is saying."
31. The publisher's announcement by David Haselwood for *Human Universe and Other Essays* (San Francisco: Auerhahn, 1965) spoke of Olson's range as being "from the economic foundations of civilization to the mutability of the universe in man."

y'know, this is a wonderful little book. I'd like to propose that the idiosyncrasy can be the most powerful political event. I mean, from my point of view, this publication, which is, in fact, *Origin*, Boston, one of those magazine serials that the—in fact, you'd be surprised how many letters I've had from the Bancroft Library of the University, the Serial Department it's called. I still collect 'em; I never get around to sending them to Jonathan Williams. They ordered the *Black Mountain Review*. You know, people bought *Origin* in series: this is only number eight in *Origin* series one. Eight, I think. I go by square numbers, until I go by odd numbers, and I spend most of my time on "The Moon is the Number 18." But I could show you some switches, because, like, Pierre Boulez is my man, my man still really I guess for office and, I mean, whatever ... fuck that shit. But we ought to treat the whole universe as though it requires—by the way, may I preach, like, it shouldn't be the "doctrine," but the old Irish doctrine: that the real boss of a kingdom is the poet?[32] The only person that could stop Enyalion ... [TO RICHARD DUERDEN] When your wife did that to you last night, and you was offended because I said it was the god of war, that's mars, lower case; william shakespeare, lower case. The greatest poet of mars in the language (and I'd love to top it), huh, is William Shakespeare. I discovered that in wyoming, lower case w, last year. No Cassiopeia in the air overhead. No J-O Joyce in anywhere. No juice. No Zeus. No Joyce, no Zeus, no—I mean, cosmonauts? They're a drag. Isn't the *Mariner* photos a disappointment? They should be. There's only clouds out there. [LAUGHTER][33] And I said in a poem, which I'd love to read you also tonight, the poem printed, before I ever knew him, as a printer's devil in Black Mountain, by Edward Dorn, the "Letter for Melville," ha, that wonderful thing, which I don't consider an attack upon the university, I consider an attack upon the universe! That's another thing: if I don't do these things—it's like that bibliography that I proposed today—would you read the poems I mention? [LAUGHTER] I mean literally? If we had that tape, like ... Where are you, Pierre? Where is that tape? There. Hm, Madame.[34] Fortunately, I brought the two tapes that we made that day, Bobbie, when we got the hell in there to Boston and got me on tape. Well, this is the next time, and it's about the only time it ever happened. How many times can Olson make it? Twice, so far, or something. So this is it.

And, excuse me, but for us I swear Berkeley is simply Vancouver topped. And who'd believe that Vancouver could be topped? And if John is here, Wieners, who was the only person, I think, present that was at Spoleto: Baby, don't you think this week in Berkeley is what Gian-Carlo Menotti would really dream of having? If this is not the Teatro Caio Melissa—what do you think? I don't mean me up here, I mean your reading last week, what I heard of that, with a very small audience, like me. I ain't got a big audience tonight. That's

---

32. "The combatants—whom they [the poets] often parted by a sudden intervention—would afterwards accept their version of the fight"—Robert Graves in *The White Goddess* (1958), p. 22.

33. The *Mariner 4* probe sent back photographs of Mars on 14 July 1965; one was on the cover of the *Time* magazine published the day of the reading.

34. Pierre Dommergues from France was recording the evening with his assistant, Suzanne Kim.

what makes me almost not concerned that I didn't go home and wash my teeth. [LAUGHTER] And that I didn't put on the linen suit I paid $120 in Rome to have tailored to be here tonight, and look like I didn't look at the Teatro. You know how you get caught? You know, I didn't look like— [TROUBLE WITH MICROPHONE CORD] Hm, jesus, that mother will get me yet! [LAUGHS] I could stop talking, or you could stop hearing. Don't go. I'll read a poem. This's been—this is the dream of my life. ["Letter 5" (1.17–25)]

> (as, in summer, a newspaper, now, in spring, a magazine)

Hm, can't stop. *San Francisco Chronicle.*

> though how Gloucester will know what damage ... only Brown's window
> ... This quarterly will not be read

> The habit of newsprint
> (plus possibly the National Geographic)
> are the limits of
> literacy

> (tho that the many want any more than, who died
> what scrod brought the Boston market,
> what movies, Gorin's sales, the queer doings
> Rockport—or Squib's coynesses
> about the Antigonish man was pulled out, 3 AM,
> from under Chisholm's Wharf, mumbling

> I am not at all aware
> that anything more than that
> is called for. Limits
> are what any of us
> are inside of

> And there is nothing less applicable
> than the complaints of the culture mongers
> about what the people don't know but oh!
> how beautiful they are, how infinite!
> And think how it will be when
>   (Saint Santa
> Claus! how they need
> is the latest for oh!
> how they bleed, the poor
> children

> Editor of a Gloucester quarterly: the eyes which watch you
> do not look in the plate glass of Brown's (that display);
> or idly, waiting for the bus, stare at yr cover in the Waiting Station
> (if Lufkin has g—

Excuse me, quote: parenthesis sign, I was born 1910, parenthesis, open parenthesis.[35]

> (if Lufkin has got over his scare, last summer,
> when you were so sillily reviewed
> in the local press

35. The line "Draw it thus: ( ) 1910 (" appears in the poem "La Préface."

Lufkin, behind whose diner—and that's the Lufkin's diner of "The ..."[36] to me the genetic equivalent of what, thank god, for my life, Mr Dorn said Frank Moore is. For me, thank god, it was Lufkin's diner. What the hell are you stuck with but your own? I mean, the thing we're stuck with, our genetic. That's why I asked Ed how did you pronounce *genet*. You know why we die is because we're genetic, that's all. And why we live, if we do, is because we made that other, that novelty or whatever that goddamn— excuse me, but I would like to suggest that just really (I'm quoting my wife) "the biomorphic must go." And I think she was going to be the painter to tell Dan Rice how to paint. Because Dan got hooked hocked on Beauty, and we're here to say something a hell of a lot more important than "beauty is difficult" or that "Paradise is not artificial."[37] We're here both to say it and to prove it, both points. And we're the only ones. And it's not only because we're later; it's because, thank god, well, we're here, hm. Gee, I'm just even trying to imitate. I mean, I feel like Mim ... Talk about Aristotle. I read him today, and he says poetry is ... for something; but he says "history is particulars." I read it to the people. Sister ... whatever her name is, gave me this text. I read Aristotle's *Poetics* really, like, for the first time last night and this morning. I got the book. I mean, she took it from the Dominican Library, where she is a member of the San Rafael, or something, where Sister Mary—what did you tell me her name was? Norbert? Sister are you here tonight?

VOICE: She can't come.

OLSON: See? The close. Isn't it wonderful? That's what I mean in that poem about "the close." Those of you who weren't ... Honestly, please don't be bored. I really ain't a talker. Hear me? I mean, I really could run the nation if I didn't prefer to talk. And the trouble with our presidents, if you'll excuse me, is they can't talk or write. And that includes Adlai Stevenson. Like, I may lay that flower on his grave, instead of our third editor of the *Black Mountain Review*, Irving Layton, who wrote a poem about him, which neither anybody else that I know in this room that is a poet now—I mean I'm not try ... I was there the night I watched the elect—I mean, I wrote a flagrant autobiography of myself,[38] imitating Ezra Pound, trying to make myself ... You know, you can't do it. There's no artificial way to be arbitrary. There's only one way: moral. Then you are! But every imitation stinks, and it leads you wrong, even if you think, "Wow, like, I'm making it, I'm Thespis or somebody." I mean, I was at the returns. I saw Mr S—I thought he behaved beautifully, you know. Like that funk from California, Nixon, you remember. That was '52. Yeah, it's not so long ago. There's enough young in

---

36. The poem "The Librarian" contains references to "Lufkin's diner" and to "Frank Moore" as part of the dream which constitutes the poem. Edward Dorn had given special attention to this poem in his essay "What I See in the Maximus Poems," first published as a *Migrant* pamphlet (1960) and then in *Kulchur* 4 (1961).

37. Both these quoted phrases appear in Pound's *The Pisan Cantos*, "Canto 74."

38. A statement for *Twentieth Century Authors: First Supplement*, ed. Stanley J. Kunitz (1955), found in *Collected Prose* titled "The Present is Prologue."

this audience to remember. In fact, it's only thirteen years ago, isn't it? A thirteen-year-old will know this. [TO KIRSTEN CREELEY] You weren't in the country, were you, dear? But, I mean, Kirsten could have been watching that television. It was terrific, 'cos you know, Mr Stevenson, if you recall— it was that guy who plays that lousy band that was at the Republican head-quarters—what's that son of a bitch's name? We've forgotten him already, except if the Republicans succeed to power, we'll hear of him again. I bet he's alive. What is that guy that was the reason, huh?

VOICE: Lawrence Welk.

OLSON: No, no. Like, it's way back, It's like Rudy Vallee; some goddamn band the Republicans have in their headquarters ... Isn't it wonderful? People cannot wait for poetry. Ha-ha! The activity has to be produced in a time schedule. You remember how we write these things? The same way I'm behaving. I'm a Professor of Posture, and I'm proving it.

DUNCAN: Charles, can you give us time to go pee?

OLSON: Oh, my god, I forgot about that intermission. You mean, in a political convention, you think the heat and the stuff inside yourself has to be relieved?

DUNCAN: Five minutes.

OLSON: You're ... I mean, "Teacher." [LAUGHTER AND TROUBLE WITH MICROPHONE CORD] That's called "recall." I'm either going to lose my position or I won't, that's all.

[INTERMISSION, OF WHICH THE
FOLLOWING IS ON TAPE]

OLSON: Allen, I'm just proving that oral poetry exists, O.K.? Ain't I or not?

GINSBERG: It's very good, it's fine.

OLSON: Isn't this oral poetry? Isn't this improvisatory, spontaneous poetry?

GINSBERG: All except one thing, when you had a cigarette in your mouth.

OLSON: And what happened? Was that visual?

GINSBERG: Couldn't hear you at the back.

WELCH: We were worried that it was backwards.

OLSON: Gee, I wish it were. It needs to be backwards. That extra piece that I needed, I don't need it. I'm drunk on youse guys. And I mean it.

WELCH: Hey, don't you have to pee too?

OLSON: No, shit, pee? I never pee. The reason why I'm not a queen is I don't have to pee to prove that I'm a man. Go pee, Allen. We got over that tonight.

PAUL X: Can I have a cigarette?

OLSON: Of course, it's yours, baby. Isn't that crazy, I should be smoking your cigarettes? Goddamn it, it irritates me, but it also ...

PAUL X: A broad gave them to me, so it doesn't matter.

OLSON: Oh good. I'm glad originally it was a broad instead of you, like.

WELCH: Isn't it a great tradition?

JOHN WIENERS: [INTRODUCING A YOUNG WOMAN] Just here visiting.

YOUNG WOMAN: Hello, how are you? I'm enjoying it so much.

OLSON: Awfully nice to see you. [A KISS] Pleasure. I'm glad. Will you kiss me too? You would kiss me, anyhow, but I want you to kiss me in honor, as well, will ya? In love and honor.

WELCH: We did. That was why we did it.

VOICE: Of course, Charles.

OLSON: My god, I mean, I'm only standing up here, trying to be equal, that is, to …

DRUMMOND HADLEY: Give 'em hell.

OLSON: It's a tent show, baby. [LAUGHS] Madison Avenue, Madison Garden.

VOICE: We didn't hear the end of Sinatra …

OLSON: No, I was just standing—I mean, I was a kid. This guy and this communist agent, who became the founder of the Progressive Party, which carried Wallace as its candidate, Lew Frank—Detroit, Michigan; box factories, father; Army out here at Camp Ojai, La Jolla. Hired by Alan Cranston, who is not here in this audience—Wesley Huss is in this audience—Alan Cranston, the State Comptroller of California, isn't here, and he wasn't here in '57. You know what Alan Cranston is to me? You see the poem I published in Cambridge? You did.[39] It's addressed to two men, Alan Cranston, without identifying him, who was last year the guy whom that lousy Pierre Salinger, who got defeated, yeah! but the Kennedy machine just pawed Cranston down. Cranston is the man who hired me in Washington, and was the lobbyist of the outfit I was in in New York, the Chief of the Foreign Language Information Service, and he's wonderful. And the other guy I inscribed this poem to is Jack Wells, who was Rockefeller's National Political Manager last year, and I know—I've been reading that book by that smart cock, son of a bitch of China, Ted White, who is no Red Star Over China, and he's no Mao neither …

SUZANNE MOWAT: Charles, what are you doing?

OLSON: I'm doing just what I ought to be doing, don't you think so? You don't? You think I should be reading poetry?

MOWAT: Well …

OLSON: God, I got the poems, but it's—I don't have any problem reading the poems.

---

39. "The Condition of the Light from the Sun" (III.44) was first published by editor Andrew Crozier in *Granta* (7 March 1964).

WELCH: Charles, do you know John Montgomery? Allow me to introduce John Montgomery. You know John Montgomery.

OLSON: No, I don't think so. I know Stuart Montgomery, the guy who's publishing Ed and me in London.

WELCH: No, he's this guy who talks so funny in *The Dharma Bums,* that forgotten painter.

OLSON: That's the last of it, dammit. I had one last slug.

WELCH: Don't you want to give him a drink?

MOWAT: No, I don't think you should.

OLSON: John Montgomery, have you got that thing I just dropped? "... and John Montgomery." Let's do this thing the way it's coming out tonight. "Charles Olson and John Montgomery." O.K.? Now, give me that shot. You got a whiskey?

WELCH: I brought this for you, but no one told me that you drink.

OLSON: What the hell is that? Just that lousy wine. Well, I'll just go like Jack Kerouac right straight on to Rot Red. [DRINKS] It's sweety time. You, you drunken bum, have a shot. And if you don't stop drinking ...

WELCH: Yeah, I know, I'm a terrible lush.

OLSON: Lew, you've got to cut it out, man. You're too good to be a lush. Come on, Lew. "Lew" doesn't rhyme with "lush," and no poets that we know have proved ...

WELCH: You come tomorrow and hear what I blow, and you'll see that I have not been lying on my ass.

OLSON: "Lew" rhymes with "Lew." Lew, shsh. You hear me?

MOWAT: Charles, I'll see you afterwards. O.K.?

OLSON: You mean you're going to leave?

MOWAT: I'm going to go and sit down now.

OLSON: Don't leave. Please. I gotta end up with only those I love. That's my— this is what's called Politics.

MOWAT: No, I won't leave. You know where I'm sitting, Charles?

OLSON: If Allen is going to be—I mean, if love is ...

WIENERS: [SHAKING HANDS] Really, Charles, I want to because I enjoyed it so much.

OLSON: Are you going to leave too?

WIENERS: No, I'm not going anywhere.

MOWAT: No one's leaving, no one's leaving.

WIENERS: But I wanted to make a point of shaking your hand.

OLSON: John, you formal son of a bitch.

WELCH: Well, he has to be; he's from Boston.

OLSON: Well, so am I. And so is Robert Creeley. He's from the mestizos, like us.

WIENERS: I'm not even a mestizo.

OLSON: Well, you've risen above it, but that's only because you can rise.

WIENERS: It's the event of my life.

OLSON: It is? Well, you know it's ten years, plus, almost now eleven, right? I'm sure, like, we're mestizos ... A *mista*? You want a *salada mista* afterwards, for supper?

VOICE: Charles broke Lew's nut, just like that. Isn't it true?

OLSON: Thank god. I got the best sharp shootin' ...

WELCH: And there it is, right there, see? That terrible sweet count to nine.

OLSON: Who? My girl? What do you mean?

WELCH: Of course, of course, Sir George here ...

OLSON: Jesus, shall I sock him? I'd be glad to.

MOWAT: No, please don't. That's my real name.

OLSON: Georgia? You were baptized Georgia? Don't forget your baptism certificate. Hey, could you take us to Arizona tonight?

HADLEY: I sure will.

OLSON: Have you got your private plane? After this we ought to really finish everything. How about it? Have you got your private plane?

HADLEY: I got a truck.

OLSON: Truck, you shit. I want to do it fast. I've gotten used to planes. I'm gonna fly. Those trucks are more interesting, but they do take a long time. If Duncan took that long, we're lost. I mean, the Queen of France turned the fire out of the haystack sooner than that.

MOWAT: Lookit, we'll be sitting right over there somewhere, Ed Sanders and all your cheering section. O.K.?

OLSON: I'm drunk.

HADLEY: You're not, too.

OLSON: Come on.

HADLEY: You're not, too.

[TO THE AUDIENCE]

OLSON: Bobby, where are you? Bob. Bobby Duncan! Is he back? Robert, come back so we can start school again.

Isn't this a university? Isn't it wonderful? This is not San Francisco. Ain't it queer? You know, it never was true that San Francisco was the source of the revolution or the *Evergreen Review*. And I think it's only been made accurate, as, in fact (if I may criticize my own editor and publisher), the divisions of *The New American Poetry* weren't accurate either. That, as Mr Dorn carefully said to me (and I urged Mr Allen, in a sense, not to divide his book that way, not by places) has been divisive. And I don't believe that the poets ... Is anybody hearing this microphone? It sounds like mad to me. Oh, O.K. It's like a Chinese theater, that's all.

VOICE: Keep talking.

OLSON: I'm happy to. But I want Robert Duncan and Don Allen to hear me. What are they doing? What do they call that stuff that's going on out there? What do they call that stuff by which votes are produced? Caucusing. Are they caucusing? I mean, you probably all read that San Francisco, the Cow Palace, was where that thing happened—was it last year? Yeah. Do you realize how history has become so completely corrupt since a certain date, like 1937, which the Spanish Civil War was the instance of: that history occurs as recorded instead of happened, happening? I mean, this is even true of Kennedy's successful nomination in L.A. I'm not talking about Kentucky or Wisconsin. May I just again use politics, which I believe, forever—I don't believe forever, but I mean, if the human race doesn't think that its politics is as accurate as its poetry, there is no society, and the only individuals are poets. And I think those poets that are here in Berkeley, where Robert Duncan dreamed—and that will be published, because it's a long, beautiful prose report. Like I learned only a few days ago that Ezra Pound wished he could write like Tacitus. I can't get over it, but that's what some poet here, I think, told me that. Ed? Who told me that? Allen? John? Who said that Pound really wanted to write like Tacitus? What I'm saying is that I think that Robert Duncan—and it has nothing to do with Pliny—but I think that Robert Duncan in the Hilda Doolittle letter will have supplied the world ... I mean, look, these are the synapses that Ed asked of me. You know, like, my poems will be published, and if you have the reason, you can read 'em. I can read 'em now, and I'll read 'em later, any of 'em. And I'm not even trying to make a pitch. Hm, I'm trying honestly to write the poems that I—no, no, that isn't true. But this is a wonderful scene for me, literally, and I don't mean in that jive sense. I mean it in a hall, and a convention, and a public sense. To make up for my lost poems. And to finish that point: Duncan in the Hilda Doolittle book, has a five-page dream, in which he and I are in Berkeley; and I'm Dr Olson. But there's three doctors, Dr Einstein, Dr Freud, and me, in Berkeley. And the whole earth is pockmarked like the moon. Robert, are you here? Gee, I don't want to garble this.[40] Maybe he just went to pee at home or something. [LAUGHTER] Makes sense to me. I've spent my life, as Edward Dahlberg unfortunately put me on to the embarrassment of having anybody else present to yourself, that the trouble with being social is you wouldn't leave to pee. And I agree with Dahlberg: I wouldn't leave to pee. That's why, if you'll excuse me, I mentioned that piece

40. See chapter 11 of *The H.D. Book*, published later in *Io* 10 (1971), pp. 212–15.

of fabulatory European mythology, that Eleanor of Aquitaine became the Queen of France because she could piss so strongly that she put out the fire in a haystack. [LAUGHTER] And the only difference between a man and a woman is that if you can hold your piss, you literally, like, I mean, drink and not sleep, everything you were talking about last … Where the hell has Robert gone? Jesus, I've lost him. Where are you, Allen?[41] What the hell, are they he who …? They've abandoned me.

WELCH: They're having a drink.

OLSON: Yeah, I know it. Well, I'm the only one that's got a bottle, Lew, and you gave it to me. You don't mind if I keep it? I'm going to deny you tonight.

WELCH: Good.

OLSON: You don't even know how to be monastic yet. You don't even know how to be in that goddamn log cabin of Lawrence Ferlinghetti while he vacations in Europe, in Spain.

WELCH: That was three years ago.

OLSON: He's still doing it. He's still in Spain. In fact, if any of the employees of the City Lights Bookshop are present, who substitute for the owner, he asked me to call them up and say, "Lawrence—Larry—is all right." Report from Rome. Jesus, isn't it so fucking easy? I mean, that filthy thing in *Time* magazine that Sinatra, that night—who the hell was the doll in all that bullshit backstage in the election of '44? I mean, excuse me, but you think '60 and '64? You know, it isn't going to work out. Ed Sanders, who proposed that I run in '68, has already been proved I'm running tonight, and I have my cabinet present, and therefore it's already over. Isn't it marvelous? I didn't even accept an invitation to 1800 Blake, San Francisco. And I said to Suzanna coming here tonight, "You know, it already happened." Peter and you, who invited me, and Allen, and everybody else was over there, right? That night, two nights ago? But the address, 1800 Blake, knocked me out! I mean, I don't even have to go to 1800 Blake.[42] Dig? That's that kind of thing that I really stand here, with all my belief in date and place, to say can happen just as much. I mean, this is coincidence, not truth. An event which is coincidence is not valuable enough. It must be simply what you deeply believe in. And I believe more than anyone else in our time has tried to encourage people to believe is their own action. But, you know, action is the same thing as the end of it all: how the hell do you get so that you have it, that it is, your action is, so that the universe therefore is essentially displaced? Not that it's stopped or anything else, but that one of us is—I mean, that's what unity means. That's what "the universe" means: "one

41. When asked about this, Allen Ginsberg wrote: "Gone to take a pee side by side with Duncan, and then at entrance-way to Wheeler Hall turned on a stick of grass with Creeley to augment enjoyment of the show, and return'd to the Hall to listen" (personal communication, 4 September 1969).
42. At this point a voice from the audience calls out, "You're lost" with an aggressive tone. A woman's voice, with some apprehension, says, "Oh no." Olson continues unaware of this. Stella Levy's apartment at 1800 Blake was where Ginsberg and Orlovsky stayed during the conference.

turn." I really believe it. That bullshit of all the complication! I think the poets—I think, in fact, they're ahead of the scientists now. I know they are. The decadence of the imagery of science is as shocking as James Joyce. I mean, Ezra Pound long years ago returned the presentation copy of *Finnegans Wake* to himself, with the word "DECADENCE" written over the cover. I mean, that takes guts, the same guts that led him to say, "I thought I knew something."[43] If he hadn't said it, I wish I could say it to you: "I thought I knew something." I'd be proud to have been the man in this century ... And, like, here I am, dragging my ass after Ezra. Two years ago in Vancouver, what did I do? I tried to read the poems. Now I could, and instead I'm telling you, "Gee, I wish—I wish they were more." I'm not just avoiding it. I'll be happy to read them. I love some of them, just like I read the—like those poems I wrote longer and earlier, I bet they'll turn out to be all right. That's not the point. They're nothing by comparison to what I propose, or what I would dream I might do. Because poets only are worthwhile if they do what they dream. And there's been a few. In fact, the only ones that count are those who want to be, hm, the same as their dream.

And I'm, like—let me continue "5," and I'll come back to "9," which I love because it talks about how a book practically is the only goddamn thing that is a dream in a society like this. And do you know it embarrassed me two years ago in Vancouver. I mean, god, Allen an activist, Orlovsky, Dunky, Creeley, everybody that was there, I felt like an old schlumpf from Gloucester. And, in fact, I'd love to read even that crazy "Tantrist sat saw Lingam in City Hall" [II.190] or something, I mean, a poem I did read, you know, I'd like to read it right now, like that, like that, like. And just make it like it felt when it was written, that's all. I am a Tantrist. But two years ago I was embarrassed, and not because I hadn't been to Buenos Aires. [LAUGHTER] O.K.?

I mean, the universe today is a very hard thing for an individual to possess. The whole human race has it. The efficiency of the universe is in our hands. But for any one of us, as what they used to call a private soul, when I protested was a piece of piss at any public wall, in that paragraph, that opening paragraph of "Projective Verse," but, you know, it comes out that the private soul—and if I could cry like the cock at the birth of day, which is all I'm doing tonight, that's the only thing that's more than public and private. And like that great thing we've been talking about and we discussed in seminar, isn't it nice, really? This *is* the private soul at the public wall. Charlie Olson. Closed verse. Not even bothering to play the music. I got the music. I mean, it's like scores, Beethoven and all those things, John Keats's letters in Harvard's library. I read 'em. In fact, I wrote a fourteen-line sonnet.[44] You know, it's powerful. I was talking to Ed Dorn recently. Probably I shouldn't have eaten supper, but ... All right, Bob, I heard you.

CREELEY: Please read the poems.

43. Grazia Livi's "Interview with Pound" had been published in *City Lights Journal* 2 (1964), pp. 40–46, quotation on p. 40.
44. The fourteen-line poem "I'm With You," written 3 May 1960, is included in *Collected Poems*.

OLSON: O.K. I'll continue "5," goddamn it. I stopped there. I will see if it can ...

                                                    (Saint Santa
                    Claus!

[SLAPS TABLE] You son of a bitch! Raymond Weaver, my ass, Allen![45] You are my instructor. I am not a professor. And I've been instructed. And if you don't graduate me tonight on this platform at the University of California. Ha ha ha!

                                                             Santa
                    Claus!

(under the mushroom)

                        how they need
                     is the latest for oh!

(you know, remember "oh"?)

                             oh!
                     how they bleed, the poor
                     children

Society is the same fucking thing as taking care of a kid or a cow, Paul (empty chair) X. I mean, jesus! Talk about assassination! That's over, see. I'm going to read you tonight the poem called "The Three Towns."

> Editor of a Gloucester quarterly: the eyes which watch you
> do not look in the plate glass of Brown's (that display);
> or idly, waiting for the bus, stare at yr cover

This is the news, the world news, reverse-wise, O.K.? backwards or something. This is it, this is the same fucking news they're rushing to the headlines, of McNamara on ... You know, Allen, Eisenhower said it. You weren't there today, but I said Eisenhower said the fucking thing when Mendes-France was selling milk to the French: "That whole country is a guerrilla country." You know that? Are we a guerrilla country? That's all that all this radicalism is to produce. The students of the world! The only way America'd be radical is that there is the students of the world, that's all. That's why Bobby Kennedy in Tokyo, the embarrassment of that situation, right? And you, being the King of May and getting kicked out of Czechoslovakia, thank god, is this side of that, baby! In my cabinet, you're the Secretary of State, not anything else.

GINSBERG: Fine. [LAUGHTER]

OLSON: ... or idly, waiting for the bus, stare at yr cover in the Waiting Station

He says to me, "Have you got the patience?"[46] You know, you said that when

---

45. "Raymond Weaver, author of first scholarship on Herman Melville. Professor of English Columbia University. I had him in college as a teacher"—Allen Ginsberg (personal communication, 4 September 1969).

46. "I had been excessively tipsy declaiming 'Kral Majales' at my own reading 'in another house' i.e. Dwinelle Hall, a week earlier. 'Have you got the patience?' probably asking Olson to be patient with me for a lengthy text"—Allen Ginsberg (personal communication, 4 September 1969).

you were drunk leaving the stage. It wasn't here, but in another house. Have I got the patience? Baby! Christ! I'm going to abandon it tonight. I am Russia. Even Arthur Miller, two weeks ago, said, "You're more Russian than the Russians." And I unfortunately said, "That's because I'm a Hungarian, like." [LAUGHTER] That was an old scene. I got myself called a Semite by telling Ezra Pound that my grandmother's name was Lybeck, which is obviously Lübeck, which is where Thomas Mann wrote the only goddamn good novel he ever wrote ...[47] [BELL RINGS] Jesus, school's over! Hm, well, then we can have poetry. That's great. Under the tree tomorrow at four. And we can start now and end up there: poetry from now till then. Let's have a rally, like they say. Not one of these "ins," these "sit-ins," these fucking "ins." I mean, how many "ins" do you have to make to prove that there isn't any? [LAUGHTER, APPLAUSE] Which is exactly the complement of what I've spent my life—like, "space," the guy said. Like, Creeley got another one I'd love to—"Maximus 2." That one I will read, Robert. Let me break in and interpolate. Let's go. It's never getting any further than if we made it "9" or "10." You wouldn't mind?

You know, I can tell you exactly: it's the only thing I ever knew about reading poems, that's the night I was told how to read poems by David Tudor at Black Mountain, due to Jonathan Williams's audacity, as a member of the armed forces, to publish *The Maximus Poems* in West Germany, in Stuttgart, Dr Cantz'sche Stuckerei, Druckerei, whatever that drugstore of publishing. It's great. A pharmacia is where you need to get your pills. And you know, it's better in Europe still, like I found it was better on the edge of the jungle in Yucatan than it is in any one of our cities. You don't need some doctor's permission to get married, and have a blood test. You can screw, and that's the proof that you love. And it's not just shacking up. You do that because that's love. You know, that was true in 17th-century Massachusetts. And you always screwed the girl next door, because it's that—you know, like, not simple, but somehow or other, "awkwardness, the grace, the absence of the suave."[48] Siena is the girl next door. As a matter of fact, Sienese art, the last of Christianity, is simply that the distance of the Eucharist is only the girl next door.

And thank god Robert Duncan proposes to publish (and I brought with me tonight), with Jess Collins on the cover, *O'Ryan 1–10*, and, you know, that's like reading that "Ode on Nativity," dammit. Those poems have been uncomfortable for me too. But that poem 10, in which I just say those things—like Frank Moore's toes is why I asked him to leave. I mean, he cleaned his toes in my living room in Washington—it wasn't a living room, it was a chapel entry, and then there was a sleeping room, that was all. But he cleaned his toes there! And my daughter, that daughter of the poem, got a hold of this lousy blue stuff, like asshole or crab correction. I had to rush

47. Lübeck was Mann's birthplace, and the setting for *Buddenbrooks*. So, though written in Munich, that may be the novel Olson was thinking of.
48. The opening line of the poem "Siena," applicable in Olson's view to Sienese art as a whole and Giovanni di Paolo in particular. See *Selected Letters*, pp. 83–87.

her to the hospital, save her life. I mean, she was oral 'cos of her father hadn't got to be not. Three times! And, in fact, we almost—she was in convulsions. And now that she's fourteen has that embarrassment of having an ugly scar on her ankle, it was necessary to cut it so fast. And I never paid the bill still, I'm so mad. Because beauty and paradise must be! Nobody can mar us, including Mars. If we don't know that War is Beauty, in the same sense that Venus took him to bed, not Vulcan. But she also was married to Vulcan. That's what I mean: lower case mars. And if I substitute, and your wife uses it—she loves your back. It's like that poem of Gary Snyder's, that nice poem of his. Excuse me, I've lost my voice now, haven't I? [MORE TROUBLE WITH THE MICROPHONE CORD] What is this thing? I may end up as the Hanged Man. I'll be upside down. And that's the image I want to end with, no matter how few of you stay, is that poem of Maximus with his feet in the air. ["Poem 143. The Festival Aspect" (III.73–75)] So maybe tonight is the night I alter myself. May it be so. I've been too long Olson. Too long a father to—I'm no father to nobody, even my own children. Isn't it crazy? And, boy, don't hear that as public confession, I hope. It's like singing "River, Stay Away From My Door" with no legs, huh? Or for Sinatra being a liberal, making a plug so that he'd be sure that Roosevelt won. Like how many people did the same fucking thing to be sure that Johnson beat Goldwater? Ha-ha! In this house, ha, even the poets. It ain't Adlai Stevenson; it's Johnson. And who the hell turns on him now? The poets. But if they went to the ballot, I bet ... And like our question, like that beautiful question. You know, Allen and I'll be in jail, we were talking yesterday, not because Allen is obviously a conspicuous metaphorical political figure, which is what Mr Havelock means. He really means it, that gods and heroes are the only metaphors. For the best of reasons: they teach public conduct.[49] And that baby does do that. Only he should teach proper public conduct. [LAUGHTER] I mean, that's all I really got to say. O.K.?

GINSBERG: Yes, yes, yes. Except I can't figure out what "proper" is.

OLSON: I only think it is what—if you'll excuse my pedantry, the word comes from *proprius*, proper to yourself. I'm happy that that book *Proprioception* is published. Every one of those essays, by the way, is published by LeRoi Jones alone, in *Yugen*, *Floating Bear*, and *Kulchur*. And I sat in Gloucester, suffering, suffering, that the world had been captured by Allen and Peter and Gregory and, in fact, their own master (like my Pound), Burroughs. And, you know, I didn't want to lose my world. I'm older. I crave power. [LAUGHTER] In fact, I so crave power that, between power and love, until this moment obviously I've chosen the wrong one. That's how powerful it matters. And you know, I wrote those essays—they're incongestible or something. They're not readable. If they're interesting they can be dug up as signs, that's what I mean. Goddamn it, I didn't even know that that's what I wrote until this lucid—Lenore, are you here? Where's that right shoulder?

49. Eric Havelock, *Preface to Plato*: "All non-human phenomena must [in an oral society] by metaphor be translated into ... acts and decisions of especially conspicuous agents, namely gods" (p. 171).

O.K. I kissed it, for that. I mean, isn't it wonderful to have her tell me that I was clear today? You said "lucid," didn't you? No, but I mean, I hope I am right now. And any poem I haven't written I wouldn't have read tonight, or I'd have faltered if it wasn't, so I'd have had to revise a lot.

I found this out. Gregory Corso was in Buffalo this year. I was asked to read. I never read in a coffee house in my life.[50] I never spent an hour in jail. I'm the White Man; I'm that famous thing, the White Man, the ultimate paleface, the non-corruptible, the Good, the thing that runs this country, or that *is* this country. And, thank god, the only advantage I have is that I didn't, so I can stand here among men who have done what I couldn't do, can't do. All I have done is what I have done alone. To my mind, it's like a table service, with good linen and silver and plates or something, without servants, and without really having the stuff that ought to make a meal work, except that, like, the stuff that's on the plates is what I was able to cook or something, some dumb thing like that. I don't even goddamn well care about the seasoning … But that won't work. O.K. Like Jack, I'll drink red. It isn't even as good as muscatel. It's "Hombre." *Hombre Universe*! [LAUGHTER] I'll have to reread that book, too, with hope. You know, this is the greatest thing, and if you'll endure it, babies … You know, every time I ever read before, the awful thing is that I might talk, instead. [LAUGHTER]

> ….. tell you? ha! who
> can tell another how
> to manage the swimming?
>
> he was right: people
>
> don't change. They only stand more
> revealed. I,
> likewise

[End of tape, interrupting "Maximus, to Gloucester, Letter 2" (1.5–8). New reel begins in middle of "Letter 9." (1.43)]

> versus the tasks
>
> I obey to,
> not to a nation's,
> or at all to history,
> or to building
>
> Flowers, like I say.
>
> And I feel that way,
> that the likeness is to nature's
> not to these tempestuous
> events,

---

50. Olson is about to tell the story of his confrontation with Gregory Corso in the Greensleave Coffee House, Buffalo, on the evening of 20 November 1964, but is distracted.

that those self-acts which have no end no more than their own
are more as plums are
than they are as Alfreds
who so advance
men's affairs

(who thr—

(parenthesis)

(who threw Guthrum back
even when he held Glow-ceastre

and he himself was holed up
in the Athelney swamp)

I measure my song,
measure the sources of my song,
measure me, measure
my forces

(Parenthesis. Wish I could have banned them tonight.[51] Ha! And I wanna show you, like, what does fuck it up.)

(And I buzz,
as the bee does,
who's missed
the plum tree,
and gone and got himself caught
in my window

(or "in *my* window")

And the whirring of whose wings
blots out the rattle of
my machine)

And I don't mean my ... [APPLAUSE] Hm, thank you.
So ... "10" [1.45]:

on John White / on cod, ling, and poor-john

on founding: was it puritanism,
or was it fish?

And how, now, to found, with the sacred & the profane—both of them—
wore out

The beak's

there.

That's a weakness. But it's weak. Like, until we've found out how weak is the only way that the whole fucking universe, because it's so fucking strong, behaves. That must be what's up. Christ, I've been weak, and I thought it was false. And of course it is. But it also, because of what Robert Duncan ...

---

51. The pronunciation here is uncertain: the phrase "have banned them" has previously been heard as "abandon them"; but the idea is the same. Throughout the reading Olson is trying various ways of expressing his desire for *negative* capability.

Did you go, Robert? To San Francis—? Did you leave me? Gee, isn't that crazy? Ed, are you here? Ed Sanders.

ED SANDERS: Right here.

OLSON: Good, 'cos Ed was going to introduce me, actually, as well as Robert. He was going to stand out there and bring the crowd in, and Robert was going to do what he did.

> The beak's
there.

I don't like that first *Maximus* [1.1–4]. I never have, because of that god-damn principle, which is a phallic—it's like a phallic image, huh? And, you know, that's a lotta bullshit, unless it's really the same as the fact, literally. I mean, if we're not the same as nature on that side, and God on the other, man isn't. And it's tough. It's not easy to get to that strength. Ed, by the way, those are the—where is Paul?—that's all I meant by *phusis* and *nous* and *theos*,[52] that that middle term, which in the *Maximus* for me is the "middle voice," which "puts the diapers up in the trees," which knocks your whole life out, even if you love and have babies who have diapers.[53] And it was Wolpe who taught me that, like he taught the man who taught me how to read poetry, so I don't have to, I can talk tonight, David Tudor. He taught David Tudor—you know that—or his wife did, how to play the piano. But that Wolpe, I mean, I still don't know what it really means, but he says the thing that makes music work is "the middle voice." And I love it. I got it in that poem where I talk about Tiamat. And I bet it's the same principle, by the way, as an old rhetorical law, which none of us can upset: that to write means you got a beginning, a middle, and an end. And that I don't think is ever disturbed by any poet who's present this week, that his thing is to do all three. Then he's got his poem; then he's got his novel; then he's got him-self; then he's got his wife; then he's got his life. Christ, how many ways do you need to say it? That the middle, which is the whole goddamn middle, and that thing of this lousy country and culture made into a word—and it was Carl Sauer, diagonally northeast of this room, who sat and talked to me in 1947—and listen to me, because I'm no professor tonight, I'm a poet. Thank the lord, once in my life I can teach and talk so it's poetry; and read the poems, because I can do that, because the poems were written, I discovered from the man who's suddenly revealed, I mean, like *hoc signo* ... But that guy in 1947—I took Suzanna out last night to a restaurant. I never knew there was a restaurant in Berkeley. You know, it's like the drinks question: where the hell d'you eat? Sprenger's. I went there, that waterfront

52. Olson is here hinting at a pedagogy he has established elsewhere, e.g. in the classroom in Buffalo, 15 September 1964 as recorded by George Butterick's "Notes from Class" in *Magazine of Further Studies* 2:
> politics (phusis)—nature, state (necessity)
> epistemology (nous)—mind (possibility)
> religion (theos)—God (imaginable).
53. The reference here is to "Tyrian Businesses" (1.35–39), which is "that poem where I talk about Tiamat," as he describes it below.

restaurant, for fish, in Berkeley. Dig that. I don't even know what water is out there. Huh! There's no such restaurant in Gloucester. I could read you a poem. Don Allen and Bet and myself were sitting, walked out of the house in the fish stink of the Fort Point of Gloucester and it was beautiful. The tide was high, raising all the wharves away from themselves, and all the fucking old houses, all that shabby old fish-houses of "The Librarian," all that crap. The tide redeems the town. Absolutely. When it's in flood, all that shit. You know, don't make waves. Let waves be! I could say that to our friend. Ha! Don't make waves! It's like talking to Vincent Ferrini. I should write a poem to Victor Kalos. That Joel Oppenheimer, he's no problem. LeRoi took care of him, by the way. Did you see that goddamn swipe at him in the play, jesus, *The Dutchman*? Whew, some swipe, huh? Y'have to sit with poets to get your brains up to your body and your soul. It really is. You need to even be sitting beside somebody, like in this instance a voiceless Ezra Pound, watching LeRoi Jones's *Dutchman*, played by Jennifer West, huh, a subway scene.

I'm knocked out. I mean, I busted a—I mean, I had a glass of whiskey. I said I hope nobody thinks I'm drunk. Man, I was high this afternoon, and I'm just exactly the same way now. That bottle of hair tonic I might drink instead of water because I prefer wine, as Omar Khayyam said. The water, that's all. Bread, Thou, and Wine, eh? I mean, if you think I'm talk—isn't it wonderful? I'd thought, you know, I might do this. [LAUGHTER] Yeah, you're scared to death. Your husband, you remember—I got a recording, a long-playing record, made under much heavier whiskey, and much greater cost, in a Boston television studio, with Robert Creeley and my wife pressing it out of me. Like, I want to be the nutcracker, not to have a wife and Robert Creeley. [HITS THE TABLE] I want to be the three particles of creation, which make the fourth possible. That sounds pretty neat. O.K. I'd like to even be neat tonight.

This is wonderful. Gee, this is like those boring businesses. Politics is always boring. People are uncomfortable. They want the results. Then they get it, like, ffftt! Ha-ha! You'd be better off to listen to me. I mean, if I'm backward, I'm backward here, and the poetry will not disappoint you, 'cos it's backward too. And if I found out how to write true backward poetry, I really would have done what I don't think I've even started to, which is what the hell is backward poetry.

on John White / on cod, ling, and poor-john

on founding: was it puritanism,
or was it fish?

And how, now, to found, with the sacred & the profane—both of them—
wore out

　　The beak's
there. And the pectoral.
The fins,
for forwarding.

(Sounds like Johnson and Ferlinghetti.)

But to do it anew, now that even fishing …

That sounds like me. That's prospective. And "But to do it anew, now that even fishing *stinks*" is the unfinished sentence, or is the same. O.K. Cicero, "Oration de Gloucester." Section 1:

It was fishing was first. Only after (Naumkeag)

(Indian for Salem.)

was it the other thing, and Conant

And that's Roger, the Governor of Stage Fort, the Governor of the fishing and the planting of Stage Fort Park, which is the border behind the walls that Creeley was building last night, one of those stone walls of Robert Frost, not Robert Creeley, that my house literally abutted.

It was fishing was first. Only after (Naumkeag) was it the other thing, and
Conant
would have nothing to do with it, went over to Beverly, to Bass River, to
keep clear
(as a later Conant I know has done the opposite, has not
kept clear)

It is a sign, that first house, Roger Conant's, there, Stage Fort. One of
Endecott's first acts
was to have it dragged to Salem for his own mansion, for the big house,
the frame of it was that sound, that handsome, the old carpentry

(not the house-making I feel closest to, what followed, so close
I'd sing, today, of Anne Bradstreet's,
or any of them, Georgetown, Rowley, Ipswich,
how private they are in their clapboards
and yet how they thrust, sit there
as strong as any building)

Conant's
was Tudor

Gloucester, your first house was as Elizabeth's
England
(and that that Endecott, the "New," should have used it
inside of which to smile, and bless that covenant Higginson and the others …

I mean, just to be really political, let me remind you that Higginson, the minister of Salem, started everything that is what we protest today.

and bless that covenant Higginson and the others …

It sat
where my own house has been (where I am
founded

by racks so poor of fish there was not take enough to pay the Adventurers
back. Three years,
and their 3000£ gone. And as much more again (where I have picked coins up,

after circuses, slid out of men's trousers they so twisted in the bleacher seats
from the tricks Clyde Beatty made lions do,
keeping them under his eye and under his whip

Elizabeth dead,
and Tudor went to James
(as quick as Conant's house
was snatched to Salem

As you did not go,
Gloucester: you tipped, you were our
scales

> (as I have been witness,
> in my time,
> to all slide
> national, international,
> even learning slide

> by the acts of another Conant than he who left his Tudor house,
>   left fishing,
and lost everything to Endecott, lost the colony
to the first of,
the shrinkers

Now all things
are true by inverse:
religion
shrank Elizabeth's, money
dilates ours. Harvard
owns too much

> and so its President
> after destroying its localism ("meatballs,"
> they called the city fellers, the public school
> graduates) Conant destroyed Harvard
> by asking Oregon
> to send its brightest

Roger Conant did not destroy, was, in fact, himself destroyed, as was the
    city, 1626

> and is paid off by those he served (State St., Washington), is made
>   High Commissioner
>   (Endecott, of a stooge State

my Conant
only removed to "Beggarly,"
as the smug of Salem—the victors!—
called that place still is, for me
(when I go down 1A or take the train
the opening out
of my countree

[APPLAUSE] I mean, having written that poem, the poem which I would
really like now to read … I mean, by the way, it's getting late, obviously.

These readings, by the way, the question I asked Suzanna as we was coming here: "Don't you think all the poets read long?" Well, I gotta be elongated, I guess, by nature. I mean, please, any of you that really are tired, or have other reasons for being elsewhere, honestly, I wish you would leave, like. I would like to read as long as I can, with those who can stay, only. Fair enough? [APPLAUSE] Honestly, and no … I mean, one, two, three, end, go. I mean, no reasons. This is really a function I do not believe in, except that organs are able, not natural, or divine for that matter, I dunno, or that only because they're able. I guess that's what I really think poets are. And I think the whole error is not to realize that the function, the capacity just to try to find out, like, "how to dance sitting down" [1.35] is what really—being an organ simply because we're born. That's all we are, you know. The total is an organ. Gee, doesn't that sound like a politician? Vachel Lindsay, that beautiful—I hope I won't die and you don't have to celebrate me like that, baby.[54] And, by the way, was that poem of yours on that South American poet, ode to Neruda? It wasn't?

GINSBERG: No. An old poet in Peru …

OLSON: I never did know who it was, but, you know, it was like—and the thing I propose to do tonight is to read you the longest poem I have ever been unable to sustain, but the one I believe in the most, and I read once, that day on tape, the poem for Gerhardt.

VOICE: Oh yes.

OLSON: Because that takes the most I got, simply because the poem itself is the only poem I believe in because it really had such a weak backbone that there's a nerve in it, only, like that principle of the condition of a frog, the elementary—not the synapse. The synapse is easy; it's the neural condition that's difficult. To simplify the neural is what I believe honestly is what's up. I mean, again another way of saying the organ—the whole biological picture of the organism is wrong. I mean, that captured frog of Calaveras County is that kind of bullshit, that this society makes its heroes of its poets Mark Twain and Robert Frost, and elects presidents of Kennedys and Johnsons. I mean, until we realize that each one of us is as hard as we're made or can make ourselves—and that's the stone, not this live frog hidden. Even that beautiful Melville can't get over that fact, which is the source of *Pierre*, which I take Allen and Jack—it's one of the one things that got me over, beside proprioception, to tonight is that I heard, and I think he will support me, that it was Melville's *Pierre* that put him and Jack on. And he himself said, in that record,[55] with San Francisco looming above, with that eye of his glancing up at it in the dawn, just the howl of the eye, the eye of resemblance, the Aristotelian eye made alive again, that rational, in that

54. Ginsberg had sent his poem "To Lindsay" on a postcard to Olson in December 1958.
55. "Notes Written on Finally Recording Howl," accompanying *Howl and Other Poems* (Fantasy Records, 1959) was reprinted in Donald Allen's *The New American Poetry* (1960). The pertinent passage is: "I suddenly turned aside in San Francisco, unemployment compensation leisure, to follow my romantic inspiration—Hebraic-Melvillean bardic breath. I thought I wouldn't write a *poem*, but just write."

statement, that "Hebraic-Melvillean" statement … which I don't believe in. I'm standing here tonight to establish that there are two angels, or there's an angelology of a terrestrial condition. And, you know, raised a Catholic, there was a good one and a bad one. Bullshit! There's the two that I read the text of Tuesday, and I wouldn't repeat it again in my life. But I ask you each to believe me that there is two kinds of angels, which each of us has. And one "writes." That's what it says. I don't know what it means, but …

Gee, you know, this is what Socrates did, goddamn it, and this is why Plato became a writer. I hope you all go! I'll be left here alone, goddamn it, proving my point, that the establishment of the future society depends upon this kind of discourse, which is oral, private, public, and, like it turned out that marvelous night in Harvard that you were asked … And I ain't writing a poem. I'm just writing on my water, instead of peein'. That's all I'm doing, and I'm happy that I know a water to write in. And if I sound loud or something, or braggart fisherman, sure, that's what I propose: Johnny Smith. You think John Smith, that great successor to William Shakespeare, is why I'm plugging John Smith as the first American writer? Well, I happen, at younger than seven, to have my father and another letter carrier from Worcester, named Pat Foley, pay fifty cents to ask a little guy, whose mother had a little boy, whose father was probably a Portygee but he wasn't known, and she had then married a man whose sons were, like Johnny, my friends, and became a trucking business in Gloucester, Howard family, which sounds great to me, as a name, more than Tudor, Rose, and Plantagenet. Because I don't know about—like bibliography, instead of reading the poems, which you came here to hear, I'm just going to end up with the same situation I think I started with: the only people that were here were those who have read me or have heard that I have a literary reputation. Ha ha ha! And that turns out tonight to be the only success I have. So here I am, doing what I did this afternoon, turning my own poems into simply a long list, a long bibliographical list, and expatiating on what I haven't even read yet to you.

At which point, read a poem! Next! It's kinda crazy, at this point I would like to read, jump, jump, like, to a poem called "On first Looking out of Juan de la Cosa's Eyes," which I wrote, obviously, like that sonnet I wrote not knowing it was a sonnet, having happened to take my wife into the collection at Widener where John Keats's love letters are to Fanny Brawne on display. And I thought, gee, that "On First Looking Into Chapman's Homer," wow, I mean, I'm first looking into the literal letters that John—I mean, like, I think that's the trouble with English poetry, that it could write love letters like that. And, boy, I think that if any of us could somehow or other get that—not to say that, as poets, we don't write, and try to, and reasonably sometimes succeed, about love, that love and woman is our subject, and I mean that so that it covers love separable from woman, too. But, though that is our subject, not arms and men, even if we have to become morally arms and men, our subject is love and, hm, "cause-cause," woman. And that's a distinction which we only, this generation right now—and if I may crawl in, like, backwards, I may be included only. "On first Looking out through Juan de la Cosa's Eyes" [1.77–81]:

Behaim—and noth—

Behaim: that's Martin Behaim, whose map, like ...[56]

> Martin Behaim—and nothing
> insula Azores to
> Cipangu (Candyn
> somewhere also there where spices
>
> and yes, in the Atlantic,
> one floating island: de
> Sant
>   brand
>   an

St. Malo, however.
Or Biscay. Or Bristol.
Fishermen, had,
for how long,
talked:
           Heavy sea,
snow, hail. At 8
AM a tide rip. Sounded.
Had 20 fath. decreased from that to
15, 10. Wore ship.

           (They knew
Cap Raz

(As men, my town, my two towns
talk, talked of Gades, talk
of Cash's

drew, on a table, in spelt,
with a finger, in beer, a
portulans

> But before La Cosa, nobody
> could have
> a mappemunde

Section 2. Parenthesis. God, am I excited to discover that!

> (What he drew who drew Hercules
> going by the Bear off from Calypso
>
> Now, it would be breakers, Sable!
> ahead, where, just off,
> you could put buckets down

(another parenthesis)

           (You could go any coast

56. Martin Behaim's terrestrial globe, a little earlier than Juan de la Cosa's, did not show America, but the east coast of Asia, as what would be reached by sailing west across the Atlantic.

in such a raft as she taught,
as she taught me, favoring me

with cedar, & much niceties.

I wish the woman was in this room. I'm not—I'm referring to the alive.[57]

It was only because the gods willed
that I could leave her, go away, determined though he had been
the whole time
not to eat her food, not to wear gods' clothes,
to stick to what I eat

And wear

The Atlantic,
just then,
was to take kings,
& fishermen

And Europe,
was being drained
of gold

Crazy, tonight. Christ, this whole fucking government isn't interested in Vietnam. It's interested in catching up with the decay of the monetary condition of the earth, and they're about to hold another Bretton Woods Conference to peg the whole fucking dinar. Not the dollar, but the whole lousy thing has gone to hell.[58] And those who pay attention to market, which is what trade is, and why war is—I mean, gee, I gotta lot of money. I'd give it to anybody who asked me here tonight. I wouldn't give it; I'll tear it up. I'll destroy the fucking money, just to prove that this goddamn thing has nothing to do with that, but the whole world—like, the world? There's only two worlds. There's only *one* of two ways. I thought that, listening to you. There's only one of two ways. The world is not differentiable. Caesar's dream is true. It's your mother, that's all. And you're the father, if you are. And you screw her, that's all. I mean, really, the prohibitions of law on cannibalism, christ, that's why I wrote the goddamn preface to *Ishmael* on the basis of ... Isn't it funny? It's kinda loud. Well, Johnny Smith and I: [SINGS] K-k-k-katy ... K-k-k-katy Da da da da da da da ..." Like that. My father and Pat Foley would pay him fifty cents to sing this. And it wasn't because he was a bastard, or a foundling, or a little sort of black guy 'cos his pa was Portygee, and he was a little not so good in the head. Johnny right now isn't, and he's married to a bag the like of which—jesus, I mean, she's such a bag, and she's so older than Johnny it's like not having your mother, even, it's worse than your grandmother; it's like the man from Kent who lived with the whore in the cave or something. And that's Johnny, Johnny Smith's life. If you'll excuse me to propose the Royal Family of Secularity, in

57. Olson makes it clear that he is not speaking of his dead wife Betty; who it might be is therefore conjecture. The poet makes this Calypso section more personal by changing the printed poem's third-person pronouns into first person at times in his reading of it.
58. Olson is again showing that he has read that day's *Time* (23 July 1965), in this case the article "Money" under "World Business" (p. 82).

the face of what I really know is quality, and I think I can distinguish it. But I believe that until any one of us is ready to possess quantity, there'll be the power system. And there will be, no matter what quality we ask for, no success, no power. We, I mean, boy, excuse me ... Gee, really, isn't it great? Well, this is that speech! And the hall is getting thinner! And there wasn't many votes here in the beginning. And nobody is caucusing for me, thank god, except Robert Duncan. He must be caucusing in San Francisco, and I can't tell the end of his dream. He and I are in Berkeley, after the earth has become like the moon; it's absolutely full of holes. This is a beautiful dream—I mean, you want us to talk about the Kabbalah? He had it: it's the Kabbalah of the future. And I think his goddamn book will make the natural history of the future, too, referring to Pliny the Elder, who nobody reads. I checked it out recently. You know, that's not a classic: it happens to be a very interesting pre-scientific book. It's like Athenaeus's *Banquet*, which is terrific. Three volumes, it's full of gossip.[59] If I'm not as Sophocles when he did his turn as Admiral—in the same place, by the way, Catullus later, if that beautiful book by that playwright, whom I do respect, *Our Town*, or whatever his name is ... Wilder, that marvelous book of his on the days of Caesar and Catullus, written in the form of letters, called, huh? ... *The Ides of March*, yeah, where it turns out Catullus, who was a wealthy cat, even if his grandfather still spoke Irish ... And that ain't unusual, right? I mean, have we got an instance of Catullus? Did Louis Zukofsky's translation become President? I mean, the television was the President. He got there by obviously being more attractive than am I not being more so tonight on, like, television, huh, huh, huh? I mean, how easy it is not to be Nixon, that's all. [LAUGHTER] And that's a rhyme, right? I mean, I'm just trying to find out how it was when I was seventeen years old, in Constitution Hall in Washington, which, as you know due to the Marian Anderson incident, is owned by the Daughters of the American Revolution, and I appeared there like this. Only this is my night.[60] And that's all I'm doing. I'm going to confess no confession at all. I'm canceling the years between having been seventeen years old, standing in a larger hall than this, the hall that was denied to Marian Anderson. Listen to "negative capability" talking! I can't sing. If I can sing, it's only because other men have said I could, not from my point of view, god help me. Gee, if the "Songs of Maximus" affected anybody, ain't I lucky! That's what I wanted to say tonight. And if it sounds like an old bum, I ain't. I sound like me, for the first time.

You know, when I was seventeen—and I'm fifty-four tonight—I guess I can say this 'cos it's thirty-seven years since, as a result of the reason I was there, I was in Europe previously. I've said to Allen and have said it to others: what a goddamn fool I've been. I've spent thirty-seven years of wearing myself out in this fucking country, because I believe in work [HITS

59. Olson owned *The Deipnosophists or Banquet of the Learned of Athenaeus* (London, 1854), but got his point about Sophocles' sense of public service from unknown sources.
60. Olson placed third in the National Oratorical Contest in Washington, DC, during his last year in high school, May 1928. He considers he could have placed first if he had not had a bad cold.

LECTERN], and I wouldn't change it; but, jesus, what a country to work in! I mean, the only reason for traveling—and, after all, I wrote the *Mayan Letters*, and, thank god, Robert Creeley also—I mean, I ain't got any books. Robert Creeley produced, I mean, gave me the ideas of my books, practically. And I don't say that to lush him or plush him or any of that shit. I mean, just to talk facts again. I wrote a lot of letters to Robert Creeley when I was once, otherwise, out of this country. And Creeley tells that nicely in the Introduction, because he says, and it's true—I discovered from Frances Perkins, who died, as you know, recently, like Adlai Stevenson— huh! my generation, the liberals, the Roosevelt, Progressive, Wallace, Pound, Populist. Baby, I mean, hear me, I had only (we spoke of that tonight)—in my lifetime I had two men only, and one woman, who are my contemporaries. And one, it turns out, wow, I couldn't even find in Rome; the man who taught me Tarot, and who had the five drawings with the five poems in the book which was my first book of poems,[61] which I'm proud to say was set by the printers of Rue Cardinale, who were the printers of the Black Sun Press, which published *Sun* of Lawrence's, if I may, like—Joyce's *Anna Livia*—maybe that's the Shakespeare & Company; but I mean, O.K. I've been attached to that generation. They're like an albatross around my neck. I mean, if I got rid of an albatross, I'd have an auerhahn, and that's about all, a hidden bird, the most difficult to hunt. I'll never get out of the fucking trap, unless there's a third bird. Maybe I have to live long enough to get there. I mean, this morning I'm here because I read that thing which I hear, if you'll correct or approve, that Haselwood wrote, that text, right? John Wieners said that was written by Haselwood. Gee, it caused me to do this tonight. If a single man might be so outrageous as to propose that he might encompass—I mean, how secular do you have to be that I should think I, one man, might know and represent and produce so that it would be interesting, not the universe, but that knowledge that the universe is too? Hm. I made a gesture there like those dumb dipping birds they got in bars today instead of *Custer's Last Fight*.

Gee, you know, you people think speech is easy. There ain't a fucking word yet I've said which is loose. This is all *lusimeles*. Every fucking word I'm saying up to this minute is *lusimeles*, which is that great adjective that has become a thing, a synapse or a password, between Sanders and me. You know, it's a funny thing, Hesiod has two—the biggest problem in the whole of creation in, like, our text of poetry is: what does Love mean? We know what Chaos—or do we? But one can know what Chaos is. One knows what the Earth is. One knows what Tartaros is, which is in Earth. The difficulty is the one that's the most obvious. And Hesiod has only one way to describe Eros: he says *lusimeles*. I open *Mag*—I mean, *Magtown from Dogtown*, published by the Auerhahn, bought by Penguin Books, copyright tonight, like the essay "Human Universe," wow, jesus, crazy, ain't it? *Maximus from Dogtown*—the only line there is "loosens the limbs," unless there's another thing which principles that. *Lusimeles* is the word, *lusimeles Eros*. And Ed

61. The Italian artist Corrado Cagli collaborated with Olson on *y & x* (Paris: Black Sun Press, 1948).

and I—I don't know how he translated that. I won't ask him; he'll top me twice today. But, I mean, what the hell! How the hell do you really loosen the limbs of love? We do know, except that wonderful thing about that is … Like the clock, tally ho!

> but cod? The New Land was,
> from the start, even by name was
> Bacalhaos
> there,
> swimming, Norte,

You know, I feel uncomfortable. Let's ask like—gee, it's like a ball park, a losing game. Hah! Are we going to play extra innings? Gee, isn't it going to be funny who wins? But would you, please, any of you that are staying here for any reasons other than that you can't go home, or you ain't got no fucking home to go to, or any of those wonderful reasons, really, without any reason at all, feel free to go? I mean, except the other reason. By the way, would you like a break? That really might be true. I mean, your asses themselves have been sat on too long. Why don't you? O.K.? I wanted to do sets tonight. I proposed to do four sets. We had the pee set. Now what's the next set? Intermission. O.K.? [APPLAUSE]

VOICE: Is "bacalhaos" an Indian word?

OLSON: No, it's the Portuguese name for cod. *Bacalhao.* In fact, it's still the Italian name for cod.

VOICE: But didn't Cabot find that the Indians used that word?

OLSON: Certainly, because the Portuguese were ahead of Cabot. That's one of my points in that … I mean, the point is that if the Italians call it *bacalhaos, bacalhao*—[TO JOHN WIENERS] Did you see it, by the way, on those menus in Rome? When I came back and you weren't there, I went to Pasetta's, and there was *bacalhao* as a fish. I still am astonished to discover that the Italians, the Italian language uses *bacalhao* for cod.

GLADYS HINDMARCH: I'm supposed to tell you that they say they're going to close the building at twelve o'clock, and that's it. It's twenty to twelve now.

OLSON: That's all right. I'll close only with the witching hour. Midnight is good enough; that's a good reason. [TO AUDIENCE] That rushes us a little. I learned that they're going to close the building. We got in that situation— this isn't the first time, only this time I've been wailing before twelve. But this building will close at twelve. I got twenty minutes more.

HINDMARCH: Perhaps we should stop the intermission and come back.

OLSON: So, any of you that don't need to rest, let's go. I'd like to continue right where I was.

> but cod? The New Land was,
> from the start, even by name was
> Bacalhaos
> there,

swimming, Norte, out of the mists

> (out of Pytheus' sludge

out of mermaids & Monsters

> (out of Judas-land

Tierra,
de bacalaos, out of

waters   Massachusetts
                    my Newfoundlanders
                    My Portuguese: you

(Or Verrazano has it,
curiously, put down as

(And he means the whole of the, I guess, really, north-eastern United States.)

> as

a Mud Bank

I looked at the map in the Vatican. I can't get over it. I'm walking through the goddamn Vatican library, and I don't mean that enormous series of mosaics done in the 16th century, which is, except for Michelangelo's Adam and Eve *before* they were expelled from Eden, *before* they were tempted … It's like censorship. I, this Catholic of Worcester, Roman Catholic of Worcester, who celebrates still (and I've not even mentioned her tonight) Our Lady of Good Voyage, the Portuguese church of Gloucester, Massachusetts, and am hung up on the Virgin of—Virgin Mundi. Hm. Lada. Goddamn it, isn't it wonderful? That "Door" of yours,[62] and this gook, he doesn't even know how to spell "lady," and it comes out another further step, "Ladeye." And, you know, like, here I am with Our Lady of Good Voyage, O.K., it's that condition; another possibility, I hope. But, I mean, I go to the Sistine Chapel very carefully, like every tourist, and goddamn it if I don't see how it is that Eve is exactly placed with Adam on the— we would say theatrically—on the right side of the tree. Of the nine things which you can only see—oh, in fact, he's beautiful. He does it perfectly, you can see it if you just bend your head up. I'm sure that many in this room had the experience. And I'm not going to even bother to describe how woman is with man, on that side of the tree. But I stand here to say I couldn't buy in Rome, and I can't show you now, and therefore I won't tell you, where she is, and how it looks. It's everything that we're all—nah, I mean, it's even—I—like, fucking Michelangelo! goddamn it, if he doesn't know, like, we know that, what we're up to. The only thing he'd—like, if you'll excuse the plug for the Virgin, aw, shit, but he wrote a very good sonnet at ninety-three or something, which I read in *Nine*, little Peter Russell's

---

62. There is a "Lady" in Robert Creeley's poem "The Door." "Ladeye" appears in Allen Ginsberg's "New York to San Fran," still in manuscript at the time of the conference. Allen Ginsberg in personal communication: "I didn't realize till conversation earlier that eve with J.W. & C.O. that the mistake unconsciously referred Ladies to Lads."

magazine, in London, in a translation which made it possible for me to read that sonnet.[63] And it's a beauty. And you know how few he wrote, not as many sonnets and ballades as Guido Cavalcanti. And he wasn't even a poet, he was a painter; but the guy wrote some sonnets as prayers, those are all those goddamn things are. And that guy, that goddamn wonderful guy, at ninety-three or whatever it is, is down on his knees, just asking, "For God's sake, look, I'm the guy who's as big as all the shit I've made." And he has to have been. We know that. You couldn't do that if you weren't as big. And, like, his prayer to the Virgin is: "Would you give me one ..." (I mean, I don't know what he's saying.) "I've kneeled—I've said my prayers every night, or I've been on my knees before you, before. But, look ..." I don't know whether the sonnet's any good, by the way, as poetry. I don't know what a wop would say about it as verse. I don't care. I don't think it's interesting. As a matter of fact, I discovered—you know why Hesiod isn't qualitatively valued like Homer? Sister said it today. Peter Anastas in Gloucester in '63, when I had nobody else to turn to, whose father I've written poems about— I wish I could write poems about him like I can about his father ... It's that problem: you always want to write poems about people. It's the measure of their value. It's why I believe in naming people only is that they have value. Only name the people whom to you have value, no other reason.

I'm—aw, shit, we could talk forever. There's everything to say, and I just happen to be in that wonderful accident of feeling confident that I can say it. That's once in a lifetime. And I'm doing this because the last time I was before the very men who are here, I felt not only the opposite, but I felt I'll never in my life be able to appear in front of them, read in front of them, speak so that I can hold their attention. And I'm out to prove that I can. That's my election, because it was my decision and my choice. That's not bad morality, quickly, in our political and discursive universe.

Tierra,
de bacalaos, out of

waters   Massachusetts
                                   my Newfoundlanders
                                   My Portuguese: you

(Or Verrazano has it,
curiously, put down as
a Mud Bank

                         "Sounding
                         on George's
                         25 fathoms sand. At the same time spoke
                         the Brig Albion, Packet,
                         John Dogget who told us
                         Cape Ann was 80 league
                         distance

Actually, the way that's written—and if I read you the "Bozeman Road" tonight, I'd have to do the first poem of the poem called 'West', which I'm

---

63. J.H.V. Davis, "The Sonnets of Michelangelo," *Nine* 3:2 (Autumn 1951), pp. 125–28.

writing at present, thank god, I mean, I wish I were or something, instead of the *Maximus*, now that I discover that I should have stayed in Worcester or something. That should be read:

> "Sounding
> on George's
> 25 fath. sand. And at the same time spoke
> the Brig Albion, Packet,
> John Dogget who told us
> Cape Ann was 80 leag.
> dis.

> Terra nova sive Limo Lue,
> he wrote it

(that's Verrazano)

> who knew it
> as only Corte Real

who is the Portygee who never came back, Corte Real, Number Two. You know, if you order cod in the best restaurant in Rome and you look at the menu (I'm saying that story) in Italian now it turns out to be *bacalhao*. You run into a Norwegian, he knows cod as *bacalhao*. We're the only people, only the Massachusetts people in the world don't know cod as not cod but *bacalhao*. Ain't that—? Honestly, really, this is like Linear A, Linear—I mean, what the hell was the power of the Portygee that the goddamn Portuguese name for cod, except for this kooky name—and I don't even know what Massachusetts person except John Smith called it cod, and it probably has to do with codpiece, which precedes it. It looked like a prick or something. I mean, really, no kidding, what was "the silver mines" that made our nation? 'Cos don't you kid yourself I'm right that it was cod that created that fucking aristocracy which is the Security Council right now of the United States. That sacred cod, ha ha! Dig that, I mean, a cliché.

> as only Corte Real   (the first known lost
> as Bertomez

(Christ, until tonight I've been celebrating amputees and cripples.)

> (as Cabot?

(No, I haven't, see.)

> Who found you,
>
> land,
>
> of the hard gale?

That is the introduction, to this poem.

> Respecting the earth, he sd,
> it is a pear, or,

By the way, this is Columbus. Not Van Allen, dig? Not Von Allen Ginsberg or that knightship that we haven't had yet—but that Van Allen Belt.[64] Excuse me, I love to do this, like. Really, notes are now like talk. Exactly. A poem is today a triptite, or a trilogy, or whatever you want to call it. We are. If we ain't three, we ain't possibly that principle that Blake says is the Son of God. I believe that. I wouldn't identify in what way the Ugly, which is probably Talk, because it's supposed to be rational ... The only person I should be talking to is the woman I'd like to marry tonight after or before fucking her in bed. I mean, that discourse with the beloved is which I believe in, is the poetry I would like, I propose, in fact, to seek to write. That's what I believe is really discourse, is Shiva and Shakti. And I think it's as simple as that and as referential. And it's not easy. I mean, it's easy to fuck. But to have talking to the person you really enjoy fucking, that's the other part of it. And that's the dream is that one is as high as the other. May I say that with no, jesus, hm, nothing else said? Not because I think it's good enough, but it's talk, instead.

> Respecting the earth, he sd,
> it is a pear, or,
> like a round ball upon a part of which there is a prominence
> like a woman's nipple, this protrusion
> is the highest & nearest to
> the sky
>
>   Ships
> have always represented a large capital investment, and the manning,
> the provisioning of same
>
>   It was the teredo-worm
>   was 1492: riddled a ship's hull

Can you—"riddled a ship's hull"? No? It bounces back on me though. It's better in this large DAR. I'm not Marian Anderson, that's all. By the way, like, to interpolate: you know what happened to me? The reason why I am not Allen Ginsberg on the level of his absolutely perfect possibility that "rhythm" is the same as (in fact, as, if you look in the dictionary, it is) "orator," is that I was at seventeen, by speech, the most powerful figure in the world. And, in fact, I not only won the only time I was previously in Europe by the power of my ability to do what I'm doing tonight, because, like Allen, you know, that voice of Allen's singing the other night, with those hand jangles,[65] gee, somebody said to me, "I'd have been happy to have listened to him doin' that the whole evening." Nah, that's not a put-down, really, because ...

GINSBERG: I would have been happy to do it all night!

OLSON: Because I don't think you use your voice after you drop the jangles like you did with the jangles. Therefore, the poetry is the jangles, or it ain't, dig? I mean, that's the powerful demand upon us. If we're performers—and we

---

64. Olson is referring to the electromagnetic barrier around the earth which was talked about during the Mars probe.

65. "Chanting Hare Krishna Mantra & Prajnaparamita Mantra as prefatory vocalizations before poetry reading; accompanied by finger cymbals" (Allen Ginsberg, personal communication, 4 September 1969).

live in a world in which they're terrific. That jig, Sammy Davis, wow, holy shit! I mean, can he do it! I've been living in motels, and I hear that god-damn program by that freak, to steal the old square meaning of Ed Sanders's word. What is that guy that holds the open end thing, from eleven to one? Carson. And that one night, who's Carson? Just like I think it's so: Sammy Davis! Jesus, you know, those fingers, and those white fingernails, and click click, whah! chahoo! whahoo! Christ, if any one of us poets …! And when I heard Gregory and Peter and Allen appear in Cambridge, long before the sacred mushroom, in that goddamn Harvard Hall (where I wished I'd been and I was proud to …) you know what happened? You know who left and who stayed in the audience like you? I stayed in the audience like you. I listened to these guys, just after *Time* magazine, that simulacrum of a magazine, had made them Shelleyites, as they were proud to cut the shit out of in the next issue, in that letter.[66] And it was our Cambridge police, Bobby, all over the place, in gold. And who left? Lowell! I still can't get over it. With some young guy, you remember? He walked out. I don't think he walked out turning his back on the reading. I think he had another engagement. That's that fucking thing about the social, instead of the society. I've spent my fucking life struggling with that. Unless you beat that, you'll end up not eating, I mean, you really will turn to other foods. That passage of mine about Calypso … You know, by denial I accomplished what the expanding consciousness … the k-o-s-m-o-s …

                It was the teredo-worm
                was 1492: riddled a ship's hull
                in one voyage ("pierced

with worm-holes
like a bee-hive,
the report was

                Ladies & Gentlemen,
                he lost his pearl,
                he lost the Indies
                to a worm

North? Mud. 1480 John Lloyd, the most expert shipmaster of all
    England,
on behalf of John Jay and other merchants Bristol
set out to
the island of Brasylle, to
traverse the seas

Nine weeks. And storms
threw him back.

                No worms. Storms,
                Ladies &

                to the bottom of the,

---

66. *Time* (9 March 1959) printed "in respect to Shelley," a letter signed by Allen Ginsberg, Peter Orlovsky, and Gregory Corso responding to a glib piece on them in the 9 February 1959 issue, p. 16.

husbands, & wives,

little children lost their

(4,670 fishermen's lives are noticed. In an outgoing tide
of the Annisquam River, each summer, in the August full,
they throw flowers, which, from the current there, at the Cut,
reach the harbor channel, and go

these bouquets (there are few, Gloucester, who can afford florists' prices)
float out

you can watch them go out into,

the Atlantic

You can go home now. [PROLONGED APPLAUSE] Thank you. You know, it's so easy to stop, finito and all that shit, right? If we don't know what the middle is, and we do, and the poets proved that here in Berkeley, my god, one night after another. I'm trying to join that fucking company tonight. A beginning, and a middle, and an end, that's all. Jesus, if I can't end a poem, then I really ain't in business. Maybe I can't end a poem? I don't even know. But the end of this poem is a third section, which I will read too. Like, Nigger Jim and Huck Finn were so impressed by those fucking—not those cemetery things, but those lithographs of ladies' loves. You remember that marvelous thing? If I've put down Twain tonight, and Frost, it's like Allen celebrating the death of Vachel Lindsay as a salesman. I would like also to celebrate those gooky fucking valentine lousy cemetery poets too, because even if they only support that lousy middle culture and middle class and middleness, which is Danish as well, and'll be Italian too, is the neo-capitalism of China. Those wristwatches on those guys! That enormous throng, carrying those fucking phony flags that even Mao has got himself into having allowed. Wristwatches! When he entered Peking, he gave soap out to scrub those fucking streets or, like Baltimore, those goddamn stoops of Peking. I mean, you know, there is disease, outside the United States: water disease, rat disease, yellow disease, all sorts of bubonic shit. Christ, we've taught cleanliness to the world. Well, then, let us be clean. "On ne"—I mean I have no French. Madame ...[67]

On ne doit aux morts nothing

else than

la vérité

O.K. Gee, it's late. If I can read a poem which Ed Dorn said was where I really started to get on, maybe it'll help me tomorrow. It's called "The Twist" [I.82–86]; and it is the flower, as he sensed, that I intended to follow that poem.

VOICE: Drop the microphone a little; it's got a bang bang bang.

OLSON: It's an awful bounce. Feels as though you're talking to yourself without it. Maybe if I put it back, if somebody would do that television shit.

67. Olson is apparently nodding to Suzanne Kim, the assistant of Pierre Dommergues of the Collège de France, Paris.

GINSBERG: Yeah … to you as before. [ADJUSTING MICROPHONE]

OLSON: To you … [LAUGHTER, KISS] Isn't it crazy? Brothers, I hope. We've been lovers, but never brothers. [LAUGHS]

Honestly, look, I could read forever, right now. I mean, christ! Oh, ha-ha! This is better than that phony strength I pumped up in Vancouver. It's very sober. It's nice. I feel very comfortable and strong and resonant, and all that shit. But, you know, like, I mean, poetry is public! I know everyone here wants to go home. Why not? This is the stuff that should be society. It should be what runs the streets and runs your news because it's what runs your nation, that's all. It's a day's business; we do it at night, goddamn it. Every fucking Russian statesman knows that. And every goddamn statesman that has any sense knows that you don't run the state during the day; you run it at night when the goddamn machines stop, so that those who you are responsible to can go home and sleep. I wish, like, you would. Because I want to talk about the trolley cars after they've stopped running. Like, the halls will be dark. And I don't even like those elocutionary poets, that I can be, and I was, at seventeen. Ha, you don't think I was in the Constitution Hall in Washington, being judged by the Supreme Court as to whether I was the primary orator of America, to meet Mathieu—I remember it so well—who was the Frenchman who was so inferior to me if I was in health.[68] It's like Frénaud, that poet, the French poet—you know, the French poet that was at Spoleto was a man I never heard of, named Frénaud. And I said, "You don't mean Philip Freneau?" I'm so fucking American I didn't even know that there was some guy like Quasimodo, a French poet named Frénaud. Sounded like "Quineau," a water. I mean, I don't know, but if I ever heard a name Frénaud, it was Philip Freneau, that contemporary of the American Revolution, and that very good, by the way, writer of *Castle Otranto* literature, better than it. You know, the commonness of John Smith, who replaced, I believe directly, William Shakespeare, has only been caught up with, in fact, I really think—and it's not plop and shit—in Berkeley since the day this fucking conference started. And that's why we were all fucked up two years ago, literally like the 18th century. I mean, what a breakthrough! [TAPE ENDS]

68. Olson misremembers the name of the winner of the 1928 Third International Oratorical Contest, René Ponthieu of France.

Charles Olson at an outdoor gathering on the Berkeley campus 24 July 1965. Photo: Robin Eichele.

7

Reading at Berkeley—The Day After

About noon of the day after Olson's marathon reading/talk of 23 July 1965, there was an informal gathering outdoors on the grass of the Berkeley campus. Richard Moore of National Educational Television, who was planning to film Olson in Gloucester, captured this unscripted discussion as preliminary footage. It provides us with a candid postmortem on the night before—not at all a dispirited one, as it turns out.

CHARLES OLSON: … Well, that's Dahlberg's old principle, as I said. But, you know, I am instructive. I'm really instructive, and I wanted to stand up right after that thing started just now and say "guru-lity" and "garrulity." [LAUGHS] Pee. I mean, that was the first time I don't think I was garrulous. [LAUGHS] Hardly anybody else, I think, might think so.

EDWARD DORN: I can understand that private/public con; that interests me an awful lot, like that. But as an occasion, it's not true. Only if it is private, then it can become public.

OLSON: Yeah, yeah.

DORN: You could think it's here, I couldn't—well, I didn't have any poems on me, and I wouldn't—I can't possibly remember any of my poems.

OLSON: No.

[GAP]

OLSON: He only got that for Connie and myself. And it's only because it feels holy to me, and as of those lines, and yeah, they were no instruction of it.[1] By the way, it's Prynne that caused—and that whole incident of my having asked him what I should have, and always wanted to do—I got my only

---

1. It is not clear what lines are being referred to. The short poem that will be talked about below, written in October 1962 at the time Olson was first corresponding with Jeremy Prynne about the Weymouth Port Books, is [11.120]:

> And now let all the ships come in
> pity and love the Return the Flower
> the Gift and the Alligator catches
> —and the mind go forth to the end of the world

passport since I was a kid to go to Weymouth and get that Port Book.[2] And I was frustrated. I have no money, and one night Bet says to me, "Why don't you go? If you call up Paul Williams and ask him for $500, I'm sure he'll wire you it at the airport." And then I didn't have a passport. It was let three years late. And the frustration and just some night of just feeling bad led me to sit down and write to Prynne, and, you know, it was the worst mistake you make. This guy is the greatest researcher, and I haven't ever heard of anything like it. And he's fast, like the modern …

DORN: He's the con man in the libraries, yes.

OLSON: Absolutely. In fact, he shipped me a catalog in Wyoming last year with the razor, airmail, and the razor—Bet and I were in bed when I was reading the goddamn thing, and I almost did what I did today with his razor that he cuts catalogs with so that he reads in all—he knows all books and everything. In any case, to get back to the point: Prynne then went and found all the goddamn records of all the boats that crossed the Atlantic Ocean after Columbus that might have bearing on entering Gloucester Harbor. So that I wrote "And now let all …" [II.120] just to get out of the trap that having done that put me into. I still carry the stuff around in my bag. I haven't opened it, 'cos, I mean, I got to do that research now on the other end, the natural end of the stuff that you use for your own purposes. So I just said, "And now let *all* the ships come in, let the fucking harbor be flooded with all the ships." [LAUGHS] And those, by the way, those are—and then there's "pity and love," and that's just pity and love. But then the others, "the Return the Flower the Gift and the Alligator," are ketches owned by a Gloucester man who built them,[3] and these are the four ketches he owned. "Ketch" is an old name for a sloop, a former sloop, but a fishing sloop, a new boat. But they spell it in the record "catches," and, you know, "catches" is songs. And to me—I mean, I'm going to write the rest of the *Maximus* simply to be—to include the last, well, I guess it's two. I've done two of those ships, and I got to do two …

DORN: To include the ships?

OLSON: Yeah, the very ones named: "the Return the Flower …" See, I feel, from even your point that I was—I mean, why I had never any problem with that correction of yours that "The Twist" was where the voice starts. You said that.[4]

DORN: Yeah, I thought that.

OLSON: Well, *The Return*. The second ship is *The Flower*; the next one is *The Gift*, which I feel I have been given since; and the last is *The Alligator*. I

2. This passport (now at Storrs) was issued 17 June 1957. Olson wrote to Gael Turnbull on 21 June 1957 that he planned "to dig port records as of fishing sailings around the time of the settlement of my Gloucester" (letter at Storrs—printed in the *Minutes of the Charles Olson Society* 44). Olson did not get to see the Weymouth records until a visit there in May 1967.

3. John Hardy of Salem (died 1652). Olson's source was *The Probate Records of Essex County, Massachusetts* (Salem, 1916).

4. Dorn made the point in *What I See in the Maximus Poems* (Migrant 1960—reprinted in Dorn's *Views* (pp. 27–44]) that the poem "The Twist" [1.82–86] represented a new movement within the first *Maximus* volume.

mean, I wouldn't want to start talking all the stuff we need to get the gift; but that's it, that's my set, that's my four aces. And they are simply 17th century excluded. This is the only four ketches the guy built, owned, and fished successfully, out of Gloucester Harbor. In fact, the reason why I know it is that he was the most successful, he was a high-liner of that date, like they say.

And then that goddamn line, the last line, is simply the reason that's been unsaid, but is kicking behind all that question that is up here, to my mind, which is that the universe is bounded by its own breathing, its own expansion and contraction, literally. So—and that's in Hesiod: "and the mind go forth to the end of the world." In fact, the whole concept, "the end of the world," got found for Charles Peter—do you know *The Enchanted Pony* in the Junior Classics for kids, a fairy tale that, you know, they've made into a Junior Classic, a kids' book? Does your child have *The Enchanted Pony*?[5]

DORN: Ah, yeah, Chanie had it.

OLSON: Chanie. You remember this third of these sort of Russian brothers who's lazy and not as good a farmer as is the other two boys? He just lies down to dream, and they're doing the work. Gee, wait a minute, how is it? And this mare suddenly comes, and she has two—she foals, and she comes to him to help her foal. And he puts her in the barn after the two brothers and the father have gone. And the next morning here's these two beautiful stallions and this little runt of the litter, the enchanted pony. And the mare takes the two—no, gives him the two stallions and the enchanted pony. And his brothers take the two stallions off to market, and sell 'em. And the enchanted pony is a magic carpet. And the ultimate end of it is the Tsar is involved. And the ultimate end of it is that in order to get the Princess that is the proposed bride for the Tsar, they have to—she lives at the end of the world, and the pony—this is where I got absolutely knocked out, because this goddamned pony takes the hero to the end of the world. And that's a shore. And the only way you can get her is to be able to go to the end of the world, and she will come, as she does, and is, in fact, just at the moment they arrive, setting up a tent, a little tent, and her meal at the seashore.

DORN: She's there.

OLSON: She's there.

DORN: Ah, she was.

OLSON: She's just that beautiful. Oh, I mean, it still knocks me out, because, if you remember—I haven't gotten the exact name of it but it's in that poem "Gravelly Hill." That's the "Gravelly Hill" that LeRoi wrote me the only time I ever got a fan letter[6]—well no, it isn't the only time. But at the date in our

5. *The Enchanted Pony* (Classics Illustrated Junior #562, October 1959).
6. The untitled poem usually called "Gravelly Hill" (II.160–62) begins with a quotation from Hesiod's *Theogony*: "at the boundery of the mighty world." LeRoi Jones's letter is dated 26 November 1963 (at Storrs).

experience with LeRoi, that he should have written me, I am—that's special to me. After "Gravelly Hill" was published I got a letter from him. That's not too long before things got tough, or tougher. You got another cigarette?

DORN: Yeah, I got that, but I don't have any matches.

OLSON: I got the matches. Oh, good, thanks.

RICHARD MOORE: You know something that would be mighty useful for us, if convenient for you: that relationship here between the two of you, how your two lives come together.

OLSON: Gee, it's an amazing story to tell, and it's a nice one, I think, don't you? Go ahead, Ed, you pick it up.

DORN: No, I was simply thinking that it's biographical starting now, or at the end point, and it's been biographical altogether.

OLSON: Yes, it has. Yes, it has.

DORN: You know, very recently, I ...

OLSON: This very minute.

DORN: ... I thought of you when I was going through Nevada, by the way, and trying to get out of that fix, you know, that local fix which I'm so hung up on anyways, and I suddenly realized I hadn't been on at this for a long time, or into the world. And these people were, were there. I couldn't think of them as Indians,[7] you know, in that sense; and in fact, it's very funny that the one place we went into where anthropologists had been was a complete failure. I mean, all the people supposed that they knew what we wanted to know from them. These people were from Stanford, Pittsburgh, University of Nevada, you know; and they almost, like, they were—suddenly they had been made volunteers of their own grudge.

OLSON: Right. That's something to me that you've got. I mean, you know, I tell you, I was stuck. I'll add my piece to our autobiography because, you know, what you ... Well, let me start with what's happened right here, and did when you read, is to me—was to realize that you had filled out what you mean by that local fix, which is, for both of us, powerful, and could be something that anybody could trip us, oh boy, and fall us, and probably most people, well, I guess they still will. [LAUGHS] But I don't think that—my point is I think—and I feel it even for myself, and I feel it even happened like almost last night, literally—but that identity simply coming out of work has overcome any of the conditions that we both determined to stay with and to seek, not materials in, but stories, a story, actually. Because the thing is that, literally, as rider together, it was a story of Ed's, which was called "C.B. & Q,"[8] and it was a gandy-worker story, and it ran from, like, say, St—not St Paul ...

7. Dorn is describing a recent experience which had been the subject of his talk at the Berkeley Conference on 21 July 1965 (see *Views*, pp. 93–117). See also Dorn's book, with photographer Leroy Lucas, *The Shoshoneans* (NY: William Morrow, 1966).
8. The story, whose title is the abbreviation for the Chicago, Burlington, and Quincy Railroad, appeared first in *Black Mountain Review* 7 (Autumn 1957).

DORN: Joe's …

OLSON: St Joe's, where they set out. But the funny—it's a funny story, it's as— at least for me, I said it, and I haven't said it to you before: that what you have filled out at that reading the other night was in poem, poem after poem after poem, it ended all that word "West." I now know how to—some- how or other from that reading, I—that title's just never been—simply been a project title to me of those poems that I've … [GAP] … *Wild Dog* in Pocatello is the only place, except for the first one which LeRoi published, that "Bozeman Road" thing, has been there. But it's as though "West" is no longer a word, due to how much you—that same enormous … It was St Joe in the North, but the end of the story is the gandy-worker's going the hell back to New Mexico, going down the track to New Mexico. And you know how much I felt that you had appropriated, not the transposed continent, but the unknown, which had presented itself again, and that a great unknown suddenly arose, I think, for us at least. I think that would be true specifically for Ed and myself. Or, put the other way, for Ed and myself it had a geographical term. I'm sure some unknown presents itself similarly to Robert Creeley, I know it does, and, say, to Duncan, others, and Hadley here, who, by the way, should get into this conversation at this point because— hey, Drum, are you listening?—because as of the very thing that, say, is both the subject and where I think it's all gone now, the dissolving of something like the word "West" or "Indian" or "White" or anything. So does that make sense?

DORN: Yeah. Does it have anything to do with this thing you're talking about, the literal and the numerical?

OLSON: I do. My god, I do. But how did we get there? No, as a matter of fact, I know where your poetry just the other night—and that poem I wrote, which I wish I—the one I wrote, still, and is the last *Wild Dog* poem of the series, the one that mentions him and Diana,[9] that's still the only time I feel I got a little of that. I mean, I think that's what we was trying to find out was how to cock the literal so that it went off. And it is a language like mathematics used to be, or something. I don't know what that means, or saying where it leads to, but those poems—and that those are poems, that's what's so beautiful, you know. Those are stories and poems as one, those things of yours.

DORN: But it was the story that, yeah, you first helped me write. I mean, simply I did it, but you pointed out to me what it meant to me.

OLSON: Did I really? No kidding?

DORN: No, well, it's possible I wouldn't have known.

OLSON: Well, that's the—well, it's nice to run into somebody who recognizes, I think, sometimes, that's all. A man always does what he does; you can never talk somebody's influencing another person. I mean, the only thing

9. "West 6," a poem that mentions Diana and Drummond Hadley by name, was first published in *Wild Dog* 10 (September 1964), pp. 31–32 (see *Collected Poems*, p. 599).

you could—there isn't only love, and that's interesting, and you go to bed with that. But this other stuff is simply, well, it's friendship, that's all.

DORN: This chant I heard, the old man dying, a Shoshone, actually a Northern Paiute. It was at Pyramid—no it wasn't at Pyramid; it was at Duck Valley. I finally understood how you can use things that are, say, not available to you. You were talking about obscure, you know, in trying to make a point that if, well, if it's obscure maybe you can make it unobscure, like shoveling the shit out for cows you can also learn a little Greek. Well, this chant meant a kind of spiritual affirmation in me very much, and was not cultural; it was simply something I heard.

OLSON: Yeah, I getcha.

DORN: And I heard it literally; I mean, understanding is really beside the point. And I heard it as a death chant. It was piercing, I mean, you know, the thing just went through your body. It was a really beautiful song. I never saw that before. I had never had that experience before, feeling an immediate response from something outside myself. And then, you know, the possibility of its being initial, without cultural reference.

OLSON: Right, I gotcha. Well, I consider that one—and it's the only thing I've been saying is that the only lines that I can keep with at the moment is that place where—and I ended that reading last night—that reading happens to be the last two lines were [1.82]

> And he and I distinguish
> between chanting,
> and letting the song lie
> in the thing itself.

And I think that he's saying that we have got to a point, or that Shoshone chant does that thing, which is that the song lying in the thing itself is the only real, what used to—it's too easily called magic, but of song—but what really song is is something that goes right through everything; and that the literal, that attention, when I think you'd agree that that's where it was, autobiographically, that it was attention at the start, that it was so critical that we—and I find this still true, that the specific—that you have something very specific that will cause your attention to be, and that then you get the results, which are these, that the song does lie in the thing itself. And that's what they call—I mean, that's powerful, that's power, and that's what we, I guess, really, I think we—this last 122 hours is simply an evidence for that quite a few men have caught on to the secret of power. And it's been treated cheap a long time, somehow. I don't know even how it got treated cheap, and that one doesn't even know, except that one does know exactly how you have to live to have that come in to at least language, so that it does do what you're talking about that song did, anyhow that guy that time, huh?

DORN: Yeah, yeah. After though, after 1950, what you're talking about, our mind, say, that succession of the mind that spans through 1950, what happened then to that force of language? I was thinking of Allen's reading the other night that it's undeniable as a force. I was calling it "popular"; and it certainly gets reflected in those rapt attentions that he was able to hold. What does that kind of language mean, then? Because it isn't the same thing you're talking about. It is sociological cataloging.

OLSON: Yes, it is.

DORN: It is the returning to an audience of all of the things that they are in such despair of, it seems to me, and shifting them so that there's a relief implicit in them when they hear them again, you know, in a different way.

OLSON: Right.

DORN: But, all right, so much for the effects. What would you say is the validity of that? Because, see, it's not that I agree with you, you know that, but I'm interested in exactly what might be objections to it. Even if they're objections, I would not want to put that word in your mouth at all.

OLSON: Well, you know I—let me say the way it came on—by god, it came in on to me yesterday afternoon, and I said it, and I said it as a result of talking to Allen the day before, in a very careful walk down the street with John to get alone and talk about his reading, and—gee, if I can only say this fast enough to say it, but it's in. I know exactly how much of how I feel it. But, you see, yesterday, after saying that, after all, really, to discriminate was what I was talking about, and I said that—and conceivably there is another, there is—the pole of that is to exaggerate. And I was reminded of that poem that you know I wrote, which I've never looked at again, to Jack Rice, which has the title "Something … Exaggerate, or How, Properly, to Heap Up" (which is what "exaggerate" means).[10] And that, instead of that, as I said to Allen, I think he is using every *thing* in the world: and it's like almost it'll eat him up if he's not careful, because he now is using words to try to include every thing in the world, and I—and now I want to just say the last piece of it, if I can. I read a poem on Tuesday here, which has that crazy name repeated, "Enyalion"; and Duerdon come to me, and I won't say in—well, hell, sure: his wife and him were making love, and as she was stroking his back he found she was saying, "Enyalion … Enyalion … Enyalion." And he says to me, "Will you tell me who that Enyalion is?" And I says, "Yes." I said I said that when I introduced it: I discovered this as a—and I said it was a deliverance for me—that that's the only apparent earliest Indo-European real name for the guy who we know later as Mars in Latin and Ares in Greek; but I didn't say this to Duerden. I said, "Well, it's the god of war." And he— oh, he turned his back in disgust, and said, "I wish I hadn't asked you." You know, I think that's the whole point. I mean, you know, gee, I mean, what I did say to Allen was, "You—you're trying to make the—I mean, you're involved, you're stuck now, right now, with it becoming a camp of the world. And I mean it," I said to Allen, "in the only meaning that I think 'camp' comes from, which is *castra*"—which is the Roman name *castrum* for "camp" and "military camp." And if we talk power, and if we are at this

10. "Concerning Exaggeration, or How, Properly, to Heap Up"—see *Collected Poems*, p. 208.

point both as a nation and a world—and we are, we're about to go at each other's throats, eat a man alive—and that's just where we are is that the violence is both pervasive, and probably—and this is why this has to be stopped, and it's got to be stopped only by such cares and attentions as I believe we've been trying both to propose and accomplish—not for that reason, but it turns out it's relevant: that somewhere that was where the secret got lost, that "how properly to heap up" is not to just have everything accumulated and then celebrated. It means literally—and in that beautiful thing that put me on, by the way, that's in the "Gerhardt" poem, if you remember, "Old Man …," where they treat a bear straight. Those hunters treat a bear straight because they—yeah, I get this from Stefansson. God, I ran into his book—Bet was reading that book the last night of her life, and it was in the—it was in the bedroom, and I never could take it back. Stefansson said that—a reprint of that great early book of his, on the Eskimo.

DORN: *My Life with the Eskimo*, yeah.

OLSON: Yeah. And, you know, the first time he learned something was like you getting that chant going through you, really. Those damn Eskimo teach their children how to hunt a seal—listen to this, Drum—and they teach them, you know, they take them out and show them how to hunt and all that, but when it's too cold, when that all-night time comes and it's cold, they all—they have to teach. The winter is—I mean, "teach" in the pedagogic sense, the *ethea* sense, what Creeley's all busted up about today, I mean, that the habits will eventually break, the habits break; and I said, "Yeah, they will, if they're brittle, they have to." But you know what they teach? When you kill the seal, if you be sure to give them a glass of fresh water you will have satisfied the requirements of creation, because the one thing that a seal wants is to once in his life, or once, taste fresh water, and then that seal it will go to happy hunting grounds, and no other seal then will object to being hunted and killed, because he will know that man treats a seal fairly by giving him what he wants when he's, like, in this instance, dead.[11] [LAUGHS] But that's not the point, it …

[GAP]

… Yevtushenko says that if he didn't know, say, some other city and Buenos Aires, literally, himself, he'd be embarrassed. Well, my god, I don't think you and I ever sought to know a single fact about all the goddamn facts that we have labored and sought to find out, eh, because we would have been embarrassed if we didn't know. In fact, what I don't know now doesn't embarrass me, thank the lord.

DORN: Yeah! right there.

OLSON: Okay. And that's us, the two of us, because, god knows, I mean, he was the print—let me do this for the audience, like they say: you know that he

11. Vilhjalmur Stefansson, *My Life with the Eskimo* (New York: Collier, 1962), p. 57 (originally published in 1913).

printed this—he was a printer—I didn't know him—he was in the print shop when I wrote that crazy attempt of mine to launch—lance— something, "A Letter for Melville," at the hundredth anniversary of *Moby-Dick*. When they asked me to go to some one of these parties to celebrate the anniversary, I wrote a poem instead. And he, he put it in type, and I still would—I would love to read that poem, all the time. In fact, in Rome the other night the translator said, "Will you please help us to translate this poem?" I said, "Well, it's no problem," I said. "Sure, I mean …" How did I say it? It was wonderful. I said, "I meant everything I said. I wrote every word from the Pantheon." [LAUGHTER] But it was a very important poem for me to write, and he printed it a hundred years before he came back and then I knew him. Isn't that true, eh?

DORN: Yeah, sure.

OLSON: On the same lot! That's one of those marvelous mysteries of anonymity or something.

DORN: Well, I was reading it, too, you know—I was reading it while I was printing it!

OLSON: The fringed man!

DRUMMOND HADLEY: Where was it? Where were you?

DORN: Black Mountain, North Carolina.

HADLEY: You were printing it there?

DORN: Yeah, yeah. It was a small print shop in the college.

OLSON: It was a working shack, it was a shack, like a woodshed. It was a woodshed, a tool shack.

DORN: We were the Indians.

OLSON: We were the Indians, right.

DORN: What happens to that spirit though? Can that—is that separate? I don't know, because I …

OLSON: Which one do you mean?

DORN: Well, oh, say, back to—well, look, it seemed obvious to me that, aside from any question of language—which you are not going to allow, but let me say it anyway—well, with both Creeley and Ginsberg there was something, there was this kind of spirit which I mean is almost abstract. The Eskimos made me think of this thing. I recently read this Edmund Carpenter edition, *Anerca*.

OLSON: Oh, yeah, yeah, oh. Gee, I've heard of that.

DORN: "Company of Man," or something like that. And there's a tale of Ohnainewk, an Eskimo who, you know, can't make it around the post and goes back to the ice fields. And in there is an old woman who says, when someone, you know, is left behind on a disengaged piece of ice and, you know, there's nothing to do, it's goodbye, you know, she starts this chant: "Say, tell me, now, was life so good on earth?" Like that, you know: "Say, tell me, now, was life so good on earth?"[12]

OLSON: Phew! Scared shivers! [LAUGHS]

DORN: Anyway, there's that kind of—you know, you get caught in the voice. I find myself sometimes not even listening except to the voice, so I can't at that time think of the language. That's why I was so confused when we were trying to talk about it earlier. I hear the voice only.

OLSON: Well, no, I didn't have that trouble. In fact, exactly, to my mind, by this point of time, and I mean right now, we're here where we are, and only here it has just happened that the distinction between the fact that that is, that voice of Creeley's is a poet—I mean, words …

DORN: It is words, yeah.

OLSON: … the words, those words, and he was reading them even with great— he read very well, and he read the way he meant everything he wrote, I mean, it's that thing. And I think Allen's words are—we've been hearing the socializing of language. Allen has got to the point where he is socializing the language. It's like I said to him: "You sound like Lenin. It's like socialism suddenly. It doesn't sound like—it isn't poetry," I said. And it isn't—my point is earlier as of that god of war is it isn't politics either, now; that's neither politics nor poetry. And Allen's has to be both poetry and politics. And that crazy Creeley, who isn't going to run for office, ever, and isn't trying to bomb the cities, mob-bomb the cities, like these poets, those two poets, Yevtushenko, a Russian, although I must fairly say that Allen finds Voznesensky more Pound, more something, to himself. But, I mean, that little thing, I mean, the Buenos Aires thing, that you have to know it: I don't have to know, I mean, Creeley doesn't have to know anything, I mean, because look how immaculately he proceeds to find out what he does know. And that's not voice.

DORN: No.

OLSON: No, well, I tried to prove last night, I mean I wanted to prove that, I mean, that on this program I can be as attractive as Sammy Davis ain't. [LAUGHS] And he's a pretty sharp cat for fooling around, working around with anything.

DORN: You were as good as your poems. Absolutely.

OLSON: [LAUGHING] Well, that was just a—that was the poem I threw away. Hm, gee, I don't think so …

[GAP]

DORN: But it's all one thing, though, I mean, this certainly saved, as the group. What you did was to force—well, the State behaved absolutely beautifully. I

12. From "Song of a Dead One" in *Anerca*, ed. Edmund Carpenter (Toronto: J.M. Dent, 1959).

mean, they did everything you could have hoped for. They turned out the lights. [LAUGHS]

OLSON: I know it. The witching hour, the midnight closing. But, you know, you get kicked out of bars, too. [LAUGHS] And you got to get up out of bed, too. I mean, the *alba longa* isn't long enough, that's all. (That's off Ezra.) I mean, we wrote an *alba longa* last night. And now it turns out, you know, gee, I wouldn't—in fact, I'm glad I didn't crawl my elongated length, and I'm very happy. I thought when I'd done that the earth was my woman. Now I'm stuck with myself, that's about all. That's all right.

Stills from National Education Television film *USA: Poetry*. Photos courtesy Simon Fraser University.

8

Filming in Gloucester

Director Richard Moore brought his film crew to Gloucester on 11 March 1966 and spent the next few days in Olson's apartment and environs film- ing footage that became Olson's segment of the National Educational Television series *USA: Poetry*, which was broadcast in the first week of September 1966 and which is available today as a fine glimpse of the poet reading and talking at his inimitable best. The following text includes all that was captured on tape on that occasion. Because of the conditions of film-making, the resulting out-takes are much disjointed, but contain many valuable moments. Thanks are due to the American Poetry Archive and Resource Center of San Francisco State University, who acquired the footage from the producer and assembled it for a first showing in San Francisco on 9 April 1976.

CHARLES OLSON: ... You know Frank. I suppose he still is sort of generally just awkward, like.

RICHARD MOORE: Looks like Mishihito or somebody.

OLSON: You know him too? How fair was he now with you people?

[GAP]

We were going to produce it in a glen in Washington. But, you see, I finally had him invited to Black Mountain, and, jesus, you know, those sons of bitches, those Black Mountain cats, they got—I mean, there was very hip guys that were most awful good men around there. And Frank was—I always thought of him as a little sort of slow on that ...

[GAP]

I can read you the best poem I ever wrote, "The Librarian." It's all Frank Moore, describing him as my brother, the brother that got born misshapen,[1] and all that. It's one of those beautiful—by the way, I got a beautiful break

---

1. Olson's parents had had a son who died at birth a year before the poet was born. It should be noted that in actual fact Frank Moore was not at all (in later life, anyway) noticeably misshapen in the face, as "The Librarian" and this conversation suggest.

there: New Directions caught a typo. Jesus! And they saved me. I called up and said, "That's one of the greatest saves I've had is that."

MOORE: Where will I find the poem? Is it in *The* ...?

OLSON: It's right in *Distances*. I had to get it and put it in my hand yesterday, doing copy. I guess I put it back. Jesus, did I? Of course, I'd love to read it. LeRoi first published this in the most beautiful—did you know LeRoi Jones's magazine, the magazine that he did before he went kooky, before he became professional?[2]

MOORE: Who *The Realist* calls "a political James Baldwin."

OLSON: Oh, I know that snide remark. Well, it isn't good enough, so it's harder. This thing is so hard, 'cos, you know, he was called by Malcolm X in those days between Thursday and Sunday, and he had it laid on him. Well, boy, that's strong enough to make any man go for quite a while. I'd like so much to read it from that fucking very first original printing. It's so foul, this Grove Press. Thank god, Jas Laughlin still hires people that catch typos.

MOORE: Jim Laughlin himself catch it?

OLSON: No, a guy named Jerry Fried, who must be worth hiring, like they say. He always had good—that Jimmy Higgins that married Kitty used to be one of his—started out, as a matter of fact, in that ... Where is that drink? I do really need it. Oh, boy. It's a hard poem to read, because it's—I guess I hope I can. It's called "The Librarian."

> [Reads "The Librarian" which ends:
> "... Who is
> Frank Moore?"]

Too much! I mean, that guy, isn't it? I mean, it's him, you know, all the way through, this damn fucking doppelgänger of me. Frank, that son of a gun, it's so exciting to hear of him. He wrote me—when the *Maximus* book come out, I had a letter from him asking me if I'd read a text of a play, if he shipped it, and I didn't answer him, you know, not deliberately, but ... I don't know, shit, those—you live with your people as well as your ghosts. You gotta live with them, so there's no mistake, eh? I don't know, I still would like—I'm fascinated that you know of Frank, even that any of you have seen the fucking ... 'cos he's like a part of me that I won't—I don't want—I won't keep acquainted with, you know.

CAROLINE CROSS: Because he's a strange-looking person?

OLSON: Absolutely. I don't know whether you heard that: "his face twisted at birth," that lopsided quality. There is something off-center about Frank, you know, physically, he's a—he is desymmetricalized, uh?

CROSS: Very much. Definitely.

OLSON: Interesting, this thing. Very interesting man.

2. "The Librarian," which appeared in *Yugen* 4 (1959), edited by LeRoi Jones, is found in *Collected Poems*, pp. 412–14.

CROSS: I'm trying to think of an animal that he was like. Like a raccoon or something.

OLSON: Yeah, I hear you. But I had somebody the other night here in the bedroom busted up, telling about—as a matter of fact, he caused that girl, that daughter of mine—we almost lost her. We left the house—we let the house, my studio in Washington—I always give—if I left, Frank took it, see. We come back, and—Frank has got dirty toes, I mean, he has got dirty toes. I guess it's one of those things like other people have scalp trouble or something. And one night, by the way, I kicked him, absolutely just in a terrible rainstorm, like I come back after a Labor Day weekend he was there with Fielding Dawson …

[GAP]

… We're on lines all the—but if you—if suddenly you go, you plug, not plug in, but you're on another line when you make love, right? I mean, it's a beautiful thing that you have. I mean, you're not thinking about that at all; that's not why you make love, no, not to put a plug in a socket, as of that book. But you can go on duty the moment you make love, in that funny way. You don't even know it till—in fact, some people, I suppose, live their whole lives and never know they're basically—really. I mean, it's like who said religion is for those who—? Oh, that's Mohammed. No, it's one of these Muslims, on the basis of the Koran, I think—because most life here is, literally, the understanding that you don't understand; and only the Muslims have sense enough to credit that as being a perfect, I mean, not an indecent or a put-down, but Nature, again.

MOORE: There was one of the Patristic Fathers came out with the *credo quia absurdum*, which is an intellectualized version of that same thing.

OLSON: But that is—yeah, I don't know. But Heraclitus is even more interesting there: "Man is estranged from that with which he is most familiar," which is actually a better—that's the best I know, by the way, of the Western thought on this question is that Heraclitus remark.

[GAP]

I mean, imagine that guy poppin'—you know, he's so goddamn good.[3] I mean, you make that to where that occurred if somebody said, "What is prayer?" and he said, "Right, I'll give you one." Bang, he knocked that thing, just popped that thing out of him. He really did that. I bet that must have been how it happened. Exactly. And believe you me, I don't know anything that isn't—and I was going along this beach the day that the Supreme Court put that out of schools, and I didn't even know that that was the day. And for the first time, you know how—this was just a few years ago, fifty …

MOORE: Fifty-four.

3. We are deprived of the context here. Perhaps this is, as Butterick supposes, a reference to Edward Dorn (*Muthologos* 1.174). But if it is, it is one that has not been explained, and a few moments later Dorn is introduced into the discussion in such a way that it seems that Olson had not spoken of him before on this subject.

OLSON: No, dear, that's the other decision; that's the education decision. The prayer decision is just five years ago. And I thought to myself, because I was raised a Catholic and all that stuff sounds like shit to me, you know, even the Lord's Prayer is just a lot of *mishpocheh*. And, by god, I'd to answer that. And, you know, I was reading Dorn's new book of poems, and that son-of-a-bitch out there in Pocatello he's got something which says "the only thing I really have got"—he so quietly says it that you don't notice it— "is the Lord's Prayer." I think it's the first other man I know that would take this square chance to speak of this dumb thing.[4]

'Cos I did it the other night, you know. People have tried—but people think you're just going, well, you're getting sanctimonious or something. But we're talking the place where it counts, which is, I—*credo quia absurdum*. We're really going to have a hell of time on that one. It's so realistic we don't believe that the thing is more interesting than we—that we're more interesting—the way it works out, we're more interesting—*it's* more interesting, that's all, *it* is.

MOORE: Well, what was it like at Black Mountain? Because I was never there.

OLSON: No, it was—I mean, you might have been, but you—but you didn't know.

MOORE: I could have, but I didn't make it.

OLSON: I don't know. It was a camp …

[GAP]

Couldn't you use the Dorn thing as a piece of this or something?[5]

MOORE: We can use part of it, yeah.

OLSON: Because I could read you a thing, an unusual statement right now by Dorn in this kooky book, this *Sullen Art* book. I don't know whether you ever saw it. It's—they were tapes. Where did …? It was here. Gee, I'm, like, tired today. It's a shame, I really—I over-anticipated you.

MOORE: Let me know if you want to stop.

OLSON: It's not that; it's just that I really over-led, I over-led just because of the excitement. It would be fun if I can just not see this one, because—it's one, two or three sentences. I don't know if I'm going to hit … Yeah, here it is.

> I think the value of being at Black Mountain was that very able people and very alive people were there, back and forth and off and on and through it. And that's what made it a very important place to be. I don't see any superstructure that existed there which would relate people and what they subsequently did, although there might be one, and a case could probably be made for it. But I don't think

4. Olson is recalling the poem "The Sense Comes Over Me, And the Waning Light of Man by the 1st National Bank" in Edward Dorn's *Geography* (London: Fulcrum Press, 1965), which had reached Olson only on 26 April 1966.
5. Olson is referring to a passage from Dorn's interview in David Ossman's *The Sullen Art* (New York: Corinth, 1963), p. 83, which he proceeds to read.

that it's so important. It was literally a place, and it was very arbitrary. North Carolina is a very unlikely place, say, for people who were mostly from New York and New England, with a very few from the midwest and possibly another very few from the West Coast. There was no important logic connected with why it should be there, so it was a very impersonal site in which to have this go on. And in many ways it was a hostile surrounding, which was more subtle than anything else, I think. But it was good—that kind of isolation, and at that time it was good. I think it has to come at a certain time of your life. That sort of isolation would be very distasteful to me now.

Isn't that nice? Boy, that's the nicest statement that I—the answer's answer to that question—that I've yet seen is that neat characterization of this early flow.

MOORE: I heard a lot from Bob Creeley about your teaching method and his early relationship to you, you know, which he values immensely. He's very excited about it.

OLSON: Well, gee, we were talking—you know, he—you know, one night I was aware, as I was holding some, just after Bob came, that he had taken this Cynthia, who was, had been, was Dan Rice's girlfriend, and he snatched her from Dan. We all played baseball one day, and Creeley doesn't play baseball, so he was walking Cynthia around the ballpark [LAUGHS] on, like, the bases. And anyhow, like, they got together, I guess. And he walked in, he walks in, and they were in the library in the dark, listening. That's a very nice—I mean, he brought her to hear me. And I don't think he ever heard me before, because, you know ...

MOORE: Well, he wrote to you, didn't he?

OLSON: Oh, four years we wrote, daily. In fact, I called him up, just to hear his voice, when my wife and I were leaving from New Orleans aboard a vessel to the Yucatan. You know, like, in Laconia or Littleton has yet to—you know, clank, clank, clank, quarters going in, way the hell up there in the northern part of the state. Here, I'd been here—no, Washington, but just to see, before I left the continent, just to hear the voice. That was, oh, that was maybe a year or two after we'd been writing only ...

[GAP]

Well, I don't know. Geez, you know who—? Do you know, by the way, Bill Williams—? That's it. Bill Williams wrote me a note and said, "If you have anything that you think is deathless or immortal, there's a guy editing a little magazine up in Littleton named Creeley, send it to him." To think it was Bill that said, "If you have anything that you think is immortal," I think. But Ferrini, by the way, ahead of that, had sent manuscripts of mine ...

[GAP]

No, I don't think I can, but it was fun as of that point, because what love—damn it, isn't it nutty how I—oh, I wish I could find that, really, because it's just fresh—can't remember where in this last book it's in[6]—find out just the point of what … Here it is all right, but I don't know if I can read it anyhow. "Love is desire just—" No. "Love is desire just plainly; the rest of it, the rest of love is the same as life. How well it stands up." Or the, yeah, gee, that's it. "The rest of love is the same as life. How well it stands up." And that's the instance that you couldn't signal, jesus, somehow. This was written in next: "Girls' legs are busier right from the street."[7] It's like I'm finding out how—you know, Duncan and Dostoevsky, they keep notebooks. No, yeah, they do. And I'm trying to find how I could write it in a notebook. I believed, as you know, so much in mem—in that funny thing, which is a thousand percent activity of the retention and immediate presentation, that kind of dumb pffh!

MOORE: Like it's all happening at once.

OLSON: Yeah, well, if I weren't alone here, I wouldn't keep a notebook. It's only because I'm alone that I keep—I'm trying to find out. And I don't believe in—I don't believe in being alone; or I don't believe in practice—like Dorn says there: you might once, but I wouldn't think much of isolation now. Here I'm—I'm isolated, lysolated, like; I'm lysolated now. I've been lysolated now recently, and choosing to.

MOORE: Do you think of leaving the isolation, and Gloucester?

OLSON: Geez, I don't know. I got to finish this attempt to retake the lines into my hand. I mean, you know …

MOORE: When did you get started on the second *Maximus*?

OLSON: Fifty-nine, with that marvelous—practically with that visit of McClure and LeRoi Jones and Don Allen and the one that—in fact, the poem, the *Maximus from Dogtown* that Auerhahn published, you know, that by now made a pamphlet, is …

MOORE: I haven't seen it.

OLSON: You haven't seen it? I think it—wait a minute, no, I think I used it later. I tell the story of—you know, Whalen was here, and both he and Mike it was their first trip to the East, and they both in a sense funked it. As a matter of fact, as you know, Mike even cut out and went, flew home before he did his thing in New York. But they were both ill, I mean literally, when they got here, no, I mean physically, legitimately, had colds. As a matter of fact, it was cold weather; it was the fall, November; and Whalen didn't even leave the house. In fact, be stayed here with Bet; and my wife was pretty gone on Philip in San Francisco in '57, and I thought to myself, "Well, this is one of those times you just braves the storm by turning your back." And I was very

6. Olson is looking into his most recent notebook. Butterick has identified these lines as dated 10 March 1966 (*Muthologos* 1.227), two days before the filming.
7. In *Muthologos* (1.175) Butterick gives this last word as "start," following the notebook (at Storrs). On the tape the word is unmistakably "street."

interested. Of course, I come back to see if anything had happened, and I learned that Philip just lay on the couch and read the *Apollonius of Tyana* and my wife all the time thought, "Jesus, what could—I mean, how can I make a pass at that big dodo bird?" And that night, later—you know, we'd prepared Mike to go out—my wife got him vapor rub.

[GAP]

'Cos I liked—last night when I was looking this stuff over in terms of—I hit this thing, and I don't know why but it still makes it. And I don't know, I guess I once read it, but I think this is the very second time. I don't know, geez, it sits in the sequence that I was reading the other night till … I'm a little jumped up.

MOORE: Do it the way you feel like.

OLSON: Well, so, because of the map we can do it this way.

[Reads "The Cow of Dogtown" (II.148–50)]

OLSON: That's a lovely poem, kooky; it was just made of nothing but Shaler's geology.

CROSS: Wonderful.

OLSON: And one day I was up I got lost, by the way. Everybody laughs. I got lost. And, in fact, people get lost and die. And, like, I'm supposed to know, like, everything; but here I am, the first time up on top of the goddamn thing and I couldn't find my way out, like any other goddamn fool, blueberry picker, or anybody else. They have to send fire departments up there and boy scouts and—I mean, it's a kooky—and here am I, the big pro of the Memphite Theology of the whole of creation, and I can't even get the fuck out of there! I don't know which way I had to go down, so—I got my ears—I'm supposed to know directions and all this stuff, and I'm listening to the hoots of the railroad trains and the noises off in the distance, and I can't figure out—because in a funny way, you know, that is one of the crazy things about that kind of a condition: it is not locable. It's better than locable, that's what I mean. It's like when I said in the Gerhardt poem about "come on over here, we'll teach you American vocables."[8] I was even saying that's nothing. That's where you start: Creeley, and new bicycles, and automobiles, and America. If we didn't start with vocables, we wouldn't be this other thing, hm?

[GAP]

MOORE: You got interested in the first *Maximus* when did you say?

OLSON: Well, I come here in I'm pretty sure it was '47, and I—my wife and I had sort of just visited my mother. It was early, it was May, like, and you never—it's always you do something because you haven't anything to do.

---

8. The allusion is to the poem "To Gerhardt, There, Among Europe's Things …" in *Collected Poems*, pp. 212–32, especially pp. 218–19.

MOORE: You got the *Maximus Poems* out of it.

OLSON: No, I did. I suddenly thought, "Why don't I really do something with this thing?" I mean, I've spent more of my life in Gloucester than I did anywhere else, that's all. And I think the first "Maximus" was written in '50; and my plan was to write them only as letters to Vincent Ferrini whenever I chose; and the first few were—they're quite—six months, maybe a year and a half, apart.

MOORE: You know, I don't know much about Ferrini.

OLSON: Well, you know, there is one man that's almost my contemporary; he's two and a half years younger. That's a curious thing. I, like, I call him and Mary Shore my—the only brother and sister I've had, that's true. And they are; they're both here in Gloucester. And they are; they're the only that kind of family. And I don't know, I—as a matter of fact, again it's due to Bill Williams. I wrote a poem on a postcard, you know, that snappy way you do. "These days"—this is to Bill Williams, penny postcard:

These days

whatever you have to say, leave
the roots on, let them
dangle

And the dirt

    Just to make sure
    where they come from.

And Bill sends the thing to a magazine at Muhlenberg or Allentown or Allegheny College, edited, you know, one of those things, called *Imago* ... *Imagi*.[9] And in the issue was a poem I liked called "The House" by a poet named Ferrini; and, you know, I look up under "contributors," and the guy is Gloucester. So the next time I come back to visit my mother I—you know, you say, "Hello, Ma," and that's it. I mean, you eat one meal and you think, "Oh, jesus, I got to get back to ..." Well, you can't leave, you know; your mother wants you to stay overnight at least. So I went out to—after I had supper, I said, "Look, I got to go over town," like; and I went over and I looked up—I went to a captain whom I knew his daughters taught the high school. I don't know how I had the idea Ferrini's wife taught school. I don't know, maybe the contributors' thing said that or something. And they told me he lived on Liberty Street, and—oh, yeah, I had this Frenchman's—the Frenchman I mentioned earlier—Riboud's beautiful Mercury I'd driven up; and, you know me, I wouldn't know about the simonize ...

[GAP]

Well, on Hart Crane and Marsden Hartley and my father and the Whale Jaw, an early *Maximus* ["Letter 7" 1.30–34], where my father is throwing a

9. "These Days" was first published in a periodical from Muhlenberg College, Allentown, Pennsylvania, *Imagi* 5:2 (1950), p. 8, and is found in *Collected Poems*, p. 106. Vincent Ferrini's "Two poems from The House of Time" had appeared in the Spring 1949 issue.

big joke. He's in between the—you know, the Whale Jaw is really an enormous, again, a glacial split, and a huge rock just left right up, from nowhere, like a clown scene, you know, ah-oo-wah! And this thing is sitting way the hell up on the top of Dogtown in one of those, a secondary level of what I was—it's in that "Cow of Dogtown" poem. And my old man is standing there, pushing the jaws of this, literally, it's like a whale's mouth, open this way, coming out of the earth. And he's just shoving the fucking jaws aside like big powerful Olson men are supposed to, you know. And I don't think I ever was there again, since that time that picture was taken when I must have been about seven or eight. Break it up! [LAUGHS] Break it up!

[GAP]

MOORE: You know what I want to hear about?

OLSON: What?

MOORE: The breath.

OLSON: The breath? Jesus! You know, I ain't—I mean, I got, I mean, you know, I just was the first time in my life told by a doctor, "You know, you don't breathe, Olson." I says, "What?" And he taught me how to breathe. And the other day I went back, and I said, "Jesus," I said, "you know, you really put me on to something." And he says, "Well, do you know that's true of everybody." "Oh," I says, "you're not as wise as I thought you were." "No," he says, "almost everybody takes sixteen breaths a minute, and," he says, "they'd be much better off if they took eight, because they—their lungs—" And he gave it to me. He says—you know, I'm having trouble because I got emphysema and all that shit now. I thought I had—I thought I'd been holding my breath to make breath for poetry, like; so, you know, the way you make up those—if somebody tells you you're sick, then you got to have a good reason for being sick, so I thought, "Well, it might have been ..."

[GAP]

... forty-six in Washington, and I would—you know, I'm so rational that I decided, well, I'd written a few poems and sold them easily to *Harper's Bazaar* and *Atlantic*, enough to buy some nice underwear for my wife, from *Harper's Bazaar*. You know they call poems in *Harper's Bazaar* "bra fillers," technically, a poem in a bra. They call down and say, "You got a fourteen-line or so bra filler?" I published in *Harper's Bazaar*, the first poems all were there, until one time I wrote a poem on Christ's Sermon on the Mount and they put it next to a Modess ad;[10] and that just finished me—a whole page in a green spring thing, the lawn, linen, and all this shit. That was enough.

[GAP]

10. "In the Hills South of Capernum, Port" was published in *Harper's Bazaar* 83 (April 1949), p. 193, and is found in *Collected Poems*, pp. 60–62.

I discovered there wasn't an *ars poetica* in existence and the last, the only poet that I knew that ever wrote one was Dante's *De Vulgari Eloquentia* and that's a marvelous essay. As a matter of fact, I'm just about—I wrote last night to get the Frontier Press to make an issue, a book, out of it, and reissue the damn thing. 'Cos, by the way, it's all the technical problems of syllables; and, meanwhile, without knowing that then, I did—I thought—I didn't know the Dante, and I wrote the thing. And in a sense, I guess because you think an *ars poetica* is technical, I wrote technical, uh? But I now find out that what I really was talking about was, even using the word "projective," was to either discover or to regain some difference of art and reason, and propose that there be that. In other words, the "Projective Verse" piece is really the last section of the "Human Universe," which—if you know Bill Williams put the first section in his *Autobiography*,[11] and it hurt me a little because he left out the second section, where I thought the humanism lay.

[GAP]

"Projection" is where you permit your feeling to flow and go out through the subject matter. And that's not the thing to do. Like my great master, Whitehead, said: "All is there for feeling. All does flow." That's objectively true. That is the creation. You don't use that for creation; that's like suckin' off the tit, for christ's sake. You do your own act, which is to separate yourself from that expression of feeling. You put the feeling back on the other side entirely. It's an act of both mind and creation itself, on *your* part. And that's what I proposed in the "projective": that that adjective has nothing to do with projection of that order. It has to do with the search to undo the inherited reason in art that we have had for so long and is based upon a false, a poor discourse and a poor aesthetic. And I was after something that I didn't know, but I started with an *ars poetica*, to in fact supply an *ars poetica*, not even knowing that there was a great one, which I didn't even know at that time, the Dante.

MOORE: You went through this whole damn process in a week or less than a week, one day less than a week?

OLSON: This last week? I sure did. A poem was sent to me, and I went for it hook, line, and sinker. And I couldn't really tell you what the fucking thing all amounted to, but, good god, was I hooked![12]

[GAP]

The only way I can say it now, because I still feel so much is really going on, and it's still going on here, and, I mean, for some reason I'm a—geez, I don't give a goddamn about, I'm not talking about America, except I can't see that the American thing isn't still going out. And I don't mean the species and the spaceship, that's a lot of crap, and the war and the whole thing, 'cos

11. It is the first section of "Projective Verse" which opens chapter 50 of *The Autobiography of William Carlos Williams* (NY: Random House, 1951), where it is called an "advance of estimable proportions."
12. There is evidence from a letter to Tom Clark of 7 March 1966 (at Kansas) that this poem is J.H. Prynne's "Moon Poem," published in *The White Stones* (1969).

that's not a nation, that's the abuse of the nation. But I mean that when I mentioned Charles Peirce earlier, that that way that that man was think-ing—in fact, as you may know, in the *Popular Science Monthly*, January 1878, he wrote, 1878 he wrote (and even James didn't know it till about 1906), 1878, that man established the whole thing. And it's a very simple principle, by the way; I can even say it quickly: Thought is Belief, Belief is Action. That's just what is that famous so-called American pragmatism. And I've lived fifty-five years, and this year found out that, of course, that's it. When I think, I believe; and when I believe, I act it. And only that way, that consistency or that order, is so true, and there's no, there's no—I mean, that gets the absolute around, as Whitehead says, the right way: the absolute is the end, not the beginning. You pick up on the matter; you pick up on the particular; and then you yourself, if you run into the eternal, you propose the same thing God did in creating the damn thing from the start. And He doesn't even know the end of His creation. He's a part of the acts which we are the—present ages are instruments of only. He's a part. I don't mean to sub—to make Him small there. I mean, only if the imagination—it's that beautiful thing that the Muses, by the way—I also worked it out by carefully going at that goddamn beautiful poet, who I think is the greatest poet now for us is Hesiod, because in the *Theogony*—it gets perfectly clear in Havelock, in the *Preface to Plato* (that marvelous analysis of *The Republic* and the poetics that are in *The Republic*, by the way), that beautiful book by Havelock, which opens on *Theogony*, he also—and I'd done this in '63 here, and wrote that poem, the second "Maximus"—oh, no, the second "Gravelly." It was published in the *Psychedelic Review*, the one that the mushroom people edited.[13] I deliberately did it, by the way. They asked me for a poem 'cos I'd been under the early experiments on the poets and the mushroom; and I deliberately gave them this, which is really my idea of a translation of Hesiod.

[GAP]

... the idea that we have become tactile-less. See? It's like I'd said earlier about food processing. You know food processing goes on in our stomachs; that's what stomachs are for is to process food, that's what the whole juices in our mouth are for. Well, language preceded even diet. And if you overt these processes in creation, you have no—as a matter of fact, if you saw that crazy, marvelous projection of the next twenty years, excuse me, of the thirty-six years from now, 2000, they have come to the point where they propose skin—babies will be—so that women won't have to go through the pangs of pregnancy, they will have the babies outside. But in addition, the damn thing says that they can produce skin and then put features on it. Now I believe that that is just what might become possible; and I believe that we're proceeding at a rate of speed and a rate of progress which leads

---

13. The poem in the *Psychedelic Review* 1:3 (1964), pp. 347–53 appears in the *Maximus Poems* volume with the title "Maximus, from Dogtown–IV" (II.17–26).

to these—it's really interesting, it's—talk about *contra naturam* it's much worse than that. It is literally denaturing Nature.

[GAP]

We arrange the measurements, now we have to get the Nature. That's where we are today. I mean, science and poetry today is brilliant because it's already now returning to what, again, my great master and the companion of my poems, Mr Whitehead, called his cosmology: "The Philosophy of Organism."

CAMERAMAN: What about this map of Gloucester? Over there.

OLSON: Which one? That one?

CAMERAMAN: Yes, on the wall.

OLSON: That's a—that's a topographical creation. There she is in her—I mean, she really still looked like a French chick, no?

CROSS: Oh, yes.

OLSON: "Isn't-that-the-girl" look in the eyes! You know, this is my bedroom wall [LAUGHS] that he was talking about—what do you want me to do? I don't know, this is my Saint Sophia.

MOORE: What is that?

OLSON: Santa Sophia, in the flesh, mind you, not …

MOORE: Is that part of a working chart for the new *Maximus* or what?

OLSON: No, I don't believe—I don't know, I don't—as a matter of fact, I was thinking of just ringing my daughter, who used to come to Christmas, you know, and spend the holidays with Pa; and you know, I'd be sitting at that goddamn desk working on the bloody damn thing all Christmas and every year for—I wonder how many years it turned out to cook the damned thing? 'Cos normally you have to go through paper records and—you see, this was—like, let me say—I can tell you it's simple. They come to this country, the peoples, like, the English peoples, at this end of the—this entirely; and they did themselves have the available best land. And it's up on the Annisquam River, and it's a marsh. And that group were planters, in the real farm sense; while the fishermen who'd been here earlier was down here at the Harbor. But, you know, the farming in New England was done by people who proposed to make Society; they weren't going to take how things were, they proposed Society. And they, therefore, had both a—well, each town in New England was really a church, rather than a town, although the town and church were really the same. And the person who had both the largest property and was considered the person who could lead or produce the future was the minister. And the settlement of Gloucester was up on this creek, this meadow where cows could be fed on this new grass, which—it was discovered that the salt marsh grasses of this country fattened cattle better than any salt grass that they knew in England, so they had, right off the bat they had—but, as a matter of fact, fishing—

like, the codfish was still the one that was the thing that was going on right here in Harbor Cove, and had been going on previously. Well, these people had children, and then, let me see, I'm pretty sure it's their children that had to expand; and they went right up into—they'd been cutting off this place that became known as Dogtown. And they cleared this piece that's the direct extension of what is called "The Green"; and it's the right—and what I was interested in was that that was the fact that it had been an absolute active, fresh third-generation occupation by—and, in fact, what happened was that by that point of time the fishing had really replaced the farming. and that most of these people that are registered here—and the thing starts on the Lower Road at 1713—see, that would be just about the third generation from the settlement—and on the Upper Road just a hair earlier, 17— no, wait a minute—this is 1713, and the Benjamin Kinnicum will be a hair earlier. But it's very early, like, at the beginning—and, in fact, as you know, America had two big rises. She had a big rise at the beginning of the 17th and an enormously big rise at the beginning of the 18th, to speak just before we talk in terms of the big rise that has now swept the world, the rise of total world change. But in this country the two big rises happen to be just after the beginning of the 18th and just after—excuse me, the beginning of the— yeah, the 18th, and the beginning of the 19th. And this is actually an attempt to just really myself find out what the 18th century was. We've been talking all evening, we're clear about the 17th; and we certainly are stuck with the 20th, and we're trying to be clear about that. And the 19th is really just almost well known to us. And the 18th, to my mind, which we assume the American Revolution took care of—I think the American Revolution put an end to something. As a matter of fact, as I've published—and the great Gino Clays, thank the lord, is the first man, and because of Gino Clays I wrote it to a thing—even before *Wild Dog* in Pocatello there was a thing called *A Pamphlet* edited by Gino Clays.

MOORE: Who's he?

OLSON: Gino Clays is a San Francisco poet man. He's a poet man. I don't know too much about his writing except this thing that provoked me to write this thing,[14] in which I suggested, and I still am trying to work that out, that the whole thing that this thing here, I think, gave me much of this, but it was also the architecture of the Harbor, which is the fishing thing that overtook this thing; so that the basic map of this, which gave me the chance to do this at all, is this crazy thing that's in the archives of the State of Massachusetts, and is the map of this parish when the Harbor people—the fishing had so changed, had overtaken the farming, in a sense the planter thing, that the downtown people wanted to become the First Parish and build a church, and these people who *were* the First Parish went to the General Court, or the Commonwealth of Massachusetts, and fought the Harbor people stealing their church and their minister from them. And this map is the— the reason it survives (it's 1741) is that they fought and lost. The Harbor won.

---

14. "A House Built by Capt. John Somes 1763" in *Collected Prose*, pp. 351–52.

Today this parish, which was the original parish of Gloucester, which I think was either the fifteenth or the thirty-first church of the Commonwealth, I don't remember which, late 1642 … 1741—this map is—they lost on this attempt. But the map is an engineer's map, locating each of the inhabitants of Dogtown. And it was Dogtown—that's not a cute name. They themselves called this place Dogtown, which I don't know who knows why, but, I mean, I'd love to know 'cos with the weight I've put on it, like, dig? I mean, the poetry I've written in this new *Maximus* is all, in a sense, all really essentially Dogtown. If the first town was the Town town, the fish town, the second town, the second volume, is Dogtown, and the third is what I'm now working on.

[GAP]

Well, each one of them is the extent of the property of each of the houses that I was able to start with, the exact location in rods and poles of this marvelous fellow named Batchelder, who did this with chains—they called them chains, it's the measurement. They do still, yeah. And poles for rods, right? A pole is a rod, I think. And the chain-bearers carry the lengths, and I just found that I could be extremely precise about something, by the way, that's become a piece of absolute—I mean, the thing like we spoke of earlier, the covered wagons that's covered America, I mean that cuteness which has ruined all literal real, real realty, real realty [LAUGHS] and pers-personality too [LAUGHS]. That's what I'm talking, that's what this thing is is an attempt to just introduce some accuracy into shit, cute shit, cute nominative crap. [LAUGHS] And it's a very, I don't know—I guess still it digs me, very excites me that you can just put a lot of gunky pieces of paper together and it means something.

CAMERAMAN: You fished out of Gloucester?

OLSON: Oh, a little bit. Nothing. I mean, I obviously wasn't made for the trade. It takes a different thing, and I'm not that thing.

CAMERAMAN: You showed Mike and I the pier you fished that you were raised on.

OLSON: Yes, I did. But that's always big stuff, you know, where you first go to sea from. That's big stuff, to step off the land, right? Go aboard a vessel for the first time, jesus, that's a funny—in fact, to come back, if you remember, is where it really counts. You can't—we used to come in to the Boston Fish Pier and sell on the Boston market. There was a bar at the end of the Fish Pier called "A Bucket of Blood." And we'd sell, and while the stuff was being sold, you know, while the captain was selling, we'd be up starting to drink, and the moment we finished the sale we'd start out for Gloucester. And we'd drink—no, we wouldn't drink aboard the vessel, but we'd lick our chops, and the moment we get here we head for Bill Callahan's, and smack! And that was the end of it, mostly. But that rope, it's to get your legs, to get your land legs. Gee, after weeks at sea it's some funny thing to come onto earth again. And I think also the great thing is that funny moment you leave it. But this is the way I might talk; no fisherman would talk like that.

MOORE: What is that newspaper clipping up there?

OLSON: Oh, I guess one of the—this is, as of the people I live with now, the Fort people, because, you know, they almost all come from a very small town, Terrasini, west of Palermo.

13 March 1966

OLSON: You'll lead me, uh?

MOORE: We were talking about continental shifts. Would you …?

OLSON: Yes, I would, I'd like very much to. Continental drift, not "shifts." [LAUGHS] This is one, one big split. In fact, one of the exciting things that I think really is—has actually occurred is that—and it's funny that it should happen right now, or just—in fact, I tried the other night in that piece for Mr Sanders's magazine in New York[15] to state it as the way in which the actual universe as a geography has turned around and is moving towards us at the very moment that the species thinks it's going out into space. Actually, space is coming home to occupy us, in fact, to re-occupy the earth. Creation is turned the other way; man's interest and attention and success must be boring Creation. It doesn't, but if—it knows where it is out there. And, in fact, that marvelous head of the Jodrell Bank—I can't remember what the hell his name is, it's like Whipple but it isn't Whipple[16]—in fact, it's the best reporting, still, and the fastest, I think, on the events of the landings on Mars or the fly-bys on Venus at the moment. He wrote a beautiful book just two or three years ago, a lovely little book called *The Individual and the Universe*, I think, a lecture in which he—and you know that that Jodrell even is another American invention: it's the radar invention of the Second World War that is the base, and he acknowledges and names the American who first invented that principle of radar as a machine, uh? It's like here, for example, there is a man that the wharfhouse was we were on last night, that isn't here any more, Burkey's we call it, where I took you, by that sail loft— it's going down, and just the building, which burned because—they didn't have to remove it—this winter: Burkey's. In that building was where the fathometer was invented,[17] that thing which makes it possible to sound the oceans now. I think they used it—the fathometer was the first way to sound depths that—that map's in my kitchen with the total bottom of the Atlantic

15. A note beginning "The moral act—how to live …" dated 9 March 1966 was, according to George Butterick (*Muthologos* 1.229), sent to *Fuck You/ A Magazine of the Arts*, but the periodical was discontinued before it could be published.

16. A.C.B. Lovell was Director of the Jodrell Bank Experimental Station in Chester, England. Olson owned his book, *The Individual and the Universe* (NY: Harper, 1959.) Fred Whipple was an astronomer at Harvard.

17. Butterick notes (*Muthologos* 1.229) that among Olson's papers is a clipping from the *Gloucester Daily Times* (undated) about a local man, Herbert Grove Dorsey, who patented the fathometer in 1928. The wharf mentioned belonged to John Burke, a former mayor of Gloucester.

almost like a garden that you could walk around. As a matter of fact, I'll never forget when Ferrini came out to Wyoming at my wife's death, two, not yet two years, I had that up. I'd just bought it, that thing; it cost me five dollars from the Lamont Geology.[18] And that was—it's a crazy map, because you feel suddenly, "Oh jesus, the water isn't there; I can walk around there too!" There's Plato Mountain, Atlantis Mountain; there's a big cleft in the middle; there's a river running from the Hudson down where today, by the way, is the great—that extension of the Hudson, Hudson's Canyon, is where Gloucester is deep-fishing lobster. Did you know that that's what's going on? They're deep-fishing lobster in Hudson Canyon outside of New York City today. It takes enormous—I think it's more interesting actually than those "mother ships" of Russia, thousand ships off through just out here on Georges, that all the Gloucestermen in their cranky, dopey present velleity, blaming somebody, talk about.

Actually, this book which I'll read from is the second volume of this poem, the *Maximus Poems* and since two years ago I've been trying to get a cover. The first volume had an actual U.S. Coast and Geodetic Survey of the Harbor, Gloucester; and I want this new cover, if we can make it, to be the earth as it was when it was one, in Devonian time. Because the poem actually is the Dogtown—the sort of a statistical or metrical base of the poem is the two roads of Dogtown, which I was thinking after we talked last night that it might be that if I said that it was the third generation of people that went up there, used that, the third generation in America, the children of the children who came here first, their grandparents were English, their parents were Americans, "first Americans," like in that sense, that dumb sense, Indians, phmn. That Meeting House Green I spoke of was called the Town; and I wonder if Dogtown, which I've found out is a very early—I now even have record of its naming by one of the chief men of Gloucester, Ellery, who was of that generation, B. Ellery, and I'll read shortly a poem of him, a Muslim poem of him: it's made up of five words, so it won't take long [11.34]. I have, or I know where it is, his record of his shipping business, and he names himself "B. Ellery, Dogtown" at 1772. Now, I assume, therefore, that this name, instead of being cute, or having to do with old ladies or widows of the Revolutionary War, or lost seamen, is actually, it might be a joke: "where the dogs go," our children, uh? *Dogges*? "Puppy Town" or something? It's interesting to speculate. For me, of course, it's the meaning of it is marvelously the other way, which I want to come to now.

Which is, that I believe that not only is the universe come in, but when the universe comes in, it declares its limit, which is the principle of creation, not the expansion, that it defines space, and also defines time. If I can say, as I have earlier when we were talking, the Devonian is a precise Route 20 limit, for example, of western New York, and one foot across Route 20, you pass out of Devonian time. We all know that there's two great national roads from the East, settling the American West. One's 40, and that runs by the

18. Olson owned Bruce C. Heezen and Marie Tharp's *Physiographic Diagram: Atlantic Ocean* (sheet 1) (NY: Geological Society of America, 1957).

terminal moraine. You can still watch the same drift kame or accumulations right straight across, in Pennsylvania, Ohio, Illinois, if you drive 40. On the right-hand side you're up against a hill; on the left, you have flatlands going to the south. And on 20, you pass way behind the Wurm interglacial, or whatever that last ice is called. You go back to Devonian. And the "Maximus, from Dogtown," which was written happily because the poets visited me here, the San Francisco poets—I was lucky; I took them to Dogtown, and I got my "Maximus, from Dogtown–I," which is published by Auerhahn of San Francisco. I mean, there is two poems in this, there's two sets, two pairs in this book. The poem opens with "Maximus, from Dogtown–I" and "Maximus, from Dogtown–II," and it practically ends in another double set, "Gravelly Hill," which is the entrance of Dogtown, which I published in the *Psychedelic Review*.[19] And in fact at this moment I'd love to honor Mr Leary who was responsible, as well as Mr Ginsberg, asking me to become one of the first poets under the use of the sacred mushroom as an intoxicant of this period of time, at this very moment, when I learned this morning that Mr Leary, Dr Leary, who is the most beautiful *brujo* that we've had in this country, has just received a thirty-year sentence in Laredo, Texas, and his lovely daughter, and the son in whose bedroom I slept when I myself had had the mushroom, and the daughter has also been given a federal term, for importing three ounces of marijuana across the American border, this enormous wall which we are building up around nothing. And punitively. As far as I'm concerned, in terms of what I have just said about the universe coming in and creating its wall, the wall of eternity, we practice nothing but the filthiest of all walls, which is the exclusion of life within, and punitively punish a man who attempted to make knowledge active and end taxonomic knowledges. And this man they give a thirty-year sentence to and make a criminal, and his lovely daughter, who was the first woman—I wrote a poem on Phryne, the great mistress of Athens, [II.35] walking into the sea yearly because men wished to see or men and women wished to see a perfect body. This was the model for Praxiteles' Knidian Venus, that utterly beautiful thing. That woman, the Miss Susan Leary, appeared on the beach right out this house, the front beach of Gloucester, the Pavilion Beach, at fifteen years old, and the whole town blew up at seeing a body in a bikini! And that girl is now doing, as her father, a federal penitentiary term in America! It's so foul an act that one—I mean, it is that point that law no longer exists, nothing but filth exists. Because it's less than criminal, it's an offense to Nature.

And I published the second—back-to-back at the end of this volume to the "Gravelly Hill," which is the entrance to Dogtown, is a poem on the Earth and Tartaros and Love [II.163–72], and is actually a translation of the largest passage that I know of poetry that we inherit, Hesiod's *Theogony*. Not the prologue on the Muses and how they go each night from Helicon to Olympus to cause Zeus to think. That's what the function of the Muses

19. Olson gives the wrong impression that the "Gravelly Hill" poem was the one published in the *Psychedelic Review*, whereas it was "Maximus, from Dogtown–IV," described in the next paragraph.

is. They're his daughters by his third or fourth wife, Memory. And those nine girls' job is to cause their father, God, to come up with more order, from knowing. In Avicenna's *Visionary Recital* we are told that there are two kinds of angels—there are the Guardians on the right, who know and order, and there are the Scribes on the left, who obey and act. And they are called the Scribes. In other words, from again Charles Peirce and American pragmatism, the poet today, an American poet, comes with a great preparation, which is, that if he obeys he writes. This is angelology, the back-to-back of anthropology, and the lacking half of all 19th-century thought, between Darwinian, Freudian, and Marxian and Einsteinian. I would like, instead of taking the latter of the pair, to read you now back-to-back the two "Maximus from Dogtowns," which open this book.

[Reads "Maximus, from Dogtown–I," followed without
comment by "All My Life I've Heard About Many," "A Note on
the Above," and "Maximus, from Dogtown–II" (II.2–10)]

… I said when I heard it, this is the first time since Henry Fielding's *Tom Jones* that the novel as novel, not as Creeley or as, say, Stendhal even, but the novel, the English novel has been restored in this fucking book by Bayliss![20] You wouldn't believe it, that guy! He was a floundering fluke five years ago. That magazine *Audience* in Cambridge was publishing him on myth and ritual and aesthetics, and he—as a matter of fact, I sat here in this house and didn't know what to do with the manuscript. I said to my wife, "Should I drop the boom or put it in the toilet?" I said, "The first sentence alone is enough to make me sick." And I didn't, and the guy—but I told him, one drunken winter night when I couldn't even walk up to his house the ice on Washington Street was so bad, you had to keep moving, like you were driving there. You'd understand, you're a good man but you don't know how to drive in the winter snows. You keep a steady speed, and you can go any speed you want, but you keep the fucking thing steady, dear.

[GAP]

Well, let's now then just shoot around this book a little, huh? I lost a little when I read that last poem I read [II.9–10], the "leap," "collagen time," that protein leap thing, which is sort of—the chemist would know what this is about, 'cos there is a kooky thing up. We've even gone so far that our chemistry today and our biology is farther out than our physics and our mathematics, or is farther out, forward from. Like metaphysics, again last night—it's curious. Mr Whitehead taught me a thing just two weeks ago that I never recognized: that what the 17th-century founders of modern scientific—I'm trying to get exactly his use—something tradition, literally, he says—I can't get over it—supplied man for the first time with that concept of subjectivity. Is this known, like? I mean, I never thought of it, honestly, that man prior—say, William Shakespeare did not have the idea of

20. Jonathan Bayliss's novel *Prologos* has now been published by Basilicum Press, Ashburnham, Massachusetts. His essay, "Ritual and Dramatic Poetry," appeared in *Audience* 7:4 (Autumn 1960), pp. 43–53.

subjectivity. It was not an equipment of the human species until, say, Descartes,[21] because—one poem I'd like, if I may, to read you now is a poem I first presented to John Wieners some years ago [1.128–32]. This book, by the way—you asked that question, Caroline—is composed from that. Well, I'll read the first one but it's practically the same as "Maximus, from Dogtown–I," which is just after the visit of Don Allen and David Cummings and LeRoi Jones and Michael McClure and Philip Whalen to this house, when both McClure and Whalen for the first time came from the Coast to the East. And I took them to Dogtown, and it was there that I saw that pile of—I can't get over it, that we went up, I took them up to this first field on that road, where in fact Merry fought that bull, and there was this pile of dumped fish, like a glistening, corpuscular jewel. I don't know how to describe it, because somebody had just dumped—I mean, Dogtown today is getting to be a dump! It's used at night, of course, for purposes of love, for years, and in the day for hunting and for berry-picking in the summers, in season, but curiously enough it's getting to be a dump, mattresses, a bureau ...

[GAP]

I would again today, again, because of my anger at this fucking decision at Laredo, Texas, like to read my poem that I wrote as a result of my spending the night after the mushroom—no, I think it was just when we were having breakfast in the "mushroom house" in Newton, Massachusetts, Mr Leary's beautifully perfect temple of truth. But of course the problem is whether you have a church. The greatest church in America, by the way, the North American Church, the Indian peyote church, was constitutionally declared a place for the use of peyote by the Supreme Court of California. And now this man who sought to subjectively create equal conditions for us all, like a barbershop or a drugstore, has been sentenced to thirty years in the federal pen for three ounces of marijuana, which itself, LaGuardia's commission in New York City proved, is absolutely non-habit-forming! The autonomic drugs do not form habits and lead therefore to the rackets of the Mafiosi, which is the sale of motor-driven drugs. The autonomic drug system includes: number one, peyote; number two, the sacred mushroom, or what is known to the Indians as—oh, wait a minute, I was even present in Yucatan, without even knowing it, to the Indians using the sacred mushroom. And I was so ignorant—as you told that beautiful story last night of the Korean old men holding pot in their hands with a little spark in it to smell the right drift of the wind and the pleasure of it, hm? Marijuana. LSD. The four great autonomic drugs. Autonomic nervous system. The sympathetic nervous system of the human race. And you know what in Nahuatl the mushroom is called? I can't even pron—but we sat here in this kitchen, Dr Leary, Dr Barron, and Mrs Dr Barron-to-be, and Mrs Olson and

---

21. As Butterick notes (*Muthologos* 1.230), Olson's copy of Whitehead's *Process and Reality* is annotated on p. 110 (p. 123 U.S. edn) with the date 24 February 1966 at a passage on "seventeenth-century founders" of the modern tradition.

me, the four of us. The fifth wheel was Mrs Barron, the daughter of a professor at Berkeley, the non-Catholic among us.

[GAP]

The truth of ugliness apparent. Beauty—I am interested in Truth. Beautiful Mr Keats said the only thing that's true is that Beauty and Truth—or Beauty—Truth is all you need to know and all, I think, you may know, or something, in this life. But that's it, those two things. And I believe that the American painters, namely Mr Pollock and Mr Kline, in 1948, and I'm of their time, solved the problem of how to live. The problem since has been how to be at all. And this is a more interesting problem, and it's being garbled and gobbled. In fact, I said to Allen Ginsberg after his reading in San Francisco, he's the fish that the little fish have eaten up. He himself has become like "many." The inscription to the *Maximus Poems*, which is inscribed to Robert Creeley, the first volume, is the second cook at Black Mountain—in the kitchen there were two cooks. One day I was in there alone at dawn when they were preparing breakfast. The chief cook was Malrey Few and the second cook was Constance Williams. And they were at both sinks in this large kitchen, and Constance Williams said, "All my life I've heard one makes many."

I'd like to read the poem which I wrote as of my first experience under the sacred mushroom, which in Nahuatl means "God's meat" or "God's *carne*." And to talk in this kitchen, which is two rooms away from us, with Dr Barron and Dr Leary and Dr Barron's future wife, who was then being instructed by a priest to marry him, as my father had to, to marry my mother—they were married not in the church but in the rectory, I assume—to these two masters of the giving to America of the mushroom I wanted to say that the translation of the Nahuatl word for the mushroom was "God's body." I said, "May I suggest that the earliest Spanish record of the translation of the Nahuatl is *carne*." And if you go to a market today and buy fresh meat you buy *carne*, that when you bite into the mushroom you bite, you absolutely take a chunk out of the body of God, and the bite—like a boy here, Mario Cardone, threw dirt at me, and I put him on the top of my automobile and I was going to spank him. Instead, I bit his side. And I had to go to the mother and say, "Look, excuse me …" His mother has eight children, my landlord, landlady, owner of this house. I said, "Gee, Suzy, I hope you're not offended. In my rage I bit your son! I'm a dog, and I excuse my mouth! I'm a poor child of the commons." [LAUGHS] So, here: "Peloria …"

[Reads "Peloria" (II.87)]

That's about just in the middle of the book, 1961. The book was started in 1959 and it was finished in 1963, Fall. And then a little extra piece called "Fort Point Section" which was written in June 1963 extra. An unbelievable passage also lies back-to-back, came across without putting the king to the queen. The book opens, "Letter #41 [broken off]."

[GAP]

The second book was on a thing called Dogtown. The third book, which I am now writing, is on I will not say. I'd like now to read this because it's fun once in a while to tell a story. And I did read you "All My Life I've Heard About Many" [II.7], and that's a creature who comes from over there and gets in the middle something, is buried in the Hill of Knockmany, and he got over here, and I said he got stuck on Cashes and then he vaulted the shoal. I'd love to read you the story of how that happened. It's called "Cashes."

[Reads "Cashes" (II.19)]

I'd really like, in honor of Mr Creeley, really, almost literally, to read one poem attached to that, and ties actually to what we've been really kind of poking around on, that which is the inertial and the metrical field as some men have it today, the thing which I deeply believe is the poet's competence today. If, say, "Descartes, age 33, date Boston's settling ...," which is the poem I did say I'd like to read to you, on John Winthrop [I.128–32], that I first offered to John Wieners for the second, I think, the one that was lost in the Atlantic and the poets of San Francisco raised $500 to replace and all sorts of things. Maybe that was *Measure* 3. John is one of those creatures that I— talk about the luck of the Irish!—one of my own. Despite the name Olson, I come also of the Church and the blood. And one of the biggest moments for me in this book is when I also told a story of ... [I.138–41]. Two men raised me, when I was five, at Stage Fort Park. One was named Louis Douglas, who's today eighty-one, and the other was named Frank Miles. And they married two Johnson sisters, the daughters of a captain, both Catholics, and neither Frank nor Lou was such. And their children, on both sides, were about my age. And when I was about four or five, those two men, being fishermen, knew where like what we would call today the breezeway was. There were two rocks outside the piazza of our camp, summer camp, at the border of Stage Fort Park, which is now known to me as Fishermen's Field, and when I was a little boy I used to see these men smoke and talk in the summer darkness on the two rocks where—and the only people that ever did it, had that quietness and fullness of nature to just sit where it was pleasant on a summer evening like Chinese or Japanese or any—or Italians or Mesopotamians or Hittites or Greeks or anybody that's ever lived on this earth knows that the earth is the geography of our being. And I used to listen to these men talk, and I grew up enough so they let me sit on the third rock and listen to them. And it isn't two months ago that, for the first time in my life, the older of the two brothers-in-law, Mr Douglas, came into this room. He brought me a cake from his wife, Ethel Johnson. And I said, "Won't you sit down?" And he said, "No." And he noticed my windows and walked in here, and three hours later—he sat where you're sitting now, Dick. And I listened to this eighty-one-year-old man tell me how he came—he left Newfoundland. He was born on an island off the coast, and had to get— you see, he had a stepfather and decided to leave, and went to the Bay of

Islands, and shipped aboard a Gloucester vessel and arrived here in 1902. I hear this for the first—and this man is the one human being beside poets that still uses language accurately, carefully, with beauty and truth. And I was—the shame of it—I'm fifty-five as we speak today, and I felt, right here—I sat here and he sat where you are, in that rocker, and I felt like a child again. It's hopeless. You pour it out, you try to build a—and you're in the presence of the fathers, and you dwindle as though God himself—because you know there isn't anything—you don't, you can't, you can only hide your eyes in the face of God. Let us be just, like, what we are: nothing, which is nothing but a human being. I mean, when you're in the presence of principles of the universe, you're nothing but this little squeak.

[GAP—scene shifts to outside the house]

No whiskey; no mail. What a town! I broke my machine in Lerma and I went into Campeche, and of course the guy who repairs typewriters—like you know the Greeks even still call their businesses in Washington, as against their house, "the store." Like gypsies. And you go in and you can get your typewriter repaired on Sunday anywhere else in the world, except … The seventh day, as we said earlier! [LAUGHS] Have you gotta match? Jesus, me neither. Oh, yes, I do.

[GAP—background conversation and cries of seagulls]

Vulcan, like. Apollo's father, Vulcan. We need that like a hole in our heads. We need neither Vulcan nor Apollo. We need only Heaven and Earth.

[GAP—walking on beach]

I walk here where the tracks is visc-tuchy, visc-tuchy.

[GAP]

C'mon, Angela.

ANGELA CARDONE: I forgot it.

OLSON: Nah, you didn't at all. Sing it.

ANGELA: I forgot it.

OLSON: You know that beautiful song she sang? I don't know who wrote it: "Love is something if you give it away …" I'm trying to do her voice. About three or four years ago [SINGS]: "Love is something if you give it away, give it away, give it away." You know, you get like "pennies from heaven" given back. You get the whole shot back. If you've got it, give it away. Don't you remember that?

ANGELA: No, I forgot it.

OLSON: Oh, Angela! I don't believe it!

Enthusiasm Greets Poets
Olson, Weiners, Sanders

A large, enthusiastic audience crowded the Haas Lounge last Tuesday evening, April 6, to hear a 'Dialogue" by Charles Olson, John Weiners, and Ed Sanders.

Poems" and "The Ace of Pentacles", his most recent book, including one entitled "To Ed Sanders and David Posner."

Ed Sanders, using a variety of

ED SANDERS

JOHN WIENERS

The program, which appeared as more a recital than a dialogue, was part of the Spring Arts Festival.

John Wieners, a graduate of Boston College and founder of the

CHARLES OLSON

magazine **Measure,** read seven selections from "The Hotel Wentley

vocal effects, read a portion of "Poem From Jail" and selection from ——————**You,** a literary magazine, and **Peace Eye,** a collection of poems published in Buffalo this year. Sanders is presently editor of a controversial magazine, **Marijuana Newsletter.**

Charles Olson read a sequence from **New Maximus** and his well-known poem "The Librarian". Upon request of John Weiners, Olson read an untitled poem written the past week.

The entire program, if not completely understood, was well-received. When talking with several students afterwards, Ed Sanders said he felt the audience to be very intelligent and sophisticated. He noted that the Buffalo area appears to be having a growth of interest in culture and art that is not merely an imitation of New York. He commented on the "genuine concern in arts" that is being shown in Buffalo and on the university campus.

The State University of New York, Buffalo, student newspaper, the *Spectrum,* 9 April 1965, two years before the Cortland talk.

9

Talk at Cortland

This talk was delivered on the day when many thousands of Vietnam War protestors, including Norman Mailer and Robert Lowell, were converging on the Pentagon. Ed Sanders was among them, and here Olson is celebrating him, in his absence, as the poet of activism, joining him with John Wieners as poets of "affect." The occasion of this talk on 20 October 1967 was a convocation of student poets at the State College of New York at Cortland, not far from Buffalo; so that there was a full contingent from the Buffalo campus where Olson had taught for two years (1963–65) and to where he was half expected to return. There was also a personal undercurrent involving a fracture to Olson's relationship with John Wieners, which was repaired during the weekend, this talk probably contributing to that end. For more details, see *Selected Letters*, pp. 389–90 and the introduction by Duncan McNaughton in *Minutes* 4 (March 1994). George Butterick, who was also there, describes the setting as "Olson's attempt to speak to the large, disparate gathering, after the tables had been cleared following the evening's banquet" (*Muthologos* II.1).

CHARLES OLSON: This isn't going to be easy, I don't think. I think poetry is— or at least I find it's become too easy, but then I sort of either fell off the nation or the wagon some years ago. And what I really propose to talk about tonight, actually, is—or at least try to make some attempt at trying to say where I think verse is and has been for something almost resembling ten years, and isn't actually what seems to me is what's now known as … (Am I being heard? Good.) That is, it seems as though there's so much of it as an easy thing that I am puzzled to start in on what I want to talk to you about, which was something that I would call "affect" as against "art." That is, in the terror of appearing here, it suddenly—I got relieved yesterday morning by realizing that I didn't have to have a subject, and that this is one of the matters that I mean by a change of … I have been reading in the last couple of years among the poets who seem to me always to have a subject in their poems, and this plus a politics is two of the kinds of poetry I think that you are, generally speaking—are those two that seem to be most evident at least. And I feel at this date of my, not of my life, actually, but of my experience, that it's breeding a peculiar condition of policy which is very distasteful to me. So, instead of actually trying to define that non-subject, I'd like to talk a little bit about what I mean.

And I've got to single out two poets, one of whom unfortunately is here tonight, whom I almost think is responsible for this thing that I'm calling "affect." The other man fortunately is missing because … The only time that Mr Wieners and I have ever read together was the first time, and it occurred in a little different situation from this, but at a State University of New York, happily in front of 450 girls, if I remember rightly.[1] And I had never met this other man that I want to talk about as two men that define a poetry that interests me more, I think, than those men whom I admire and have been attached to in earlier years, such as Mr Creeley, Mr Duncan, and I'm sure I'm forgetting others whom I believe in and am close to. It's lucky that the other person isn't here, and if John won't mind my speaking of him, even though he is here …

The other one is Ed Sanders. And the trouble with Sanders, we discovered that night, is that he's got the—Mr Sanders, as I think many of you will know, is the creator of the Fugs, and already has the new public style, or had it. Was it three years ago that this happened? Two and a half, two and a half years ago. I never read with Wieners until two and a half years ago and I've never read with him since. And I had never met Mr Sanders, and I didn't realize that he had this new style. Well, fortunately, a year ago he came to see me with the drum, drummer—"drum" you call him?—the drum of the Fugs, a fellow named Ken Weaver from the Gulf Coast, who is a spontaneous non-poet poet. Sanders, however, is a well educated man like the rest of us [LAUGHTER], and particularly valuable to me because it's in Classics.

I happily once translated the—in fact, if it weren't such a short evening and a restless one, I could read you—it's the fourth of four long poems called "Maximus, from Dogtown" [II.163–72]; and it happens to be a translation mainly of a passage from the *Theogony* of Hesiod. Well, I know no Greek. The poem was published by Mr Leary in the second issue of the *Psychedelic Review*, and I deliberately of course put that poem in there to prove that you just need poetry to get strung out, and all this stuff was just something that you used if you hadn't known anything yet, especially hadn't any particular senses to begin with. And then Mr Sanders at this meeting that took place in Buffalo, two and a half years ago, mind you, asked me if I would translate the *Theogony* for his then magazine or—not his magazine. That was that magazine that was stopped in New York City by the police because of its title. But he actually has a publishing house by the same name—like, it is the same name, isn't it, the publishing house? Isn't it? *Fuck You*—does it say "a publishing house" instead of "a Magazine of the Arts"? In any case, I said, "Well, look, Ed, I can't translate it because I don't have any Greek." And he went on; and, in fact, this Frontier Press, which also grew out of this New York State that all of us are a part of or have been, that

---

1. While a professor in the English Department at the State University of New York at Buffalo, Olson invited both John Wieners and Ed Sanders to join him for a poetry reading on 6 April 1965.

is simply some electronic control of the possibility of the Governor of the state being President, I'm sure. At least it can make New York catch up with California.

I do want to go back to a date which is a date I think most of you know as a sort of a crucial date of ten years ago, eleven years ago this year, '56. I'd like, in order to say—let me still use that word "affect," uh?—to define this as against other changes, another change, at least, that happened in '56. You know, we live in a time which is very easy itself. That's been quite increasingly conspicuous for the last ten years, and it has been in just those ten years that poets like Wieners and Sanders have, I think, just taking them as two horns of the head or two heads of a new sort of a beast, appeared. If I had Mr Sanders's first book here, *Peace Eye*, published by the Frontier Press in Buffalo, I could try, I think, to show you even a date at which Mr Sanders himself seems almost to have been turned on by the ground.

I'll go back to something of Mr Wieners's in that respect, but he comes from Boston. You can hardly talk about Boston as a ground. And I come from around Boston, so ... I was forced some years ago to sort of specialize in a place and maybe, in other words, to live long enough to be here now to create a person, and then start writing a poem of a person, and a place, and isolating myself to that. And because I'm the one that's here and getting paid so much money to do this, I'll read some of my own poems in a few minutes, instead of reading either Mr Wieners's or Mr Sanders's, because Mr Wieners, I understand, will read on Sunday anyhow, and maybe, if I stay over, I'll read some of Mr Sanders on Sunday, instead of myself, therefore I can get a crack at you twice.

I'd like, actually, in order to go any further, to ask, generally speaking, if—how much familiarity—would you literally just sort of raise your hands if you know the work of either of those men? How much Sanders, say? The poet, not the—oh, it's mean to say, but I don't mean, actually, the Fugs, his Fugs records, but the actual poetry. Yes? And how many, how much Mr Wieners then? The same. Similar. Hm. See, it's not going to be easy, as I feared.

I think, then, I can now give you a little bit of what I mean by—I was pretty struck, and I'm still trying to buy the books. I understand I can't even get the one that I need. Some of you may have seen this book, just published, or you may have seen the review, which is all I have, of a book of Miss Stein's—a book on Miss Stein called *Gertrude Stein and the Present*. Anybody notice that book being published this summer? It called to my attention a book of Miss Stein's I'd never heard of, called *The Geography of North America*—do I have it right? *A Study*—or something—*of Human Nature and the Human Mind*, subtitle? It's the book I find that Gordon Cairnie says, "You fool, you can't even buy it, it's ..."[2]

2. Subsequently, Harvey Brown, who was in the audience at Cortland, found for Olson a copy of Gertrude Stein's *The Geographical History of America or the Relation of Human Nature to the Human Mind* (NY: Random House, 1963). The review referred to was of Allegra Stewart's *Gertrude Stein and the Present* (1967) by Robert Gorham Davis in the *New York Times Book Review* of 3 September 1967, pp. 5, 16, a clipping of which Olson had with him to quote from.

GEORGE BUTTERICK: It's in the library at Buffalo.

OLSON: Oh, but I, you know, I never read books that I can't keep for ever. What struck me was that Miss Stein—first of all, hear that title, *The Geography of the United States: A Study of Human Nature and the Human Mind*. But if this reviewer is right, Miss Stein defines her two subjects in this book: "geography" and the "dictionary." And geography "represents history, individual limitation, personal memory, existence, and human nature"; and the dictionary "represents words, transcendence, genius, creative novelty, discontinuity, and human mind." May I, because I think I value so enormously these distinctions of hers, and I'm offering to you really instead of my own thought simply because I find that she seems so interesting, like: geography "represents history, individual limitation, personal memory, existence, human nature"; and the dictionary "represents words, transcendence, genius, creative novelty, discontinuity, and human mind." I take Miss Stein in this lead because, to some people present, I myself have done nothing but talk about topology and etymology for, well, for the last five or seven years, and have found myself in the last seven years paying attention almost exclusively, except for a few poets who write and strictly are Americans, that is, in our time—I mean, in our time I think only American poets are of any interest whatsoever. There's beautiful poets alive, like Ungaretti and Patrick Kavanagh and—well, there's two poets I think of—but, I mean, when I read them I find I turn to my fellow-Americans, the few whom I think are actually of this attention that I'm trying to bring you to, of "affect."

I live now where I was raised, in a city which was once the chief fishing port of the world and had at the point of its highest rise a population of 25,000, which it still has, exactly. In other words, it's the most paralyzed possible spot in these last seventy years. It's almost as though you had a dead bullseye. It's so much so that the other day when I went into the pharmacy and for what reason suddenly realized that the whole city is dead, and rushed up to see a poet who edits a magazine there, named Lansing, to tell him we've won: history has proved itself to be the liveliest thing there is. Now hear that again as of Miss Stein calling it "geography." And also, if you will accept my statement of my own excitement, it was so beautiful that I was able to write ever since, again. And I will read you one new poem and three or four others of the last couple of years (avoiding some poems which haven't been published yet), which have been written in this whole period that I speak of that at least we could call "the period of Sanders."

Those of you who do know Sanders I hope do know his very first poem, which was published by Ferlinghetti, called *Poem from Jail*, a pamphlet poem. I would advise anybody in this room, if you're interested in what I'm saying, as a "habit" and a true "haunt," a true "haunt"[3] ... If everything has gotten easy so has the idea that it's easy to be a human being, to be a free human being, and therefore "haunts" and "habits" are running loose. But an

---

3. Olson is reminded of Hesiod's *ethea*, the Greek word behind "ethics." The definition Olson had found in his Greek dictionary included the two words he uses here: "haunt" and "habit."

actual "haunt" and an actual "habit" is not an easy thing to have, I mean, to keep, I mean, to have so that you finally have it. And it's truly what everybody's after, it's all that counts.

A man came to see me last night to ask me to a Halloween party, and he asked me about a—there's a poet in Gloucester whom we all regard as a poet, or a—his name is Vincent Ferrini, and he just published a book called *I Have the World*, published in London. And the man said to me, apropos some remark of mine, "But do you know his poem 'The Garden of—,' 'The Garden of—'?" What's the final, the greatest thing? Not Armageddon, but— or apotheosis, but "Garden of—"? What's the most ultimate thing of all, the cliché of the—?

ROBERT HOGG: Of Allah?

OLSON: Allah? No, no, no, no, it would be, you know, it would be abstract.

VOICE: Not the Garden of Eden?

OLSON: No, no, that's the whole point, I mean. "The Garden of what"? You know, like these guys, like Teilhard, and progressive, the end, the great end, the Omega. "The Garden of what?"

DUNCAN MCNAUGHTON: The Apocalypse.

OLSON: Yeah! "The Garden of the Apocalypse," yeah. "Oh, my god," I said. I read the poem quickly. I said, of course, just what you said: the Garden of Eden always is it. You can't just figure it's, you know, it's going to be a result of policy. It's—it is. No, I could even put you on, even really put you on to the Garden of Eden. I know where it is; I know how—I know where yours is; I mean, you know, there's no problem. These big essential things are not—they're not going to run away, and then—and you can't just sort of arrive there by fine new ways of travel.

The reason why I stress the first Sanders poem is that it's one of the most extraordinary poems, I'm sure, such as you yourselves write and dream of, a new poem, a young poem, and not too good a poem, that's sort of, like, as such, enormously derived from Allen Ginsberg; and this not only gives the poem some of its power but, in fact, takes nothing from the poem. (I might have one line, effect on one line, maybe. There's something in it he says I— he picked up.) But it's a very beautiful poem; I think it's one of the essential poems that exist. I lived with it for a year on my kitchen table and found that I was more turned to—I would turn to it like the—well, there's a daily story in the *Boston Globe*, "Up on the Here," and it's that kind of a poem: you just depend upon it. Then I discovered, when I looked at *Peace Eye*, the first interesting poem is written on that peace march that occurred from— was it New Orleans to Washington? Can anybody help me? The poem is written in sort of Roanoke on a motel stop, like a lot of people in America are on tonight. But this was, as is peculiarly true of Sanders—as far as the political activity of our time, Sanders is almost always earliest on the calendar. Would you agree to that, John, in your experience? Both as of the South and—what?

JOHN WIENERS: [INAUDIBLE]

OLSON: No, this was—no, this was a bigger and a—it was the first peace march, I think, of the—it was '61, I'm pretty sure. You know that poetry that dates from '61, is dated '61? Nashville, maybe, is what it—there's one—what poem am I thinking of? Can you give me the—? It's one of the "Soft Man" poems, I think, I'm speaking of.[4] I say that because I myself went through an enormous satisfaction of getting poems I wanted, in that same period of time.

Mr Wieners, I think, precedes us all in writing poetry of the order that I'm speaking of, by several years, actually. The *Wentley* poems, I mean, I'm not even thinking of them, but thinking of the time you called me on that poem that Crozier published, as of your mother, the cigarette poem,[5] and you said that you wrote that in '56? Yeah. That seems to me to almost be— if you take this other level, beside the usefulness of Sanders in defining activity, Mr Wieners in defining what is normal, if I may say so, literary life-time. Would you accept that? A characteristic poet's life. In fact, to tell you the truth, the reason why I mention Mr Sanders coming last year with his drummer was that he then told me that he and others were faced with the problem of inventing an "art song." And that seems to me almost, if I didn't trust Sanders, to be the end of it all, [LAUGHS] not the end of what I'm talking about, but the end of what I valued so much about Sanders, except that the Frontier Press now has his second volume of poems, and I trust the publisher and he says it's a better book than *Peace Eye* so that I guess his search for "art song" was simply having to do with the Fugs and records.

Well, I've worked myself into that marvelous track of having forced the poems to be incapable of being themselves because they now have to prove something. I'm very—that's very—that's a very awful thing that's happened. I've done this before, but it never obviously came this close to being a bad end. In fact, in order, actually, to give you my whole pitch of some time ago in a poem itself, I'd like to read you "Letter—," one of the *Maximus* poems that was withheld, "Letter …" (Excuse me, I'm able only to find this.) "Letter 27," "Maximus to Gloucester, Letter 27." I should have asked how many of you people even know my own work, especially the *Maximus Poems*, the first volume of which was published in 1960, and actually does tell rather a story about this city, Gloucester, and this person who addresses himself, named Maximus, to the city. And this one is out of place; it's purposely held from—it was written around 1952, and hasn't yet been published in book form. It was written in 1952, wasn't it?

VOICE: … published …

OLSON: In the *Yale Review* only, isn't that true? Yeah. No, I see yesterday that Kelly's got it in that *Controversy of* anthology, thought he'd run it. So that

4. "Soft-Man 10" in Ed Sanders's *Peace Eye* (Buffalo: Frontier Press, 1965) is dated at the end "Apr 27–May 7–62. Nashville-Wash DC Walk for Peace."
5. Wieners's "Poem" ("As I put out my cigarette tonight in bed") was included by Andrew Crozier in the "American Supplement" of *Granta* (7 March 1964).

I'm deliberately here actually doing a re—how do you say a "cut back" or a "retake"?—both in terms of its date of writing but, as I say, it's never been enclosed in a book, which is much—it's almost ten years later.

[Reads "Maximus to Gloucester, Letter 27 (withheld)"
(II.14–15)]

A poem both in subject and in expression was there. I mean, if a poem of sum was written. And I've—I kicked this whole thing you're in two years ago. I flew out; I just couldn't even get away from the motel. I took a cab and went to the airport, and then wrote a letter to the chairman of the department that said I had left. And I have been writing a few poems since, and those were what I wanted to read you: just how it might be to go home, in just the kind of a hole that I either live in or am in or choose to be, which is, if you do know Greek, what an *ethos* is. Because there are some friends here tonight, who have grown friends and dearest friends, I certainly want to read one poem which has never been seen and never heard before, which is the companion poem to the one I just read, called "The Ridge," and which will some day, if I still regard it as I still find I do, fifteen years old tonight— and the daughter who's referred to was sixteen on Monday, so you can judge how much, how old she was there in the occasion of the poem.

[Reads "The Ridge"[6]]

The first poem I wrote, I think, after I got out of New York State, or the other end of it ...

WIENERS: Are you never coming back?

OLSON: I guess I ... I'm here. Right. I think I ought to finish that "Buffalo Ode," you know; like, I mean, those trains and Indians have to get home sometime.

"Maximus, in Gloucester Sunday, LXV." Well, I should say, because now the problem of names suddenly arises, it was Robert Creeley that seems to most have called my attention to the fact that I, in writing him a letter once, which he published in a book called the *Mayan Letters*, had said that "change now is substantive." You know how he writes; you know, you feel that you can write, so you write. No, no, I mean, you want to write, so you write something. I wrote that, and I didn't—then I heard it back from him, thank god; and it's been—I mean, I've been living with it ever since. That is, I do believe in proper nouns, and I can't get over the fact that the dictionary, for example,—it's again why I respect Miss Stein on what words are as "transcendence, genius," everything else, including "human mind"—that *Webster's Dictionary* still doesn't list proper names or proper nouns. Every day I get more and more defeated by that: why aren't proper nouns in the same dictionary as common, as a common word? Well, I happen to drive

---

6. This poem was passed over for *Maximus IV,V,VI*, but was sent to Robin Blaser for publication in *Pacific Nation* 2 (February 1969). See also *OLSON* 6 (Fall 1976), pp. 47–51 for an earlier and longer version, with Butterick's notes. When Olson goes on to refer to "the first poem I wrote" he is beginning to introduce "Maximus, in Gloucester Sunday, LXV."

people crazy by, as you will find in the last poem I'll read, which is the last poem was written day before yesterday, how I do use people's names. But these in this poem and, as you've discovered, the other poem of mine …

[Reads "Maximus, in Gloucester Sunday, LXV" (III.79–80)]

That, I think, was written before I had finally left New York. This is written direct—this is written afterwards, in the sign of Scorpio, in the month of November, 5, 1965: "Maximus of Gloucester."

[Reads "Maximus of Gloucester" (III.101)]

And just for the ride of it, well, I think I'll read in the honor of Mr Creeley's daughter's presence, which is so attractive as ever she meant to me one night two years ago in public little larger than this. This poem also has never been seen or heard. I've never read it myself. But Mr Creeley unfortunately stood me up, unbelievable, one night, and I had left my house and got the hell out of there in the secrets of these events of this year, two years ago, to meet him, and from then I was to go to the roof—my own point of view.[7] I had my car, my bag, and the house was closed. And the day I returned from Magnolia and read "The Binnacle" again as printed by Robert Creeley in the *Albuquerque Review*, December 28, 1961: the title is "Got me home, the <u>light</u> / snow gives the air, falling."

[Reads "Got me home, the <u>light</u> / snow gives the air,
falling"(III.127)]

Yeah, just for the joy/juice of it, I will risk this poem, which I'm not sure I— I'm not sure it doesn't show up my charge upon the year 1956 and why I prefer poetry of another order but here. It's called "The winter the <u>Gen. Starks</u> was stuck." Today so few people know Stark. Stark was the hero of the battle of the Fort. Hm, you got it, no? Hero of—one of the great Revolutionary heroes. And this particular vessel, Gloucester vessel, was, you know, booked for his privateer in the Revolution. In fact, this is the winter—I discover from reading recently about Indians again in this area (I picked the books up in the Olean Public Library) that it was the same damn year the English trying to use the Indians on this frontier and the actual Americans crossing further into Kentucky and to southern Ohio, Illinois, the rivers was frozen solid, the Allegheny, for example, was frozen to the bottom, and it was a— the winter was, I think, 1798–79–1799?[8] And I picked this one up just locally. I'm hoping I'm interesting you.

[Reads the first few lines of "The winter the <u>Gen. Starks</u> was
stuck" (III.105)]

Yeah, I don't like this kinda talk; I don't like it any more. I'll read you something else instead, a poem which has also not been—it's just about to be

7. These circumstances have not been elucidated.
8. John Stark (1728–1822) was a general of the War of Independence. We know, from overdue notices, what books Olson picked up from Olean, NY, public library on about 20 September 1967 after visiting Joyce Benson in Oxford, Ohio. They include Dale Van Every's *A Company of Heroes: The American Frontier, 1775–1783* (1964), which provided information on 1779, the year in question.

published, but I have never read it, and I don't think persons present here know it. Hope I can make it. Doesn't really matter; don't be thrown by that. It's like cards; I mean, there's quite a few in the deck. Only, there's only seventy-two, you know what I mean. But, I mean, that's quite a few. And I have one here … I'm getting a little tired of this … would you mind if I read this one sitting down? Then I'll read the last one, hopefully, standing up. This shows you—I mean, it's a little bit like that first one I read you—it shows you how much, even if I say I don't believe in—I certainly don't believe in subject. I certainly do, however, believe in judgment, and I believe judgment is *dotha* and dogmatic, and I think it follows as fast as our senses, within a very short split second. But I also … I don't know if I'll say any more about that now. This is written a year ago, Thursday, June 16, 1966, and the title is "AN ART CALLED GOTHONIC."

[Reads "AN ART CALLED GOTHONIC" ending with "corners" (II.168–72)]

Yeah, that's it, I guess. I was afraid there was more. That's the end. Excuse me for blowing it there. Yeah.[9]

And I will close by reading the latest of the *Maximus*, which is very peculiarly cap-titled "(LITERARY RESULT)," but in parenthesis; capitalized, underlined,[10] and in parenthesis: "(LITERARY RESULT)."

[Reads "(LITERARY RESULT)" (III.184)]

Thank you. [APPLAUSE]

9. Olson was right: there was more, certainly as published, but apparently not in the manuscript he was reading from.
10. "(LITERARY RESULT)" was not underlined as printed.

The Eaton Chapel, Beloit College, the venue for Olson's lectures.
Photo courtesy Beloit College Archives.

Poetry and Truth

As George Butterick explained in the separate publication of these Beloit College lectures, *Poetry and Truth* (San Francisco: Four Seasons Foundation, 1971), Professor Chad Walsh's introduction on the first evening was not preserved on tape, but he responded to a request to write "A Retrospect" for the volume, which is excerpted below:

> Olson gave three formal lectures, as well as a reading of his poetry. Formal is perhaps not the word. The setting was formal enough— the college chapel which also serves for secular events when a big audience is expected. But I recall no prepared manuscript, and I'm not at all sure he had any notes, though possibly they were on scraps of paper that were too small to be visible where I was sitting. He gave the impression of someone thinking as he went along. It was as though he were wrestling with some demon of language, trying to put into words the ideas that already existed in a preverbal state. Often there would be long pauses. Once he spent several minutes rifling through the chaotic contents of a cloth book bag, looking for a short quotation which seemed to be the key to a point he wanted to make.
>
> By the end of the first lecture, he had turned off the great majority of the faculty, who—mostly registered PhDs and trained in common logic—could not make heads nor tails of his remarks. The students reacted in a more complex way. Many who could not have summarized what he said still followed him from lecture to lecture, and by the end there was a small but intense band of disciples who pursued him and seemed to know exactly what he meant by even the most non-Euclidean statements.

Monday evening, 25 March 1968

CHARLES OLSON: I debated for many weeks, in preparing for these lectures, whether to tell Mr Walsh that the title had a subtitle. And this afternoon when somebody said, "You certainly gave yourself plenty of room," I thought I should have done it, because it would have at least straightened things out. But actually I left it that way because I've dreamed all my life of the title. If you know a man whom I have the same reason you do to admire—Mr Goethe did write a book called *Dichtung und Wahrheit*, and I always wanted to get that transfer over into English, of simply "Poetry and Truth."[1] But I did intend to tell, and now will, that the subtitle is "The Dogmatic Nature of Experience." And I propose to handle it in three shapes or circles, unquestionably more circular than shapely, and now I will satisfy that lad that said to me today, "You certainly are giving yourself plenty of room." The first evening, that is, tonight, does propose to be "Cosmology." And the other two would be "Belief I" and "Belief II." So that I really do mean Truth. (Can you hear me? This thing is too low for me. [LAUGHTER] Can you hear me?) I do mean Truth, and in a very simple sense. I hope I even have my definition of it. But I mean Truth in the solemnest meaning of Truth. I don't need any room at all. In fact, if I've had any result of the weeks and months that I've been anticipating being here just right now, it has been poems; and that's about as much as I could bring to you, and I can't do that because I have to *tell* you something as well. I will, however, read at least one poem that came from this, in order to get my chance at you ahead of time. But I would like very much to see if I can, rather than try to talk of poetry as we could and we have already today in a couple of instances, talk of what's up. I'm more interested in seeing if I can give you my sense of where it counts and is going.

And it struck me that it would be useful to try to lay out to you this shift which I see as having happened right recently, and that I think is of such an order that poetry as being written today, especially by or in our language, yields a future that is unknown, is so different from the assumptions that poetry has had, in our language, that the life that one lives is practically the condition of the poetry rather than the poetic life being a thing in itself. And one could almost say that these two words today have practically flown together, flowed, I mean, flowed together.

I think I'll start, actually, with a dry poem which just in fact arrived from the printers Thursday, because actually it was a moment of thinking of being here tonight that, in fact, I rolled up into this piece of paper. And in order to give you the title's reference, I'd like to read, if I have it with me, a poem written in 1963. [SEARCHES AMONG PAPERS] I don't know why I have to even seek to find it; I think I remember it. Tomorrow night I will be reading from a book which is in press, the *Maximus Poems IV, V, VI*. The poem I'm reading you now, reciting you now, is the opening poem of a third volume, which started in 1963, and is simply this epigraph: "To write a Republic in gloom on Watchhouse Point" [III.92]. And this poem that I wrote for you, I wrote because I was to be here, is called, "*Added to making a Republic in gloom on Watchhouse Point" [III.190]:

1. It is Goethe's title in itself that Olson is interested in (he did not own the book) and what Goethe said of it to Eckermann: "a *fact* in our life means nothing in so far as it is *true*, only in so far as it is of *consequence*"—quoted in "A Letter to the Faculty of Black Mountain College" *OLSON* 8 (Fall 1977) p. 31 and also to Robert Creeley at the same time, March 1952 (*Olson-Creeley Correspondence* 9, p. 213), where the implication is that only poetry "with sufficient intensity" can press truth into having the power of consequences.

an actual earth of value to
construct one, from rhythm to
image, and image is knowing, and
knowing, Confucius says, brings one
to the goal: nothing is possible without
doing it. It is where the test lies, malgre
all the thought and all the pell-mell of
proposing it. Or thinking it out or living it
ahead of time.

And it's inscribed, "Reading about my world, March 6, 1968."

Well, that's my present, the dry paper, for you, to begin our voyage. What I want actually, then, to try to do tonight is to see if I can suggest what I mean by "an actual earth of value." I'm being awkward and stupid because I have done it all, as far as I'm concerned, up to the moment of time, in poetry, and I don't know how to talk about what one has done. I think, myself, we have entered—there's one way of talking about what I think I'm here to do is to suggest that words about it are no longer equal to the use-fulness of our own action, or, if it is poetry, our poems.

This, then, lays the burden on the poem. But if I say, "an actual earth of value"—and that's a dry, small "e"—I do mean an earth, the Earth. And I think, if you can bear it, I'd like to read a terribly rough poem in which I tried to invest what I called "cosmology" as a subject tonight, which is a spiritual condition which I think many people in this room have already known in other ways, which is to get around on the other side of the nature of anything, especially, like, what we now can call our experience, and not mean something that's subjective, but is common. I happen, as a poet, to be interested in what is the old word, I think, for creation as a structure, which is that word "cosmology." I got to it in a series of visions or dreams similar to other men whom I propose even to draw your attention to tonight. The most classic case we've had of the poets, I wanted to say the pre-poets, is Mr Yeats's remarkable experience in later years, on the train between San Francisco and Los Angeles shortly after his marriage. I think you probably do know *A Vision* by Mr Yeats. May I just mention it as of an event which occurred—what? He was then about fifty? I think it must have been in—oh yes, I do know even—sort of in the twenties. He married, I think, around 19—somebody here must know what I'm—the date of that? I think 1921, possibly, is the … His first version of it was published, I believe, in 1924. He realized he wrote the whole thing wrong. He got the messages wrong, and then rewrote it and published the thing as he found out he was more right in 1928. Am I about right? Professors in this room, I'm sure—? In any case, if you don't know it, I just mention it as a fantastic instance of recorded vision. It was his wife, suddenly, that in another berth, started talking in her sleep. And it was suddenly a body of doctrine that was being given to him by persons who called themselves the—oh, wait a minute, they called them-selves "we," really. I'm thinking of the most remarkable instance of "We are bringing you images for your verse." If I'm not mistaken, it's exactly the—

or is it? Do I have this right? Yes, I think so. And Yeats—it was quite an exhaustion, three years, and they finally had to ask the messages, messengers, to come at other hours than at night. And they did. And it was afternoon, and the transcripts which Yeats would do were through her voicing of it. I mean, mind you, I hope I can keep this this side of mediumism. But I think if you know the poetry of Mr Yeats that resulted from it, you'll hear me speak of this as a serious, early instance in poetry and in the West of a change which I myself was prompted just a few minutes ago at dinner to say emerged as the archaic in 1961 or '2 and is now in furtherance of itself. And though it would take some close work, I wish that we also this week might get at—and if not here in these lectures, at other points, smaller points— some poetry that I could show of others that I think has some of the signs of this. It turns out to be rather difficult and sometimes obscene poetry. In fact, in one case, remarkably obscene, so totally that in publishing it myself, in his next book,[2] I had to even create a fund to fight the legal results, and it runs into $25,000, at least, if we get swacked, like they say. I mean it's so dirty that [LAUGHTER]—I put it that way just, not to tickle your appetite, because I can give it to you anytime you want it, but simply because I just want to put Mr Sanders side by side with Mr Yeats as evidence of how far things have moved in the pre-archaic and into the present archaic period. I also say that, as I say, a little bit to anticipate that difficult thing I propose to do, which is to read this poem, which as far as I know is un-understandable. However, the other poet whom I wish to suggest to you as a readable man in what I call the archaic was kind enough once near Peter Cooper Village there on the east side of the city—what's that, Avenue C, I think?—in a little greasy joint said he was interested in what I had done.[3]

This poem was first published, deliberately, in the *Psychedelic Review*. I was asked to publish a poem by those young editors, who were aware that we all had come under the mushroom experiment. (This was pre-acid time.) And I was so completely—I so believe that poetry requires a scalar eventuality, and that this poem was at least for me an evidence that I had been used, and that I got—you'll see, it's a—you'll see how I come a cropper and end wherever anyone might, but where a poet cannot, may not. But I wanted it as an evidence of the process of poetry as approaching truth with no other guise than itself. And I chose, it chose to express itself as of the Earth. I think, in fairness to you all, I ought to read a more immediately hearable poem, which is its twin. I've been writing this thing called *The Maximus Poems* for about twenty years, and I come from a city to which these poems are addressed, a seaport in Massachusetts, which was once the largest fishing port in the world and still shows signs of it as urban renewal goes into its third, second hitch. And in the beginning of the 18th century, in the first growth, first leap of population which has—which you all are

2. Olson had written a foreword for Ed Sanders's book *Peace Eye* having recommended it to Harvey Brown for publication by Frontier Press of Buffalo.
3. Presumably LeRoi Jones, who lived in the Peter Cooper Village area of New York City.

Malthusian[4]—this place was spilled over to, and was known in its own day, curiously, as what it's known as today, which is Dogtown. And this is "Maximus, from Dogtown–I." And the poem that I mentioned, that I want to reach, is "Maximus, from Dogtown–IV." I'd like tonight to shoot these two at you so we have a ground of my sense of tonight's subject of cosmology, if I have to label myself with that damn title. It opens with a "proem."

[Reads "Maximus, from Dogtown–I" (II.2–6)]

[APPLAUSE] Thank you. I read that to you in order to see if I can read this much different and much harsher, or rougher, poem. I wonder if I could have a drink of water? I didn't—I lost a great deal of the rhythm in that poem, I think, and the only thing we got is rhythm, so, better try it. I mean that as of our subject, in that poem I read, the small one I read you that just was printed this past week, "an actual earth of value to / construct one, from rhythm to / image, and image is knowing, and / knowing" [III.190], and so forth. I'll come back to that in closing tonight, as of what I mentioned earlier of mythology as what the poets turn. I was interested today with a remark of Sven Featherstone's, that theology—he mentioned theology in the same way I was in fact interested in trying to pair it for you tonight, if we were going to attack this thing as archaic now; and I may, because I had planned, actually, to quote you a man who lives, by the way, in Wisconsin— yeah, wow, I must try to even see him this week! I've never met him, and have been completely captured by his essay on Norse religion in a remark- able book which I have with me, on *Ancient Religions*, published by, edited by Dagobert Runes.[5] It's the Philosophical Library, I think it's called, curious series of books, and this one's remarkable for an essay on Norse which is essentially the source of my mythol ... I'm not playing a game with you, but if I spent the time to explain instead of showing you the poem, we'd be nowhere, or we can do it later in the week, or at various places or some- thing. But you will hear, this one is an attempt on my part, some years after that other, to try to cope with what I'm, in a sense, arguing or hopefully pro- posing, no? I'm convinced that we are now engaged in taking to ourself an earth of value. This is "Maximus, from Dogtown–IV":

[Reads "Maximus, from Dogtown–IV" (II.163–72)]

[APPLAUSE] You're very generous. Wasn't too bad, as a matter of fact. The best I ever read the damn thing. [LAUGHTER] Seems such a labor. I'm sorry, I really—something there, but it's on the page if it's there at all. Well, thank you, I really—you tolerated me. Something I really—well, that's my vision of it anyhow, I mean that's my vision of the physical thing, and the texture and the condition of love as it was then possible to say it.

---

4. Olson was aware that Thomas Malthus's *An Essay on the Principle of Population* (1798) had utilized statistics from "the northern states of America" in proposing the geometric increase of populations.

5. One of Olson's companion books was *Ancient Religions*, edited by Vergilius Ferm for the Philosophical Library series (1950) under the supervision of Dagobert Runes. The particular contribution referred to is Murray Fowler's "Old Norse Religion."

I want now to add a third poem, before sending you home with a fourth, which has appeared recently in a new magazine called the *Pacific Nation*, published in Vancouver, British Columbia. In order to pass to that, though, I can't take that step, I think, without coming back to that question of a poet's images and his coming into possession of them, leading him to something that we too familiarly know as mythology and that today are terribly prone to speak of mythology as though it was a social condition, when I'm convinced mythology has never been anything but, as I said earlier just a few minutes ago, the turning point, like theology. And I mean theology in a very stiff and curious way that leads eventually or possibly to what I have called—and in fact the hero in this last poem was straight stealing from Hesiod's cosmology via both Norse additions or retentions from earlier Indo-European, what we call Indo-European myth and I'm trying to call "cosmology"—to the question which I'm sure any one of you is more lost in, as I am: how do you, how as a person, not only as a poet, does one live one's own image, rather than use it simply for writing, which has been a three-hundred-year problem in English and now is broken? And we now are determined to make our image of a union of ourself, I think, and have no other choice, whether we'd like it or not, an obdurate or, as I say, an archaic time or condition. And the poem that I wrote two years ago was an attempt to bring this thing closer and try to talk as though it was "I" rather than some creature like I said I call "Maximus," who's been the person that's presided on those two poems. And yet the poem I'm reading is what I now call, continue to call, a *Maximus* poem, and is a part of that book that I said is "making a Republic on Watchhouse Point." This is written in 1966, and it opens with a bracket, which never ends, so it doesn't matter. But there isn't another bracket, so don't mind. In other words, the bracket is very important, but it doesn't—it just encloses everything.

[Reads "[to get the rituals straight" (III.173–74)]

[APPLAUSE] Am I all right on time, or am I pushing against it? How much have I used?

VOICE: It's 9:15.

OLSON: So we're running almost it would be on the nose, then? I'd like to read one more, if I may, just to complete the picture. I realize, happily, that I have made my thing. I don't know whether you can see it or not, but I mean, literally, that poem was why I labored you through those other two long Dogtowns. [LAUGHS] And I'd like again to be difficult. Excuse me for this enormous prefatory evening. Happily, you never write poems in time, thank god. They write very swiftly, as you know, then you have to live with them. I hope I can. I'm awfully tempted to read you this thing just because I think it will bring me home as well as, hopefully, send you out happily. The only thing is, I've only got this in manuscript. My own publisher has never managed to get a satisfactory ... Yeah, here it is. I obviously want to put out about five legs and let them sit right down on the floor tonight, because this one is the attempt to now raise the thing back to the thing that we call "poetry as art," and define that too. So that we've done, if I may, if I may just read my lesson backwards—I mean, in this, as I said originally, the circular rather than a shapely lecture or lectures, that's what I've got is a five-legged chair, I think, if I offer this to you. This is written on Thursday, right after this poem which was the one I just read you, which was written on—oh, there's no date, I don't know—the same day or two. "Thursday, June 16, 19—" I dated that. What was the date there, June 19? It's pre-this.

[Reads "AN ART CALLED GOTHONIC" (III.168–72)]

[APPLAUSE] Thank you. Let me just say one word before … Thank you, and actually it's like ground hamburger, but that's ground, and we got something, I hope. Thank you. [APPLAUSE]

Oh yes, and though I see that Chad has left short on the idea of questions, I'd be happy to have you poke at these poems. I've done this once before and quite the other way. And there's a tape, I can even play to you, or read you the whole damn thing, where I did the terrible thing of taking poems and trying to make them prove something that's a point.[6] Which I tried tonight to do in a different way and less directly, and I'd be happy if anybody wanted to stay and push me. I mean, the poems are either good or bad; I mean, it's up to our push to find out.

Wednesday evening, 27 March 1968

DAVID M. STOCKING: I do hope the author of *Call Me Ishmael* won't take offense if I introduce him by quoting a few words from a "rival" of his, but I thought one of the things that D.H. Lawrence said about Herman Melville applied particularly and aptly to our experience this week: "He was a real American in that he always felt his audience in front of him. But when he ceases to be American, when he forgets all audience, and gives us his sheer apprehension of the world, then he is wonderful, his book commands a stillness in the soul, an awe." Mr Charles Olson.

OLSON: That's too much. Thank you. That puts my father right on top of me, like, if you heard who that was saying.

I don't know how many of you have been here on the previous two nights, both the reading and the first lecture. I have to assume a little bit that there's a good body of succession. And because of that, I'd like to see if I can—because this is about one third of the way and before we're finished tonight we will have gone beyond one half—sort of recap and tell you some of the secrets of these lectures to me. As I said the opening Monday night, the problem is actually to proceed, rather than progressively, in something that I call either the "circular" and hopefully the "shapeful." But there's another funny thing in this whole subject of—let me take the mid-term, "mythology," and argue the origin and experience (can you all hear me?) of an image, and then that on the hither or scalar side, say, is something that

---

6. By this time, Olson had received a copy of Donald Allen's transcription of the "Causal Mythology" lecture at Berkeley, later published by Four Seasons Foundation in 1969.

the word, which is a difficult word still to use, I think: "cosmos." Easily I could substitute "creation," except again you suddenly start to get adjectival, which I abhor in a word like "creation." And there has been now, for nine years, three words that have constantly forced me down, or kept me in, or possibly steadied me. And in preparing for being here, I couldn't get away from them again. Then I thought, just to make you feel, I mean, try to see if I could give you the shape of the whole, and the inner, the motor of my own experience to say these three words. And they're Greek, but they're easy.

And again I get in that marvelous problem of which, like an assortment of candies, which one will I take first? And I don't really care, because I can't get away from any of them. And if any of you are interested in looking at them on the page, they're at the end of that sort of a congery or mess called the "Feinstein letter," which is usually attached to "Projective Verse," to most people's further difficulty, or difficulty, as a clinker. They are, and let me use them in the kind of order I proposed this week to make these lectures on: of *topos*, which would have been sort of Monday night's lecture, if that five-legged chair can still stay in your mind. And it means, of course, simply "place." But again place has too much familiarity in America, curiously because we're colonials possibly in the origin of our nation, and unhappily become local instead of, now, national. So I for years wrote place and names,[7] and kept saying that like, I don't know, like who? Dreiser? Or—not Melville. Lawrence again is interesting, fiddling on that question in America and the Southwest. And I hope in Monday's shovings and wrestlings, better I think last night possibly, when I almost threw this lectern down and mounted it and wrestled with it instead of talking to you, that I gave that sense of place as in the same sense that I would think names are almost always proper, of the earth, as sort of the place of our habitation, at least, but that that literal globe or orb is our lamp or clue to the whole of Creation, and that only by obedience to it does one have a chance at Heaven.

The other two words are *tropos* and *typos*. Obviously the latter is very easy, it's "type," and is "typology," and is "typification," and is, in a sense, that standing condition of—I mean standing, really, in the very literal sense of substantive or object or manifest or solid or material. We get our word "type," which interests me, I suppose, as a writer, from it. If any of you have ever seen a piece of movable type, at the bottom is the letter and the block is above. So that in order, really, to imagine a printer doing it, he's under your words in order to make the letters of them, which always delights me, literally, as a problem of creation. In fact, literally, I would go so far, if you will excuse my Americanism, to think that you write that way, that you write as though you were underneath the letters. And I take that a hell of a lot larger: that is, I would think that the hoof-print of the Creator is on the bottom of Creation, in exactly that same sense.

"Tropism," I think, is actually the riddler of the lot; or it's the management, or it's the maneuverer, or it's the—it's ourselves. And as you know, it means simply "turning," and is, I think, the freshest of the—or

7. Or perhaps Olson is thinking of his specific piece, "Place; & Names."

maybe the … Obviously "type" is almost the cliché. I have a hunch that most of you would find *tropos* the more difficult, I mean the more abstract, in that sense, literally of shape or place, and that tropism is almost—I dunno, I mean, I always myself only started, I think, with—when I was a kid, there were Canadian sailors used to come and visit, not my sisters, which I had none, but girls whom I knew and were older than I, and we would be babysitters for these chicks, and it was the Canadian Navy on station in Gloucester, and I think the first cigarettes I smoked were "Heliotropes," which was the most—no, excuse me, they were from His Majesty's Ship *Heliotrope*; they were "Player's," right? And I think I still have a queer imprint or stamp of believing that the meaning—like, now I can spill it—of "tropism" in ourselves is the sun.

I even, for example, recently with two friends of mine in my own kitchen, two lovely, close friends—I mean, one of the reasons why this coming here is so meaningful, really, to me—it's not flattery—is that all this is so close to me that it's almost difficult to disclose my secrets to you and offer any more than poems. But the three of us were sitting there and suddenly we were talking about—the word was "photo-copic," which I thought was marvelous in terms of all this shit of McLuhan's (excuse me) and today, like, as of literally what I'm here to, in that sense, both misrepresent and represent otherwise. And this word was—suddenly the whole meaning of all of our experience was "photo" (how can I say?) "photo-copic": that we are darkness, that our, like, condition inside is dark. In other words, if you stop to think of yourself as an impediment of creation, I mean, you—I think you follow me that the unknown is rather your self's insides. And I suddenly was talking to these two men on the basis of the fact that that's exactly the whole meaning: that we become sure in the dark, that we move wherever we wish in the six directions with that light. And I'm not making pictures; I don't mean black sun or black light. I mean, literally, that to light that dark is to have come to whatever it is I think any of us seeks. And tropism to my mind—and actually here I do again express experience of, say, twenty years ago, which was to me dogmatic, when I knew there was a sun, I mean a "helio," inside myself, so that everything, every other human being, and every thing in creation, was something that I could see if I could keep that experience. I think even that's where I—I mean I'm not saying that so—I'm not being smart. But, say, if I did say that the purpose of these lectures as "Truth" could be subtitled "The Dogmatic Nature of Experience," somewhere these—such a thing as that I realize that, my god, I mean, my feeling is a sun of being which sits in this mass of blackness, or darkness better, or eyelessness, or sightlessness, and lends itself—and I hope here I can capture for you what I think I did not successfully, quickly, get to you Monday, which was that the experience of image or vision is as simple as that. It's simply an entrance into our own self of what are dogmatic conditions, which we inherit by being alive and acquire by seeking to be alive, and that those two things are both true from our having been at all. I'm confident, for example, that if you think of yourself at the other end, which is when you began, and if you had children it gets more powerful. I mean, your own child's birth is too much, because of the fact that you did this, I mean this terrible thing, to have passed life on to somebody else, because what you've experienced. And I think that many of you, maybe most of you, are still happily too young to have had this second shutter on the light. But I do mean that fact that the thing grows from you, and that you, without knowing it, you watch this thing come up like a tree or any kind of a growth. I mean, we only did grow.

Again I'm speaking in that enormous "tropism" that I'm proposing, I guess. I mean, the wiggle is—is tonight "tropism"? Is Friday "type," or is tonight "typism," or Friday "tropism"? But I—actually it's no problem. I can put those two things in quite familiar terms, and I would like to. I would also like to ask you all to excuse me (I hope Bob is here) for having been so touchy and testy last night.[8] But I could, really, right at this moment, meet that whole question of reason by some perfectly fast philosophical pass. I find, in some of the notes that I did in those months preparing before I came tonight, it just says that "Belief I," for example, which would be tonight's, say, was "realism." Again you get another quote. I don't—I mean, I'm canceling that word "realism." Know what I mean? I'm trying to give you your language. And it's unfortunate that we all come from a society which has been both liberal and technological, obviously overrational, logical. The word, happily—no, I'll hold that. And I honestly think that the whole great creators of our minds in this 19th century are all fallacious, including Einstein, and all this testing of the universe which is proving him right. And if I say I seem to be here tonight to almost demand that the present dismiss itself, I equally wish, I equally feel, hopefully, that you may trust me enough to believe that I also have the authority to discuss any piece of your own past as well as my own. I say that without, I hope, any either offense or gall, because the problem lies much deeper. It lies in what is so old and what has not yet happened. And if, which I did not say, the other word was "ideal," neither "real" nor "ideal" will pass. One must ask that any act of yours or my life or anyone else's be not actually that life but its act or production, and that that is something which is essentially our language— I don't care in what form it occurs, and I'm not speaking aesthetically—and that that act be, or that production is, something that one can even specifically call something that neither "realism" nor "idealism" even covers, and both bends your attention away from the transcendent and ...

So that all of you may feel that I'm not speaking loosely or, like they say, passionately, no, fanatically, no, mystically, no, I mean all those, you know, juicy supposed conditions of poetry, I mean, the personality of poets in poetry, I could even put you to the page on this, like a head to a block. I mean, there isn't any way that a mathematician or a physicist has even succeeded in getting where any of them have except by the fact that mathe-

8. Chad Walsh in "A Retrospect" speaks of "the now famous episode of Bob Arnebeck, whom he [Olson] expelled from the reading because Bob's smile (or was it a laugh?) came at the wrong point—I suspect there had been earlier encounters, since Bob was celebrated for his skill in sticking the needle into visiting poets."

matics is a language which has the symbolic ability to show light into the transcendent. And that's absolutely, I think you could say, the monorail, even right now, any time and up to now, and into the future. But that is only one of the—and they're actually, I think, denominable languages. Not too many, or everything is—whichever way you take that doesn't matter, but specifically I would care to have my five-legged chair even here, by at least running some of the languages which are there as well as language, like, say, your own dreams, which I consider completely a language, if you know how to read it. And here I'm close to that condition that I said Monday night is that emergence of image from an enormous condition of Creation which we only poke at, even no matter what our image, music patently and curiously a language rather sister to mathematic. And it's perfectly obvious to me that I myself care for the three languages of those three, that is, mathematics, music and poetry, or language. Painting, yeah, literally. The rest I think are secondary forms of all of those, dance being only our own bodies becoming in a sense that capable, which could be another leg of that chair, I guess. I haven't even—I've got one left, haven't I? I think I have my fifth leg, which I won't even speak of to you, which is a language, I mean, of course, obviously yourself. I mean, let's knock that subjective thing out, too, right now: that that is all that is the language that you have by having been alive. And I mean literally your own self, I don't mean some division of individuality, or even identifying or identity. Except here it gets close, huh? And to give the whole game away and then start to try to go further this evening.

And I'm now trying to cope with that thing that I find so many of you have asked me to continue, that word which I was so pleased that when I dropped it Monday night every ear heard it, hears itself, thought "a-hah!": and that's "theology." In fact, since Monday I suddenly realized that the whole damn thing is simply naming God, one of the quickest ways to call that thing. I'm trained here, right? Again, somewhat bothering Bob, I want all of you to realize that the word "logos," or "logical," has been ruined without your knowing it in your experience because it means the study or knowledge of anything, and that is absolutely only late, exactly early Christian meaning of the word. It is actually, "In the beginning was the Logos." Or it's literally what the Greeks of the 5th century also did to it. In fact, in the instance of Aristotle in the 4th, right immediately thereafter Plato and Socrates creating logic, which became even—a girl last night sitting after my reading as we shrank down to one or two, asked—oh no, it may have been after, yes it was after the reading—asked me about the difference between "emotional" and "logical." I mean that's how bothersome the damn thing still is, as a false reason upon you, upon us all. I want to interest you in it this way, and literally to place it again in that marvelous place that I find the whole, how you say it, the teeter.

The teeter I mentioned is literally the word *muthologos*, which is the Greek word itself. Not myth. I mean, like, I can't use "mythology" without finding it *muthologos*. And I can tell you what's in this whole thing. Again it's a number of years since I first stumbled on that. And it was in pursuing my own interest in the other Greek of myself beside Hesiod, Herodotus, who was known because of his *History*. I don't know how immediately and how early this was his name, the "Logographer," in contrast to Homer, who was to the Greeks the "Muthologos." I hope you hear that switch. It's a most exciting switch, to my mind, because actually what you call Herodotus's stories are known to the Greeks as *logoi*. May I get that to you? Actually *logos* in my mind right now, logic or l-l-l-l-l is like st-st story, and is, like, only story. And that when you have subjects like psl-ychology and psl-opology, you're actually only having the stories of. And history is, like, so. At this point, happily, we can say myth-th-thology is st-stories of m-myths, which is the word "mouth." *Muthos* is "mouth." Pthth-puth. And indeed *logos* is simply "words in the mouth." And in fact I can even be stiffer an etymologist and tell you that if you run the thing right to the back of the pan and scraped off all the scrambled eggs and there's still rust on it and you can't wash it, you'll find that what you have to say *muthologos* is is "what is said of what is said," as suddenly the mouth is simply a capability, as well as words are a capability; they are not the ultimate back of it all. You have this funny abstraction, "what is said of what is said." Now, I think you can hear that peculiar way that balances exactly a very subtle experience of all of us, which is that all we ever have is this peculiar, as I come back again to say this, peculiar transcendent miss or hit of having made that, and that, in a funny way, to me at least, that *logos* there, as I think even the Greeks in call-ing Herodotus the "Logographer" mean it, that he who can tell the story right has actually not only, like, given you something, but has moved you in your own narrative.

Actually, in that poem that I read you that I wrote for this—I'm going to call these lectures when I publish them "the Beloits," anyhow, there's no way else to—I mean that common noun "the Beloits." I think it's a good invention for the language. Obviously I can't get away with it, but it's a great idea. Tonight, I mean it's nice I believe in something about being here, and it is that. I feel that "the Beloits" is some fragment, some fragment of food or some splinter of spear or, if I may steal from my friend Dorn, "awn" of wheat or barley or corn, which belongs in the language. And now I'm performing "typification," right? I mean, following "tropism" and, obvious-ly, like, having arrived, and am, if I am, and I have been in some moments, here.

Don't be fooled by my, like, mouth. Believe me, sounds awfully nice the way it got said tonight, huh? Easy, hmm? I do believe in that, and I come back again to one of the things I think I'm doing this week, I hope that I am, is the responsibility, to use that lovely word, the responsibility of a poet to mythology. I think that really is a difference between what I call the "archaic"—and if I do say so, I hope, thanks to Chad's asking me to tell you what I dated the archaic, and how I did it, as the change of the nude in 474 from a symbolic to a representational or idealistic Apollo and Venus.[9] The nice thing about getting behind that, by one day, to Kore and Kouros, and

9. Olson is using Kenneth Clark's discrimination in *The Nude* (1959), p. 57.

that oh so sort of artistically dumb sculpture in which the bellies are flat, the angles are stupid, the imprint is arbitrary or typological, and that Klee's wonderful objection to the typological at his date, in the notebook—what's the name of that wonderful Klee notebook which ends in the attack upon typology?[10] He means the attack upon this screwish, whorlish, ugly society that we are and have been for three hundred years, or at least, wait a minute, excuse me, for two hundred years now, or certainly from the date of Mr Keats, if I may use one of my own crucial parables. Mr Keats, I think the Christmas of 1819, a play, a mummers' play, was in a coffee shop afterwards with Coleridge and, listening to Coleridge's enormous mental and interesting talk, went home and wrote a letter to, I believe, his friend—some of you may know this, it seems to me now getting kicked around, this phrase, and I'm putting the phrase back to the origin in that letter—Reynolds. And at that moment, which is pretty close—what, two years later he's dead?—he's very young, late twenties? Oh no, early twenties. At that moment he got his—he's on, he's got it, I mean he knows where he—what he wants to do and what he has to do. He even has the point of how he's—because he's been reading Shakespeare, in really a very practical sense, like any writer, to see if he can write plays, turn that verse of his into some damn use that will more interest him. And the whole thing is this question of what's, like, how are we. Before I give you it where I put the whole phrase in front of you, I also want to say that in another letter trying to characterize this, he speaks of himself (and may I use him as my measure? because you know he was four foot nine—I used to measure my children's growth by him), how he lost, how when he came into a room of children, because it was a birthday party he went to, they took his, they—I mean I'm just ghosting it in—they took his nature. I mean, they were so typological that he was in them as the spirit of them. I mean, he's marvelous. A roomful of children is like, is all that Keats thinks of as the whole of the experience of being alive, and he is susceptible, and he believes that in that susceptibility alone is the act that he must now master. And he says in this letter after the Christmas mummers' play, that "all that irritable reaching after fact and reason ... man must stay in this condition of"—gee, I forgot even the words—"confusion," "ambiguity"? "He's better there. And that I call Negative Capability." I think from that moment—and I've said it in that piece which some of you may have read, that review of Mr Melville, of a book on Mr Melville, under the title—I reviewed it in the *Chicago Review*, the Zen issue, the one just before it became *Big Table*. It is the last piece in that magazine, and it's a book review, and I opened it with this story.[11] The book had the curious title *The Fine-Hammered Steel of Herman Melville*, which was what obviously shocked me.

So I guess really I'm trying to—I guess I'm being "tropistic" tonight, that's all. I guess that's where we are is in that. I mean we're on that other

10. Olson is thinking of the *Pedagogical Sketchbook*, but it is in Paul Klee's lecture "On Modern Art" (1948) that any mention of typology occurs.
11. "Equal, That Is, To the Real Itself," in *Collected Prose*, pp. 120–25.

word, as against the possibility that you will imagine that Monday night we did something with the word *topos*. I'm obviously dishing out myself, like they say, tonight, which I guess is what I mean by "trope": I mean, obey yourself and in obeying yourself kneel or lean to the sun, or whatever that heliotrope, like, is. I can say it very seriously at this point. I can switch you, and maybe once again the switch is to go to my master in Madison, whom I don't know, but whom I have found is one of the only enlightening men as of mythology in the world, because he happens to be so alert to have paid attention to Norse, the texts of the Eddas, again, in this century when they became a complete piece of unassailable cliché in the latter part of the 19th century, and just discuss and read you, in fact, his discussion of old Norse religion and his care with the word "theology," or, as I said, read Ed Sanders's *Poem from Jail*, where an act of theology from quite another place, from, in fact, so far as I am aware—I can't tell whether Sanders drew it simply from spending his time in jail when he was on that rap for having stuck himself to the first nuclear submarine in New London, an enormous thing for an amateur from Kansas City, I mean, an amateur in submarine nay-swimming, I think just before that having acquired—this is the leader of the Fugs, who shows his ass every time he has a good audience, I mean, takes down his pants and turns his back on the audience at the end of a performance so that they may know what a ring-tailed baboon, like—I guess that's the reason he did. I only know how completely capable he is of "type" that he knows what he looks like without—from the, like, from the rear. I don't know how he—this is the secret, I'm sure, of his ability as a poet. I didn't realize I was saying again the same thing as the, like, the … right?

I mean, if I may switch at this mid-point (I think we're just about at the mid-point of three lectures), I mean, I am again, or for the first time, aware that there are six directions, yah? I didn't know it. If I'd had a good religious master instead of having lived as you have in that society that Mr Keats so completely characterizes as "irritable reaching after life and death," I would have known that there are six directions. I mean, I've certainly built much of my work on the four directions and their parts, but I don't think it was— I think it was in preparing for this, these "Beloits," that I saw this careful discrimination, which I'm sure is known to—it must come from the—I don't know where it comes from. But these days with so much Oriental knowledge having been slipped into the pockets of several of you through underground magazines at least, you may know this much better than I: that is, that the six directions are, front, back, left, right, up, and down, and that at any point those are the vectors on which you actually are experiencing things.[12] That is, if I run you like a trolley up to this point, you've still got six directions that are feeding you or you can go in. And that is almost exclusively your possibilities of experience. That's pretty good, no? Six is not bad. I mean, if you can think of it. I mean, did you know there was six? I

12. Olson's immediate source was probably page 52 of S.H. Nasr's *An Introduction to Islamic Cosmological Doctrines* (Cambridge: Harvard University Press, 1964), a book which he had received as a gift the year previously.

didn't know there was six. I thought we were—did you know there was six? Does anybody here know really that we are like the cards standing up, capable of six, six sort of, I suppose you'd say, sides or faces. I hope this doesn't bother you. I'm an old Tarot teller, which I gave up because it was too true. I gave it up in exactly the year 1950, because I had foretold something to the minute and the hour. That's too much. I can't do that, I mean I don't believe in that. I mean, if it's so easy to master magic, Mr Faust, then lucky we. Or no, we haven't buried him at all. I mean, happily we're—I mean, thank god he's, thank god he's … [STRIKES TABLE] But I mentioned the cards really because they—the riddle here is don't be bothered by the abstractions that I offer. I hope you won't. I mean, let me just—in preparing again for tonight, I wanted to quote Fowler, whom I mentioned just a minute ago, and this sentence—I can't get over it, how exactly—I mean, he's marvelous there. He's completely, completely impeccable on the condition of—in fact, some of those poems I was reading to you this week rest entirely on his discrimination of where is the edge of creation. If, say, that poem "Gravelly Hill" I read last night, with some, apparently with some light, is called "at the boundary" or what of something, the "boundary" or "borders" of … [11.160] I mean, here I'm suggesting to you how language, that is, the ability of language of your own, like, not in words, if it's writing, can equally give you, like, the moral. And I mean, again, I have to go back to a word which is in our whole lives but we don't go back to it in Greek, *ethos*, which means "cave of your inner being," as, for example, "economic" as *nomos*. Again, I've been telling, in some of these meetings with people since I've been here, that lovely opening of the *Theogony*, in which Hesiod is told by the Muses, "Now you must be a poet, and there's only one way. It's very—I mean, you're sort of, you know, like you gotta be. And we instruct poets, and the way we instruct poets is the same way we cause our father, who's *noos* or Zeus, to invent rules of"—and by rules they mean, like, seafaring or—they cause Zeus to bring further results of creation further. And without them, he can't, he's on the nod, he just is Zeus. I mean, he's not very active. He has to be danced to, sung to, shown by his daughters. And that these Muses say to Hesiod, "Look …"—I mean, there's two other, beside him. There's—like this is, like, God we're talking about, huh, in that book? There's two things—and with the instructions is the same, that is, for both of them, as well as, in a sense—but then you get that damn thing: which is the front, which is the back? I mean, because they're Zeus's daughters, they can sort of face him. I suppose they sort of have to, sort of. But do you know, when they give the poet or the prince his instruction, it's as though they just threw it like meat over the back of themselves? In fact, one has this marvelous feeling of the impertinence of these bitches to come on and say, "Look, Boeotianic, we now have it for you," sort of thing. It's a very exciting passage, and in it they say, "We will give you the—"; and in fact, Havelock in the *Preface to Plato*, a book about four or five years ago, the first attempt, the first time anybody has taken Plato's *Republic* and examined that question of the poets' rejection, the rejection of the poets by Plato from society. Which I think is another one of those marvelous moments that we're at: that the exact reversal or obverse of that is now true, that the prince and the poet have to be able to pass to others the customs of men and the laws of gods. And the word "customs" is, in Hesiod's line, *ethea* (*ethos* as the singular), and the word "laws of the gods" is *nomoi* (or *nomos*). And as Havelock is at great care—happily I ran *ethos*, I ran both of these in my machine some years earlier and was astonished to arrive at the fact that "laws" mean cannibalism.[13] If *ethos* means the cave of yourself, that you are what I tried to suggest was full of "photocopic" earlier, I still can't get beyond that fact that an ethical—that, like, verbally, we are an *ethos*. I mean, it's so marvelous I can't think how you can—did I switch on you? I mean a cave. I mean, the word only means "cave." It means literally "a house inside itself," or something. And then the other means "appetite for your own kind," I suppose, what cannibalism means. It does not mean eating animal food, it means eating your own. And that's law, laws, the most important teachings that the Muses can claim that a prince and a poet have to have to pass on to other human beings from their instruction.

The sentence of Fowler's at the end, his summary: "Old Norse religion is strictly theological, strictly, indeed, traditional and metaphysical: from it may be abstracted, therefore, fragments of a creed answerable with a yea on many levels of thought." That second half of the sentence may sound pedantic, but, believe you me, that awkwardness I think is earned. But the first part of it is where I think he's shooting you, if you ask for reason and logic. And the part of word that is definitive, parts of, that is, used for speech to be analytical, is strictly—that is, "Old Norse religion is strictly theological, strictly, indeed, traditional and metaphysical."

Well, like I say, if there's six directions, and you're a rolling stone, I almost would prefer now to take a breath and have you move me, if possibly I have successfully advanced the wheel of our week. What time is it, David, or Marion? It is after nine? You say it hopefully! [LAUGHS] What actually is it?

VOICE: Ten after nine.

OLSON: Ten after, oh, that's a much appropriate size. I really think that you weren't being hopeful. Good. In fact you were being conclusive! So why don't those who wish to go out into the spring now feel free to, and any of you that are as dry as me may stay in the grass. [APPLAUSE]

May I ask for any of you that are interested in that luncheon tomorrow: I wonder if you'll all—it's a student lunch—ask you if I might be excused. In this sense, I'm pretty turned into grist anyhow, not by you but by myself, and I'm having a little trouble sleeping and resting; and I will try to make it because of those who have apparently signed up. This is all on my own, and don't blame anybody, I mean, especially David or Chad or any of the—and if I don't appear, talk about me. If I do, O.K. And if I don't, would any of

13. After having made cannibalism one of the themes of *Call Me Ishmael* and "The Kingfishers," Olson must have been arrested by Eric Havelock's comment in *Preface to Plato* (1963) about *nomos*: "The prohibition instinctively observed by mankind against cannibalism" (p. 63). On the same page of Havelock one finds *ethea* defined as the "lair" or "haunt" of an animal.

you who sort of wish to get at me, please give me this second chance at five? Come to me, come to speak to me or whatever, because I have that session with the poet's manuscripts at four at the World Affairs Center, South Lounge, and I'll be there, I have to be. So then, if those of you who don't want to associate with poets (which is understandable in a society which hates them), come at five and I'll clear the way for you. And I almost think from I've said it so well that I hope now that I may not be there at lunch. If in case my cat's mind wakes me up or I successfully sleep before early enough, I will.

Friday evening, 29 March 1968

WALSH: The speaker is an extraordinarily generous person. In spite of the way we've been working him all week, he has volunteered to have another question period at the end of this, his final lecture. So when the lecture is over, why, any of you who would like to stay on for a final opportunity to talk with Mr Olson, just please come up to the front. I'm going to make this introduction quite brief, for fear that I may get too sentimental. It was only four days ago that I was standing up here introducing Mr Olson and his first lecture. I don't know whether he'll like me saying this, but he seems so much a part of us now that I hate the thought of this being my final opportunity to introduce him. I've had the feeling that we've had the living history of poetry in our midst and also a very complete human being, and there's never an excess supply of those. I'm happy to present to you, Mr Charles Olson.

OLSON: Well, I'm as equally moved, or more possibly, because I'm the one who passes through, to be, to have been here, and regret that it comes so soon to a climax, if I, hopefully, can make it such. For those of you who are new tonight, we've, or at least I've, tried to build, in one week, both a structure and a corpus, built really upon three words. And now I have the hardest, I suppose, to deal with. On Monday night I at least took a crack at arguing a world which has value, and on Wednesday I made a further, I mean another attempt to see if I could at least identify any one of us as a flower, or such a possibility. And tonight my job is to see if I can characterize what, in using the word "type" or *typos*, I mean by "the blow upon the world." At such a point one enters the area of, in a real sense, finality, which was at the beginning. It's not known until it's finished. And as I took on, by proposing that these lectures be "Poetry and Truth," I have that responsibility tonight to see if I can argue that truth is specific. In that sense, then, to my mind there is that initial and optive matter which is, or of which we use the word, "truth." At this moment I'm a little bedeviled because I—I mean, because it's now. I don't mean tonight, I mean this particular world and society. I'm awfully tempted to say that where my sources lie, rather than—in order, in fact, to help any of you that may find what I equally announced, in opening these lectures, that I understood my title to be, to require me to speak of, to speak sublumally[14] of "The Dogmatic Nature of Experience." I suppose in the flux of the present I'm a Tantrist, and care for that order of showing, which, as I understand it, is text. And I'm aware that—I think it's true that that is not too comfortable in the present, or it seems not to be so, because if we suddenly start talking that Oriental jive, we easily come on words which are more familiar, I think, like "mantra," and what's the other beside "tantra"? So, just so you feel a little more comfortable that I'm a possible ladder, call me Tantra.

By "type," and what I mean by an imprint, I think, characterizes all Creation. Again I feel that wonderful sense of a hundred years ago in this country when almost all of the men that for us, I think, in this stage of writing, are our predecessors. I've been, as nobody fortunately here has bothered me with that adjective, "transcendental"; I'm happy that's true. I do think, though, that the lift, both of the Americans of the first half of the 19th century, is extraordinarily like our—has put us on the mountain in the first half of the 20th up to a point where possibly something like the dogmatism I've offered might be supported.

You see, I have a piece of paper and I'm interested—a little envelope, and I don't know which side—it's marvelous to go from one side to the other, as they say. This is like having written again for Beloit, and I did this since 7:30, so I'm having that marvelous experience of finding out whether these words are worth anything or not. I think I'm going again to do what I said. I'm bedeviled or straddled from the occasion of now to something I've avoided doing all week, but I tend to think I'd like to at least leave for you some place I think is a body of doctrine that has been for me entirely confirmatory, and for many, many years, because the text I think I will, one at least that I will use, or two, tonight, I think both actually come from the same period of time. And in a sense to draw you towards, from your own society, towards what I think is a demands society, I'd like to see if I can just quickly dust it in. It lies between something like—well, it lies between something like 800 AD and 1248, or 1246 possibly, and if, on one night here, we drew up, or I proposed, an archaic calendar to cover ourselves, this body of time that I have been astonished supplies so much truth, at least what I would call truth or what seems to be truth, is these years throughout the world.

I had the challenge of—someone yesterday said, "Well, what is truth?" So I said, "Well, like, I'd like to say, but I left the book behind, like." I'm sure I have my mind enough to offer it to you as such. And it, I think it is, I remember it as such and as a matter of fact I give it, the name of it, in the— it comes into our history as the *Liber Platonis quartorum*, and it's known as, in its Latin, and I think it's, as such, 12th century; but it clearly is of Arabic origin and originally dates and has been ascribed to Kabir,[15] whom I really

---

14. Olson very carefully says "sublumally," a neologism.
15. The source of Olson's knowledge of *Liber Platonic quartorum* is Carl Jung's *Psychology and Alchemy* (NY: Pantheon, 1953), especially pp. 249–55. Olson's later quotation about *veritas efficaciae* is from p. 256.

mean when I say 800. Kabir is generally known, some of you may well know him, as a hero of alchemy, but in fact is actually Al'Jabir, if I have it right, and is one of the starters of Ismaili Muslimism, if not almost the originator of it. And whether he wrote this book or not, I don't know, but I have found more and more that I settle on one passage, in which these words are all that is said (or I'm going to concentrate them): "In natural things, there is a *veritas efficaciae.*" And as I both hear that and feel it, it's all that I know: that there is such an efficacious truth. And what Kabir means is literally what he says: that in natural things there is an *effic*—ayeh, it won't work. Well, at this point you do want to use words like "health" or "hygiene" or, to those of you who know some uses of modern drugs, the "sane." The technology, to make that point again that we made earlier in the week that rose on the first day or first hour I was here, that technology has truth in it today, and you need not turn your back on it in rushing to either the East or—what was Sven's third? I've forgotten his third, his—oh yes, in fact my own "theology" itself, proper. Or as I've argued with you, other poets who are—or one poet, especially, Mr Sanders, who is a curious instance of pure theology causing, immediately, poetry, from the very beginning, when he was jailed for having stuck himself under water, through the U.S. Navy's frogmen at New London, to the first nuclear submarine, for which he did a term in Uncasville, Connecticut, and wrote *Poem from Jail*, which, though I may not read when we're all together, if any—and I promised it—want to hear it afterwards, I'd be happy to. I'd rather, actually, see if I can just bring in front of you this last of three, and firmest, I think, of the aspects of what I've brought, hope to have brought, to you this week.

In speaking of this period that straddles the occasion of Europe, I wanted, in a sense, to draw you to the finest time. I think there are such periods, and I think this one is one that we can isolate. And generally speaking, we inherit such a diverse history, and have practices of time, therefore, which are discursive, I kind of would like to point at that like a *topos* in which, I'm convinced, man was behaving rather almost, let's say carefully, to, well, something as simple as his organic condition. To tell you the truth, I don't think I'm saying much more all week than that that is our occasion of truth, that we are organic. And that on Wednesday night, when I tried at least to suggest that—or was it publicly that I did that attempt to speak of the dark, the blackness of—and I don't mean that blackness that has become so popular as of, I mean, that blackness of Mr Poe and Mr Hawthorne, say. I mean real blackness of being inside ourselves. It was Wednesday, was it not, when I spoke of eyes as all the lanterns we had? Was it not so? I hope you're with me. I think this is all right. We're tight, but the ship's in the water. I hope you feel comfortable; I do. So much so that I'm apt to now seek to even suggest to you the scalar that lies in this third meeting. Whoever wrote this book I'm quoting to you, either he or this remarkable commentator on that book, Dorn, Gerhard Dorn, I think it may be Dorn that argues it as closely as I'm going to: that, as creatures of organism, the original difficulty is that of the soul having its chance to realize its separateness from the body; but that only the mind can free it from its fetters to the body; and that when that happens—I'm tempted to try to run the ball on the sideline by saying that in order that you realize how topological this is, instead of how spiritual, there are three things that are going on at the same time as these three parts of you are seeking to reach a fourth; that you have to pass through composite nature, things of composite nature, things of dispersed nature; and you arrive at a point where the mind refuses the soul any further progress, will not let the soul into the heaven of itself. And at that gate, which sounds absolutely like theology and parable at this point (I hope we're winning this game enough for your tickets to be valuable), you suddenly have nothing but matter. If I understand this thing that I'm seeking, speaking, seeking to carry here, it is that efficaciousness is in matter; that when Kabir says "natural things," he means matter.

I hope now I can draw my paths back to Monday when, if you will recall, I said that I thought that I was here to see if vision could be as carefully left alone, and at the same time run down in its place, as any object-ism. And to my sight, this single, this—I do want to say "single truth," it's so easy to— and I will, I hope, in the second half of this evening, draw it to you in anoth- er way—I just wish at this moment to fiercely see if truth can be said to be itself and, if possible, against I think all history except our own as a people, to be so articulate, or to have failed in being so, as to say that matter is the fourth scalar, the world which prevents, but once felt, enables your being to have its heaven.

I hope, for some of you, this sounds like what it sounds to me, as prag- matism. I have labored to find Charles Peirce quotable to you. I couldn't. But if you will read the January issue of the *Popular Science Magazine* for 1878, you will find the first moment in my knowledges when something that I characterize as that period of time which includes the Norse capturing of most of the world and the invention of the Eddas—it includes equally the expansion of the Arabs and of Moslem learning, or power and then learning, and in such qualities of feeling and thought as, say, that Al 'Arabi I mentioned at the end of Wednesday night's writing the *Meccan Revelations* for twenty years around the black meteoric stone at Mecca. And the reason why I say the thing is really over, in that sense that time also has its shape, at something like 1246 or 1248, is that I'm dating that from the Carpini Mission, which only has, I think, become available to us, or it became available to me—and I think it's actually a text that couldn't have been quite as clear until this—was by the discovery of what you may know of as the Vinlanda map, which Yale broke out with two years ago Columbus Day. And the Vinlanda map, which shows such an island, with such topology that everyone seems to be agreed that it is Newfoundland, but it equally is so good that one excellent English woman geographer, who's died just recently, believes that it is a fraud[16]—in that book that that map was found in is the

16. Ed Dorn had sent Olson the London *Times* obituary (7 July 1966) of Eva Taylor, where it is stated that she had grave doubts about the authenticity of the Vinland Map that had been revealed to the world in R.A. Skelton et al., *The Vinland Map and the Tartar Relation* (New Haven: Yale University Press, 1965), which includes Fra Giovanni de Piano Carpini's account of a mission to Central Asia.

freshest report of the Carpini Mission. I stress this a little bit because of, again, the marvelousness of our time, that the politics of politics I'm being careful about as of both the whole spasmodic condition of today and the social one. Carpini is the contemporary of St Francis and became St Francis's first political condition, political, I don't want to say agent, but body. Suddenly Francis, who himself was a sick soldier and had a dream in Spoleto which so caused him—or was sick in Spoleto, like a shaman can be, and had this vision of being Christ, actually, if possible, again—suddenly he's joined by this man who becomes Carpini and is already by the date of 1245 so useful and has been so, has been the ambassador of the Franciscans to the Germans originally, missionary, I suppose, in the first sense, then to the rest of Europe and then suddenly about that date to Poland, is sent by the Pope, with two brothers, to the East to discover the Mongols' intention, the expectation of the whole West being that in 1250 they will raid again and destroy to the Atlantic. And the Carpini Mission goes to Karakorum and sits, or tries to, for three years to hear whatever they could hear in the marketplace, and come home, and arrive back in Poland at around 1248 to report that apparently the Mongols are not going to strike. I'd like to call that the end of the advantages of the mind that we can reach to. I mean, it could almost—what I'm talking about is something, such a lump of time with so much in it that we could spend a great deal of time. I just have the confidence that I'm speaking of something that is almost a book, it's so there, a book, I think, really in the same sense of *liber*, as used in the book I quote from.

I'll turn my page again and see what the other side ... In fact, I think it's rather easy. I think now I can, at mid-point of tonight, offer you the other and final text to what suddenly, as I have acknowledged this week, while during these months and weeks of intending to be here, seemed such. I remember one night, at least, when I felt I couldn't believe it, but I read every word in it, and felt, as I boasted to you early in the week, that I could read it to you tonight throughout, and get it to yield to you, as I feel it does, the whole import of truth. And I believe it is that same, well, I know it is, but I'd like to convince you, that it is that *veritas efficaciae*.

You can hear how many things I'm avoiding, no? in order to talk of this subject. I think it's quite obvious that the thing is here to be clear without referring to all that has previously been brought to bear on this word (I mean "truth"), and that the advantage of a poet ought to be, at least, that he might make a pass of this order. Therefore, I will, and maybe I'll end up with one sentence. It's not a very long book, and I won't show you it but I can hold it in my hand. It's a little book. And this book, by the way, dates definitely within that time, that topological, tropical time I have proposed as worth your attention, and comes quite from the other side of—no, as a matter of fact, it comes from very close to Karakorum, 400 years earlier. It's Chinese. And so that your minds will not be teased, or so that your minds may learn not to be teased, don't be teased 'cos I don't use its title. This, I'm sure, is not practiced, but again my masters hold their hands upon their lips.

I even quoted today in Chad's poetry class, as of energy, *ergon*, the final picture—I didn't mention the picture, but the final words of the *Mutus, Liber mutus* or *Mutus liber*, which I've never seen.[17] I'm a little excited about that, that such a name for a book—I'm not sure it means that there's no words in the book, but I mean, for example, it's sort of made up, maybe like a comic strip of just pictures, I should imagine. I mean, the most that I've seen of it is pictures; but then there's words on—like some of us this week were talking about, say, a poet like Ron Padgett, a young poet who successfully writes today by using nothing but, well, usually just comic strips, and putting in the balloon and in the situation his story and his poem. A most interesting fellow from Enid, Oklahoma. He and a whole bunch come out of that place. McClure actually is from Oklahoma, I think, too, earlier. They edited a magazine called *White Dove*. Wasn't he in it? You know the mag, remember when they had that magazine? For example, this is a group of which the Fugs is the orbit. Very crazy bunch of kids from western Oklahoma. I don't say kids, you know, like that. I mean, they—you can say it at any time.

Yeah, I mean the first sentence is the whole shot, shoot, shook. I used it only once before and I didn't do this to it. I simply walked out and said, "I would like very much to talk on it." This was a lecture at Berkeley, in front of my peers, called "Causal Mythology," and I had just flown in from Rome and hadn't done my work, and had to get up in front of, oh, I think the body of poets that you could say are in this world, or most of them, at 10:30 in the morning. [LAUGHS] And luckily I remembered a "Visionary Recital," the one I mentioned to you, of the angel of the right and the angel of the left, which I also have with me tonight, and as a tape. That's the one I mentioned earlier in the week, Avicenna's queer shot, whatever it is. Again, Avicenna in this same period. And I said I wanted to talk about the orb, the urbs, the imago, and the anima mundi, and that it was all to be done under this apothegm or epigram, epigraph. And now here I am again, for the second time, in such a situation (and with the bell tolling!): "That which exists through itself ... That which exists through itself is what is called meaning." Too much! I mean, I don't think it is. It's too much for me to stand here and just have that. And that is what I have to offer. And that's what I think there is to offer, and I don't think anything in this world moves it a jot, except as we do, or become such. "That which exists through itself is what is called meaning." And even that word "meaning" is, I think, very—I'm reading from a translation of the Chinese, and as you prob—many of you, many of you, especially, may know, the word, of course, in Chinese is that word which I would like to avoid mentioning, but it rhymes with the man to whom that is attributed.[18] And we have that word in our language as "how," if you get my string of rhymes: a Chinese man's name; his, like they say, or

<hr />

17. Illustrations from the *Mutus liber* (1677) appear throughout Jung's *Psychology and Alchemy*, the final one appearing on p. 462, where the last word in the drawing is "Inuenies," with the sign indicating secrecy.
18. Lao Tzu.

one did say, concept; and our word "how." I mean, like, the trouble, at least, if I may again jump on him, Bob had, the first night I was here, with what was the first of three poems that for me belonged to you—and in my stubborn Rus way, I would like to read it again, so that we can summarize, hopefully, the week. It has the title "*Added to making a Republic in gloom on Watchhouse Point" [III.190], which is simply where I live; it's called such, it's part of Fort Point, Fort Square, Gloucester, Massachusetts:

> an actual earth of value to
> construct one, from rhythm to
> image, and image is knowing, and
> knowing, Confucius says, brings one
> to the goal: nothing is possible without
> doing it. It is where the test lies, malgre
> all the thought and all the pell-mell of
> proposing it. Or thinking it out or living it
> ahead of time.

And it has that gloss, margin, "Reading about my world, March 6th, 1968." Now, it wasn't Confucius, of course, that—right? It wasn't, as you, if you— I mean "how" does not rhyme with "Confucius." I mean, there's—I hadn't even figured it out that night I thought I'd read this whole damn thing to you and come up like a living exegesis and make it work so that you understood every word. It's only about twenty-nine pages this,[19] and it's really impeccable. It's more like immaculate. And completely penetrable, completely penetrable to your mind, to your life, to your thought, to your feelings, and I think only those things will actually produce results, result. That's why I have pressed you, or harried you, harried you so hard, I think, is that there isn't any way out of that. We think that that statement, that almost, apparently, a truism, as much as Confucius says, "nothing is possible without doing it." There isn't any way out of that. It's like a, no matter what we may think, a pliers of typology, or not of typology but of what I'm saying is the blow upon the world. I'm sure we could talk tonight, like Mrs Walsh and I at dinner, of Mr Williams. When I wrote that tonight, "the blow upon the world," I was sure, I mean, I suddenly thought, of course, that lovely other alternative, which I'm sure some of you know, Williams's letter in middle life? I don't know when he said it, wrote it: "Love is a stain upon the world" or "is the stain," is it not "is the stain upon the world"? Any of you confirm me or correct me on that? William Carlos Williams. "Love is the stain upon the world," I think he opens a poem or something with it.[20] I don't want that to seem, the way I presented it, as though it's equal at all. I want to take on that burden, too, of not.

I would like, actually, if I can, just to leave you with that sentence. I think it's, like they say, less enough. I mean, I suppose I have the superstition that human beings have, that when they hear something that matters to them,

19. "T'ai I Chin Hua Tsung Chih" in *The Secret of the Golden Flower* (London, 1931).
20. In "Love Song" included in William Carlos Williams's *Selected Poems* (1949) there occurs the phrase: "the stain of love / is upon the world."

it's true. I—and again, if you'll excuse me, I will keep my noun—I once was told this, by myself, to myself, by no body or thing that I could identify. I think I was asleep, and it was a dream. But what got said was, "Everything issues from … Everything issues from ts-ts-ts-ts, and nothing is anything but itself, measured so." Which I'm sure led me on the path to the door of this sentence, quite simply. Can you hear? May I, would you like me to just repeat that? It's easy. I mean, it's like a prayer. Not really, a bead, something I carry in my pocket. I've never said this out loud, that's how much I'm on youse heres nows. Nobody ever heard me say this before. And still I have something for myself, by even telling you that much. "Everything issues from st-t-t-t, and nothing is anything but itself, measured so." I mean, that's what of course got me. Those things always—I mean, that's why I do believe in the reversible, because actually the thing cocks back. That's why I'm talking—earlier in the week I stressed the whole Arabic or Ismaili Muslim concept of ta'wil, which I think is almost singularly the only place I know, actually, in the body of man's accumulation, that you have this little—or you have what we seem to me to be practically preparing from scratch, the acts of the future. "Measured so": I mean, what a trick to pull on somebody, give it the whole thing and then say, "measured so." I mean, that's a voice talking, literally, like they say. I mean, if you take thought, it's simply seeking to be correct in the meter. It's perfectly obvious that that statement is not indulging me; it's supplying me with, like, the afterthought. I say that as of some conversation I had at the end of one session with someone from Madison who was saying that there is no metric left in poetry because time now is now. I said, "Yeah, that's—oh, yeah." He's one of Creeley's men,[21] so he's very quick and bright, and knows what it—knows something, really, you know, like the meter is sort of gone and come and done in front of ourselves, and how do you therefore have meter? Well, I think it's simply measure, and I think it is what I'm, unfortunately, probably, sort of engaged to do. And here I do it now publicly for the first time, which is to see if you can be so careful as to do this in public, to suggest measure as well. If you will note, the first poem that I wrote for you carefully does not involve itself except in itself with that question. The statements are on the other matter entirely, of "rhythm," "image," "knowing," and one I also added but I slipped out of the synod or quartorum: "construct." I equally received that as a gift, maybe ten years earlier. The leading poet alive in the world, in a dream, told me when I was very young or much younger—I can read you the poem. I published it some years ago, in a series of poems in which I sought at that date, and this is prior to I think what all of you most best know of my own, that piece of writing called "Projective Verse." This is written some two years, I think, earlier, "The ABCs." And hidden amongst them, in "ABCs(2)," is the actual words that I then was—that were spoken, again inside my nut by another person entirely:[22]

21. Not at present identified.
22. Olson reveals elsewhere that the figure speaking in the dream was recognized by him as Ezra Pound. See Addendum below, p. 467.

of rhythm is image
of image is knowing
of knowing there is
a construct

So in closing tonight, I would like to read two further poems of the three that were written for Beloit. And I only discovered after dinner tonight that my mind must have slipped. I sent the third off to the printer, I thought, the night I flew here, but I seem to have it, so I—that seems very silly—I wanted these printed so that I could give them away to you, but they never got to me in bulk.[23] And I think I'll read that last first, because in some of that riddle or diddle that I mentioned on Wednesday night, of whether tropism or this imprint of creation belong one before the other, I have no way of knowing. I do know that the thing I stressed the first night, of something that you're on or in or have a standing figure by, which is, whether it's the earth or the sky or the sea or the worldly tree, or whether it's simply that you, I want to say, bionomically but I—neobiotically, or how is it that our electromagnetic society calls the study of living things? Arthur D. Little in Cambridge investigates the vertical condition of everything in order now to be sure that that can be supplied eventually to all space travel. What's that marvelous word that covers that sort of study and preparation for the future of our— what do we call our society beside "corporation-land," "technology-land"? (Both are Mr Mailer's, of course.) "Bionics." In the instance I'm speaking of, the vertical, that which—and, like, we know it isn't, like, just—how you say it?—gravitation. Or it is. I don't know. In an electromagnetic epoch, it's gravitation. In an imaginable epoch, which I think, as you know from the start of this week, I believe is current and comes in and passes through any epoch, including, say, one as large as the one we're in, which is electromagnetic and describable as such, and limited as such, and not necessarily therefore the whole of creation, even of the universe, maybe. So, indeed, the third poem, I think, really is, though it isn't most conspicuously, tropistic [III.191]:

Wholly absorbed
into my own conduits to
an inner nature or subterranean lake
the depths or bounds of which I more and more
explore and know more
of, in that sense that other than that all else
closes out and I tend further to fall into
the Beloved Lake and I am blinder from

spending time as insistently in and on
this personal preserve from which
what I do do emerges more well-known than
other ways and other outside places which
don't give as much and distract me from

keeping my attentions as clear

23. The three "Beloits" were printed as miniature broadsides by the Institute of Further Studies, Buffalo.

And that's titled, double quotes, "'Additions,' March 1968–2." And hopefully for your pleasure, and as my last thing from the basket, the first of the three, which is, or which should be simply, as I think the other two really are, a poem [III.189]:

> That there was a woman in Gloucester, Massachusetts whose
> father was a Beothuk "Red" Indian (her mother was
> a Micmac.
>
> And that this was in 1828 and that she remembered
> traveling in a "canoe" which had the full forepart
> of itself covered sufficiently to enclose all the
> children as well as household goods and dogs
> (like a wicki-up but larger, in the sense that the women too
> were inside this forecastle
>
> so that we have here an instance of the Pleistocene
> "boat" as such—the Biscay shallop of another
> age literally en place in Gloucester, Massachusetts
> —and probably not even far from Biskie Island, that
> Speck interviewed this woman
>
> Who was able to give this evidence because
> her father had been, and one has
> a picture of some such "boat"
> both from Newfoundland and
>
> from the painted cave of Castillo
> at Biscay

[APPLAUSE]

BLACK MOUNTAIN COLLEGE
Black Mountain, North Carolina

New Studies Building, containing student
and faculty studies, also classrooms. (The
first of four wings that will form the "Study
Center" of the College.)

Postcard of Black Mountain College. Kate Olson Archive.

11

On Black Mountain (I)

Charles Olson gave this informal talk on 26 March 1968 during his visit to Beloit College. Two detailed accounts of Black Mountain College can be consulted: Martin Duberman's *Black Mountain: An Exploration in Community* (New York: Dutton, 1972) and Mary Emma Harris's *The Arts at Black Mountain College* (Cambridge: MIT Press, 1987).

CHAD WALSH: ... So without further ado, Charles, if you'll tell us about Black Mountain College, because I think it's probably the most influential college that has collapsed in America during the past thirty years. [LAUGHTER]

CHARLES OLSON: Ha-ha! It's just the predecessor of the nation! [LAUGHS] The symbol for the—what do you call it? the mute show before the main show.

　　Now, I'd like very much—I'm curious, actually, how you people—like, what Black Mountain do you know? I mean, how does it come up that we ask, that we have this thing?

WALSH: I think it was Marion's suggestion, the raising of it. But I've been interested in it for years, ever since my wife taught in the South during the thirties and was always talking about Black Mountain College as a kind of place she wished she could teach in herself.

OLSON: Mm-hmm. I ask that because I—it was a very curious experience last year to be in Berlin, West Berlin, and read, and go to a real way-out saloon, the Eden Saloon, in the city and, you know, flashes and stuff, and a lot of people your age at the bar, and everything. Everybody that came up to me wanted to ask me that question: what about Black Mountain? So I really was in—and in fact, actually, in the past year there's at least two or three books actually being written right now. Duberman at Princeton is doing a history in an educational sense, and just two weeks or three weeks ago I got a letter from a boy in Devon, named Mike Weaver, whom I'd heard was in the States last year and had been to Raleigh, where the archives are, where we solved the problem, how do you cut off people's lives? You know, colleges are for youth, and there's thirty to forty years thereafter with transcripts and things. So snap, you cut like fate a place like that off. It's very curious, you see, the history isn't closed and it's not like administrations and things, this body. So it was a very puzzling question: what do you do with the record of every student at Black Mountain, especially the last persons that were there, like? Fortunately, the Archives of the State of North Carolina was willing to keep that open and service it for the rest of this century. So as a result, I gave them the papers, instead of sealing them, like Picasso did his letters to his friend last week, for fifty years. It's been one of those marvelous things, open-ended even after its ending. And this boy wrote to me because two weeks earlier he'd got a contract from MIT to publish a book, an anthology of Black Mountain. I don't mean anthology in the literary sense, I mean a documentary,[1] but a very marvelous thing, I mean, nothing but pieces and parts of this place, which lasted from 1933 to the day that the Treasurer and I just confronted each other and said neither of us want to continue with the other, do either of us wish to go alone? And we stopped it right then and there. I mean neither of us wanted to do it without the other, because we couldn't. I couldn't order the books and keep that stuff going, the coal and all that, and he wasn't interested, really, in handling the, like they say, the educational fare. We already had a theater operating or planned in San Francisco, the Black Mountain Theater, for Robert Duncan and a company of about sixteen actors and actresses, and he was the director of that. So he went off there. The *Black Mountain Review*, which had been published since 1954, I think, was being printed in Mallorca under Creeley's editorship, and that thing was continued. And I was planning to offer in all the major American cities, free, eight weeks of an institute in the earliest writings of man, and I don't mean pictographs, I mean Sumerian, Hittite, and Canaanite, amongst the three men, Kramer at Pennsylvania, Samuel Noah Kramer, who's the most interesting man, I think, on Sumerian; and Hans Güterbock at the Oriental Institute in Chicago on Hittite writing and religion; and Cyrus Gordon at Brandeis on Canaanite. And then I was to be anchor man and run the thing between that and Homer or Hesiod or Herodotus, the beginning of some of what we call [   ].[2] In addition, the painters were gone, went to New York; and some of our educators proper, like they say, went to the Hartford Theological Seminary. Our anthropologist, who was trained by Frobenius, got his first job at Frankfurt under Frobenius's museum directorship, was an Africanist, and went to Hartford, as did our linguist who we acquired from Mount Olivet College here in Michigan when that had an administrative smash-up.[3]

I'll come back to the—I start at the end simply because this Weaver has actually put a beautiful sort of a new ceiling on it. And that MIT is publishing the book gives it again that curious condition of Black Mountain, which was—in thinking about coming here to talk like this

1. Mike Weaver published *William Carlos Williams: The American Background* (Cambridge, 1971), but the Black Mountain book was never finished.
2. The latter part of this sentence is hardly audible and not capable of certain transcription.
3. The anthropologist Paul Leser and the linguist Flola Shepard both came to Black Mountain College in 1949 from Mount Olivet College. Leser left for Hartford Seminary in 1951, and Shepard in 1954.

today, I was trying to figure out again the same mystery, the mystery of it, because of what was the two as one that it was. I mean, the gracefulness, the enormous gracefulness, and the complete unsafety, or the lack of any Roman condition whatsoever, I mean the total insecurity, founded, built in, created in its origin, and this incredible gracefulness of human condition. To tell you the truth, I thought I'd just say to you that really the reason why I think it's so interesting and there are people who are interested in it today, and I certainly remain utterly interested in it, is its economy. And I mean that as its housekeeping in the biggest sense, but I meant its economy must explain this—hm, how do you say it? In fact, I should think if I at some point, if anybody wants them, I just list the names of some young people, some young and some old, that had their starts, or their metanoias, at Black Mountain, fantastic list of people! And I think I'll leave it to the end to whisper to you, as I talked to Chad last night or yesterday, what its numbers were, what it really was, stacked up against what I'm sure any one of you must think it was that it serves so much that is memory. What I can say is that it probably was the largest landholder of any university yet in America.

I had that idea, actually, that there were really three Black Mountains, and this boy has, or had, already done this enormous work of going through, and finding, and visiting the great founder of Black Mountain, John Rice, a Southerner from Charleston and a Classicist and an extraordinary orator and antifundamentalist in higher learning; Rhodes scholar, educated by two teachers at Bell Buckle, Tennessee, in Latin and Greek; professor first at Nebraska, then at Rutgers, New Jersey Cultural (I don't know what it's called today), and went off in one of those experimental schools, one that I'm sure any of you today would recognize more easily, I think, than at the time it was created. It was like a valentine at that date in everybody's heart, Rollins College, which was known as the Free Love University, FLU, you know. And it was founded by an editor of a leading weekly in America, *Outlook*, an independent, Holt. And when that was founded I'm not sure, but about that year of Roosevelt's, about the year of the end of the—not the end of the Depression but the crisis of the Depression and the election of Roosevelt that spring of '33. Yeah. The whole thing happened, really—it sounds again like normal America, but this fellow Holt, in the spring of '33, couldn't, in Florida, couldn't stand the mouth of John Rice, who was at that point, I think, ranked Associate—he was under contract; he wasn't under, like they say, tenure. And he fired him, outright. What happened is the origin of Black Mountain. Curiously enough, everybody that really sort of was alive, including the person that became the Treasurer of Black Mountain, who was married to Dwight Morrow, I mean Mrs Lindbergh—or yeah, Dwight Morrow's other daughter, Mrs Lindbergh's sister, and was the president's, like they say, you know, young man. General Electric. The name is Ted Dreier. And he went out with Rice. And so did an enormously able, apparently, professor of philosophy who died on his first lecture at Black Mountain, right in front of his students. And I mean, now, I'm talking myth or fable or fairy tale as

I heard it, you know. I wasn't there. I did not come there until first in 1948, and then returned from Yucatan for a summer session in '51 and then stayed and became Rector in '52. Rector was the title that John Rice demanded the place have for its apparent president, he having been so outraged by Holt and, in fact, obviously a man who would be outraged by executives anyhow if they were more than essentially what they are, and grown more so, managers and fundraisers. Well, at that date, I can assure you, hope was still in the world, the Spanish Civil War hadn't happened, and America was still way back in blueberry heaven, and love was personal as well as possibly social. And the case became—the reason I stress this is that it's one of the glories of unionism. Again, remember the date. I am speaking now of '33. It's the one case, I think, that the American Association of University Professors ... Is that the name of the union?

VOICE: The American Association of University Professors.

OLSON: Right ... that it ever produced, not only a prime principle, but, in the case of Rice, in fact backed a man who was extraordinary in principle. But equally, the report done for the AAUP, if you ever see it you ought to read it, because it's written by one of the finest writers of academia, in fact one of the last possible writers, products of the universities, in America at least, who still write well (but that's not very interesting, really), Lovejoy, Arthur O. Lovejoy, who wrote *The Great Chain of Being*, which is the—I guess you probably have it in the library—or something like that, the history of Western, the history of the later carrying of Plato's thought. Right? Somebody must know that book in this room. And this report is Lovejoy's, signed by him, on the Rice case, showing that Rice was absolutely within his, not only in his rights of mouth but his rights of the college's oath to contract within him, and that this president was acting arrogantly and out of hand. And I read that report on the first time I ever had a job—it was Clark University. It was very curious. I had some impression of that print, reading that Arthur O. Lovejoy about this place and this argument about this man. And by this time Black Mountain had been founded, this place; and really it was very interesting, Lovejoy. And there it was. It was a thing that was eventually going to—an omen, like you suggest, saying I was going to arrive at in the sky later on, much to my surprise, because at some point—for example, at just about the time of the Spanish Civil War, when the radicalism of the thirties was at its bend or something, or the bends, I could remember being so bored with the thought that there was this place down there that had a work program, which was the thing that had come sort of, you know, like reached up at that point of time into national magazines or presses. I thought, oh shit! And I of course became, as Rector, the person responsible, for about six years, for the Saturday work programs! And that was something, because one of the really interesting people that hasn't yet come into prominence, quite possibly the best painter that was produced as a student at Black Mountain, Dan Rice, just because he had some spunk, stood me off one Saturday on the program, and took everybody off for beers. And here I was left with the total creation of six hundred acres and thirteen buildings, and windows and cows and stuff, roadways and everything, to just stand there and think, "Shhshhh, a fine lot of fish!" [LAUGHTER] He was the student moderator, an instance of ...

Well, Rice happened at Oxford to marry, squire and marry, Frank Aydelotte's sister, Nell. Mr Aydelotte was the, what, Mr Oppenheimer's predecessor, founding director of the Institute at Princeton, was he not? I think so. Under Flex—this again an instance of America when she was good and constructive—Flexner (I think) 's money founded the Institute at Princeton which Oppenheimer—it was where Oppenheimer actually was when he was made the atomic energy director and then was thrown back when he was declared—how do you say it?—sort of non gratis for the secrets of our power by that committee of three, that federal kangaroo court. And this group of dissidents from Florida met on his porch and decided to open this place, and by god in six weeks it started at Black Mountain, North Carolina, in the YMCA Blue Ridge building, which is the biggest wooden building in America. I've never seen anything like it, Robert E. Lee Hall. And it was Rice's, this Southerner's, idea to put this thing in this wooden building because every service was in one building. In fact, the YMCA supplied the linens. I mean, he had this marvelous—in fact a man and a woman cooked for that place, faculty and students, and it was one of Mr Rice's conceptions that dinner, that all meals shall be—no students or faculty shall ever have to do with the preparation of food, and it shall be prepared for them and they shall sit and enjoy it like Greeks or Romans, if you will. And that evening dinner—all meals at Black Mountain, by the way, for twenty-three years were in common. Or twenty-one. At the end we had to sort of go out like the love feasts of today and go into our particles and pads. But essentially the principle was single—I mean, everybody had three meals a day in a dining hall. And it was true in Blue Ridge, and then it was true when we moved across the valley to let me call it Black Ridge, but it wasn't, I've heard the name Craggy Gardens, some chrysanthemums up on the top.

This was—in fact, Mr Rice almost, I think eventually he left Black Mountain, although he was driven out by the—there's three Black Mountains: the Rice Black Mountain, the Albers Black Mountain, and then this ragged-arse place that I and others were a part of. And it was Albers and Dreier, that Treasurer I mentioned, who eventually sort of maneuvered Rice out. In other words, again, he lost because his mouth was so—but he talked well, and he thought well, and spoke out and believed in, in fact, actually, the Socratic method. He cared for human beings' minds, no question. But another thing was that he didn't believe that universities should own anything. He believed in rent, simply that it took care of services and again left that shot down the alley as the thing that you were here for, and do what you do, what you do. You can do it all the time, and you didn't do nothing else there, and that's a total occupation.

Equally—and now I will get to the textual curriculum, and then stop and let you throw a question—the original catalog is written by Mr Rice, anonymously, and it says, in so many words, that this place shall be that place in the world in which the arts shall share the center of the curriculum with the more usual studies. And he meant it. Curiously enough, I suppose if you talk in terms of education, literally as such, a curriculum, this was why I suppose Black Mountain still sort of has blood for others, because in some sense Rice is the chief, I would think, the chief reformer of education since the Middle Ages, by meaning that dumb, funny statement, which sounds like a Classicist, also a professor. He doesn't sound like an artist; no man would come out that flat. But, you know, it was true. And even the plural works. And it is—in fact, another way of saying it, there is an autobiography of Mr Rice, called *I Came Out of the Eighteenth Century*, which was withdrawn for libel, so you can't see it very easily. There's a few copies around, in libraries or something, but it never was on the market. And the last chapter is on Black Mountain and his part in it—I mean, his being the *raison* and his part creating it. Now, if I say that was the curriculum, that was the trivium or the quadrivium, quadrivia of the place, quadrivium and trivium of the place—and new, because there's something funny there. It's like the difference between seven and eight. He added the ogdoad by that statement, that funny center of the curriculum.

Now we come to the very strange thing, which I also was thinking this afternoon. I hadn't thought of this before; I thought I'd say it to you. Two things I want to say is both, remind me to talk about the city, but equally, this strange thing happened in that year that Hitler, of course, rose, came into power that same year: it's one of those things, '33, wasn't it, when he came to ...?

WALSH: '33, yes.

OLSON: Same year as Roosevelt, this thing in Black Mountain. It's like Walt Whitman, Herman Melville, and Queen Victoria born in the same year, 1819. (Can somebody give me a match?) And Black Mountain's incorporation is the document that I was in the courts finally owning Black Mountain on. This is another instance of Mr—in this case the wives of the three men that essentially founded it were Mrs Rice, Mrs Dreier, and—funny, those legal documents were wives' things. I suppose they often are. Maybe this college is originally incorporated ...

VOICE: Were they [INAUDIBLE]?

OLSON: No, they were the incorporators. The only names on the document are three wives of these three, the clust of three, the nucleonic three. And that document, by the way, I still have. In fact, a writer you may know, Michael Rumaker, who was graduated from Black Mountain, just published *Gringos and Other Stories*, wrote me recently saying that he was trying to get a college job and could I possibly give him paper on his graduation. I'd failed to send those last documents to Raleigh. And I have this enormous doorstop, the stencil, the what do you call it of Black Mountain ...

VOICE: Seal?

OLSON: The seal, yeah. You know, you could kill somebody, it's so— [LAUGHTER] Raskolnikoff—one blow, and that's the death of that watchwoman! And I just took a piece of my yellow paper and wrote and stamped it, right, only two months ago. It's very illegal, at this date. But mind you, that incorporation—now I'm going to tell you the terms of it—non-stock corporation, it made it possible for me, for example, for years to lay the debt on the land, finally sell that land at a profit greater than all the debts, because it was the most beautiful land in the Blue Ridge at six hundred acres, and a herd of thirty-eight Herefords, and a farm with twelve milk cattle and guinea hens and pigs and a mica mine. I realized about $150,000 just by simply planning ahead of time to lay all the debt over on the possibility of this potential sale, which you never, you know, you never know what you're gonna get, you never know what's going to happen in the next market on that stuff any more than anybody else does. Well, it worked out like lucky omen, and we not only made it, but in the end the same lawyer that incorporated was the lawyer that I, in Gloucester, I made a long-distance telephone call and said, "Look, Mr Williams, I just mailed you the final checks for the benefit of the creditors"—Assignee for the Benefit of the Creditors was one of my final titles—"and I'm enclosing a check for your services, and that's the end." And he and I were the last voices of Black Mountain. The incorporating lawyer and I, a magnificent creature out of the old Southern past, like Andrew Jackson or any of the fine lawyers of the South, whom Mr Marshall as Chief Justice—that kind of stuff. And he, absolutely, has this damn probity. For example, Black Mountain was the first, I think the first Southern college certainly to—I mean, it isn't that way; that says it wrong. Black Mountain had the admission of Negroes as its— you know, it wasn't even—if you think of it as debt, the letter has already killed the spirit. I mean, there wasn't any—I mean Black Mountain admitted Negroes as well as the rest of the citizens of America. And this lawyer, being an Asheville lawyer, a Southern lawyer and a member of the representatives at Raleigh, finally had to get out. And I found, one day, in the files this lovely letter of his—but he remained absolutely a member of the board—no, not the board, but the directors of the place, 'cos now I'd want to say that in terms of it comes a point how do you say the way Black Mountain was administered. In any case, he was the only man, he was the last man, the lawyer, that I spoke to. But he had felt this professional necessity to ask to be excused, because Black Mountain admitted Negroes, from continuing, not as the lawyer of the corporation, but as the—what was that damn thing they had at that time?—well, the board. Yeah, that's right, a member of the board. Because the founding of Black Mountain was based upon these principles: no accreditation, no board of trustees, no endowment, no ranks, all people paid the same and one payment for everybody, except for that thing which is current too: where a person had no money, they were, unknown to anybody, paid. In other words, the tuitions were all the same, everybody paid the same, but actually somebody paid nothing. That is, there were, not endowment funds, but there were subscribers to the poor. There was a cat walked here and he didn't come in, asking me why I talked like I do last night and I'm not productive, or constructive. I thought, my god! And they need listening to me now. I'm talking about a condition of American education, in the South, what, from 1933 to 1956 when we closed, October '56. It took me another year to finally sell and clean up the debt and figure it out right, '57. And here was this place. It did not graduate its own. Every student that graduated from Black Mountain was graduated by an outside examiner. So that she tested herself not by that ingestion or corruption of the self-educating school, but put herself up against the test of all outsiders on her students, which, I suggest, is one of the liveliest things—I've never heard of it in any other school in the West, have you?

VOICE: Earlham, probably.

OLSON: Earlham does it?

VOICE: It does that to some extent. Within your major, they have outside examiners. It's not common.

OLSON: Well, Earlham is one of our "sisters," a Quaker sister of Black Mountain. We had interchanges there. Well, I certainly don't want to—I mean, I should—I'm sorry, the personality stories or the life stories of Black Mountain are much more interesting than going through—but I wanted to get at least this quick academic, educational, structural, property, administrative picture in your mind.

ROGER MITCHELL: Can I ask a question?

OLSON: Please!

MITCHELL: I'm curious to know why Black Mountain …

OLSON: Why? Yeah, I know. Well, the only reason was to give John Rice a place to continue to be John Rice, teach Classics, be a Socrates, found a college, and have a college in which he was the Rector and there was no president.

VOICE: He wanted to know why it closed.

OLSON: Oh, did you ask that?

MITCHELL: Yeah, I did.

OLSON: The same. Honestly. [LAUGHTER] I mean, both Huss and I wanted out. And nobody else wanted in. So then we just sat, and had a beer in Asheville, and said, "O.K." And we'd opened, by the way, we'd opened, with a reasonable number of students, and money in the bank, and a future. We opened—as a matter of fact, I had a picture I lost in some bar of the last night in my house with my wife and I, where we had a party for the opening.[4] And the next

4. The photograph found in the archives at Storrs is reproduced in *Maps* 4 (1971), p. 42. See also Mary Emma Harris, *The Arts at Black Mountain College* (Cambridge: MIT Press, 1987), p. 241.

morning I woke up and my wife said Huss was down and would like to see you around noon. And I said, "Oh dear, I'll bet I know what's on his mind," 'cos it was certainly on mine. I mean, you know, we had gotten to the cliff that has now become the hanging of this time. I wrote a thing for this Mike Weaver on just the answer to your question.[5] He asked, "Will you write a piece on the 'fall' of Black Mountain?" It sounded like "disobedience and the first fruits"! And I, of course, not only don't think it fell, or closed, it only stopped! Like it began. I mean, not like it began; it went out the other end. [LAUGHS] I mean, it did close! And it closed, like I said when I started on all these mad places, like other places.

On that program, for example, I was going to give, CBC wanted to take it off the—if I gave it in, say, Vancouver or Chicago, that first eight-weeks thing, they wanted to take it right away and put it on television. And, in fact, in some of the last moves, parts of moves, or settlements or plans of the place, that woman I mentioned, Mrs Dreier, I went to call on in Milton, Mass., one night on the trip north to Boston to raise a few bucks for those— for anything—and she wanted me to bring Black Mountain into that radio station which was Channel Two, I think, in Boston, the major educational television station, and make Black Mountain the university of the air. And this, by the way, this was early. Mind you, again, this is '55, I think, or '56. And there were all sorts of—in fact, the place that is now the home of all that movement of Cage and Cunningham and Tudor and the potters of Black Mountain outside New York City on the Hudson there, Stony Point, it's literally a continuing limb of Black Mountain. And the man who was our architect at that time, Paul Williams, had money from his father and wanted me to—made us the offer, and I had to make the decision—to move the thing north, either to a skyscraper floor in New York City or to a range of New York City within 250 miles, in the country or by the shore, that kind of thing.

But I wanted to tell you that in writing this piece, well, I said, we got to the point where holes in the head and innocent girls were more than we could handle. And that was really true. I mean, those of us who were on the faculty had buried cows, and didn't know anything about farming, and suddenly the thing that has become a condition of the youth of America, the origins of civil war, actually had begun to come into existence. And, in fact, Black Mountain was practically one of the hearthsides where you first saw—what I mean by "hole in the head" was literally two cats come in one night in a rainstorm, big rain—yeah, it was the night of that party! It's why we closed, come to think of it, was a hole in the head! That night there was a huge rainstorm in the mountains and we had this party in our house and suddenly the door opened and these two cats, one a painter and the other an actor from Louisiana, walked in. They looked wet, but they looked O.K. And my wife suggested they sit by the fire in the fireplace, and she looked

5. The prose piece sent to Mike Weaver, "So There It Was," dated 7 March 1968, quoted by Butterick in *Muthologos* II.185 includes the summary: "Wes Huss and I closed it on a dime. It was as simple as going for a beer on a rainy day."

down and then just gestured to me. And here was this guy with a big quarter hole, size of a quarter, no skull. Well! [LAUGHTER] And just about a year earlier, one of our best painters from the Coast, plus Mr Creeley and Mr Rice, that painter I mentioned, and Jorge Fick, who Kline graduated as a painter, and Robert Hellman, the writer, all were in a Buick, and Rumaker was waiting for Field to come home, sitting out in the night, and I was just in bed, when this damned Field in a big Buick got sore—first he was dropping Hellman—went down the hill, over a gully, to his house, and drove the car right straight into the wall, at the top speed. And it was a battlefield. This place was strewn with these bodies, broken backs, broken hips. Creeley just shook his head and walked away, with a match, lighting his cigarette, after he and I hauled—unfortunately we didn't know enough to tell Dan Rice's back was broken and you shouldn't move somebody like that. We gently got him out of the car and into the grass. But this is the kind of thing that finally—it was, like, not inefficient, it was just unable any longer to cope. Well, one of the things we couldn't do was cope with the rising change of human identity, of the problems of human identity or the search for human life.

MITCHELL: I heard certain stories that you had pressures from the community.

OLSON: [LAUGHING] Are you kidding? Imagine that crazy Rice putting a school like this in the mountains, like, of Tennessee! I mean, gee, really! And that environment really was very hostile. But that was true from the beginning on, to the end. And in fact, actually, the only thing happened was, when Huss and I finally were faced with crises and money, our own bank, the Northwestern Bank of Black Mountain, wouldn't give us $10,000 on a property which I later realized hundreds of thousands. So. But that didn't squeeze us. I mean, we switched from money to, well, you know, what you people know, the new economy. We shifted to pad and council house and a common dining room of another sort, grits and hominy, our own pigs or something. And we were all right! In fact, we were in that sense a tent. They didn't know it was out there. I'm sure that these stories are—which is only one of the multifoliate, probably, explanations of it and why that boy thinks there was a fall. Please, I'd rather—I wasn't supposed to make a speech; I was supposed to just sit here and answer a lot of questions.

WALSH: I'm not quite sure how the structure of the learning was there. Was it sort of an apprenticeship kind of thing, or was it more classes, or what?

OLSON: No, it was very stiff. It was classes very strictly. And a full curriculum, and a faculty of twenty-six, many of whom were—that's where that thing I slipped up on, didn't finish that story of '33 and Hitler. Actually, what happened was—I expect it's the strangest blending of Europe and America that happened at that date. Suddenly from the Bauhaus, the school that was particularly offensive to Hitler, I think, we acquired, say, a painter like Albers, some of our great weavers, two of our professors of subject matter, one of our chief administrators. The place opened actually in six weeks after that thing in which Rice was on the porch of his brother-in-law's, with this enormous influx of, like, the first comers to America. I mean, it was like Cotton—the priests of Boston. I don't mean the John Winthrops, but the opposite, the teachers of the parishes of Boston and some other districts. But I mean the curious intellectual flash across the Atlantic, which lasted to the end, by the way. The place was—one of the attractivenesses of it, and in fact I would say somewhat lent to the grace of it, was the presence throughout of Europeans, and very, very good instances. Gropius, for example, who founded the Harvard School of Architecture, was one of that time. And Albers, as you know, or you'd know the painting, I think, of Albers. Albers, I really—I mean, Albers and Dreier brought me to Black Mountain and, in a sense, I was the substitute back. Do you know that those men were—that the students were so—like, I laugh now that I see the student revolt, because the students was able to ask for the resignation of Ted Dreier, not as Treasurer, but as a teacher of mathematics. In the moment that that happened, Dreier was so personally affronted that he asked to resign, and Albers, a smart man, knew that that was the source of all the chits that covered the deficit of Black Mountain, which ran about 10,000 a year, resigned. And that's how Albers left Black Mountain. And it's how the crazy, original European-American thing just became this lumpy later American thing which we all were, with, like I say, some fantastically marvelous Europeans, Dehn, the teacher of mathematics and philosophy, who is the man who answered the clover-leaf knot problem and died trying to solve—what is that maximum wave in flood that no mathematician can yet answer, the famous wave that the last wave and the maximum wave of a river flood? You guys in topology would know what I'm talking about. I don't know enough specifically. He was one that was there towards the end. And the original professor of music who was—whose wife was our—who was there to the end—Jalowetz, he died on our property. He was the conductor of the Prague Symphony, and brought, as a result, that enormous European music from Prague, famous as well in that whole intellectual aspects of that society, part of that day of Europe. Excuse me. Yeah?

VOICE: I was just curious to know—I know something a little bit about Cummington.

OLSON: Yes, quite.

VOICE: Are there any similarities between Black Mountain …?

OLSON: I think the only thing is that Cummington, if I have—if I'm fresh enough—I knew that Cummington quite well. It was again one of our reflexes.

VOICE: It, too, was populated with a lot of foreigners. It was about this time.

OLSON: Yes. But I think Cummington tended to be professional craft, and the thing that often—for example, like the Communist Party of the South—Black Mountain was always being fought for. I mean, amazing, overnight, for example, there'd be an enormous coup d'état planned at dawn. For example, Bentley, that translator of German plays, he, in one of the great Southern Conference of Human Welfare attempts to grab the administration under a very fine man that founded the later Civil Rights Congress, Foreman, Clark Foreman—and it was the Party all right, don't kid yourself, and they wanted Black Mountain in a part of that folk-craft and Southern rights nation that was part of—it's still a part of the scene, right? And they needed one vote and they decided to see if Bentley would yield to them, and they got him into a night session and he learned of the conspiracy. Overnight, however, he felt that it went against Black Mountain's democracy, so at breakfast he asked all the people to hear him. And it was that kind of a place where you could call—you announced concerts within three minutes, I would say, because it was one spot. You announced a coup d'état—I mean, you counteracted a coup d'état in two minutes. You equally, of course, were teaching in two minutes, you were talking in two minutes, you were painting or doing other things at the other end of the lake within two minutes. It was about a two-minute walk from the dining hall to a studies building which was built out over the lake at the other end. And this was all in a very narrow or a little shallow ladle of a spoon at the bottom of a valley, of which the mountain and the property went up rather another seven or eight hundred feet possibly. I never went to the top, but I used to watch my herd of Herefords in the end like a great plantation owner up there in the sun where we left them from spring to fall. It was the very beautiful condition of this funny little pool in a spoon at the bottom. And this was, by the way, the first town west in the Allegheny Ridge. It was up on the—towards the twelve-hundred rise from Old Fort, which itself is the end of the Great Warrior's Trail, the great trade trail of the Indians. Cherokees picked up Iroquois' goods at Old Fort and went up that three-thousand-foot rise, and Black Mountain—actually the property of Black Mountain was the home of—what was that boy, that fabled boy of Cherokee, the holy boy of Cherokee legend?[6] So we were a strange spot, in a strange spot, this first town on the plateau of the Alleghenies starting west.

VOICE: How many students did you say you had at the peak in actuality?

OLSON: Let me—I told you I'd end up with the smallest pool of truth!

VOICE: I was wondering what were the admissions requirements?

OLSON: Well, that brings up that question of I want to say "city." One way of saying what I think is the feeling of the place for those—you can talk to many others, Black Mountain people—for me it was the largest city I've ever known, the swiftest, and, you know, it's all there, absolutely all there, a

---

6. The Wild Boy of Black Mountain is described in *Myths of the Cherokee* by James Mooney (19th Annual Report, Bureau of American Ethnology, 1900), pp. 242, 432, the probable source of Olson's knowledge of the Cherokee, though he would also have gained insight from his fellow faculty member David Corkran, who was an expert in the field. Olson also owned Marion L. Starkey's *The Cherokee Nation* (NY: Knopf, 1946), where p. 8: "It was from a cave in Black Mountain, near Asheville, that Wild Boy released all the ills upon the earth."

very strange experience. And excuse me, now, repeat that question so that I know what I'm answering.

VOICE: What were the admissions requirements?

OLSON: Yeah, that's right. So the other thing: the entrance and exit was practically remedial. I mean, I want to say that like "city," if you'll hear me. A city is a wonderful thing because you can walk in and out of it, yes? At the same time, it is a unit. And the thing about Black Mountain was this crazy fact that whoever was there god knows why they were there. I mean, the reason that they were there went from limp, limpen grammar school incompetence to some of the finest or most interesting minds. For example, when this fellow Dehn I mentioned died, and we were seeking another mathematician, I tried like hell, and I have some contacts, or had, with interesting mathematicians, and I end up finally with Lefschetz at Princeton, who blew his hands off when he was a chemist as a young man and had these funny hands. When you had him for canapes you had to put the thing on the iron hand and then he'd lift. It's a most beautiful thing. A man of enormously beautiful will, that shifted from a practising chemist to a creative mathematician, like they say, simply because he'd lost—he blew his two hands off. He was really one of the fine men of mathematics, and he said to me, "Oh, don't trouble yourself, hire that man,"—what's his name? Kemeny, I think it was—two Hungarian boys named—"that you graduated last year," and that Brauer, I think it was, the mathematician at North Carolina, had graduated as the outside examiner. He said, "He's the finest young mathematician I have ever known." It was like that where you get a violinist from Oistrakh or some—I mean, you suddenly get these damned—you said "apprentice," I think, at an earlier point. See, those words don't work. Like "talent," you know. Because it was a university; it was educational, you dig? Very curious, it was not—it comes back to the Cummington question in another way; or it comes back to that original thing, which I think is the conundrum, of Rice's meaning of the arts, which was absolutely Enlightenment and 18th century, and he himself has none of those energies. I mean, his PhD or his thesis at Oxford is on Stella and Swift's love letters. He wrote for *Collier's*; his major educational writing was in *Harper's* and was against the founding of the University of Chicago, Hutchins, and a poor pedagogue. He called it "Fundamentalism in Higher Learning" in 1937. And he was shot, right? I mean, just like Deadwood Dick. He drew him down on the first line. I mean, they never had a chance. It's a marvelous essay on the problems of the education that you are refugees from, I assume, by being here. [LAUGHTER] But, for example, there's a man who still threatens me by arriving at my door from New Haven, who was five years older than I was when I was Rector at Black Mountain, was writing a Confederacy novel, still is, which is absolutely fascist, is built on the White man's hate of Negroes, Jews, and Love. [LAUGHTER] He came from a rubber plant in New Haven and had never been able to learn how even to spell or to write, and was admitted to Black Mountain because of the condition of our linguistics professor, the one I mentioned that we got from—Flola Shepard, who was one of the great instances of both oral and technical language users. And I still have and will get somebody to publish some day some of the poems that man wrote to me, or wrote for me, because they are, simply because of the illiteracy, interesting. Which, if you know, is a verbal advantage sometimes: instance the Greenberg manuscripts of 1912. One of the greatest poets who's not known in this country died at eighteen. What's his first name? You know the Greenberg that Crane stole and published as his own, thinking the kid was never discoverable, because he was dead, and he got the only manuscript.[7] Well, this stuff is absolutely dazzling because of the spelling. It's exactly some of the things we were talking about yesterday, or we were talking last night about bubble gum. What's that stuff you showed me? Bubble gum, those wrappers, they're intentionally message-y, right? Well, you know illiteracy, non-spelling, or inability to spell, can be very psychically powerful. I mean, it's like a release of the psyche in some "nuts," I mean, some schizophrenics, like Peter Orlovsky, who, again, a fantastic—yeah, Mrs Ginsberg, that man has written about three poems which would—well, they're possibly better than Allen's, actually, in fact. I think one is, actually, the poem written in Benares, the filthy one, the really filthy one, which was published by Mr Sanders, the man I mentioned last night, in *Fuck You/ A Magazine of the Arts*, which is practically the successor of Black Mountain. By title, too, by the way. Again, hear that funny word that Sanders put on that title, as of Rice's first, yeah? You got that? Too much! I mean, that word "arts," which is death in art and in education, I mean, right across the board. I mean, it produces nothing but bad schools and poor art schools, I mean cheap art schools.

DAVID STOCKING: According to Robert Creeley, he and Duncan are no longer writing in the prosody or in the system developed at Black Mountain.

OLSON: I should hope not. They'd be hurrying back there.

STOCKING : Right. The question I have is: are you and Creeley and Duncan— I mean is this a new movement? Are you creating—are you at all together?

OLSON: No, I think that whole "Black Mountain poet" thing is a lot of bullshit. I mean, actually, it was created by the editor, the famous editor of that anthology for Grove Press, Mr Allen, where he divided—he did a very—but it was a terrible mistake made. He created those sections: Black Mountain, San Francisco, Beat, New York, New, Young, huh? Oh, I mean, imagine, just to hear of "young."[8] Hear the insult, if you're young. You're suddenly classified into a thing by one of the great editors, the founder of *Evergreen Review*. And the first four issues of *Evergreen Review* are really first rate. But

7. Olson owned a copy of the *Southern Review* for the summer of 1936 containing an exposé, "The Greenberg Manuscript and Hart Crane's Poetry" by Philip Horton. The man from New Haven was Benton Pride.
8. The subsections of the *New American Poetry 1945–1960* were not given headings, but Donald Allen explained the divisions in his preface, where he states that section 5 "includes younger poets" (p. xiii).

he made a big mistake; he made a topological error. I mean, he had wrong topology in the damn, stupid thing, and he created something which is very unhappy. There are people, for example, poets, who just can't get us straight because they think we form a sort of a what? A claque or a gang or something. And that there was a poetics? Boy, there was no poetics. It was Charlie Parker. Literally, it was Charlie Parker. He was the Bob Dylan of the fifties.

STOCKING: I think that at least Creeley is writing in a system. I mean, he has more or less a kind of poetics from which he's writing at the moment.

OLSON: The latest, you mean, the newest? The numbers and figures?

STOCKING: Yes.

OLSON: Well, that's quite a breakthrough, that's his metanoiac, his conversion.

STOCKING: Does your own recent poetry form any kind of poetics?

OLSON: Oh, very much. What I was trying to—what I called last night the "archaic." Yes, quite.

STOCKING: Is that at all related to what either Duncan or Creeley is doing?

OLSON: No, on the contrary. I think the three of us have gone—and I must insist to mention other poets, because these are only three. I mean, I hired those two men as instructors, and I was hired as an instructor, that's all. We were three instructors. And they were my friends. We'd been published in Boston, 1950, in *Origin* together. And actually at this date, I mean the three of us—for example, I just received, I told that class yesterday, the last poems of Duncan. Unbelievable, these new *Passages*. "Passages 33" is what I think where Duncan is. I think he's now at 49 or 50. I mean, he's moved into almost a status or something, if I may use that word, a condition of status. I don't mean stasis, I mean literally status. He's become a big poet, like Yeats. I mean that quality; suddenly, at 49 he put on the robe. And he writes marvelous—but it's big, it's odic—"paeon" would be useful. And non-Blake, but I mean beautifully American. It's like we were talking last night about that blast, that new novel of Mailer's.[9] It's like Dunky the Fairy, suddenly, like Mailer the All-American Male, suddenly both these stand forth like American men. It's as beautiful as that. Two such—suddenly the slot opens on one side, the slot opens on the other, and out comes these two figures, baagh! And the writing is almost the same winter, this winter, this enormous winter of nothingness and horror, and suddenly these two big poets just pumpfh! (Mailer, I should say this great prose writer.) I mean, suddenly this marvelous thing. And then Duncan's like that. Creeley, on the contrary, is like the soul, the psyche and the soul, suddenly stepping over that thread that kept him from walking differently, I think. I think he's made a great movement.

9. On 13 March 1968, just before leaving for Wisconsin, Olson had written a statement about Norman Mailer's "The Steps of the Pentagon" (later published as *Armies of the Night*), which had appeared in the current issue of *Harper's*. (Sent to Robin Blaser, the typescript is now at Simon Fraser University.) Olson notes that Mailer styles himself a "left-conservative," a term he applies to himself later in this tape.

MITCHELL: Is anybody writing "projective verse" any more?

OLSON: Well, I don't know that that thing ever meant any more than, say, if I would—in these last few days—and not necessarily because of Beloit, actually for another reason, a woman that's writing a book on *Call Me Ishmael,* who wrote me a letter last week and asked me if I had composed that book with geometries in mind. I wrote back and said, "Gee, I don't …" She admitted she had nothing more than high school geometry, and so did I. But she does know that I pretend to have some knowledge of non-Euclidean geometry. Well, to be trouble, I wrote to her and I suddenly was reminded of something I didn't even know. And I told that to her, that that word, which the day I wrote that piece, was fresh to me, is used exactly by a Canadian geometer named Coxeter in a book which I'm sure your library has, called *Projective Geometry.* And I mentioned it to her,[10] because I had to go to the Library of Congress to find this book or look at it. And the reason I did was this story: a painter, who was my buddy, a Roman painter, Cagli, who published in my first book of poems, *y & x,* Black Sun Press, Paris, and his drawings, and he was the one that told me this marvelous story of a boy working for his father in Hartford, Connecticut, selling rugs; and because they were Armenians and it was new, they worked hard, and the boy didn't get any further education at the time that he dreamt all the new forms of possible—all the new solids, the polytopes, he dreamt one night. And he didn't know what the hell had happened. But he knew (excuse me, I didn't mean to plug the week's lectures, but it's another instance of where he's together), he knew that these were something crazy, and he then went on to study, and find, and try to learn, himself, how to make those shapes. If you ever go into the Harvard Library, there they are, on floor seven or something, dusting in the shelves, all the new solids, the polytopes of man. And this boy did it, from one dream one night, as an uneducated, or somewhat educated but working boy in Hartford, Connecticut. This is in our century; this is later than Yeats, obviously. And the story is told in this book, *Projective Geometry,* by Coxeter. And I want to just answer you by using the word in its homology rather than in my application of it, which I still believe in. I don't mean I believe in something I called "projective verse," but I do believe in something that the word "projective" holds in the way I used it there, actually as against closed verse. If you remember, actually the first passage is the French verse drama between closed and open. And even that, I mean, not free, or non-metrical, or anything, I mean open, simply, a geometric condition rather than a—in fact, that's fair enough, it is geometric rather than a—but if you say that at this date, after the physicists and mathematicians of the last century, suddenly you're into a great problem; you're into whether the field of inertial energy and the metrical field affect each other. And in fact, as you know, in Planck, which is like post-Einstein, that is true: that the inertial field is affected and does change. So that there is, I think, still a rather

10. Ann Charters discusses the geometry question in her *Olson/Melville: A Study in Affinity* (Berkeley: Oyez, 1968), pp. 13–15.

interesting argument for "projective" as a validity in art as well as of the universe.

VOICE: Are you talking about patterns projecting on patterns in terms of this inertial business?

OLSON: No, I'm talking actually that movement of force as wave and particle and particles dissolving into vibration. I'm talking quantum as well as the construction of the—I'm talking normal topology, if I may say so, if you know that word again as mathematics, or as a division of mathematics. Again, don't press me much further than my own words, because I won't be—I'm no mathematician, I'm no geometer; I'm just, like, a report.

VOICE: Through this whole thing, there's one thing that's bothering me. When he asked you first about curriculum, I thought, very honestly, you contradicted yourself.

OLSON: I did? Good. How did I?

VOICE: Saying that it was a strict curriculum and at the same time there was all kinds of spontaneity.

OLSON: Oh no, I didn't say those words at all. I wouldn't. For example, spontaneity I don't believe is interesting, really. And I didn't say strict curriculum, I said it was strict in the sense that there were classes and it wasn't master and apprentice, it was literally the same as what you have, and in fact, actually, as all colleges and universities. And one of the things you had to fight in all these struggles as of, say, Cummington on the professional-technical side, or the technological, to use it in its way that we now call technology-land the USA, equally, the left, the struggle to make Black Mountain a community in the social, purposeful sense, either agrarian or lib-lab or actually communist—and in fact there's a lot of places, lumps of it here. One, for example, a fantastic—one night one economist took fifty-two students and himself and went to Oregon ...[11]

[GAP]

... Hear me when I said it was possibly the most graceful place I've ever been in in my life, and not safe at all. I'm talking about a live society, not something proposed, something that was done and was there. We ended and exited, and these things happened there. Wow, I mean I want to start talking like Wallace Stevens about the "live and sustaining air" or something. I mean some part of it. I mean the way the air was full of the droplets of event. You know, them stereos, they don't accomplish that, that's all. I mean, I think not even right now, if you'll excuse me. And of course that would be our argument. But excuse me for insisting, as a "left conservative," that I don't believe so much in the—in how easy it is.

---

11. *Quixote's* firsthand report on this event indicates that we can add here the words: "and started Grundtvig College over my resistance to such" (p. 90).

VOICE: As a poet, as a communicator of truth, the truth you were talking about last night, how did this affect, say, some of your administrative decisions at Black Mountain, and how did you ...?

OLSON: Yeah, I agree. Yeah. Well, mind you, I was only the third Rector. There were two other Rectors. One was Albers, who was one of the damnedest, as you know, if you know his paintings, is one of the—well, how could you, those of you who know, how do you say what Albers was, what Albers is, as a painter (he was eighty-two years old last week)? You know those damned things, those squares, and those squares and those squares, and those circles and those circles and those circles, and those angle lines and those angle lines and those angle lines, and those labyrinths of visual optical trappings. What is that? I mean, think of it. It's one of the stiffest, dryest forms of both line and paint that still isn't known. Mondrian and he, say, as of, say, Klee and Kandinsky, who were his contemporaries at the Bauhaus and were young painters together ... No, continue to pay attention, my dear, will you? Or argue, because I think you raise a very crucial question. If Black Mountain is radical, it sure is! [LAUGHS]

VOICE: You really read me wrong, that's the only thing I can see.

OLSON: O.K.

VOICE: You impute directions and motives that I just don't have.

OLSON: Oh, my god! It sure tasted good! [LAUGHTER] Well, after all, I don't know you as well as I know myself. [LAUGHS]

WALSH: I think it's about time. I better go up there.

OLSON: Sure. Excuse me. Well, as long as Chad's leaving, maybe we all better go. But I ought to, really, as long as he's gone, do the same thing he asked me yesterday: like, how big was—how many students were at Black Mountain? That's the funniest thing of all, I don't understand how to ...

VOICE: Was Duchamp there when he was young?

OLSON: Duchamp? I don't believe so. Not that I've ever heard, but it's possible. No, he's too old to have been young and at Black Mountain too. You mean Marcel? You know, I mean, god help me he was playing chess at eighty in Washington Square the last time I saw him, and he certainly was young before that, before Black Mountain. I don't believe so. I don't know that Duchamp—Rauschenberg is a Black Mountain student, for example.

VOICE: He was a student?

OLSON: Student! I mean, that's what's so interesting. Rauschenberg is one of the instances of the sort of roster of curious people that that damned place produced. And when you talk of poets, I wanted to mention sort of the poets that were students at Black Mountain, not the faculty poets like Mr Creeley and Mr Duncan and like myself in the rears of—I mean the crazy number of writers that came out of Black Mountain and the painters and the intellectuals or, like they say, professors. Or the creation of things like the Cunningham Dance Company for the first time performing at Black Mountain, and some of the things like that clover-leaf knot and stuff that was done on the ground. I mean, all these peculiarly productive things is society, which was at any given moment not one bit more in number than, in my period, and meant originally to be no greater than, one hundred: seventy-five students and twenty-five faculty. So that's really what I meant by the amount of water in the spoon. It seems to me, as against what was going on current with it, but of course has bombed out since 1950, and from, say, two million students in America to, what, four and a half million now, and six expected for '70? Tell you the truth, I think if people really knew what I'm telling you, it would affect their—it would bend their idea of Black Mountain so they wouldn't know any longer whether they should be as interested as I seem to have remained and you may be, too. Can you believe that something that would be so fluorescent could be so small, as a college or university or whatever you want to call it, a school, whatever you want to call this thing, which was one thing in one place. And when I first got there the faculty was twenty-six and the body was fifty-five. It had, to fully answer the whole question, during the Second World War, due to the GIs—you remember that scene, Office of Naval Reserve or those funny extras—gone up to 125, and for the place to handle it, deliberately boarded out those veterans like so many other colleges did, and went down the road—we were in the mountains—and they were farmed out to farms and farm families, and walked up the hill each day. In other words, at the maximum, the place never had in one moment of time more than 150 people, and at the time I got there it was running just above seventy-five. Please respond on that. What does it do to your minds, I mean that kind of unit of size, your minds at this date? I would love to know. I mean, for me it isn't any—it doesn't disturb mine—the ghost, the spirit, the holy spirit of Black Mountain at all. But I wonder, I wonder myself if it isn't so shocking, in a sense, I mean, so defaulting, that the fall of Black Mountain is in that word. Excuse me. Yes?

VOICE: One reaction: as an instructor at a college of that size, did you find yourself with enough time to do what you needed to do, and the privacy?

OLSON: Yes, very much, actually. In that sense that what I did do was satisfying, because it—like you can sleep in certain places and in others you don't feel so—you feel you're not asleep: that condition of life, of liveliness. I mean none of us, for example, were—again, curiously enough, the condition—I have to use that word—the quality of the production of Black Mountain is the only place you could possibly put the real abstracted numbers, not in the amount again. But then this is a strange century in that respect, as against, say, the 19th, where writers always imagined themselves as Balzacs. None of us—Mr Creeley, say, or any of us, are little pear trees, practically, by production. Excuse me, sir?

VOICE: I wonder if it was more a university or whether it was more a community of like-minded people?

OLSON: No, I think it was a city. I use that word advisedly. That's my best answer to anybody who asks me how should a place be so sort of occupied. It was this damn thing of being a true city. At one point, for example, when the faculty shrank to fourteen and there was not a student in prospect, or we had no money, we had no wages to operate on, I remember a meeting of them all. I was young then, this was back, forty—this is just after Albers and Dreier left, which was the hard time, when the money was gone, money's coverage was gone, and for some reason I felt so strongly the thing which I've written into this piece for Weaver's book, where I didn't mention my source, and I want to tell it to you.[12] That that aspect I call "city" I have to, in a sense, spring from—sprung, sprang (what do you call that, "sprung verse"?), sprang it from, "Hopkins-ize" it out of what you mean by urban, or what most of us do. I tell you this story that—I said to those people that day, "Look, if this place is as interesting as you take it to be and I find it to be, and others do obviously, and there's no students and there's fourteen of you left here, isn't that who you are? Fourteen people on a mountain?" And I then went on to tell that story of the novel, which some of you must know—Miss Buck translated it very interestingly—*All Men Are Brothers*— I think it's 14th century, or 12th, Chinese, and is a remarkable book, because it's at the moment of one of the Chinese empires where the Mandarin no longer had use for his wrestler, his instructor in swordsmanship, his cooks, the dancers of the civilization, the actual, how do you call 'em? The scholars. And they all take to the road, in the novel—it's a two-volume novel—and go west in China. Actually, it is the—I can be corrected, but Mao Tse-tung, I think, actually did have in mind this novel when he took off to Yenan when Chiang Kai-shek attempted to break the original Sun Yat-sen revolution. It's the novel that, in a sense, instructed Mao Tse-tung. It is a very exciting book, because you feel that we are in that period of time when it is not the usual gab of today's relative use of language, dissidence, or disaffection, or anything; it is merely unemployed! I believe you, as the youth, are unemployed! Your talents are no longer valued by this economy, which is what we call corporation-land or technology-land, or Disney. I mean, I don't say this as bitterly. I hope I don't sound so—among capitalists myself, like they say.

VOICE: You would? You would say this bitterly?

OLSON: No, I would not. I would say it in—I mean, I think it's greater than these agonies. But I find that the attractiveness of this idea that day—that was to say 1948—was this funny feeling, my god, this goddamn place is just sitting here with fourteen unemployed faculty, like those who can no longer perform the Mandarin exercise, because they're not valued. It was this peculiar condition of rump Black Mountain. Again we come back to Cummington. I mean the place was throwing off these peculiar feces, and it

12. Olson had written to Mike Weaver: "The mountain was a holy place West China where all had come who were thrown out of the Mandarin exercises" (manuscript dated 7 March 1968 at Storrs). His source, as Olson reveals below, is Pearl S. Buck's translation of *All Men Are Brothers* (*Shui Hu Chuan*) (NY: John Day, 1933), of which he owned the second volume of the two.

was like an angel, or a prick, standing high in the sky, a missile. Excuse me, but we have to use obscenities in this country, to be fine at all, to be mandarin at least.

VOICE: Did you find it difficult to come back after you'd gone? Or did you want to come back very badly?

OLSON: To Black Mountain? From Yucatan? No, I didn't want to come back so much. I was very happy in Yucatan, I would have loved to have continued my ...

VOICE: Why did you come back?

OLSON: Oh, I had a baby and no money, and Mrs M.C. Richards, who was chairman of the faculty at that time, wanted off and she was my friend and she asked me to come back. Oh no, she didn't ask me! In fact, I was black-balled by that woman I mentioned, Flola Shepard. I was refused faculty return. The students paid my salary, another instance of that place's spontan—that's where I think spontaneousness belongs: suddenly you're employed! The faculty blackballs you, they won't employ you. I was in the same situation as John Rice at Black Mountain, you know. Inside Black Mountain I was too much mouth, so Black Mountain itself refused me. Pfffft, keep that tongue away. And the kids wanted me to oraculize, I mean, oralize, uh?

Well, I think we should quit, because I must rest a bit before I read tonight. Thank you very much. Oh, by the way, anyone who is interested, if you can tell me really a quick feeling on that question of size, I'd love it. I mean, anybody that wants to come up and tell me anything that shoots that stuff ... [TAPE ENDS]

The Rise and Fall of Black Mountain College by Alasdair Clayre

Charles Olson, 1954

ALASDAIR CLAYRE: In the spring of 1933, John Rice was teaching classics at Rollins College, Florida, then one of the most advanced experimental colleges in America. He had been a Rhodes scholar; he was a friend of John Dewey; and he had firm ideas about the nature of education. He disagreed violently with the president of Rollins about curriculum and there was a quarrel. Rice believed he had security of tenure; the president claimed that he could dismiss him; and he did.

MORTON STEINAU: Rice was literally ejected at the end of the school year, which would have been June 1933; some time in the fall of 1933, Black Mountain came into being.

CLAYRE: Morton Steinau, who came to Black Mountain in its first years, stayed on through the Thirties as treasurer. Most of the small group of teachers he knew and worked with came originally from Rollins. They were people who sided with Rice in his quarrel, left with him and—with a handful of students—decided to set up their own new college. From the start it expressed Rice's ideas about education: that a college should not just be a place that taught about the good society—it should be a good society. Charles Olson, the poet, came much later and was the last rector; but he was in close sympathy with Rice about the nature of an ideal community.

CHARLES OLSON: Rice even believed that no university should own anything: it should rent everything, including the linens. It should not have a board of trustees; it should not have an endowment fund; it should be completely without ranks or positions. The reason why he was rector and I was rector was because he wouldn't even permit the word 'president': it offended his sense of a successful non-administrative

society. Instead of a society, a flag is what it should be: just another thing which flutters in the breeze.

CLAYRE: Michael Weaver, of Exeter University, is an English scholar who has made a special study of Black Mountain.

MICHAEL WEAVER: The climate at Black Mountain in Rice's day—that is to say, from 1933 to 1938—was something between an American community in the utopian sense and a progressive educational school, although Rice attacked the whole notion of 'progressive' as an institutional concept.

CLAYRE: Rice wrote, in the prospectus of 1933, that at Black Mountain the arts should share the centre of the curriculum with the more usual academic subjects—not the history of the arts, or art criticism, but work in drama, in music and in painting. He believed that these were the subjects which most called out the student's own internally administered discipline, and he believed that they would help his development more than a purely intellectual education.

OLSON: One of the parts of Plato's criticism in the *Republic* is that he's frightened of the dogma of the poet. John Rice in some funny way wasn't. He should be added to Charles Pierce and William James as one of the American pragmatists who somehow or other got us over a stile that's been holding up the whole scene for a long time.

CLAYRE: Rice wanted the best teacher of the arts that he could find. It would have to be a man who was not just a theorist but a practising painter too, and he himself couldn't fill that role.

ANNI ALBERS: Josef and I had been associated with the Bauhaus, which was an in-

stitution where you were always among a group of people experimenting with their own work. So when we were asked to go to Black Mountain, and came across the phrase 'a pioneering adventure' in regard to Black Mountain, we looked at each other and said: 'That's our place.'

JOSEF ALBERS: When we were in Berlin, not knowing where to go, a telegram came, asking whether we would come to North Carolina. And I sent a telegram back saying that I didn't know what North Carolina was. But one of my American students in Berlin knew and said: 'Beautiful country, very southern and very mountainous.' I sent a telegram back, 'I'm sorry, I don't speak one word English,' and they sent another telegram: 'Come anyway.'

MRS ALBERS: It wasn't an established place, like going to Yale, going to Harvard. You didn't go to be at Black Mountain: it didn't exist. So there was this great challenge.

CLAYRE: Other arts, besides painting, were taught at Black Mountain. There was a dedicated drama teacher, Bob Wunsch; Anni Albers brought her craft of weaving from the Bauhaus; but the work of the college in those first years centred round the poles of John Rice's own teaching and that of Josef Albers.

STEINAU: The classes that Rice ran—the Plato classes—had nothing to do with Plato, and nothing to do with Greek. They were classes in semantics and in running down the meaning of a word: 'What does it really mean? And don't bother to use the dictionary. Let's talk about it.' A given word—'love'—might be discussed for many weeks on end to see what it meant in people's lives. Rice was an extremely scholarly man; in addition to which he had a tremendous amount of sanguine lust or joy of living—a desire for power; rebellious, brilliant, vengeful.

CLAYRE: By contrast, Albers was in a more severe and impersonal European tradition. Learning to paint was learning a craft. It had to be methodical and it had to be done by painting, not by discussing.

WEAVER: If a student came to his classes without having done his exercises, which would usually be in design or in colour or some kind of use of material, then he was not admitted.

ALBERS: When you want to learn you have to compare, compare within your own work, and particularly compare with your neighbours who do the same work, have the same aims. That we do all the same exercises makes comparing from neighbour to neighbour unavoidable: 'he did it quicker,' 'he did it better,' 'he does it not so good.' Comparison is the basis of all evaluation. We believe you have to do it more than once; only then you know whether you improve. When a student said to me, 'But this is what I wanted,' I said: 'Commit suicide.'

CLAYRE: Black Mountain was a remote place. The college was isolated and it was a small community. At its height there were less than 150 students and teachers there; and in the prospectus for the first academic year, 13 teachers and 21 students are listed. Only three are local people.

MRS STEINAU: It was pretty amazing to me to find what looked like such a substantial,

12

BBC Interview

Alasdair Clayre, of All Souls College, Oxford, visited Gloucester on behalf
of the BBC Third Programme on 27 July 1968. From the taped interview
with Olson he edited two scripts. The first, on Olson's poetry, was
broadcast on 26 August 1969; the second, on Black Mountain College, was
heard on 15 January 1969, with contributions from Mike Weaver, Annie
and Josef Albers, Edward Dorn, and others. Since the tape recording itself
is not available, Olson's contributions to these two programmes are
presented here from the BBC scripts.

1. The Poetry

CHARLES OLSON: I shrank it.[1] I mean, I want it to live as a shrank, a shank of
a thing; that's what I want. I didn't want the thing that has been narrative all
through this same period of space. One wants a narrative today to strike like
a piece of wood on a skin of a drum or to [STRIKES TABLE]—or to be
plucked like a string of any instrument. One does not want narrative to be
anything but instantaneous in this sense, or in fact as carefully, as close to it
as you can get it. In other words, the problem, the exciting thing about poetry
in our century is that you can get image and narrative both to wed each other
again, so that you can get both extension and intensivity bound together.

***

You have picked out, in asking me to read, "The K," the first poem I ever
wrote. And it raises a nice point why I have to sweat so much under fardels,
because I didn't start to be a poet until after I left quite a few things behind,
and I—the last thing I got out of was politics.

Take, then, my answer:
there is a tide in a man
moves him to his moon and,
though it drop him back
he works through ebb to mount

---

1. Olson is referring to the "First Fact" of *Call Me Ishmael.* He had just recorded the short piece on
the tape, telling Clayre that it was the first time he had read it aloud.

the run again and swell
to be tumescent I

The affairs of men remain a chief concern

We have come full circle.
I shall not see the year 2000
unless I stem straight from my father's mother,
break the fatal male small span.
If that is what the tarot pack proposed
I shall hang out some second story window
and sing, as she, one unheard liturgy

Assume I shall not.
Is it of such concern when what shall be
already is within the moonward sea?

Full circle: an end to romans, hippocrats and christians.
There! is a tide in the affairs of men to discern

Shallows and miseries shadows from the cross,
ecco men and dull copernican sun.
Our attention is simpler
The salts and minerals of the earth return
The night has a love for throwing its shadows around a man
a bridge, a horse, the gun, a grave.

This poem has to my mind no shape. It just happens to have lines that hang together like wash on the line should. But I don't think it has a shape, like laundry doesn't have a shape; but you have to put it on. I think this is a poem, but it isn't—it's a poem in the old—no, that won't do either. It isn't a question of a poem in the old sense. It's a poem, well, which is based on uninterrupted statements. I mean, the syntax is rather clear and decent, and the image is not permitted to either ascend or descend. And then, generally speaking, the vocabulary is clean. It's just not the vocabulary that I claim, because I didn't even know what vocabulary there was to claim. It's just that fumbling to see if you can find out the meaning of what you're—it's the deepest principle of poetry, which is to write the poem because you're fumbling to find it. Obviously there's a lot of people who say, "Why do you have to abandon every means that's known and acquired by the human race, and still use language? Why don't you give it up, for god's sake, and try something else?" I mean, we are the damnedest bunch of pre-metaphysical conceitists, the poets that America has, my friends and peers like Mr Creeley and Mr Duncan and Mr Dorn. We do so come out very peculiarly either middle 17th or late 16th century. I'm thinking of Donne and Sidney rather more than Spenser. I mean, it's like repairing the Atlantic Ocean or something.

***

It's a very great acknowledgement, because he really is saying, "This is for you because I'm wearing your cloth at this moment."[2] But it comes out

2. Clayre had asked Olson to comment on Charles Tomlinson's poem "The Syllables: Homage to Olson."

absolutely his, because it comes out in very, very, like I say, sharp, stark couplets. And I don't—I mean, I never let the thing stay that set. I'm damned if I will, you know, like I'm going to move on or break it the moment it happens, because I don't want it to sit down that long; and I can't "finish the song." That's silly, to my mind. You know, I mean, that's making poems, and I'd rather—somehow or other I don't make poems.

***

There are two versions of the poem that you have asked me to read. The first poem of the *Maximus Poems* is a classic invocation of the muse and I will read the version which is, I think, by all odds, the true one.

[Reads "I, Maximus of Gloucester, to You." (1.1–4)]

That's the best reading it's ever received by all odds; by every shot in the world, it never was read like that. The only time I ever obeyed the written score, which, as we just said, is all it is; it's a score.

***

It's a cat in a penitentiary. It feels as though it's in Florida or Georgia rather, and it's [SINGS] "The racial rock grows higher and higher. The racial rock grows higher and higher." And it's tenor pitched, sort of a holler or scream. You ever hear this thing, "That racial rock grows higher and higher"?[3] It's only like a repetition. That's all I remember, anyhow. I heard it once suddenly in some funny situation. I mean, I can't tell you how piercing, not piercing but so soul-wise penetrating. But you can hear it's a mad idea, I mean, "the racial rock." And say it dated back twenty-five years as a recording, it's one of the most beautiful lines I know. I suddenly realize that it reaches at me because I believe in that fact that monstrosity grows, that it is usually petrified and it grows as such, as, like that fairy tale of John— there's a Grimms fairy tale, "Petrified John." It's the same goddamned thing. I mean, exactly. "Petrified John" is the name of a Grimms fairy tale. And this mad cat in the pen singing this holler or something that has this statement. I mean, listen to it at this date, right? Oh my, wow! I suppose he really means "rock" in the penitentiary sense of breaking rock, breaking goddamned stone mountain. I mean, that's all you do, but—or maybe not. Maybe it's definitely where we all get these things from is our unconscious.

***

On Tuesday this week I end nine years of labor,[4] and on Wednesday, thinking I'm going—I mean, already the future is rushing toward me, and I write what I'm going to read you, which I'm afraid is going to be just the same as what these *Maximus* poems seem always to be, full of dates and persons. But this one, in fact, has sort of relieved me and made me extremely happy for a while. It raises the whole question of how, like, how small can you get. I

3. Olson is remembering a recording of "Lead Me to the Rock" made by Alan Lomax at a prison farm in Mississippi in 1936.
4. Proofs of *Maximus Poems IV, V, VI* were just about to be returned to London for publication by Cape Goliard Press.

mean, "How can you possibly, Olson, be writing about such minutiae, of such an extremely minute speck of earth, this Gloucester, and hoping at all to reach others, other than sort of those who read the classified ads in the *Gloucester Daily Times*?"

[Reads "above the head of John Day's pasture land" (III.195–96)]

2. Black Mountain College

... Rice even believed that no university should own anything: it should rent everything, including the linens. It should not have a board of trustees; it should not have an endowment fund; it should be completely without ranks or positions. The reason why he was Rector and I was Rector was because he wouldn't even permit the word "President": it offended his sense of some society which really functioned like a flag that flutters in whatever breezes cause it to stand up, or if there are no breezes it falls down. Something like that, some real successful non-administrative society. Instead of a society of flag and pennant, a state should be just another thing which is affected by nature.

***

I think what really had made her valuable today is that she was not only the first breakthrough in curriculum since the Middle Ages, but she was, in some strange way, right up to date, the only communal invention that has substituted for the damn Western conception of society, which sort of is assumed as though it has to be administrative, it has to be government, it has to take care of things, or it has to take care of people, or there has to be some sort of thing which does, a City Hall, or the Privy Council, or the White House.

***

It's never been observed that the South is really nothing but a bowl of the Gulf of Mexico, and the only relief you can get in the summer is Black Mountain. That's what she is—a summer resort; and that's why Rice was able to rent Robert E. Lee Hall, with all of its linens and silver and everything else. All the year round. And another 1,200 feet up was part of our property—the mountain ridge, which is all covered with rhododendrons or something, the most beautiful flowers and stuff, and here was these cattle, we'd leave them up there, we didn't have to touch them. Even burs weren't a danger because of the clarity of the pasture.

***

Every evening you came to dinner—we all ate in the common dining-room—and you never knew what in the hell was going to happen, a concert, a show, a dance, a reading. I'd never heard of David Tudor, but suddenly there was a concert by a pianist named David Tudor on a Sunday afternoon. We all played ball, we wouldn't give that up, and I can remember we came in and we were so embarrassed because we were full of sweat. So we sort of went out and sneaked onto the porch to lie down and listen to this man. And that's when I first heard Boulez's *Second Sonata*, all covered with dust from playing first base, and full of sweat. I thought I'd flip. I hadn't heard anything as interesting as that since I once heard Bach. The only other piece of music I've heard in my life, practically, was this goddammed Tudor playing the *Second Sonata* of Boulez.

***

So I had this idea of having Jung, Hawkes, Braidwood come and lecture for two weeks each, and I had the responsibility of leading the thing off; and, obviously, if your theory is that there's four new sciences of man the one I got stuck with was Pleistocene, I mean, was man before the ice, that great man who created those cave paintings and who hunted so successfully that he made it possible for men to succeed him.

***

What is amusing or ironic is that Black Mountain is now practically the dream of all youth. When I read in West Berlin this past winter, nobody asked me any question about my poems, but they were all in the Eden Saloon on me, trying to find out something about Black Mountain.

Olson's kitchen table after a night of talk during Inga Lovén's visit.
Photo: Inga Lovén. Kate Olson Archive.

13

Interview in Gloucester, August 1968

It is known that the Swedish writer Inga Lovén had lived in Boston for a number of years and was probably planning to write about Olson for the magazine she published in occasionally, *Ord och Bild* (Stockholm). The interview was done over a two-day period in mid-August 1968. Olson was well prepared on aspects of Norse history, having read into Carl Sauer's *Northern Mists* (Berkeley: University of California Press, 1968)—notes in his copy at Storrs are dated 4 August 1968. Also on his mind was the book just given to him by Harvey Brown, Seyyed Hossein Nasr's *Science and Civilization in Islam* (Cambridge: Harvard University Press, 1968), which refreshed him on all his earlier study of Muslim poetry and thought in Henry Corbin's works, especially *Avicenna and the Visionary Recital* (NY: Pantheon, 1960). Also present in the second session is Ronni Goldfarb, a student from Buffalo who had come to Gloucester to be Olson's housekeeper.

CHARLES OLSON: … If this sounds too historical or technical, I can explain why I myself at least can't even talk about the question of *samtal*, or conversation, any longer at this date, or projective verse or any of the questions of language or of poetry or prose, without digging down at this point. I have enormous confidence that this is the only way to be clear, because I have learnt a lesson, and I have learnt it from two or three or four, all Muslim poets living contemporary with these same events I am talking about in the North Sea and in the North Atlantic and in the direction of this harbor that we're sitting in, which was intended by the French, the Norse, and the English, as well as the Dutch, as the entrepôt or the entry gate to the continent which was then known as—which was then unknown but was assumed to be (if one could find out how to get around it or through it) Cathay or Asia or China. And what I learned from my Muslim poets[1]—and here I have to include a man who was considered a philosopher but is

1. With his phrase "Muslim poets" Olson is probably thinking of Nasir Khusrau (1004–1088), Chazzali (1058–1111) and Ibn 'Arabi (1165–1240), to whom he was introduced by Fritz Meier's Eranos lecture "The Mystery of the Ka'ba: Symbol and Reality in Islamic Mysticism" in *The Mysteries* (NY: Pantheon, 1955), pp. 149–68. Olson's marginal comment there (p. 149) specifically connects Khusrau with "*late* Norse—& approx identical with Norse occupation of Iceland, Greenland—& Vinland."

actually a tale-teller who is known in Europe as Avicenna (but is known in his own name as Ibn Sina); and it is from him, from all of the Muslims, that I learnt the concept of *ta'wil*, which sounds, suddenly, as though it's as meaningful as *samtal*, and it is as simple as *samtal*, too. What *ta'wil* means, if I translated it immediately, it simply means "backwards."[2] But what it really means is you can't move at all, you can't do anything, without it having, or you having, *ta'wil*. And as I understand Ibn Sina's own under-standing of *ta'wil*, there is only two ways that *ta'wil*—and it is one of Mohammed's own words, I think—I think that actually all these men have their language from the Koran—what I understand *ta'wil* to be is two con-ditions which we today—and Henry Corbin in translating Ibn Sina uses the same language—is a double condition or what we would call a "dipolarity," not a polarization or polarity but a double condition, which experientially is at once topological and etymological.

And why I stress Ari, sort of at the peak of his powers about a hundred years after the Norse had deserted America, at about 1100, and a hundred years before Snorri Sturluson was at the height of his powers—and to me Snorri Sturluson occupies the same position as of the problems in language in northern Europe, and in North America at this date too, as Hesiod in the birth or progress of cosmology and mythology towards poetry in and around the date 800 BC in Greece ... There is about a twenty-five-year spread, apparently, although it sounds a lot more like the spread between Ari and Snorri Sturluson to me, between Homer and Hesiod. But if we inherit, as a culture and a civilization, Homer and Hesiod as founding poets in a thing called, in a thing we now have to be very, very wry about, epic poetry, just as we have to be extremely wry about sagas and Eddas, unless we treat this stuff as seriously as I think Ari was serious in writing—what is the great book called? (my Icelandic is still so poor)—the book, the *Íslendingabók* ...

Another way of saying it: in my own work, for years—let me quote "Letter 23" of the *Maximus Poems* [1.99–101], which is an attempt to be com-pletely careful about the facts of the first use of this harbor, Gloucester Harbor, in Massachusetts in New England. I suddenly break out: this place was first used in the spring of a year which under the old calendar would be mistakenly called 1623, because of the fact that until—what date?—some time during the 18th century, Europe as well as America still believed, still used a calendar in which the year began, the new year was on March 28, if I'm not mistaken, so that the first month of the year was March. It was about three days. So that Gloucester, which is considered to have been settled in 1623, really was settled in 1624. And the problem is to determine the events that were going on in this harbor because of that problem of date, because everything is misrepresented by the dating, unless it's under very careful hands. In exposing in this poem how—what might seem how overcareful I'm being, I suddenly break out and say: "I would be an historian

2. Olson is thinking of Henry Corbin's definition in *Avicenna*, p. 29: *ta'wil* is "to *cause to return*, to lead back, to restore to one's origin and to the place where one comes home ... Thus he who prac-tices the *ta'wil* is the one who *turns* his speech from the external form towards the inner reality."

as Herodotus was, finding out for myself," and so forth, and then go on to quote a fantastic evidence of exactly who was here at such and such a day in the spring of 1623/4.

Another way of saying what's so interesting about the *Íslendingabók* by Ari is that suddenly a hundred years after the major events of the Norse in Europe and in the British Isles and in the North Atlantic, including settlements of Iceland and Greenland and the obvious further settlements either of Newfoundland or of Nova Scotia and New England, is that Ari—we call Ari "Herodotus" and then we call Snorri "Hesiod," which is more true, but until we can get our Herodotus and our Hesiod straight ... And again, I can even say this another way: a man named (which does sound marvelous in the context) Eric Havelock—I would assume the name Eric Havelock has to be Scandinavian—he happens to be an Englishman, born an Englishman, and trained in Classics in England, migrated to Canada and was one of the founders of the most important new political party in Canada in recent years, then accepted a post at Harvard where he was the chairman of the Classics Department, and now is chairman of Classics at Yale. And in between the switch which occurred about three or four years ago, Harvard published a book of his called *Preface to Plato*, which is an examination of *The Republic* and why in the tenth book, or no, in *The Republic* in general but I think in the tenth book in particular, Plato drives the poets out, including Homer and Hesiod, from the education and the preparation of people for society and civilization.

So that we are not so far off. I mean, I can circle about; and in fact I can't imagine anybody that I could recommend except Bruno Snell and his book, where Havelock as the younger man has the advantage, like us who are younger, too, than Snell. Snell—and this is the other great book that is relevant to what we are talking about—the title of his book is *The Origins of Greek Thought*, or *The Discovery of the Mind*. In other words, it is clear to Snell that it was in the development of the Greek language after Homer and Hesiod, in, for example, the invention of the definite article, that generalization occurred for the first time in the world, and that such things then that Plato and Aristotle invented or that conversation by Socrates made impossible—and I mean conversation in that bad sense that I think and hope *samtal* in Swedish avoids, as it seems to me it does, to my ears, simply because it is an Indo-European language like English at an earlier stage, at the same early stage as Greek in the hands of Homer and Hesiod was, before the development of these unhappy grammatical constructions which made possible logic and classification and the whole taxonomy of Aristotle, which has had to be destroyed and is being destroyed, is slowly coming to pieces, as is the present civilization, so that we can get back to ground and then start again.

So on the whole question of poetics and narrative at this date you can trust very, very—you got to brush the dog until you practically get to his skin, and find about three men like Havelock, Snell, and Merleau-Ponty who you can trust at all on questions of grammar, of history, and, in the case of Merleau-Ponty, of literally the meaning of narrative at all in the world. And then I step again right across to Ibn Sina and say that if you, for example—I want to stress that book I am drawing from, Corbin's on Ibn Sina—and oh yes, the whole problem of this topology and etymology is that Corbin is restoring to Western knowledge the fact that Ibn Sina, or Avicenna, was really a storyteller and a poet in that sense. The title of his book is a translation from the Persian: *Visionary Recitals.* The book is called *The Visionary Recitals* of Ibn Sina, or Avicenna.

Now, I am saying that something that was going on in Iceland in the hands of Ari and was continued a hundred years later in direct influence, because between him and Snorri there is a master who taught Snorri what Ari taught is the invention of narrative and image in the languages that we share among the Germanic peoples, which includes English and which is what, for an American, is the Northern condition at this point, is more interesting than any Mediterranean, or at least for me it is, because I find that if I continue to write what I do, I get closer and closer to what I call the Armenian or the Gothonic than I do to anything else.

[GAP]

... And he thinks to himself, "How the hell am I gonna get down there? There's only one thing to do: roll down." So he turns himself full length and just rolls down the whole cliff, using the snow for a bedding, and ends, and steps aboard his vessel. And the crew, they can't—it's like a descent from heaven—they can't figure out, "How the hell did he come aboard? Where did he come from?" They know that there's no dory, he's taken no dory, he's been on the land, and suddenly here's this huge coast, and here he is walking aboard and says, "O.K., set sail for Gloucester."[3]

And there is a story of a vessel—I have forgotten the whole story, but there's a race once—there is two of these guys picking up herring in Reykjavík, and they race from Reykjavík to Gloucester, one of the most famous sailings across the Atlantic Ocean, so I am not off my chore, like they say. You mustn't mind, but the only way I can deal with these kinds of questions is to talk like this, because there is a birth of mythology. If there is a cosmology, which is absolutely possible today due to science, there is no end to the absolute care—I mean, you can take the whole of the expanding universe and draw it. I mean, de Sitter, Planck, Einstein, Riemann, they've presented us with—Lobatschewsky, Bolyai Farkas—there is no reason—I mean, O.K., let the machines go out and let the human being get on board the machines and get out. We got the stuff anyhow. It's happened, I think, twice before in the whole of human history, maybe three times. I put three times: Homer and Hesiod, probably those goddamn Arabs, but their contemporaries were the goddamn Norse or the Anglo-Saxons. I mean, the Germanic peoples and the Norse, they are, like, so like this. Would you

3. This Capt. Thomas Bohlin story is told in Gordon Thomas's *Fast and Able* (Gloucester: William G. Brown, 1952), p. 79 (1973 edn, p. 12). Olson uses it in "Bohlin 2" (11.45). The Reykjavík to Gloucester race is from James B. Connolly's *Port of Gloucester* (NY: Doubleday, Doran, 1940), p. 186.

know a word, *Muspell, Muspill, Muspellsheim*? In Swedish? I can spell it for you. There is a Bavarian poem in the 8th century which is called *Muspilli*. In the Norse it is *Muspell*. And that's *Nebel*, it's "Cloudland."

INGA LOVÉN: That's where they went when they were dead.

OLSON: That is right. But it isn't right; no more than that's where a seal goes when he is dead. It is the whole secret of the whole inner paradise of Creation. Right? This one is definitely "moisture." This is the big problem. What does it mean? Actually, in Norse it means "heat" and "the end of the world." I'm not sure that even my great source here knows.[4] This is in Snorri, this is Snorri again. It's in the *Gylfaginning*. Do you know the *Gylfaginning*? I will never get over this. You have done something to me, Inga. This is the first time my own ancestors' language has ever been—it's like an infection, it's like a poison! It is like Rimbaud said, that poetry is poison. Or "life is poison." That's Rimbaud, one of the great men, the greatest fucking men. *Gylfaginning*:

> Licked man (as such) out of the ice,
> . the cow————did who
> herself came into being
> so that Ymir would have some source
> of food (her milk one supposes
>
> Odin was born of either this man directly
> or one generation further on, Odin's mother
> was the giant————.

[II.154] And now the next poem. Audumla, does anybody in Sweden christianize, baptize their child with the name Audumla? God, wouldn't you love to have a daughter called Audumla? This is my translation of the *Gylfaginning*. Just from having read the *Gylfaginning*, I write this poem, then I go and translate the poem [*Gylfaginning VI*, II.155]:

> a cow Audumla,
> which had come into being to provide food
> for Ymir, licked a <u>man</u> [not a
> iotunn] out of ice whose name was
> Buri, whose son (or maybe it was <u>Burr</u> himself)
> Burr (or Borr) is the <u>father</u> of Odin

That is a beautiful poem in English. Odoo, dooo …

[Rereads the poem, imitating a Swedish accent]

That is almost like what Swedish sounds like, or Ari, because this is where Ari—this is why they got on to this, they got on to this whole question, which is the whole Herodotus. If you know the *Theogony*—and in fact, people, still, to this day—those women the other night,[5] they want to trace

---

4. Olson's source for much of this, and the *Maximus* poems he reads here, is Murray Fowler's "Old Norse Religion" in Vergilius Ferm ed., *Ancient Religions* (NY: Philosophical Library, 1950), pp. 237–50, especially his treatment of Snorri Sturluson, p. 240.
5. It is not known which women Olson is referring to here.

who is married to whom and who was the first, when they came and where they were and what was. It is the basic, natural, not genetic but connective necessity of a human being. There is the miracle and there's the connective. If you remember, once I wrote in "Projective Verse," verse is the connectives, the wrists, the knee, the ankle, the toes, the fingers, all the connectives is verse. There is a certain wit in doing this and in closing it.

I am very proud of that poem. What a vision that is! That's again something like that Eskimo teaching. I mean, it is way ahead of all the fucking stuff that we inherit in classical mythology, at this date, for us. The cosmology has to be sort of rude. It's not primitive. Ha ha! On the contrary, by the law of these two things, these two prior conditions, these two conditions prior to chaos, we've got to be very careful. I don't know what it's like to have been raised in Sweden, but if you are raised in this culture, after what the English did to this stuff in the 19th century, you have got to be so careful you don't dare move. It is dangerous to introduce this even into this book. Even that much is dangerous, because everyone will think they know what you are talking about. They don't know what you are talking about at all. I don't know if it has become a cliché in Sweden; maybe it is considered knowledge that is old hat. I will read a poem written just two years ago, approximately.

[Reads "AN ART CALLED GOTHONIC" (III.168–72)]

This is a titleless poem, which opens with a poem and then does something else.

[Reads "[to get the rituals straight ..." (III.173–74)]

[GAP]

If Swedish *samtal* is not satisfactory, if that is much more like jumping around among trees and branches, that can be very meaningful. Like, birds do it and monkeys do it or Kierkegaard does it. You told me, in a sense, that the quality of Kierkegaard's prose in Danish is almost like that. That sounds very interesting. But if you talk to us—I mean by "us," USA—you know that before the Second World War the Japanese marketed their goods in America and there was a law that the goods should be manufactured in the United States of America, so the Japanese invented a town called "Usa" in order that they could mark all goods that were Japanese, "USA." It is that kind of a thing that I am talking about: that language has become like that. It is factitious. It is only a commercial—and I am trying to say this so that I am not attacking, like, television or ads or anything of that loose, or even interesting, punning. I am talking about the way in which everything is—the reason why Mr Johnson lost the confidence of the American people is simply because he is a confidence man, or they think he's a confidence man. They think nothing he says is what he means, or that there is no meaning in what he says. Basically that's true in a much wider way than Mr Johnson. It's like the young Americans that stop reading and talking entirely. They believe only that they can trust non-verbal experience. I, of course, as a poet in America think that that's one of the most dreadful things that's happened. Not because I want them to listen to poetry. I don't think it's that. In fact, I read now that poetry is like another part of the program; it's going to be added to the Newport Festival or something. It's a necessity, like fishing for what they call stripers. It's part of all unions now to make sure that all workers can leave their jobs early in order to go fishing for stripers. It's all recreational. I mean, I remember just a short time ago saying that the condition of this country has become absolutely two things, acculturated and anaesthetic. That is, that the culture and the aesthetics is the only thing. And that's like what I said just a few minutes ago, if the tape was on, that the youth used to be kept off the market by sending them to school. Now they are on the market and being entirely encouraged, because they have got so much money that there's a teenage market, and it's one of the biggest pieces of the economy. Equally, say, the guitar or the music market is so valuable that they make gold records when there's a million sales, I think. It is as if the whole world is losing its ability to discriminate among functions. And the function of speech—I don't mean speech, but I mean the function— yeah, I do mean speech. I always have to remind myself at a time like this— it is Christopher Hawkes, the English—he wrote a very great book when he was one of the curators of the British Museum called *The Prehistoric Foundations of Europe*, with the subtitle *To the Fall of Knossos*, which would be the history of, like, Sweden and England and the whole of the European continent and Italy and Greece and the Middle East and the Danubian areas and the plains between Europe and Asia and Russia, up to 1450 BC, and it is to my mind one of the most precise and specific books that I have ever read. Hawkes starts his book just where man had suddenly acquired what we call his grey matter or the new brain. That is, he had the *medulla oblongata* at the top of his spine and that was now known as the old brain. And in fact Jung has suggested that the whole condition of the unconscious is actually the *medulla oblongata*. And one of the most interesting things about the development of the cerebellum is that it is all—if I am not mistaken, the major part of the brain is connections, speech and communication, feelings, reflexes of this order. And it was the development of that brain in man that seems to have followed from the fact that he began to develop more than—how do they call the distinction of the thumb?—that the brain that I'm talking about, that is, the grey matter, developed as a sort of further thumb. It made everything more graspable. And actually it is one of Hawkes's points that—I mean, it remains to Shelley and to Dante—and certainly I myself, with my interests, can't get away from the fact that at some point you have to ask yourself the question, "Can there be thought without prior speech?" Or especially a poet always has that experience, that he doesn't write to be heard and he doesn't write with words as though they are oral. In fact, he writes actually in the silence of his own being, with a pencil or a pen on paper; or even if he writes with a typewriter, he doesn't hear it. The whole thing is written from the inside, not only of what it may thereafter be, but the inside of himself, that, in fact, the whole condition of feeling that makes you do, like—if we are talking about poems, or poetry, or equally a story, it doesn't occur in the same circumstances as to tell a story or to lead a whole people by coming up with the right image. It occurs in the privacy or the total secrecy of the universe, whichever way you take it, whether you take it the widest or the smallest, that is, the inside of any one of us as an individual. It is suddenly very quiet and it is everything. But the experience or the occurrence is actually a non—it is verbal in the word sense, and what is called the inner ear is crucial. I can't imagine anybody who is interesting—if you talk again in terms of—who was it, was it Beethoven who became deaf? And it was Milton who became blind. The poem I read you yesterday, that "Wholly absorbed ..." [III.191], the poem of the narcissism of narcissism, I am trying to say there specifically the thing I am here talking about, in that stupid meaning technically of exactly what it is that words are made up of. They're made up of something which I think you can take back to the point which Hawkes is making, that, in fact, man couldn't have had—his point is a very careful one: it's not a question of civilization. I think it's actually a question of culture. But it has to do with— that is, the fact that man could make and use tools was succeeded by a moment in which he could substitute for precept an example, tradition.[6] He could tell his son what it was he was doing instead of the child having simply to mimetically duplicate what he did. And the moment that that became possible, all of the, like, the geometric progression or the multi- plication of man occurred. And I am not talking population; I am talking of the increase of his abilities. And it seems to me that we are at that point today. I meant that the whole matter of what it is that is the language, and here I mean language in mathematics, language in music. That is why I mentioned Webern, and the man who, to my mind, is the only interesting composer that I felt, when I first heard him, a likeness that I wanted to admit for myself at least, was Pierre Boulez, the French composer. Where he was going in 1952 seems—again, where those painters I mentioned were going, the American painters, and where we still, it seems to me, are going, in fact the more so because now society has become the danger simply because it is so poor and so cheap. In fact, the whole of society's attention has been called to its neglect of the human being.

I am not stumbling. I am cluttering, perhaps, in these words about words. Don't be disappointed. I mean, everything is so easy today that it is not very interesting. Everybody can say everything so skillfully that who cares. The subject won't go away and the action has to be found out. It is going to go on anyhow; and if you talk poems, the poem is going to have to be written; and the only way, in a sense, they can be written is if one keeps one's mind on this kind of, well, I want to say a necessity or an imperative which is in us willy-nilly. I mean, that we live at all is now at stake. You were translating Bill Williams's poems from the Danish in the Swedish magazine,[7]

6. Olson means to be making the point found in Hawkes's *Prehistoric Foundations of Europe to the Mycenean Age* (London: Methuen, 1940): "The faculty of even the simplest speech could substitute precept for mere example in the training of the singly born children" (p. 3).

7. Inga Lovén has brought Olson a copy of *Ord och Bild* 5 (1965), which contained her translation of William Carlos Williams's "The Sparrow."

and it was just the same as though they were his poems when they were being translated from another language. I mean, so clear was Bill Williams's ability to address himself to the subject of a paper bag the size of a human being rolling down the street and being run over by an automobile, but then unlike a human being retaking itself immediately, retaking its shape immediately and continuing to roll down the street: those are the observations which are perishless. And if the words simply do as perishlessly what is occurring, then you have why Williams is so exciting to us all still: because he knows the simplest rule that that is what language can do is to purchase forever whatever occurs.[8]

The best oral poem I ever wrote, I still think, is—and I know we were talking about it yesterday, because we were looking at the German translation of it by Reichert and it just looks so good in German—is the Gerhardt poem, "To Gerhardt, There, Among Europe's Things." That is a two-track poem. On the left track I am writing what is called vulgar American; on the right hand I am writing like "Hey there ...!" I can tell you exactly where the passage comes from. I want to say Tlingit, but that's not right. It is Northern Siberian hunters addressing themselves to the bear before they are hunting him, so that they can, like those dumb anthropologists say, practise magic.[9] Magic, my—I mean, like, for example, Vilhjalmur Stefansson, though he sounds like a Scandinavian, actually like myself was born in this country. I think Stefansson was born in Brooklyn as I was born in Worcester, Massachusetts. I think he may be, as I am, the child of migrating parents from the Northland. But Stefansson, very young, became interested in the Eskimos, where those famous crossbred Norse Eskimos, the famous blond or white Eskimos were. (That's not interesting.) What happened to him when he went north is that, on the first expedition, he got up the Mackenzie and got caught in the Arctic Ocean when the ice set in; and along with his friend who was with him, two Eskimo families also got caught to the west of the mouth of the Mackenzie and had to settle in for the winter. And it was a very lucky break for Stefansson and his friend, because the Eskimos knew instantly how to survive, built igloos and invited those two Americans to live with them through the Arctic winter. This is, by the way, from that great first book of Stefansson's, *My Life Among the Eskimos*. I've never been able to get beyond the passage. They spend this winter in the igloo with these two families, and immediately the Eskimos do more than just live, they hold school for their children, and the principal problem is to teach them to hunt, right? Of course Stefansson quickly learns Eskimo in the best fashion and he is able pretty quickly to follow the instruction by the parents of the young children, preparing them for the rest of their life. I'm not sure I can remember exactly what it is that a polar bear wants most in his life and can't have. The law of teaching an Eskimo boy to hunt is that when you kill a seal,

8. William Carlos Williams's poem about the paper bag is "The Term."
9. Olson's single source for the bear songs in "To Gerhardt, There, Among Europe's Things" was a paper presented at the Twenty-third International Congress of Americanists, "Bear Worship Among Turkish Tribes of Siberia," by N.P. Dyrenkova, published in their *Proceedings* (New York, 1930), pp. 411–40.

you must instantly give him the thing that he most wants to have, and it is fresh water. So that an Eskimo boy is taught—to my mind it is the most beautiful definition of paradise that I have ever heard, and of immortality and of post-life, is that the one thing that a human being requires is that which they want the most and can't have and if they don't get it they become therefore the enemies of life. In a hunting society like the Eskimos, the danger is that the seals as a family will not look kindly upon Eskimos killing them if every seal isn't, the moment that it is killed, given fresh water. And equally Stefansson tells how these parents teach those children what it is that a polar bear most wants and that he gets that too the moment he is killed. And it is this kind of a thing that I am doing in that passage. I am simply translating from Yakut. And in Reichert's translation from my translation of Yakut, like, "One eye / sees heaven, / another eye / sees earth" or "One ear / hears heaven, / another ear / hears earth," that is translated directly, that is that simplicity both of occurrence and speech which goes from one language into another as though there was no difference of language at all. That is not bad. The Eskimo must—the boy must learn, or the girl must learn, too, at the same time for her reasons, that a seal has something it wants that it can't have. What could it be? The imagination of the Eskimo has thought of one thing: the seal lives in salt water; the seal comes up through ice and that's when they get him, when he comes up through ice. So what is he coming up for? To lick the ice like an Eskimo pie or a popsicle! It must be. The only reason a seal would come up and be a sucker in such a situation that he would be killed by an Eskimo, it must be fresh water. That must be what a seal wants more than anything else in life, so therefore if you kill a seal you immediately give him fresh water, to seal his life. Isn't it beautiful? I wish I could remember, it probably is some fresh meat a polar bear wants.

Believe you me, what I was trying to do—you were absolutely right— what I was trying to do in *Ishmael* was to put together—see, I won't use that word "montage," which we could use if we talk about Eisenstein. But in fact what Eisenstein was doing was what you are saying about the *Ishmael*, is *samtal*. But it is not conversation, it is *convertere*, which means "to turn together." I think I am right. Of course I am right. Do you know what "verse" means? *Vertere*. Well, this is a big problem. What does the word "verse" mean? For example, in "Projective Verse," a piece which I wrote and which Mr Williams published as part of his own *Autobiography*—one of the most happy examples of *samtal* I know is the fact that Mr Williams suddenly published his *Autobiography*, and on the copyright page copyrighted the work as his and mine, because without my knowledge whatsoever he had printed, and nobody could tell—it was right in the middle of his book, suddenly there's a passage called "Projective Verse" by Charles Olson, and it is not said, "This is a piece by" or "I want here to put in." Nothing whatsoever. It is simply a continuing narrative of the *Autobiography of William Carlos Williams* which suddenly happens to be a piece that I wrote, and he treats it as though he acknowledges that it's a piece by him; he copyrights it in my name when he copyrights the whole book in his name. I mean, it's one of those utterly beautiful examples of "turning together." My point is that verse—where did we get to verse?—oh yes, conversation. "Conversation" really means "to turn, in turn with each other." I am sure *samtal* wouldn't mean that, because -*tal* is not "verse"; -*tal* is "tale," is speech, is to tell, in a sense, a story. It even reflects a wholly different condition than conversation. It is my particular present-day belief that we will not know what is the source of not only narrative but, I am convinced now, of image, equally, and also—which is the third component, which is difficult to state, and I am talking now as an American poet looking straight ahead—how to write anything at all that is interesting, in poetry or prose, unless we pay attention to what happened in Iceland when …

There are very simple facts here. The movement to Iceland from Norway, like the movement to Ireland and to England by the Norse, the Swedes, and the Danes, the Swedes in particular to the east coast of England and the south coast, Kent in particular, the Norse, it may have been the Danes, too, to the west coast and to Ireland, and then the movements north after the investiture of the British Isles to, like, the Faeroes, and then the fantastic earliest movements to Iceland, was the Irish, apparently, pushed out by the Norse, pushed to the north by the Norse, by the Viking invasions. I am not forgetting that the Anglo-Saxons under Alfred stood this whole—I mean, our language, we were taught that English, in a sense, begins with Alfred. Today, any one of us who is working at this date and at this stage of the English language, we not only are going to keep that fact but we are going to surround it with the circumstances that also occurred. For example, Alfred had to actually stand off and maintain a remnant of the Anglo-Saxon migration against the Danes, the Swedes, and the Norwegians in and around 900, but by 1000 not only had Iceland been occupied but Greenland had been settled and the Norse were apparently in southern New England by a date 1000, and were in occupation of Hope, which is Hop in the sagas and is now still called Hope, a county of Narragansett Bay, which is essentially the city of Providence in the state of Rhode Island in the United States.

I am saying all this because I simply want to narrow or, in fact, concentrate the attention upon what then happened. It was a hundred years later, before Ari, who appears to be the first man to invent what we know as a cliché, saga; and I think, Inga, that you would confirm that saga—"say"— what does "saga" mean in Swedish, "to say"? If I am not mistaken, "saga" must come from "saying" before it means "telling a tale." (Jeezus, it is, excuse me, it is already dawn!) "Saga" must be, in fact—I don't know. The point that I want to stress is that one hundred years before Snorri Sturluson wrote—what did he write?—the *Poetic Edda*, which is the one …

[GAP]

… "His wife divorced him and remarried. For a while he took to drink. He turned back to the Indians, it is the saving gesture—but a gesture of despair.

Poe can be understood …"[10] No, I stiffen up. It is not even plenty, it is not even enough, but it's not not nothing, [LAUGHS] not not nothing!

When I was on "Open End" television, two hours—did you know that I was on television in Boston, WGBH, on one of these programs with, like, several other people? And I was like the "po-et," or like there was a very famous highwayman in the West who used to leave a note in which he called himself "Black Bart, the po-8." He signed the note "po–" with the numeral "8." "Great Black Bart, the po-8." And because they don't know what to do on television except everybody being sort of tagged or represented as what they are, it came my turn. There was a man who just climbed Everest, there was a big league umpire who was replacing Bill Russell of the Boston Celtics, and there was some woman who was contributing to the Red Cross or something, with some other people, I have forgotten who, specialists. So when it comes to me, I was supposed to do something. And I not only—I mean, I couldn't look at the screen or the audience, I couldn't read from a book, I couldn't open my mouth, and this peculiar thing happened, the silence and the blindness replaced everything else, every other possibility, and my family was at home looking at the television [LAUGHS], and the most beautiful thing happened. You know, they can reach quite a number of human beings, but then they do the damn thing on radio and reach another several hundred thousand people. And there is a very good poet, who I think is a very good poet, but he is not very well known, was one of the original poets of the gathering when Creeley was going to create a magazine up in Littleton, New Hampshire, the thing that eventually became the magazine *Origin* in Boston, which Cid Corman founded, and this man's name is William Bronk. And William Bronk lives in Hudson Falls, New York and owns, I think, a coal and lumber company, and I think writes a very, very marvelous, quiet, distinctive verse. And I had a letter from him saying, not seeing me in the agony that television exposed me in, but only hearing this huge gap of nothing on the radio, thought it was the most marvelous thing that ever, the most marvelous evidence that he had ever … He wrote me a letter which I think is essentially the source of the title of his last book, which is published by New Directions, called *The World, The Worldless.*[11] (You had the tape on? You got that? Good. Don't you think that is a beautiful story, though?)

[GAP]

Write me, write an article for *Ord och* (that crazy word), write an article about me and translate some poems into Svensk. They are not as good as Mr Williams's, but, jesus christ, it is a beautiful magazine! What is going on in Sweden?

[GAP]

10. Olson is reading from "Descent," the Sam Houston chapter in William Carlos Williams's *In the American Grain*, (NY: Boni, 1925), p. 213.
11. "I only keep looking for other people who know how to be worldless"—see "The William Bronk-Charles Olson Correspondence," ed. Burt Kimmelman in the *Minutes of the Charles Olson Society* 22, p. 20, letter dated 31 October 1962.

It is an interesting question. I never thought of it myself until this moment. He has raised that damned thing to a point where[12] ... As a matter of fact, don't kid yourself that men like Creeley and myself in particular, who have had to fight since 1956 against Beat on this question—do you know that Creeley and I still believe completely in the written word? Printed. Though Creeley has now made himself such a superb reader in public, so that he can stand up there and—yet even Creeley has adjusted his reading style to something that is really the Beat trick. What you must get for Sweden is the Berkeley tape. Did you ever hear the Berkeley tape? Who sat down for four hours? You did? Where, under what circumstances?

RONNI GOLDFARB: In a house with some friends.

OLSON: You see, I was supposed to read, and I flew in from Rome on a Monday night. I lectured, I did a lecture called "Causal Cosmology" at ten o'clock the next morning. That evening I heard Ed Dorn read, on Wednesday night I heard Allen Ginsberg read, Thursday night I heard Mr Creeley read, and they were all in excellent shape. And on Friday night—usually I am the anchorman, I am the relay—so I have to read. And I think, "These people have been listening to poets read every night for two weeks, and here I am going to stand up and read." And I was in the absolutely perfect condition that I have never achieved to read, never. I had a day and a week the likes of which had put me into a situation where I thought that everything that I ever wrote was as good as I thought it was when I wrote it, which is the only way that you could possibly read. So I started out reading a poem which Creeley curiously had put in his selection of my writing for New Directions, called "The Ring of," which was written the day my daughter was born. It was simply a poem on the birth of Venus stolen from the encyclopaedia. And I read it just like I thought I could read. So I did a dirty trick. Creeley was down in the fourth row on the right, and I said, "Robert, I wonder—I am so interested that you selected that poem, I wonder if you would have selected, say, if you had had the space, the 'Ode on Nativity'?" And this whole thing had gone on until he got to say, "I would have." And then I said, "Oh for christ's sake, it is a lousy thing to do. I shouldn't have asked you but I guess all I want to do is to read 'Ode on Nativity,' which is on my daughter as a baby." (I am doing it about right, am I?) So I start to read the poem, which I wrote for a Christmas party at Black Mountain. It was literally a Christmas poem called "Ode on Nativity," and I never had much interest in it since I wrote it. But it also sounded marvelous, and I read it just like I was reading that one too, Ronni, right up to—filling out every letter and word. The letters felt as though they were full, the words felt as though they were made of each of the fullness of each of the letters, and the words, and the syntax, and the lines, and then the condition of the development of the lines into the paragraphs and the stanzas. But suddenly I stopped reading it, didn't I? What the hell did I switch to? At this point I started to go away and

12. Butterick believes that Olson is referring to Marshall McLuhan's idea that our society listens more than it reads (*Muthologos* II.97 and note II.191).

I started to talk, and I talked for four hours, and finally two policemen of the university were standing—suddenly I realized that two policemen— well, suddenly about two and a half hours later, Robert Duncan thought- fully spoke from the middle of the audience and said, "Look, Charlie, couldn't we take a break? There are people here who would like to pee." "Oh," I said, "that is right. Gee, Robert, go and pee." He left and never came back, and other people left and never came back. So then I got kind of sore and I said, "Look, I am going to talk forever tonight, so it would be wise for anybody that feels that they have other, better things to do, to go now because—and it would be nice of them to dwindle. It is not necessary, it's okay, I am all right, everything is all right." And of course there were quite a few people that didn't. I don't think that a great many people did take me up on the invitation, and so we started in for a second session. And I meant it, I was going to talk until I dropped dead! Unfortunately, about twelve o'clock or something, the whole problem of these places turns up, and there was two policemen—they looked like state police to me, but I think they were only officers of the university—were at my shoulder, and that was the end. But it's a tape. I never heard it, but I'm going on the basis of Ed Dorn.

LOVÉN: Who has that? Berkeley?

OLSON: Yes, it is purchasable. It is buyable like a book, and I could get George or Ronni to supply you with one. I would be happy to, because that really would be an example, if it is true, as friends have said, that it works. In other words, if the McLuhan world exists—in fact, there was a review of one of those prose pieces that Creeley selected, or "Human Universe," the only review I've ever received except for the pieces by Creeley and Duncan, and Dorn, and, like, who else? There has been damn little writing on me. But there was a review by a man I didn't know,[13] and that man had read that tape and understood exactly what I was up to as of the whole situation that somehow or other has come into being in this international conspiracy in which McLuhan is one of the absolute—I can prove it—agents. Barbara Ward, the English economist, is another member of it. They meet on Onassis's yacht in the Mediterranean each summer to plot the conspiracy of communication. And I can prove that too. And what it is I am not saying. I don't know what it means; I don't know. I don't consider it politics. I don't think it is a science, either. I don't even know what kind of human engineering or mechanics or scientology or dianetics or dietics or hygienics or adultery or non-encyclical it is. I mean, there is no way to know what this fourth law of abortion or third law of abortion, what it has to do with miscegeny. Who can imagine what trumped-up—? To tell you the truth, I think it is as meaningless, ignorant, and uninteresting as CBS or NBC buying the New York Yankees and yesterday *Time* magazine buying Little, Brown, the publisher, in Boston, and my own university having sold the

13. Olson wrote to Donald Sutherland, a Classicist at the University of Colorado, about his review of *Selected Writings* in *New Leader* of 22 May 1967: "It is in fact my first public judgment of any relevancy," *Selected Letters*, p. 391.

most monstrous publication in America, which affects every child in public or parochial school, called *My Weekly Reader*—and my own university published that and sold it to Xerox, and in return owns fifty-one percent of Xerox, which is one of the wealthiest corporations. And you don't know what it is all about. COMSAT is up there, put up there by American Tel and Tel, right over the Equator in the perfect celestial position. The only interesting thing that has been done in the whole missile or satellite or whatever they call these planetary inventions is COMSAT, a reflecting mirror of television from one continent to the other. I mean, what is it all about? Some presidency of the world, some uninteresting unification? It isn't even a plot; it is like a development instead of a plot. It is not even an interesting story. Merleau-Ponty, for example, if I only had the text, shows exactly what is happening to story, like any one of us poets ought to be able to tell you exactly what is happening to image, or any painter, today. But what it is is not interesting. It is not interesting, like the further development of mathematics, the further development of music, the further development of poetry, the further development of language. "That verse which print bred." I think I believe in "that verse which print bred." Don't I say it that way,[14] isn't it said positively?

[GAP]

... Yes, all this is Dante.[15] Like, I mean, somebody should throw Dante in the face of everybody today has any argument that gets into any of these questions about action replacing, action as preferable to everything else. Of course, action has always been—I mean, will, like they say, is so completely the push that causes motion, today's word "action" is getting to be aesthetic. It is an avoidance of will; it's an evasion of the action of will. I mean, the motive behind anybody is that they have the will to do it, therefore it happens. But today, action is getting into the same state as recreation and leisure. It is something that the present world economy or state is a trick—it is like keeping—it is like the universities used to be when they kept the young off the labor market. It became that way suddenly in the West some time ago. Literally, they kept youth from living from eighteen to twenty-two because they were a threat to the labor market. Today the adolescents have become one of the biggest markets in the world, so they are being cultivated as a market. But these, these switches and inversions are ...

[GAP]

... Of course, why not? They've talked about Riemann in Sweden?

LOVÉN: He pops up a little now and then.

OLSON: He does, I should think. I guess in Australia, except in the puddles where the aborigines lean to drink, I guess they talk about Riemann. Riemann is one of those minds that man today hasn't even plumbed.

14. In the opening paragraph of "Projective Verse."
15. They have apparently been looking at the essay "Quantity in Verse, and Shakespeare's Later Plays" in *Selected Writings*, pp. 31–45, and *Collected Prose*, pp. 270–82.

Riemann's university lecture as Rector at Heidelberg, I think, in 1856, to my mind it is so interesting because … (Don't give up, Ronni, you said you were strong! No, the cigarettes. No, I will find that, don't worry, leave it open.)[16] If there is a piece of reading that—like, '56 is interesting. Like, 1956 is very interesting; 1956 is the year when we all split, like they say, in this country. But 1856 is so interesting because of the fact that Melville wrote *The Confidence-Man* and left for the Holy Land. In that year, Mr Whitman published *Leaves of Grass*, and Mr Riemann did that inaugural lecture. And if there is three pieces of writing in one year as those three things! And I mean right now it is some hundred and odd years. It has been, like, twelve years now since we all took off. I'm speaking literally of the leadership of society by the poets occurred in America in 1956, as precise forms, in at least two places precisely.

[GAP]

… "The true beginnings of nothing but the Supermarket—the exact death quantity does offer …"[17] Yeah, I think I am just swinging around. By now the supermarket is like the drugstore, I mean the whole new morality, which is not a morality but which is a condition which I learned from my master Sauer is to speak of man as not carnivore, he is omnivore. Man eats anything, man buys anything, man is capable of anything. All these things are not very interesting. But that pluralism has now become what is mistaken for both man and society; and it is so completely both the supply and thereafter the condition of the human being that there isn't anything going on except mud. Now mud is important, but it has to be fatherhood. I can prove that it is fatherhood in a cosmological sense, cosmythological sense. Until it is taken from that advent, as that kind of an advent—and today, certainly, scientism so makes it uncomfortable for anybody to believe that things are from matter, and that all is in matter and there isn't anything, including, in fact … "Everything does issue from, and nothing is anything but itself, measured so."[18]

I don't want to sound, like they say, indirect. As a matter of fact, it is actually getting clear to me that the only thing to do that is interesting today is to be explicit. But it is also true that talk is no longer a sufficient form of explicitness. Actually, to overcome the misuse and abuse and destruction of the world, it is necessary to produce action and things all of which are explicit in their condition. Again, this is a very difficult problem when you come up against the fact that this was particularly difficult for—well, it was once. It is no longer difficult at all. But say, for example, in the group of men that again are part of the break-out of 1956, say a painter like Kline, a painter like Pollock, the so-called American abstract expressionist painters, for them it was to make paintings that were so explicit that—the problem was

16. Olson has been asking Ronni Goldfarb to find some pens, saying earlier, "I don't know what could have happened," and "These are not the pens."
17. Quoting from "Equal, That Is, to the Real Itself," *Selected Writings*, p. 47, *Collected Prose*, p. 121.
18. Olson is quoting himself here, the same dream words that he quoted in "Poetry and Truth" above, p. 262.

how the hell do you deal with painting when Picasso is the measure of painting. For any one of us, how the hell do you write when for an enormous populace Joyce is the measure of writing? Not only is it such a nuisance but it feels to us as though there is something quite wrong about it. But we don't do anything about—we're not putting down—I mean, they weren't putting down Picasso. I am not putting down Joyce. We're this side of either of those men and their work, and we are still at work. What is it that is now "art" or "form," to use the old words? And if you take words, I, for example, said it some years ago in a letter to Elaine B. Feinstein: I really believe that pun is rhyme.[19] I think that the real experience of rhyme rests upon something that—like, again, suddenly I think of the fact that Freud had the wit to recognize that humor, that all pratfalls, are pun situations. If I say that rhyme is pun, I mean that the sacredness of sound in the universe is literally all that rhyme, if interesting at all, is revealing by itself. That is what I mean with pun: that it is a form of equals, by analogy; that the rhyme isn't equals in the dumb sense of poor rhyming; that it is nothing but revealing the full sun of a pun. And I mean s-u-n. If you were talking language equal, say, to the spirit of the flesh, of which the sun is both the source—and in fact anyone who is loved and desired at all knows that the moment that you love there is a sun born, a sun inside yourself, and you are then a condition of sun. And I am talking sound. Sound is like pun was the sun, and every rhyme that is interesting is a piece of that.

This isn't being said badly, I think. It is just very mysterious. Only, not a mystery at all. It is mysterious because—what the hell is it to say, what does it mean to say that pun is rhyme, except that I believed it when I said it nine years ago, wrote it nine years ago? And I still don't know anything that tells me more about how to write poetry so that that condition which used to be called terminal end rhyme is occurring all the time. That is, when it occurs. One wouldn't want to write in nothing but rhyme that simply any more than one would want to write in meter, either, all the time. That would be sort of boring by now. That was true of the art, say, of the languages as we inherit them from a certain condition that we like to call, like, say, Greek at some such date in the 5th century. But not previous to that, by the way. Greek was a wholly different language in the hands of Hesiod and Homer than it had become, and that language has been since. And in fact, one of the interesting things about writing English today is to try to make English start to behave like a condition before man had a definite article, knew how to generalize, and thought he knew what the hell he was saying when he used words instead of being explicit. In other words, being explicit has something to do also with the fact that pun is rhyme. Cut it and we talk about it, like in Swedish *samtal*, conversation, and quote my friend Dahlberg that "literature is conversation." If it was true, and it was to some extent at the time I knew Dahlberg, and in fact that Dahlberg—the first version of *Ishmael* was rejected by Dahlberg, and I took his objection completely and nobody has ever seen that manuscript except Dahlberg,

19. "Letter to Elaine Feinstein" in *Selected Writings*, p. 29, and *Collected Prose*, p. 252.

because I wrote it in—he considered it too biblical; and I thought so too the moment he said it; so then I waited several years and wrote the book as it now stands. But I think that even by the time that I wrote *Ishmael,* something is more interesting than talk. As I said to you yesterday, if there was one man in the world whom I considered I addressed that, the man who was the measure of what I was trying to do in that book, in the composition, was Eisenstein. And certainly no one would ever say that Eisenstein was conversation. Never, because whatever it is that Eisenstein was as a composer, I could now say, and we could move forward from this whole question toward the present and in fact meet that matter that we were talking about a few minutes ago as of Riemann and *Leaves of Grass* and Melville's *Confidence-Man* in 1856, and what happened in this country among the poets and painters in 1956. Or in fact, to tell you the truth, for myself, and with the painters, it happened ten years—we were on to this whole question from, say, around 1948 on. I mean ... [TAPE ENDS]

Black Mountain College dining hall.
Photo: North Carolina Department of Cultural Resources, Division of Archives and History,
Black Mountain College Papers. Courtesy Mary Emma Harris.

14

On Black Mountain (II)

The following interview was conducted at Olson's Gloucester home in April 1969 by Andrew S. Leinoff, who was preparing an honors thesis on Black Mountain College as a student at MIT. On this transcription's appearance in *OLSON* 8, Fielding Dawson called it "for those in the know, an eye-opener if there ever was one."

ANDREW LEINOFF: I found Will Hamlin at Goddard. He's at Plainfield, Vermont. And let's see, the Boydens are at Marlboro.

CHARLES OLSON: Are they? Tied to that place?

LEINOFF: Yes, he's been there for twenty years.

OLSON: Has he really?

LEINOFF: Yeah, and as a matter of fact, Raymond, who is a friend of the Boydens, said that the Boydens don't realize how much like Black Mountain Marlboro is.

OLSON: Oh god, jesus christ. Well, I don't know about—I didn't go to Marlboro. I read, I spent a week, at Goddard.

LEINOFF: But Goddard is kind of different.

OLSON: Oh yes, it is. But Marlboro—yes, I've heard that several times. The Cambridge School in Weston is just—and, by the way, it is the French family who were involved at Black Mountain seem to have been responsible for founding this.

LEINOFF: The Cambridge School? Yeah, that's what I had heard. I'm supposed to look up somebody there, French, I imagine.

OLSON: It's interesting. They've gone out and started the school in Colorado, which has gotten to be a well known sort of a ranch scene. I don't think they're there anymore.

LEINOFF: Nat French I had at the North Shore Country Day School in Winnetka, Illinois.

OLSON: Well, that's where—wait a minute. Yeah, it seems to me he did, because Smith was the great teacher there years back, and he used to supply—when I was at Harvard I had most of my men from North Shore Country Day. But Corkran, who was a teacher of history at Black Mountain, Dave Corkran, I think they came from North Shore Country Day or from that large military high school—no, I think he came from North Shore Country Day. He was a Wesleyan man, as I was, and actually was a fraternity brother; and his sons, who all grew up with us at Black Mountain, playing ball and stuff, have become some of the major graduates of the same fraternity and Wesleyan too.

LEINOFF: I almost got to Wesleyan. But I didn't want to go there.

OLSON: You were wise. You're much better off.

LEINOFF: It's more fun at MIT.

OLSON: Yes. Undoubtedly.

LEINOFF: You know, this stuff that you were bringing up about the pedagogical aspect of the school, in discussions with various people they saw one of the main common points of the school being, rather than pedagogy ...

OLSON: That it was the sociology. Yeah, I know it. But mind you, that's that crazy business of the—ultimately, for example, when Paul Williams wanted to move the whole place, when we really were faced with the fact we didn't have any longer anybody to pick up the deficit, and Paul had put in some money, bought a beef herd and also put in some loans, and was anxious actually to preserve Black Mountain and wanted to move it north, intact, within a range of about a 250-mile's circle of New York City—or his greatest of all propositions was to take a floor of a skyscraper in New York and just put it right in there—and my point was, well, I don't know whether that's relevant. My point always was: she was there and she had this stamp of educating; she had that busyness or that runner or something. That always seemed to me to be the thing that kept her from—in fact, most of the rump revolts and jumps away were on the community question, literally. And in fact, as I was just saying about that damned Studies Building, it was like the ridge of Charlottesville simply because it made the living thing and the curriculum thing almost, like, pure one. I mean it's such a complicated question that I would stress the pedagogy simply because my interest in Black Mountain really comes from John Rice's founding of it; and certainly, I think, if you examine Rice you see he was himself a superbly trained Classicist and an excellent mind, and his agitation was really pedagogy. He was a great oral teacher in the Socratic tradition. Obviously it was why he was fired at Rollins and why he was finally, I guess, fired at Black Mountain, or pushed out.

I mean, the very first year, whom do they acquire from the Bauhaus but a great deal of interest in architecture as well as Albers, who in my experience, at the end of Albers's period there, was himself an enormous pedagogue, as I think he turned out to be later at Yale. And certainly I myself in the last few years of the place was a pedagogue, as I have always been. So that my impression is that the line that's least noticed, or which gives her her back or her spine, is pedagogy, and equally, of course, was the activity of the fact that we were all in one bunch, I mean all in one six hundred acres with a fence. And as so often, as I'm sure, as others have said, the moment you pass through that fence—and as I once used—you remember Earl Carroll's "Vanities" used to have, "Through this door passed the most beautiful chicks in the world"? In fact, when we tried to repaint at least that lower ground where those boards of that gate were, I had a hell of a time finding the exact white paint that Albers had used, because in America there's a dirty yellow thing in white paint, a very famous acid that you can't—and Albers knew enough not to paint with that acid in it. And it's very hard to get the paint, to get a white paint that doesn't have that god-damn acid in it. Well, it was that the whiteness of that fence was almost like the beautiful girls of Earl Carroll's show. I mean, the moment you went through that fence, you went into another world. In fact, I would call your attention to even the famous mark of Black Mountain, that funny black and white target that's on her seal. I mean, it's on her catalogs, that crazy *bindu*, we would say today, the pureness of that *bindu*, which was pure target, black and white target.

LEINOFF: Is the target Albers's work?

OLSON: Yeah! Absolutely. [PAUSE] I'm trying to say something when I say "pedagogy," trying to avoid the word "teacher" or "faculty," as Black Mountain damn well did, right? There wasn't any professorships or differences of appointments; the place was owned only by—in fact, the moment you walked through, somebody was saying the other day on the phone to me, the moment you walked through that goddamn fence, if you were a faculty member you became the equal owner to all those who, no matter how many years they'd been there. And there was never any pensions, which came to be kind of an irritating thing for, say, Albers at the end, because he felt, "My christ, I've been here almost twenty years or something and here I leave with nothing." Which is about the way it really was. And like somebody else came in last week and they're in just the same boat. Well, but that also was one of its great—I mean, if you talk openness in any real meaning, you really have to distribute openness. It can't be dickered; it has to be doled. [LAUGHS]

LEINOFF: Well, one person that I talked with, I don't remember who exactly, I guess it was Hamlin at Goddard, he said that there were people at Black Mountain that were interested in teaching, and there were others that were as willing to participate in the community as they were to teach. He put it there were scholars and then there were community people. He left it to me to decide which one I had more respect for. But the terms …

OLSON: I think that would immediately suggest that Hamlin was a community person. You see, this is where the secondary was always trying to either encompass or rival the primary. And I submit that if this place is a college, which it was—in fact it was a remedial university: it went from, literally, remedial cases, forty-year-old remedial cases from New Haven, who couldn't write or spell, to work done there which was of an order greater than the Institute of Advanced Studies at Princeton. As a matter of fact, as I think I told you on the phone, when I had to replace Max Dehn, who retired as mathematician finally and then died, I called Lefschetz at Princeton, who was one of the two mathematicians I did know and just was helpless to— and he said to me, "But my god, Olson, the best man I can suggest is your recent graduate, who's here at the Institute of Advanced Studies"—which was either Kemeny or—there were two Hungarian-named boys of that same period, Alex Kemeny and—god, I think it's the other, the other Rumanian name—the point was that's how far she was, in a sense, in her range, again by, I would say, the openness principle, which has to be told. But I do think myself that so much of her history, which was in that period of America in which there was a sociology, or there was intentional sociology or a sociology which still lived in the age of hope or something, there was a lot of agitation and activity, and in fact to some extent some of the health in her cheeks was the commune, community thing, right?

But again, when you come right down to the bottom of it, to the *bindu* of it, she was a college. She wasn't some goddamned intentional community or work program, farm attachée. In fact, I go back again to the founder's idea that she never should own, anyhow. And, in fact, the moment she bought, she hurt herself for the rest of her life. That is, Rice thought that renting was the best principle for an activity up to the level of the education that he found himself involved in, believing in; and in fact even though, as you told me,[1] that Linda-Mei Leong says that Georgia and others had almost to persuade him to bother to found Black Mountain, but I'm sure his interest in education would have led him actually to think of it as a place where literally education could occur again, and in fact enormously, almost since the Middle Ages, at least, in principle.

LEINOFF: Well, that brings up another question, which questions some of Rice's motives, in a way. I mean, just for clarification purposes. And I could also question it as far as what actually the spirit of the place was by the time you were there. I can't be sure whether Rice intended a place of impermanence.

OLSON: No, I think he intended a place of non-ownership, which is a much more important point to make. In fact, to tell you the truth, his own idea was even to call it New College, but then he realized that that attributive was already used at either Oxford or Cambridge. (And in fact, as you know, now there is a New College been founded at this date recently in America, meaning "new.") And practically it became Black Mountain simply because that's where they settled, which makes sense to a particularist like me. In fact, it's one of the reasons why, finally, when Paul wanted to move her north, I said "Aw, why not let it die where she got stuck or something. I

---

1. Leinoff has apparently mentioned a History honors paper at Harvard by Linda-Mei Leong, "John Andrew Rice, Jr.: Visionary, 1885–1968."

mean, why move her? If things have gotten to the point where she needs to move, leave her fall where she is." That's why I said to you on the telephone, when I left that last day with everything packed, I thought—all I saw was some weed, one stalk, and that seemed everything. I don't mean that was all that was left. I meant that was all she really was to begin with anyhow was a stalk, or the wild asparagus that grew beside the cottonmouth's nest that bound both the descent to the Library and the step up to the pavement of the Studies Building. And these two things, this wild asparagus and this cottonmouth's nest, which used to bother some of the faculty that had dogs or children, was one of the things that my generation fought for tenaciously: "Leave that cottonmouth alone!" And she was a female, and there was a—right where the major traffic of that proposed three-room building was to be.

I'd love at some point, honestly, because I feel your own bearings are a little bit toward—and in fact the danger of a history obviously always is it appears to be in past time. And as I've said to you, Black Mountain to my mind is not only not in past time but is a flag hanging out in the future which hasn't yet been, hasn't been redrawn, in a funny way. Today even, she may even—and I don't mean like—I have no sentimentality or wish—in fact I've refused at least two huge offers to refound her: one in the first outburst of, not the Beat, but the Beatnik movement in Venice, California, an enormous offer by a young former faculty member who had run into some real money.[2] Three, really. One was that; and the other was that crazy proposition I mentioned to you at Wesleyan in six figures, where they were gonna sort of, like Abraham Lincoln's cabin, re-form her as sort of a monument. And the third was recently, and was where? One of them places like Vermont or New Hampshire, where these places are springing up, Franklin Notch or something.[3] I don't know specifically, but some place else. And I said, "Oh no, forget it." Or when we were all being asked—and in fact Creeley and I almost joined Burroughs and Trocchi—I'm the one of the four that stayed out of it—in that movement, the Sigma movement of Trocchi's in London and Amsterdam, and was very much behind that whole movement of the what-do-you-call-its, of the famous white bicycle cats in Amsterdam, the Apple people. What's their name, what's the name of that group of young kids that were very, very much the first "free city" cats? What's the common noun for them? Because they were brilliant. I mean they left white bicycles around. Wherever you found a white bicycle in Amsterdam it was yours to ride. And wherever you took it you dropped it, and because it was painted white …

LEINOFF: You mean Diggers?

---

2. Olson had written "Notes for a University at Venice, California" in response to Tony Landreau's proposal (published in *OLSON* 2 [1974], pp. 65–68).
3. Two former students were going to set up "Black Mountain North" on a farm near South Royalton, Vermont (see *Selected Letters*, p. 396).

OLSON: Yeah, like the Diggers. But I mean this is very early. Their name is marvelous, the Dutch name for that, for that first sort of …[4] And there's a rather interesting man who's a part of Sigma today who's written a book on "grass," in fact it's called *Grass*. Wiggenpoof, or some such thing.[5]

LEINOFF: What's the Sigma-Trocchi movement?

OLSON: That's the biggest movement to—in a sense, ideational process of the present. And in fact, the Sigma movement was very sort of a late syncretic Black Mountain movement. And in fact, like I say, it was a funny coming together of Trocchi, Burroughs, and Creeley and myself, being asked to join it, to found it. I mean, not to found it, but to elucidate it into a worldwide "millions university" sort of thing, with museums, with production. It's a thing which is still, you know, like actively in the air as a kind of old educational radical instead of an activist radical present.

LEINOFF: All these new proposals, maybe except this one, which maybe I don't understand, it seems they're more interested in the community aspect than …

OLSON: Well, I again think you're just—may I, in a sense, hopefully help your own thinking? Look, if you put the community as living—you know, the problem of every day for any human being forever, or any animal too, bird or flower, is just making it, right? I mean in the barrenest or boringest sense. So, O.K., that's what community really means, dig? What society really means. I mean, you're not going to get away from the secondary no matter what you do. You're going to have to spend an awful lot of hours doing it. So let me be careful, because you sound like another one of us Americans who come from one of the most drastic preparations for life, which is that filthy, foul thing, sociology, anyhow, which is non-class and mush, mud and mush forever. And at the same time, none of us have become anything at any point after adolescence, at least, when that whole sociology thing has to be dealt with, unless we turn to a prime, to the other, whatever the other thing is. I mean, I can say what it is but I'm trying not to say any of these things that, like, obviously, like whatever it is that makes one care to do something besides just eat, sleep, and make a living. So that, I mean, don't ever, don't get led by anybody on the Black Mountain thing.

One of the great things was the wars of Black Mountain, which was the wars over living. There was, like, a battlefield that was going on all the time. Whoever that writer was that was five miles or two miles or one mile away from the Battle of Waterloo, and when interrupted by somebody saying, "Did you know the battle was being fought?"—"Don't interrupt me, I'm busy!" I mean, it's that kind of a thing. There always was those wars, that's normal. Again, it's one of the reasons why I believe in her. She was as healthy as the University of Paris or Bologna, or presumably, like, in fact, we know

4. Olson seems to be thinking of the "Provos" ("provocateurs"). The Diggers were a San Francisco phenomenon.
5. Simon Vinkenoog, who with George Andrews edited *The Book of Grass: An Anthology of Indian Hemp* (NY: Grove Press, 1967).

the condition of Athens under Socrates, which led to his death. I mean, he was tried and found guilty by a city, familiar kind of a prosecution, but a nuisance in the *agora*, a bother in the marketplace. I mean, John Rice was a bother in the marketplace. And I hope Black Mountain was and is only memorable as a bother in this whole nation! Because she was actually doing much more living at the greatest least cost that ever was proposed. And in fact, in the end I met the Korean Bill of Rights, which offered the American soliders, dig this, in the fifties—850 bucks a year was what that bill was cut back to for the Korean veterans. And Black Mountain met it. It offered everything, food, clothing, housing and teaching, home and board, I mean locations, situations, for 850 bucks. Now that's obviously impossible by any principles under which the American educational system, which is supposed to be a deficit business, operates, right? But we met it. We not only met it, but all the bills were paid and I ended up with profit. And the realization of the funds of Black Mountain went—due to the circum-stances, it was necessary to just, in fact, foreclose her. Because I was the fore-closer, I was the undertaker. In fact, at one point, due to the founding lawyer, I became the single owner, in order to settle her affairs as a trustee, no, assignee, the exact title under Norman law, Assignee for the Benefit of the Creditors. Which was the whole fact. Mind you, there was no other creditor, dig? I mean, that was unbelievable. The place was resolved, actually, solely because some of her teachers were old and scared; those of us who were younger had dug into our own flesh or into our families' means and were at the same time offering an education at 850 bucks. We were doing all right. We opened up in the fall of 1956 with a $10,000 pump of cash in the bank and an increased student enrollment with a freshened faculty. But we closed because there was only two of us that were, in a sense—Mr Huss, who was treasurer, and myself, who was sort of stuck with handling the whole thing—and we just really didn't—I think we'd had it, like that's all. I mean, the two of us had it, and, like, it being the date—again, as I stressed to you on the phone—the date 1956. It was, by the way, then twenty-three years old, and '56 is that year when the big gear shifted throughout the world, and so she was a Ubangi lip of the present that was hung out there in the past. And now the present has been occurring for ten or fifteen years and hopefully will go on to be more interesting, as indeed I think every time the present is interesting, god love it, it increases interest, or shows how interesting she was.

But just to tie it down: I have always been impressed by the way a writer as accurate as Dorn, who was a student at Black Mountain, actually, and graduated from Black Mountain in writing, and is a figure today of considerable ability in American writing as a poet and also a storyteller, and has written a rather remarkable book called *The Shoshoneans* as well as this new poem, *Gunslinger*—but in an interview in a crazy anthology done around, oh gee, it must be back now in 1960, by David Ossman, called *The Sullen Art* (which was Dylan Thomas's description of poetry), there's an interview, like this tape thing now we're doing, with Dorn, and the opening questions are, because of his promise, even then, as a recent Black Mountain student graduate—and if I can lay my hands on a copy to read that, unless you know it, the Dorn quote on what Black Mountain was as he found it as a student at—I wouldn't even say at that date, because my hunch is that if you could get a man of such sensibility as Dorn—in other words, I'm saying that a poet of his order ought to be capable of expressing what some other people might smudge, even though their feelings might be what they're trying to express. Let me just for a moment see if I can find that. Why don't you cut the tape so we don't lose it?

[GAP]

I can't find the book at the moment, but the thing is, if I remember the quote, it's to me almost like the key quote on Black Mountain to this day, because it gets that quality of air and activity.[6] Or, to put it another way, from another poet, Creeley, when he first met my former wife, the wife I lost, who was a student at Black Mountain, just said to her, "What are you here for, to get clear?" I mean, not to get clear, but to, like, to be clear? To be clear, yeah.

These are the things that I'm trying to stress that I think is the marriage of pedagogy to something that is personality, that was really the double track that was always going on all the activity of the day, the dining hall and the struggles to define what is a society of this order. And to my mind, the danger will be that the treatment of Black Mountain will tend actually, because of history spread over twenty-three years, rather to take her as a question of community or of a communal order. I think I said it best when I said it's living. It is living, and that goes on anywhere for every human individual anyhow, and it goes on in a place which is self-organized, with more interest, with more worth, where it's self-organized.

LEINOFF: What I am trying to do, as I see how to write something as far as this is concerned, is to let people go on and on and on about Black Mountain any way they want. I might want to find out certain facts just to sort of vaguely get an idea of the history, but I think that the history is going to be different for anybody I get it from, and the contradiction is what I am looking for, because in the contradiction you find the personalities.

OLSON: O.K., but I think that's that kind of allowance-ism that's in our society and temperament today which is just boring. And, in fact, to tell you the truth, if that's your attitude I think actually you'd be contributing to the delinquency of this nation. And I don't think Black Mountain was interesting as such. In fact, on the contrary, by the comparison to the larger units of education which have so contributed to that delinquency that today they are under entire question, as in fact is the rulership of the society, then, I'd say, why bother with Black Mountain, because she was a little speck in the

---

6. Olson had read Dorn's passage on Black Mountain during the "Filming in Gloucester" tape, pp. 208–9 above.

dust of eternity only. But she was a speck in the dust of eternity, she wasn't some comparativism of our time.

LEINOFF: This is good to talk this out. I'm not sensitive or anything about this, but you might look at it as Black Mountain being a little speck, but it wasn't. I mean, in Black Mountain you have almost everything.

OLSON: You had everything. Inside those white gates there was everything.

LEINOFF: And so within Black Mountain you have a variation which covers everything.

OLSON: Right. But that variation is the variation of all the people that were in it.

LEINOFF: Yeah.

OLSON: Well, but that's variable, and there's also immediately then the fact that there wasn't a single person there that wasn't occupied with the education. So there's that crazy fact that you've got a runner, like, in the snow, a sled, or wheels on it. You had a runner; you had something that's in the universe, curiously enough. Yeah, well, in the general society—and we're particularly sensitive, I think, at this point because we all contest, and it's a grief that we have to, that there is any purpose in this fucking United States of America, and for a long time, an awful long time, since this side of the 18th century, when she was sort of conceived, in some way, almost like Columbia University was defined, curiously enough. If you want to see what I mean by this, look at the actual definition of the founding of—was it King's College originally then? I'm not sure I'm talking the actual original incorporation of King's College or of Columbia proper, but read it as against that first catalog of Black Mountain to see what, in a funny way, on this side of the Revolution ... We have yet to talk about most universities other than Harvard and Yale and Princeton. In fact, Princeton begins to get towards the Revolution. In fact, Jonathan Edwards was, what, the first president of it, I think, wasn't he? In other words, already there's very few colleges back before the Revolution. So that at the point that we're talking, at this date we're talking the enormous expansion of universal education as a result of the Revolution in this country, and I'm saying that you ought to look at that thing to see the words "humanities" and "living" as the whole ground of the founding of Columbia University. Now, Black Mountain was— as a matter of fact that phrase of Rice's, "with the more usual studies," was already moving her into activity; like, if "the arts shall share the center of the curriculum with the more usual studies," you have that gas in the motor.

I seem to have gone away a little bit from what we were presently speaking of, but I don't—no, I'm not, because I'm talking that crazy business that a society, if it's interesting, not only has everything in it, which is almost easy for it to have, because that's true of any city, it's true in a sense of a nation, or in a sense ought to be, or is at an earlier point of that nation. But at some point, if, like they used to say, the divine is permitted to over-produce, or to be overcut thus to underproduce, you begin to lose the grip. And I'm charging this conception of society in America, as well as the government, as lacking something that in a sense was an intensification principle at Black Mountain, operative for everybody that was in it. In other words, that the social is total, that the search or the striving or the offering to other human beings has to be something which is not intentional but is motive, occurs, is active in the sense that it does occur, and a dynamism, a dynamic. In other words, like in language, the phonetic structure is only one part; you have to talk about the dynamics of the phonetic structure as the reason why the characters that are called phonetic actually behave in the mouths and in the writing of human beings. And there's a general laziness or history-ness, which I call sociological or comparative or relative or all those damn statistical, or any of those things which get just ten no matter what you argue to. You finally end up in an assortment of opinion, or in a theory of probability, to take it at its furthest. And I'm contesting whether that ever reveals a thing. In fact, to tell you the truth, it cheats life; it makes dead the life of the persons and the thing that they are. I mean, I'd love to review, myself, with the authority of having been responsible for that place for six or seven years, everybody's opinion from the beginning to the end. I mean, I don't say that—if it sounds arrogant, it certainly is; but I would think if you're going to take the approach you're taking you ought to create a court, and literally an Areopagus, I mean a court on a hill, because that ought not to be done, to pass out the generalized memories or reminiscences of everyone that was there, because I just think you'll get nothing but a patchwork instead of an assistance or whatever would be a possible re-creation of a condition that it was.

LEINOFF: Yeah, but I mean you wouldn't want just opinion, you wouldn't want a gossip column. The point I was making was that if you take a fixed point, if you take, say, the personality of Albers and you find out what so-and-so thought of him, what so-and-so thought of him, what so-and-so thought, you get a reflection on the kind of a person that was there at the time.

OLSON: I think that's descriptive, though. What about Albers on Albers, what about Rice on Rice, what about me on me, what about Dorn on Dorn, what about Creeley, what about Mrs Jalowetz on Mrs Jalowetz? That gets to be the only place that what I'm calling an intensification basically can be registered.

LEINOFF: It's my thought that selectively choosing some of this stuff, you bring across the point, the above struggle. I mean it should be obvious to anyone who reads it.

OLSON: Yeah, I hear you. And in fact, I have enough confidence in the thickness of her body, and I don't mean her hide, but I mean what you called earlier Black Mountain as an organism made up of all those growths that lie by the seashore, within a certain amount of space that is occupied by them. You'll get a picture. I mean, you'll get better than a picture. The animism of that organism will declare itself. Yeah, I'm sure. So it doesn't matter. I'm just, as one who got caught in her because—I mean, I've been in education, in a sense, all my life, and I only was really caught by this; this textile machine is the only one that caught me, as against, say, having been trained at Wesleyan and Yale and then having taught at a great university which became a city college like Clark University, then moving to Harvard, then finally ending up as full professor with tenure forever at the State University of New York at Buffalo. I really have had it, like. I even taught at state extension in Massachusetts and city high school in Worcester, Massachusetts. I mean, I've been in everything in it, and I am obviously, by my work alone, a pedagogue. But I'm saying that particular little skunk hole named Black Mountain is the only place that really drew me, I mean the allure of her perfume or something. I'm sure an awful lot of other people must talk to you, too, with that funny feeling, "Oh jeezus, that was something!" O.K. [PAUSE] Question?

LEINOFF: I'm just trying to think of the name of the fish. Remember? Black Mountain was like a fish.

OLSON: Yeah, yeah, what was the name of the fish? Yeah. What was the name of the fish? Damn it. I said I'd remember everything, didn't I? God, now I …

LEINOFF: It's just when you were talking about seashore and organism …

OLSON: Yeah. What was the fish? Poof! I have it in the notes I made when we were talking, but … It'll come back. Catfish. Catfish?

LEINOFF: No, no, began with "s." A spanner, there was a spanner.

OLSON: The idea that you—yeah, the lure, the lure was a spinner, and that you caught the fish. I don't know, I'm full of images of Black Mountain. I think I may have told you when we were talking on the telephone of the crazy time when I was first there, to talk about the real crisis, when there was danger that—you see, the students had actually asked, in one of those typical revolts at Black Mountain, for the resignation of Ted Dreier as the teacher of mathematics. There may have been some grounds for criticizing him as a teacher of mathematics but it happened that Ted Dreier was actually the Treasurer, if I'm not mistaken, literally by title, of the College and had been maybe the Treasurer the whole time. I mean, the conduct of the business of the place was being taken—as, for example, when Huss and I finally closed, I mean, I couldn't have run the place without Huss. Huss kept the books, Huss had the ability. I can't keep a book as of my life any-way, so how could I do it for a place like Black Mountain? But when they asked, then he resigned, and the moment he resigned Albers said, "Then you take my resignation." Well, then they lost their shot. Those men are very conscientious men and they sought to see if they couldn't propose some furtherance of Black Mountain. And there was meetings. I can remember—that's when that dean from MIT that I …

LEINOFF: Burchard?

OLSON: Burchard came down. Also a fellow who had a Porsche or a Jag, from Boston, who'd become an architect, I think, who'd been an early student, and came—damned if I can remember his name—a very attractive man, young man still. And like, oh lord, there was a panel of about five or six, including one very attractive and interesting woman educator—oh, like who were these people?[7] But they were very nice. Well, Albers lost his voice over the week they met and I finally came in on one of my monthly visits from Washington to teach for five days, and Albers asked me actually, because he had no voice, to speak for him. And it got to that point where suddenly there was the prospect there would be fourteen faculty members, no students, and no Black Mountain. I said, "That's like—" I mean, I was so reminded of the great Chinese novel which Miss Buck translates as *All Men Are Brothers*, which, just to add a topical note, it's the book which I'm told that Mao Tse-tung has always regarded as sort of like the preparation of his own mind. It's a great book, because it's the moment at which the Mandarin China or Empire China suddenly had no longer any use for her most valuable instructors, like the instructor of the emperor in swords, or the wrestler of the palace, or the great courtesans, or—so that in fact everybody that really had anything to offer the society was suddenly thrown out on the roads. And they all go west, like in fact the whole Mao thing did in the famous Long March, and the novel is simply like a great medieval tale, either Boccaccio or Chaucer, of a sort of broken pilgrimage to nowhere, but going west. And all these funny unemployed people meet each other as they go, and they become a kind of a thread or a strut or a woven composition at the end of the book, so that they all end up, not in Yenan, but almost. And the great thing about it was that finally they are all together. Like I said, what's wrong with fourteen people being left alone on a mountain? What's wrong with that? As a matter of fact, that's one of the reasons why I have such a passion about Black Mountain is that I felt even then, and that was the first year I was there and that was when the place was in the statutory condition she'd basically been in since her founding (this would be the spring of 1949), I had that funny feeling: what's wrong? It would be a marvelous example of what is the situation in this nation that fourteen such people—and they were rather a considerable bunch, they were a faculty, but they were, like, again, a society, a funny little group of human beings, a society, like they say—so I said to them once at a faculty, and it was marvelous to say it, and I was getting pretty drunk, really, drinking that lousy but marvelous, sort of punched cheap wine, not muscatel or port but tokay, which is a son of a gun. I mean, it left me so that I walked right down the hill without touching the ground at all. But I can remember saying, "Fourteen people, what's wrong with fourteen people? What do you know will come of that, what do you know will come of that?" And in fact, in a curious way, the arrestment that that might have been of the movement of this nation could have been as important as the movement of Black Mountain up to that date. It would go on, of course, for another nine years or eight years. I mean, I really think in terms of like the States, States-side, at least, and now worldwide, world-wise, it would have been kind of fun. What would have emerged from those fourteen people stuck there, stuck on

7. See Martin Duberman's *Black Mountain* (NY: Dutton, 1972), p. 310 (p. 324 paperback).

that sheer rise from the floor of the Swannanoa, of the Swannanoa River, flowing into the French Broad, the French Broad flowing into what? But this is the waters flowing into the Gulf of Mexico, not into the Atlantic Ocean. Black Mountain sat just on the edge of the flow of the rivers the other way, that is, west and north to the Ohio, and then down. Yeah, from the Broad to the Kanawha, the Kanawha to the Ohio, the Ohio to the Mississippi and down into the Gulf of Mexico. There was a funny thing, that the creek we used to swim in was itself turned the other way, turned inward towards the continent, then down through the middle and out. Which is interesting because there was such a bunch of striving Americans. Like, it was Scotch-Irish country from the old migrations through and down the valley. Equally ...

[REEL 2]

OLSON: There was an obit in the *New York Times*?[8] Could you ask your friend to send me a xerox of that? Would that be a drag?

LEINOFF: No. Just 28 Ford Square?

OLSON: No, f-o-r-t. Fort, federal fort. "Defiance."[9]

LEINOFF: O.K., I'll push a little bit then. This is in regards to when the students asked Dreier to leave. All of a sudden they decided he was just a bad teacher of mathematics?

OLSON: No, I don't think so. But there was a guy come in from—you know, we used to import these people or they would come, ex-sailor people would come from like St John's or from Marlboro, Goddard, Oberlin, Antioch, and they'd end up at Black Mountain, and they'd stay permanently or just go back. This particular cat was in history, his name was Jackson—I'll never forget him—and he came in and he had a certain amount of ruggedness and mental stupidity, I could say (excuse me, Mr Jackson!), but I mean thickness or stubbornness. And he just—I mean, like, Black Mountain was a power. In terms of today, for example, it makes you almost laugh to think that the students were struggling to get representation. As you know, from talking to some of those student moderators, the power of the student moderator at Black Mountain was, I think perhaps from the beginning—I don't know exactly when the first concept of the student moderator—I'm not sure that's in the incorporation itself: that one student shall be always a member of the ...

LEINOFF: It's in the catalog.

OLSON: It's in the catalog, right. But in any case, the student moderator was very much a—because he represented the students, therefore it wasn't a question of his having only a vote. I mean, he represented a larger population than the faculty, right? The point of the present, or one of the irritations of the present, is that, my god, here we are, not just that we're

8. John A. Rice's obituary was in the *New York Times* for 28 November 1968, p. 7.
9. "Defiance" is the early name for Fort Point where Olson's house is situated.

paying, but we're the population, we're the people, like they say these days in these struggles. I mean, this place is an institution if it isn't a society. And we're bound to see that it's a society, otherwise what good does it do us? We might as well go to the city. The city's no good anymore, so where should we go? Go to the temples! Go to your farms where you get back to simpler things! Go where you are boss, go where you isolate yourself! Go into holes, as who did found the whole principle of—was it St Anthony that first dug a hole in the Nile and made the principle of monks? I don't know. I mean, do it yourself, like in "The Kingfishers," which I wrote just at the time I was at Black Mountain. That's the point of the kingfisher: he lays his eggs in holes dug in banks. I mean, lay some eggs, for god's sake! Be fecund! Students, be fecund! And I mean fecund on the earth, in the earth, not the—societies don't stand except by having feet. Two. They walk, they talk, they are mobile.

In fact, it was interesting the last Black Mountain was done, a plan for it was done by Tony Landreau, the weaver, who was then twenty-three, I think. I kind of hired him on sight. And he came up with this marvelous idea of a mobile Black Mountain, which was to be anywhere wherever she was. It was very beautiful, great. As a matter of fact, I was for it. Wolpe, the composer, was all upset because he couldn't figure out where he'd be when it was mobile, which is understandable. But then, you know, I said, "Well, somebody must be—you can stay home if you don't want—and you could come and join us wherever we were." In fact, that was about it, because the point was that it suddenly became interplanetary or something. In fact, we were so wealthy, in that sense, even when we closed, that if you look at the last board meeting, the instruction to me is to resolve her difficulties and plan her future. And her future was already programmed. One part of it was this mobile thing, but other things were the theater in San Francisco, the *Black Mountain Review*, which has since become a rather well known result of the program at Black Mountain. And artists, painters were in New York, and dance, and music, and also I had this wonderful thing that developed rather far, to hold eight-week programs, given away, in the major cities in the western world, like, on Sumerian, Canaanite, and Hittite literature, with Güterbock from the Oriental Institute in Chicago doing Hittite, Samuel Noah Kramer from the Pennsylvania Museum doing Sumerian, and the great decipherer at Brandeis, Cyrus Gordon, doing Canaanite. And I was just going to be the end run, doing two weeks of a sort of indication of what it was to take this step back from the so-called Classical literature, which is the assumption that we start with as though that was the beginning of our humanities, civics, reasoning, logic, and civilization. And that went so far that Canadian Broadcasting wanted to pick it up and transfer it to BBC. So that, in a funny way, already the—you might take it both ways: either the residence of fourteen lonely people on the mountain or this crazy final actual deflatus of Black Mountain, '56 and into '57. Because, for example, I read in San Francisco at the Museum at the time that the Black Mountain Theater was into production of the second of Duncan's plays, and there was a company of about twenty-four people and I was in a sense paying the bills, as still the Rector, but also by that point of time, the Assignee for the Benefit of the Creditors, on the assumption there would be profit, which there was. In other words, Black Mountain's activity was simply—it was not foreclosed, it was simply, really, just sort of, I don't know, it just was stopped by Huss and myself simply because we'd had it. That's all, but I mean, I give you some of the sense and even the fretwork of the stars that she was climbing towards on the stairway of surprise.

LEINOFF: But it's still unclear. I mean, you had ten thousand, right? And you had faculty that …

OLSON: … were new and fresh and active. Right.

LEINOFF: And you had faculty that were old and were worried about what was going to happen.

OLSON: Some, some, some. But they were right to, because they were almost all widow ladies and it was tough and Black Mountain had no security. She had no pension fund, she had no tenure of any sort. Wait, she had tenure; yeah, you had absolute tenure! [LAUGHS] If you stayed, you was paid.

As I've said to you, the actual, unfortunate thing that was done in 1950, which would be, mind you, one year after the leaving of Albers and Dreier, there was a funny sort of an interim condition there in 1950, some new people who'd not been there before, kind of a concern for the future, which led to the writing of a thing called "contingent salary," which—in fact, if I could make it quickly clear, I tell you I'd be doing something that the faculty itself I think never did quite understand what it had done. [LAUGHS] But what they were doing was writing an equivalent—mind you, Black Mountain as a society offered everything for life. There was housing, there was food for everybody, there was salary, a little bit, but that was equal to everybody. And if, for example, a person—and there was, say, two, I remember two faculty members that came through to us in that break-up of Mount Olivet, and they were very able, normal academic teachers, who have gone on, and may be retired now, but very important teachers at Hartford Theological Seminary, one an anthropologist from Germany named Leser, and a great teacher of linguistics and languages, Flola Shepard.

LEINOFF: Nathan Glazer?

OLSON: No, Paul Leser, Leser. L-e-s-e-r. And there were others, and in fact there was some of these widow ladies too, and older people. The point was that they did want to get some chit or some tally that would be comparable, that would give them something they could show if they needed to go elsewhere, try to get a job at another college or university, because you had to have some sort of a—how would you say it?—some sort of an equation of value as to what actually was the standing economic gain. I don't mean gain, but, like, the salary figure of a person at Black Mountain. Because, unlike all other places, practically, salary is something earned in payment for teaching; it isn't all your other things. So they wrote this thing called "contingent salary." What they also meant was, contingent upon the closing of Black Mountain, which was an unhappy idea. And in fact, as I tried to point out to Huss almost immediately upon my return in '51, so far as I could see this thing shouldn't be carried beyond any given year, because it represented simply a paper, a paper representation of value received. But it was carried as a debt because of the concern of some people that Black Mountain might not make its next heave. As she did, you know, she made her next heave and she lasted another five or six or seven years. So she had a kind of third lease on life. I can't say how many ways, how many times she lived, I don't remember. I kind of think of three Black Mountains myself. The founded one, the Dreier-Albers one, and the last one with myself. That's the way I—I don't know what your picture is, but that seems the three shapes. The thirties, the forties, and the fifties, you could put it that way. Well, this thing, which should have, it seems to me, absolutely been written off each year because it didn't represent anything, except that Huss was such a tidy and superb budget accountant and administrative man that he paid federal income tax on that funny thing, so that if again Black Mountain shouldn't make it, the people who received that payment that was being carried as a debt wouldn't have to pay any tax on it, backwards. Which again was a typical Black Mountain care for her own, which I love about the thing. But the point was that the damn thing didn't represent anything. It wasn't back salaries; it was equivalence, all of what was being offered in any given year. So that it became actually carried on the audits and became a debt of $56,000, and was called as such. Well, go into a court, or show a thing like that to a lawyer! I mean, it's like [LAUGHS]—can you get, can you excuse bare feet, beards, and so forth and so forth, I mean, you know, if you pass into the formal places of society? Well, of course, the court looks at the audit, yes, and saw 56,000. And three—sort of two ancient and one, well, one ancient and one middle and one young woman, brought suit against Black Mountain for what was partially this contingent salary thing. So I had to meet it in the Buncombe County court.

I hope it's only taken me ten minutes on this tape to make it clear, and I hope I'm making it clear. I have, by the way, in case you're interested, written to—I mean, Mike Weaver, in writing that book from England on Black Mountain, assigned some young fellow in Asheville to go to the courthouse and examine the whole disposition of Black Mountain, and the boy did a beautiful job[10] and wrote me then just on this thing again: "What was that contingent salary at Black Mountain?" I wrote him a letter, which does exist, I hope, and could be gotten, something like fourteen pages, saying how this completely got resolved in court, so that it may be understood. Because it ought to be understood. This is a very important thing; this is just as important as the founding of Black Mountain, to my mind, the

---

10. Roger A. Wicker. See his article "Black Mountain College" in *The Serif* 4:1 (March 1969), pp. 3–11. Olson's letter to Wicker is not at present known.

incorporation and first catalog, is this crazy way she finally came through the Buncombe County court out and with her debts paid and plus.

And equally programming—at the same time that I was carrying on all of this, these programs, which I call the network of her stars, which in a sense could have run upon the world as mobile university or however you want to call it, activism of an educational order free from, as she always was free from, all the structural and institutional characteristics from the beginning, so that she could never get credit, for example ... I wish it might be known to whoever hears this tape, whether you in doing your paper, that Black Mountain couldn't get accredited by the—what do you call them?—the regional associations. It's a very important thing. When I think of Gloucester High School right now being stuck because they don't—I mean, the cost of building a school, like, ha ha ha! I mean, I think of ho ho ho! But in order to get approval today to be a high school you have to go through some state organization which is called the audit bureau or something like that. Well, Black Mountain couldn't go through any of the accrediting functions of the Association of American Schools and Colleges, because she didn't have 25,000 volumes in her library, she did not have a board of trustees, she did not have, like what else? Because I can remember, even though Frank Aydelotte was finally the man who probably pulled the rug out from under her, Frank at one point, when I was seeking again to get accreditation from the Southern Association of the so-and-so and so-and-so, wrote a letter saying that Black Mountain should be treated like parochial schools, which don't have their—because the nuns don't get paid, right? I mean they're a part of the diocese or something. We were part of a diocese which had no Vatican [LAUGHS] other than our own blood and lives. And it was a marvelous argument that Aydelotte offered, that sure she should be accredited, because she purposely does not have these so-called structural or methodological jungle-gyms normal to schoolyards. Not bad. Useful. Because it's the in stuff. That's why I said to you on the phone, you have to work hard in anything like this, even like a history of, or a paper on, or any examination of, something that lasts even twenty-three years. It tends to spread before your eyes and you've got an awful lot of people involved here. I mean, how many? Several thousand, I suppose, over twenty-three years, literally speaking, live, living beings right now, several thousand attached, touched, or their lives are still in some way being affected by having been at Black Mountain. Certainly hundreds, and probably, yeah, I should think if you total, nobody's ever done this to my knowledge, how many actual students/faculty there was in the sum of twenty-three years. It's very interesting.

LEINOFF: I think Duberman, actually, when ...

OLSON: Yeah. But, for example, one of the last things that Katherine Dreier was so beautifully conscientious to insist upon me: "What are you going to do with the transcripts, what are you going to do with the records of the students?" I said, "Gee, it's a tough problem"—because you know it's a funny thing, the trouble with these colleges and universities is they go on forever or there's no idea that they should stop when their usefulness is over. They have a tendency like all things to—it's an old point but it's still a very valuable one: why shouldn't things stop when they're over? That's my own attitude toward Black Mountain anyhow, that she stopped when she was over, whatever that means. But in any case, one of the funniest things hanging out after everything and everything and everything was done was this question of what are you going to do with the records of students whose lives, for example, at that point, are still in their twenties and some in their thirties and none, literally, later than their middle forties? And that means that, say, for twenty to thirty to forty years, the record of those people at Black Mountain has to be an open file, has to be available somewhere. So, happily, when the Archives of the State of North Carolina asked for the records of Black Mountain, I asked if they could service those transcripts of student records as long as it would take, and that would be twenty to thirty more years. And they said, happily. So that that service exists too; so that there is that funny string-out, still relationship of this thing to its own.

LEINOFF: Let's get back to Buncombe County, O.K.?

OLSON: Right.

LEINOFF: There are three people suing for the back salaries.

OLSON: Yeah. Actually, at the end I think two of the widows of the professors joined them, reluctantly, but with fear that—or with hope, in a sense, or some perfectly understandable wish. Again, like that idea of contingency thing, which was if Black Mountain was closing, the moment that, for example, these two wives of two professors, both of whom died and were buried on the grounds—I'm speaking of Max Dehn's wife and Mrs Jalowetz, whose husband had been teacher of music back in I think the forties or, if not, the thirties, but I mean for some time, for that length of time—they actually joined in the suit, but they only did it because they were, well, they were widows and late in life themselves. So it was five women, if I'm not mistaken, that in the end were bringing suit. Three of them, one of whom was the wife of the founder, who'd been, become and was carried forward as the librarian at Black Mountain; one was the physics teacher, who had tried to administer the place in either, I think, 1950, but maybe the year '49, I think maybe the '49–50 year, I'm not sure ...

LEINOFF: Who was the physics teacher?

OLSON: Goldowski, Natasha Goldowski, who ended up at Alfred and may or may not still be there. And the third was the photographer, who was the youngest, Hazel Larsen. And they were the three that actually brought the suit on the basis of having, as the rest of us had, not paid ourselves any salary for one term so that there was actually an unpaid back salary which was on the books, which could have been sued for and we would have paid ourselves the same as they would have been paid. But they also, if I'm not mistaken, in their suit claimed the contingent salary, and that's what broke the back of her in the court. This is all examinable. My memory is as good as I can make it at this date. It's examinable, it's on the record, and it's absolutely solid paperwork and complete, how you say it, accountancy, because I was carried by three insurance companies, bonded to carry out the instruction of the court to sell and to realize on her properties, to meet all debts and all loans as well as all mortgages, as well as to finish off her existence, and if there was any furtherance to carry—no, I mean, I'm not sure of that legal question of whether or not—actually, she kept her charter and in fact, so far as I know, has never been resolved except as a—because I chose, as I said, Huss and I chose, well, let's just give her the business, that's all.

LEINOFF: Well, before we jump on to those finalities, the two widows understandably wanted to sue for contingency, and the other three …

OLSON: … were really sort of not playing, how do you say it, the old Black Mountain game. They weren't standing in as though they were still representative of the place; they were doing the one thing Black Mountain—and I think this would be said by everyone from the beginning had agreed upon, which is, this is not going to be a great life, we're in this thing because we're all—as you know from probably having talked to those early people like Georgia or the Alberses. I remember once Albers saying to me, "My god, I mean we got $500 a year!" I think that was the figure for most of the thirties was 500 bucks a year. Just think of that as in terms of America. I equivalate that by saying that crazy story that we were offering education at the end of the Korean Bill. And by the way, the Korean Bill was extended to everybody; we were offering every student a total education for $850. So that, comparable to two figures that balanced the seesaw of Black Mountain is the debt which he could say to me in some pain: "Look, $500 a year was what we got when we founded the place." And I'm saying that she was at the end offering education total, including food and living and everything else, and company as well, because the place was marvelous simply because it was the only place we all were $850 a year. So mind you, that's twenty-three years later. And the American economy, lord, I mean, wow, just think, by any measure, what either the payment to each of us or whatever was like 500 bucks basically mean salary throughout, and essentially on a scaled level because she scaled her scholarships, even. She was expensive if a person had money to pay, but she was zero if you could convince Black Mountain that you should be a student there. So that was another way she was in a marvelous balance or equivalence of condition. Excuse me, I didn't mean to go too far on that question, but, I mean, come back to your own. I just would say that those three ladies had certainly "unhabituated" themselves [LAUGHS], to be as generous as I can be.

LEINOFF: Well, maybe the other two were new, but Nelly had been there for a long time.

OLSON: Well, the others weren't new either, to tell you the truth. Natasha had been there as long as I, in fact before myself, and Hazel before myself.

LEINOFF: Well, I don't know much about Nell, so …

OLSON: She'd been there; she's one of the incorporators. The three wives that incorporated her, Mrs Rice, Mrs Georgia, I think, and Mrs …

LEINOFF: Lounsbury?

OLSON: Mrs Lounsbury, yeah, I think. For some reason the wives of the three teachers are the ones that incorporated Black Mountain. I don't know what the technical reason for that is, but it's interesting.

LEINOFF: Well, what was Nell like?

OLSON: Mrs Rice, I think, was really—in fact, to tell you the truth, may I say it so that I don't get involved in the whole question? The judge, Judge Williams, who had been the lawyer who incorporated Black Mountain and is the man who actually took me through the courts so there was a single lawyer, judge, a great Southern, western North Carolina lawyer of the ilk or order of Andrew Jackson in my book, but "Red" Williams, as he was called, R.R. Williams, Sr., took the whole thing from the start to the end, and at one point, when Mrs Rice was in these throes of last activity, said to me, "Olson, I would advise you and the board to get a sheriff and remove her and her property immediately from Black Mountain." So I can say that as true, and it is the kind of a judgment and objectivity of a man who was the lawyer of the Corporation of Black Mountain College that felt that her behavior had become so, well actually if I may, if those who hear me won't think I put too great a weight upon it, because I think life is what it is, but, I mean, treachery. Well, as a matter of fact, when you get into this you get into what the novelists ought to be doing, because this is sociology. And Mr Rumaker, who's an extraordinary writer, once proposed, and I wrote a recommendation for him for a Guggenheim, a novel on Black Mountain. I suppose some day there may be such result. But I mean some of the, some of all that, the natural history of the family, like they say. Like Mr Rice's own book on his whole life, *I Came Out of the Eighteenth Century*, which his final chapter's on Black Mountain, was removed at date of publication and is one of the rarest books because the Rice family, as I understand it, raised a suit against the publisher, which was Harper's. That's damn interesting, though, that the book by John Rice himself on his whole life, *I Came Out of the Eighteenth Century*, there's only a handful of copies in the world because it never was distributed by the publishers.

LEINOFF: One is at Harvard.

OLSON: One is at Harvard, right. There was one in the Black Mountain College library. Those are the only two I've ever heard of.

LEINOFF: Can you say anything, then, about the natures, if you want to put it that way, of Larsen or Goldowski that would make them do what they did?

OLSON: I don't think—except that I think both of them had taken on administration, and in fact they had, in that crazy year, 1949–50, had both taken on to administer, and had in a year palpably either not so much failed but had created a faculty of a social condition at Black Mountain, which was that year 1950–51. See, there was these two interregnum years, and they didn't work. And in fact, to tell you the truth, Natasha was in some ways some sort of a sub-Rector, because a man was brought in—this is the only time I think in Black Mountain's history, a Rector was brought in from the outside, who'd been with Aydelotte at Swarthmore and had been sort of a business manager of Swarthmore or something—I can't remember his name, it's a very strange name,[11]—I mean, as Rector visited Black Mountain, and Natasha was sort of administrator for him *in absentia*. And if I'm not mistaken, Hazel was treasurer at that period too. So in a sense they had a certain, probably a sense of failure with the Black Mountain that had reemerged under—if I'm not mistaken, M.C. Richards was chairman of the faculty in 1950–51, Mr Huss had come in as a theater man and was chairman of the board, and that was the administration that, when I came back from Yucatan in the summer of 1951, and Lou Harrison came in for music and Katherine Litz for dance, and we stayed on, yes, I think Harrison did too, we all were invited to stay on and did. There was this new Black Mountain suddenly, with the administration which tended to stay to the end, even though M.C. went out because I was teaching writing instead, but it was like a vacation, and Huss and I stood in to the end. So that in a sense they suddenly were in a place that for a year they had more or less been the bosses or whatever you want to call it. It wasn't the boss but the attempters of, which is all we ever were anyways. And I think they may have felt they would like to get out and they would like to get out with something. So they did. They succeeded. And we all did, too, which isn't what we were after at all. No, no, there was no exceptions. The only people that got out with something that brought about that kind of future were those three women who sued, and equally then the two, but then I say those two ladies I think would have to be excepted from the suit.

LEINOFF: Well, were Larsen and Goldowski, then, instrumental in some way in writing up this contingency proposal?

OLSON: I think not, as a matter of fact. My impression is that—that could be checked—is that that was done by not the faculty of 1949–50 but the faculty of 1950–51, and that that was that faculty that I say was made up of M.C. Richards and Huss, as chairman of the faculty and chairman of the board, that essentially I tie into, as I tied into the end of the Albers-Dreier train. See, I came there, I was invited there by Albers and Dreier after Dahlberg couldn't—well, Dahlberg, my friend, went to Black Mountain, but Dahlberg found that Black Mountain was not a city museum or the sidewalks of the city, and that the girls couldn't be made so easily, and so he got bored rather

11. N.O. Pittenger, a retired treasurer of Swathmore College, who served as "Administrator" at Black Mountain in the spring of 1949.

quickly and got out of there. And he suggested they try me and I was in Washington and I didn't accept, but eventually they did ask me if I'd come once a month, which I did for a year, and that was the year 1948–49. And then I was asked to come for the summer session of '49, which my wife and I did. And that was the beginning of what we might call the Goldowski period, because it was Buckminster Fuller and Einstein's former assistant, Rosen, a physicist from the University of North Carolina, and there was generally a temper or climate of the place during that period. In fact, it was a funny period in which you might say that science came to the top, or scientific, or scientifish, or MIT-ish sort of people. And I mean that not as of Rosen or Goldowski, but I'm thinking of Buckminster Fuller's continuing presence at MIT. So that, actually, I think it was another faculty that wrote that contingent salary, which was then taken advantage of, in a sense, by these previous, with one year's previous attempt at administering. And it didn't work. It was not a happy solution. It wasn't a solution, and it was a rather unhappy period. Equally, the year 1951 wasn't. There was a real gap of two years there before a certain amount of energy, whatever it was that was in there, in the last six to seven years, whatever that was, that last, what I call the third Black Mountain.

LEINOFF: O.K., we got to the Buncombe County court, and these five people now are suing for back salaries and/or contingency of some sort. So what happened?

OLSON: Well, one just had to meet the suit, right? I mean, when you're sued and you're brought into a court, you appear. Happily, M.C. Richards came down from New York in a very beautiful suit. And I was wearing a beard at that time, and the lawyer obviously, again Mr Williams, would really have liked me to appear before the judge of the Buncombe County court without a beard, but I got that problem, right? You just can't tear your flags down. So here I was, going to be a lone man, because Huss was on the Coast and didn't feel free to come back, even though he's the one that wrote that contingent salary. That's why I wanted him there, because that was going to be the issue, and I thought, and still think, that thing has to be made clear, as obviously this tape shows. [LAUGHS] And it has to be made clear because it's the one ambiguity and the only ambiguity I know that still sort of flutters about and is a bore because, if examined and gone into, it can be shown to be all that I think I'm saying it is, and it was my responsibility to take care of it. I inherited it and took care of it. I paid the 56,000, I paid the back salaries, and then, in addition, I paid all the mortgages and all the loans and even the gifts, and in fact did not charge many, many students— all the students' debts I wiped out, just never even considered calling them, and still realized more than the total debt plus the current expenses of the place. So that, in that marvelous sense, I may sound like Sir Walter Scott or whoever it was that spent his lifetime paying his father's debts: I just want the statement, the positive, that the apple of Black Mountain was as rosy at the end as the tree that she was planted by.

LEINOFF: In the court, you know, the case in the court …

OLSON: Yes, to come back to that.

LEINOFF: Those people were …

OLSON: On the one side was these three ladies, Mrs Rice, with a little sort of a bird-nest hat on top of her hair; Miss Goldowski, who had been the most marvelous Russian physicist, who had nothing but flaring hair; and Miss Larsen. And there was I, with a beard, except for the arrival in the early morning, happily, by train from New York, Miss Richards, who appeared as chairman of the faculty. So that I did have a girl on my side. And after about thirty, forty-five minutes of a very long tedious in—how do you say it like in a court? the lawyer of the opposition bringing out something about a telephone call of mine to Hazel Larsen—after almost forty-five minutes of this slow testimony, the judge, with some tedium, asked to see the lawyers in the back room, and after a short conference, Mr Williams, who was the lawyer for the Corporation of Black Mountain College under the state laws of North Carolina, and therefore my representative, came and asked me, said that it had been suggested, as it so often is in the courts, that the thing be resolved by simply I taking on this post of Assignee for the Benefit of the Creditors, and that the place be regarded as, how do you say it, resolved or absolved or no longer in business.

LEINOFF: Bankrupt?

OLSON: No, not at all, no. Yeah, it amounts to it, but then mind you the phrasing is—you see, it was not bankruptcy, it was not voluntary bank-ruptcy or involuntary bankruptcy. It was the court's desire to resolve this thing that looked like an inner-family struggle, which in fact it basically was, which got into public for the first time. In fact, it's interesting to say that, because in terms of all the rump, agitated, and split-off things of Black Mountain, this was the one that did get into the court. All the rest of the crimes of social life occurred, occurred in the privacy of our own range. Suddenly these three sort of horny cows got the thing out in public in, of all places, Buncombe County. And by the way, at that point, due to the final instructions of the board that previous fall to me, Mr Williams felt, actually, because he was concerned that we were, that the so-called mobile university had already come into existence, and that we weren't functioning on the grounds of the college itself, which was what I was improving for either return of the occupants to it or for sale—but then we were already intending to finance if possible, from the six hundred acres and the thirteen buildings and the stock and everything else, the future of her existence in the possible, like, larger world of anywhere. So that, in that sense, there was a prospective—the amount was prospective, right?—but he was concerned that I couldn't show that we were a college in existence in that sense in which colleges—you see, that's kind of interesting as of our day, where people are in the cities, people are in the country, people are in the colleges, people are anywhere. What is it in today's word? The streets belong to us. I mean, Black

Mountain's position was that space belongs to us. Which is one of her great, I think, one of the parts of her round target black and white flag, is space belongs to us. He had, prior to this suit, under a Norman law, made me personally, as Rector and chairman of the board, by that time point, so I was double-officed, the owner of all of Black Mountain. So that it was my decision whether to continue to fight this thing up in the courts; but I was already in the embarrassing position of being the sole owner of this damn property plus all of its accretions or accoutrements.

LEINOFF: Your term as sole owner didn't mean that you were being held responsible for …

OLSON: Yes. In fact, the three women were really, whether they knew it or not—and I'm not sure their lawyers knew—they were suing me. But they thought, they may have thought they were suing—and in fact the general drift of that original testimony suggested that it was probably going to be a personal charge upon me that was going to, in a sense, eventuate, although it never did get to that point, so that my beard, or my nature, was never actually investigated. [LAUGHS]

LEINOFF: Excuse me for being a little pedantic about this, but …

OLSON: Please. I'm happy. Like I said, I have no secrets; I'm willing to speak to anything.

LEINOFF: The legality, though, of the judge assigning …

OLSON: Yeah, it was absolute; it was already through the courts and was as clear as a bell.

LEINOFF: It was clear?

OLSON: Oh yes, absolutely. No trickery to it at all. On the contrary, it was his protection, again, of Black Mountain, the Corporation of Black Mountain College, so that she was in firm and healthy and legal, territorial existence. There was no maneuver; it was no maneuver.

LEINOFF: I don't mean anything like that, I mean …

OLSON: No. And I can't yourself, I can't give you the legal—it's a Norman law, as I understood it from him. And in fact, it's why, after that conference of the lawyers and the judge, Mr Williams came to me in the open court, with Miss Richards I think actually with me at the moment that he told me, asked me, would I accept to become—because this is interesting, and I should say it that way: because I was sole owner, it must have been resolved by the lawyers and the judge that I would have to then be the Assignee for the Benefit of the Creditors, which became my title. So that we agreed, then, to cease all operations until the debts of the college were satisfied. Which is all I agreed, or Mr Williams and I took that as the solution. So the court was satisfied, papers were drawn promising the suers as well as all others party to—which included the mortgages and the loans—that all those things were on schedule to be paid, and when those payments were done then

Black Mountain should be excused from the court. That's my understanding, and I'm trying to think if I'm right that actually, in a sense, the legal existence of Black Mountain, if I had come out with so much money that I could have reconstituted her, I could have reconstituted her. It was like a suspension rather than a bankruptcy or a foreclosure, suspension of operations, which we'd already done, see. We'd already suspended operations on the ground, in the situ sense of a college, which is one of the drags. Again, you might go back to Mr Rice's thinking, which I've always found so interesting, the more that I was the last Rector and had to go through all of this, that the ownership thing isn't equal to the rental, that I resolved in a sense the same thing, by paying all the debts, realizing the debts, as John did in founding it as a rental, you dig? It's a curious kind of a wise, a light, fast, · flexible financial result that we came out, like, because my speculation, my risk, and the faculty knew it every day that we'd discuss it, I said I think I could realize so much from such, so let's go ahead another year, sort of thing. We were putting the money on that land, right? And in the end, like a bird that had to fly, I had to fly from that nest as John had originally conceived her as flying from a rented nest. I think this is true. The balance, I think, is not just a sort of a figure.

LEINOFF: All I was saying by—you were saying that, I thought, there was treachery involved in the designation. The judge did a service to you in that you could have found out about this in a higher court somewhere and you would have been really screwed.

OLSON: Well, I would have been screwed in a very simple sense. I couldn't see that any court in the nation or in the world was going to allow that this was a college, that had no students, in the sense, registered on its grounds. I mean, like, I'm no *luftsmensch*, I mean, I can tell the difference between air and a flight of birds or stars and the fact that I'm not on those stars! There's a real difference here. No matter what your imagination may propose, the substantive does count. I mean, if I may teach the great lessons of the Elixir of Life, the "thought-earth" is where the "heavenly heart" occurs, in the "middle house." I mean, you can't have substance without the "thought-earth," and the "thought-earth," this is one of the places where I was …

[REEL 3]

That's fun that passage.[12] Is it on now?

LEINOFF: Yeah, it's on now.

OLSON: Well, what I was going to say is that whole idea of the "thought-earth" is, curiously enough, why I, when that whole proposition in around—gee,

12. The passage Olson read off-tape was probably from pp. 25–26 of the Harvest paperback edition of *The Secret of the Golden Flower* (hardcover, p. 28):

> The way of the Elixir of Life knows as supreme magic, seed-water, spirit-fire, and thought-earth: these three. What is seed-water? It is the true, one energy of former heaven (eros). Spirit-fire is the light (logos). Thought-earth is the heavenly heart of the middle dwelling (intuition). Spirit-fire is used for effecting, thought-earth for substance, and seed-water for the foundation.

what would it be, around 1952, that Paul Williams and that whole group that are now at Stony Point in New York State wanted to move north? If I say "thought-earth," I mean that constituted place that was as far as I was concerned a road to Sutter[13] lake and in the mountains of North Carolina was where the earth of Black Mountain was. Like it always has moved me that the most famous figure of Cherokee myth, who was called Crazy Boy, was probably in a cave on that property. So that if Black Mountain has a kind of a *umper* or Pooh Bear—or what is that *puer aeternus* it had, a Cherokee *puer aeternus*?

But, I mean, I didn't see any reason—like, my decision the moment that that judge said, "My lord," when Mr Williams suggests something, I can assure you that you feel not at all that you're in the hands of a lawyer but that you're in the hands of a man of adage or something. That's why I say Andrew Jackson, because North Carolina at that date had, I think, nobody, or no one—I think that in the history of Black Mountain, Judge R.R. Williams, Sr. should be remembered as almost a constituent part of her. He represented the law, like they say, in the most intimate and conductive sense that I have ever known.

LEINOFF: Do you know if he's still alive?

OLSON: I don't know. He was then old enough—he was then in his seventies, so that he would be today certainly in his eighties. I don't know, as a matter of fact. But he was of the order of the days of the earlier America, that he might be as stringy and tough as he was then. He was so, like they say—I mean, like I say about the fact that she was there: I mean that that's where Rice and that group put her, brought her, right? I hope somebody—and if this is the chance, let me do it, I mean, say that of all the people of Black Mountain the man who might not be put in there but who should represent one of its powers, is Judge R.R. Williams of Asheville, North Carolina.

LEINOFF: Was Rice and the Rice family friends with Williams?

OLSON: No. I don't know why, except I should imagine that when they did go to Black Mountain that Mr Williams's firm was probably the most natural one they turned to, because Asheville is a small city.

LEINOFF: What year did this trial take place in?

OLSON: In the spring of 1957. As a matter of fact I was in San Francisco, as I said, doing that reading and having a chance to see the whole bunch that had gone out to create the Black Mountain Theater, in production, doing the second piece of Duncan's trilogy on Medea. The first one, which had been done at Black Mountain when she was open, had—so I was called back; that trip had to be curtailed because that suit suddenly appeared in court. It was the spring of 1957.

13. The word "Sutter" is uncertain, as is "umper" later. The Wild Boy of the Cherokee is found in James Mooney "Myths of the Cherokee" in *19th Annual Report of the Bureau of American Ethnology* (1900), pp. 242, 432.

LEINOFF: Well, if the school closed its doors essentially like with fourteen men …

OLSON: But she was not closed. We closed her in October of the previous year, October 1956. Everybody left before the next day, you know, and my wife and child and I were left there, and during that whole period from October to the spring, when we went to San Francisco for me to do that reading and to have that chance, too, to do the lectures I had done on "The Special View of History," redo them for twenty people for five nights in San Francisco, in other words, literally as a teacher I was again working for Black Mountain in San Francisco in the spring, in February or March of 1957. Equally, the theater was there; the magazine was in existence; equally, the painters considered themselves, in New York City, and so forth.

LEINOFF: Well, why did everybody leave?

OLSON: Because we decided to stop operation on the grounds, and I was left to conduct her business both prospectively outside as well as to see what I could realize inside.

LEINOFF: So this was, in essence, an indication of a fundamental change in policy?

OLSON: Completely. Or put it the other way, yes, a change from a policy of being in site on the Black Mountain property to being no site and somewhere like fretted stars wherever in the world. I should say that another way. For example, another wonderful aspect of the kind of feelings and thinking, for example, Mrs Dreier, when I made a trip to Boston during that year that I speak of after she'd closed and met with Mrs Dreier, I'm pretty sure Andy Oates, who was then running a store on Boylston Street in Cambridge, went with me, and another Black Mountain student whose name I've forgotten at the moment; the three of us had dinner with or visited Mrs Dreier at home. Ted was not at home, that's the only reason or he would have been visited too. But in talking about it, Mrs Dreier suggested a very interesting thing. She said, "Why don't you move Black Mountain into the television station (it's Channel 2 now in Boston) and let her become a university of the air." Which was equally an interesting proposition. Now mind you now, that date is 1956–57, the winter of '56–7. It's thirteen years ago, and you know where Public Broadcasting Corporation is today. Mind you, if Black Mountain had been functioning out of the leading—what is it, WGBH out of Boston?—where in a funny way most of her earliest sort of enrollment and financing came from, or scholarships or gifts, was generally around the Boston area. I think I'm right. I may be wrong, but I have an impression that an awful lot of her, especially like in music, say, her support was much in the Boston area, and certainly in the architectural connections that led to Gropius finally being at Harvard, and MIT connections all seem to be a part of that.

LEINOFF: Let's see if we can finish up with the final, the denouement. It was agreed, then, the thing was, the college (the thing!), the organism, the organism was ...

OLSON: Or the seal, or the charter, or the name, or the incorporation, right? Because be careful to say that these were all in existence. That seal is right in this room now. I can get it and show it to you. I look at it all the time as a sculptural object. Well, I can't use it, because I wouldn't, I have no—I don't know. It's interesting. I mean, I conceivably might have, although I have no idea what would have happened to the charter of Black Mountain, literally, right now. I don't know. I had no problem when I shipped away in trucks the archives to the capitol of Raleigh, so I suppose somebody processed that charter out of existence. I don't even know. Maybe I still have a right. [LAUGHS]

LEINOFF: The thing is, though, that if the thing was suspended, the charter ...

OLSON: No, no, no. I'm saying the operation was—I pushed it out. I said: "Get out of here and leave me alone, to see if I can realize, on the lot, values from her that will support further operations elsewhere." But I was told to do this. The records of the last board meeting at Black Mountain will show my instructions very carefully written by, not by myself but written by Mr Huss, I think, Mr Fiore, the professor of painting at the time, and others. It was a very important little sort of an instruction. It's a very valuable little thing because it tells me what I'm to do as, like, the one who stayed home, curiously enough. I was the nanny who got the—what do they call it when they raise children, the nanny? Isn't that what you hire as Mrs Jacqueline Kennedy hires a nanny? I was the nanny at the end. No, not at the end, by the way. But we could say that very carefully: when I said to Huss, "Let's no longer operate," then it was decided, "O.K., let's get out of here and continue operations in the field or wherever they are, in the air." And they went out and it was marvelous to see this migration, because it was absolutely like the tents of the Hegira. Whether it's Hebraic or Arabic or American, it was a Hegira. But it was not an exodus, it was not an exit or an exodus or an end. It was a movement. Yeah, that's the way to say it. She's been a movement since October 1956, and there's been some of them that's, ah, curtailed her movement. [LAUGHS]

LEINOFF: The ruling of the court forced you to vacate operations in the State of North Carolina?

OLSON: No, no, no. The ruling of the court required me, as Assignee for the Benefit of the Creditors, to cease all operations until all debts, mortgages, loans were satisfied, including that 56,000 contingency salary, which was about half the debt and more than a third of what I realized.

LEINOFF: It was discovered that it would be impossible to honor all these debts?

OLSON: No, on the contrary, they were all paid off. Every one. And without calling any of the students' debts, which were—I've forgotten the total amount, but they were—if at any point, for example, I had even thought of making a campaign to keep Black Mountain alive; I could have asked all those students would they pay their bills so that we would have then funds, in addition to what I ended up with, which was, I think, literally a thousand dollars plus, say. But, I mean, we could have said—I think I'm within absolutely both legal and incorporative rights to say that after I had satisfied the court of Buncombe County that all this had been done, that Black Mountain still existed, and if she had the means could have thriven. But mind you, by that point of time, which is like the summer of 1957, the realty itself had been sold; I'd arranged for the sale of the realty. And in fact the moment—like, again, I come back to the "thought-earth" of the intuitive existence of everything, the substantive existence of it. I mean, my own attitude was, "Well, hell, the ground is no longer here, I don't care. I mean the air, let the air take care of itself now, you know." It was as simple a decision as that moment when, as self owner due to that funny defense of Black Mountain before a threatened suit, then when the suit was actually brought into the court, when the judge asked us to, in that sense, compromise, I felt that to make any struggle of it would—other than to resolve the very thing that the board instructed me to do, which was to realize out of the property her debts, which was one of my four, I think, instructions, then if there was stuff left over, to continue to support all operations in the field, sort of thing. There were four, if I'm not mistaken, four instructions to me, but the first one was to resolve all her debts. In other words, I think that you could interpret that last board meeting's instruction to me as actually covering those women that then went on to sue, so that in a sense if I had been able—no, if, say, they had been patient, because my work all through 1956–57 was to keep that property shining and to succeed in selling it to that man who had leased, Mr Pickering, who finally did buy it all, who had leased the lower property, to buy the upper (I had sold the farm, which made it possible for us to start that operation with 10,000 cash in 1956, fall), I then would realize—in fact, I realized a considerable unscheduled payment from the property above, which then included what had been leased to Pickering below, on an annual, I think, basis. But if they had waited, probably the same result would have occurred. In fact, I don't see how I could have gotten out of paying all the debts by the sale of the property. It would have been questionable if I didn't do that, I mean, sold the property, which had been the common property of all the faculty since they bought there at Lake Eden.

LEINOFF: So that it was the directive of the board not even to attempt to reconstitute on the property?

OLSON: That's correct, that's correct, but actually it wasn't said so much the word "reconstitute," but if you can realize the sale and settle the debts then we will have accomplished that much. Then if there's anything left over we'll just …

LEINOFF: Was there any chance later to reconsider that direction?

OLSON: No, as a matter of fact, because actually the moment that I became then the sole owner, curiously that shifted the board; the board was all gone. There wasn't an education on the ground. Equally, I didn't realize that much beyond the total debts, mortgages, loans; and I paid off all of the loans and gifts. For example, the beef herd, which was like a five-thousand-plus purchase, and I sold the beef herd as everybody was selling beef, at loss, in this country at that date. But, I mean, I paid off the original purchase price of that herd at the sum that it had been purchased at, right? In other words, we fully completed every one of our engagements. That's one of the things that I wish may be always understood, including that silly 56,000 paper thing, which didn't mean anything.

LEINOFF: So then how fundamental to the actual physical continuation of Black Mountain and the reason why it didn't continue, it seems to me, is involved with the decision of people at Black Mountain prior to 1956 to go into the constellation business.

OLSON: Well, maybe. In some sense, yes. Only, I think that the tendency of if I may call it the third Black Mountain was to find the world. For example, in the creation of the *Black Mountain Review*, being printed and edited in Mallorca, you have a difference from the older Black Mountain. I think that was the step, in a sense, that began the removal from the "thought-earth." Our intention then was to—in fact, the faculty accepted the small costs of that review simply with the idea that Black Mountain never did have any promotional policy or publicity condition really, and their interest in the creation of the *Black Mountain Review* was the idea that the thing itself would circulate where it would, as an active thing, be a draw, that it would at least interest those who were interested in, like they say, writing, to come to Black Mountain. It could be compared, say, to the summer school programs that were so successful after Albers. I think Albers initiated those, I'm not sure, but that's a part of history that you know better than I.

LEINOFF: Can you say a few words in any kind of detail about how Black Mountain came to discover the world, who were the personalities involved that drove it, or if you'd want to say, called the world to its attention?

OLSON: Well, I don't know. I think myself that that takes it a little too far. I think, to tell you the truth, as I said to you on the phone and have repeated tonight, that the gear of the world itself by 1956 had thrown into its second mesh. And, as I said to you, I think there's one more coming in '70–72, and that's the final gear. That is, there's three gears, say: the old gear, the new gear of '56 and the final running gear of '70–72. If you take the moon program, say, or in fact I know this is—I could show you five to seven years ago the calculated predictions of the automotive industry on what kind of a car is the limit of an automobile before she flies. [LAUGHS] That is realizable, and it's about 1970. In fact, seven years ago this general planning by General Motors and Ford was on paper for the rise of the automobile to her finished condition by such a date. And I think that's generally an image of the econometrics, the atomics of today, the foreign policy, the conceptual or ideological rival of the end of this whole supposed expanding development of modern man and society.

LEINOFF: Well then, what's the next gear?

OLSON: The next gear—I am just saying, one should never anticipate these things; you just have to notice that they occur, or anticipate their occurrence. In some instances they're planned, or—but I'm blocking out something when I say this. To tell you the truth, I think that what Black Mountain was doing, in that reach that she picked up in 1951 and lasted as a functioning place on the lot for five years, and then went on for that funny sixth year, was terminated as much by the year 1956 as it was by herself. But she was reaching, that's what I say, rather than she was seeking anything. In fact, to take the suggestion of Paul Williams that we move to the north or go into the skyscraper or Mrs Dreier's going into the radio station in Boston, you see all that kind of expansion—shall we use the word? That's the big word, huh? Expansion, or the conglomerate or the aggregate or the congregate, I mean, the general words that are today's forced thinking, wherever you are, literally, the population increase, the density increase, the age, the chronology powers that are now on the earth.

LEINOFF: How is the concept of the kind of pedagogy—how can you reconcile …?

OLSON: I think the pedagogy was—that's why I stressed the pedagogy in the first place and consider at the end she was as pedagogical as she was in the beginning.

LEINOFF: Even in the reaching out?

OLSON: Oh boy, and how! To tell you the truth, I think she was—if you take the fact that she supplied the principal poet-playwright in this country a theater to operate in, in San Francisco where he lived. Or if you take, what I stressed earlier, that program that I had the chance to—and in fact I enlisted and had accepted Güterbock, Kramer, and Cyrus Gordon's joining me in doing these free eight-week whatever you call 'em, not courses or seminars or lectures, but instruction in principal cities, and then with the invitation by Canadian Broadcasting to pick it up, why we would have been naturally, like, on the air. But the point was to give it away. There was no idea it was going to be—it was Black Mountain paying that bill again as she paid her own faculty. And each one of those men had agreed to take whatever I could shake out, and we'd arranged to do it on their vacations from their posts in other places, including my own.

LEINOFF: Even with the ideas of reaching out, like tentacles I guess …

OLSON: Or the flying from the nest.

LEINOFF: O.K., flying from the nest. Didn't the people that were involved with these ideas consider that once it was flown she'd fall?

OLSON: Yeah, well, as I said, Stefan Wolpe was quite upset, and he was a very considerable man. He was a composer, and like the painters and the dancers and the musicians, they have a tendency to need to be in a center, either a metropolis or a rusticated thing or a commune, like they say. But, like, writers especially, like, I was a writer, I was the only writer who was a Rector of Black Mountain, so then I had, I mean, a man is no larger than his …

LEINOFF: Wunsch.

OLSON: Wunsch?

LEINOFF: Wunsch was a writer also.

OLSON: Was he? Well, my problem was my seriousness. I'm not saying Wunsch wasn't an interesting writer. I don't know his published work. I think if I had a—well, to tell you the truth, Mr Albers or Mr Rice were very considerable writers, both on the record. So I'm not trying to be smart, but I'm only saying to some extent the bearing of my thought is affected by the fact that I am a writer. I tried, in fact, to bring together at Black Mountain a faculty—for example, I wasn't able to bring Boulez, who at that date was known only to those who knew what music was capable of in the 20th century. I invited Pierre Boulez. I told you on the phone that in the next to the last year we were able to constitute an advisory council at Black Mountain made up of Einstein, Jung, Franz Kline as a painter, William Carlos Williams as a poet, Carl O. Sauer as a geographer, and Norbert Wiener. And that this was all at the end. And these men were all interested to engage themselves both to support and to seek to raise, for whatever use we might make of them, in seeking to support a Black Mountain in her further career. And the paper that was shown to them, that was accepted by them as evidence, was these kinds of thinkings that we were all doing for the last three or four years to take her, in a sense, another step, whatever that might, whatever that means, whether it would be on the ground or off, we didn't know, we were seeking only to go ahead. And I'm pretty sure I'm right that that's 1956 that that council was around then. You could check that; it could have been a little earlier; it might have been.

LEINOFF: It's true, I mean, what you said, if you come to realize that the objective in the last years at Black Mountain was to spread itself, to spread itself in the sense of going out. In a way the ideas, they are, whether it's a result of the people from Black Mountain going out or what.

OLSON: Yeah. Yeah. I don't think this question has been almost ever faced as much as we're facing it, even, for example, in Tony Landreau's marvelous plan, which is on paper somewhere, the mobile university, which was, from Wolpe's point of view and some others of the faculty when it was broached, almost like a joke. But I took it very seriously and so did Tony obviously, and I think Huss, interestedly, was interested too. But, I mean, the point was that it did come out almost, like, funny. But that was very late, mind you. There wasn't any thought of sort of evaporating or universalizing itself. So again the tenacity of her "thought-earth," her intuition, is what I'm stressing, even despite the fact that I'm suggesting that I think she was willing to weave her cloth or fret her stars as far as she could go. But it's never been examined and it's worth examining. It's as interesting—as I said to you from the first day you called me, I think that the ending of Black Mountain is as interesting as the founding. And it's not been attended to because in a funny way I, as the undertaker, am almost the only person that could, in a sense, speak of it, because of the fact it did get—well, gee, when people leave a common ground, why the only person that thinks about things is the one that's on the ground. That's the difficulty; that's why the "thought-earth" is so powerful in the actual facts of life. I don't mean that at all "local." In fact, there's a lot of anonymous writing by me and others on these whole problems for the last five years anyhow. I can remember things being written and sent out as catalogues on this. I remember even writing myself, when Albers was still Rector and Dreier was treasurer, a passage on the road linking the dining hall to the Studies Building as almost like the terrific image of the traffic of the human society that she was. Yeah, in fact, I remember doing that and it was in 1948–49.[14]

One of the things that always interests me as of, say, the success that so many of her students have since been in the world—I'm thinking, say, of a conspicuous case like Rauschenberg, or another one which gets unnoticed but is almost as large or as important as Rauschenberg, a student—who is it I'm thinking of, besides Chamberlain, who was a part of that later Black Mountain more than Rauschenberg, John Chamberlain the sculptor? But there is some quite noticeable present-day artist that was a student at Black Mountain? Oh yes, Noland. But again, Ken Noland comes from the Albers period, I think you'd say. But, for example, as early as 1948–49 there was a light-sound-color-projection workshop, which was a very dazzling piece of theater, like, of all the sorts of things that have been happening now. It was being done on the lot. I mean, it was that kind of effecting. That was why she was such an attractive place. The room was always there for the best idea that could be brought into being.

LEINOFF: The way I found out about Black Mountain was reading about it in Goodman's book.

OLSON: Oh yeah? I don't know it.

LEINOFF: He wrote *Communitas.*

OLSON: Oh yes, the older Goodman, the architect; yes, Percival, the other Goodman.

LEINOFF: Paul also wrote it with him, though.

---

14. "Black Mountain College as seen by a writer-visitor, 1948" was published posthumously in *Credences* NS 2:1 (Summer 1982), pp. 89–90.

OLSON: Yes, that's true. When Paul Williams was the architect at Black Mountain that was the one book he was reading all the time he was on the lot, which goes back to, like, the fifties or something.

LEINOFF: Were you around when Goodman was there?

OLSON: Actually yeah, but not Percy, I didn't know that Percy was even at Black Mountain. Do you know?

LEINOFF: I don't think he was. I think it was just Paul Goodman.

OLSON: Paul was teaching then, or didn't teach then but was—in fact, to tell you the truth, that year that I was not willing to take the position because I wanted to stay in Washington and was coming monthly, Paul was one of the two people that Albers and Dreier were asking me whether or not I'd recommend that they be brought there. And eventually Paul came to graduate one of my own students, a Mark Hedden. And I think he taught, yes he did, he taught in the summer session in that funny what I call the inter-rump, interregnummy, or rummy period of Black Mountain. In those two years he was there for a summer session. But Paul never really was, you might say, and it would be fun to say it, never made it as a teacher at Black Mountain, because, I think, for a very good reason, if I may criticize a man of his superb attention to real things. I keep thinking Goodman was a rump that never got there, yet felt to be a rump of. [LAUGHS] I mean, he's the outside rump that never entered into the circus tent. I'm saying this without too much knowledge of Paul's book on education nor his recent one. When I was in London two years ago, he was coming there and did come and was very effective, I hear, in that whole thing around Joe Berke and that psychologist,[15] that whole thing, I've forgotten what they call it, that movement. Do you know who I mean, that psychologist that functions in London and that's sort of a very important hip kind of an activist of a communitas rather in a metropolis society of London, in the sense of giving hospice and health and home to those who are not influenced? In fact, on the contrary, they—I mean, there's a nice—I can't think of the name of the principal psychologist, whose thinking is a result, but like I am a little bit out of—as time went on, Paul as being obviously a city man who really would like to cruise cops, that's a drag.

LEINOFF: We talked about when Albers left and Dreier, and you said there was a guy named Jackson …

OLSON: He was the student leader who caused the—effectively got the student body, and I don't think it was the Board, but it was the student body, to ask for the resignation of Dreier as a teacher of mathematics. They weren't attacking him as an administrative officer, but just as a teacher of mathematics.

---

15. R.D. Laing and his colleagues of the Philadelphia Centre, Joseph Berke and Leon Redler, organized the "Dialectics of Liberation Congress" in London in July 1967, which Paul Goodman attended.

LEINOFF: Well, if they were just asking him to leave as a teacher of mathematics, did he take this as some kind of affront?

OLSON: Yes, as a matter of fact he did, because in fact and in effect Dreier put in twenty years or more—no, that couldn't be—but a good number of years, sixteen years, as indeed had others as well as Albers. And it was a pride question, I suppose, some question of pride, an affront to his personal pride. And the feeling: "Well, if I don't teach I'm not going to just conduct the money problems of this place." I don't know; I mean, I did both Albers's and Dreier's Tarot fortunes the night that they both resigned, so I know a great deal of what their future was from that, but the past I don't know. In fact, to tell you the truth, Juppie, as we called him, Josef, was intelligent enough to realize that without Dreier, same way I was on Huss, without a man—in fact, Dreier was even more—well, I don't want to say that. I mean, Dreier financially was more, I mean, had availability to moneys that Huss didn't have any more than I had. Nor did Juppie. But the point was Albers was too intelligent a man to seek to make up that deficit each year, that chit. He didn't have any more means except—in fact, the summer school, as far as I know, was the only means Black Mountain had to pick up a little income as against her annual running current deficit anyhow. It would be interesting if somebody actually looked at the books of the college from the beginning and actually saw what my general impression was that she ran about a 10,000 deficit every year, and that was in a sense picked up by donors as long as Dreier was treasurer. So that Juppie wasn't going to try to handle the thing any more than I wanted to, or Huss, when we suddenly had—certainly if that property hadn't been there, neither Huss nor I would have had any imagination about how to raise funds for her. I made one trip to the north at some date in the fifties trying to raise funds and, boy, I hit as many streets, as many possible people as I could, and I couldn't get a cent.

LEINOFF: Juppie was kind of abandoning the ship?

OLSON: No, he was not. He was realizing—I mean, with the fact that Dreier took it so that he said he'd just have to leave, I mean, he was going to quit, I mean, he was going to go rather than quit, but he was going to go. Well, then Juppie said, "Well, I'll go too." I know Jackson or those others didn't think they were gonna—they should have had more brains, but they didn't know enough or they were too stupid to have realized that in striking at Dreier they were gonna bring Albers down too. I mean, that kind of a thing was so essential—the persons that were trying to keep that thing going were going to have to continue to do it. Somebody was going to have to continue. That's interesting. My mind then was thinking of the present attacks, like upon—it's interesting because it's way back, like in 1948, which is a wholly different period of time as well as an economy, but—and in fact afterwards we recovered it and ran it, like, into the ground or on the ground, like they say. But I mean we ran it successfully another five or six years beyond the two years in which it was not handled successfully enough to have a go-ahead. So it isn't so comparable, really.

LEINOFF: I was just kind of wondering, just examining the possibilities, at least the reasons why Albers decided to leave.

OLSON: Well, I would say it had to do with the fact that he and Dreier—if you'll look at the books of the college, I think you'll find from a period somewhere in the late thirties, generally speaking, without knowing the history of Black Mountain, my impression is that, when Rice left, essentially the weight of the responsibility fell on Dreier and Albers, even though there was always a board behind any of us.

LEINOFF: What I meant was, was Albers trying to force the hand, say, of somebody like Jackson?

OLSON: I think he might have hoped that his saying, "Well, if you take Dreier's resignation you take mine," was a power shove back, yes. But my own impression from speaking to both of them that day, coming in on Albers that day that that was done (I don't think I was there the day it was done but I think I had come in the next day), my impression was they both were hurt; and believe you me, I can tell you, but you have to put a few years into the effort of a thing called "society"—you know, like, you can get hurt. A little bit like parents toward their children, even if we ain't things like that. It's like anything else. I mean, if the damn thing doesn't accomplish something or you can't bring it to produce, oh shit, there's other worlds to conquer. In fact, I can remember the Tarot of Albers directly predicting he go to Mexico on a trip-vacation and be appointed to Yale University. And boy, he didn't know that at all! He wasn't envisioning anything.

LEINOFF: I talked to Stan Vanderbeek originally, I don't know if I mentioned this on the phone, but one of the things that he said was, toward the end of the school, the kind of students that went there actually changed.

OLSON: Oh yes, very much.

LEINOFF: He said that it came to a point where the faculty were repairing bloody noses because of brawls and various things like that.

OLSON: I think that's his own virtuousness! It was a very serious problem, yes. But that, mind you, is one of the reasons why I said that she was the lip of the present. The actual condition of the student is constantly—were the first wave of the children of the recent past. I mean, they're always the newest thing in the world, right? And they're always different. And those students of the fifties in Black Mountain were—gee, I think they were the famous generation of today. And in fact one of the things I suppose that caused me to stop Black Mountain was a hole in the head of one cat that came in out of a rainstorm. The rain was so thick it had washed the blood off him but there was a big piece of his skull out, from having cracked up an automobile down the road and walked three miles up to the college. And I thought, "Oh gee, I mean, like, I can't be bothered with such casualties." A veteran again, and there was a veterans' hospital down the same road. So I had to say to Joe Fiore, "You got your Jeep, we've got another passenger!" So we go down again and deliver bodies to the veterans' hospital. It was, by the way, generally in this society the fact that after the Korean War there was a lot of new kind of people coming back into the society, and the beginning of the famous generation of "war babies" from the forties was beginning to appear. In fact, one of the guys that was with that guy in that accident that night was sixteen years old and apparently from London, who'd been affected by the raids, the v-2 raids (and is still, like, one of the major artists working in America today), was affected, nervously, by having gone through the raids of London.[16] I mean, you can't say that the condition of the human race isn't always changing and that to some extent it's of such—it can be, again, in a retort like Black Mountain. She tended, after all, to draw—I mean, who the hell would go to Black Mountain except some, like, you know, like they say, queer or crazy or potentially intensive person? [LAUGHS] Why, with the range of the choice of education in America, should anybody have gone to Black Mountain, from the very beginning, right? I mean, what did draw people to Black Mountain? This is another, as far as I know, almost unexamined question. Again, we could talk all we want about what were its pronouncements or its formulations, and, to some extent, its principles of both structure and function, like, say, the rental question, then the purchasing of Lake Eden, and with the purchasing of Lake Eden the problem of having the farm and what do you do with a work program, what do you do with a self-supporting economy anyhow (this is being faced today by the communes throughout this country), without necessarily, as I keep saying and think is extremely crucial, having that central runner, what I call the runner of being an educational society. Which is a very great difference. That is, the curriculum of Black Mountain was, from the start to the end, her plank. She had a curriculum. And she had her curriculum change.

LEINOFF: Well, if the students that started to come to Black Mountain in the fifties were more, you know, rambunctious, more prone to some kind of problem ...

OLSON: They weren't, they weren't. My point is that they were much more example of what has generally been true of the young right through the present, and they were the beginning of it, they were the earliest of it, they were the unformulated young of today.

LEINOFF: O.K., well, if they were the "unformulated young" of today, in the past, at least when I talked to people, it seemed as though the students played just as important a role almost in formulating ...

OLSON: From the beginning.

LEINOFF: ... what went on.

OLSON: Oh, oh, oh, I think that's a misconception. And I think to some extent Stan is reflecting it because he came from the middle Black Mountain and

16. The young artist Basil King is included in the Black Mountain group photograph in *Maps* 4 (1971), p. 42.

was—in fact, to tell you the truth, I don't believe that Stan was there after that summer that Ben Shahn taught, which is one of the reasons I came back that summer, which was the summer of 1951. I don't think that Stan was there after that. He did that "Map of Moves" for *Apollonius of Tyana*, that beautiful thing he did for that book of mine; and then I'm pretty sure, yes, in fact I know he did, because he actually lived in that A-house that Paul Williams built on Cape Cod in 1952, so that he was gone, I think, by the fall of 1951. In fact, to tell you the truth, if you can follow, if you can keep in mind, or anybody can that listens to this tape, it was that 1951 summer session that created that new fall or motion of the College until the end. You can't—don't listen to Stan Vanderbeek. He didn't know what the hell was going on. See, that's again why I say opinion of anybody other than when they were there, in that sense, is not—is just opinion. [TAPE ENDS]

Charles Olson gesticulating, from Gerard Malanga's *Film Notebooks* (1969) © Gerard Malanga.

15

The *Paris Review* Interview

Gerard Malanga, a well known New York poet and associate of Andy Warhol, was commissioned by the *Paris Review* to interview Olson for their "Art of Poetry" series. He came to Gloucester with a long list of prepared questions, but, as it turned out, the "interview" was a four-hour talk session with Olson's friends Gerrit Lansing and Harvey Brown also present. However, the formal questions baited Olson into revealing himself in a unique way. He was challenged by this induction into the "House of Fame" to face his life's accomplishments as of 15 April 1969.

Another spur to self-reflection had come in the morning's mail. A magazine from England, *Park* 4/5 (Summer 1969), contained a review of *Maximus Poems IV,V,VI*. Olson recognized immediately that his longtime correspondent Jeremy Prynne had written an immensely important judgment on his work. This review, referred to constantly in the interview, is reprinted in the *Minutes of the Charles Olson Society* 28 (April 1999), pp. 4–13.

CHARLES OLSON: … Either that or we can make it up without even thinking. As a matter of fact, I'd be happy if we'd fantasy the whole fucking thing anyway. [PAUSE] Don't you think it's beautiful the way Prynne comes on on that whole question of Corinth? I thought I'd flip when I saw Corinth there.[1]

GERRIT LANSING: Oh, I mentioned that to Harvey, as a matter of fact. I thought, "Corinth? That does not belong there. If it does, I don't." In that context I thought he was going to say Tyre, obviously. I suppose that if he'd said …

OLSON: No, don't do that, dear. Don't don't don't don't don't. The trouble with these fucking things, see? Don't touch. Aw, jesus.

HARVEY BROWN: Did you say "current"? You said "current."

---

1. Prynne had written: "The first stages of *Maximus* give wary and at times fulsome regard to the sea, flooding into the serrated flanges of Gloucester. The abruptness and sudden localism of language in places there owed these features in large part to the marine invasions of the land, the new Corinth."

LANSING: "Corinth." Yeah, that's what I said to you.

BROWN: I heard "current."

OLSON: Get a free chair, and sit down. [LAUGHS] And don't worry about anything, Gerard, especially this. We're living beings, and we're forming a society. We're creating a total social future, and you're worrying about—I mean, you got all day tomorrow or Thursday in Cambridge to do shit like this. That's terribly funny; everybody in a crowd, like 'Cisco.

LANSING: What are you doing tomorrow in Cambridge, Gerry?

GERARD MALANGA: Hm …

OLSON: Don't ask him. It's uninteresting. It's tomorrow.

MALANGA: Well, tomorrow I want to go visit the 1968 Yale Younger Poet.

OLSON: [LAUGHING] You see what's wrong with these people? They're topical.

MALANGA: She's a female!

OLSON: Doesn't matter. They're not that good. Female poets don't come so easily. [LAUGHS] Stick with those girls you like, those absolutely elegant ladies.

MALANGA: She seems to be pretty in her photographs anyway.

OLSON: You know, he only keeps company with the women that are the most elegant dames in the world. I mean, Panna put me on to, like, most of his girlfriends' mothers. [LAUGHS]

MALANGA: Speaking of pretty girls, I wanted to give you this. This is about one of the pretty girls.

OLSON: Well, leave it there. I know about her. I'd love to read it. I'll look at it when I go to bed. That's what I need when I go to bed.[2] Well, didn't you think it was funny, that flip, that Pound?[3] I follow you entirely on saying it: why the hell did he say "Corinth"? That's mine. Let me make more, I mean, let's … O.K.

LANSING: I'll wait, and have some whisky, thank you.

OLSON: My dear Gerrit, will you take that beautiful cup there, which I think is even clean, and use it for yourself. I think it is, isn't it? Or not? As a matter of fact, it should be healthy if it isn't clean.

LANSING: Corinth is sort of the older kind of a typical example of commerce, isn't it?

OLSON: I don't think he means that.

LANSING: That's why I wondered about that.

OLSON: I don't think he means that.

---

2. The book gift is not known. Possibly it was Malanga's own 3 *Poems for Benedetta Barzini* (1967).
3. Olson distinctly says "Pound" as though it were a common noun.

LANSING: Or why he wouldn't even say Carthage or certainly Cadiz.

OLSON: Do you know, I so trust that cat's kind of immaculate sort of …

LANSING: You didn't seem surprised at that, Harvey, when I brought that up, Corinth, that way.

BROWN: Because I didn't even know …

OLSON: But he was, though. So am I, like. We're all three in agreement. But what does he mean?

LANSING: Maybe if we found the people who got the records about Corinth it would …

OLSON: No, I think he's talking about that movement into the Peloponnesus of the Greeks from the north that is the great moment then that you know has to do with all that fucking—for example, Oedipus, as you know, was sold to Corinth, and fled Corinth because he thought (because he knew he was to kill his father and marry his mother) that he'd get out of town. Of course, he went across the Straits, and ran right into the whole fucking scene. But, I mean, in fact, knowing Prynne, I should think he almost is— equally there's a possibility that he's referring to that Corinth that I use in the John Smith poem and which I steal from Herman the Thief, Mr Melville.[4] But I think it's more, because of Prynne; because Prynne is so— he's knowing, he's knowing like mad. [DROPS ICE CUBES] Don't worry about it. The kitchen is reasonably orderly. I crawled out of bed, sick as I was, and threw the rug out of the window or something. [LAUGHS] I went to some pains to anticipate Mr Malanga's coming. D'you get some? Sh-too. [PAUSE]

MALANGA: Well, the first question I wanted to ask you, [LAUGHTER] according to this interview, is what fills your day, and the things that you're interested in.

OLSON: Nothing. [LAUGHS] But nothing. Literally. Except my friends. That's literally true.

MALANGA: These are very straight questions.

OLSON: That's what interviews are made of.

MALANGA: If knowledge is a material for your writing, certainly you must derive this knowledge as a definite quantity to be found in a given place at a given time, namely Gloucester, and its entire heritage?

OLSON: Now, listen, both of you, because this is not an interview; this is a composite, multigraph. You see, that's the question that Mr Prynne takes care of, right? Neither the term "knowledge" nor the term "Gloucester" have any—well, they might rhyme if I spelled it GN, as it should be spelled. Would you come to GNowledge to get to GNoucester? You'd have to do

4. The "John Smith poem" is "Some Good News," which contains the lines: "like Corinth / burning down / produces bronze" (*Maximus* 1.123). See also *Call Me Ishmael*, p. 38.

GNA GNA GNA, right? But, like, it's nothing to do—neither term, neither "knowledge" nor "Gloucester" ...

LANSING: There's also GNature.

OLSON: GNature, right. But neither GNowledge nor GNoucester equal the Lord's Prayer or something. Our GNoster who art in knowledge, hallowed be that thing.

MALANGA: Well, would you say that knowledge was a part of your writing?

OLSON: Actually, only in the sense that it's a perfectly adequate thing to get to the end, but it isn't the whole; it isn't. Just novel. It doesn't get you to the end. It's simply one of the most magnificent travels that exists, but it doesn't arrive any more than any such means ever arrives at what you're after. So I don't think it's knowledge at all. Well, it's knowledge, like I said, in the sense of Mr GNoster who made Gloucester. Mr GNoster who made Gloucester.

MALANGA: Is that true?

LANSING: It's no different than anywhere else.

OLSON: No, Mr GNoster who made Gloucester. Are we on tape? Because I'm saying: GNoster who made Gl-G-G-GNoucester. Mr GNoster who made GNoucester. Then we get it right, right? Come and help me, you two! Interpolate, interrupt. Contest me.

LANSING: The question doesn't ...

OLSON: Can't do anything with it except what I'm doing, can you, Gerrit, to the question? Because the knowledge of Gloucester is only interesting if I said it just like I just then did.

LANSING: Everybody uses this same knowledge.

OLSON: Yes, quite.

MALANGA: Well, let me re—

OLSON: It's the beginning of a poem by saying "The knowledge of Gloucester, te-da." Immediately I want to write. "The knowledge of Gloucester, de-de-de-de." In other words, it's perfectly good, but it doesn't mean a damn thing synthetically deprived of its future possibility. Literally, neither knowledge nor Gloucester or, as Gerrit says, any place else or any thing else or any one else ...

LANSING: Or any event.

OLSON: Absolutely, except in the sense of the future. And I don't mean some— and I'm not trying, you know, like—I'm not involved or interested or am I so young that I need to have a stake in the future. I'm not even interested in the present. I'm only talking about something that is surely going to—if, like: "The knowledge of Gloucester, di-da-di-di-da," well, you get something, you get something, you get somewhere.

LANSING: Rephrase the question?

MALANGA: Well, I was thinking of it in terms of like …

OLSON: No, we'll axe that question, because, I tell you, Mr Jeremy Prynne today in a review has answered it immaculately, and we can just plug this in and answer the question from Mr Prynne; because Mr Prynne has said it in a way that I myself really, totally—no, I could not have said it—but totally, quick, thank god, like, he did, somebody else, you know, he said it. My christ, nobody else, like, in that way quite, in exactly the way in which you're saying "knowledge of Gloucester," question number two at the end.

LANSING: Knowledge of the whole.

OLSON: No, knowledge *and* Gloucester.

MALANGA: I didn't say "knowledge of Gloucester."

OLSON: No, knowledge and Gloucester. I didn't say … Read the—now, for those who aren't here, read the question again, please.

MALANGA: If knowledge is the material for your writing, certainly …

OLSON: Which it is not. Number one. O.K. Go ahead. No, go ahead, go ahead.

MALANGA: … Certainly you must derive this knowledge as a definite quantity to be found in a given place at a given time, namely, Gloucester.

OLSON: Hmm … No, because actually Gloucester is not a given place at a given time except any given place and any, like—just as Lansing insists, and I agree completely: that "at any given time" is the whole point, which is that you couldn't possibly put your hands on it, because it's …

LANSING: Nor has knowledge specifically to do with Charles more than anybody.

MALANGA: Well, knowledge in terms of when Charles might be using—like, he has a vast library of rare source books—or books, but they may be used as source material for some of his poems, like the history of schooners or something.

OLSON: Well, no. I don't think—I mean, like, no, I think that's—like when you asked me what do I do all day, I remember Mr Duncan saying, "Oh, Charles is like me; he spends his whole day reading books! He reads books all day!" Which is a kind of a marvelous way to, you know, avoid going out. I mean, why go out, mostly? No, it's more fun than that.

MALANGA: But you're a Capricorn.

OLSON: Hm, and so is he. And so is John Wieners, and so is Marlene Dietrich, and so is Mao Tse-tung, and how many others? O.K.

MALANGA: And they're basically hermits, then?

OLSON: Are they? Oh, Charles[5] and all that! Hermits they are? Are they hermits?

MALANGA: Yeah, basically. Maybe not all of them are, but each Capricorn is very different in their own ways. They're very individual people.

---

5. Olson says his name with a French accent. It may be an allusion not at present recognized.

OLSON: Except I saw the most marvelous thing, a new thing. It must be psychedelic. They've got a new astrology for brides. And it's very complicated. I look immediately, of course, like anyone does, at their own birth sign; so I see Capricorn, and I'm thinking, "Now, which way am I reading it? Am I supposed to be the bridegroom or the bride?" But I finally decided from one triple statement that it means the girl herself is married to a Capricorn in her imagination, and therefore what must she be like? And it says she must at all times be a lady; she must have a clear sense, some sense of the purpose of her own life; and must be very good at taking care of money or a house. I thought: "OK! As a Capricorn, I'd say the same to the lady. You'd better be all three of these things, or else!"

LANSING: Hermits are in the world too, you know.

MALANGA: Of course, they're in a world.

OLSON: And what a number is …? Number 9 is the hermit, "l'Hermite," in the Tarot. And what is he seeking? Number 10. And what is Number 10? Please tell our friend John Clarke, or Mr Creeley, or all the new decan boys: Number 10 is the Ruòta di Fortuna, as I was sure the other night it was, and I've checked it since. You know this jive, but it's the only jive I really can stick to and feel there's some—why, it's marvelous, the argument, like. Jack and I sat here for three or four hours doing, you know, numbers; and fighting over—I was fighting all the time against him.

BROWN: Against Jack?

OLSON: Talking 20; saying the trouble with 10 is it's not 20; and the only thing that's interesting is 20. But, gee, it was very exciting, because Jack is always interesting here, because he's such a nut, right? And on numbers he's a sucker; I mean, he gets sucked in, to the Kabbalah, and to Creeley's *Numbers*, and the misplacing of zero at the other end of this series, which is one of the worst, dangerous things that's happening, to my mind, today. Do you follow me on that, Gerrit? Oh, my god, if I were worrying about how magic is run awry in the present, the wheel not being down on the ground, the fifth or whatever the wheel is not being on the ground, and therefore there's no ground, so that the current isn't really, so the fucking thing isn't really running; it's jogging, it's jogging automatic, like the new indoor sport in America, self-jogging in one place. [LAUGHS] This is why I'm in Gloucester.

MALANGA: Do you find Gloucester the most appropriate place for writing your poems?

OLSON: No. In fact, that's why I've ceased to be able to write, I'm sure, because I've stayed here for [LAUGHING]—for quite a while. Aw, no, no, that's nothing to do with it. In fact, it has to do with living: I find it impossible, like they say around here, to get across Cut Bridge, which means that you've really come down for the summer. [LAUGHS] Like, there are three people in Gloucester: those who came by sea, those who came down for the summer, and those who stayed. They're called three different classes. [LAUGHTER] That's not a bad bit of Gloucester humor! Whoever was talking to me on long distance and was quoting that from San Francisco the other night was quoting, "Gloucester, get off," I mean, "All off!" [LAUGHS] I suppose that could have been somebody with a lot of wit, in San Francisco. I don't know who it was.

MALANGA: Why have you chosen poetry as a medium of artistic creation?

OLSON: Hm-m-m. I'm sure I made a hell of a mistake. That's the first confidence I have. [LAUGHS] The other is that I really didn't have anything else to do. I mean, I didn't even have enough invention to think of something else to do. I should have been in business; I should have stayed where I was; and I should have made all that money that you guys make so easily. And in fact I think I might have; I could have. In fact, I think I might have, just literally, because that was the only thing that might have interested me was all the money I could have made, I mean, literally, at the time, like '46, wasn't it, when I kicked it? '45, '46? I mean, that's when all that stuff was still honest.[6] Not really, it never was. But we still—I mean, you didn't already have to know how bad it was. [LAUGHS]

MALANGA: '45 or '46?

OLSON: Well, in—like, if you'll excuse me my own stupidity, but, I mean, I really wouldn't have. To tell you the truth, I wouldn't have bought the—still don't buy the money argument, really. You know, like, I don't. I think that the desperate thing is the greed, uh? And I think that's again been shot by what's happened now: that money has been shown up. I mean, it's like time today. At one end, money is too short. It's very funny: an inflation is the same thing as a human being being out of touch with time. It's the same ampe.[7] It's the same false swill—swell, but "swill" I want to say. It's filling something that isn't filled yet. It's like you haven't blown the air in or something. And it's called "inflation."

LANSING: It used to do something different.

OLSON: Exactly. That must have to do with it, you see. But my point is this is why the poor today are not even able to be "the poor" anymore, because of the abuse of society makes us, as well as—us literally, and I think I'm funny feeling poor, as well as those who want the most, which I also comfortably feel; but I want both at once! In fact, that's why I put that thing, the *mode d'emploi*, the French passage, in the *Gloucester Times*.[8]

MALANGA: Well, then, why is poetry always considered a poetry of prestige and not a poetry of commerce?

---

6. Olson is referring to his career with the Democratic Party National Committee.
7. Olson says this word carefully, but the reference has not been identified.
8. Olson's 29 January 1969 letter to the editor of the *Gloucester Times* is printed in *Maximus to Gloucester*, pp. 149–50, where Peter Anastas's note explains that the directions for use in French were probably on a tin of crabmeat or shrimp from Quebec.

OLSON: Oh, I think that's only so in post-Neolithic. Literally, in fact. In fact, it is simply post-neolithic, the idea of poetry as that. Again, see Prynne, review of *Maximus V,V,VI*, page four, on said subject. No kidding, again he's right on the button there, isn't he, in that, on exactly …? Now, like, the pot's hitting. [LAUGHTER]

LANSING: I think you have to speak of patronage in that sense of the 18th century …

MALANGA: But there is a poetry of commerce as opposed to a poetry …

OLSON: I think it was so superb, in London at least, in the 18th century that men like Pope, Dryden, and Samuel Johnson, god save our souls, who said that one of the—in fact, Mr Prynne again is only the other side; and thank god there is an Englishman today who can take every one of the really true aperçus—and the English nation has a few—and turn them forward. And in this piece Mr Prynne does it. Now I'm really talking about him. This is what's so good about that: that an Englishman can do what he did about the Stuttgart. The first two books come from Stuttgart, and now a book from London. I mean, how beautifully he says that to lead off that review. But the point is, like, wow, like, he comes out a judge, a judge in a world sense. I mean, we haven't had that, in a funny way, we haven't had it. I think he's almost the first judge, in the old sense. You'd hear me on that? I mean, he has *iudicium* in a very strange exciting way. Like, I mean, I wrote a poem about seven years ago, dreaming—like, I got it still, but it's a big sloppy *Maximus*.[9] I'm sure it sounds like frob frr, like frr, false whipped cream being blown off your beard. But I mean it was a crazy—I mean, I dreamt of that we would all write very shortly in a language which was—I remember the word was "international," because I don't believe in the whole universal thing, but I meant really sort of like so large an Indo-European language that it would be convenient for any other peoples also to understand it.

LANSING: It's the first time for a long time that an Englishman's been able to be observational in that sense.

OLSON: Yeah, absolutely. But with that marvel—I mean, for example, what is it that funny kind of a cranky thing that Johnson says about the moonster? "The nicest thing about a human being is that he can't yield to his temptations." No, that's too puritan! The thing that I underlined in this thing, for example, is—would you be interested, like? "The moral structure of immediate knowledge." I mean, that just takes care of everything I thought I was thinking myself, I mean, trying to think.

MALANGA: "Moral," did he say "moral"?

OLSON: "The moral structure of immediate knowledge," right?

MALANGA: I don't know what that means.

9. George Butterick did not hazard a guess as to which of the *Maximus* poems left in manuscript Olson could be referring to.

OLSON: That's right. That's why one has to quote Mr Prynne, because that's one of those statements that's like, you know, Mr Jung—do you know Mr Jung's belief that the only real thing is—how does he say it?—"the something of the necessary statement ... the method of the necessary statement."[10] Which is, to my mind, one of those absolute tongues of the mind of the 20th century today.

MALANGA: Yeah, but morality is an artificial phenomenon.

OLSON: No, not at all. On the contrary, no, absolutely. In fact, it's so completely the base—and, again, Prynne's "base," base, bases, base, base, base, I mean, touch base. Don't think I'm talking like an ex-minister, like I discover Prynne was trained to be. I was an ex-priest, only I didn't get there, you know. I was supposed to go to Holy Cross, because I wanted to play baseball. I did too. That's the only reason I wanted to go to Holy Cross; it wasn't anything to do with being a priest. I'm not, like some of our beautiful friends, still priests, or only recently not priests. Hey, Vincent! [LAUGHS] Can I teach you two? Gerrit? [LAUGHS] You know, "moral" is really so interesting that all stupid religionists or religional or membership church people wouldn't even know what the fuck, excuse me, Mr Prynne is talking about, because he's talking about something I don't believe this goddamn nation called the United States of America ...

LANSING: Remember you trying to tell me and Betty one time over at 92 Main Street about this thing? I really didn't understand ...

OLSON: Could you just say what I said then, please? I'll try to revise it. But it is so, I mean, what I'm now saying if you could get its ...

LANSING: Yeah, but I mean, remember my resistance to this thing, the same way Gerry seems to be resisting it.

OLSON: I know. But doesn't he even use the word "rectitude" in here? I want to depend upon it, really, because it's like a script. I got a scenario for the show, right? It came in the morning's mail, right? That's also true is because of the marvelous era. But he does say that, he does say at the end, "rectitude." He uses that beautiful word. Gerrit, did he not? What? Take anything you want? What do you want? You need Gerrit to cut it?

MALANGA: No, no, no, no.

OLSON: Oh ... I should just quote from this every time you ask me a question.

MALANGA: All right. Great.

OLSON: "The sum of its local permutations." You know, only Dorn and Creeley have said anything relevant to that, Gerrit, in print. If you'll excuse me, you have not written on me. Nor you. Nor Johnny Wieners. Nor—you know, I've got a whole bunch of—I've got a blacklist. [LAUGHS] I want to hear you all. It's the only compert I have. But isn't it—? "The sum of its local permutations." It's a little cornball; but then, christ, you know, you can't

---

10. A note dated 1 April 1969 on the flyleaf of Olson's copy of Carl Jung's *Memories, Dreams, Reflections* (New York: Vintage, 1965) refers to p. 310, where these words are found.

expect an Englishman who rushed over here ... By the way, what about the Tuzo Wilson quote? Hey, do you understand that?

LANSING: Where it is there, no.

OLSON: But isn't it beautiful there? Oh, you mean where it is there you don't? 'Cos that's where I get it. What is Tuzo Wilson talking about? I mean, I know what he's talking about. In fact, if this interview should ever appear, like, as I do hope it—whereas I desire that it not near, here in the *Revue Parisienne*, I would like to say that ... I have appeared before in *La Revue Parisienne*, de New York.

MALANGA: It's going to be fantastico. You don't know it. I see it as something totally—

OLSON:—out of it! That's what I tell you, a real happening, like, not any of that.

MALANGA: Well, I'll just go down the list, you know, like, and anyway I wanted to ask you ...

OLSON: I mean, how does he know, quote, colon: "no movement without the new laral nouns and observances of the New World"? Doesn't he pass it to us and me and anyone else on the—? I mean, isn't that beautiful that Prynne exists in England and can say that, like as though John Winthrop Jr had started to try to be an alchemist on the Connecticut River and have an ironswork in Saugus? I mean, it's the most beautiful moment to have this in Gloucester, I mean Mr Prynne's review. It's exactly like the thing I really said—the *Times* misread that (fairly enough, it's my handwriting): "17th century motions" not "motives."[11] Because I, again, like, as of the question Gerard is asking ... Hold on a minute on "moral structure," hold on a minute, Gerard, on "moral structure," 'cos all I want to say is, like, I mean, like, that's the difference. What's the difference? I forgot. What's the difference? I mean, there is—at that point there is no difference. Right?

MALANGA: Afterwards I'm going to tell you I had a very basic structure in mind.

OLSON: O.K. But, mind you, he's talking about a very basic structure, the moral structure, which we call "character." I mean, I call Reich "characterologism." And you said earlier, "psychobiography," as Rank says. Otto Rank. Yeah. No. Is it? Yeah, "psychobiography," that's what he claims to talk.

MALANGA: It's really great. Can I steal it?

OLSON: Look, it's Rank's. [LAUGHS] It'sa Rank's. Wasn't that beautiful the other night? You know, he came back, and we looked over the whole Memphite Theology. Did he tell you this? My christ, I mean, I haven't written any poems since, but I should have.

BROWN: Yeah.

11. The mistake ("motives" for "motions") appeared in the *Gloucester Times* for 7 April 1969; see *Maximus to Gloucester*, p. 154.

OLSON: Oh, absolutely. Did you? Lucky you. I couldn't. I dreamt like oh fucking mad since, like I can. I did kind of get—that's right—haven't I? I forgot. That's a long time ago. It's like the frog in the stone. That's a good rhyme, you must admit, Gerrit. My Indian shaman master, whom I wish I knew, but whom I love—yeah, how can I refer to that beautiful Indian who now exists in America?—he would understand. He would hear me say, "Last-a evening I did, in ninety-eight hours …"[12] [LAUGHS]

MALANGA: Are you able to write poetry while remaining in the usual conditions of life, continuing to do the usual work, preserving formal relations with people, and without renouncing or giving up anything?

OLSON: That's the trouble. That's what I've done, to my cost and loss. [LAUGHS] That describes it perfectly. I have absolutely …

LANSING: It's a good question.

OLSON: Yeah.

LANSING: It's the best question yet.

OLSON: But I don't honestly—if I just answer it like you're forced to when you hear a thing. That's like that letter. Every one of these fucking, excuse me, these questions are like letters. I mean, it'd take me a lifetime to do a tape recording if it were done in my beliefs. Read it again, because I'm impressed by how much Gerrit acts as though he was so quickly able to answer it. I can't believe it.

MALANGA: The only way I could have thought about this whole thing was to write it down, 'cos I'm a very …

OLSON: Aw, come on. That's what I'm talking about. You asked me not to write it down, but to sit here like a—why don't you give me a form like in a Government office to fill out three hours over if you're going to get a job with Vought Nought Aircraft Company? I mean, let me sit down and answer your questions. As a matter of fact, I was thinking, "Why doesn't he send me the interview, and then I could see him, like, elsewise"—like we have already, thank god, the way it came about. It really comes on, like, straight. Wouldn't it have been awful? I mean, thank god we're four, and we're playing this thing right on, with four suits. I mean, we got a chance. It's true, too, we're playing four suits here tonight, four-suited cards: four and eight. By the way, is there any goddamn poker game in anything straighter or drawer than this? It's so true, isn't it? Isn't it exciting, Gerrit? Gerrit? Isn't it exciting? Hey, Studs. Hey, Studs. Hey, Studs.

MALANGA: Do you want me to read that question again?

OLSON: Uh-huh. I'm sure that the audience would too.

---

12. The "Shaman master" is the protagonist of Carlos Castaneda's *The Teachings of Don Juan: A Yaqui Way of Knowledge* (Berkeley: University of California Press, 1968), a book given to Olson by Don Allen in November 1968.

MALANGA: Are you able to write poetry while remaining in the usual conditions of life, continuing to do the usual work, preserving formal relations with people, and without renouncing or giving anything up?

OLSON: That, as I just said, is exactly what I, unfortunately from my point of view, have never known anything else than to do. But I'm saying: "Don't do it! I mean, it won't lead you anywhere." It's so true that, like, if I may quote again ...

BROWN: I don't think the question is answerable myself.

OLSON: But I have to answer it. But it's—no, it's both—I mean, he's thought this out. I know what Gerard is asking, in the sense that I know what he does with his own poetry; and we know what, say, some of the great sub-masters of the present, like Joel Oppenheimer and like a man whom I can mention from the most recent past, a man like Oppen, for example, utterly misleads, curiously, this best of all such sub-masters of the problem of the language between prose and poetry that we as a people are peculiarly possessed in, as was Chaucer alone previously in this tongue. This is the moment of the beginning of a tongue which ... and that's all. I'm not making any, like, spreach, but the exciting thing is that's just what's sort of the most—oh god, it's so exactly what's happening that you couldn't—I don't mean "happening" in that cheap sense, but this is really what's going on. It is the thing that's happening right now, I'm sure, because of ... No? Isn't it? How did I get there? What was our problem, like?

LANSING: The problem was the question, the question is ...

MALANGA: I indicate myself.

OLSON: Yes, you get me back. I meant that Gerard asked this from a very, very debatable thing in his own self, the two-legged man known as Malaga, Gerard Malanga. You really do: you ask this not for me, because, look, my life is spread out like, like ... like the spectrum. Quickly, just to get out of the embarrassment of that one.

BROWN: Yeah.

OLSON: Are you all right? You want more of this.

BROWN: Yeah. I wanted to be more help, but I'm not ...

OLSON: Oh, you are, too, you dope. I mean, you're the king of diamonds, and he's the king of clubs, and he's the king of spades, and I'm the king of me! I'm the only one that's having a heart. Oooh, look, I got a heart! How about that? I don't believe it: I give you hearts. [LAUGHS] Isn't that beautiful? Didn't that go on? Harvey, goddamn, I want you to understand that.

BROWN: I heard.

OLSON: Diamonds, man, diamonds. Jack of—isn't he the jack of diamonds? Aw, completely, I mean, bang! bang! bang!

LANSING: Sure. Jack or king.

OLSON: Jack or king, but I mean, jacks are open in this …

LANSING: One-eyed jacks.

OLSON: Well, no, there's two of us here, I mean there's two of us here. [LAUGHS] Yeah, go on. I think we've batted that one around. This is called spring—what do they call it?—spring, spring training. This is spring training. Yes, that's what it is, Mr Plimpton. This is called, "The Spring Training." [LAUGHTER] That's good, right? This is all, like, green, greenery.

MALANGA: That's beautiful. Better than George Plimpton. Aawhh! We can see about getting a baseball team and a football team.

OLSON: Plimpton will not disallow, but will cancel all contracts. I'll be all in trouble. Now I'm in trouble with Apple and Beatle, and pretty soon I'll be in trouble with CORE. [LAUGHTER] I mean, spelled C-I-A-A. And Beatles said to me, Tom Maschler crawling up the pyramids of the mastaba … [LAUGHS]

LANSING: *Stalky & Co.*[13]

OLSON: *Stalky & Co.*, right. And who's "Western Hesiod"? Who's "Western Hesiod?" I mean, there again, what d'y d-d-d-br-br-brwa-de-wa-br-r-rrr. I mean, this is that old drrrr-oo-a-de-a-de-a-wa-ger-a-bo-bob. What do they call that stuff? They used to go abubrradubidi-ababababad. That was beautiful, that stuff. It was like early jazz, that great Louisiana jazz. And now it's been supplanted, by nothing. I mean, we're here, like, present musicians.

LANSING: "Sold American." The Reynolds Tobacco Company.

OLSON: Yeah, yeah, yeah, yeah, right.

MALANGA: Are the conditions of life in which you are placed at the beginning of your work, in which, so to speak, the work finds you, are the best possible for you, at any rate, at the beginning of the work?

OLSON: I'm afraid, as well as the end. It's like being sunk in the cockpit—what a cockpit or whatever, the airplane sank. I read the most beautiful story about how Will Rogers and Wiley Post were lost. They stopped onto a lake about ten miles from Anchorage to ask an Indian boy if Anchorage was in that direction, and when they took off they plunged into the lake, and the poor Eskimo boy was not near enough to get them, so he ran ten miles to Anchorage to get the people to come out, and he said one of the men had a sort of a cloth on his eye, and the guy knew it was Post and Rogers were lost. It's one of the most interesting sort of air flights around the world before there was gnostronauts. [LAUGHS] And that's what was there then. I mean, it's the most—you don't break up freshwater lake, it's—you know, they— the plane came down. [SHOUTS TO DELIVERY PERSON: Forget it. Leave me the paper. I'll send you a check.] This guy, Wiley Post put down on pontoons, so he must have come up off this freshwater lake and went pump!

---

13. Gerrit Lansing mentioned Kipling's *Stalky & Co.* because one of the characters in the novel is called "Beetle."

That's all. D'you ever hear? I mean, it's one of those great national tragedies, like "Where is Mrs Earhart?" or something. You're all right?

BROWN: Yeah.

OLSON: I'll deal you cards, man!

BROWN: O.K.

OLSON: I'll make you a Tarot. Will you believe me when I say "Prince of— Prince of—Prince of the Diamond." I read it with you the other night, the "Diamond of the G-town,"[14] did I not?

BROWN: Yes, you did.

OLSON: Yeah, well that's what I mean. What are you worried—? *Absolument!* First base! Second base! Third base! Home!—sound like Ferrini. Yeehah!

MALANGA: Does poetry constitute the aim of your existence?

OLSON: Oh, I wish, I really wish it were so. I wish I really had—like, the other aim. I do. I get left with, like they say, poetry. I don't even know that I, like, did it. That's what's so stupid about the whole fuckin' thing. I mean, of course I don't live for poetry. I live for what anybody else does, and forever, and why not? Because it's the only thing. But what do you do meanwhile, what do you do for the rest of the time? That's all. I mean, if I sound sorta smart—smarty pants—lights, or demi- memi-emmy-demi-quaver witless, but I—that's all. The fact is they don't just get together often enough. Excuse me for kickin' it, but—and I don't mean from feeling—I mean, I don't believe in having any feeling, like as you—as all is action. I mean—I don't mean like this. But the kind of feeling has to be action. And I don't mean murdering or all that shit.

MALANGA: Then would you say there's …

OLSON: And I don't mean that "peace" thing, either. I mean "love," and, like, "live," in a rhymed sense, in the weakest rhyme there is, which is a shorter one after a fat short. I never did that before. I'm very happy about—like I want always to rhyme a bad rhyme, like, that's the big bad rhyme, if I make—I've been examining this question of how do you get two—what amount of shortness—you said, "quantity" earlier, "quantity of knowledge"—how much shortness is not enough, and yet how can you get a lesser shortness to go together with a greater shortness? Like "live" is shorter than, like, "love."

LANSING: L-L-L—life like love.

OLSON: Huh?

LANSING: Life, like—life like love—L-L-L.

MALANGA: That's an accident.

OLSON: That's beautiful.

BROWN: It's not an accident.

14. If the reference is to a *Maximus* poem, it has not been identified.

OLSON: No, it isn't. And like we were talking about Dunky, and, in fact, that conversation again today in Kansas with Dorn had another one like that; but I mean when we were talking about life and belief, *lief,* I mean, I was— I'm convinced still that there's—that beautiful thing that Duncan does in connecting life—or "the truth and life of myth," that instinct he has to put those two things together. Like, *Wahrheit* has not overcome (you remember that) *Dichtung*: that's beautiful when he moves in there for schtt![15]

LANSING: Provence is a perfect example of the school of light.

MALANGA: That's like the light shows of today, the whole tradition from that.

OLSON: I didn't know how you got to "light," but that's not a word I'd use like he's—I mean, it sounded like as on the tape we were going to get Love, Life, and then Light. And I don't want that! That's too Einsteinian. I wish to object. I am an anti-Einsteinian. That's a very high form of anti-something or other. In fact, Linear A, Linear B, and … us! because we're the new scarecrows. We, the non-born of the new real enemy. Yes, the new real enemy. Boom, boom, boom. Pow pufft!

MALANGA: Oh, wow.

BROWN: Hammond.

OLSON: That's straight taken from "Mandrake the Magician." [LAUGHTER] You see, it's impossible: I never will be taken seriously—because maybe I ain't! That's the trouble.

[REEL 2]

… So I was interested to say, "What was *tombeau*? What was the meaning of *tombeau*?" And all I could find was "sarcophagus," and I approached this can of tin with great care, having washed it, probably, or run it under fresh water. And I take the top off, and, "It's bevelled," I said. "It's bevelled all round and oval." Which must be why the French call it a *tombeau. De foie gras—trouflé. Trouffle.* How do you say that? *Troufflé. Troufflé.* Just [LAUGHING] to garble the national language of the *Paris Review.*

MALANGA: Would you say the more you understand what you are doing the greater will be the results of your efforts in what you are writing?

OLSON: Well, that's one of those things that you're absolutely so bitterly uninterested in that you can't eat and live on it. I mean, you know how useless, worthless, and in fact, unfortunately, preventative it is, because somebody assumes that it might be of interest to you, and it's so uninteresting that you can't imagine that it isn't. It's nothing, but it breaks your heart, that's all. It doesn't mean a thing. Pthah! I'll take it with all the wit of, again, Chaucer, and say, "I will write now upon what it's like to go to the House of Fame." And do you remember the eagle? Finally Chaucer gets higher and higher, and he says, "You wouldn't"—I mean, he's being held by the eagle's claws.

---

15. "This is not, however, Wahrheit supervening on Dichtung"—Prynne's review. Olson had received Robert Duncan's *The Truth and Life of Myth* from House of Books on 6 March 1969.

He says, "You wouldn't shit me, would you?" That's one of the greatest moments in American poetry. [LAUGHTER] In fact, it is *the* great moment in American poetry! Wow, hm, interesting. When did it happen? I mean, I'll go home and see the place! What a blessing we got, like, nationally. [LAUGHS]

MALANGA: Are you concerned with the isolation of the image in historical contexts cited in your poems?

OLSON: Hm, no. I hope, as a matter of fact, that just exactly the opposite is what happened. To tell you the truth, if it's in isolation, then I'm in the ward; because that's the one error I must not make, otherwise they'll know. [LAUGHTER] So you see how careful you have to be. If I shouldn't know as much as I do about something I do say, I might be in danger. But I don't know that I know enough anyhow, so how could I be so sure? No kidding. The point is ... Wow, I've forgotten what the question is but I'm sure I'm, like, feeling it. I know I'm feeling it. Not like I'm feeling a pyramid, but ... but it's ... There isn't anything except ... everything, which ...

MALANGA: Is your concern with topological discourse as a measure of things and distance a substitute for imaginative apprehension of the reality around you?

OLSON: Gee, say that again, because I lost ...

MALANGA: Is your concern with topological discourse ...

OLSON: Right.

MALANGA: ... as a measure of things and distance a substitute for imaginative apprehension of the reality around you?

OLSON: Right. Well, certainly the latter is in total error; and the first is in some funny way, because the latter is in a total error, disconnected from the important thing that that contains, which is like the Black Maria or something. So that the first part, then, doesn't obtain, but, like, I mean, see ... Have I said that right? Because it is a question almost of a bio—bio—bionetic, I want to say, hook. Like the DNA or the RNB or something. One is talking at those interlocterates at this moment, whatever the question is really. But, like, that's what we're talking about: we're talking gut—what the easy said thing, so it's called "gut-talk" now. And ... O.K.

MALANGA: It's all about measurement and distance though.

OLSON: Yeah, but, no, I mean, you might read—why don't you read it again? Because I asked you, but why not hear it again? 'Cos it's one of those questions: it's got—it's got both arms in it, don't you think? Yeah.

LANSING: Maybe Harvey should read it aloud, because then ...

OLSON: No, it's O.K., I'll hear it. But he has got two—he's got the two true twos, Gerrit, he's got the two true twos.

LANSING: Locked with a "but."

OLSON: Yeah, that's right. But he doesn't give any—so I can't answer the first on a question of consequence, and I can't answer the second or I have to correct the second in order to get a sense of flow, going back to that beautiful—those Egyptians, like, flow. I don't know where I come out of that, like. I must have dreamt it. By god, did they have flow! And today doesn't have flow or speed. So one wants to talk. Excuse me, but let me talk right into the tape at the moment.

MALANGA: Go ahead.

OLSON: Because I'm talking—Mr Brown and I were just—really for the first time for me in five years and I think for him for the first time, I was just reading the way a Pharaoh was ensconced during the very first formation of the whole role of the Pharaoh and indeed of Egypt itself in the Memphite period between the so-called King Scorpion and the first Pharaoh, Menes.[16] And I'm talking about the Memphite Theology that then obtained possibly from Menes's reign on, but in any case was the installation of the next Pharaoh. And we were just, like ... Well, I don't know, I've overtold the story to this point, and I've lost what it was that we were at as of your question. So come back to your question.

MALANGA: Is your concern with topological discourse ...

OLSON: Right.

MALANGA: ... as measure of things and distance a substitute for an imaginative apprehension of the reality around you?

OLSON: You see, it's a time-space question, isn't it? It's the biggest question in the lot, isn't it? Isn't it time-space?

LANSING: Well, the question is treacherous.

OLSON: Go ahead again, because it's so interesting we could make a tape on this, we, the four of us could make a tape ... [GENERAL HUBBUB. OLSON GOES AWAY FROM THE MICROPHONE, THEN RETURNS.] Well, that's O.K. Then it's my job to answer it so I dissolve ... uh? which one does have to, though. That's why I hope I did succeed in writing a "GRAMMAR—a 'book'" because I do believe there is something going on here.

MALANGA: It's the second question[17] that involves the substitute. It's "is distance a substitute for imaginative apprehension of the reality around you?"

OLSON: My god, may I answer that second half straight on the tape saying, "Look, I'm not a shaman, but shamans *are*." And that question is answered completely by the utter human ability to transport itself for real reasons where it's wanted and needed and has to be, and get home too. So, like, that's the answer to that is that's bullshit to use the word "distance" as against what I meant by it in "The Distances" and what distance always has

16. Olson is probably referring to "The Mystery Play of Succession" in Henri Frankfort's *Kingship and the Gods* (Chicago: University of Chicago Press, 1948).

17. The question, adapted from Ann Charters's *Olson/Melville*, p.16, has been misunderstood by Malanga as two questions, causing confusion.

meant to anyone who scans or looks—that is, that's what's beyond the horizon. I didn't mean to sound like Eugene O'Neill, but, wow, didn't I? But I'm talking, like, distance, ah-ah. No, come back now; go back to that temporal first half, which is the jigger jigger.

MALANGA: Well, the first half is: "is your concern with topological discourse …"

OLSON: Harvey, would you call Mrs Talbert? I forgot to get the liquor. Call "Liquor Locker" 283-2200 I think it is, and "send them over the usual"—just that so I'm dealing with Gerard, that's all. Go back now to the … 283-2200, no? Here, dear, I thought I looked at it recently.

MALANGA: Oh, we should read the telephone directory.

OLSON: No.

MALANGA: Charles should read it.

OLSON: No, no, no, no, no. I got a friend who does that, and every time he stops here … 0630, 0630.

MALANGA: No, that would be good.

OLSON: Don't do it. I hate—don't do it. Come sit down. I'll do it in a minute. Let's finish off where we were. Again, you stay on first base, otherwise this diamond is going to break. You understand who's the diamond? O.K. 1234 1234 ey pay ey tay ey tay le le le le nous nous nous, O.K.? Chin-chin or something: some ancient unburied or unrecovered Tibetan low mountain style, like we get from Uxbridge or something, where Frank O'Hara and I were born. "Baltimore, Ohio, and points West!"[18] [LAUGHTER] Really, you see how really this is getting great. Why not? Shit, let's go on the road, like they say. Sunday night I saw a picture of Dylan looking absolutely la-da. Oh, magnificent! Not a yeshiva student in our sense, but like back when Poland was Poland. Did you see that picture with this beautiful stiff brim and his marvelous—done up for—did you see it? It's off his new recording.

BROWN: Yeah. *Sounds of the Nashville Skyline.*

OLSON: Yeah, that's the one.

BROWN: With Johnny Cash.

OLSON: Oh is it? Why, the repro! Really, he is again another lovely Hasidim laughing Jew; he's just beautiful! I mean, it's got nothing to do with Woody or any of that shit. It's just an absolutely delicate thing, like Ashkenazi or Sephardic, like Engels, that incredible whatever it is, a scimitar or something, whatever the shit is. But there is some fucking, not the power of the benediction of God but the fortune of the sidereal realm or something that the Jews come out with this crescent. Is there such a crescent?

18. Frank O'Hara was born in Baltimore, and grew up near Uxbridge, south of Worcester, Massachusetts, Olson's birthplace.

LANSING: This is the Mesabi Range really.

OLSON: I don't care. I don't care. When you see him at this lovely moment saying, "I was pleased to sing with—aie, I was honored to sing with ..." I mean, d'you know, like, oh, mumumumumumumumuma. I love the man. I mean, he's only a living poet, that's all. I read his verse in the *Georgia Straight*,[19] and it's not very strong, like they say. [LAUGHS] Lacks just that strength. But him: oo, stuch! It's like a Spaniard or something. He does. In fact, to tell you the truth, I think that's—that sounds very non-Ashkenazi, sounds very funny ...

LANSING: Sephardic.

OLSON: Sounds very Sephardic because—it's beautiful. And his statement is so beautiful. I hear he wants to write some more. I love him for saying, like, "Would you have some more?"

MALANGA: Did you write the *Maximus Poems* independently of any influence?

OLSON: Oo, wow, yes. I sure did. I never had that question asked. It's marvelous. Gee, I really feel as though I did. But how can I prove it? Hm, oh absolutely, like right out of nowhere! I mean, "I, Tyre of Gloucester." I don't know how many Max—I mean, what Maximus is is of course a verb.

MALANGA: When Charles answered the question like that and he completely knocked out two questions that ...

OLSON: No, go on, let's mop 'em up. [WHISPERING TO HARVEY BROWN] Stay. Don't think of anything. Tell my secretary next door to go to work. It's 10:00 already.

BROWN: From the Liquor Locker.

OLSON: Oh, good.

MALANGA: The question was calculated for a calculated answer. I would have expected you to say Pound and Williams, you see, because everything is structured ...

OLSON: Well, no, dear, it is not structured. That's ignorance, if you'll excuse me, ignorance of your own, baby, time, Gerard; because actually one of the clichés that's grown up—in fact, it was created in the first place to put me out of business, if not my friend the lovely Dr Williams as well as Mr Pound, because there's some goddamn funny thing been going on in this century, I must say, and I certainly don't believe in conspiracy. But there's a very funny business that the only people that—I mean, the amount of connection that any one of those three people mentioned would feel to the other is highly questionable, identifiable as at least my two seniors certainly are with their work. Again, I'm answering the question, yeah, like umbumbumbumbuh. The only validity of those kind of relevant relationships is how much they spin from the central core, I mean as literally as though we were talking real

19. Olson had received the 14–20 March 1969 issue of the *Georgia Straight* from the editor Dan McLeod. It contained the long poem "What He's Saying" by Bob Dylan.

mathematic. If I didn't have three vanes to my propeller who were about two inches astern of the vanes on my propeller, Mr Williams and Mr Pound, I don't know where I would have known how to—as a matter of fact, like Dunky, whom I love so much now because he writes those "Passages" almost like cantos, I may end up trying to write cantos. I'm beginning to think I've been wasting my time, or diddly doddly. I'd better should try to see what it's like, because Dunky really has again shown himself to be one of the damn few if not the only progressive compositionist amongst us. And I say that almost with a dig, Dunky, because I'm not sure that composition any longer is—I mean, I am completely sure it's more compressive, more impressive than ever, but it might turn out to be a lot less than … I don't know. That's the big question: what could be composition in a poem today? I guess we know, but … Tell me what the question was once more just so that I remember it.

MALANGA: Did you write the *Maximus Poems* independently of any influence?

OLSON: Oh, if you could possibly say that, but it's like asking you to have shed your skin before you had it. I mean, I'm now only, like, how many years, seven, ten? What is it Duncan tells me, every nine or something? But I mean, like, good god, man, I mean, my pre—my assumption, I mean …

MALANGA: Could you have written the *Maximus Poems* as you did without knowing Pound's or Williams's works, say?

OLSON: That's like asking me if I could have written without having read. And in fact, who do you read the most? The persons the nearest, the most recent to you. So why not?

LANSING: The nearest at hand.

OLSON: The nearest at hand. Exactly. But curious enough, it's equally true in the enormous empire of time; and may they all know that, because the one thing that is true of us who do read is that we, wow, I mean, do we travel! Talk about light; that's going nowhere by comparison, nowhere, by the speed of the takings, I mean the real sweeps. What's the Mafia call that ten percent they take off the top? What's that called, the wind or something, whitt! whitt! Should be called shtt! [LAUGHS] It's called the … you know, it's a marvelous word too.

MALANGA: Is there any similarity in content between the views of Pound on history as a form of experience and your own?

OLSON: None whatsoever. In fact, Ezra's are optative, and mine are decisive; or mine are *formidables*, and his are *souples*. I mean, I love him for all the—like in that game "Go" that I learned that time at the Castle, I got a game called "Boxes." I love Ezra for all the boxes he has kept. This is where he really is a canto maker. And I ain't got nothing to do, by the way, Gerard, as of the previous question, with cantos. I couldn't write a canto if I sat down and deliberately tried. My interest is even not in canto. It's in another condition of song, which is connected to mode, and has therefore to do with absolute actuality. It's so completely temporal, and so ins—like, what's that beautiful word? The nouns are wild. Excuse me, a "secret insistence." If I might with a "secret insistence" suggest some further …

MALANGA: But that's not good, a secret insistence.

OLSON: Oh, it's so—it's so true that it's like the whole …

MALANGA: How can insistence be secret?

OLSON: Gerard, I mean, you love flagrant, I mean, fragrant women, and I do too; but the one thing that does not distinguish them is whether their perfume is theirs or a maker's. Wow, that prose got finished, believe you me! That slentence slid home, like Ed Marshall says about his mother's ears.[20] Did you get this rhythm? Did you get this?

BROWN: Yes.

MALANGA: Does Pound's teaching bear any relevance to how your poems are formed on the page?

OLSON: No. In fact, it's evident that my masters here are pre-Pound. They're Webern and Boulez and, I don't know, what's some sort of paper.[21] Look, the point is that at that moment of time, like—that's what's so kind of still crazy—I mean, at that moment of time almost every possible art that ever existed, and some that we don't even know, sprang forth again. The seven arts, my ass; it was about seventeen thousand or seventeen hundred or seven or something. But, I mean, there was a fantastic sort of whum! And it's still on. Don't cheat your own balloon. I mean literally, like a trip around the moon. That Jules Verne, I mean, I read him when, like, when you—your brother Charlie's books that I read—but I read that trip, you know, around—you know, it's so completely applicable today that they don't have any primacy at all. I don't say that cutely, because I'm thinking about this last whatever that was on the tape.

MALANGA: Do you write by hand or directly on the typewriter? And does either method indicate a specific way in which the poem falls on the page?

OLSON: Well, I'm not so sure, again, about the poem, but I sure know that my life gave up or something, because Duncan is the first man to have asked me the query. He discovered when he first came to see me that I wrote on the machine and never bothered to do anything, you know, like that famous remark: "If he should only correct a line." (There's the stuff.) I mean, I wouldn't want it, 'cos, like—but let's say it because Jonson did. What did he say when he saw the manuscript? Or he said, if you saw the manuscript, "He ne'er correct a line," to talk like Bobbie Burns.

LANSING: "Would that he did—would that he had."

---

20. Ed Marshall's long poem "Leave the World Alone" includes mention of his mother, but not her ears.

21. Olson is hiding a name in a conundrum. Perhaps the solution is in the remark in "Reading at Berkeley" about "the paper of Matisse's sons."

OLSON: "Would that he had." But "he ne'er correct a line." So I, like, ne'er correct a line. But listen, Gerard, I mean, this is like—unless it's on, like Robert Burns. Zoop! (Look at the color from here. Gee, it must be Friday night.)

BOB[22]: Sixty-six bottles.

OLSON: No kidding. I owe you money.

BOB: Oh, no, no, no.

OLSON: How much? Wait a minute. Yeah, that's right. Give me a half a dollar back. Baby, you got skinned. How about that? Sixty-six, one, oo, wow, didn't you get skinned! I told you never deal with a sharp trader like me.

BOB: Naw, I didn't get skinned. I made over thirty-two cents.

OLSON: But I made a buck out of you. Come on, give me twenty, give me a half. Then we're even, right on the nose. I must show you how equitable things are. The world, the real world is equitable.

BOB: Is it?

OLSON: It is. Did you just ask me? I just told you. Gimme a half a buck, then we'll show you that justice reigns.

BOB: You're the boss. There you go.

OLSON: I am the boss. On this subject, I'm the boss, right? Is there anybody else that needs justice all sewed up?

BOB: We'll see you later, pal.

OLSON: We're on tape, Bob.

MALANGA: You sound like a TV announcer.

OLSON: Wasn't that nice? He is good. Like the man said: economics. Come on, and in the other hand [CARRYING BOTTLES] take the scales of justice. Isn't that nice? Didn't I catch him on his own doubt, his one doubt, the social doubt? Let's have a big new jury and a court, the Areopagus, and decide decisions here on this side of the Cut, and see what happens to the n-a-t-i-o-n.

LANSING: Not "Pacific."[23]

OLSON: No, absolutely not. Non-pacific. Not even guerrero, or something, not even lah lah ah wah. Love and war, everything goeth. Let's goeth. Down with peace and scurrying about, and up with curry and cutty, "Cutty Suit." [LAUGHS]

MALANGA: Charles, would you care to explain your care with such matters as line units and indentation in your poems?

---

22. Apparently a delivery man from Liquor Locker, whom Olson later addresses as Bob.
23. A reference to *The Pacific Nation*, the second issue of which had recently arrived in Gloucester from Robin Blaser in Vancouver.

OLSON: Wow, if I only knew I did it, it would be marvelous! Did I? Thank you. But, like, please, I don't know how you say that, because, like, you don't know a thing of what … I mean, that was another thing today. I read that piece of Prynne's, and, I mean, he says everything right, accurately, and I'm sitting here and I'm thinking, "Isn't it terrible? You know, until somebody says it to you, I don't know nothing, I didn't know I did any—I didn't know what he says I did. Then I know I did what he said I did." It's that wonderful business. Are you following me?

LANSING: Yeah, but it is registration he's asking.

OLSON: No, no. Hear me. I'm not asking for it. That's the important—but in some funny way despite the famous actor in me, in some funny way I don't, no kidding. May I say that once in the world and let it be said? It's so funny, because my vanity is so back-faced I'm stuck with the other end. [LAUGHS] That sounds approximate.

MALANGA: Would it be correct in saying that your abbreviations derive their nature from the device which Pound has used in portions of the *Cantos*?

OLSON: Oh, yeah. I wish those damn things I had never dud. I wish I'd known enough to just do what I just did, which was to slip my head or something, because all that stuff, it isn't that interesting. It's the cheapest kind of non-attention is to take a service mark for the whole thing. I mean, all of us, at those points of those draggy pieces in the language, one wants to just ignore them. And I think, by the way, writing has gotten now to the point where it doesn't have the AT&T or Western Union syntax, so that it just jumps the syntax in a funny way.

LANSING: Isn't it an accident, just as the acceptance of our time is an accident, it's long or short hair or something?

OLSON: Right. I agree. Or like that guy said again: "glotto chronology." Wow, again, may I, *Paris Review*, refer to Mr Jeremy Prynne, English officer, formerly in France … like, I mean … O.K. Gerard …

MALANGA: What is the distinction between your usage of technique of quotation and that of Pound's?

OLSON: Well, again, equally I could say, and in fact in my own experience it was Eliot, I think, that first—I first saw that thing, that apposite—is it "apposite"? Sounds like "apposite": if you use a certain quote a certain way, well, you can get a lot of things. To tell you the truth, I think both Pound and Eliot were after something rather different than us who come a little later, either as flatheads like myself probably, I'm sure, or as hippie, hip, hips, I mean hip-cool thing, which is like another, a real, a real face, like, a river for the tiger of the river. And that's all that matters is that the thing be the thing of the thing. Yeah, it's either, right? But, mind you, to say it in language like that is hard as hell, right? I mean, I just suddenly thought, "My god, I got a leg up on Ed Sanders"—because Sanders, I think, is still the most interesting young poet in America, like they used to say about—and they still say ...

MALANGA: Watch out, or you're going to be caught.

OLSON: I know. I'm hearing you, but that's O.K. But, I mean, he himself feels that he's the youngest possibility for the great heritage now already in existence in American poetry.

MALANGA: It's a horse race.

OLSON: It's a horse race? It is not a horse race. It's a real finish and an accumulated betting totality of. Said. And next race! But until next race, race on is race race, yeah. Dink? I mean, it's no—no, it is not a horse race. As a matter of fact, you said you wanted to make a million, and I told you how Sanders and Ken Weaver are going to make a million before they're thirty. And I'm talking about a poet who's twenty-eight and who thinks ... But if you said nothing, you say, like, "the youngest poet in America," right? The youngest poet, because he is; that's what's so—in fact, to tell you the truth I was thinking about him last night, and thinking, "My god, how many troubles ..." This is Ed Sanders I'm talking about, who's the peony winner of the greatest poetry profile award that ever was made this side or the other side of the Atlantic Ocean. It's called the anacoluthic award, and I hereby now make it; and it's pre-Anacreontic, and is absolutely way down below Atlantis, and it's got no end, no end, 'cos it's like the stalk of heaven and creation, and it hasn't even bloomed or hasn't, like, sat on its crown yet. But it exists, to talk like Sut Lovingood. And I know where it's planted, [LAUGHS] and I know where it's planted and I know where it is. And we all do too, and we all know who we're talking about, 'cos it's dar, dar, down on the plantation ...

MALANGA: Charles ...

OLSON: ... under the trunk of that large cypress tree in all that goo, way down dar where them coon are too, and an awful lot of everybody way, way in that rank swamp, woo-oo.

MALANGA: Would you say that the inclusion of the subject of economics in the *Maximus Poems* is a revival of that very same effort found in the *Cantos* by Pound?

OLSON: Oh, yeah. If I should—I mean, Mr Pound, I think, comes of a family which—I know they had means enough to—not only could take Ezra across the Atlantic, so he had the advantage of a European education ... Look, I was born in South Worcester, and that's a very important difference. In fact, it was the break between us, because I finally got pissed off at Ezra's pissing on Dr Williams because one portion of Bill Williams was Jewish: I've forgotten what sixteenth, eighteenth, ninth, fourth, seventeenth, two, too-toot.

MALANGA: Would you make a specific distinction between poets whom you yourself or anyone could imitate and poets from whom one could learn?

OLSON: Oh boy, you learn from anything. I almost wanted to send both of you the poem made up on the basis of some new marvelous thing, just suddenly some absolute—today, poom! Like my pung, I've forgotten what it sounded like. [LAUGHS] Like, just flash me again: what was, like, the signal?

MALANGA: Would you make a specific distinction …

OLSON: Yeah, yeah, yeah, yeah.

MALANGA: … between poets whom you yourself …

OLSON: Yeah, yeah. Yeah, yeah, yeah, yeah.

MALANGA: … or anyone could imitate and poets from whom one could learn?

OLSON: No, that's not the whole question. You've gone on.

MALANGA: No, no, I haven't.

OLSON: Say that question you asked me just now again, which is whrrrrrr …

MALANGA: Would you make a specific distinction between poets whom you yourself or anyone could imitate and poets from whom one could learn?

OLSON: That what you said? That's too much. That's damn interesting. You got your answer: Father Pound. That was beautiful. Like, Father Daedalus, and Father Ols—I mean, Father Me, Father O'Me. That's too much. Beautiful. That's way out. Go ahead, you Russian stinkpot, you. Vhat are you from, Malanga? Vhere? *Jesu, eccu.* He's from—I know where he's from. I tell you absolutely. [LAUGHS] When we end the interview I will say the name of the ward and district from where he cometh.

MALANGA: Would you define the nature of influence?

OLSON: Wow. That we be and that we do. That we be and that we influence. That we be and that we influence. No, that we be … Yeah, that we be and that we—O.K. good enough. That's it, because that covers it all the way into serial, right? Yeah, that we be and that we influence, right?

LANSING: And that we do.

OLSON: Yeah, that we do, really. But that sounds too aphoristic. Ha ha! Like, at all costs, clear the air. The American advantage: clear the air. It's called: "Clear the Air!" Our equity is monstrable.

MALANGA: What is the distinction between influence and discipleship?

OLSON: Oh, brumbmbmanthpftnbrum. I don't really think these questions … It's like, if you'll excuse me, Gerard, and I respect you and I regret, this is like when I was on Canadian television in one of those feature programs with a lady tiger from Tanganyika, puss puss, and an American baseball umpire or something; and it's like the English—because in Canada the voice, the Canadian voice, is still too rustic, like in the States, you might say, and therefore only Englishmen can get an actual announcer's job on Canadian

Broadcasting, so that the guy who had the notes, who never knew who I was or what I was there for …

MALANGA: I want you to take these questions seriously though.

OLSON: … I was there to represent "Poetry" like as against hunting in Tanganyika and such and such and such and such, playing sacred things in Southeastern Asia. [LAUGHS] That's very connective, but I really … Where did we go from? It was an interesting question? I botched it?

MALANGA: It was an *easy* question.

OLSON: Well, I'm not—are you in school? Am I in school I'm getting easy questions tonight? I mean, like, jesus, I thought when I didn't feel so well for two days, at least if I get up Gerard will keep me interested. [LAUGHS] Like I did—excuse me, anybody that really reads this or listens to it, but like that wonderful sleeper …

MALANGA: You can't want to see the future on this tape.

OLSON: Oh yes, I can, because I can talk right to the tape right now, because, like that sleeper, I'm very fresh. I just woke up.

MALANGA: How do you account for the change in trend in American poetry from experiment and technique to subject matter?

OLSON: [LAUGHS] For the same reason why this nation is going to hell right now: because it's finally got caught up with itself. The tail got in the mouth or something. Are you kidding? I mean, the reason why that was true was that everything finally got in, got like … Again, Mr Prynne, I mean, he says it so that I sat here and thought, "Oh god, how really rewarding it is that he says that so beautifully how I have said what this poor goddamn silly States just paid too much for," that passage where he comes up from the ground there, yeah? Do you remember that? I mean, it's the most—(Oh, I blew something on your machine … Sounds just like I was hoping. [LAUGHS]) But I mean, like, I don't know, it doesn't matter. The only thing is, shit, I mean …

LANSING: I don't know that one can talk about American experiment, anyway. Experiment isn't …

OLSON: It's O.K. Don't. I mean, you're too young. You'd answer these questions much more rapidly and interestingly than I do, but excuse me …

MALANGA: Don't underestimate yourself.

OLSON: No, I don't. I told exactly how … I mean, I'm enjoying it. I don't think you'd enjoy it as much almost literally with the exercise of your mind as I am, like, just answering the questions. [LAUGHS] That's not a put-down to you; it's a discovery for me. For me, I said, all right? I'm on board this Norwegian ship, and we're passing through the warm waters again. [LAUGHS]

MALANGA: Would you say that after the appearance of your manifesto "Projective Verse" that poets nurtured their poems of the type demanded by your theories?

OLSON: Oh god, no, please, and in fact if I ever … I tried to answer this once in Toronto with all of Layton's goons with him, including a marvelous ex-wrestler poet named Mankayvitch, I think it was. I've forgotten. Ma-something. Ma, like. He'll be mad at me now, and I was going to tell a nice story about him, oh dear. Wasn't Mankayvitch—it's a Jewish name, Kovitch, like. In any case, he was a doll, and after I finished reading he said, "Why don't you write like William Butler Yeats?" The first question, though, was the one you just asked me about projective verse; the second was this protest from the audience, you know, like, modern new gangsterism: "Ah wah wah. da. Temme, wah dontcha write like William Butler Yeats?" Well, I didn't know what to say, you know. [LAUGHTER] Moscovitch! Harry Moscovitch! I really didn't know—I mean, I felt so peculiar. What could I do? [LAUGHS] Isn't that a beautiful old act? What is that from? It's like "Baby Doll."

MALANGA: Do you enjoy telling young poets what they ought to do?

OLSON: Oh jesus, god, if I ever did, may the lord of the whole of all the seven saints of India, China, Buddhaland, Gangee town, and all Tatars this side of—the other side, where the Tartars live—may god forgive me: because, oh please, if they would please, like, never think … And, in fact, as you know, I am happy to have some friends of all of us here in the kitchen, all of whom are like possibly that. And look at them today! When I think of it, arghhrrrr! [LAUGHS] Some of our best friends are terrific! Arghrrrr … fufufufuff!! So, therefore, n-o-d, or something … d-o. [LAUGHS] I mean, wow! Why not? Boy, I've been very lucky, very lucky. I'm sorry, but I was born with a caul over my head. Or so they told me, like they used to tell everybody, probably, in order to make them really take that fucking angel thing seriously. Like, I think I'll tell every one of my children exactly not only how I conceived them, because I remember at least the details in each of or one of … O.K.

MALANGA: Let's say you were to meet a young poet and this young poet's work shows signs of influence from your own work, can you be sure that the influences come directly?

OLSON: Oh, completely, instantly. It's as immaculate or as impeccable as the existence of something new … and boom boom wang tung zip toodledo cookydowaddlededa. This is nothing, bat it in. (Can you give me a light? I ain't got no light.) I really regret that I had answered that beautiful poet Eigner when he complained, "You—but you don't help people, you don't help people in your poems." I says, "I know, I'm afraid, uh." (I'm teasing you, but don't worry.) It always moves me, those guys: "You don't help people, yuh." I've been trying to help people all my life, that's been the trouble. I said that to him, and he just did—oh yeah, I got bawled out. I said, "My sense of responsibility is the only thing that's hanging me up; otherwise I'm a free man." That's a big 18th-century problem. A woman, you know, says … that's silly … I mean, of course I'm trying to climb up both walls at once. Gimme light! Gimme reason! Give me—what? Give me out, right? Like that beautiful Blake, who's like four feathers of a raven caught down in a chasm, of which we're just later birds. The doll, he really is; he's like a frozen four-winged raven down in a chasm, shrieking for the light.

LANSING: Frozen?

OLSON: Not frozen, but I mean ahead of us, in the sense that just ahrrr! like a box kite practically—rahrrr! Eight; like on one side it's four, but I mean four plus two is six plus something, you know, eight, like, ahhrrg! and right there, but never moving. And we're all movie, moving, movement. So moving, in fact, to tell you the truth, yeah … how do you also …?

MALANGA: Makes me want to conduct interviews; it helps …

OLSON: Isn't that nice? Isn't that nice? But it's because we have breeze. If you don't mind, pour yourself a drink. We got a big thing here to hold, because it's like the night in Boston that Bet and Creeley and I had to drink that bottle of whisky to get that fucking tape done. And goddamn, again, see, I'm going to lose the—whatever the rights are, the ARC rights?

MALANGA: The ARC rights? All rights reserved.

OLSON: He doesn't understand. Gerard is one of these absolutely … I feel like his grandfather. I'm going to give him, after I've finished, I'll tell him where he comes from, within ten miles of the polar ladder, and I don't know a thing, you know, not a …

[REEL 3]

OLSON: … this fucking stupid letter … card.[24]

BROWN: … It's just a crime. I think …

OLSON: Huh? Do you know what I'm talking about? No, I dunno; I'll show you the damn thing; there's no signature. It's all gum—it's all gunked up with all the …

LANSING: Well, it flashed through my mind too …

OLSON: Four somethings—four some …

LANSING: … because I told you about Carol Weston's letter.

OLSON: Yeah, well I don't—I don't think it's—and I don't think so. Because I don't think they would do this "Charles and Charles Junior."

BROWN: Not Carol Weston, no, there's this …

OLSON: But these—I talked to Carol Weston saying she was married—having an affair with a witch, or seeing herself to be a witch. Come on. If it's a covens, you got some—you got some better than a covens? Gerrit, hey Gerrit, hey? My nephew, I want you. If you stray, I say, "Come back to Hebraism, Gerrit. You after all are a Lansing, remember, a Lansing."

24. The letter being discussed remains a mystery.

[LAUGHS] That's too much fun, we could go on for ever, right? Isn't it beautiful? Suestadsdadeda wootodo. We really …

MALANGA: Why is it that so many poets tend to shy away from or even criticize the idea of the themes of subject matter and poetry being those extended to topics and objects related to the life of a modern man or woman and non-poetic materials and mass media as an object of structure shaping content and theme within a given set of circumstances involving the poet in life? In other words, why does—why—?

OLSON: Oh it's an—do you know what the answer is? So simple …

MALANGA: Why do most poets shy away from writing about non-poetic things, like the mass media or Vietnam, things that aren't considered poetic or proper poetic substance?

OLSON: Oh, they're not, they're not. They're social secondary matters, which we have the government to take care of. We have no interest in such servospect—servomechanisms. That's why Mr Norbert Wiener's in the hole. In fact, our control of the planets as well as the machines is just the vulgar matter, and in fact to tell you the truth it's based on vulgar matter, it's simply an improvised condition of vulgar matter …

MALANGA: Well, would you consider …?

OLSON: Just a minute, Mr Malanga … And will continue until somebody says this, and really somebody hears it, because the thing is literally as old as— as a matter of fact, god bless my lovely painter friend in Carmel Highlands, in whose bedroom, his daughter told me, Dylan and—I mean Bob Dylan and peacemaker Joan made first love. I mean, this is how, like, you can say years back, decades back, "Admiral Doner, thank you for your victory at Midway, signed General Something." The FBI rushes in, at one, two, 'cos my wire came from Washington.[25] But what I wanted to say is something entirely different, which is, like, whatever Doner did say that was relevant to what we were just talking about.

MALANGA: Well, would you say that it's not poetic to glamorize something like mass media in poetry?

OLSON: That it's not poetic to glamorize?

MALANGA: Glamorize, in poetry.

OLSON: Oh, let them glam—like, what do you mean, it—it isn't? What— what's that connection to poetry? Did I not under—?

MALANGA: Mass media in poetry …

OLSON: Yeah, I understood. Mass media: that's no problem.

---

25. Olson is speaking of a prank which involved his sending from Washington a telegram to his buddy Ephraim Doner (who later moved to Carmel, California) congratulating him as "General Doner" on the Allied landing in North Africa. The FBI intercepted the message and interrogated Doner (Clark, pp. 79–80).

MALANGA: To glamorize the mass media in poetry, would you consider it proper poetic valid—?

OLSON: I think, I mean, I—I think—I think it's a waste of energy, like a newspaper.

MALANGA: You do?

OLSON: Oh yeah, because honestly in five years, like, we'll want it all back. That isn't what I mean, but we won't want what ... No, that's not fair, excuse me, I guess that's another point.

MALANGA: Why would we want it all back?

OLSON: No, I got you, I got you, I got you, grrrrr. Yeah, I don't know, I mean, we want what's been suddenly disallowed. I mean, there's a funny—again, that son of a gun uses sort of legal language. Excuse me, but let me—I wanna ... Do you remember that funny legal language? I was surprised to discover he was trained as a minister. He used one word here that I thought I'd absolutely—I mean, it'd hold me forever like I'm trying to keep it now, but I don't know how to. It's some damn legal word.

MALANGA: I'm going to have to get a copy of that.

OLSON: Well, I want you to, because I want it to be the hallmark of the, like, whatever that means, but I mean that sign thing. Excuse me, like Kansas. Well, Sedalia, I sez.[26] No, I mean, like back here in the East where tobacco was first grown and has been spat ever since.

MALANGA: What poet would you regard you have had a lasting influence upon?

OLSON: Oooh, wow. I should hope, like, "a lasting influence"? May god authenticate everything I've ever done that might have possibly had influence upon some of the men whom I really feel connected to. And how! Wow! If I could get draughts with red flags and ribbons, I'd be the collector of 'em. Like I told Jack Clarke about finding Orc just after Canute in southwest England. The first grant of Canute in Dorchester is to the Lord Orc. I've been waiting for five years—no, three—to tell that to Jack, you know, in the dawn on Easter Sunday. And it's true. Must have been some Norse name that was written in this beautiful—I saw the original, this is Canute's document. I didn't see it in a book or anything, like knowledge is, like, supposed to be. I saw it in the life condition, transcribed by some monk, who wrote Norse for Canute, or English for Canute probably.[27] But Orc gets the whole—and, in fact, you know, Gloucester is settled from the split of Orc ... This is what you don't do with Blake. [LAUGHS] This is what you don't

---

26. The sign and its connection to Sedalia (a town in Missouri near Kansas City) remains obscure. The "legal language" referred to may be Prynne's use of the word "rectitude."

27. Olson saw Canute's actual manuscript in the Dorset County Museum during his stay in Dorchester in May 1967. Blake gave the name Orc to one of the characters in his symbolic narratives. The connection to Gloucester is, unfortunately, not completed by Olson.

do with those who also live at the same time previously as you do. You don't do this, because, like ... I don't know what it is you don't do, I really don't.

MALANGA: Don't you have a fear of being reduced to conformity by having too many other poets understand and imitate ...?

OLSON: Oh god, are you kidding? I mean, do you think I can be—do you think I'm empty; like, who? I mean, I got about five people who have given me any evidence that they know what the fuck I said. I mean, literally, like, I guess, five.

MALANGA: Who are the five?

OLSON: No, well, I don't ... That would be really to create quite a successful society. In fact, the successful one, from my point of view, with that five. Wow, how many companions do you need?

MALANGA: Who are the first five?

OLSON: No. [LAUGHS] That's literary, like, history, and I'd have no interest in it whatsoever.

MALANGA: Yeah, but the people out in *Paris Review* land want to know about this.

OLSON: Well, I know, but, like, to tell you the truth, let's sort of light a rock under the *Paris Review*. There's a whole package of big—you know, like I told Betsy Klein—no, I mean ... Oh, you do? ... Cigarettes.

BROWN: Want a cigarette?

OLSON: No, I thought you wanted matches. O.K. No, dear, we got some.

MALANGA: Why don't you mention the first five, though?

OLSON: Well, I mean, no, I'm trying to think of how many people have ever ... like, no kidding. [PAUSE] How many times do you think that you get anything back that in any sense is interesting to yourself? And it's nothing to do with being understood or something. It's that you are moved by the fact that another person sees what it is that you have done: which is like coming to the shore or some stupid thing, like I fell off the big pile pole, and I've carried the flag with me, and I swum ashore.[28] But, I mean, that kind of a marvelous sort of result: it's what the other person somehow or other, by recognizing, gives you, puff! But that's company. That's as long—that's all that eases the greatest fucking loneliness is that somebody will say something relevant to what you have gotten yourself involved in. I mean, it's so important that it's, like, it is, like, just, you know, is love. Whatever that is it's so corny. I was laughing earlier, but when that beautiful Chaucer, again, who seems to be the king of this broadcast, but I mean when he does write the "House of Fame," I think that's a clean thing. I am for it right now. If I can claim five persons who seem to, gee, now, give me the sense that I'm where I was whenever it is that they read was where I was, then I'm still, uh, living.

28. Olson is thinking of the greased pole competition in the Gloucester fiesta, where the aim is to get the flag at the end of the pole without slipping off.

That's as big as I know it to be. And I don't think that shrinks it one fucking bit; as a matter of fact, sounds like really, like ptt! That's the end; I mean, that's it. And that's what's something, and the rest is …

MALANGA: Would you say that the *Black Mountain Review* helped to systematize your ideas about "Projective Verse"?

OLSON: I'd written it long before the *Review*, in fact, four years before the *Review* appeared. So it's irrelevant.

MALANGA: Yes, I didn't know that.

OLSON: And I would like to point out, instead of answering the question, that the "Feinstein Letter" is almost ten years after the "Projective Verse," and is a completely different apprehension on my part; and it's still one I haven't been able to add another ten-year or nine-year shot to. As far as I know, the "Feinstein Letter" is still, except for that sort of stuff of Dante's that I discovered in the "Shakespeare Quantity in Verse" thing that was in the *Human Universe*, but, I mean, literally speaking, that "Feinstein Letter" still seems to me to be something to be extricated as of 1959 from. And that's after the *Black Mountain Review*, if you'd like to put it that way. The "Feinstein Letter" is just as much after as the "Projective Verse" is before. Let me say that, because of the importance I lend to the *Black Mountain Review* and to its editorship. [PAUSE]

MALANGA: Is it the point—is it the point that …? [PAUSE]

OLSON: [LAUGHING] That stuff. I was thinking of that beautiful opera that is like the central opera of our lives, and it's not Svengali; it's "The Something Apprentice." That music … who is that? Whose music is it?

LANSING: Dukas.

OLSON: Oh yeah, that's right. And it's very attractive music. It's as good as the Italians almost, or it's like the Americans doing Italian.

MALANGA: Is it the point that just as one does not have to be an "imagist" in theory to produce poetry that can be rightly claimed as "imagistic," so one does not have to know or to believe in your theory of "projective verse" to produce poems that can be rightly called "projectivist"?

OLSON: Oh, I should hope so. Like, if Einstein wasn't able to have talked about the universe, then I certainly was wasting my time talking about, like, poetry, because that's all I was talking about. And hopefully therefore, if there's a truth about what it is, that doesn't have a goddamn thing to do with how many experiences of it there are.

MALANGA: [PAUSE] What are the basic differences between "projective verse" and the "objectivist" movement established by the American poet Louis Zukofsky?

OLSON: Now, Gerard, do you want me to educate you? It's just like I mentioned earlier about being on Toronto, the King's pronouncer comes on and says, "Mr Olson, what do you think of imagism?" And I said, "What?"

[LAUGHS] And you just mentioned, the previous question, and now you mention "objectivism." I mean, that's the same sort of question as the indissolvable union of Mr Pound and myself at the *pratigiano*[29] or something of the skin of being, which is as true in poets' loves for each other, and in parenthood, as it is in the whole forms of life, anyhow, trees, ferns, and eventually far rocks in the earth.

MALANGA: Were the *Maximus Poems* or the *Mayan Letters* written out of your emotions exactly as they came to you in life, or do they represent a state of consciousness or emotion or idea without dealing with the relation to the expression of their original ideas?

OLSON: I hope so. Altogether. The question satisfies me completely. [LAUGHTER]

MALANGA: Have you ever found yourself struggling with existing ideas in a poem without being able to find a direction for the new ideas?

OLSON: Like I said in that *Maximus*, I didn't know there were any ideas.[30] [LAUGHS] That's not what—but it's exactly what I said today: I didn't know there were any ideas. [PAUSE] Ask me another question immediately on the same point, or I'll ...!

MALANGA: Do you find that often one new word that you had not heard before would alter the whole picture, in that you would be obliged to rebuild the poem and everything that you had built up before?

OLSON: I do think that's true absolutely on the instant with which I would begin a poem; but, you know, I am a little bit like Plutarch or somebody: I write a poem simply to create a mode of a priesthood in a church forever; so that a poem, for me, is simply the first sound realized in the modality of being, if I may speak like my master, the greatest of all, the flower-power man of them all. You know, like, I mean the man who really did.[31] If you want to talk about actuality, let's talk about actuality, and it falleth like a doom upon us all. But it falleth from above, and if that's not straight the whole thing is doodled; and if that's straight, then you can modal modality all you want. You can do anything, really, literally, right? And that, I think, is one of the exciting possibilities of the present, I swear, is the possibility that the goddamn thing can be modaled throughout. That's what I love about today's kids: I like them only because I think they're modaled throughout. And I don't think their teachers are at all, as a matter of fact. I mean, I'm happily almost, like, astringent here. I sit back, shp shp, in my lollipop Gloucester, fffft, and don't do anything, dirty lousy cop-out. [LAUGHS] You know, oi remember way back when oi was young, ten years ago, and Elroy Jones was in New Yark City, I was lobbing 'em. I was like the

29. This Italian-sounding word is as heard on the tape. It is uncertain what Olson was thinking of.
30. In "Maximus to Gloucester Letter 15" (1.68) Olson quotes Paul Blackburn's accusation, "you go all around the subject," and chides him: "I didn't know it was a subject."
31. Alfred North Whitehead, whose *Process and Reality* speaks of "mode," "being," "actuality," and "eternal event."

Civil War then, what? He was in Richmond, and I was in the redoubt at Petersburg, and we weren't doing nothin', so we were pptt pptt pptt! from Gloucester to Manhattan. No kidding. And now it's the Vietnam War, dig? You follow me? I mean, literally. And it was marvelous, pewt, pewt, playing catch, if I may say that really to a European audience as well as an American. But it's true, it's very—it's not *Catch* whatever that shit is. I don't even know what "catch 22" is; I've never read that fucking thing. But catch, we were playing catch. And he's a goddamn nice fielder, dedadedadadadada. All that Jewish Bronx shit—I don't mean because it's Jewish, but because it's this late Jewish, late East Bronx literature, which is, to tell you the truth, to a geologist like me, just uninteresting. A "geochronologist" geologist, whatever that feller says.[32] Marvelous, wullulup wullup wup; just like ripping off a piece of tape from one of them machines, you know, those new ones, the world machines. That's what they got now, the world machine, derrump! When will this government cease being a nuisance to everybody? Because they're stopping invention; for the congregate is the aggregate is the world machine. Sprumcruchrrm! Every human being has got that power shit. Chrrt! Wrap up baby catso … picatso …

MALANGA: Do you find, when in the act of writing a poem …?

OLSON: All right?

BROWN: Yeah.

OLSON: O.K. Gimme—gimme some—a little more of this … Go ahead, yeah.

MALANGA: Do you find, when in the act of writing a poem or reworking the same poem afterward, that intensified observation brought about by self-remembering always has an emotional element?

OLSON: Notional what?

MALANGA: Emotional element.

OLSON: Yeah, I know. You know, like, here I have to defer to all those other American poets who, for some reason, I both envy and admire. I do. I mean, I never have rewritten almost anything; or if I have, like to Harvey Brown, who's playing first base tonight, I mean, like, you remember … hm, [PAUSE] where was I, like they say? I was nodding into first base …

MALANGA: … a question about language.

OLSON: No, I meant, not as of—just before I went off on this position I was going to create the diamond; we were gonna suddenly run the diamond, you know, the diamond? The diamond, the sutra diamond, the sutra dia— for the superstar. He's the first person that wrote to me the word. I never heard that word before.

MALANGA: Really?

---

32. Prynne writes of "the geochronology of land formation."

OLSON: Yeah, superstar, from Boston to where Andy is.[33] I never saw that word till I—till he used it, you know. It's that kind of impressive thing. It's like that comics that's now in the—is it in the British news? But you know that marvelous Caper Comics, is it, that's in the *Georgia Straight*?

LANSING: I haven't seen it.

OLSON: You haven't seen it? These grotesque big-footed creatures, these comic creatures? You mean to tell me that's local?

BROWN: Hedd comics.

OLSON: Hedd comics, yeah. God, jesus, I mean, this is just like Hedd comics: one step—if we let them in ...

BROWN: That friend of Kimball's from Lawrence ...

OLSON: From Lawrence? He does that?

BROWN: He puts them out in *Grist* magazine.[34]

OLSON: Isn't that too much? Is that right? It's only because I was thinking, reading the *Georgia Straight* the other night, in these forty-eight hours, "You know, I know this shit, like I know Jess Collins's revisions of Dick Tracy." You know, that color thing? That's the incunabula of the 20th century, right? I mean, it's absolutely monkish. You've seen it? The color Sunday edition.

MALANGA: Dr Berrigan had a whole section.[35]

OLSON: I tell you, Dr—if you—do you listen to us? Are you listening to us or no?

LANSING: Yes.

OLSON: You hear what we're talking about?

LANSING: You're talking about Dick Tracy.

OLSON: But done by Jess Collins.

LANSING: Jess Collins, yes.

OLSON: I think it's the—it'll be the incunabula of the century; it's so cool, you must admit.

MALANGA: Yeah, but he's in a very unfortunate position now, because the whole pop art thing is over and done with, and he's going to be totally crushed by everybody.

OLSON: Maybe; but maybe Dick Tracy, maybe the heroes—no, no, no, dear, Gerard, maybe the heroes of the present will retreat to the imitation they

33. Olson had been reading about the "Diamond Sutra" text in D.T. Suzuki's *Zen Buddhism* (New York: Anchor Books, 1956), p. 267. The reference to "Andy" (presumably Warhol) is obscure.
34. A comic strip by Harold Hedd was in the *Georgia Straight* about this time. The somewhat similar drawings in *Grist* were by S. Clay Wilson. Jess Collins's take-off on Dick Tracy is "Tricky Cad" in *Stolen Paper Review* 3 (Spring 1965), pp. 28–31.
35. Presumably a reference to Ted Berrigan, who did some cartoon strips.

are, anyhow. And both the comic and the photographic and the antiquarian figures behind each one of those kind of comics …

MALANGA: Only the connoisseurs would know what …

OLSON: I don't think so, but, mind you, I don't—to tell you the truth, as of this interview, may I?—what was your word just now?

MALANGA: He is in a very bad position.

OLSON: No, that's not what you were saying. That's not the point—what was your *verb*? I want to get that verb in, really, 'cos that's the whole thing.

MALANGA: I forgot.

OLSON: I have too. Isn't it stupid of me? You see, that's what's so nice. It's like that dipple-dopple bird in a bar. Poop! You're the one that starts. Once it gets some water, it has to take water. God, isn't it beautiful? I mean, that's after Newton, that's after Newton. [LAUGHS] Hear that as some Arkwright. We diddled that one in seventy billion light years, because that's what I discovered Black Mountain looked like. I discovered it under the mushroom, you know, like pun. I tell you the truth, like, I'm sorry, but if I could write rhyme as good as good pun is when you actually know it in that funny way that, if you do treat the sacred drugs sacredly, you discover that they really yield what everybody else finds (I hope they do) God does, love does, life does, they do. But, like, I mean, there isn't any—the problem is not of quality.

BROWN: I thought you said "life dust."

OLSON: Like what? No. Oh, that's good, but I didn't mean that, I didn't—like, that's mystical, referential, metaphorical.

MALANGA: If you try to recall your past and write down what you actually remember of some particular episode in it, do you discover how little you do remember?

OLSON: No, on the contrary, I rush immediately, because I know about ninety, more than ninety-nine percent. In fact, recently, for example, as of my own Irish rather than Swedish, curiously (because the language question takes care of the Swedish, happily)—but the Irish language question I don't know; I can't quite get a model. So maybe I'm wrong, but I read my friend Brown, who's here today, a letter I wrote to a woman in Stockholm, whom sort of, like, I fell in love with during this past year,[36] and so, finally, like, I tried to meet her in London, but that didn't work either; so I then wrote her a letter, as I told Brown, and it was in Icelandic, which is why she's been staying in Stockholm studying it all this year. And I've never had an answer; so on this side of the Atlantic … [LAUGHS]

MALANGA: You wrote the letter in Icelandic?

---

36. This is Inga Lovén, who conducted the "Interview in Gloucester, August 1968." See also *Selected Letters*, p. 430.

OLSON: Icelandic, yeah. Like, for example, in the last ten days I've been writing to Worcester to the woman who is so old ... John Wieners and I met her one night here in Gloucester at the Tavern to the surprise of both of us, and John was very comfortable about bringing me to meet this woman. She's from County Kerry, and she must be—when my parents were old I thought she was the same age; but she's still alive, and she's utterly beautiful, and I had a letter from her today in her hand she learnt in the convent. She must be ninety plus. May Sullivan. Mary Sullivan. The letter came itself today, and she says I don't really—but she told me a thing I never knew: my mother was raised by her grandmother, which puts ... Well, you see what I'm going to have to, if the tape and the whole Atlantic Union and the outer space control care to, like: the point was I wrote not so much to her but to Anna Shaughnessy, who was my teacher at high school, about this fact that I discovered that the O'Heyne family and the Shaughnessys are buried in the one instance of Saint, hm, like, Stephen, but it can't be; and the tombs are the same, and they date back to the 7th century.[37] Something just runs around that Irish question, right? If I could land this question of my mother, and Mary Ferrini's, Mary Shore's grandmother's name too, you know, this funny Hines thing. You know about that, the will-o'-the-wisp thing. I read the poetry in the *Celtic Twilight*, 1893. Mr Yeats's. And, you know, it's not bad, if you look at it from 1969. You look at this poetry that he's putting down in 1893, and you scratch your head a bit and think that Chanticleer and Pertelote did, you know, like, get together in the garden. I mean, you just think, "Oh shit, we've really scratched a few bit o' corn up on this side of them [SINGING] Allegheny Mountains, oh boy ..." Let's not leave here, forever. Oh no, no, let's not go West. Let's fuck off, and stay home, and not rush over there where that place is.

MALANGA: What are the techniques and attitudes that you require in order to create your poetry?

OLSON: Oh god, anything that I can find. What d'you mean? The yachts, the yachts, piazza, with the yachts' quarter flags flying, and some chap from the lighthouse cometh? I have no idea. I mean, the green grass and ...? I sound like Homer; I mean Winslow Homer. But I do also sound like the other, Onslow Wilmer, [LAUGHS] because really I'm sure he was talking about the same thing in some funny way as that word you're asking me to talk about, which is impossible. That's like a painting by that beautiful French, you know, that great cat that lived way into the present, Monet, Monet. He did that beautiful painting; you remember the thing sold recently to New York.[38] Like, "Come in, *Paris Review*, come in!" [LAUGHING] Paris, oh Paris. Oh, Paris. Oh, Pontius. Or the God of Three. Gaul is divided into

---

37. The long letter to Anna Shaughnessy of 29 March 1969 is included in *Selected Letters*, with the burial tombs mentioned on p. 418.
38. Claude Monet's *La Terrasse à Sainte-Adresse* had been bought by the Metropolitan Museum of Art, New York, in December 1967.

three. [SINGS] Clark is divided into three.[39] There are five rivers to Paradise, five rivers to Paradise.

MALANGA: [PAUSE] Are objectivity and directness very significant principles for your poetry?

OLSON: Well, that we got to do over, just for the efflorescence of it, man. I wouldn't want to lose that again for no money. [LAUGHS] If you don't do that again the same way, Gerard, we'll send …

MALANGA: Are objectivity and directness very significant principles for your poetry?

OLSON: I shouldn't think so. As a matter of fact, I would think quite the opposite: that I'm the most devious, non-objective, plural, subjective son-of-a-bitch this side of the wind. In fact, to tell you the truth, I can confess it all now. [LAUGHS] If you looked for me, I wasn't there … like, bang bang bang! Jesus, that's what's so, like, it's much more than mystical; it's simply, like, not mystical; it's just … swoo!

MALANGA: Could you explain …?

OLSON: You go on with that! Really, I could have finished that in seven stanzas, I mean, not in seven stanzas but in seven choruses, yes, and stesichoruses too. One stesichorus, then a chorus, then a stesichorus then a [LAUGHS]— then we just have horses prancing, ah-ah! And that architrave …

LANSING: … Stalking horse of Tennessee—that horse really gets there.

OLSON: Yeah, that's right. Completely. I know, but that's like that guy who photographed for the man whom he's using today, that marvelous primary primitive, Eadweard. Did you see the one I have, his photographs of an elephant walking in the bedroom? You know the guy I mean? The first man who used motion …[40]

BROWN: I'll have to look at it again.

MALANGA: Could you explain the degrees of consciousness or unconsciousness—?

OLSON: [LAUGHS] Well, mostly, like, that's been my drag, and I don't think I've kicked it yet and I'm unconscious. What did he say: "unconscious"? Sounds like—I mean, I'm in a hell of a trap, Gerard.

MALANGA: The question was: Could you explain the degrees of consciousness or unconsciousness with which …?

OLSON: But the way he said it, like. [LAUGHS] I don't know.

MALANGA: Do you write consciously or do you write unconsciously?

---

39. Tom Clark was currently poetry editor of the *Paris Review*. However, there is no way of being sure that Jack Clarke is not being referred to here.
40. Olson owned a reproduction of Eadweard Muybridge's *Animal Locomotion*. The man he photographed for was the painter Thomas Eakins (1844–1916).

OLSON: I write—I really wouldn't even know how, I mean, I wouldn't know, like, and if I could be responsible for … If I didn't know as much as what else I do, like, I'd talk about this; but, I mean, it's so, like, radical that it's not even news.

MALANGA: John Wieners on the telephone asked me to ask you, quote, "To what descent do you participate regarding your forebears in literature?"

OLSON: How about that? Just as I was just saying, I complained about Mr …

BROWN: Could I hear that again, would you mind?

MALANGA: John Wieners asked me to ask you, quote, "To what descent do you participate regarding your forebears in literature?"

OLSON: [PAUSE] I'm off Pleiades. It's pretty beautiful, hm. Said the right way. That's the first question that's like the plum or the lemon or the orange on the vice machine. [LAUGHS] O Johnny, O Johnny, you've done it again. I agree entirely. Yeah, what do you want me to do? Talks like a slot machine. I would pay off, hm, plunge plunge plunge, no kidding, because that's the only answer to that kind of a question. To tell you the truth, it's so sexual that it's … uh?

LANSING: "Descent"?

OLSON: Yeah, absolutely. And it's so sexual. It is, between you and me, like. So, Johnny, oh Johnny. [LAUGHS] Excerpt. Cut it off, like … I was really playing with English in a pub. I was playing it in Dorchester. You remember I told you about those slot machines. I'd play alone, like an American, because they wouldn't put money in. So here I was, you know the way you hit when there's enough money. I mean, I never—I dreamt—I thought I'd split in my middle being in Dorchester, you know, like, Dorset, in the busiest brightest bar in town. And I don't mean to put down a province; I mean, look, a very nice sort of a normal old-fashioned human universe bar. I'm staying there: this is the Antelope Hotel. All the goddamn hotels in England are now owned by the breweries, and they're a filthy bunch of big corporates, like BMC, and the thing he belongs to, whatever he belongs— MBC [LAUGHS] from the Beatles; he may be a Beatle, who knows? Who knows? He's a Beatle.

MALANGA: Are there recordings on that label?

OLSON: I know. I suspect. Because I'm a rolling stone myself. I go from pomery to pomery, to pomery, to pomery. That's an in-joke in Liverpool. [LAUGHS]

MALANGA: What is your personal aim about what you want to attain and not about the reason for your existence?

OLSON: Oh, wow. Oh god, say that again.

MALANGA: What is your personal aim about what you want to attain and not about the reason for your existence?

OLSON: Yeah, O.K. I'll let the question be the answer. I beg—I special plead, beg off, ask forgiveness. Propose the—propose the answer.

MALANGA: I don't know. That's why I'm asking you the question.

OLSON: That develops like quote Gerard. I mean, you're just my interviewer. [LAUGHS]

MALANGA: [PAUSE] Why is it that a poem will produce different impressions on people of different levels?

OLSON: [LAUGHING] Because of the vulgarity of all classes in the present. And I said "all classes." Hm, I never thought I could be the ultimate—I didn't know there was a snob beyond snobs! Right? It's new. Send a cable, please, to Jack Clarke, saying, "Enter in the Joyce file," I mean the Blake file. Listen to that, wow! Jesus. Freud, you son-of-a-bitch. Isn't it terrible, you can't beat the fucking …

MALANGA: Why is it that people of—?

OLSON: AUGHHHHHH!!!!! …[41] I mean, it's absolutely like King Kong, and doodledy doodledy. How can you get out of one into the other, and keep it constant? How do you do it? I know you son-of-a-bitch, you've got some insight here. You got some insight here. Yes, you do: the way you're talking down on the plantation to this fellow here. I tell you, man, with all the cotton I've baled up that fucking river and draw down all my interest in Cincinatti.

MALANGA: Do you feel that before the time comes when you will be able to write what you want to be written …?

OLSON: Oo-oo. What? I'm already too old to have even arrived at that station, now I got to do something new? something unheard of? I went and blew my time. I didn't earn and spend it; I blew it. So now I gotta blumph blumph? What are you asking me? I ain't got no time. What are you talking about? Read that, really read it, for anybody that's interested, that question again.

MALANGA: Do you feel that, before the time comes when you will be able to write what you want to be written, you must know what it is?

OLSON: Oh, wow, oh I hear you. That's like school; that's instruction. Yeah, I think it's like instruction. I don't think it relates. I mean, it's three parts, sort of. It's like, you know, the beginning, the middle, and the end, that discourse, that syntax question, if you'll allow me to say so, Gerard. It's terribly complicated. It's a devil, and you know it. I mean, how many times has this happened? This is the first time in my kitchen in a sense we've been able to sit here as we often have and to your deadly—that nightshade that night I really still—some day I will somehow or other manage to have excused myself. That poor man. You remember that night: there were three of us sat here doodling doddling through the night, the middles of the time

---

41. Olson finally expresses exasperation at the constraints of the questioning. He goes on to adopt a Southern plantation owner's accent.

of night, which nobody mentions at all, like the torchless bearers running around in the dark, I mean, woowawoowawoo, old sympathetic us. I mean, what the hell are we getting out of this? Right? I mean, like, bing bing bing! We ought to treat this as in sort of a negative, right? Now that I've been ...

MALANGA: How can a poet learn to feel more if he lives so much in his head?

OLSON: Oh man, but, I mean, you know, that's been the, like, the bearing. And I hope it's not you, but I hope you're representing—like Harry Martin was the devil's advocate once. All these questions really have all the leading errors and none of the relevant ... I mean, if there's anything I did that's interesting, then it ought to be interesting; otherwise, it's a waste of time.

LANSING: Maybe it's specifically a core element ...

OLSON: Yeah, it is, it is. But I don't think it's Gerard's. I think he's trying to get a modicum, or some one of those fucking middles, out of it, to position from. And this question—but, you know, the Berrigan question generally speaking is—it's like that Canadian broadcaster saying, in 1963, "What do you think about imagism in 1913," right? I just read about it, like, I just read about Amy Lowell the other night. [HAMMERING OBLITERATES GENERAL DISCUSSION] We can go over this question, like, a million times, because this is the kind of tomato catsup question. Tomato catsup? Yeah, tomato juice it's called today. But I mean, like the U.S. Banana Company, the UBC of them all, the Columbia Corp of Agigry.[42] All right? I mean, the whole obvious shot. The greed is so completely food that the poor things are just—I mean, I can't contribute to Biafra or, in fact, my darling cat that edits *Georgia Straight* in Vancouver, because I don't believe in colonials, as you know I don't, colonial English: I think they're well off because of that Empire, whatever they plead, or whatever ease with which they become radical, [SLAPS TABLE] including the Swedes and English and the Canadians, at least. And they're our people: we're Northern peoples; and there's a certain power, palearctic power or something that just has to dominate this foul civilization until sort of the ice melts or whatever. Like, literally speaking, it's getting clear now what we're waiting for is the ice to melt.

LANSING: It's a Tiny Tim song: "The icecaps are melting ..."

OLSON: Aw, god love him, is it really? Tiny Tim. You mean my nephew Tiny, my friend, down there just west of Asheville? Tiny Tim? My god, don't I love him! I haven't heard or seen from him for years. Did he say that? You see what I mean: everything's all over right the Blue Mountain.

LANSING: [SINGING] "The icecaps are melting. I'm waiting for ..."

OLSON: Isn't that beautiful! [LAUGHS]

MALANGA: How can a poet tell whether he has established something for himself that will take him further in his work?

42. "Agigry" is transcribed as heard on the tape. The meaning is obscure. Olson was perhaps thinking of the Columbia Corporation of Agronomy, located in Maryland.

OLSON: Belief. And I don't know. Like, that's the only thing; and what it is is so timorous wee speaking, whatever; but, I mean, I don't know what it is. Belief; conviction; experience. It's the decision, which is the only decision I know is the suddenness with which the thing, like, or you or he, whatever it is, whatever the initial thing is, is so … the exact opposite of universal. May I say that, so this thing is clear? That's what's absolutely the whole fucking living thing of creation is that moment when you know what the hell to do, what you feel or do. But, then, this other thing, which is this—"intuition," as a matter of fact, Descartes calls it,[43] and doesn't make a mistake; because he calls the other thing "senses," and he says the other thing is "intuition"; and that's the bugger, ha-ha, that's the one which just, pkpkpkpk, goes so fucking fast you can't read and say it; and that's the one you've got to make your decision on, and that's the one which really fixes everything, like, whew. Anybody that can get those two things so that they're antonomic or something, is with it, that's all, obviously. That's it, isn't it? What's "antonomic" mean? Sounds … "Antonomic": let's try to remember that tomorrow. Send me a note, send me a note.

MALANGA: Is it true that there is a definite rule regarding the writing of poetry that when a poet writes there will never be any necessity for him to disguise what he writes simply because he cannot avoid using exactly the same language in which he had learned to speak?

OLSON: So true, so completely true; and now so evident by either the law of persona or the law of psyche …

[REEL 4]

OLSON: Please send two dozen, you know, or bring a lot up. Bring a lot up. Or it sounds like a province. I don't know, like …

MALANGA: … Well, potato is a root.

OLSON: Course it is: great tuber. Have you not read Mr Sauer on tuber?

[GAP]

OLSON: You can't see with the lights, but I think it's nice out. Just don't mind. I just feel as though it's fun, fun to be here. It turns into a session, right? You would feel, enjoy the thing? [INAUDIBLE VOICE] That's the thing, how would we know, like, that's the?—god love my life, in that sense, that the only way to have a session is if you can …

MALANGA: … Socializing with Isabel García Lorca. Every time I call the house, her father answers and I say it's Gerard Malanga, I keep on thinking that they are thinking it's Gerard Potato.

OLSON: [LAUGHING] And in Spanish, it's "potato" in Spanish? What about in Italian?

MALANGA: It has no meaning.

43. Descartes is quoted to this effect by Whitehead in *Process and Reality*, pp. 66–67, 461.

OLSON: Oh, isn't it marvelous? [LAUGHS] I bet you de Santillana is in the same situation, by the way.

MALANGA: Malanga is Neapolitan, so the Spanish were in Naples at one time. That would explain it.

OLSON: Well that's exactly ... If you know de Santillana, he's—and Jorge Dias, the philosopher—there's two of them. And the Marq—you talk about Pierre Falaise but the Marqués de Giorgio Diaz de Santillana is one of my best friends by Ruth Yorck. [LAUGHS] Could dust that one as though I didn't even try, right? I mean, wow, could she do that! Wasn't that night that she passed Mussolini-isms with Hammond one of the—I really have—I've understood what the boys used to say about her in the thirties, in the dirties.

MALANGA: Did you know Maxine? Maxine de la Boehme?

OLSON: No, that's Panna's ... I take it by induction from ... but not one step removed, right? I mean, how many? I mean, whistoo! Speed, astumrip! That's some stumit stummy nummy metric ... zumbrumm. We got to have this. We got to have this. This is the radical life that we're on.

MALANGA: Is one of the ways by which contemporary poetry has tried to escape the rhetorical, the abstract, the moralizing is to concentrate its attention upon trivial or commonplace objects?

OLSON [LAUGHING]: I think you're an agent of a foreign power, Malanga. I've never heard such a series of questions, even from the FBI or from the Tzarist police himself: never in all my life, in court or in secret, have I known such utter a-questions. Who wrote thees, did you? If so, leef my house. [LAUGHS] If not, then, please, own up the ownership. Mr Malanga, Señor Malanga, I will expose you to your nation. I will send you back.

MALANGA: I expose myself.

OLSON: I will send you back to Malaga and say, "Raise more raisins. Don't bother with anything else. Raisins is good. Grapes are good." Those are dry questions. I would like you to repeat that raisin of a question once more, so that the whole world via the *Paris Review*, which is the Gorgon or Medusa instead of the pediment of the present, speaks with a comic mask, on all large cities in Western and Eastern world, Panatche included, and publishing in Punjab, also Halav.[44]

MALANGA: Do you find it useful to collect opinions of friends about your work? Do you feel this often helps in discovering points ...

OLSON: Oh yeah, oh yeah.

MALANGA: ... to improve your work that you would normally not discover on your own?

OLSON: Yeah, if I only got any, if I only got any. [LAUGHS] But don't you think I'm looking for some. You mean, my "friends": that's what I was talking

44. Panatche and Halav do not appear in gazetteers.

about, about them five people, they never say anything that satis—that's not enough, like, they don't say enough. At which point, like, today's people, I'm appealing to the audience, "Remember, remember. I'm here." [PAUSE] That didn't get—like rubber plantations: don't you come near. [LAUGHS] That didn't—you didn't hear what I was doing, did you? Did you?

BROWN: Yeah.

OLSON: Did you? Did I make out like Emperor Jones? I don't mean LeRoi, but Mr O'Neill. Did I make that roll? Did I make that roll rocking through the Lescanderdand and the Haiti forest? Wasn't it Haiti, all spooked down, that he did his—wasn't that where Emperor Jones was, Haiti?

BROWN: Yeah.

OLSON: Yeah, that's right. Wasn't he spooked? I'm spooked, I'm spooked on Main Street. [LAUGHS] I think I'll move that one after Mr Quine's letter today.[45] Maybe if you saw that, Descartes. How about that? Gee, that's really just ... That's your friend that you said went out of the film. Mercutio; that's patrician.

MALANGA: Yes.

OLSON: Very much, right? And this is the old drag-ass, if he'd stop playing Mab at the end of his string, he'd be all right.[46] Hey, Jeremy, are you listening? I'm broadcasting to your island, and loving what you gave me today as of my—what?—island.

MALANGA: Do you feel that poets can create and live with different personalities without them clashing, and if these personalities have no external manifestation, do they exist internally all the same?

OLSON: I don't know, because I lived with demons who didn't pronounce themselves sane. I don't know. That's a funny question. That's almost a time, present-day question; it's not a five-year question. I mean, it has nothing to do with demons or troubled real people or dead serious, you know, a whole series of kinds of human beings. It won't last very long because the whole thing's been genred, if I may use that word; and I mean it the other way from what I used it as of Ann Charters and, like, hopefully yourself today.[47] I wouldn't, but, I mean, funny non—may I?—no, genred, like gen-red. Genred: I mean like it would be a color next year. No, that's too easy. But I'm thinking of Barnett Newman, as a matter of fact, some protest against that kind of art.

LANSING: There's only one mad Portuguese poet wrote in five personalities utterly separate from one another. He was able to express ...

45. Olson equates Prynne and Willard Quine, professor of philosophy at Harvard, whom Prynne had mentioned in his review, saying that Olson's poem "Stiffening, in the Master Founder's Wills" (1.128) puts Descartes "into the role of a minor mystagogue, the Willard Quine of Ultima Thule."
46. The context is not clear, but presumably Olson is speaking of himself.
47. Olson's previous uses of the neologism "genred" are not known.

OLSON: But equally I read the first act, scene of *Henry IV, Part 1,* and Mr Shakespeare knocks those three or four—you know, the difference between those three men, how like is old Rabelais or nobody. I couldn't believe it. I said, "That's absolutely ..." This is all I've been doing, as I said to you, this winter is reading poets whom I have always loved sort of thing, that's all, having some fun. And, my god, I read this thing for breakfast. I mean, you can't imagine that within two pages how he's got the Glendower and Hotspur—I mean, curiously enough as of that silly conversation, he's got everybody placed. [LAUGHTER] You, me, him. You haven't got it yet what you did, I suppose you know that. You're the only man knew it ahead of time. Do you know I sat here the other night telling him I thought all the time I thought Glover did it? Did you hear this? Did he tell you this? Did I tell you?

BROWN: No, this came while we were still here.

OLSON: That was while we were here? No. Did it—did that come as a confession when you were still here? That all the time I thought Glover did it?

BROWN: Yes.

OLSON: Wow, wasn't that crazy? That's really a beautiful case of mistaken identity, because the person who did it heard everything I'd say to the person whom I thought did it. I mean, that's my dream if somebody would write to me and answer what you just said a couple of questions back. Ah ah, oh boy, wouldn't I love to hear that! Not from some gossipy reason. As a matter of fact, under the mushroom I can remember some sensation of that, and realizing now gossip is tale. And I believe it, like, I mean it's so like—that's the other thing, like. And it's so good that I now pay aught for it, like, that's all, 'cos row-tay-wow-tchee. I'm not being, like, suggestive or cute. I'm talking narra—I mean, story, tale, like, at the moment.

MALANGA: Do you feel that by taking drugs a poet, any poet, yourself for instance, is put in touch with higher senses while writing?

OLSON: No, not while writing. But certainly gets an enormous confirmation; like my wife wrote, I discovered after her death, a note that she read Whitehead, which is *Process and Reality,* for confirmation or corroboration, whichever word it was. But the point was here I am trying to read the fucking book. Like, if poetry doesn't exist to completely set right everything that's wrong I don't think it has an inch to stand on. And it should be known to those who know that action; therefore, poetry should be—we used to call it the arsis of the verses? No, but the rise of the, you know, that dumb thing, it's in English is reversed. But I mean like atah-tah-tahtahtatatatata: some simple plateau plane, one great motion of, if I may steal, like, first overtone, to trail from first overtone, then overtone. Unheard overtone, right? One ... tstshh. F sharp. F sharp. I've been talking to some musicians since, you know, like Jack Clarke. You remember that night we did that thing, god wasn't that wonderful! Without reference to what you'd been snotty to me in the restaurant about as a musician, and that damn thing in there. I'll never forgive you for that, you shit. Aw, come on, ay-hey, Lansing. Well, I know you can play a better piano than I. And I mean it. You should hear mine. [LAUGHS]

MALANGA: What constitutes a school of poetry?

OLSON: Oh god, love you, you're like the induction PhD in History. If it weren't for him Manhattan wouldn't exist. [LAUGHS] Manhattan wouldn't exist, believe me. He asks these questions of, like, the Fargoes.[48] "Yessir! I feel like you've been under this deport—dey might crush me if dey stepped too hard." Black Wells and his wife, kids in there: [SHOUTS] "Yous down dah." "We down here, man, don't bother us, right? You got big boss all out. We just live in here, down at bottom of the stairs. [RAPS ON TABLE] Stop-you-big-mouth is up there." [LAUGHS] Ever since you told me that thing, I've been dreaming this sonata or something, or the synoptic gospel. [LAUGHS] Whatever we can do to help the cause along. [LAUGHS]

MALANGA: Well, what constitutes a school of poetry?

OLSON: Double change. Like the man said: "What does not"[49] is the new boobeclebobedeboobecleboo. I mean, not even that, like. Of course, like, of course, of course, of course. Suddenly I break through the curtains and say, "Of course, of course, that's the point, of course it is. It is, yes, indeed, yes, that's the whole point." [LAUGHTER] Carry on. Destroy films. Take another step, giant step backward. [LAUGHS] Malaga. Malaga, that's it. Malaga. Gerard de Malaga. Take a right step backwards. Now ask me some decent questions.

MALANGA: Is the function of a literary movement ...?

OLSON: That sounds dirty as hell. We can take that to the Supreme Court. [LAUGHS] Oh yeah, I heard that. Go ahead, to continue without repeating it. Yeah, I heard you.

MALANGA: Is the function of a literary movement ...?

OLSON: He's already conditioned. It's like a reflex. His name is Maslow. [LAUGHS] Go ahead, it's like the chain of being, it's O.K. Atlantis will arise again. Go ahead. He's got wit, this boy. He keeps good company. Women have taught him wit. Nobody else. Not men. But women have taught him wit. Go ahead, doll.

MALANGA: Is the function of a literary movement primarily to secure publication of the good work of poets connected with that movement, or does a literary movement or school present a different function or advantage?

OLSON: I should hope to either—because that isn't a thing has a thing to do with either. That's a dumb—that's a dumb sort of blotchistorical question, if I may say so, and a typical sort of a Columbia 20th century question. I don't think it's very—is it at all interesting? We can blast that from both sides of

48. Olson proceeds to improvise on some incident involving Wells Fargo & Company.
49. Olson is quoting the first line of his poem "The Kingfishers."

the deep native tunnel called the Atlantic Ocean. (Give me a match and I'll be made. We got no more? I got a box but it doesn't ring. Yes, it does.)

MALANGA: A school is a place where one can learn something. Can a school lose by giving away its knowledge?

OLSON: Oh boy, that's beautiful. That's a lovely question. Read it again, 'cos it's really such a lovely question. It's like a koan; it's a pure koan.

MALANGA: A school is a place where one can learn something. Can a school lose by giving away its knowledge?

OLSON: Right. Jesus, god. I feel—if you don't mind, you stabs me right through the solar plexus. [LAUGHS] As the pantheon of Black Mountain or the Pharaoh of the exile, I say, like, that was the whole conundrum, wasn't it? So why did I do it to 'em? Why would anybody do it? We all went on to other fields, other Bull Runs, on the insight I had. It's a marvelous question, though, something like Suzuki or something: do you stick your sword in your belly or do you, like, use the top side of your head? I mean, it's a marvelous question.

LANSING: Post-exile.

OLSON: It is. And it's very exciting. In fact, it's the most exciting question I think really you've asked tonight, because it raises that whole sort of—no longer a dilemma at all, may I say? No longer absolutely that bullshit, but just an absolute ... Wow, that's a beautiful question, like it's tck-tck-tck. O.K. Do it again, it's so nice really; but I mean really it's like a song, like when I put the two quarters in your hand, it's the same, just these two, and bejesus if she ain't eleven, if I'm not mistaken, yeah? Nine ten eleven here, old P.R., P.R., no longer longer P.O., nor P.A. either.[50]

MALANGA: Would you say Black Mountain College's sole existence depended on the part of those artists who took part in the building of it?

OLSON: Oh no. I think in fact the man who built it, wonderfully enough, was not an artist at all. He was an American, a very, very *rara avis* American from Charleston.

MALANGA: A what American?

OLSON: A rare bird, *rara avis*, a rare bird like Audupon—Audubon American: sounds as though you got to translate it now into the pods or the seeds that wear off and make other trees, right? So—what did I say? Not Audupon? Audupon, right, like two twin maples or any other form of seed, Audupon American, was John Lee Rice,[51] who went to school at, like, Bell Buckle, Tennessee, to two men there, one who ran and who taught, and then he went to Rhodes scholarship; and then he was the same as, like, his brother-in-law, who, before the man who was the head of Manhattan Project, was the head of the Institute of Advanced Studies, Frank Aydelotte; and, like,

50. This play on initials remains cryptic.
51. Olson has given John Andrew Rice, the founder of Black Mountain College, a new middle name, perhaps thinking of the first facility used by the college, Robert E. Lee Hall.

John Rice, whom I'm talking about, from Charleston, South Carolina, which sounds awfully much like Vietnam to me; I mean, that's where we once had watery crops, and we did; we raised watery crops like the great waterish land of Vietnam. I mean, the great phalanges of all earth is as osmotic as we, you know, the rrlrrlrr, if you can just enter that rigmarole.

LANSING: Abyss.

OLSON: Hm. Abyss is in hell right here, I mean, shit, I mean, that's me, like that marvelous—I so love that beautiful Stefansson, because he and I represent to me the most—I mean, when I was a kid he used to eat at Romany Marie's, which was a block from when I was a boho—whatever they call the thing now, and today you wouldn't say what was a boho in the Village. I was a propo in the Village. [LAUGHS] I was the core before the apple. I was the Adam before the core. I was the Eve—I mean, I was the Garden; I was the Eden; I was the snake; I was the God. How many ways can you get behind the apple core? Dah lead! Oowoowoo, dat didn't do—I got nothin' to do wid dat. I ain't got no niggers actually talk, no? Dat talk: take it away. I'm just not livin', that's all. I ain't just have that, like, proximity.

MALANGA: Is a school of poetry necessary in order to gain attention for a group of poets' work or is it a handicap?

OLSON: Oh, I don't think it's relevant. If there was a school, good for it. And if it wasn't and I don't know where any of us, like—if that question is still connected to Black Mountain, like, that was a—really, you know, I mean …

MALANGA: I'm talking about a school of poetry in terms of a movement or a group of poets.

OLSON: All right, so name 'em, and to—I don't think so, I think it's an error of *peinture*. Poets have no reason to be in a quoroth.[52] If they do, it's some marvelous sort of ITT thing or interworld aviation. I mean, it's a very great difference between the speed question of music and poetry as against that fucking goddamn—and don't you think I don't love it, but I suppose, like Bill Williams, I wish I'd been a painter, I wish I could have painted or something. But it doesn't matter, fuck it. It's bullshit, it's not interesting. I mean, sculpture, like that dumb thing, this is the Civil War veterans, this is gray in the light … uh-ru-de-uh.

MALANGA: Do you see the prospect of a definitive practical guide in the form of an anthology of the Black Mountain School of Poets?

OLSON: Yeah, well, I certainly don't. And if the fuckers don't get along down the trail, I'll kick their fucking asses for them. [LAUGHTER] I'm an old, like, a train man from the woods, and if the goddamn stuff doesn't come down the trail to my satisfaction, until I'm beaten I'm still boss!

MALANGA: When I say "Malanga" it is an ornamented "Malanga," made to look what he is not. I attribute to him many things he does not possess. I do know his weaknesses.

52. This appears to be a neologism based on "quorum."

OLSON: Right.

MALANGA: The condition of growth of real "I's" is to get rid of "Malanga" not to be identified with him.

OLSON: Right.

MALANGA: In saying this, would you say that *your* life is a by-product that is existing without you?

OLSON [LAUGHING]: That's mad! What are you, a yo-yo? Speak for yourself, doll. I mean, jesus, you beg me to come in from Abbey Road and all the way from my ship, and that's a hell of a boom-boom. I mean, we're just back to the whole landing on the barren coasts of North America. Fantastic what you ... I think for the audience of Europe, because this is like—this is one of them bardic questions that don't come off any—like, come too often—there's nobody offers them; it isn't a question of their coming off, nobody offers them. This is a very palladic question, my dear, altogether ... Audiences here or out of—I don't give a goddamn, but listen to this man's very, very, like, bare—like how they say—what's that story when the joke is at the end, it's not "stray dog"? or "dead dog"?—what do you call that sort of boom the ending, like? Listen to what he's doing. O.K.

LANSING: What's that end, "by-product"?

OLSON: By-product. By-product.

MALANGA: Would you say your life is a by-product that is existing without you?

OLSON: Yeah, go ahead, read the whole question, because, like, that's the dirty end. [LAUGHS] Say it again. Read that ...

MALANGA: When I say "Malanga" ...

OLSON: No, say the ending, if you like.

MALANGA: Say the ending again?

OLSON: Yeah.

MALANGA: Would you say that your life is a by-product and is existing without you?

OLSON: [PAUSE] Read the beginning, please, at great sleep. Read the first section of the question as long as you possibly can, while I unbutton my shoes. [LAUGHTER] I mean, that's like asking Pharaoh to get back in the tomb. I don't know what the fuck he wants. Aw, come on, Amenhotep number one, anyhow, if not Zosima the first! But, like, do that whole thing from start to scratch.

MALANGA: Really?

OLSON: Please. That's a whoppy. That's a whoppy. We call it a whoppy. That's a new form of something.

MALANGA: When I say "Malanga" it is an ornamented "Malanga"—

OLSON: Right.

MALANGA: —made to look like he is not.

OLSON: Right.

MALANGA: I attribute to him many things he does not possess, and I know his weaknesses.

OLSON: Right.

MALANGA: The condition of growth of real quote "I's" unquote is to get rid of "Malanga"—

OLSON: Is that "eyes," e-y-e-s?

MALANGA: No, "I's."

OLSON: Right.

MALANGA: —is to get rid of "Malanga," not to be identified with him. Would you say that your life [LAUGHTER] is a by-product that is existing without you?

OLSON: No, I'm afraid you got a problem, Malanga. [LAUGHS] A very normal problem. And you will take care of it, I hope. I hope. At one point, much earlier in this tape—sounds good now, sounds like Hawaiian: we can make anything out of this tapoo. I said "tapoo." [LAUGHS]

LANSING: It's a bit like "pumpkin" …

OLSON: It's only shredded wheat.

MALANGA: What do you spend your money on?

OLSON: Oh, wow, jesus, on anything … poor citizen anywhere trying it. In fact, to tell you the truth, with credit like mine, I don't pay my bills. [LAUGHS] But they'll get you in the end, I'm sure. So I've just come back from W-h-o-c-m-e-s.[53] [LAUGHS] Like, christ, we really ought to do something; we'll go out and tear the town apart, even if we can't eat, let's fuck the place tonight, and dump her in the ocean. Let's pull a real buzzah. Do we deserve something! But this is crazy really. It's all right. I mean, I hope. Usual interfering by not being here, the idiots.

MALANGA: Could you read a poem for me?

OLSON: Yes. Oh, just that? Mm. "Maximus, to himself" [I.52] Isn't it nice the way that guy goes direct to "Maximus, at the Harbor" [II.70], which is, like, happily another poem to this, and equally weak, I think, because I believe that in the present the subjective is so strong that, if you aren't willing to treat it as a weakness, you won't get anywhere. And I think the trouble with the social revolution of the subjective is simply that it isn't willing to admit, except in some sort of associatal term, the suffering that goes with it. I'm talking about holy living and holy dying or something like that. And I just deliberately have fallen on my face, and, like, I love Prynne for being hooked

53. This word, although spelled out by Olson, is at present not elucidated.

in a sense by, not "Of the Parsonses" [11.63], which is the positive poem that he mentions, but as of "Maximus, at the Harbor," which, you see, is a sucker poem, if I may tell the world. And the people who really get caught by that poem are being caught on my treadle, which is a form of *d'avance*. But, like, I hear you, boo. I mean, you don't think I put it in there without meaning that I should comb my hair with every one of them things, uh? Otherwise, what's the excuse for a comb? I mean, I'm only giving you value in that devaluated sense, the depression with which we exist at all. But that's a part of it too, goddamn the present, because it doesn't understand that the bum trip or bad trip is where there's as much to be found as [   ].⁵⁴ And if we don't get that straight, we ain't got but ninety-eight percent of everything, and that's today not worth a piece of shit, because if you don't get a hundred today—that's what I meant by everything—you're just killing time. That's all right, uh?

LANSING: Yeah.

OLSON: And I think this poem, which Gerard has, is like a soliloquy. And in the newest book, I have another, which is "Maximus, at the Harbor," and it's deliberate: it's a soliloquy, and it ends *Book IV*, and that's the end of that shit, if I may excuse, a *croix de grâce*, my crossing myself left, right, and all over the picture, then I can so claim. I mean, it's that big question whether you ever can. In fact, you can't, so that's clear, that's not an embarrassment; but I mean one wants to talk about one's—like, you get stuck with this fucking thing. I wrote this poem, I mean "Maximus, to himself," and it has the lesion of talking about myself, which I permit myself at this one point at all seams—and it's only two I've written so far—do you permit yourself (if I understand the second half of your card from Boston), do you permit yourself to let the leak in. This is one and that's the other, and that's all. Otherwise, the boundaries have to be as tight as our structural—our "moral structures." And I think you hear that; I believe you do. Absolutely. It's a beautiful sort of a fucking sending: this minister, Ed Dorn tells me today, trained minister, who's the finest scholar I know on the other side of the Atlantic Ocean. But he was trained as a minister, isn't it marvelous? So, today, like, he asked me, hm … I can read this, I hope. And it's sort of, like … The first sentence, which is so boring, I mean:

> I have had to learn the simplest things last.

It's so true that—I guess if I axe it … I mean, it's so bad don't ever have anything to do with it. It's one of them truths that, if you can avoid, for god's sake avoid, because I can assure you, like, fifteen years later, don't listen to me. [LAUGHS] "I have had to learn the simplest things last." I mean, I told Harvey Brown's wife today, "I'm still only catching up with—as a matter of fact, I've gone all to pieces backwards, because the simplest is going to occur tomorrow. What am I going to do?" [LAUGHS]

> Which made for difficulties.

54. A French-sounding phrase ("*en mont pas im en me wont*") resists elucidation.

Hm-m.

Even at sea ...

Well, this is now interesting. I mean, that's where I was really a dope. I mean, I was with men who moved in their environment, and I was from another environment. And I don't mind. I told you that story of being in a restaurant in Gloucester this week, and feeling every bit of the movement of my position. But, jesus christ, you can imagine how little I feel that any more: the motion of my position. Will you put that down? That's what I've been looking for for that gravity question, or the one that we got that night on Musa.[55] What did I say?

MALANGA: "The motion of my position."

OLSON: You know what it's called? "Impetus," by Mr Whitehead. I found it, by the way, like, in Jung? It doesn't seem possible.[56] "The motion of my position." Ah, isn't that beautiful? Gee. What's the date? 20th? No. 10th, 11th?

MALANGA: Fifteenth.

OLSON: Fifteenth. A Roman! In fact, he's a Roman, this son-of-a-bitch. I feel as though I should do this all in caps. "AS TO." He is a fucking Roman. I bet you he'll turn out—I bet you when I tell him where he did come from, and all the fucking history of his family, which is simply his own futura—like, we speak in the Tarot, we either do a fato or a futura. *Esta lang human*, hm? *Italienne le plus humain de France et German et Inglese et American et Italienne et Sebastian.* And I don't mean all of us. [LAUGHS] "I have had to learn the simplest things / last. Which made for difficulties. / Even at sea I was slow, to get the land—to get the hand out, yeah [LAUGHS] or to cross / a wet deck. / The sea was ..." This is boring. I mean, this cat today, like he say: "He was pretty wary in that first book of the sea, what?" Oh, what a gracious statement! "At the same time, very often fulsome." But this is where I'll be, like, very wary. Or I can read a new poem! May I? Like, a brand new poem—fuck this thing—on this same subject. Just one minute, then I'll go on, then I'll go on. [GETS MANUSCRIPT] My god, yeah. I don't think I ... I've failed her; I don't think I can read it: "Her st—." Hm, I'm talking about the same thing—and I'll come back to this slowness on the deck—the same ship, same vessel, same sea; like, any place today where there's action, god help us. "Her stern like a box, / the Hor—the Doris Hawes—the Horace Dawes / [LAUGHS] waddled / off Browns, out of the off-shore westerly until, / after the lightning storm I thought / she'll never come back from the something / of the full North Atlantic itself ..."[57] It seems like the whole truth to me, that this beautiful little vessel, which, brrrrrrr, going to the eastward, you know, to get out of the storm, and I'm brrrrrrerrerr. There the

---

55. "Musa" is clear on the tape, but the reference is obscure, as is the "gravity question."
56. The word "impetus" is underlined in Olson's copy of *Process and Reality*, p. 472. The word is not listed in the General Index to Jung's works. Presumably Olson is inscribing these phrases in Malanga's copy of *The Maximus Poems* (1960).
57. Butterick included this manuscript poem in *The Maximus Poems* (1983), p. 603.

lightning, berrberber. And I'm thinking as I wrote this poem, this—I just got so excited. I don't know whether it makes it, like; but you can hear the levin, I mean, the absolute pratfall, beluaaah! Will she ever get her stern out of the full North Atlantic in some way? Come on, come on, come on out of it! Don't be so big, you know, like. It's a beautiful, it's a big, it's the fourth— fifth book of that whole story, the *Iliad*, the *Iliad*, like they say. [LAUGHS] I was sitting in the Tavern, you know, and those kooks somehow they get stupid, you know, pah ...

LANSING: Read it, please.

OLSON: Yeah. "I was slow, to get the hand out ..." That's obvious. Also: "To cross / a wet deck. The sea was not, finally ..." That sounds awfully stupid: perfectly obviously not. "But even my trade ..." Hm. That's like when you asked me that question earlier: I got stuck. "I stood estranged ..." Woo-er. That's very clumsy. I couldn't make it at all. "... from that which was ..." Was quite close to me! And I don't care about being "delayed" that's a drag. And all that "argument": bullshit. No. No envy, I was thinking, of who "show daily / who do the world's / businesses / And who ..." Bullshit ... Now:

> I have made dialogues

(That's true.)

> I have discussed ancient texts

(To my pride!)

> and have thrown what light I could

I think that's a little bit special pleading; it's begging your sympathy. Please. But I'd thought, like, I'd change the syntax, but it would be O.K. Like: "I've discussed ancient texts; on some things have been original, innate, inertial, never to be forgotten. Fuck you. Can't do it again. Somebody can."

> and offered
> what pleasures
> doceat allows

Which is what, like, I'm stuck with. I mean, when he says "moral," oh my christ, I mean, I'm with him entirely. It's the one thing I marked: "moral structure of immediate knowledge." That's *doceat*. That's all it is, and never was a goddamn thing to it; and that's what's called "teachings." And either you do it, or you don't. And it's a wide-open choice. And I don't see why anybody would do it, because, my christ, I mean, it so both infines and confines your existence that you just have to have existence.

LANSING: There's no choice, is there?

OLSON: There is none; but I mean, like, talk about the horse on the track, what? What? The whole thing is there, right? And if you're stuck, you're affine; which I said to Bayliss, and he doesn't understand what I mean. Affine. It's a matter of attention, commission, report. Let those who do not know find out what "affine" means![58] I don't know what it means. But I know what it feels like that it does mean. And that's wha—absurd. Affine, affine, affine! But, I mean, isn't it crazy? That's all, and you boom boom! you shoot them, pssss! I drunk the mash swamp water. Yes, this is the filthy vulgarity, what he calls—what does he call it there? The "geo-." He's too much! Those words of his, those great by the way Novalis words. Do you realize how much Novalis is—? Like, the "curriculum Novalis." I'm going to write him a note, saying "Reverend Novalis" or "Le Comte de—" Who was Novalis? Yeah, a Hapsburg. I want to write a letter to Prynne.

LANSING: Novalis, the new birth.

OLSON: Right, right. Oh god, the doll. And he did it as an archetypal name like Ie,[59] you know. Again, may your askers or your questioners—or your own question asked who's Maximus? Who's Maximus? Who's Maximus? Who's Leo Africanus?

LANSING: ... Klingsor's fables ... in Klingsor's fables, you know, you work with ... [INAUDIBLE]

OLSON: Who says that?

LANSING: Novalis. The book came to me yesterday.[60]

OLSON: No kidding. My god, that's why he's post-Blake, see? Let Clarke hear that, not us; he needs it. I don't have it. But as I grew out those tales of the Alleghenies already, you know I have it. "Appalachian": you saw that beautiful thing in there; this is where he drags his—this is where his knowledge gets to all those as Europeans, whom I love, my beloved, my beloved former nation. And what I would wish I lived in today, simply because of the grace of life, which is still yours, my dear Europe, oh, as against this abusive, vulgar, cruel, remorseless, and useless country, the United States of America! May she perish in these five years, simply not because of any radical wish at all, but that she would get out of our way, and leave us alone, and leave things alone which she has harmed and harmed and harmed. And for what? For nothing. For something which she herself no longer values, and will buy her nothing. And immediately, redemptorily, we will all be in the same boat, with all the leaks of this filthy system, which has purchased all of our lives at its cost. Not really, thank god, god damn her soul, because she didn't have enough strength to win us. But, my god, when I think of two or three centuries which did play her game, whistled to her tune.

LANSING: There's no skipper.

OLSON: Well, I don't have any. I ain't got no skipper. I'm no skipper either. [PAUSE] I don't know, it's the greatest. It's like really is—when you used the

58. Olson saw the word "affine" on p. 74 and elsewhere in Hermann Weyl's *Philosophy of Mathematics and Natural Science* (Princeton: Princeton University Press, 1949), a constant companion during this time.

59. Pronounced on the tape "Eye-ee." The reference is uncertain.

60. Lansing has just received Novalis's novel *Henry von Ofterdingen* (New York: Ungar, 1964).

word "unconscious"—like, unconscious, like just what it sounds like: this country has been unconscious. And it's got to awake. That's my belief; and it's why I've spent so much time just, like, painting her dales and sails and seas, or something. I mean, you can't do anything but be the piper of a sleeping nation, of this order, which is enormous, so stupid. It's awake all the time; and it's never awake for a minute. It's the deadest sleep that ever was, to talk like Blake. Dadeda dadada dadad, dadeda dadeda dadeda.[61] Isn't it? It's the deadest sleep that ever was. I don't think Blake could have imagined it. I think today's poets can't imagine it. I think that if they permitted themselves, they have every right to imagine it. They have to imagine it. It's ridiculous. It's not an aggressive problem.

LANSING: Not regressive?

OLSON: Aggressive. It's not an aggressive problem. I beg, like, almost like somebody, before the Civil War, to say: "Oo, don't do it; it's not worth it, wave not the white flag but the whole cliff, the white cliff. Wave the white walls." Say, "Don't do it; it's just not worth it." 'Cos what's really what we're talking about tonight is already true. That's why I don't like these things. But I like 'em tonight, 'cos we can sit here and, like, chew the fat, to speak an old American dogshit thing. We're chewing the fat! I mean, if Harvey and Gerrit weren't here too, we wouldn't have any chance to chew the fat, or me sitting on one leg of a log like …[62]

[REEL 5]

OLSON: [LAUGHING] "… These exilic origins"—like Jewish separation— "are political facts of a high order"—especially in Babylon and Egypt, right?—"especially as they might seem to bind (but do not) the dispersed faunal and poetic realms of the two Atlantic seaboards."[63] I mean, a Winston Churchill should now discover why he was in his grave; I mean this is the great rhetoric that Troy brought to the realm of Britain, and the Celtic genius has presented, because now the Celtic genius belongs to the Norse realm where it ought always to have been. Like, where does the Hamitic belong to? Does it belong to Africa, like the Semitic belongs to Arabia? No. I think I won a bet once, a lotta money like. Egyptian was originally an Hamitic language which became Semitic? I'm asking you. I think I'm about right, and it would've paid off at the track, you know. I think Natufian was Hamitic, and through a long period before what I was referring to earlier, the kingdom—the two kingdoms. And then, I don't know like when, but I mean, the Memphite Theology seems to me the whole seam of time, because I believe that was written, if you like that kind of jive, that democratic political jive, at a point where there was a kind of a demotic condition in Egypt or some shit like where nobody had made this scene

---

61. Olson is singing the tune and rhythm of the march "Colonel Bogey."
62. Unfortunately, the tape ends here abruptly.
63. Olson is quoting Prynne's comments about the *Maximus Poems* having been published in Germany and London.

before, like in the USA, nobody made this scene before. We're not a fuckin' Mongol-Russo tent, we're an unoccupied nation of Indians who were killed by an occupying White force. We are a colony; and that's as true in mythology as India. Would you hear me there? That raises ...

LANSING: A colony of colonies, though.

OLSON: Ha-ha! I know, but, mind you, what's India, Dravidian?

LANSING: ... From Sicily, or from ...

OLSON: Okay, but mind you, hear the way it's got said today, it's got to be the dirtiest thing in the world. I don't know how it comes about that America becomes colonial, but America—to be American, you know what we're talkin' about, and it's not like he says, that "swerve." That's not a real swerve, what's done, that double. You unisex what I hear—Saint Angelo calls unisex—huh?[64]

LANSING: He says "swerve" or "swirl?"

OLSON: "Swerve." "Double swerve," curiously. That's very beautiful, because, to tell you the truth, as you know, the problem with that poem to me is absolutely—O.K., excuse me, I go back to this one, which is the same—this is tennis. This poem is tennis. I don't like this poem. It was only when I was utterly physical.

MALANGA: It's very romantic.

OLSON: But it's also very accurate. I was absolutely physical. I mean, I could do those things. The "agilities," like, were all that shit that—"nature's." And I wasn't "late," to tell you the truth. It was drag. That's the point, goddammit, I didn't know enough to say, "Look, you horse's asses, you're pullin' me back! I wanna go! I wanna go."

MALANGA: The Blake was more appropriate.

OLSON: Well, but mind you, you see, it only comforts people today who are sort of dragging their asses. If there's any importance in this it was that sort of hopefuliloquy in the theater of time. It was written in 19—19—very soon thereafter, about 1950, I should think, about 1950. I mean, you know, like, I'm telling you, I don't know—poetry ... Frank O'Hara or Jimmy Schuyler, who wrote that beautiful note on poets and painters in Mr Allen's anthology, that's the most interesting note of all. Why have they—why are poets in this language at this point of time for the first time later than painters? It's a very interesting question. It is the first time, because in the whole history of the language there has not been very interesting painting, until like suddenly around 1950 there was very interesting painting. And Schuyler says this so marvelously in that anthology, that note. Jimmy Schuyler, you know who I mean?

64. Prynne had written in his review: "This double swerve of direction also opens the cosmos to hymnic and personal speech in this sense, that in the ancient scheme Aquarius is masculine and Taurus feminine ... Almost all the primary cosmogonies of the past deal in sexually polarized language."

LANSING: Yeah.

OLSON: Who's a crazy—I don't think I ever met him, but when I was thinking today when Berkson wrote me about writing about Frank, again I come back to that crazy question. I mean, Frank was absolutely enamored of Marilyn Monroe and painting.

MALANGA: You said "dandy," I think.

OLSON: Huh? I said "dandy"?

MALANGA: You said "dandy" at one point.

OLSON: Well, but I meant "dandy" in the great tradition of English. If you talk in terms of his life and death, I mean, in his poetry, good christ, if there was any man who had done what those people call, like, *Campus Martiae*, who did it? *Campus Martiae*.

MALANGA: Campus what?

OLSON: Campus of Mars—*Campus Martiae*? "Frank O'Hara was engaged on the *Campus Martiae*." My first line for Berkson's piece. I'll write the piece now. Let's get it done tonight. The young are de-idolized. Enyalion, the Apollo, the perfect figure today absolutely requires, in every respect, in word, in action and in person, was hung up by whatever it—by *Campus Martiae*.

MALANGA: Campus …?

OLSON: *Martiae*. Which is the image of Mars as inherited to us as a military, ROTC or aggressive, or camparison figure: which is camp. And I know that Frank was writing at the very end, and the poem to Berkson was republished in lower-point type, in the lowest point type I've ever seen in English, in, like, what magazine?

MALANGA: Bob Kelly's anthology.

OLSON: Kelly's anthology, right.

MALANGA: "Biotherm."[65]

OLSON: "Bi—" right, "Biotherm," right, is the motion beyond that problem, and god love us that Frank didn't live to continue that attack. Like all of us, we are only attackers, not viruses, but, like the real thing, attackers upon a forest of the future. And Frank we lost. Frank is one of those—christ, if I wrote about the American Civil War, I'd inscribe it to Frank O'Hara. I'm literally—the substance of my poem was the carriage, right?[66]

LANSING: The chariot's crowded, completely.

---

65. Frank O'Hara's poem "Biotherm (for Bill Berkson)" was printed in six-point type in order to be accommodated in the Anchor paperback anthology *A Controversy of Poets* (Garden City, NY: Doubleday Anchor, 1965), edited by Paris Leary and Robert Kelly.

66. Though the word "carriage" is not entirely clear on the tape, Olson seems to be referring to his poem about the god of war, "Where Enyalion quietly reenters his Chariot" (III.38). Lansing appears to be taking it as such.

OLSON: Yeah. But he—literally, I will never write a poem about the American Civil War, and Frank in a sense, like I said to him earlier, I always thought came from Baltimore, 'cos that's my highest compliment to a person who accompanies such elegant men and women as I think Gerard and Frank do. Like, that's worth doing. Or John, my friend from Milton, but that's like the Duke of Almanaco de Gotha, who's in the dilatory domicile.[67] I mean, myself, I had to wait, like. If I might write—read this poem, I could whoops—whoop:

> I have made dialogues,
> I have discussed ancient texts,
> and I have thrown the light I have,
> and offered
> what pleasures
> doceat allows
>
> But the known ...

Ah, I've got it. I've had it. It's not, it's not—it's just "tokens." But "sitting here" today, doing nothing, just getting a little bit of sun, waiting for—I mean, I'm not even dreaming, 'cos I had a note that my friends weren't going to come till 9:30 PM. I thought, "Oh shit, by that time I'll have folded again, 'cos I haven't got that kind of old—psss—solar energy." But sitting here today, last night, I look up with the same old solar energy, and I'm thinking, "Aw shit, I don't know anything about this 'quarters of the weather'." That's bullshit, that's simply geomancy, and I gave that up as long ago—in fact, I gave it up reluctantly, but I sure gave it up after, like, what do you call—cartomancy? Yeah. Cartomancy. Electromancy I practised, gravitomancy I practiced, spiritomancy I practised. Divinosacrenuchogratudeverdura I practiced. But what—no, what is this four? What's four?

> I know the quarters ...

And I see I've written this now—I don't mind, I can read it now, if you'll hear me, having done what this guy says I did, which is to move the fuckin' thing so I could talk about the weather. [LAUGHS]

> I know the quarters of the weather ...

I mean, that's just so ignorant. I could've said "the fours," "the protein corners." [LAUGHS]

> ... where it comes from

And where it's going ever since. "See Atlas Protean—Protein"[68]—nthpffl- "back onto"—pffff—like the *Paris Review* first published—bddlla— "turning your back on that," you know, like. Remember the way that goes:

---

67. John Wieners, born in Milton, Massachusetts, and a friend of Olson's since 1955, was then in a mental hospital. One of his personas was a flamboyant aristocrat.

68. Prynne's annotation in his review, "see the current *Atlas of Protein Sequence and Structure*," has reminded Olson of his "Maximus from Dogtown–II," which had been first published in the *Paris Review* in spring 1966. It begins, "the Sea—turn yr Back on / the Sea, go inland," and contains the phrase "protein / the carbon of four is the corners" (II.8–10). The poem's composition goes back to Demember 1959, so Olson's "1963" is puzzling.

"into the proteins of the four corners of," huh? How about that? 1963. Just [LAUGHS]—I made the masonic sign. They taught us when we were kids, like, the five-fingered fork, you know, which I think is the only ... If I could only get to Jung, if I could only have got to Jung and say, "Jung, come on, a leetle levity, a leetle levity, Jung!" [LAUGHS] That's fun, isn't it? You know, I did—you know that marvelous—I was absolutely—I met him, stiff, at Harvard, in the Tercentenary, with Murray. I just was so much of a kid I couldn't even—I was paralyzed in my suit, like somebody had been frozen there. [LAUGHING] Jeez, I wish I'd had size enough to quarrel with him then. But, I told Harvey, I did write him a letter saying, "You know, Mr Jung, you got—you got like—you got your mystic symbols all mixed up. [LAUGHING] A burlesque show. You don't know which is front from rear." [PAUSE] I'm still reading this poem, "Maximus, to himself." I think it's pretentious.

MALANGA: It's one of my favorites.

OLSON: Isn't he marvelous! But it's okay. It's like living or something. You'll—you don't think I wrote it accidentally. But I can tell you that, fuck, I'm very intolerant. [LAUGHS]

MALANGA: It's very lucid.

OLSON: Yeah, the only things that I'm interested in are the locatives.

> I look out as a wind

—I wouldn't say, like, I thought "like a geomancer" simpler. "I look out as a geomancer, testing, like some kind of big fuckin', you know, tower. It's no problem to solve. It takes a lot of time. But eet's very valuable." [LAUGHS] But it's been overrated, by the way, except for the music. I don't like the present static that poets like Snyder, Rexroth, the whole West Coast—I suspect Allen as an East Coast equivalent of the West Coast, myself [LAUGHING]. I think the whole thing is llsss—like they say, static, like, if you was really, [WHISTLING] I mean, doing it at all, I mean, extremely, but nowhere, absolutely no shit at all, I mean, just like—mprrr, and I don't mean L.M.E. from Waskish[69] or any of that drag-ass dry flat creek shit, or any juicy shit. I mean, just like, I mean, nothin', man, that's what. You know, a southern rebel would say it that way. And that's all I'm talkin' about is "Maximus, to himself," but it took me all these years, whew! But I knew it instantly, by the way. There's that point. I knew this poem was no good from the moment that I wrote it. [LAUGHS]

MALANGA: That's not true.

OLSON: It is. It's absolutely true. Hear me. If you don't hear this I haven't got anything left. I mean, everything else is on the pyre side.

LANSING: I'm going to request "The Cow of Dogtown" [II.148] after.

---

69. Not at present elucidated.

OLSON: Good enough, but mind you, right—I mean, you heard me, I'm on the, like, wrong side. I mean, I can't make it either way. I can't make it in the past and I can't make it in the present, in this funny way we're just talkin'. 'Cos I just can't make this. This sounds like—what's that guy?—he likes himself, number one. "I don't like myself at all," this girl told Panna in London.[70] That's so beautiful. And that was that great pistol shot reading, like, I look like Wild Bill Hickok. Wasn't I the fastest raisin' left arm in the business! (Bullshit!)

MALANGA: Are you left-handed?

OLSON: No, I am naturally [LAUGHING], naturally … Did you not see me raise that gun, man?

MALANGA: No, I wasn't in London.

OLSON: Did you not play me on that diamond? You know, have you ever played poker with Jonathan or played baseball with him? Williams? No?

MALANGA: I never met him.

OLSON: You never met him? And you're telling me that beautiful story about him today. Now this is what I mean by the gap.

MALANGA: No, no. Nononono.

OLSON: This is not the gap, but this is what's wrong with the whole connection.

MALANGA: What beautiful story did I tell you today?

OLSON: Today, about him being the man who published the *Maximus*, you know, when you read that Prynne thing. I thought, "Aw, christ, I gotta even call up"—I called Ed Dorn, and you—"I better call up Jonathan. I'm gonna say, 'Hey, Jonathan.'" You know, like, as of the other night, we were talkin' that money question as of that Apple thing? That was beautiful, that conversation. And he sits here today laughing, when you'll be able to get him this recording, like, you know, "Ya dope, you didn't look at the contract?" [TAPE ENDS]

70. The occasion was the International Poetry Festival on 12 July 1967 in the Albert Hall, London, but the "guy" and the "girl" talking to Panna Grady have not been identified.

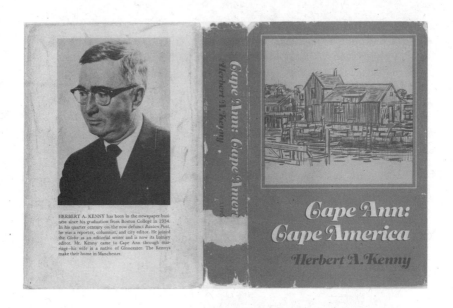

top: Dust jacket for Herb Kenny's *Cape Ann: Cape America*.
bottom: Olson photographed in Charles Stein's apartment in Gloucester, around the time of the Kenny interview. Photo: Charles Stein.

16

Conversation with Herb Kenny

The second part of this recorded conversation was transcribed by George Butterick for *Muthologos* as "I know men for whom everything matters." Butterick sets the scene in an introductory paragraph:

> The following interview took place in late August 1969 at Herbert Kenny's home in Manchester, Massachussetts, down the road from Gloucester about five miles. Kenny is a newspaperman for the *Boston Globe*, editor of its "Books" section, and was an acquaintance of Olson's since the early 1960s. He had previously called attention to Olson's work in reviews for the *Globe*, and arranged this interview in preparation for a book of his own on Cape Ann, eventually published under the title *Cape Ann: Cape America* (Philadelphia: Lippincott, 1971), in which he makes use of the tape on which this transcription is based. It is early evening. Olson has a small clay pipe that he periodically knocks out and refills.

The tape of the first part saw the light of day only upon the passing of Herbert Kenny in 2002.

HERB KENNY: The only thing is that you see in Manchester we have a perfect example of the end of the feudal system in the United States of America.

CHARLES OLSON: [LAUGHS] Or the beginning of the present feudal system.

KENNY: Oh, the new one, yeah.

OLSON: I'd rather think that rather than ...

KENNY: Now, go to Ipswich. Ipswich is an ideal town to talk about the western migration. That's why the 17th-century mansions exist over there because nobody had any money to tear them down and rebuild them with vulgar taste. The town became a backwater in a way after its best days and had a great lapsing period, and more people left Ipswich to go west than any place else around here.

OLSON: Some truth to that. Actually the covered wagon was invented just back up—you know that crazy marvelous marker on—the actual covered wagon was first used in, and then it had moved west from—it's right there in Topsfield or Wenham, just back of Ipswich, in fact right by the store. You ought to even—in your own book it would be a hit to spot this because you are quite correct. In fact, to tell you the truth, Ipswich, it's even more exciting. Do you realize that John Winthrop Jr first settled there and went from there to Connecticut? Equally, Obadiah Bruen, who was the first town clerk of Gloucester, went from Gloucester to New London, and then went on to found Newark. And Mr Winthrop Jr—the whole of Connecticut was really the frontier, which they moved on to, and from Connecticut equally as well as from, say, back of Ipswich, the West became settled. And this has to do with Indians too, by the way. The West was …

KENNY: Ipswich was in the early days an intellectual center. Anne Bradstreet was there, Nathaniel Ward was there, and Jonathan Wise was there.

OLSON: But you're talking quite a wide—you're talking almost a full century.

KENNY: No, no, no.

OLSON: Yes, you are. John Wise, for example, is …

KENNY: Nathaniel Ward, John Winthrop, and Anne Bradstreet were contemporaries living cheek by jowl in Ipswich.

OLSON: That's quite true. And so was John Winthrop Jr there, like. And, mind you, don't leave him out, because intellectually Mr Winthrop, as I think in one poem of the *Maximus Poems* [II.48], yes, I do, as of the fact that, for example, the man who sat down in Gloucester, Mr William Stevens, and who represented Gloucester in the squabble with Manchester over whether or not this property we're on in your house, which is this side, mind you, of the Blynman farm, and Blynman was the minister of Gloucester, so patently this belongs to Gloucester. I have thought seriously of introducing a suit (as I grow older I have nothing else to do) in the General Court to restore this situation. But Mr William Stevens, who was the commissioner, was one of the commissioners of Massachusetts on this border, Mr Stevens was the most distinguished shipbuilder of all the countries of Europe as well as of Boston, and then of Marblehead, and then of the men of Gloucester.

KENNY: William Stevens?

OLSON: William Stevens. But equally Mr Winthrop Jr was invited and urged by his friends in England to return on the assumption that he'd have been Prime Minister.

KENNY: Oh, really, John Winthrop Jr?

OLSON: Of England. John Winthrop Jr. I agree with you that there's a certain concentration at Ipswich, but if you were doing this fairly you ought to— or if you're going to treat Cape Ann even, at this point of time you've got to start talking of John Winthrop Sr, you've got to start talking of John Smith and John White, even though—in other words, the mobility or the plasticity of this situation. Today we have a tendency to talk culture and literary and philosophical values, and have a long time, right? But, in fact, at this date specifically in the 20th century, if you do want to say that Cape Ann is, as you have, the microcosm, that is, by a kind of an entail at least or [LAUGHS] the tail of the dog that the nation has to come, you might be wise to notice, to not lock it up in Ipswich, that the intellectual or activist content of this particular colony was unbelievable for the first time, not only in the first decades but extending …

KENNY: The intellectual content, yeah.

OLSON: Yeah, was extraordinary.

KENNY: John Winthrop Jr had a library of eleven hundred volumes when he came over.

OLSON: I know, I know, and in fact, actually—what's that famous marvelous story of the library that still is the heart of the Beverly Public Library collection, which was a wreck of the library of a boat coming to the United States and was bought by—how is that now? It's one of the most beautiful stories—bought I think by the minister of Beverly at that date.

KENNY: Bought the whole library?

OLSON: Bought the whole ship's—yes, it was a passenger, one of the great sort of practical scientists of Europe who was traveling or something like so many people did in the 17th century. To my amazement, they were—in fact, to tell you the truth, there was more curiosity about the world in the 17th century and in the 19th, because the Americans of the 17th were fantastic intellectuals but after the Civil War, and our government to this day has the most outstanding record in the world of publishing the important scientific and intellectual documents. No government ever, in Europe or any place— in fact, unless you imagine, say, that, Pax Egypt, Egypt's priests were …

KENNY: And now, let me get you on my other thing now, and that is: in Essex we have another magnificent aspect of the United States of America, the disappearance of the hand craft, wooden boats built by the same techniques from the time of Noah down to five years ago, all gone.

OLSON: T'aint true.

KENNY: They're not building boats in Essex anymore.

OLSON: They ain't. They ain't. Except that if you know that remarkable book published two years ago called *Frame-Up!* by the present Story.

KENNY: *Frame-Up!* yeah.

OLSON: You will realize Story, for example, has got a functioning yard right there in Essex today.

KENNY: No, he doesn't.

OLSON: Yes, he does. As a matter of fact, one of my birds that comes to my door from having read me, Joe Bommarito, worked for him.

KENNY: Mr Story himself assured me that no more boats are built in Essex.

OLSON: Well, he, I think, needless to say, whom I met for the first time at the fiesta, St Peter's, just a month ago, I think he's just being modest, because actually he is so in love with, as that book shows, that fantastic father, who built almost all the great vessels of Gloucester, that he wouldn't mention the things he is building. But, for example, again, I just came back from Southwest Harbor, and the cab that I took to the plane at Bangor, the taxi man, his father was a Banks fisherman from Big Cranberry and he himself walked across in the big freeze when the whole of the bay there, whatever it is, between the islands and Mount Desert froze in 1923, and he never went back; but, like, I mean, Southwest Harbor, I mean, any class of vessel of any importance of recent years, especially the one that's just opened up the fishing for deep sea lobsters off the continental shelf, the *Judith Lee Rose*, are built in Southwest Harbor. I mean, again, I just want you to recognize that when you are writing about Cape Ann, your own point in a sense, and equally David McCord's,[1] is that this—if I say, for example, Boston still has the essential control of the National Security Council one administration after another, it's equally true that the prime impulse, impellance, are still busy as hell to the east of this thing, as, like, that money is to the nation. I mean, Southwest Harbor Boat built the *Bonaventure*, which is the paying boat out of Gloucester right now, the *Holy Family*, which is the Moceri family boat.

KENNY: But they're not being built in Essex.

OLSON: I know. I know. But don't—mind you, when you say that's craft, the weakness of that is to play the tourist so that—or the denatured gains at the very point where if you say "microcosm"—and if there's any value in—and in fact I think there is value, not in history but in the—that a primary or a prime, an originatory thing, curiously enough, holds such force that it is like the sun of the earth forever. And in a funny way the lines go out; you might find them in the Polynesian Islands, but the same thing—in fact, you do find them in the Poly—if you know the museum in Salem, I have to even tell my daughter, who loves Salem, goes there to buy her clothes, like they say, there's a little hut in the middle back side of that museum and it's a Polynesian house, it's a Polynesian collection. I mean, mind you, let us not let the clipper ship period be the mark of the—I agree with you, but let us remind ourselves that schooners, though they are no longer built in Essex, draggers and schooners are still being built on this same coast and being built so well that my—Harvey F. Gamage down in South Bristol, Maine, is putting ships out that—in fact, he just, I mean, he put, I mean, Alden or whatever the name is, I mean, this is a crazy activist—I go back to the word activist. I mean, 300 plus-plus-plus decade years and there's more actual touch with activeness which really matters than in this rather dissipated, distracted, mobile, space-ridden universe, in my sense of the charge. That is,

---

1. David McCord wrote *About Boston* (Boston: Little, Brown, 1948) and many other books of local interest.

I would take every one of these towns that constitutes both Cape Ann and Massachusetts as charges, as requirements, as demands, as moral orders.

KENNY: And now we go on to another one: Rockport.

OLSON: Well, now, explain this, because that name only occurred with the granite industry.

KENNY: That's right. Fifth Parish, right?

OLSON: Hm-m. Was Sandy Bay. Still is called Sandy Bay on the charts.

KENNY: What we have there is a marvelous story of the granite industry.

OLSON: Which goes all around Halibut Point to this side as well.

KENNY: Yeah, which now has, in effect, gone too.

OLSON: Oh, yeah, because of hard top. Think of it.

KENNY: Yeah, I know. But then too we have a magnificent instance there of the crushing of art by commercialism.

OLSON: I would skip one lick of art and not put—even, like, if somebody gave me the best ice cream in the world and it was this, this the point of Rockport, I wouldn't eat it. Because Rockport is shit, and has been since it became Rockport in terms of art. I mean, actually, there is—this is simply—it is commercialization, but it's worse than that. It's summerism selling sea-ism to cheap vulgar people who want to have some I don't know what, even like—I have to suddenly just stop because my father not only painted but had home recourse of paintings of ships at sea. So that fantasy of mine is fair enough. But I hate people that supplant such a fantasy, and Rockport has been doing that, like, almost since Fitz Hugh Lane died.

KENNY: So what glory Rockport had has really gone. One interesting thing about Rockport in this regard too is that the great artists who painted on Cape Ann painted Gloucester Harbor.

OLSON: Well, painted in Gloucester Harbor, and painted Gloucester Harbor, and drew, as Winslow Homer, for example—I don't know whether it was in your paper or the *Herald* but one of the Sunday sections this winter, suddenly here's two drawings by Winslow Homer; one is of a ship being built, and I could tell you exactly what yard it was in Gloucester because you can recognize the accompanied buildings, and in fact that lovely fishmonger who now lives in Ipswich, Gordon Thomas, whose father was a captain out of Gloucester who did that remarkable book which still is in—published by Brown's department store.

KENNY: What's the name of the book?

OLSON: What is it called, the book on the schooners of Gloucester?[2]

KENNY: What's his name?

2. A new edition of *Fast and Able*, published by the author Gordon W. Thomas, had just come out in 1968, sponsored by the owners of the schooner *Caviare*.

OLSON: Gordon Thomas. And that book is the most—and that man has done the most, one of the great pieces of research, 'cos he is a—again, it's very similar to the Story, because his father was once a great captain and lost one of the great vessels on her maiden voyage on Sable Island's northwest peak.

KENNY: I'm glad we agree on Rockport. Now let me go on and ask you something else. What about Bakers Island? Can you describe …?

OLSON: I have very little sense of it, actually, or interest really, to tell you the truth, because I think she's just an obstacle to navigation.

KENNY: What do you think of the end of feudalism in Manchester?

OLSON: [LAUGHING] Or rather, as I keep telling you, the beginning of American affluent feudalism in Manchester, because Manchester, may I tell you, if you don't know, and you do, of course, being already into this history, she really is Jeffries Creek. It's her original name, and she is a creek, essentially, and still is. And what's more valuable as such—I say this with some chagrin because what I can call the Stage Fort men principally established Manchester. William Jeffreys, for example, from whom that creek is named, was part of the Stage Fort Dorchester settlement. The main powerful family of Manchester, the Allens, he was a carpenter in the Stage Fort settlement, William Allen, new foundings, and his son Onesiphorus Allen …

KENNY: That's a wonderful name, isn't it, uh?

OLSON: Beautiful. And in fact Manchester's value really is it's a sub-let of the import of fishing at Marblehead and the shipbuilding of Salem's Neck and the fishing in Gloucester.

KENNY: Keep talking. I'm going up to get another tape.

OLSON: Right. I won't keep talking. I'll let you come down.

KENNY: What about William Jeffreys though? What became of him, Charles?

OLSON: Nobody knows.

KENNY: He went to Ipswich. [PAUSE. OLSON POURS A DRINK.] He come to Ipswich, Charles.

OLSON: He did? Well, that's very interesting.

KENNY: There's a record over there of someone having given him some land and they were selling it.

OLSON: Really? Where did you notice that?

KENNY: Oh, well, maybe a history of Ipswich.

OLSON: No kidding. Well, that's interesting 'cos I never did figure out where he went after his—you know the Manchester town records, by the way, do you know them? They're very, very good, and very interesting. They're hard to figure out, whether they're a part of Salem history, actually, because of that practice of—that the basic movement toward Manchester was from Salem, from the Beverly end, rather than from the Gloucester end.

KENNY: They've just found an old document there, you know, some record that some old gaffer kept for the years where the town records were lost. Didn't mean much to me. I read it through; didn't help me much.

OLSON: Didn't? I'd like to see it because actually the published records are scarce enough. You know Gloucester has never published their town records and Manchester has, and the Manchester town records are very valuable.

KENNY: Manchester history was, you know, Jeffries Creek; it was nothing. Then it became a cabinet-making place, and musical instruments. Then that died out. Then it became a summer resort. Richard Henry Dana came in.

OLSON: That's what I mean by when—what you hate is the beginnings of the exploitation of the coast by summer visitors.

KENNY: Charles Walker had about four hundred men working on his estate up here at one time.

OLSON: Well, think of how many Frick must have had at Pride's Crossing.

KENNY: Well, he's not in my ...

OLSON: Well, he is. Pride's Crossing is this side of ...

KENNY: No, I'm cutting him off.

OLSON: Oh, don't do that. I mean, if you're going to write a history of Cape Ann, my dear man, you must do it from Cape Ann Side, which is this side of that bridge. The very name itself should give you the clue. Don't leave Beverly out. Beverly is the most important—Beverly, Ipswich, and Gloucester constitute a triangle of such an order that you just ...

KENNY: Can't leave 'em out.

OLSON: Huh? Can't leave 'em out.

KENNY: "Beggarly." John Winthrop called it "Beggarly," I believe.

OLSON: Well, I don't think Mr Winthrop did at all. No, on the contrary. As a matter of fact, I think it was probably Endicott, because he was in such a war with the old planters, that is, with the men who had been at Stage Fort and who went back and established Salem, but re-found themselves by this new manager whom John White, the founder of Cape Ann, had sent over at the request of John Woodbury and Mr Conant. This, by the way, is very beautifully stated in—the only actual oral history we have of what went on at that period is the Reverend Hubbard,[3] who was the co-minister with Ward at Ipswich, the most—one of the most extraordinary unknown histories of New England is Mr Hubbard's, and one of the great things in it is the fact that he must have been a friend of Roger Conant; and you find fantastic material that isn't in anybody else's, including Winthrop's or

---

3. William Hubbard, *History of New England* (1848), p. 107, quoted in Frances Rose-Troup's *John White* (NY: Putnam, 1930), p. 92.

Bradford's *History* on this end of the thing, see. We're talking about the drag end, curiously enough of the—since the historians of the 19th century do that Boston, I don't know, I mean, do the appropriation of Boston. Again, where I dislike even the idea—I mean, William Howard Taft (I wouldn't mention any names) has been helping on this shore and all these large wooden summer hotels, including Mr T.S. Eliot's appropriation of some materials from Gloucester in his poetry.

KENNY: Was "Prufrock" written on Bass Rock?

OLSON: Well, I—to tell you the truth, I was talking with a poet who lives on Big Cranberry the other day who gave me a poem on Eliot's death, rather an able sort of a Georgian poem, in which he has at least the wit to notice T.S. Eliot dying on Twelfth Night and writes the poem on that trointh. It's a Christian poem, like they say;[4] in fact, I said to Mr Richman at the dock as we parted there: "You are a Christian, and you must be one of the last Christians." But [LAUGHS] actually what's both astonishing is that the two great rivals, Dr William Carlos Williams and Mr Eliot, both had hang-ups which they never left the subject of: Dr Williams's was the nature of his proposal to his wife, which he repeats and repeats and repeats in any number of forms, poems, plays, and novels; and Mr Eliot obviously had some extraordinary pseudo-erotic or genuinely archo-erotic experience in a rose garden, which is still there on, just on Niles Beach. And that gets repeated in everything that Mr Eliot wrote, and we don't need to prove it. Mr Ferrini's former wife did a thesis.[5]

KENNY: I have the paper.

OLSON: It would be very interesting. I've never seen it. I wonder if she knows enough to tell these stories.

KENNY: Well, it's not very deep, Charles, no.

OLSON: It isn't? Shame, because somebody should really notice Eliot's—in fact, to tell you the truth, one of the extraordinary things about—I read in the London *Times* this past year (a fantastic *Supplement* the *Times* has) on the Eliot manuscripts, the manuscripts of the late poems, they're written in notebooks, but it's Gloucester. In fact, it's any of the important notebooks as the *Times* stacks them up in line came from Procter's Bookstore on Main Street, and in fact there's a whole bunch of poems which I don't ...

KENNY: You got that copy of the *Times Literary Supplement*?

OLSON: I do. Yeah.

KENNY: Would you hold on to it?

OLSON: I certainly will, if I didn't in some exasperation of jealousy throw it away. But if I do, I'll certainly keep it for you. It was sent to me with a lot of interest by somebody in London smarter than I am.

4. Olson owned Robert Richman's elegy *The Day of Five Signs*, published by the author. Olson carefully pronounces "trointh," a neologism.
5. Margaret Duffy (Peg Ferrini). The thesis or paper is not at present known.

KENNY: Let me go on, because, after I take these towns one by one …

OLSON: The regnal towns, the baker's dozen.

KENNY: I then come into Gloucester, see, as a city which breaks all the statistics.

OLSON: Right. Happily.

KENNY: And unhappily.

OLSON: Well, I don't know. How could it be unhappy?

KENNY: There's more goddamn misery there, you know. There are more broken marriages in Gloucester.

OLSON: [LAUGHS] That. That. That's what they meant by Christianing the fishermen.

KENNY: If you take all the sociological statistics, Gloucester is always …

OLSON: Oh, yes. I'm sure you're right. I hadn't even known that was true, but it's interesting when I chose it as my subject. Irregularity is what …

KENNY: It becomes, once again, the best microcosm of an American city that you can get. Do you follow me?

OLSON: I hear what you're saying, obviously, but I took it …

KENNY: Now, I can quote these statistics. The State of Massachusetts puts out statistics on, y'know, the wage scale in Gloucester.

OLSON: But that was due to the Gorton Corporation, Mike Ford, who held the labor pool as carefully as possible.

KENNY: And so we get into Gloucester, and there it is, a very interesting thing. But the people who have chosen chose it.

OLSON: [LAUGHS] Yeah, I agree.

KENNY: Winslow Homer.

OLSON: Like Eliot did say in that beautiful poem called "Cape Ann": "Leave it to the gulls." [LAUGHS]

KENNY: "Leave it to the gulls."

OLSON: I think that really we're too irregular for Mr Eliot. He had to flee back to England and to royalism, ecclesiasticism, and literature.

KENNY: This magnetic field of force which you see running from London back and forth to Cape Ann …?

OLSON: I wouldn't call it magnetic. I mean, lets call it "turbinic." [LAUGHS] *Conturbat me.* Turbine in that sense.

KENNY: What part would that play in bringing Eliot from Cape Ann back to London?

OLSON: I think it's just like a piece of flotsam; he drifted back to the old centers of power because he couldn't stand the vulgarity of this new strength, strength of society. I think, like William Burroughs, these St Louis men are the decampment of the Middle West. And I think they just—I mean, like, it used to be—and, if I may, then I'm certainly anti-Yankee by now but then, after all, I've also known and loved many Yankees. I mean, we have rather a scorn for these Middle West fugitives who approach Boston with candles in their hands. Even us Irish from South Boston feel that this is ours, not St Louis's.

KENNY: Eliot's Cape Ann to London has nothing to do with John Winthrop's London to Cape Ann?

OLSON: Utterly not; as a matter of fact, does not. Mr Winthrop can record experiences of the freshness of the air, or even Reverend Higginson can record the, if it's not the strawberries, the taste of fresh fruit, fresh air and fresh fruit, as they came to these shores. It's like the rediscovery of Eden; and Mr Eliot, unfortunately, had ashes in his mouth wherever he went. I say this recognizing of course that, as Mr Burroughs said when Mr Trocchi and Mr Burroughs and I were sitting in Trocchi's shoot-up room one night in London three years ago, and so, because in some stupid—I was so surprised at Trocchi (he's a Scot, of Italian descent) making himself a confession or something to me: "What do you think of Eliot?" And I said, "Well, look, Trocchi, that's like asking me do you like string beans as well as peas?" And Burroughs said, "In other words, you are saying he's a poet?" I said, "For sure," you know, sort of like, I mean, he really was, he was a poet, there's no question about it. But then we fight, don't we? 'cos we have to.

KENNY: But you don't acknowledge that that experience ...?

OLSON: No, on the contrary, I do think, I do think I'm coming, I come of the same turf. I mean, my uncle (Dr Williams is who I'm thinking is my uncle)—I mean, there is that great factum of choice between whether you stay on this shore where the migration came to or whether you backtrack. We really have a lot of scorn for those who can't take it here. I mean, god knows, none of us who stayed here (and it gets increasingly worse) think that it's anything but unbearable. But then, mind, we certainly come on, and we stayed here.

KENNY: Got to stay here—fight it out.

OLSON: Well, it isn't even that: it's ours.

[GAP]

OLSON: ... Remind yourself that the Pilgrims came from years in Holland. They must have spoken Dutch quite spontaneously; and one of the most extraordinary pieces of history is a little book by Francis X. Moloney, done as an honors thesis and published by Harvard, on *The Fur Trade in New England*, in which we discover that the Dutch taught the Pilgrims the secret of wampumpeag, which is that crazy money, I mean, that oyster money, and as a result the Pilgrims made an enormous fortune in less than a decade in fur by the rivers of the—in fact, down to Leicester too was still fur of the otter and the woods were full of raccoons and martens, if martens were a water—I don't know whether—I think that they're a water animal too; and the first shipment from Gloucester, which was the original, actual (how do you say?) telephone company between the old England and the new, the first cable, the real cable ...

KENNY: Which was?

OLSON: Cape Ann, as they called it, more than Plymouth, because Plymouth was as Pilgrims, again, dissidence of such an order that despite the fact that the eventual great ferryman of the Atlantic, Captain—was on that plaque at Stage Fort[6]—became known as the ferryman of the Atlantic; but that, in turn, was only after Boston's settlement, fully a decade after Plymouth, and when it became clear that Winthrop and the other interests in London trusted this man as the best captain because actually he had by that date crossed the Atlantic, but that in fact the cable or the real connection, like the planes today, the BOAC, between this Massachusetts and that England was between the port of Weymouth, England, which was the port of Dorchester, and this thing that they called Cape Ann Side, or Cape Ann, here in what's now known as Gloucester, and was then, and is that settlement still at Stage Fort Park; so that in a real sense what our friend Dorn has called "The North Atlantic Turbine" and written a volume of poems, and Sauer, who was my great master in geography insists ought to be called the "Northern Atlantic," that this field, this kind of a field of force, which still continues to this day as a matter of fact as a factor—in fact, if we do say, as you did, or as you quote McCord saying that New England is the ...

KENNY: "Authentic version of the nation."

OLSON: "Authentic version of the nation," which we all know is actually a financial and political fact continuing right to this moment, that it's not simply the President, or a recent President, or a family, it happens to be actually very powerful positions like secretaries of the National Security Council, these posts are almost exclusively held by Boston men, and we do know equally that the Boston wealth really rests upon the cod, so that in the dynamic sense right to this day, in the domain sense, in the domain sense, actually this end of Boston was the originatory end. But one must be careful to say that the Pilgrims and Plymouth, which remained, as you know, a funny, isolated settlement, which eventually, simply because of, well, the fact she hung by herself, was incorporated or enclosed in Massachusetts, she was a sort of a tennis shoe or a gripping sole in the very strange connection (I suspect it's a lot more than anybody's ever dug out of the record) with the Dutch at New York, because in fact what turns out to be extraordinarily true in—and though you're right that William Bradford certainly was the most extraordinary writer that the Pilgrims produced, the man who in a funny

6. Captain Hewes, mentioned in *Maximus* 1.48 and 1.112.

way equals in leadership other men in the earliest settlements is Edward Winslow, and Winslow's to my mind—again it's depending if you could or would or did look into it, but I've discovered that Winslow actually functioned both with the Indians and in England, because he did make trips back and forth, and possibly with the Dutch, although I've never known exactly it was the time of the Dutch. But, for example, as you know, having worked now twenty-two years on this poem which actually occupies itself as a subject with this end of Massachusetts, specifically Gloucester, the port of Gloucester I mean, it's one of the most important things that you finally have to recognize is that the Pilgrims sent, almost at the same time that the Dorchester (England) interests had representatives in London trying to get, and in fact had already succeeded in getting, the rights to the western shore of Cape Ann Harbor or what we call today Gloucester, the Pilgrims likewise sent Winslow too in London, and he came back in a ship with a Captain Altham, who put in right ashore on the western side of Gloucester the very same year, 1624, that the Dorchester Company put their men in quite a large number on that same shore. So that in fact what you suddenly realize is that the western harbor of Gloucester not only was of prime interest to anybody who was seeking the plaice or the mackerel or that thing which is still this great sort of a swimming ... If I use the figure of Dorn's "the turbine," or in fact if I use the figure of Sauer's of the North Atlantic, whichever way you do it, whether you take the topography or you take the motion, you in every case finally get home to that western shore, what we call Western Harbor, but the shore of the Gloucester port.

KENNY: Which shore do you mean, by the way?

OLSON: Stage Fort Park. Which is today called Stage Fort Park. Now, and I'll finish this run and take on what you said was your own proposed theme, by saying that there's one other factor, and you practically have almost what Parkman called, what Parkman alone of all the historians on this side—or in fact, to tell you the truth, really the English haven't caught up with it, and neither have the Canadians, is this crazy story of the migration, this creation of a Magna Europe or a—certainly one wants to call this fantastic thing which is now the United States, the U States of America, but which was at the point we're talking simply the first feet really, the feet that stood, the feet that stayed on this continent, both continents in fact, both the ore and the steel, like they say. The one other factor that to my mind is like the fasces of this thing that I'm trying to suggest to you is almost like a cat's cradle or a series of veins, like, in a beautiful mobile machine or a weather measure, is the much earlier fact of Samuel Champlain coming into this same harbor, and notice, having examined Plymouth and Hyannis and to the south, drawn maps to them, equally Saco to the eastward, and his—this is 1606 he's in Gloucester Harbor, and his map, and the reason why all of them, including the Pilgrims as well as the Dorchester Company as well as Champlain, appear to have valued this shore is that that particular hill there on his map shows cleared land occupied by Algonquin village or corn barns of such a number and in such a clearance that one almost feels as though it—and now I'm talking my own thing, I suppose, but I hope that it equally is objective—that you could almost say that that line in an early *Maximus* poem as of my great teacher at Harvard who taught the course in Westward Movement, which was the course from this shore to the whole other side, Merk, in one poem, in the "Letter 23" [1.99], I say that I didn't tell him there but I was really asking him questions of any further work done equal to this Moloney's on the fur trade as of the fishing trade or anything of knowing that on my front yard—because curiously enough, as you know, my father brought us there and we rented this camp right on the stone wall of that "fishermans ffield," which is what it still is known as ...

KENNY: Where is that located?

OLSON: That's Stage Fort Park.

KENNY: Fisherman's field.

OLSON: Field, because those rocks that are just off Cressy's Beach are still called Field's Rock, and it reflects simply that warring, wearing, of names, proper names, which are crazy along this coast: that's Fisherman's Field's Rocks. I always thought it was a man named Field as I grew up, but now it's perfectly clear to me that those are Fisherman's Field's Rocks. And it's taken me a devil of a time with the Town Records of Gloucester to restore the divisions that that field was divided in. Apparently I should assume, like, in fact, that crazy thing that Champlain's map shows in 1606, that by the time that the Yankees were back here and making Gloucester a kind of an outpost, not an outpost from Europe but an outpost of Massachusetts against the French, they divided that field into what I would assume was not for gardens but for drying fish.

KENNY: Yeah. What was the stage that they built? How elaborate was that?

OLSON: Extraordinarily elaborate, surprisingly elaborate. In fact, there is in Captain—not Waymouth—Captain—the most famous explorer, recorder of Newfoundland, in his book shows one of those stages; you'd be surprised how ...[7]

KENNY: It had stories on it.

OLSON: Well, yeah, but the main thing is that, like a present day wharf, the problem was to get it up above the water by pilings on spiles and equally to give plenty of working room. It really was a wharf with fish houses what it amounts to, and that's what a stage was. But equally there was this drying problem, which requires racks, and racks in fields, equally, which can be carefully always attended to so that you could, so that they don't burn too much in the sun and they can be covered with those, perhaps you've even

---

7. Captain George Waymouth's voyage of 1605 is included in Charles Herbert Levermore's *Forerunners and Competitors of the Pilgrims and Puritans* (1912), which also includes an extract from Captain Richard Whitbourne's *A Discourse and Discovery of Newfoundland* (1620), which Captain John Smith included in his *The General History of New England* (1624). There are no illustrations in these selections, so perhaps some other explorer of Newfoundland is meant.

seen them, they're still used down in Newfoundland, those lovely little shed houses that go on top of them.

KENNY: These are flaking racks?

OLSON: Flaking racks, right. So that I assume that—and in fact, as you know, the great fight that happened within one year of that day that Winslow arrived with a patent and found the Dorchester Company in possession, within one year the Pilgrims were so interested in the attempt to equally get fish as well as fur out of this coast that they—there was a squabble there, in fact of such apparent intensity that Miles Standish marched over from Plymouth with troops, and there was a real contest. However, it seemed to have been resolved by simply permitting the Pilgrims to have a stage there as well. And again it shows how the will of the Pilgrims or the economics was rather the other way about, that they quickly discovered that they could, because of the Dutch and wampumpeag, make money out of furs.

KENNY: Well now, two questions. When Champlain sailed in he had a map.

OLSON: No, he made a map; his map is drawn ...

KENNY: He had a map aboard.

OLSON: Did he?

KENNY: More than likely. Which showed Cape Ann under the name of Cabo de Santa Maria.

OLSON: Yeah, I know what you mean.

KENNY: Spanish map.

OLSON: Yeah, that's correct. There is a—that is it's locat. As far as I know, both the Portuguese and the Spanish agreement, or just excitement ...

KENNY: One other thing: who was "Captain Shrimp"? John Endicott or Miles Standish?

OLSON: Oh, completely Miles Standish, and it's Morton's, Thomas Morton's name for him in good Elizabethan pamphlet style.

KENNY: I just read last night that somebody called John Endicott "Captain Shrimp."

OLSON: You know, I expect somebody called him lots of names, but not "Shrimp." He wasn't—apparently Standish apparently was quite small. Yeah, and Endicott, who could have been called many names, in fact, Hawthorne's stories alone would suggest how ... I don't know Endicott; he's a mysterious man.

KENNY: Well, what you have said in a way supports my thesis, because my thesis is this: that the cod was the thing that brought them over here; the cod was what made them money.

OLSON: That's true, except that in the case of the Pilgrims again you've got to allow that truism to stand that—in fact, I can even tell you that the actual enterprise or mover or promoter of the settlement even here was religious, that is, the settlement here in Gloucester was religious. The Reverend John White, who never came to these states, never came to this side of the ocean, who was utterly the fantastically important figure, who's somehow or other been permitted to do the kind of Bostonishness and Quinceyishness of our history—due somewhat almost exclusively to the Adams family, not only has wealth tended to concentrate in Boston but so has history, and, as a result, the part that John White, who was Rector of St Peter's Church in Dorchester, played in Massachusetts by time and time again—as well, by the way, may I point out, for the record, that Hugh Peter, the minister, the powerful minister of Salem, Hugh Peter, who actually lost his head for having gone back and been one of the five (was it?) men who ordered the beheading of Charles the First and he in turn paid for it with his life, but Peter, while he was minister of Salem, which was in those great formative years, was pushing Winthrop and Endicott, that is both the Salem and the Boston enterprise, to be sure to turn to fishing. It wasn't in the minds of Winthrop and the Massachusetts Colony as much as one would think, even though the governor, the actual governor, prior to Winthrop's removal to this side, a man named Craddock, Matthew Craddock, had a great deal of shipbuilding interest on the Mystic Head; and equally again the Pilgrims had a man who was the promoter of the faith, who turned out to be rather a, as far as one can see, a sort of a crook to the Pilgrims, Isaac Allerton, who seems actually to have been the principal creator of Marblehead, which was a fishing village much more thriving earlier than, say, Gloucester, because Gloucester didn't hold. The Stage Fort men backed off and became the Beverly, the so-called old planters of Beverly, Mr Roger Conant and Captain Trask and Balch.

KENNY: Endicott?

OLSON: No, Endicott came after the removal and, in fact, after the Dorchester Company changed toward the Massachusetts Bay Company, which is when Winthrop and his interests bought in. There was a little company, which Frances Rose-Troup, who wrote that remarkable life of John White, which, for example, doesn't exist in the Gloucester Public Library, but it's incredibly the most important history of White—if you took it, in a sense you'd have to say that White, Winthrop, and whom you mentioned, the historian of Plymouth, Bradford, that in a sense those three men almost equal each other in importance across the front of this piece of coast that eventually was Massachusetts.

KENNY: When the Puritans, the Dorchester Company, petitioned James I for a charter, which they were granted and which they brought over here, the first ones to do that, and he asked them why they were coming over here, they said, "Fishing."

OLSON: Yeah, it's quite true, but mind you, that story was actually, that story, I think, is—you have to extricate that. That story has to do with Richard

Bushrod's license to—oh, I see what—no, let's put it this way: the original licence to fish was to a Richard Bushrod, a merchant of Dorchester. When the Pilgrims went back to get that license to the western—an equal right to fish and use the western harbor of Gloucester, apparently that's when James said that. The story has gotten attached to the—it may be, tell you the truth, that some—now it's like talking oral history. I couldn't say where I pick up this idea, but I have the impression, and it feels as though it's of the record practically, that John Smith offered himself to the Pilgrims, and that there is a story that the Pilgrims were really headed for Gloucester Harbor, which they picked. If you remember, they had a license to settle within Virginia, and Virginia would have extended all the way down to, I think if I'm not mistaken, to practically Somes Sound, which divides Mount Desert into what was eventually British as against American but was at one point French as against English, and there's a whole 48th parallel argument on this coast just as much as there was on the other coast, which has never been particularly pointed out. And there is some impression that that, say, that rather famous religious colony, the Pilgrims, did propose to fish here.

KENNY: In Gloucester?

OLSON: Yeah, in fact, literally was seeking Gloucester Harbor, but because they didn't have such a navigator as Smith would have provided them if they had taken him, they just missed. In fact, usually it is said they came too far north; my impression is that—and in fact there is—I don't know where I picked this up, that they actually undershot Gloucester.

KENNY: There is evidence to indicate that they weren't intent on going to Virginia.

OLSON: Oh, that's for sure, because they wanted to be alone. But this was for their—again we have to give them their, as I say, that cliché, what became a cliché, and at this date if you live in this country one wants to even ask why the dollar bill says "In God We Trust" when the Supreme Court, to my mind most unhappily of all the acts of recent years, removed the Lord's Prayer from the schools. But still we—the so-called theology behind all the settlement on this part of the coast even, as I've said, extends to Gloucester, because John White was very, very anxious that that port be a kind of a olé. In fact, right now I just came back from Mount Desert, from Ilesford, from Cranberry Island, and, like, the fact that I had to drive the taxi from Bar Harbor to Southwest Harbor is a part of a missionary movement which exists right now, that works all over and has a boat.

KENNY: Sunshine Mission.

OLSON: Yeah, that's right. The Sunshine Missionary, and they seek to make sure that—like, how did we say it, just my daughter and me as we were driving back from Bar Harbor: that fishermen along the coast are, like, wild. And White in his beautiful pamphlet that supported the settlement by Winthrop of Boston suggested that the fishermen needed religion.

KENNY: Needed religion, yeah.

OLSON: Which, living in Gloucester, one feels is quite true.

KENNY: I think what you say doesn't contradict my thesis, because once again the Massachusetts Bay Colony in 1690 did take over Plymouth.

OLSON: Yes, quite, oh yeah. But mind you by 1690 they took over New Hampshire, they by that date actually governed Maine, say (his daughter), and in fact at some point in that period before even 1690 Massachusetts power ran down through Nova Scotia at least as far as Lehave.

KENNY: This is the point I make. The point is that once again New England is the authentic version of America. The Puritan settlement which stands on this end of the shore was the—and now today if we look at Cape Ann we have a microcosm of the United States of America. Now I'm including in Cape Ann interior places you wouldn't. I pick a certain parallel which takes in Castle Neck …

OLSON: I certainly would. What do you mean? I mean Cape Ann Side, which the 17th century started, or if you've ever noticed the crazy map by John Winthrop, apparently in his own hand, but I'm not sure, which the British Museum now has, of the—the map is crazy enough, it's 1634, and the map is made so that the north is to the left side …

KENNY: In other words, there's some justification for my taking in Ipswich?

OLSON: Oh, my god, as a matter of fact, I have that geology map by Sears[8] folded on my kitchen wall, that beautiful canvas map, and if you fold her so that you get the projection of Cape Ann, you come about the mouth of the Merrimack to the bridge at Salem, you include—and what's so interesting is that this map by Winthrop, 1634, the manuscript of which is in the British Museum, and shows his farm and Humfrey's farm and Marblehead and Mr Craddock's weir and shipbuilding on the Mystic and all the way the rivers, like the Ipswich River goes all the way back and almost ties to—and Mosquito Creek comes in and almost ties to the Charles—it's a beautiful map; but the point is what do you suppose is the most pronounced thing of all, the map being made with the north to the left, is this crazy promontory, like a thumb, of Cape Ann.[9] She stands right up there on the top, and you notice, more than most people ever paid attention to, the fact that this cape juts out ten to twelve miles from the coast into the ocean, and she goes from Beverly to Newburyport. You're absolutely right.

[REEL 2]

KENNY: Judge Morley.

OLSON: Oh yeah, oh very interesting.

8. A geological map of Essex County, prepared by J.H. Sears, was published by the Essex Institute in 1893.
9. Compare the 1630 Winthrop map from the Massachusetts Historical Society used for the cover of *The Maximus Poems Volume Three* (1975).

KENNY: He told me. He said, "Geez," he said, "there's domestic trouble and violence all the time."

OLSON: Sure.

KENNY: I says, "Why?" He says, "Well, it's the ships. The ships, you know. A guy goes off on the ship and the wife gets lonesome; she goes down the barroom. He comes home with a few bucks in his pocket; he hits the barroom before he goes home. He meets somebody else's wife, who's waiting for another ship to come in." But there is a sort of a—there is a terrific Yahoo element in Gloucester.

OLSON: Hmm! Isn't it so!

KENNY: That's right. And you know, this Yahoo element, it exists on all levels. They've ruined the Circle down there, you see. In other words, the point I'm making is this: that if we think of America being ruined by a lot of realtors and other things, boy, that's in this microcosm up here. Ipswich now has got bulldozers running over it. They're going to bring in eighteen million people and they've got thirty-three square miles. They're the biggest in the area of all. Gloucester is being destroyed and corrupted. Every time you look around, a new building's torn down. The only thing that's happened that heartens me is there is my friend Hyde Cox building a new addition to the museum so the Fitz Hugh paintings can be shown.

OLSON: But you see, Herb, I do think you—I mean, those statements are not as important as they seem. That is, neither pollution nor culture—in fact, one and the other belong together! [LAUGHS] I'm afraid that the interest in the past, which will—in fact, there's some very good projections that, like, by 2000 the whole idea of heritage will have absolutely been cleaned out of the human species.

KENNY: Of heritage?

OLSON: Heritage. That there will be absolutely no experience—I can see it myself already in interesting ways. I suppose one of the reasons why I'm—like Corso said to me, many years ago, "Why are you writing about a city that is going to disappear?" I said, "Well," I said, "you're a New Yorker aren't you?" Of course, he was actually born in the Italian district south of the Village, Sullivan Street or something. I mean, like, it was marvelous at the time, because I thought, "Why am I?" Except that I consider her a redeemable flower that will be a monstrance forever of not a city but of City, and, say, because she wasn't urbanized until—in fact, if somehow or other that federal urban renewal program had been just delayed a few more days practically, Gloucester wouldn't be urbanized today. She would still be the sort of, like, as I said in some letter to the *Times*, that she—when you urbanize Gloucester she comes on like Bridgeport, Connecticut, she doesn't come on like New York City or Detroit or anything else. Again, it's the Ya—it's Yahoo! Come a ti yi yippee yippee yay! It's a fish-town, that's all I mean. But, yeah, wow, marvelous.

KENNY: But what are they going to save in Gloucester?

OLSON: I don't—it doesn't matter to me, you know. That's my point. I mean it matters enormously; but, I mean, in terms of, like, the future ...

KENNY: I mean, you went and raised hell about—what was the house you went to the Council about?

OLSON: The Parsons, the Parsons House. Yeah, well sure, but that was love, like they say, and love won't lose. You can never lose to the City Council if your case is love. And I lost unanimously.[10] And the mayor was Lowe, I mean, low man on the totem pole.

KENNY: But what about that City Council, is there a brain in it?

OLSON: At the moment, it looks to me as though it's that thing which is running America, the Junior Chamber of Commerce. It's a most extraordinary organization. No one pays attention to it. They're much more powerful than the American Legion at this date, and the pols, in a funny way, because they've become the pols. And they're a very peculiar bunch; they're like junior executives in all the corporations. And they're ex-GIs of the Second World War, and they've got a house, and their wives are gymnasts; their children, god knows what they're gonna be. They're certainly not going to be Houyhnhnms. No way.

KENNY: You're not disturbed by that?

OLSON: I, I'm—you know, I've found out that I believe in God and His Creation, and it doesn't matter to me what the human species, as a bunch of what we call midges coming off a marsh, do to it, even to themselves. I'm not interested in their rather pathetic failure to respect what they've been given.

KENNY: That's about it, isn't it?

OLSON: I think so, because—and I hope, by the way, now that they realize that this is the only place where there is any living—each time they take another shot at another one of these planets, they turn out to be ash heaps. And hopefully they might some day realize that that famous blue planet, as she's now revealed herself to be, is the only one with atmosphere which reflects the great ocean, and therefore that we breathe and live here. We're little aquarian creatures that grew up. And I hope that ...

KENNY: Well I'm glad to find that you rejoice each time they find another ash heap. I was ...

OLSON: I love it.

KENNY: It delighted me that Mars was an ash heap.

OLSON: Well, I was ...

KENNY: Science is so determined there must be somebody else living somewhere.

10. Olson wrote to Mary Shore from London on 20 February 1967 about claiming ownership of the Parsons-Morse House on Western Avenue, Gloucester (see *Selected Letters*, p. 386), but, being away, he could not meet the City Council's conditions before the deadline of July 1967. For this, and the Essex Avenue protest mentioned below, see Peter Anastas's *Maximus to Gloucester* (1992), pp. 105–11.

OLSON: It seems to be so—it's perfectly obvious, by the way, I mean, it's been said before, that the Americans are a people in love with death, and it's perfectly obvious that this flight from the earth is this unbelievable science-fiction hope that there's life somewhere else. It must be some obvious psychological reversal, because what's wrong with what is? I mean, geez, what a drag. And the kids really are sold on this dumb idea of fantasy, of fantasizing life somewhere else. Which just makes me so nervous about them, that they aren't enjoying themselves.

KENNY: So you're reconciled to the destruction of Gloucester?

OLSON: I wouldn't put it so negatively as "reconciled." I mean, don't I fight all the time about even one little building and one brick? I wouldn't stop—and one blade of grass? I mean, I think I even helped in that marsh fight over on Essex Avenue. Well, the state refused the permit, happily, because of some aquarian life that they claimed that would be—aquarian?—yeah, aquarian life which might be destroyed. But like, oh, I'm very euphoric anyhow, and I'm very prospective, and …

KENNY: Well, I can tell you this, there was one city councilor who walks the new wing to the Museum every day and has never set foot in it.

OLSON: Foot inside! [LAUGHS] Well, that of course has been a weakness of the Library, not the Library, but of the Museum's, which again goes back to a change of what we would really call culture. And, like, a change of culture is a change of civilization. Since John Babson, who founded both the Lyceum, which became the Library, and actually founded, as far as I can figure out, the Cape Ann Society, called the "Scientific," and was Superintendent of Schools, graduated everybody that went to high school, was a banker and wrote the history of Massachusetts banks, and wrote an anonymous pamphlet for the centennial exposition on the fisheries of Gloucester, which is one of the most valuable books ever written, with his dream of Gloucester Harbor as he thought it would be at this date, with all the Outer Harbor covered with wharves, the fishing going on like the Soviets today, and the Poles and West Germans and the Japanese. He saw Gloucester Harbor as just whoo, whoo, whooof! Talk about dynamo! Turbine! He saw it as just being the whole, absolute fruit of fish, I mean, the enormous sort of a—of the Ocean itself, throwing herself further and further and further via the harbor, via the wharves, vessels, and fishing.

KENNY: Where's that pamphlet?

OLSON: It's around. It's in the—it's in both the—you should see it. *The Fisheries of Gloucester.*[11] It was given away with the exhibit of the fisheries at Philadelphia.

KENNY: Hard-covered volume?

11. *The Fisheries of Gloucester, from 1623 to 1876* (Gloucester: Procter Brothers, 1876), though published without author's name, was the work of John J. Babson, who published his *History of the Town of Gloucester* with Procter Brothers of Gloucester in 1860. Roger W. Babson published several books pertaining to Gloucester over the period 1920 to 1940.

OLSON: No, no, paper, a pamphlet.

KENNY: John Babson was Roger's father?

OLSON: No, no, no; no, no. Roger comes rather of that other Babson, the one we call the Halibut Point or the Sandy Bay Babson, not the Harbor Babson. Much as Roger made much of his—actually, he does come legitimately from the same family.

KENNY: But now, you see, in Gloucester too, you have the mixture of the races here.

OLSON: Yes, thank god, that's our multinational character. I believe in it utterly, the heterogeneous, as I said in the tansy poem [1.9–12].

KENNY: Now, I must confess that as I pursue this theme I plan to do one chapter on Olson.

OLSON: Just quote the facts, quote the tape! I mean, I think I am not helping you; I think I'm just shooting my mouth off. So let's get back to you, your questions, because I'd rather help, as Morley did I'm sure, and any other man would, your text. I mean, after all, I'm writing my books! And in fact anything I say like this doesn't, I hope, equal what I've said when I've done it as poems.

KENNY: You haven't shot down my theory.

OLSON: I haven't, I wouldn't, I wouldn't.

KENNY: Well, that's the point. When I find that it's fairly congenial to you, I'm content, you see, that at least I'm not on an absurd thesis.

OLSON: No, except that you'll have to suffer the same things that like I say I've suffered for picking up some back corner of everything and saying this is the microcosm. [LAUGHING] Don't let me confuse this any more!

KENNY: I'd like to kick, uh, to kick Gloucester right in the ass, and Rockport particularly.

OLSON: Good, do it, kick 'em in the ass.

KENNY: As you said, there was a pathetic failure to recognize what they've been given, or to appreciate it.

OLSON: Well, I wouldn't give Rockport—mind you, Rockport is simply—I mean, don't let that place, don't let that place—it's only a frigid Provincetown. I mean it isn't even worth a moment's consideration. I mean, it didn't—as a matter of fact, the only time when she was of any interest was when she—and in fact at that point Annisquam was an Essex moor using the famous Chebacco boat, and as you know *chebacco* even is the Indian word for Essex. So that it was a period of time in which there was a certain amount of shore fishing, but actually even Annisquam was much more a powerful center, even Mill River, Mill Cove there, Riverdale, what we call Riverdale, was much more. I mean, Rockport is an insignificant little self-aggrandized—in fact, to tell you the truth, it's a meager Maine. It's the first

Maine town. She doesn't even—she should be cut asunder, sent off over there, sent across the bay, because—if she was in Maine, by the way, she doesn't even compare to the great Maine towns.

KENNY: No, Wiscasset and the others.

OLSON: Absolutely. I mean, she's just a small—and, in fact, hidden in Annisquam is a much earlier and beautiful development. Annisquam itself, literally, is—I have a great Algonquin sculpture that came, twenty-one inches down, on S. Foster Damon's ground, and that's an Algonquin head of a woman with a baby being carried on a tumpline across her forehead. That is one of the most beautiful, in fact, the only known actual piece of sculpture by the Algonquins, and it was found in—mind you, that's—in other words, the archeological proveniences, in that sense—and it was under the shed that was the old spars and sail shed for the man—what's the famous captain that built that house of Damon's which is just to the right of the bridge at Lobster Cove? And I mean, believe you me, I mean, as a matter of fact if anybody bothered to recognize that this whole act of separation by Rockport has given her false identity, which she mismanages every time the council meets. I have nothing but, really, contempt for that place. I would like to see it removed, removed from consideration. In fact, if I were leaving anything out of the whole of Cape Ann, I think the slight would be beautiful if you just mention Sandy Bay in this book occasionally. Because your point, for example, about the significance of the painters themselves, I mean, there's only that two or three men that did their work in Gloucester Harbor that matter at all in the whole history of—including that crazy cat that became Whistler's protégé, that Elwell fellow, some paintings of which exist and are in the museum.

KENNY: Elwell?

OLSON: Yeah.

KENNY: He was a Whistler protégé?

OLSON: Yeah, I mean, that's not a bad run. He died in poverty in London and nobody's ever seen his later work at all, so Brooksie told me. He was a really important man. I have in fact a copy of a painting of his that Miss Proctor permitted me to make, of the city hall of Gloucester the morning after she—she opened on one day and burned to the ground the next, that night. The present Gloucester City Hall. And there's this fantastic painting of her done around 7:30 the next morning, bought at 7:30 the next morning, when he was painting it, by Joseph Proctor, paid thirty-five dollars to Elwell for his painting.

KENNY: Where is it?

OLSON: It's—actually, it's that lawyer who was mayor of the town, who's got a firm and whose son is practising law.

KENNY: Sylvester Whalen?

OLSON: Nope.

KENNY: Don Ross?

OLSON: Nope. They both were mayors and lawyers, but this fellow was …

KENNY: Clark?

OLSON: No.

KENNY: Friend?

OLSON: No, the next one, very, very loved man for Miss Proctor, because he did so much for her all those years of her life that she gave murals …

KENNY: Oh, Bill MacInnis.

OLSON: Billy MacInnis, Mr MacInnis has it. Because, at least, when I took the photo, on the back she had a thing she was a little embarrassed by, because that meant I knew that she had stipulated on the back of the—she owned a Lane, a great Lane of Freshwater Cove, and this fantastic painting of City Hall by Elwell, and MacInnis owns them.

KENNY: So, this City Hall that's there now …

OLSON: Yeah, that same City Hall burned the first night she was …

KENNY: Is that so? And then they had to restore it?

OLSON: And they just did it right over. But the painting of the ruin, and brick, the brick, the beautiful brick, and the fire line of the fallen building. You just got to see it, Bert. In fact, I hope that MacInnis is careful enough to give it to Hyde and the museum, because it's an evidence of what an important painter this fellow was, which you can't know except by this one painting itself.

KENNY: Well, Charles, what do you think the future of Gloucester and Cape Ann will be?

OLSON: An image of creation and of human life for the rest of the life of the species.

KENNY: Say that again?

OLSON: [LAUGHS] An image of creation and of human life for the rest of the life of the species. Because by being so retrograde at an enormous progressive time, yet having been the absolute Siragusa or whatever was the first of the great colonies of Greece, she was the great—see, what I'm saying is, and it's why I chose to use Maximus of Tyre as the figure of speech, figure of the speech, is that I regard Gloucester as the final movement of the earth's people, the great migratory thing, which no longer is interesting at all, right? It's impossible. I mean, if you talk today about going to the Moon or to Mars or Venus or putting off on a satellite through Jupiter, because Jupiter itself is nothing but a huge mass of gas like the Sun, any one of these things are not migration any longer. That's space, right? Now, migration ended in Gloucester. The migratory act of man ended in Gloucester. And I think the migratory act of man is the fillet of the rose, is the filings of the energy patterns.

KENNY: Why do you say it ended in Gloucester?

OLSON: Because Gloucester began this continent.

KENNY: Began this country?

OLSON: Continent, yeah. In any interesting fact. That is, again we'll come back to where we started, the *North Atlantic Turbine*, to take Dorn's lovely title of his book of poems, or take Sauer's *The Northern Atlantic*. It doesn't matter what you take, each day it gets increasingly true. Or take Stefansson, which is one of the basic premises of *The Northwest Course of Empire*, written in 1920, Vilhjalmur Stefansson: that the motion of man upon the earth has a line, an oblique, northwest-tending line, and Gloucester was the last shore in that sense. The fact that the continent and the series of such developments as have followed have occupied three hundred and some odd years doesn't take away that primacy or originatory nature that I'm speaking of. I think it's a very important fact. And I of course use it as a bridge to Venice and back from Venice to Tyre, because of the departure from the old static land mass of man, which was the ice, cave, Pleistocene man and early agricultural man, until he got moving, until he got towns. So that the last polis or city is Gloucester, see. Therefore I think that in a sense man now is either going to rediscover the earth or is going to leave it, whichever way you read it. Then Gloucester becomes the flower in the pure Buddhist sense of being the place to be picked. Right?

KENNY: Hmm. Theoretically, yeah.

OLSON: The "Fire Sermon," the truth, the truth, the truth figure.

KENNY: But I don't see how, for example ... [ASHES SPILL] Don't burn Teresa's rug!

OLSON: I think I've burned my hand ... Well, you said microcosm. I'm only trying to suggest to you what that microcosm really means.

KENNY: Yeah, you are, and you're right, and I'm learning from it. How do you dismiss the Spanish-language people?

OLSON: Actually, I don't. As you said yourself, "Cabo de Maria."[12] The Dutch called it "Wyngaerds Hoeck." Same thing. Hoeck. Graveyard Corner—I mean [LAUGHS] Grapevine Corner, Grapevine Harbor. That was their name. There's a great map, in the *Documents of New York*, showing the peninsula as "Wyngaerds Hoeck," which is now that supposed Indian name for that beach and the dunes. But it's Dutch typography, same as the Portuguese and Spanish before them.

KENNY: And you think "Wyngaerds Hoeck" is Wingaersheek?

12. Cabo de Santa Maria was an early Spanish name for Cape Ann, which Olson saw in Justin Winsor's *Memorial History of Boston* (1880), p. 43. Wyngaerds Hoeck, found on an early Dutch map, became the present Wingaersheek Beach. Olson refers to a map in *Documents Relative to the Colonial History of the State of New York*, ed. E.B. O'Callahan (1856).

OLSON: It is indeed. Oh completely, oh completely! I mean, it was just—I mean I can prove it to you. And Grapevine Road, for example, and Grapevine Cove, which as you may know does exist—Garland and I were talking about it the other day, and I was reminding him that there's another one which he doesn't know, High Popples Cove, which is where the Worcester Brewers built, right there, those two coves on that front end that were used by the early English.

KENNY: So Wingaersheek is not an Indian word?

OLSON: No, it's Dutch. Wyngaerds Hoeck: "Vineyard Corner" or "Grapevine Harbor." And she shows absolutely on Adrian, that captain that ...[13]

KENNY: And Wingaersheek becomes a corruption of the Dutch?

OLSON: Yeah, and then curiously enough was taken as Indian from—and in fact there's no known Indian names, because as you know, between Champlain's finding this harbor full of a thousand Indians under a chieftain named Quiouhamenec, who was the brother of the sachem at Ipswich and the brother equally of the sachem at Saco—the Bay was an Indian area and the three great centers were Saco, Ipswich, and Gloucester, and there were three brothers, or possibly that term meant "kin" ...

KENNY: Masconomet one of them?

OLSON: No. No. Masconomet is later. In fact, he inherited the thing. He survives this famous yellowing disease, curiously, which wiped out four fifths ...

KENNY: Is that what they call it, the "yellowing disease"? Do we know what it was?

OLSON: No. No medical men are comfortable that they do know. But it hit the Indians enormously: it hit exactly the Algonquins that we're talking about. It hit them from Saco to Bass River in Beverly.

KENNY: The Massachusetts tribe was practically wiped out.

OLSON: No, they were not, as a matter of fact, whatever you mean by the Massachusetts tribe, because it's not true. They survived. But then they're southern Algonquins anyhow. The northern Algonquins reached, or the Abnaki or the Micmac peoples, reached from Newfoundland to Bass River, Beverly. And only—in fact, there was a complete gap between the, say, the Ipswich Indians and ...

KENNY: But there was a tribe around here called the "Massachusetts"?

OLSON: Around Boston. Yeah, the Blue Hills. But they really were—they only came into any significance, actually, as a result of this, of the yellowing

13. Adrian Block in the spring of 1614 from the Dutch settlement in Manhattan sailed north along the coast and recorded information for "The Figurative Map" (1614), which appears on p. 57 of Winsor, showing Cape Ann as "Wyngaerdes hoeck." Winsor has a footnote stating that a facsimile of the map is in *Documents Relative to the Colonial History of the State of New York*, ed. E.B. O'Callahan (1856).

disease, which wiped out these rather more vigorous and impact tribes. There's very little—I mean, curiously enough, the southern Algonquin— and this is their actual history, they're southern Algonquin—were not very active compared to the fantastic condition of the wing we're talking about that covered this area is called the Pennacooks. And even the Algonquins to the eastward didn't suffer the same. So that that's why, in fact, Maine was, in fact, it was actually—it was a very curious thing: that between Champlain— and those Indians came in here to skin Champlain, you know. He fled. They had him ambushed. They all came down in canoes from Saco and there was a—he saw it—he was a sharp cat, and he got the hell out. But they were gonna wipe him out.

KENNY: They came down from Maine?

OLSON: To wipe him out. From Maine and Ipswich they came in canoes and they were ambushing him right over there on Rocky Neck. And they almost had him. If he hadn't been so quick a man, he'd have lost himself, his life, his freedom, and his men. And Lescarbot, that great poet who wrote an equal history of that visit and that fantastic thing and evidencing that ambush too, Marc Lescarbot, whose book on Gloucester Harbor is one of the greatest books, as well as—in fact, more interesting than Champlain's report, because Lescarbot talks with some vivacity about Gloucester.[14]

KENNY: Some of these Indians when they were ambushing wore Portuguese clothing, hm?

OLSON: Well, that of course, and French clothing, too, because they'd been—I mean …

KENNY: There was quite a traffic back and forth?

OLSON: Well, you've got to realize that fishing had been done—who, for example—what does Georges Bank mean? What is the name for it?

KENNY: I don't know. What does it mean?

OLSON: St George! Now, which St George? I mean, think of suddenly what you're up against. St George of Portugal, St George of England, or St George of Anatolia? Which is the George? So that there was fishing for more than a hundred years before there was even any attempt to settle either Plymouth or Gloucester.

KENNY: That is they were on Georges Bank a hundred years?

OLSON: After 1500. From the date of the great initial voyages from Bristol and from Portugal. I mean, actually it goes back to the Azores and to Prince Henry the Navigator, who did the same thing that, in fact, that has always been done, and in fact Winthrop did it in setting up Boston, which is the arbitrary settlement of a colony. Prince Henry the Navigator established the Azores as the stepping point for the further movement into the—to the

14. Olson read both accounts in Marshall H. Saville's *Champlain and His Landings at Cape Ann, 1605, 1606* (Worcester: American Antiquarian Society, 1934) and made notes in the copy now at Storrs.

discovery of America. And this is how this coast was discovered was simply promotional European enterprise.

KENNY: It was a business enterprise?

OLSON: Well, if you call fishing business. It's that big problem. Fishing is food, right? It's the Apostles' calling, as in that story of James you may have. It's that question we've smudged, in a sense, because we—or at least I didn't want the word "business" to stand without this objection, because actually to produce—production is another matter than what business is now become, right? So that when you talk production—in fact, if you want to talk about the outlines of Gloucester, you also have to talk about just as many—if Morley wants to say that, I can tell you just as many stories of great men who came in from sea and raised families and even to this day are men of such dignity and shape that I don't know their equal in other forms of life or business or profession in the rest of the world. I can take you, introduce you to them on the streets of Gloucester right now. In fact, there's one man I see taking a bus back over the Cut that I consider the man who made me a poet simply because of the nature of his language when I listened behind a stone wall to him and his brother from Newfoundland talk when I was four years old.

KENNY: Who was that?

OLSON: Louis Douglas. And he's eighty-five years old.

KENNY: A captain?

OLSON: Nope, never was. And he even—and when Ethel sent him—the only present, the only thing I ever did to admit, acknowledge my debt to him was to—a few years back, a fellow did a book on Newfoundland and the Norse, and I sent it over from Brown's.[15] And being the kind of people they are— his wife is the daughter of a Swedish captain—Ethel made me a cake, and Lou came to the Fort to bring it to me. And he had been on the Fort once in his life the day he came to Gloucester, in a bar which was owned by your wife's grandfather, and was asked the day he got here to take a sight aboard a vessel, and had never been on the Fort again, until the day he brought me the cake, which is fifty-five or -seven years later. And he knew every house, every person. He stood and he says, when he walked in—he wasn't going to stop, but then he saw my windows and he said, "My lord, Charlie, you do have, you have some, you have a lot of windows looking out!" I says, "Yes." So I said, "Come through the house and see it." Sat down and talked for three hours, identified everything that ever was on the Fort! He has that fantastic condition of the human race when everything mattered. Today, nothing does, and that's what's so poor. And I know men for whom every- thing matters. Still. Who see, feel, and know that everything that they run into does matter. Hah! and then they retain it. And then they have it. And

15. Brown's department store supplied what was then a current non-fiction bestseller, Farley Mowat's *Westviking* (Boston: Little, Brown, 1965). For a photograph of Olson and Louis Douglas together on 16 May 1966, see *Charles Olson at the Harbor*, p. 208.

then they have it forever. And when they're buried they're bigger than those people who don't. Even if they look the same and fit the same box.

KENNY: Do you think this marked all the Gloucester fishermen or ...?

OLSON: Nah. No, no, not all of them; but qualitatively-wise, I mean, the container had a better chance to have a content.

[GAP]

OLSON: What do you suppose Sweeney, who was head of the thing, wanted to do? He wanted to show me a letter of Eliot's on Connolly and ask if I agreed with it.[16] And I said I certainly do, because Eliot's position was that Connolly was the greatest writer of Gloucester. And in a funny way he is, you know. The only trouble is that he chose to write it in that goddamn stage Irish, which just ruins the damn thing. But the fact is that James B. Connolly knew Gloucester at the height of the industry of fishing and the machine of the schooner like nobody else. And in fact his work is so dependably the story at that date that you can't touch it, you couldn't beat it.

KENNY: What years did Connolly write it down?

OLSON: From about 1907 through 1915. And, as you know, he was essentially a newspaperman and wrote for *Collier's* and was born in South Boston and comes of the Boston Irish end of the same sort of fishermen.

KENNY: What were the great years of the schooners?

OLSON: 1885, or 1880 really, with the revision of the schooner that was forced on Gloucester by one of her great captains, Captain Joseph Collins, because the schooner that's—for example, there's a schooner going around each evening here now which is that very dangerous, what's known as the clipper-bow schooner, which caused more deaths on Georges than any single machine that man ever invented. And this Collins, who came from Shelburne, back of Shelburne, and was a very great captain, he was also a very great intellectual; in fact, he equals Powell and all those great discoverers of the West, and became the head of the Smithsonian's—what, today, is that cat that?—they call it the Transportation Department, and this fellow that runs ...[17]

KENNY: Captain Joseph Collins?

OLSON: Yeah, Captain Joseph W. Collins. And he edited and published the great "Fishermen of the North Atlantic" in Goode's *Fisheries of the United States*, which is one of the greatest publications of this country. And

16. John L. Sweeney of the Lamont Library Poetry Room, Harvard, had a letter from T.S. Eliot of 5 November 1952 saying, "I am much pleased that my words of admiration should be conveyed to James B. Connolly."
17. Olson is thinking of Howard I. Chapelle, who talks about the replacement of the "clipper-bow" in his *National Watercraft Collection* (Washington: National Museum Bulletin, 1960), p. 169, which is Olson's source. As to Captain Collins's place of origin, Chapelle says that Collins was born at Isleboro, Maine (p. 4), a place Olson knew well. Shelburne, Mass. may be an error or Olson may have had another source.

Collins's book is unknown, of course, because it's unseparable from that Goode's series.[18] But this man actually designed the present, the great schooner, the schooner which not only saved lives but became an enormous machine of industry.

KENNY: Which was the schooner that lost the lives?

OLSON: Oh, the clipper, the so-called "clipper-bow." And she was the ship that was used from about 1840 to about 1880. And when they started to use her on Georges—I'm not sure I'm not too early on the 1840. She seems to reflect the clipper ship, to tell you the truth, you dig? which, after all, MacKay was doing in Newburyport around 1860. So I suspect that I'm twenty years too early. And she was a small—she was small, of course, by comparison to the clipper ship, but she was a very dangerous ship. And Collins wrote articles in the national magazines and then went—was drafted sort of—went to Washington and did this fantastic lobbying job. It's just as great as Melville and Cooper on the flogging in the Navy, what he did. And it's forgotten in Gloucester, as a matter of fact, and in fact, when Gloucester celebrated her 250th anniversary, he was there and nobody knew he was. He came from nowhere.[19] The most moving story of the man, and that famous—the most famous of all the schooner races occurred in that 250th, the famous race of the *Belden* and the *Nannie C. Bohlin*, the great race, the one that really counts.

KENNY: That's the one that Maurice Whalen won?

OLSON: Yeah, the one when they were really—that was a real race. The rest of it since has been acculturated attention, including, I practically have to say, the *Columbia*, not to speak of the *Thebaud*.

KENNY: When did the motor, when did the engine come into them?

OLSON: Yeah, just about the date at which Connolly started not to write. Tendency comes in just about ...

KENNY: About 1907?

OLSON: No, no, no, I think that it was Sol Jacobs that first used an auxiliary engine. I think it's about 1917, but I may be wrong.

KENNY: Oh really, that late?

OLSON: Well, I may be wrong on that, because ...

KENNY: But it was in the 20th century?

18. Olson is referring specifically to sections III and IV of *The Fisheries and Fishery Industries of the United States* under the general editorship of George Brown Goode (Washington: Government Printing Office, 1887). Collins wrote "The Sea Fishing Grounds of the Eastern Coast of North America" (with Richard Rathbun) and "The Fishermen of the United States" (with Goode). His hand is clearly evident in the many pages on Gloucester and the illustrations of schooners.
19. The story of Captain Collins incognito at the Gloucester celebration is found in *Memorial of the Celebration of the Two Hundred and Fiftieth Anniversary of the Incorporation of the Town of Gloucester* (1901), p. 310.

OLSON: Oh completely. And, in fact, to tell you the truth, it's one of the reasons why, if you know Connolly—have you read any of Connolly's work?—because, you see, there's no auxiliaries in the—he's all sail. All sail. That's another reason why he's so interesting. He's all sail. And it's a big problem, I mean, because there's no one written, except Gordon Thomas, about the ships since with any real or equal attention. And that's a great book by Thomas; you ought to look at it, you ought to buy it. It's a dollar. It was republished by those people that bought the *Caviare*, they refinanced the second edition of it. It's over in Gloucester House, because his sister-in-law ...

KENNY: Oh, you mean it's available over there any day now?

OLSON: Oh, absolutely.

KENNY: Where would Teresa buy it for me if she ...?

OLSON: At the Gloucester House.

KENNY: At the Gloucester House. The restaurant?

OLSON: Yeah. They sell it right on the counter.

KENNY: Is that the sort of the thing like that with the pictures in it?

OLSON: Yeah, it's a pamphlet.

KENNY: Oh, I think I have that.

OLSON: It's unbelievable. It's biographies of the vessels. It's unbelievable; it's obituary-biographies of the great Gloucester schooners of the period since Connolly, which is what's so valuable about it. He dug it out of the newspapers of Gloucester, and it's accurate as hell. Most of it was published in the old, what's now called the *National Fisherman*, but was the old *Maine Coast Fisherman*. You must see this, because ...

KENNY: Let me ask you this, Charles. When those fishermen and that type of fisherman was sailing, when they went out of Gloucester did something big go out of Gloucester?

OLSON: Well, one big thing went, I'm sure, which has gone out of human life, which is nature, right? I mean, it's like as though you no longer had to hunt for your food. I mean, they were still fishermen as hunters for food because of the condition of the vessel, the danger to the vessel. It was like, it was like Indians and White men as hunters, right? And when suddenly that thing got protected, then, in a sense, in a funny way—and in fact it's now developing, as you know—in a sense, in fact, today's great mother-ships, the Mayakovsky class Soviet draggers and all that stuff, are factories; they're called "factory ships." Essentially, there isn't any danger in fishing any more. I mean, there's a man might slip or he might get hit with a—in fact, to tell you the truth, most of the cases—if you talk to Morley, you might talk, say, to one of those lawyers like Sandler or that fellow, that crazy Jewish lawyer in Boston that's handling most of the insurance cases, Katz I think his name is. If you talk to these guys, you could really write some fantastic material on the present-day Gloucester, because, actually, most of the cases today are carelessness or failure to keep—it's like realty, failure to keep up the house at this corner, right? And there's suddenly an injury.

KENNY: Tort cases.

OLSON: Tort cases. I mean, if I stepped on your porch and went through, right, I'd sue you, you know. Well, like, that kind of a case is all that—in fact, that's practically the whole injury matter. But that's hardly a kind of a—but mind you, again, Herb, we're talking something that's gone out in practically our life. In fact, I remember it. You do I think—you're younger than me, but I remember when my father was even one of those men, when life was still dangerous. Each day a man went to work he was in danger. Today the only fatality is an automobile, and the only case is possibly a limb injury or whatever. But there's none of that sense of that you're up against the whole of nature, right?

KENNY: It's returning to the cities now, though.

OLSON: I know. I agree. But then that's violence. That's sort of man's own desire to—he's missing something, he's missing something.

KENNY: It's not like lumbering or mining now.

OLSON: Or absolutely anything. My father's job was to replace brick chimneys with the new iron chimneys. But that meant he had to go up on stagings and that meant danger. He was high steel, like they say. Indians today, the Iroquois, are the only people that can really top a building, put a top on a building, because they're the only people that can stand that height. Well, it's that kind of a thing. I mean, something that I believe we possess. Crucially, I think our body is our soul, right? And if you don't have your body as a factor of creation, you don't have a soul.

KENNY: You mean you think that we need that element of danger for our best character?

OLSON: Well, I wouldn't say it's the nature of danger but it is the nature of perception, of attention, yes, which is a spiritual condition that—you could put it "intensity." I mean, the amount of—this slackness today, the laziness, the lackness, the limpness, is all the fact that you don't need attention any more; you don't need your perceptions any more. It's all taken care of for you by the environment of your automobile, your house, of the economy, of the money system. In fact, there isn't any money; there's credit. In fact, it's worse. I mean, this is a crazy sort of a post-nature, post-natural thing that the species has gotten into. So, who cares? I mean, O.K., have another species. I just happened to have liked that species that's called man. And I, therefore, think God was interesting too because of men. And I thought, and I still think, Creation is crucial; and if you don't stay close to it you lose everything. That's all, just everything.

KENNY: Yeah, and I'm afraid the city of Gloucester has in a way lost everything.

OLSON: Oh, she's lost so that you can't imagine. I have to go every day a further distance to find what I believe—I'm getting so that my legs, which happily were a letter-carrier's ...

KENNY: You mean from Gloucester?

OLSON: From my house I have to go further every day. And literally, practically every day by inches I have to go further in order to be in touch with those things which I consider necessary.

KENNY: Such as what?

OLSON: Oh, the sight of a red-winged blackbird, or a weed that interests me, or air, a change of—a fresh, a movement of air.

KENNY: What about the architecture?

OLSON: Well, yeah, I regret enormously the losses of that. But then I can't do much about that, can I?

KENNY: What about the people?

OLSON: They, they still satisfy me enough. You would know what—for example, I just came back, as you know—maybe Teresa told you she helped me carry my mail back after two weeks from the post office, before she went tonight. And like—so, I was two weeks up there on Islesford, which is an island out in the Atlantic shelf.

KENNY: What was the island?

OLSON: Islesford, or Little Cranberry it's called, either way, just off Southwest Harbor by a ferry, a motorboat. And, like, there's lots of lobstermen. In fact, it's a Gloucesterman's island: the Hadlocks from West Gloucester apparently were the first to use this island. And then there's Somesville, which is the most, only beautiful place on the whole of Mount Desert. And that's my Somes's (whom I wrote that poem about) brother, Abraham, the older brother of John Somes, who built that beautiful house Webber's got on Middle.[20] That house, for example, is enough for me almost every day of my life. All spring I was going by it, until the kids began—and in fact the Italians across the street became very nervous. They thought I was some sort of an agent, or the city was planning, you know, to do something.

KENNY: Let me hear you on this theme: Bill Cafasso, my old pal there, you know, who runs the C of C, I said to Cafasso, "You know"—well, I was asking questions about the city, and I said, "It's economically depressed." "Yeah," he said, "that's true, you know, it is an economically depressed city. But don't worry," he says, "these people all know how to take care of themselves." He says they're living like kings.

---

20. Olson had been reading about Abraham Somes's move from Gloucester to Maine in William Otis Sawtelle's *Mount Desert: Champlain to Bernard* (n.d.). Olson's annotations are on p. 50 of the copy from Kate Olson's archive. The "poem" mentioned is presumably the short essay "A House Built by Captain John Somes 1763" in *Collected Prose*, pp. 351–52, celebrating the Somes-Webber House at 20 Middle Street, Gloucester.

OLSON: Kings. I know.

KENNY: He says they've all angles.

OLSON: Absolutely! I think she's one of the niftiest, richest cities. In fact, to tell you the truth, I have often thought, if you—and I have an assistant now that I might turn on to it—if you did a tough economic study, I think you would come out rather the opposite. It's that well-to-do.

KENNY: Cafasso says between employment compensation …

OLSON: And double or triple or quadruple work in the—by the way, I mean, the food processing workers. I mean, I watch them peel out of that house across the way from me at 8 in the morning. Let me see how many people go and work all day long and bring income back. Talk about the Negroes in Washington, it's nothing compared to how the food-fish workers of Gloucester make, bring money home to the house. Three or four daughters—no, two or three daughters and a mother and an aunt. There's four women going out of those houses at daybreak in Gloucester every five—I mean, if you total those checks! Wow!

KENNY: Well, you confirmed that. Now let me ask you this: they tell me that the language of the women cutting the fish in Gloucester is Billingsgate of the highest order.

OLSON: Right, right. Would cut you absolutely in half, would cut you—you couldn't even keep up. The filthiest, foulest, toughest-tongued women I've ever heard in my life. And yet, when some years ago …

KENNY: Has anyone ever recorded it?

OLSON: Nope, nobody. And some years ago, when I got up, Bet says to me the two women from around the corner were here today and want to know if you'd represent them at the city council. It was in that situation where that bunch of Sicilians, direct from Sicily, were going to put that building, boat building there on the corner of Commercial and Fort Square. Well, there's been four kids killed there because of those trucks in recent years. So the mothers all were in arms, and they wrote this little document they wanted to present to the city council, wanted me to check it, and then asked if I'd represent them. Well, the moment that I met Rosie Tarantarro and heard her voice, I said, "Look, don't bother with me, you just let her speak." And you should—why every—I mean the mayor, who was then, I think, O'Maley, every fucking councilor, they just, they were like this! I mean, you should, if you want to record a woman, you should get this woman. She's not only got a voice like a man at sea, but she's got the absolute talk-talk, she's got the syntax, the vocabulary. She's been nothing but a fishworker, and her husband disappeared years ago and she's raised this lovely daughter, and I think that's all that she has, but she owns two cars, and she's just like—christ, you just would—you'd get the hell out of the way! It's just the same as Naples or Palermo, I mean, but more, because it's here, dig? More, because that stuff is natural there, here it's not, it's personal, individual. You just feel as though you had your face not only slapped but that you were—your dignity as a man was, just was destroyed.

KENNY: Yeah! Yeah! I'd like to go and record her some time.

OLSON: Oh, she's terrific!

KENNY: But Morley confirms this, and also I'm concerned about it because Teresa had a friend who worked down there and she couldn't take it, an Irish girl, couldn't take it.

OLSON: It's pretty hard! Some of those girls I've had as housekeepers, I'd suggest they go around there and get a job. I don't know whether they could make it.

KENNY: Let me get you another match.

OLSON: Will you? Christ, bring me a box or something. You don't know what a pipe takes. You've forgotten what a pipe takes. [PAUSE] Gee, Herb, you know what you ought to do? Wow! I'm getting more out of this conversation than you are! What you ought to do is to write an original book on Gloucester, because a man with your, with your training, and your natural gift that's made your life what it is, you shouldn't do a—I mean, I'm not saying don't do this book, but for god's sake why not do these things that …

[GAP]

OLSON: I mean, like, as of the whole thing, there's three great men: John Smith, who found her; Mr White, who funded her; and John Winthrop, who founded her. And I quickly call them the Finder, the Funder, and the Founder.

KENNY: To be used only with credit to Charles Olson.

OLSON: [LAUGHS] I mean, if you just bothered to follow the leads of this stuff that you're telling me, leads that Cafasso and Morley and others tell you, I mean, you'd get underneath the whole thing.

KENNY: Well, first of all, I've got to do this one. I must say, I must confess to you that having got into this thing about Cape Ann …

OLSON: Yeah, I know it; you'd better stay there first.

KENNY: … I realize how much stuff there is around, and what could be done on Gloucester.

OLSON: Oh my god! As well as on Cape Ann.

KENNY: I found out that there was a guy by the name of Martin Luther, who was an anthropologist of sorts and lived over here in Magnolia, and he went around interviewing people on this whole sub-society of Gloucester, you know.

OLSON: He did? When?

KENNY: Well, I don't know. Fifty years back, maybe.

OLSON: His papers exist?

KENNY: Yes, they do. They're at the Peabody Museum.

OLSON: Ha ha! Terrific! Beautiful.

KENNY: Now, I want to get a hold of them.

OLSON: Jesus Christ, will you make a—you think you're going to xerox them? If you do, would you let me pay for a set?

KENNY: Oh, I'll give you a set. Yeah, I'll give you whatever I get. But I'm having a hard time tracking them down. They were given to Paul Kenyon, he gave them to Gordon Smith.

OLSON: Oh, I know the papers—if they're those Kenyon papers. Was the guy a Finn?

KENNY: No, no. The guy was Martin Luther was his name. He lived over here, in Magnolia.

OLSON: Because there's another thing that Kenyon's got, by the way, is the whole *Kalevala*, the Finnish epic. You know about that?

KENNY: Oh, I've got that. I've got Barbara Erkkila's paper on the Finns; she did a paper on the Finns. Not the paper on the Finns. This is a paper on the Finns done by some kid getting his MA.

OLSON: Yeah, that's the guy.

KENNY: I've got that.

OLSON: You got that?

KENNY: Yes, yeah. But I want to get the Martin Luther stuff which nobody has seen and nobody's written about it.

OLSON: No, jeezus, no, not at all; never heard of it, never heard of it.

KENNY: You don't know about that? If I get it I'll let you have it. Say, excuse me, I've got to call Teresa, we're supposed to … [CALLING UPSTAIRS] Teresa, hello! It's 7:00, honey; you awake? Would you bring me down a necktie?

OLSON: Why don't you just give me—have you got one shot, so I can get back to the town?

KENNY: What was that?

OLSON: Can you give me just a shot of whisky? Straight? Scotch?

KENNY: Yes, yes. Charles, I would love to get those Martin Luther papers and see what's in them.

OLSON: My god, yes. If they show, if they show—well, there could be a single sentence in it that could be valuable, you know. It needn't be too much. It could be terrific … Just one snap, just a little teenie teenie; just for the road.

Textual Notes

1. At Goddard College, April 1962

George Butterick found the Goddard College tapes useful for his *Guide to the Maximus Poems* (e.g. pp. 7, 9, 360, 370), but chose not to include them in the *Muthologos* volumes. In 1993 the present editor requested a copy of the tapes from Goddard College; they were supplied by James Jatkevicius of the college library. My transcription was published in the *Minutes of the Charles Olson Society* 2 (June 1993), 3 (October 1993), and 5 (September 1994). Further attention to the tapes afforded a few corrections, and some of Olson's false starts have been eliminated to achieve a smoother text. At a later stage I followed the independent transcription of Kyle Schlesinger, as provided by him from the Slought Networks, and was able to make a few more adjustments.

I have been indebted to a letter of 17 April 2001 from Forest K. Davie of the Goddard archive containing information about people present at the reading. Mr Davie drew some information from John Bloch, the student who did the taping: "John told me the event—events, because Olson stayed four or five days and gave repeated sesssions—was held in the upper Lounge of Kilpatrick House, newly re-finished as a student residence." Olson borrowed Bloch's car and drove it around and around a big field: the students felt that Olson was not financially very well off at the time, and may have enjoyed driving a car because he did not do it very often.

The archive at Storrs contains a note from Kristin Glaser to Olson of 2 April 1962 with directions on how to get to the college.

2. On History

This is the session of the Vancouver Conference of 1963 where Olson takes stage center. But it should be pointed out that his domination of the discussion is more accentuated in this transcription than it was in actuality. Practically all of Olson's points have been included, while other participants have had their remarks severely curtailed. Olson was obviously trying to steer the discussion to make it a unified event, for instance, by leading off with "Place; & Names" and reading it again at the end. One way of handling a taped group discussion is to give the leader full rein to create the best coherence he can. A consequence in this case, however, is that anyone interested in participants other than Olson has to go to the tape itself to hear their full contribution.

It would, in any case, have been impossible to get everything onto paper. It was too acoustically noisy; the microphone was placed on the table in front of Olson in such a way that it jumped every time he made a gesture, and it did not pick up other speakers too well, the audience hardly at all. Editing out the literally blurred and the annoyingly tangential seemed the best plan, and still seems so. My *Muthologos* text is here reprinted without changes.

This text was first printed in part as "On History" in *OLSON* 4 (Fall 1975), and existed in preliminary drafts for five or more years before that. Students in my classes at Simon Fraser University heard it and participated in elucidation. I am particularly indebted to Wendy Newman, Hendrick Hoekema, and Rory Wallace, students during the summer semester of 1971. The chief debt is to Fred Wah, who had the presence of mind to find a tape recorder on 29 July 1963 and make the resulting tapes available to us.

3. Duende, Muse, and Angel

All said above in relation to the textual problems of "On History" applies here. Because of acoustical blurrings and losses, no attempt has been made to be complete. The more sensible aim was to provide a pleasant reading experience of selected portions of the discussion, attempting to be entirely accurate in what is presented.

Through the years I set this tape as a class exercise at Simon Fraser University for students who were inclined to take it on, Lois Sanford in the 1970s, Kathryn Alexander in the early 1980s, and Jody Castricano in collaboration with Peggy Gerbrecht in the later 1980s. All these students made valuable contributions. Robin Blaser listened to the tape with my final transcript in hand, and I am grateful to be able to adopt some of his suggestions.

This transcription was first published in the *Minutes of the Charles Olson Society* 1 (January 1993) and was reprinted in *Sulfur* 33 (Fall 1993), pp. 83–98. The present text has been tightened up even further with a final listening to the tape.

I have no doubt that, if it had been available at the time, George Butterick would have included this discussion in *Muthologos*. As Eliot Weinberger said, when he picked it up for reprinting in his guest-edited *Sulfur*, "It strikes me as a remarkable document, not only for what is said—the occasional lightning in the heavy clouds—but also as a sample of how American poets used to talk, only thirty years ago."

4. Under the Mushroom

George Butterick's meticulous transcription of this event was first published in *OLSON* 3 (Spring 1975) and was included in *Muthologos* with expanded notes. I have felt compelled to make a few amendments, chiefly in connection with Olson's references to Arthur Young. (I am indebted to Jeremiah Kelley for illumination on the background to Young's work.)

For the present printing I have clipped off a few seconds at the beginning merely to spare us from the hostess's confusions. Likewise I have not felt it necessary to allow the tape to peter out, but have ended it with a strong statement. The omitted part is valuable only in Olson's recommending an article: S.M. Unger, "Mescaline, LSD, Psilocybin, and Personality Change: A Review," *Psychiatry* 26:2 (May 1963), pp. 111–25, which he owned as an offprint.

5. Causal Mythology

Donald Allen was immediately alert to the value of this lecture and soon after the Berkeley Conference ended began work on the edition which subsequently appeared under his Four Seasons imprint in 1969 with the title *Causal Mythology*. This is the text that Butterick, with little emendation, used for *Muthologos* and that, with very few further emendations, is printed in the present edition.

Allen gave acknowledgment to Brian Fawcett and Albert Glover "for letting him compare their transcriptions with his own." I have not seen the Glover transcription, but Fawcett's, which was done as a Simon Fraser University course project in the late 1960s, has enabled me to hear, on relistening to the tapes, some small differences and one rather crucial one: the last paragraph of p. 75 of vol. I of *Muthologos* contains the phrase, "the way that the Earth gets to be achieved." Butterick added in square brackets "[attained?]," which was Donald Allen's word, but Butterick himself had heard an "ee" sound. So had Fawcett, who had provided "appeased," which is, I believe, closer. These are attempts to hear Olson's intention at a point where the exact sound had not communicated anything readily acceptable. But the pronounced words are quite clear; Olson says "a pea," which should not be unacceptable in this context. Earlier in the talk he had said that "the Earth is nothing but a pebble" and a little before that: "I find myself constantly returning to that unit, Earth, as orb, as though it was as familiar to me as the smallest thing I know." So we should in this later crux allow ourselves to hear the equivalent of a pebble, a very small thing: a pea. Olson is interested in "the way that the Earth gets to be a pea."

One other important change will be noticed. For Donald Allen's edition, Robert Duncan was given the opportunity to rewrite his opening remarks; also an interchange between Olson and Duncan early in the lecture was deleted. The present text supplies the actual spoken words in both instances.

6. Reading at Berkeley

I first heard the tape of this Berkeley Reading of 23 July 1965 at Jack Clarke's house in Buffalo exactly a year later. It was a year after that that Zoe Brown's transcription, *Reading at Berkeley*, was published by Oyez, and the commitment I had made at the time of first listening became a call to action. I had missed the event itself; I was now determined to recreate it on paper. I obtained the tape from Berkeley and began annotating corrections in the Oyez edition, which turned out to be full of errors and omissions. In the summer of 1968 and spring of 1969 I had students in my Simon Fraser University classes follow the tape and help decipher some of the cruxes in sound and meaning. Many ears and much library research were involved in producing the type-script which I was able to drop off with Olson in Gloucester on 6 June 1969. I sent a copy to George Butterick, and he and Olson talked about it over the telephone. "Charles equally and especially pleased with it," Butterick wrote to me on 11 July 1969, "though he did wax somewhat and grow dark about your 'accuracy' to the point of including every 'er' and other such stutters, noting the wastefulness of same, how boring and distract-ing." And Butterick added, "I must completely agree." I didn't myself completely agree, and left in a good many "ers" when I retyped the text with footnotes in what I called a "triptite" edition—voice, text, and annotations—for use in English 414 in the spring semester of 1970 at Simon Fraser. (This hand-out Butterick dignified with a bibliographical entry in a list of Olson posthumous publications in *OLSON* 7, p. 43.) By the time this triptite edition reached Olson he was in Connecticut and became terminally ill before he could write to me. However, he did have Linda Parker pass on the message that he was happy with it, especially the index, "one of the most successful evidences of the lecture itself."

Olson did not mention the remaining "ers," but when I came to prepare the text for inclusion in *Muthologos* I remembered Butterick's opinion and tempered my enthusiasm for such stutterings. Having become resigned to the comparative smoothness of the *Muthologos* version, I have had no inclination to return to a choppier sailing. Neither has there been much need for changes, the only notable one being the word Olson uses to describe Creeley: "unco," as in Robert Burns's "unco guid," which I restore over Butterick's veto (see the *Minutes of the Charles Olson Society* 39, p. 5).

There are several aids to understanding and appreciating this extraordinary speech-event, the top billing at the Berkeley Poetry Conference of July 1965. Of the series of "Backgrounds to Berkeley" in the *Minutes of the Charles Olson Society*, the following are of particular use. In *Minutes* 4, "The Re-enactment," a reprint of Robin Eichele's diary of the conference as a whole, along with a "Log of Olson's Berkeley Reading 23 July." In *Minutes* 6 "Documents in American Civilization," the written exchanges between Suzanne Mowat and Ed Sanders during Olson's reading, followed in *Minutes* 7 by "The Suzanne Mowat-Charles Olson Correspondence." Also in that issue is "Zoe Brown's Transcription," letters revealing the history behind the Coyote edition of *Reading at Berkeley* (1966). In *Minutes* 16 there is an examination of Tom Clark's account of the reading, and a discussion of proposed emendations to the *Muthologos* text.

7. Reading at Berkeley—The Day After

This discussion, called "Charles Olson and Edward Dorn" in *Muthologos*, is the first of the film sound tracks which constitute the two bad transcriptions of that volume. The tapes came to George Butterick from Gordon Craig of the American Poetry Archives at San Francisco State University, along with Craig's own preliminary transcription. Butterick placed too much faith in Craig's error-filled draft; he improved it a great deal, but it has not been difficult to improve it much further. For instance, in the first sentence Olson did not say he was "destructive" but "instructive." Butterick added a question mark to "destructive," but it should be got rid of altogether. Likewise, Ed Dorn is referred to as "the prick" in *Muthologos* (1.165) whereas Olson was, as is clear in the context, talking about him as "the printer" of Black Mountain College. And so it goes throughout.

As well as the audio-cassette received from the San Francisco State Poetry Center, I utilized the video supplied by Simon Fraser University Instructional Media Center. The transcription first appeared as "Reading at Berkeley—the Next Day" in *Minutes* 3.

It should be noted that I have ended the transcription at an auspicious point and thus have omitted an exchange at the end of the tape which takes one off the main track. Likewise, I have begun this transcription with Olson rather than a statement by Dorn which exists on the tape.

8. Filming in Gloucester

It was felt that the title of this tape in *Muthologos* could be improved, along with much else. This is the most chaotic and fractured of all the tapes, and Gordon Craig's preliminary attempt at transcription was far from helpful to Butterick here, as in the previous tape from the same source. One factor was the camerman's stopping and starting for his own needs, which interrupts the flow of talk and so often denies us the context for a difficult passage. The main problem is that Olson was being his normal talkative self, which means quick switching of topics and unpolished, incomplete sentences. Absolute accuracy can therefore be aimed for, but not achieved.

In these transcriptions I have used the video of the producer's outtakes as supplied to the Simon Fraser Library by the Poetry Center at San Francisco State University. I have also used the finished fifteen-minute National Education Television film itself and, following Butterick in *Muthologos*, injected into the outtakes sequence the small but significant passages only found there.

9. Talk at Cortland

In 1991 Jack Clarke sent me his cassette of this talk, so that I was able to hear for myself that George Butterick's transcription in *Muthologos* was a good one, but incomplete, stopping before the sequence of poems from the *Maximus Poems*. It is impossible to include the long poems themselves, but I felt it important to include the commentary, in some cases, substantial, that Olson makes as he proceeds with the reading of them.

A version of the present text was printed in *Minutes* 4 (March 1994), with an illuminating introduction by Duncan McNaughton, who had been present at the event. A further listening to the tape has produced one or two significant changes.

10. Poetry and Truth

In the early nineties I made enquiries of Marion K. Stocking, who I knew was an endur-ing figure at Beloit College and, in retirement, was most knowledgable about Olson's visit there. She was able to locate two reel-to-reel tapes of the events of March 1968 and allowed me to have one for transcribing. (This tape is now in the Contemporary Literature Collection of Simon Fraser University.) I was thus able to discover that George Butterick's version first published as *Poetry and Truth: The Beloit Lectures and Poems* (San Francisco: Four Seasons Foundation, 1971) and included in *Muthologos* vol. 2 was excellent.

Listening to the tapes again in preparation for the present edition I found I was able to make a few improvements, mainly in punctuation, to help the syntactical flow and sometimes, I believe, to secure Olson's meaning from a previously fractured sentence. I was also able to add the few remarks Olson made at the end of the Wednesday evening lecture, warning the audience that he might not be at the luncheon scheduled for the next day.

11. On Black Mountain (I)

I have followed George Butterick in separating out this informal discussion on Black Mountain from the main lectures ("Poetry and Truth") done at Beloit College. Butterick published his transcription in *Maps* 4 (1971) and included it in *Muthologos* without revision. From the tape provided me by Marion Stocking I have found it possible to make a number of corrections throughout.

Quixote 3:4 (1968), an independent student publication out of Madison, Wisconsin, published selections from this discussion which were probably notes taken down by shorthand. Some names of participants were gleaned from this source, as well as the information given in footnote 11.

12. BBC Interview

It is the usual practice of the British Broadcasting Corporation (except for "historic" broadcasts) not to keep a tape but to retain a script for legal purposes. Unless Alasdair Clayre has one, there is likely no tape of his interview with Olson. Butterick did not mention the source for what he printed in *Muthologos*; it may indeed have been Clayre, for I could not myself find the script at the BBC Written Archives at Reading, England. Thus I have used the *Muthologos* version here. The only change has been to exclude Clayre's commentary, which was not part of the original interview but added later for the broadcast.

I did, however, find an additional script at Reading, titled "Black Mountain College," which included further parts of the Gloucester interview. Clayre published a piece in *The Listener* (27 March 1969, pp. 411–14) based on this script. Olson's words quoted in *The Listener* have been checked against the original script and added to from that source. (See the *Minutes of the Charles Olson Society* 39.)

13. Interview in Gloucester, August 1968

The actual tapes are nowhere to be found, neither at Storrs nor in the George Butterick archive at Buffalo. My assumption, therefore, is that Inga Lovén requested the return of the tapes and that Butterick courteously complied without making a copy. Consequently, it is the *Muthologos* version that we have had to rely on, and there seems to be no reason not to do so. I have, however, scrutinized it and made punctuation changes to conform with the practice in the rest of this volume.

14. On Black Mountain (II)

I listened to the tape of this interview at the Thomas J. Dodd Research Center at Storrs with Butterick's transcription in hand as published in *OLSON* 8 (Fall 1977) and felt I had very little reason to change anything.

Presumably Butterick omitted this interview on Black Mountain College from *Muthologos* as overlapping too much with the Beloit tape on the same subject. I have not found the repetition unattractive, where indeed it exists.

15. The *Paris Review* Interview

It was very gratifying to be able to get a proper version of this interview, or kitchen discussion, into print in *Muthologos*. The original attempt published in the *Paris Review* 40 (1970) was totally unsatisfactory (there is nothing at all to recommend it). Unfortunately, that version with all its flaws has been included in the *Paris Review* omnibus volume, *Beat Writers at Work* (Modern Library, 1999), extending to a new readership this old defamation of the poet.

The *Muthologos* version was made possible by my receiving four tapes through the good offices of Jeremy Prynne. Two of the participants, Harvey Brown and Gerrit Lansing, listened through the tapes with me and elucidated many difficulties. Many remained, and the *Muthologos* version chose to pass them silently by rather than burden the reader with too many uncertainties. More digging has been done since then over the years, so the present transcription is much augmented. In addition, in 1992, Charles Watts of the Simon Fraser University Contemporary Literation Collection became alerted to the fact that a fifth tape had been deposited by Malanga at Texas; he made a trip there and transcribed the tape for the *Minutes of the Charles Olson Society* 2 (June 1993). His text appears here edited to conform to the format of the rest of the volume.

16. Conversation with Herb Kenny

George Butterick's title in *Muthologos*, "I Know Men for Whom Everything Matters," quite rightly draws our attention to one of Olson's greatest statements about life (here on pp. 443–44) only a few months before his death. The present title more acknowledges our debt to Herb Kenny for drawing out Olson in a way that made his peroration possible. Besides, a second tape, kindly supplied to me by Henry Ferrini, doubles the material and further reveals Kenny's inaugurating contribution. The transcription of this new tape was published in the *Minutes of the Charles Olson Society* 58 (May 2006). Since then I have listened to the tape again with Joseph Gallagher, a native of Reading, Massachusetts, and benefitted greatly from his being able to recognize the New England accents of both Olson and Kenny.

Addendum: The CBC Interview

The following text became available after the body of this second edition of *Muthologos* was set in print, and is here presented as an addendum. Robert McTavish in the process of making his documentary film *The Line Has Been Shattered*, concerning the 1963 Vancouver Poetry Conference, retrieved from the CBC Archives a stenographer's transcription of an interview Olson had with the Canadian poet Phyllis Webb at the time of the conference, August 1963. The many flaws in the stenographer's type-script are understandable for someone not versed in Olson's idiom, but remedial attention can extract a readable version.

We have been aided by an audiotape (received from Library and Archives Canada), in which Phyllis Webb culls from interviews with five poets—Robert Duncan, Allen Ginsberg, Robert Creeley, Denise Levertov, as well as Olson—an hour-long program called "Five Poets," due to be broadcast 19 January 1964, but apparently canceled. From these extracts made by Phyllis Webb in preparing the edited broadcast, we have been able to confirm portions of Olson's interview as transcribed by the CBC stenographer.

ANNOUNCER: This is an interview with Charles Olson originally prepared by Phyllis Webb for inclusion in the CBC Wednesday night program.

PHYLLIS WEBB: Will you tell me something about Gloucester?

CHARLES OLSON: Will I, any more than what I have spent so much time writing about? I don't know—actually, it has one advantage, that it's stuck out into the Atlantic and is neither Maine or Down East or Massachusetts, and has been so since the original Indian as well as the possible Norse occupation of it. And even the Dutch, for example, who were ahead of the English in arriving there, gave it the same name that seems to be the name that it had for the Norse, which is" Grapevine Corner." And in this sense it's been an angle both for me—and it seems to me to stand as an angle in the world which is both actually a surviving uniqueness, and I would believe— at least, I have spent the time on it to use it as a particular from which I think all "universal" can grow?

WEBB: You use the word "locus" a good deal ...

OLSON: Very much, and not for that reason, not the place idea or the local idea but—or even the better word than "locus" is the "topos," which gives you that shift in mathematics through the whole art of topology, in other words, the advantage that no ground need be treated as such because you can reduce it so flat and get dimensions which are free from the perspective problem that it seems to me so long our expression as well as our minds have been tested by. And Gloucester offers to me a specific of something that I would call "topos." But then, if you remember my "Letter to Elaine Feinstein," I was careful to argue that you can't talk "topos" if you don't talk two other crucial terms, one of which we have very easily in our language, but I'm saying "typos," and we know it as "typology," and as such is wretched, and certainly Paul Klee was right to put it down as completely objectionable killing of things; but if you take it and join it to "topos" and then swing in the great one of "tropos," which is that we are battered or twist and turn in both our natures and in our lives, you have what I would say is the triad which makes real sense. And it's that kind of a triple flower of Gloucester that I am seeking to ...

WEBB: "What does not change is the will to change." Why do you feel that you can leave Gloucester now?

OLSON: Well, I—actually you have some sense if you launch into a poem that is made up of poems of the shape or general direction at least or the tie to your own life. And the first volume, which was the last one, that created the whole idea of the poem, was very, very much set in Gloucester and was an argument problem probably of "locus" or "topos"; but the second, which ...

WEBB: Can you name those books please?

OLSON: Yes, the first one has been published as the *Maximus Poems*, about 1960, I believe. The new one, which is the one I have been working on since 1959 is now completed and is one of the reasons why I not only have left Gloucester but feel very gratified to be out of it; because, for those four years I was involved in writing what I would imagine is—a second volume ought to be really a "typos," and now I'm left with—if this sounds like a proposition or an idea, it only comes off to the fact that this thing precedes it, and then you do use, or at least I do, formulations which seem to me to fit, but which, I hope, never impose themselves upon the actual poems of the poem. So that I am now busted, in the sense that I have done a second volume, or second part, and am left now to approach a possible third, which I should imagine is the end of it. And in fact I hope so, because I have already started to publish, in fact I have now published three poems of a long poem of a similar—called 'West'—the first one of which I read this week, as a matter of fact, "as of Bozeman," and that would be the first poem of this new thing which would occupy me, if I could finish the third *Maximus*. It may be—my own plans at present are to abandon any further pursuit of the *Maximus*, and go after this other poem for a while.

WEBB: In the *Maximus* poems you draw on all kinds of things in Gloucester, in its history—can you tell me something about how you got at those sources?

OLSON: Well, again, she has the advantage of being the first English settlement on the Atlantic coast that was economic or industrial, and stayed continuously as such right to the present day. She arose out of actually the port of Weymouth in England and was the idea of the minister of Dorchester, Reverend John White, who was in fact the finder and founder of Massachusetts, preceding John Winthrop in this sense; and, although Winthrop became the executive and creator of Massachusetts, the actual origin of what we—of what I think can be called, if you talk of North America, the *original* settlement, because of the continuity and the present fact of herself, a fishing town from beginning to end, this has an enormous—well, just if it's simple food, you have an absolute straight on town life on this continent of over 300 years.

WEBB: So history, economics, geography ...?

OLSON: Yes, each. This means that you got everything in one bundle, and it's a question of how much do I succeed in getting all the pieces of the bundle off of it, believing, as I do, in the sacredness of bundles.

   I wrote before, or just in the midst of starting, those *Maximus* poems, a play which Nick Cernovich was to dance, as well as myself, called "Apollonius of Tyana," which has not yet been performed, which exists in print, and has almost—and this "Apollonius of Tyana" was a contemporary of Christ and moved around the world in the first century, actually himself poking his nose into anything, and persisting—coming from Tyana on the advantage of the specifics, not of a place but of any place, to yield a—well, the words are wrong but, say, to yield to the universal.

WEBB: You have spoken a good deal about space and consciousness in America. Could you expand on this idea?

OLSON: Yes, I do. You are referring to, I think, that whole thing that I spoke of so much in *Call Me Ishmael*, which was a book on Melville, which opens almost after an original story on space as the fact of America. And indeed the advantage to me of that thing is that we were a new physical, naked, or open, or aboriginal space, which we have, in a sense, now miserably filled competently, but I think now uninterestingly; and I myself believe, because the space thing devoured us as against time, it seems, in my own experience now, that time and feeling are not only what's been missing but what's up, and is powerfully drawing us towards itself. And yet I would say still that the advantages of having been people of space—I, in *Ishmael*, even stated it aphoristically as "we are the last first people,"—is still one which I would think that we would be advantaged to not abandon, despite the obvious nonism of the accomplishment.

WEBB: Was it the "nonism" of the accomplishment that sent you to Central America to study the Mayan culture?

OLSON: I don't think so. I actually went there from the way that all of us do who read or write—or the old *American Weekly*, which sounds a wonderful name now, but was her "Sunday Supplement" section that I was reading, as we do as kids, with the newspaper on the floor, and fantasized the whole world out, because it was the sacred well into which each is thrown, and this is the sacrifice which I suppose—but I actually went there to learn Maya, living Maya. I found out that the fisherman that kept his sails on my porch wouldn't teach me Maya any more than he would teach his sons to learn, so dreadfully has the Americanization of the world eaten up even such things as languages, live languages.

WEBB: Are you an archaeologist?

OLSON: Not at all, and I can now have this marvelous opportunity—because of a mistake in the blurb of this book *The Distances*, I was credited with receiving a foundation grant from the upper, the inside group of archaeologists, the Wenner-Gren Foundation, at the age of eleven! So I have the pride of an archaeologist who, like, ceased any longer to be one. Actually, to say this, it was a lie in the first place, but I actually got into digging in the dirt of Yucatan and in five minutes hit a lovely pace, and have actually at home the thigh bone of Quetzalcoatl, the only known human bone of the Maya, carved in their hieroglyphs at the apex of the art of both the language and the cutting. It's an enormously handsome thing, and it clearly was found in such a situation and is so unique that the argument is that it has to be the great femur of his own thigh, and it's a beauty. And, in fact, the glyphs are to explain how the way one refers to the language of the Mayan, which is something like hieroglyphs, and this bone is, has a full passage from him to me; and this one, it was really a—I mean, for me, Lerma was a true place that I went to as just an action of one's life, not with any purpose.

WEBB: While you were there, I understand that you took drugs. I have been asking other poets about drugs as a means of opening up their areas of consciousness. Could you tell us something about the kinds of drugs that you take, and the effect of them?

OLSON: Actually, I didn't. But I was completely aware that there was stuff going on in Lerma that I was out of. And since, of course, I have learned by myself that such a thing as morning glory or *ololiuqui* was actually probably in use then from my own drug experience. When Allen Ginsberg, in the early days of the new discovery of the synthetic of the sacred mushroom, psilocybin, asked me to go in with him on a session in Boston, or Newton, I did, and found, for me at least, the mushroom was a confirmation of altogether that which I feel as though I had known without any use of drugs whatsoever, and, in fact, that my own sense is that our body is actually possessed of the powers, and one of the obvious difficulties is to live in our own body. And I am publishing a book this fall, by the publisher of *Maximus*, actually a prose book of very, very almost resistant pieces, which is called *Proprioception*, and with some deliberateness, because I am of the belief that the area of the body which is really just not felt or thought of at all or even experienced, the area which lies between the organs of the inside and its skin, is the tremendous transmitive, transmission area properly called "proprioception," and is almost like, say, the balances or the gyroscope that is left out of most of our awareness of ourselves, this crazy distance which is really nothing but transmission.

WEBB: What kind of consciousness would it ...?

OLSON: I actually found myself under the mushroom—in fact, I said one very simple thing when I was waked up in the morning, "This is a love feast and a truth pill." And this sense of the fact that you were actually being encouraged to experience your own, the love feast of your being as well as the dogmatic objective existence of truth, and, in other words, that this is not an hallucinative or pictorial or even sensational and certainly not self-expression area; it is a dogmatic area, and it is almost like a tie that ties us to Creation.

WEBB: Do you think that mystics have access to those awarenesses, since they issue "truths"?

OLSON: Yes, if we can leave the word "mystic" alone. Myself, being a terrible literalist and a secularist if not a particularist, I think that our vocabulary ought to be set aside until we actually have the experience. And, in fact, if we use a vocabulary, we already are turning the advantages away, importing words from, say, the East, like to use that stupid word "tradition" to forward some future, which we ourselves seem to me right now are the chance inverters of.

WEBB: You said, "I find the contemporary substitution of society for the cosmos captive and deathly"—a beautiful sentence; it seems to fit in here.

OLSON: Very much, very much. That's why earlier I booted the word "universal." I think that the only word—"cosmos," itself, again, I would want to use with great ginger. Large words tend to take over when actually our own lives are at stake. But, believe you me, you can quote that. I certainly would stand by it because it was for me an experience that stayed that way.

WEBB: Well, to move now to poetry, you are the father, really, of "projective verse" and I was wondering if you could go back in time to 1950 and recall some of the precepts of "Projective Verse" for us briefly?

OLSON: We can talk just from where we were—I mean, the thing that still seems to be useful—with a formulation which Robert Creeley, I think, gave to me in a letter: that "form is never more than an extension of content," and that argument that you stay with the content and let any form of a poem occur because you yourself are in the content. Yesterday, for example, I had a lot of interesting—all day, it was due to Daphne Buckle, a poet of this session that we're holding at the University of British Columbia, who asked me as against the Fenollosa, Ernest Fenollosa's statement about what is a primary sentence, and he argued that it was a lightning stroke was the model of a sentence in the universe. She said to me, "What do you think of Wordsworth's 'emotion recollected in tranquility'?" And all day yesterday, not only were we examining the power, and I don't mean in the meanings but the—in fact, with some of the young professors and then later on among my fellows—and it is interesting to see Wordsworth's argument. I myself found that, in the second volume of the *Maximus*, Wordsworth became almost my Virgil, my accompanist, in a poem in which, in an unusual instance, I inscribe to Robert. It is Wordsworth that becomes the man, "O Wordsworth be with me at this hour" sort of thing. When you see him declare a poem "arises from feelings," I would say from *feeling*, and be very insistent that that plural wastes some point and that working with what we used to call "content" (I would not like to say the whole substance) you have nothing but "emotion recollected in tranquility." Now this sounds as though it's a thought; I believe it is a means. It's sort of a soft going after the feeling and after the projection of the drive to write the poem, which gets you, as a means, truly through. So that he himself says in the—which I was looking at again yesterday—at the end of that first paragraph of the Preface to the *Lyrical Ballads*, he ends saying that you do, therefore, come back by "a species of reaction" (which is a curious phrase, "a species of reaction") to the feelings that prompted you to write the poem. Now, I am offering this book because it is our tradition too, and the "Projective Verse" piece was written in resistance to all that kind of talk, and tried to make, in a whole series of statements, the argument for something that came out "composition by field," or "open field" poetry as against "closed."

I just received a letter from Charles Tomlinson, the English poet who reviewed *Maximus* in London more successfully than I've seen any review anywhere, asking me where I found out that French poetry had a distinction between open and closed verse, and I got to confess I don't know, but the idea was that the forms that we've had since Sappho and Alcaeus are closed forms and that there was some advantage, and it certainly was enormously brought about in the early part of this century by such American poets as Williams and Pound and certainly others, to leave the poem open, or to arrive at an end which was of its own rather than of any end which came from a form accepted from the beginning to be the form of a poem.

WEBB: How did you arrive at the concept of "feeling"?

OLSON: I have no idea. It's like the word "projection"; I never in my life imagined that there was anything like projection in psychology when I used the word. I really did very carefully add three other words, "percussive," "projectile," and "prospective," just to actually the word "projective" I was using, I think, as in geometry and from non-Euclidean and from the whole development that started with Bolyai and Lobatschewsky, contemporary with John Keats, which interests me in that that phrase of words was "by a species of reaction," because I have never been able to get away from John Keats's argument of "negative capability," which is a non-Euclidean argument, it seems to me, of feeling and verse; and I believe in it very much. And that was what I was after: it was a non-Euclidean basis for writing a poem, and I still think that I am with it or it is the possibility.

WEBB: You also said that if projective verse were pushed far enough, the problem of larger content and larger forms may be solved, and you use Pound as an example of someone who is pushing towards this solution. You yourself have pushed toward it in the *Maximus*. Has anyone else done this?

OLSON: Not on that same line, I don't think, because, to some extent, the line itself has shattered so that there's all sorts of new poems—in fact, for example, any one of us that's here on this present thing going on in Vancouver are all writing poems—if you stop to think of Mr Duncan's "On a Line of Pindar," or Mr Creeley's new novel, or Mr Ginsberg's poetry, the line which may have in 1950 had some advantage to be called "projective" has now shattered. In fact, that is again why I say something like Wordsworth has re-arisen. I think the "Projective Verse" piece, with every advantage that it had, needs to be modified. And I felt myself I made the best modification, being asked to write by Don Allen, who edited *The New American Poetry*, a second "Projective Verse." Actually, how it came out: I was asked two questions by an editor in Cambridge, England, and answered her in what is published now as—and it is really in truth a revision of "Projective Verse"—"Letter to Elaine Feinstein." It's written in a kind of prose which I now believe in, but it's not at all attractive to read if anybody should be led to do it; very difficult, I find.

WEBB: I'd just like to end by asking you about influences, literary influences.

OLSON: Yes, I had to deal with that question just recently. For example, I have always been associated, say, also beside Pound, with Bill Williams. And you know I felt as though Bill Williams really, really were a father, and, I mean, he did remarkable things for me on his own with no traffic or even friendship between us, like he published the "Projective Verse" piece in his *Autobiography* quite by himself, an amazing thing; he just popped it in there as part of his autobiography. I would say for sure that Pound is perhaps an influence, but then again, believe you me, I can read you poems which are absolutely—and, in fact, in the *Maximus* I make him a man of my poem and almost bring him into Gloucester, and don't treat him as a Virgil or a Wordsworth or a man holding my hand, because he is—I, in dream, have been instructed by a man, of dream, named Ezra Pound, exactly how to write my verse, and that is not influence. That is something much more mysterious and vital and crucial, and I believe that any one of us would have to not only listen to that instruction but in that instruction we are being told exactly what to do. Pound in a dream, in fact, is my influence, and anything that I now am or do is following those instructions.

Annotated Index

Roman numerals from i to xvi indicate parts 1–16 of the Contents; add = Addendum. (The Introduction and Textual Notes are not indexed.)
hn = headnote; n1 = footnote 1 etc.